LEARNING BIBLICAL HEBREW

A NEW APPROACH USING DISCOURSE ANALYSIS

B. M. ROCINE

SMYTH&HELWYS
PUBLISHING, INCORPORATED · MACON, GEORGIA

For My dear Catherine.

Smyth & Helwys Publishing, Inc.
6316 Peake Road
Macon, Georgia 31210-3960
1-800-747-3016
© 2000 by Smyth & Helwys Publishing
All rights reserved.
Printed in the United States of America.

Bryan M. Rocine

The paper used in this publication meets the minimum
requirements of American National Standard for Information
Sciences—Permanence of Paper for Printed Library Materials.
ANSI Z39.48–1984   (alk. paper)

Library of Congress Cataloging-in-Publication Data

Rocine, B. M.
Learning Biblical Hebrew: a new approach using discourse analysis / by B. M. Rocine
p.   cm.
Includes bibliographical references.
ISBN 1-57312-324-2
1. Hebrew language–Grammar. 2. Hebrew language–Discourse analysis.
3. Direct discourse in the Bible, I. Title.
PJ4567 .R56 2000
492.4'82421–dc21   00-063748

CHARTS

The book's charts are listed below in the order in which they appear. Not all the charts are listed because the paradigms are built gradually during the course, and there is no need to list charts until they are complete.

INTRODUCTION

Our many quality English translations of the Hebrew Bible are worthy accomplishments. However, there is no substitute for reading the Hebrew Bible *in Hebrew*. In his book *Hebrew: The Eternal Language*, Wm. Chomsky quotes historian and orientalist Ernest Renan:

> A quiver full of steel arrows, a cable with strong coils, a trumpet of brass crashing through the air with two or three sharp notes--such is the Hebrew language...the letters of its books are not many, but they are to be letters of fire. A language of this sort is not destined to say much, but what it does say is beaten out upon an anvil. It is employed to pour floods of anger and cries of rage against the abuses of the world, calling the four winds of heaven to the assault of the citadels of evil. Like the jubilee horn of the sanctuary it will be put to no profane use; but it will sound the notes of the holy war against injustice and the call of the great assemblies; it will have accents of rejoicing, and accents of terror; it will become the trumpet of judgment.

This volume is a one year course in Biblical Hebrew requiring roughly 300 hours of study time to complete. The student will learn the Hebrew alphabet, the basics of pronouncing Hebrew, and about 400 of the most common words in the Hebrew Bible. By the end of the course the student will have read approximately 1000 verses of Biblical text.

The rationale for this book

There are many carefully prepared teaching grammars for Biblical Hebrew already, some quite new and user-friendly, but there are several reasons why another approach is needed First, existing texts focus on teaching only the parts and pieces of the language from the sentence level and smaller. How the parts and pieces function within a system in a larger context, such as a Biblical story, is left a mystery. On the other hand, modern linguistics, computer-aided Bible research, and the experience gained from translating the Bible into hundreds of languages world-wide have worked together to give us new, powerful and perceptive models for describing Biblical Hebrew. We have learned that a writer's choices at the word, phrase, clause, and sentence levels are influenced by larger context in systematic ways. In other words, a writer guides his reader through his text with grammatical signals. In this course we will study these signals, referring to our study as discourse analysis.

No teaching grammar prior to this one has incorporated the work of the many discourse analysts of the Hebrew Bible since the landmark work of F. I. Anderson in 1970, *The Hebrew Verbless Clause in the Pentateuch*(New York: Abington). It is my sincerest goal to help people understand the Word of God more richly and intimately. I have found the discourse analytical approach to the Hebrew Bible to be the most powerful grammatical tool for gaining this intimacy. This book is therefore written to teach the exegetical power of discourse analysis right from the start.[1]

---

[1] Several Hebraists of the 1990's have called for an incorporation of discourse analysis into beginning Biblical Hebrew studies, among them Dawson, *Text-Linguistics and Biblical Hebrew* (Sheffield: Sheffield Academic Press, 1994), 218, "However, it is clear that the most immediate—if not the greatest—benefit from text-linguistic research will be for students and teachers of the language. In the same way that checking the cards in a deck to determine which (if any) are missing is far easier if the cards are arranged in numerical order by suits, so also learning (and therefore teaching) *any* language is greatly simplified if its forms are systematized—all the more so if it is a dead language. If the system of text-types were presented to students (I do not mean the theoretical parameters, but rather the simple existence of these text-types), and their associated mainline forms, then this much, in one stroke, would give the learner a handle to begin sorting through the various distributions and functions of the Hebrew verb." Also Longacre: "...discourse analysis emerges not as an option or as a luxury for the serious student of a language but as a necessity" (quoted in Waltke and O'Connor, *An Introduction to Biblical Hebrew Syntax* (Winona Lake: Eisenbrauns, 1990), 53. And *Joseph: A Story of Divine Providence: A Text Theoretical and Textlinguistic Analysis of Genesis 37 and 39-48* (Winona Lake: Eisenbrauns, 1989), 42: "The whole legislates the parts, while, in turn, a study of the parts is necessary to the comprehension of the whole." Also van der Merwe, "From Paradigms to Texts. New Horizons and New Tools for Interpreting the Old Testament" *Journal of Northwest Semitic Languages* 22/2, 179: "It appears that in the very good old days Jewish scholars knew relatively much about the grammar of BH as well as how it was used to communicate in the OT. Divorcing the study and teaching of BH grammar from rhetoric, concentrating on the forms of the language

The second reason this course is needed is because the study of Biblical Hebrew needs to be made more relevant for today's student of the Bible. As already mentioned, we have numerous excellent translations, exhaustive concordances with number-coded lexicons, and powerful Bible-study software. Can only one year's study of Biblical Hebrew be worth the effort? With such helpful Bible-study resources available, there is definitely no need for most of us merely to translate the Bible all over again. Yet this is exactly what most first year courses in Biblical Hebrew are teaching. The student learns that if he can translate the Hebrew Bible into something like the Revised Standard Version, he is succeeding. Today's student knows it is a lot more efficient to simply purchase a Revised Standard Bible and a good computer program for Bible study. Also, first year courses are traditionally designed as though they are nothing more than a prerequisite to Biblical Hebrew II and III. However, students who take only one or two years of Biblical Hebrew often quickly forget almost all of what they had worked so hard to learn. It is therefore the goal of this volume to teach, from lesson one through fifty, useful nuances of meaning, especially those related to the discourse analysis of Biblical Hebrew, that are not accessible through English translations. This course seeks to stress the worth of reading the Hebrew Bible in Hebrew. Although this course in no way discourages additional years of studying Hebrew, it does seek to teach some of the subtleties of the Biblical prose that students can remember and use during a lifetime of Bible study even if the they do not continue with formal study past one year.

The third reason this book is needed is to provide a course that can truly be used with *or without* an instructor's help. Of course, it is definitely best to study using this or any other book as a class with an instructor, but often this is impossible. There are relatively few colleges and universities in North America that teach Biblical Hebrew. It is assumed that many of those who may be interested in learning Biblical Hebrew cannot, with reasonable convenience, access these institutions. Synogogue or church classes in Biblical Hebrew are also non-existent in many communities. This book is therefore written suitably for independent study. It takes an interactive approach in which the student and the text are in a kind of running dialogue in a workbook fashion. The book constantly reviews and tries to anticipate the students' questions by constantly cross-referencing the students to earlier lessons.

The organization of this book
The following three teaching guidelines control the organization of this book:
1. Teach what is most needed first.
2. Use a Hebrew Bible text as the basis for every lesson.
3. Teach discourse analysis from the start.

On teaching what is most needed first: By giving higher priority to the vocabulary and grammatical constructions that actually occur more often in the Biblical text, the student will progress as efficiently as possible, surprisingly quickly. To reiterate an earlier point, many students of Biblical Hebrew will only be able to spend one year studying the language. This book is therefore designed to teach, in one year, the most useful information about Biblical Hebrew that is possible in that given time. There is no attempt to learn everything there is to know about Hebrew. However, there is no need to wait until the second or third year of study to begin learning some basics of exegesis of the Hebrew Bible.

On the commitment to using only Biblical texts: This commitment keeps the lessons relevant, and the student confident that he is progressing. A particular Biblical verse generates the concepts covered in each lesson. Memorization of charts and paradigms does not occur until the second module of the course. This writer does not believe that it is necessary for the student to know all the grammatical paradigms before he can enjoy actual texts. In fact, the goal in this course is to keep the student as involved with actual text as possible. Learning Biblical Hebrew is not treated as an end in itself. Rather, learning the language is always treated as a means to greater understanding of the Bible.

---

unfortunately resulted in a very reduced picture of what constitutes a knowledge of BH. A recent shift in the study of language from the message of communication to the recipient of communication draws attention to the entire range of variables involved in a communication process. Apart from revealing how little we know of BH, it emphasizes the inadequacies of the grammar-and-translation method of language teaching. Though we know relatively little about BH pragmatics, I am convinced that introducing it in introductory courses can no longer be delayed."

Lastly and most importantly, on the choice of a discourse analytical theoretical base: A discourse is a text, a group of expressions linked together from a beginning to an ending so that they develop an idea in some orderly fashion. A story, a song, a thesis, an inaugural address, a friendly letter are all texts or discourses. As alluded to above, linguists have recently been able to study hundreds of living languages around the world, not only at the level of word, phrase, and sentence but at the level of discourse. Linguists have come to realize that language users signal their audiences what they are doing in their discourses by the grammatical constructions they choose. For instance, when writers are telling a story, they indicate story structure, what is more and less important to them, how events are related, what is foreground what is background, when tension is greatest, and so on, all by linguistic signals. Largely as a result of organizations such as Summer Institute of Linguistics, and their effort to translate the Bible into the languages of hundreds of indigenous peoples around the world, the pragmatic approach of discourse analysis has proven to be an extremely fast and efficient theoretical base from which to learn a language. Since there is no reason to believe that Biblical Hebrew would behave differently than any living language, we seek to utilize the advantage of discourse analysis as we learn Biblical Hebrew.

It may seem like a student just beginning the uphill climb of learning a new language has enough of a burden to simply learn about the language at the sentence level and below. The addition of the higher, discourse issues may seem as though it will overload the curriculum. On the contrary, the addition of discourse issues organizes and systematizes the presentation of the introductory material *with a system that is inherent to the language being learned*, and in fact, that is already a part of the student's own experience with how language works. Since the system used to organize the material is inherent to the language and familiar to the student, the student is then able to learn more information more easily.

A couple last points
The emphases in this book will *not* be on composing and speaking Hebrew. Those who are interested in learning modern, conversational Hebrew are strongly advised to find other better-suited materials. A secure, automatic pronunciation ability for Hebrew is very important for being able to read and enjoy the Hebrew Bible. Otherwise, the student will be so preoccupied with pronouncing the text, his comprehension will suffer. However, an undo emphasis on perfect or "native" pronunciation is not necessary either. The book does not promote a sloppy or carefree pronunciation of Hebrew, but it does not put the stress on pronunciation that would be appropriate for a course on conversational Hebrew.

A first year teaching grammar is not usually footnoted, and although this one is not annotated as extensively as a dissertation would be, there are numerous notes which point to the literature which discusses the topic at hand. These notes are not intended primarily for the first year student who can easily ignore them without compromising his course-work. Rather, they are for the benefit of instructors who may want to use this book, but find they are unfamiliar with some late studies. In addition, they should prove helpful to the student who has finished this course and wants to continue his studies. Or the notes may help someone who has already taken some Hebrew but wishes to learn more about the discourse analysis of the Hebrew Bible.

Acknowledgments
I am, as mentioned, indebted to the Hebraists of the last thirty years whose research inspired this work and whose work is, I pray, done justice in the text and its notes. I must thank especially Robert Longacre and Alviero Niccacci, for it is on their work that this project most fundamentally rests. I thank them both for the personal time and interest they both gave me and this project. This course has developed over six years of field use in a variety of settings, academic and informal, from high school level to the mission field to college and I thank all the students and instructors who had valuable insights and suggestions for improving the lessons. I must express my gratitude to those willing souls of The Church of the Living Word in Syracuse, NY, most especially Richard and Linda Ludovico, who ventured through the first drafts of many of the lessons as we discovered together the merits of this new approach. I also appreciate the assistance of Stanley Bray, Dutch Schultz, and Paul Bailey in providing me so much technical support in using the computer for this project. I am also indebted to Rodney K. Duke of Appalachian State University for his constructive criticisms. I claim full responsibility for all the errors that remain in this present work.

Materials required for this course

In addition to this text the student is required to have a Hebrew Bible with Masoretic vowel markings, preferably the *Biblia Hebraica Stuttgartensia* and a good English-Hebrew Lexicon of the Hebrew Bible, preferably *The New Brown-Driver-Briggs-Gesenius Hebrew-English Lexicon* (Peabody: Hendrikson, 1979). Both of these books are available through Eisenbrauns, Inc. (phone: 1-219-269-2011, e-mail: orders@eisenbrauns.com) among other places.

PRONOUNCING HEBREW

A brief history

If the beginning Hebrew student looks at any page of the Hebrew Bible, he likely does not see a thing that looks familiar. As a result, simply learning the Hebrew alphabet often seems intimidating. And then there is the matter of Hebrew proceeding from right to left. Students often ask, "How come Hebrew goes the wrong way?" If we take into account that Hebrew went from right to left thousands of years before Geoffrey Chaucer wrote "Whan in Aprille with his shoures soote" in Middle English, which language, if either, goes the wrong way?

Actually, a student, knowing neither the phonetics of English nor Hebrew, and all else being equal, would most likely far prefer learning the Hebrew. Unlike that of English, all Hebrew pronunciation makes sense and operates according to a relatively small set of rules. There will be none of the kind of thing that happens constantly in English: for example, a different pronunciation of the *o* in words like *love* and *rove*. Or the classic: seven different pronunciations for one letter sequence, *-ough-* as in *rough, though, bough, ought, through, cough,* and yes, even *hiccough*!

Originally, the Hebrew Bible was written in a different alphabet than the one you will be learning. Scribes did not begin using the "square" Aramaic alphabet that is used in the Hebrew Bible today until the Babylonian Exile in the Fifth or Sixth Centuries BCE. Originally the Hebrew Bible was written with consonants only, i.e., without vowels. Many scholars believe that over time some of the consonants began to do double duty as vowels and were then added to the consonantal text as aides to pronunciation and clarity. You may wonder how any one could make sense of a language written without vowels. Can you read this sentence without any problem?

Lts g swmmng n th lk tmrrw.

Does the *n* mean *on* or *in*? You will see that the same type of interpretation must often be made in Hebrew. You may also be interested to know that most Modern Hebrew is written with a bare minimum of vowels.

However, in the Tenth and Eleventh Centuries CE, Jewish scholars called the Masoretes /MAS-or-ites/ desired to add an apparatus to the text of the Hebrew Bible that would leave the consonantal text unmodified but would also specify the exact pronunciation of the Holy Text. The result was the system of dots, dashes, and other symbols that are written above, below, and in between the consonantal text.

> DEFINITION: The system of dots, dashes, and other marks added to the consonantal text by the Masoretes is called the text's **nikkud**. The nikkud consists of two parts, the vowel markings and a system of accent marks.

In this course you will spend a great deal of time learning and using the vowel marks and much less time on the accentual system.

The consonants

You will learn more about the nikkud shortly, but let us begin where the Hebrew Bible began, with the consonants. As you learn each letter of the alphabet and later, each vowel symbol, you need to associate two things to each symbol just as you did back in the first grade or two of your elementary education when you chanted "*B* says /b/ in *ball*." Of course, you must learn each symbol's name so we can later refer to the letters in the lessons of this book. Learning the names of the symbols gives us the linguistic lingo we need for instruction. Much more importantly, however, is that you learn the sound each symbol makes. Although we are not studying Modern Hebrew this course will use the pronunciation that is most widely heard in Modern Israel, also probably the simplest dialect to learn, the Sephardi. You will not likely become automatic in your ability to pronounce the Hebrew alphabet before Lesson 1, and that is not a problem. But you must eventually gain this automaticity if you will ever unburden yourself from "thinking" about pronouncing the Hebrew Bible and enjoy comprehending it instead. If you take the time to pronounce all the Hebrew verses, drills, and examples given to you in this text, you should approach this automatic pronunciation of Hebrew by the end of this course.

THE CONSONANTS:

Letter	Name	Sound		Letter	Name	Sound
א	aleph	silent		ל or לֹ	lamed	/l/
בּ	bet	/b/		מ מֹ or (final)ם	mem	/m/
ב	bet	/v/		נ נֹ or (final)ן	nun	/n/
ג or גֹ	gimel	/g/		ס or סֹ	samekh	/s/
ד or דֹ	dalet	/d/		ע	ayin	silent
ה	heh	/h/		פ	peh	/p/
ו or וֹ	vav	/v/		פ or (final)ף	peh	/f/
ז or זֹ	zayin	/z/		צ צֹ or (final)ץ	tsadeh	/ts/
שׁ	khet	/kh/		ק or קֹ	koph	/k/
ט or טֹ	tet	/t/		ר	resh	/r/
י or יֹ	yod	/y/		שׂ or שֹׂ	sin	/s/
כ or (final)ך	khoph	/k/		שׁ or שֹׁ	shin	/sh/
כ or (final)ך	khoph	/kh/		ת or תֹ	Tav	/t/

Notes:

1. Most of the letters have sounds that correspond nicely to sounds of the English alphabet as noted in the chart.

2. The *aleph* [א] and *ayin* [ע] are thought to have originally represented a guttural stoppage of sound. We will, however, after the modern practice, treat them as essentially silent in and of themselves. We will see that both of these letters may be accompanied by a vowel in which case the consonant itself is still silent, but the vowel is pronounced.

3. Five letters have final forms, the *khoph, mem, nun, peh,* and *tsadeh.* The final forms are only used when these letters happen to be at the end of a word. Otherwise, the regular form is used. Keep in mind that Hebrew is read from right to left as you look at these Hebrew words as examples of regular and final letters (the vowels have been left off):

מה (regular *mem*)
שמה (regular *mem*)
שם (final form of *mem*)

x

צַדֵק (regular *tsadeh*)

מצא (regular *tsadeh*)

אֶרֶץ (final form of *tsadeh*)

4. Many of the letters can take a dot, called a ***dagesh***, within them, but only in a few cases does the *dagesh* have any effect on the way the letter is pronounced in Modern Hebrew. The affected pronunciations are within the *bet* [בּ vs. ב], *khoph* [כּ vs. כ], and *peh* [פּ vs. פ]. The presence or absence of the dagesh in Modern Hebrew does not affect the pronunciation of the other letters that take the dagesh.

5. There are several letters, called the **guttural letters**, which cannot or very rarely take a *dagesh*. These include *aleph* [א], *heh* [ה], *khet* [ח], *ayin* [ע]. *Resh* [ר] is not technically a guttural letter, but it acts essentially like one it its usual refusal to accept a *dagesh*. You will later learn that the refusal of these letters to accept the *dagesh* has some important effects on a word.

6. One sound in Hebrew that we do not have in English is the sound of the letters *khet* [ח] and *khoph* (without the *dagesh*) [כ or the final form ך]. The sound, symbolized in this book /kh/, is made by shaping the mouth in a manner similar to the way we do when we make our *k* and then blowing so air passes by the tongue at the back of the mouth. It is similar to the German *ch* in *Bach*.

7. A couple of Hebrew letters make sounds which we have in English, but which are represented by digraphs in English. These are the *tsadeh* [צ צ or ץ] pronounced like the *ts* in *hits* and the *shin* [שׁ or שׁ] pronounced /sh/.

The vowels

The nikkud, as you remember, are vowel and accent markings added to the originally all-consonantal text by the Masoretes. Below is the vowel part of the nikkud. Each of the vowel markings is shown with an *aleph* [א] so you can see how the vowel marks are placed in spatial relationship to the consonants.

THE VOWELS:

Nikkud (with an *aleph*)	Name	Sound
אָ	qamets	/a/ as in *father*
אַ	patakh	/a/ as in *father*
אֵי	tsere (plene)	/e/ as in *prey*
אֵ	tsere (defectiva)	/e/ as in *prey*
אֶ	segol	/e/ as in *met*
אֱ	khataf segol	/ɛ/ as in *met*
אִי	hireq (plene)	/i/ as in *machine*
אִ	hireq (defectiva)	/i/ as in *machine* or /I/ as in *pin*
אוֹ	holem (plene)	/o/ as in *hope*
אֹ	holem (defectiva)	/o/ as in *hope*
אָ	qamets khatuf	/o/ as in *hope*
אֳ	khataf qamets	/o/ as in *hope*
אוּ	shureq	/u/ as in *rude*
אֻ	Kibbuts	/u/ as in *rude*
אְ	silent shewa	silent
אְ	vocal shewa	shortened /uh/ as in the first syllable of *McCoy*
אֲ	khataf patakh	lengthened /uh/ as in *amount*

Notes:

1. Several vowel marks may make the same sound. This is often no more than alternate *plene*, meaning

full spelling versus *defectiva* meaning *shortened* spelling of the same sound. Notice that the same symbol [ָ] is sometimes pronounced /a/ and sometimes /o/. This symbol's pronunciation is determined by a reliable rule which you will learn in Lesson 3.

2. Two of the letters which you have already encountered as consonants, namely the *vav* [ו] and *yod* [י], can also be used as vowels. You will see shortly that the use of these symbols is not ambiguous. For instance, whether the symbol וֹ says /v/ or /u/ in a particular Hebrew word is determined by completely reliable rules.

3. The marks *khataf segol* [ֱ], *khataf qamets* [ֳ], and *khataf patakh* [ֲ] are often referred to collectively as the *compound* or *composite shewas*. They make the same sound as their full vowel counterparts *segol* [ֶ], *qamets* [ָ], and *patakh* [ַ], only shorter.

Open syllables

The basic rule of Biblical Hebrew spelling is that every consonant except for the last one in a word or the silent letters *aleph* [א] and *ayin* [ע] must be accompanied by some vowel. To pronounce the text then, the reader proceeds from right to left, a consonant with its vowel, a consonant with its vowel.

An open syllable is one which ends with a vowel sound. Pronounce the following open syllables (every *qamets* [ָ] is a regular *qamets* pronounced /a/):

טוּ טֹ וֵ וְ רִי רִ רָ וֶ וַ זְ זִ הַ הֵ הֶ הֶ הֹ דָ דַ גִי גֶ גֶ בִי

בָּ בַּ נִ נַּ נַ מִי מֶ מָ מֶ מִ מִי לְ לָ לֵ לִי כ כוּ כֹ כֹּ כ

יֻּ יֻ יֹ טוֹ טֹ קוֹ קֻ קַ צ צוֹ צָ צַ צַ פֹ פוּ פֹ פִי פ ס

סִי סָ סַ סַ נְ נִ נָ תְ תוּ תֹ תֹ שׁוּ שׁוּ שׁוֹ שׁוֹ שׁוֹ שִׂי שִׂי שָׂ

שַׁ שַׂ שָׁ רוֹ רֹ רְ רַ רָ תָ תֹ תֹ תֵ תַ תָ

Remember that the letters *aleph* [א] and *ayin* [ע] are silent in and of themselves. However, they may be accompanied by a vowel that is pronounced. In addition, some words may have an *aleph* or *ayin* that does not have a vowel, and so the two silent consonants are present with zero pronunciation value. In such a case they still provide an important clue to a word's meaning. Pronounce the following open syllables that have *aleph* and *ayin* incorporated into them:

הַעַ גְעַ גַּע בַּא בָא עִי עִי עֻ עוֹ עֹ עַ עַ עַ עַ אוּ אֹ א אִי

אִי אֶ אַ אָ לוּא לְעַ זְעַ זָע זַא חָא חִיא חִיא הוּא הָע וְא

פָא פַע פָא וַא דוֹא דְעַ צָא צֶא נָא נַ נָ נֶע נַ מָא מֶ מָע מ לוּא

Closed syllables

Closed syllables are those which end with a consonant sound as opposed to open syllables you learned about above which end with a vowel sound. Unlike open syllables which often contain only one consonant, closed syllables usually contain a minimum of two consonants, the one which begins the syllable and the one which ends it. Pronouncing closed syllables will give you an opportunity to practice with the final forms of the letters, so watch out for final *khoph* [ך], *mem* [ם], *nun* [ן], *peh* [ף], and *tsadeh* [ץ]. Pronounce the following closed syllables:

אַל אֵל עָם חַג אָב יוֹם יָם דֹר יָד דָם רַם רָם בָּם בּוּז רַב
כֹּל קוֹל אִישׁ חוּץ פּוּן רוּץ מוּל מוּת אוֹת זֹאת שָׁם אֶת אֵל
אַף לֵךְ לָךְ דַּן חֵן הֵן מִן צֹאן פֶּן סוֹף סוּס אוֹף כּוֹף טוֹב
גַּן שֵׁם שָׂר עַד כֵּן רִיב גַּם אִם עַם בִּין בֵּין בֵּן אָח דָּג קַד רַךְ
תֹּף חַף טַף כַּף אַף

Multi-syllable words

Proceeding to multi-syllable words is a relatively simple matter for most words. Multi-syllable words usually have their emphasis on the word's last syllable. This is such a prevalent pattern that you should always pronounce the Hebrew words in this text with their emphasis on the last syllable unless you are directed to do otherwise by an accent mark [<] in this book (The accent mark do not appear in the "Assignments" sections of this book).

Another detail to learn here is what to do with a *heh* [ה] that ends a word. If a *heh* ends a word and has no vowel with it, i.e. if the *heh* closes the last syllable of a word, it is silent. For example, in the word הָיָה The first *heh* is pronounced /h/, and the second is silent. On the other hand, the word-ending *heh* that has a vowel is pronounced /h/ as in the word פִּיהָ Once again, observe the difference:

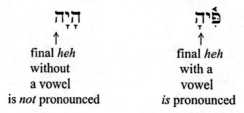

הָיָה	פִּיהָ
↑	↑
final *heh*	final *heh*
without	with a
a vowel	vowel
is *not* pronounced	*is* pronounced

The one exception to this rule is when a *heh* has a dot in it. The dot is not the *dagesh* you learned about earlier. It is a special dot that is only found in final *heh* called a *mappiq*. *Heh* with *mappiq* is pronounced as an aspiration or breath of air at the end of a word. We will not stress or practice with the *mappiq* until Lesson 19.4. All the syllables in the following words are open except for the last syllable which may be open or closed. Pronounce the following words.

אֹמֶר אָמַר אֶחָד עָלָה עָשָׂה עֹשֶׂה דָּבָר פָּנִים בַּיִת אֲשֶׁר
מֹשֶׁה אִשָּׁה לָקַח אֶחָד יָשַׁב אֶרֶץ אֱלֹהִים הִנֵּה הָאֲדָמָה תַּעֲשֶׂה אָמַר
שָׁלַח כֹּהֵן מָלַךְ מֶלֶךְ אֵלֶּה דָּוִד

Silent and vocal shewa

Discerning between silent *shewa* and vocal *shewa* may be tricky for a little while. First we will examine the problem by examining why the silent *shewa* is required. If you recall, every consonant except for an occasional *aleph*, *ayin*, or the last letter in a word must be accompanied by a vowel. However, the need quickly arises for consonants to close *interior* syllables, that is, syllables that are not the last syllables of a word. In the case of a closed interior syllable, a silent "vowel" must be used. For instance, look at the word *Israel* in Hebrew: יִשְׂרָאֵל Let us divide it into syllables:

xiv

יִשְׂ | רָ | אֵל

The first syllable is closed because it ends in a consonant, but the rules of Biblical Hebrew orthography require that the *sin* [שׂ] be accompanied by a vowel. The Jewish scholars who added the nikkud to the consonantal text would use the *shewa* [ְ] in such a case. Basically, because this *sin* closes the interior syllable, the *shewa* is silent, and the syllable is pronounced /yis/.

The next two syllables are easier: one is an open syllable pronounced /ra/ and one is closed, pronounced /el/. Assembled, the entire word is pronounced /yis-ra-EL/.

We can also solve the problem of distinguishing between a silent and vocal *shewa* from another angle by listing the occasions when a *shewa* should be vocalized.[1] Remember that its sound is a brief /uh/:

1. When a *shewa* is under the first letter of a word, it must then be a vocal *shewa* as in יְהוּדָה which is pronounced as three open syllables: יְ | הוּ | דָה

2. When there are two *shewa*s in a row, the second must be vocalized. (It then represents an open syllable made with only one consonant) as in יִשְׁמְרוּ which contains one silent *shewa* and one vocal *shewa*. Once again, the word is pronounced as three syllables:

יִשְׁ | מְ | רוּ
    ↑ ↑
vocal silent

When you pronounce the following words notice how the *qamets* [ָ] is slightly raised inside the final *khoph* [ךָ] as compared to the *qamets'* position with other letters:

אַבְרָהָם	מִצְרַיִם	יְרוּשָׁלַיִם	מִשְׁפָּחָה	שְׁלֹמֹה	פְּלִשְׁתִּי
יִשְׁמְרוּ	יִשְׁמְעוּ	לְמַעַן	וַיְדַבֵּר	וְקָטַל	וְלֹא
וְהָיָה	תִּשְׁמֹר	בְּרִיתִי	תִּקְרָא	יִחְיֶה	אִשְׁתְּךָ
וְיִשְׁמָעֵאל	מַמְרֵא	צָחָקְתְּ	גְּרָר	שְׁכָבְתּוֹ	וְאָמַרְתְּ
וָאֶרְאֶךָ	וַיָּלֶדְתְּ	יִפְגְּעוּ	קֹלֶךָ	גְּחֹנְךָ	יְשׁוּפְךָ

---

[1] Some grammarians teach a third case in which the *shewa* is vocalized, namely, when it follows a long vowel (either *qamets, shureq, hireq, sere,* or *holem*). Our technique will follow more closely the Modern Israeli practice.

xv

Letter combinations

One last detail which we will cover in this brief introduction to pronunciation is letter combinations whose pronunciations cannot be derived from the rules above.

Combination			Sound
יַ	as in	אָחַי	/ai/ as in eye
יָ	as in	אֲדֹנָי	/ai/ as in eye
יו ָ	as in	אֵלָיו	/av/ as in lava
הֶ	as in	רֹאֶה	/e/ as in prey
יֶ	as in	תֵּעָשֶׂינָה	/e/ as in prey
וֹי	as in	גּוֹי	/oi/ as in boy

MODULE ONE—THE HISTORICAL NARRATIVE GENRE AND THE SYSTEM OF VERB FORMS

OVERVIEW: Two of the most repeated terms in this book are *discourse* and *genre*. Recall that a discourse is a self-contained text, maybe long or maybe short, but the text has its own plan, purpose, and meaning. A *genre*, as we will use the term, is a *kind* of discourse.   Because this book has only the modest goals appropriate to a first-year course in Biblical Hebrew, you will not be required to learn all the interesting but technical notional and structural features that distinguish one genre from another. If you are interested you can learn more about the theory behind this approach in Longacre's *Grammar of Discourse* (1983) or in the work of other discourse linguists.   For our purposes, we will distinguish one genre from another quite simply by two features, (1) the GENERIC TASK a writer/speaker performs by using the discourse, and (2) the set of GRAMMATICAL CONSTRUCTIONS that characterize the discourse.

GENRE   = TASK + A SET OF GRAMMATICAL CONSTRUCTIONS
  a discourse type

The study of Biblical Hebrew prose genres is one of the main organizational concepts in this book. To give you an impression of where we are headed, look at the following list of genres you will learn in this course and the tasks they perform.

GENRES AND THE TASKS THEY PERFORM:

GENRE:	TASK:
Historical Narrative	Tell a story about the past.
Predictive Narrative	Tell a story set in the future.
Instructional Discourse	Tell how to do something.
Hortatory Discourse	Influence the behavior of someone.
Procedural Discourse	Tell how a procedure was done in the past.

This first module will be devoted to **Historical Narrative**, the most common genre in the Hebrew Bible, accounting for approximately forty percent of the Hebrew Bible. As shown in the chart above, Historical Narrative's task is to tell a story about the past, so it is the dominant genre from Genesis through 2 Kings and elsewhere such as Jonah and the books of Chronicles. In this module, then, you will learn the set of grammatical constructions that are found in Biblical Hebrew Historical Narrative and how they function to tell a story from the writer/speaker's past.

This is a very exciting module because you will receive the greatest returns on your study efforts for any module in the course. You will learn the most common verb form in the Hebrew Bible the **wayyiqtol** (pronounced /va-yik-TOL/), used over 14,000 times. The wayyiqtol verb form functions as the **mainline** of a Biblical Hebrew story, like a skeleton from which the rest of the story's details hang. The equivalent mainline function in English Historical Narrative is performed by the simple past tense, e.g. the *said* in *And God said*. You will then learn several other verb forms used in Historical Narrative, called as a set, **off-the-line** verb forms. The off-the-line verb forms serve the mainline of the story by giving detail, background, and clarification of the mainline. Finally, you will learn how the one mainline verb form and the several off-the-line verb forms work together in Historical Narrative to give a particular text its **discourse profile**, sort of a "discourse shape."

1

Lesson 1

וַיֹּ֫אמֶר יְהוָה

Genesis 2:18

How the lessons work

As explained in the introduction to this book, each lesson begins with a specially chosen "verse" from the Hebrew Bible. The verse illustrates the small number of topics for that lesson. The fifty lesson verses, taken together, cover much of the material that a first year student needs in approximately the order of its frequency in the Hebrew Bible (To learn *all* the material in this one-year course you will also need to complete the readings that run concurrently with Lessons 15-50). We call the lesson verse a "verse" as a handy name, but to be perfectly accurate, the lesson verse is not always an entire Biblical verse. For simplicity' sake the Biblical verse often has unfamiliar material edited out. Or it may be shortened to allow us to isolate our topics for a particular lesson.

Within any one lesson, you will learn about a small number of topics in basically the same order that the topics appear in the verse as we read from right to left, Hebrew-style. Be advised, however, that all the topics in one lesson can hardly be considered of equal value. Some information is critical to master quickly, other information may be of a less important, explanatory nature. To aid you in identifying the most important information in a lesson, the main goals for each lesson will be given at the start of each lesson.

One of the most common goals for a lesson is to "identify and read" a particular construction. The reading part is a very important concept in this course. It does not mean merely to pronounce the words or merely to translate them. It also means to understand how a particular kind of construction helps a writer achieve his goals. Considering how a writer is pursuing his goals is where discourse analysis comes in. As we begin this first module, remember that you will begin learning about the Historical Narrative genre and how the Hebrew writer uses his language to the best advantage for telling an effective story. [1]

Goals for Lesson 1:

- **Identify and read the Qal wayyiqtol 3rd masculine singular verb form.**
- **Learn the terms associated with the verb analysis chart.**

Pronunciation

1.1a. Pronounce the lesson verse from right to left, a consonant with its vowel, a consonant with its vowel. The last syllable of וַיֹּ֫אמֶר is a closed syllable, so called because it ends with a consonant. It is pronounced /mer/. Most Hebrew words have their accent on the last syllable of a word, but the wayyiqtol form of verb is often an important exception. The *vav* with its *patakh* is so influential upon the word that it often "attracts" the emphasis in the word from its natural place at the end of the word towards the beginning of the word. וַיֹּ֫אמֶר is therefore pronounced /va-YO-mer/. We will refer to this shift in emphasis again later.

To clarify pronunciation in this book, whenever a word has its emphasis on something other than the last syllable, we will provide an accent mark.

1.1b. The nikkud of the second word of our lesson sentence have been left out intentionally. This word is

---

[1] Sternberg, *The Poetics of Biblical Narrative: Ideological Literature and the Drama of Reading* (Bloomington: Indiana U. Press, 1987) 256-257. As the title suggests Sternberg asserts that the Biblical story-teller stretches the Hebrew language's linguistic code to develop the special literary conventions which will communicate the ideals of Biblical faith to best advantage.

the four-letter name for the LORD called the *Tetragrammaton*. For religious reasons, the Masoretes would not pronounce this name of the LORD. As a result this word may appear in the Hebrew Bible without nikkud or with the nikkud of *Adonai* or *Elohim* as a reminder to substitute *Adonai* or *Elohim* when reading aloud. It is very unfortunate that we are not sure how to pronounce this name. Many Christians pronounce the name <u>Jehovah</u>, based on tradition, but some think that the original pronunciation was like /yah-weh/. If you do not wish to pronounce the name, you may substitute *Adonai* whenever you see the Tetragrammaton.

The wayyiqtol

1.2a. A *vav*[ו] at the beginning of a word may mean *and, but,* or *or* no matter what vowel is with it. It will most often appear וַ   וְ   or   וּ   So the concept *and* (*but, or*) never appears in Hebrew as a separate word. It is always found at the beginning of another word.

1.2b. We will begin by noticing something special about the *vav* at the beginning of the word וַיֹּאמֶר
Let us stretch the word out so that we can isolate the special *vav:*

וַ   ·   יֹאמֶר

The word's *vav*, its vowel which is a *patakh*[ַ], and the dot that was in the *yod*[י] have been removed as a unit from the word. You will see momentarily the significance of this unit, but first let us learn more about the dot that comes from the *yod*. The dot that is sometimes seen inside a consonant is called a *dagesh*.

> RULE: If there is a full vowel immediately preceding a consonant with a *dagesh*, it is a **dagesh forte** (strong dagesh), representing a **doubling of the consonant in which it appears**. A full vowel is any vowel other than shewa [ְ].

By the way, the other kind of *dagesh* is a *dagesh lene* or weak *dagesh*. The *dagesh lene* does *not* follow a full vowel. The *dagesh lene* may alter the pronunciation of a letter (for instance, changing a ב to a בּ), but it does not double the letter like a *dagesh forte*.

The י of וַיֹּאמֶר is preceded by a vowel, the *patakh* under the *vav* [וַ]. As a result the dot in the י is a *dagesh forte* which represents a doubled *yod*.

1.2c. When we see the ו at the beginning of a sentence followed by *patakh* and *dagesh forte* [וַּ], the construction has an important effect on the way we understand the attached word.

> [וַּ] indicates:
> 1. The word is a verb which we call the **wayyiqtol** /va-yik-TOL/ **form**.
>
> 2. The subject of the verb is a prefixed pronoun which is indicated by the consonant following the *vav* [ו]. In וַיֹּאמֶר it is the *yod* [י] which is a prefixed pronoun that means *he*. Let us once again stretch out the word so we can better view the *yod*.

וַ   ·   יׁ   אמֶר

To reiterate, the *yod* means *he*. Just for comparison purposes at this point, Let us look at some of the other prefixed pronouns:

תּ-- = *you*

נ-- = *we*

א-- = *I*

There is no need to memorize all of these right now. We will only be dealing with the 3rd masculine singular prefix meaning *he* for a few lessons.

3. Most translators usually use the English simple past for the wayyiqtol verb form.

RULE: **The wayyiqtol verb form functions as the mainline of Historical Narrative discourse. The *vav* + *patakh* + *dagesh forte* (a doubled pronoun consonant) [וַ] indicates one event in a string of events.**

Verb analysis

1.3a. We will now explain the following *Verb analysis chart*:[1]

root	stem	Form	person, gender, number	function	basic root meaning
אמר	Qal	wayyiqtol	3rd m. s. *(he)*	h. n. mainline	*say*

1.3b. **Root:** To understand a Hebrew word, we must figure out its *root*. Most Hebrew words contains a *tri-consonantal* (or *tri-literal*) root. The word's three-lettered root gives the word its basic meaning. This basic meaning can then be modified in a number of fairly patterned variations of pronouncing the root.

Remembering that most Hebrew words are derived from tri-consonantal roots, we must now divine from וַיֹּאמֶר which three consonants constitute the root. Generally speaking, the three consonants of a root will appear together. We will have to decide which consonants from the beginning and/or the end of the word are *not* part of the root. Since we have already accounted for the consonants represented by וַיּ we are left with the three letters of the root אמר which means *say*.

1.3c. **Stem:** The basic meaning of a root is altered by vocalization or pronunciation. Patterned variations in the nikkud or additions of other letters to the root indicate this variation of meaning called the *stem*. We might say that the stem in which a verb is written flavors the root's basic meaning. The basic, unaugmented stem is *Qal* which means in Hebrew *easy* or *basic*. So we can write Qal or Q in the "stem" column of our chart since אמר appears without any augment. There is a good chance this business of

---

[1] The verb analysis charts in this book are adapted from those used in Kittel, Hoffer, and Wright, *Biblical Hebrew*(New Haven: Yale U. Press, 1989) and Ben Zvi, Hancock, and Beinert, *Readings in Biblical Hebrew: An Intermediate Textbook*(New Haven: Yale U. Press, 1993).

4

אָמַר being "unaugmented" is not entirely clear to you. Just trust that it is so for now until you learn some other cases for comparison.

1.3d. Form: In this column we write wayyiqtol. The name of this verb form comes from וַיִּקְטֹל To repeat, it is pronounced /va-yik-TOL/. The *w* of wayyiqtol comes from the thought of some Hebraists that the *vav* was pronounced like our *w* (some Hebraists call ו *waw*), but we will pronounce it /v/. וַיִּקְטֹל is simply the Hebrew root for *kill*, קטל put into the same form, person, number, and gender as our lesson's וַיֹּאמֶר Grammarians have chosen the root קטל to name this verb form because the root conjugates regularly in all forms and stems.

1.3e. Person, Gender, Number: In 1.2c.2 we learned that the *yod* in וַיֹּאמֶר is a prefix that represents the pronoun subject of the verb. More specifically the prefix indicates a third person, masculine, singular ("3rd m. s." on the chart) subject, which in English is *he*. There are only masculine and feminine genders in Hebrew; no neuter as some other languages have. For this reason, a third person, masculine, singular subject may have to be translated as *he* or *it*. A 3rd f. s. subject may have to be translated either *she* or *it*.

1.3f. Function: The verb form and its function within a genre or kind of discourse are closely related. This is the case in any language, including English. The wayyiqtol verb form has the most specialized function of all Biblical Hebrew verb forms. It carries the main plot line, or simply mainline[1] of the Historical Narrative genre in the Hebrew Bible in over 14,000 cases. As the mainline verb form, the wayyiqtol pushes forward a story. The English verb form that performs the same function is the simple past tense. This is not to say that the wayyiqtol verb form is the Biblical Hebrew's simple past tense. It is not exactly. Biblical Hebrew verbs do not bear time signification the same way English verbs do. However, we will usually translate the wayyiqtol using our English simple past tense.

Another key to understanding the function of the wayyiqtol is the *vav*. The *vav* configured with a *patakh* and *dagesh forte* tells us that we are in a string of events. We may, as a result, want to translate the *vav* configuration *and then*. You will learn later when and when not to translate using *then*.

1.3g. Summary: וַיֹּאמֶר is a sentence in Biblical Hebrew, all compressed into one word! Read the following from right to left, Hebrew style:

אָמַר	יְ	וַ
say	*he*	*and* or *and then*
		+ past time translation

Translation: *And (-then) he said.*

Word order

1.4. Not only is the *yod* in וַיֹּאמֶר the subject of the verb, but in Biblical Hebrew another separate word

---

[1] Longacre, *Joseph: A Story of Divine Providence* (Winona Lake: Eisenbrauns, 1989)64, "Discourse grammarians are coming to recognize more and more that in the telling of a story in any language, one particular tense is favored as the carrier of the backbone or storyline of the story while other tenses serve to present the background, supportive, and depictive material in the story," and "A chain of (necessarily verb-initial) clauses that contain preterites[our wayyiqtols] is the backbone of any Old Testament story."

can also specify the subject. In our lesson sentence, this is the case with the tetragrammaton יהוה The concept <u>he</u>, embedded within our lesson's verb refers to יהוה In Biblical Hebrew, the word order is usually verb-subject or V-S. When we translate a Biblical Hebrew sentence that is in the usual V-S word order, we will use the usual English word order which is S-V.

Complete translation: *And (then) YHWH said.*

Assignments:

1.5a. Learn all the particles, and the first fifty words on your vocabulary list which begins on p. 411. For now, you only need to memorize the gloss or "meaning" that is boldfaced. You will need these particles and fifty words for the first eight lessons, but you do not need to know them all "cold" before you go on to Lesson 2. Review the first fifteen proper nouns a couple of times.

1.5b. Below is Genesis 44:22-26. You should be able to find and circle five wayyiqtols based on what you have learned so far. Even though you cannot understand them yet, you can find them. Each one represents another event in a string of events. Keep in mind that the letter following the *vav* is not always a yod. Your only obligations are to a *vav* with a *patakh*, followed by a *dagesh forte*. By the way, any *dagesh* which follows a *patakh* is a *dagesh forte*.

וַנֹּאמֶר אֶל־אֲדֹנִי לֹא־יוּכַל הַנַּעַר לַעֲזֹב אֶת־אָבִיו

וְעָזַב אֶת־אָבִיו וָמֵת: וַתֹּאמֶר אֶל־עֲבָדֶיךָ אִם־לֹא יֵרֵד

אֲחִיכֶם הַקָּטֹן אִתְּכֶם לֹא תֹסִפוּן לִרְאוֹת פָּנָי:

וַיְהִי כִּי עָלִינוּ אֶל־עַבְדְּךָ אָבִי וַנַּגֶּד־לוֹ אֵת דִּבְרֵי אֲדֹנִי:

וַיֹּאמֶר אָבִינוּ שֻׁבוּ שִׁבְרוּ־לָנוּ מְעַט־אֹכֶל:

וַנֹּאמֶר לֹא נוּכַל לָרֶדֶת

6

Lesson 2

וַיְדַבֵּר אֱלֹהִים אֶל־מֹשֶׁה וַיֹּאמֶר אֵלָיו אֲנִי יהוה

Exodus 6:2

Goals:
- **Identify and read the Piel wayyiqtol 3rd masculine singular verb form.**
- **Identify the speaker and addressee of a speech introduction formula.**
- **Identify and read a verbless clause.**

Clauses

2.1. Read the lesson verse. It is actually three clauses. *Clause* is a critical term in this book, so we must have a clear definition.

> DEFINITION: **A** *clause* **is a Biblical Hebrew statement, the heart of which is a subject and predicate unit.** Usually the predicate is a verb, and each verb identifies another clause. There are a couple exceptions, the most important of which is learned later in this lesson called *a verbless clause*. Clauses that can stand alone as Biblical Hebrew sentences are **independent clauses**. Clauses that cannot stand as complete thoughts and must be grammatically tied to another independent clause are **dependent clauses**.

The first two clauses in our lesson sentence, as you can see, contain wayyiqtols.

Piel stem in וַיְדַבֵּר

2.2a. To analyze a verb we begin by removing the "appendages" from the beginning and/or end of the word until we are left with the three letters of the *tri-consonantal root* (see 1.3b).

What verb form does the initial [וַ] indicate?_____ (1.2c.1)

What genre of discourse does the [וַ] indicate?_____ (1.2c rule)

What kind of *dagesh* is in the *yod* [יְ]?_____ (1.2b)

What kind of *dagesh* is in the *bet* [בּ]?_____

2.2b. After we remove the sign of the wayyiqtol form from our word we are left with דבבר from which to determine the root. Why two *bets* (ב)? Remember that a *dagesh forte* doubles the letter in which it is found.

> RULE: **The doubling of the middle consonant of a tri-consonantal root by a** *dagesh forte* **is the sign of the** *Piel stem*.

So דבר is the tri-consonantal root, having been augmented by the addition of an extra *bet*, and

7

consequently, made Piel stem. The Piel stem refers to the causing of something to be in a state or condition. דבר means *to speak*, or to be consistent with the definition of the Piel alteration, *to cause to be verbalized*.

Although דבר is used almost exclusively in the Piel stem, we will later study roots that are used in both the Qal and the Piel stems. At that time it will become clearer how the Piel stem modifies the basic meaning of a word. For now let us be satisfied with *speak* as a meaning for דבר

2.2c. Fill out the verb analysis chart:

root	stem	form	person, gender, number	function	basic root meaning

2.2d. As we translate the verb, let us stretch out the word as we did in 1.3g.

דַּבֵּר   יְ   וַ

speak   *he*   *And* or *And then*

                                  + past tense translation

Translation: *And (then) he spoke*

2.2e. Our lesson word will usually appear in the Biblical Hebrew texts <u>without</u> the *dagesh forte* in the *yod*, וַיְדַבֵּר instead of וַיְּדַבֵּר as in our lesson sentence. In pronunciation, the strong influence of the *vav-patakh* unit at the beginning of the wayyiqtol verb form is overcome by the even stronger influence of the doubled middle root letter *of the Piel stem*. It is as though the Piel stem and the wayyiqtol verb form compete for the pronunciation emphasis, and the Piel wins out. Even though Piel stem verbs in the wayyiqtol form will often have no *dagesh forte* in the prefix subject, we will still label them wayyiqtol. You must be able to identify this exceptional form of wayyiqtol.

אֱלֹהִים

This Hebrew word means *Elohim* or *God*. What is the relationship of the word to the verb before it?

_____ (1.4) This word has the masculine plural ending יִם -- The word can means *gods, mighty ones*, or *judges*, as well as *God*. Most often it is used for *God*, with a singular sense and hence, the 3rd m. s. prefix pronoun in וַיְדַבֵּר

Translation: *And (then) God spoke*

The addressee

2.4a. אֶל is a preposition which means *to, unto*. It appears twice in our lesson verse, both times after a verb that can introduce speech. It identifies the person to whom the speech is addressed, the **addressee**.

2.4b. In the first instance אֶל־מֹשֶׁה the dash, called a **maqqef** is not a punctuation mark strictly speaking, even though it looks like one of ours. It is part of the marking system introduced to the Hebrew Bible by the Masoretes. It indicates to the oral reader that several words are to be pronounced as one pronunciation unit with one emphasized syllable in the unit. However, because phrasing in oral reading naturally tends to coincide with grammatical phrasing, the *maqqef* usually indicates close grammatical relationship as well as pronunciation

2.4b.1. מֹשֶׁה is the name Moses, but it is pronounced /mo-SHEH/. You will find that our traditional English pronunciations are often quite different than Hebrew pronunciations of the same names.

Translation: *to Moses*

2.4c. In the second instance of אֶל in the lesson sentence it has a suffix attached to it אֵלָיו A ו or וֹ at the end of a word means *him* or *his*. **The same suffixes can be either objective** (e. g., *him*) **or possessive** (e.g., *his*). Since our lesson suffix is attached to a preposition, it is the object of the preposition. The object of a preposition would translate into the objective *him*. Here is another way to think of it: Would we say *He said to him, "..."* or *He said to his, "..."*? Context is very helpful for knowing whether the ו or וֹ means *him* or *his*.

2.4d. Notice that the addition of the suffix has caused the vowel which is normally in אֶל to change. A word's vowels normally change when a suffix is added. The י between the word אֵל and the suffix ו connects the two and has no meaning itself.

Translation: *to him*

2.4e. Our lesson verse is the typical way for a Biblical Hebrew writer, or English writer for that matter, will begin a dialogue with ***speech introduction formulas.*.* He makes it clear who the participants in the dialogue are by naming them both. *And then God spoke to Moses* tells us God and Moses are probably about to have a conversation. Less specification is necessary in the second half of our lesson verse because both dialogue participants have already been identified. God is then referred to as *he*, and Moses as *him*.

וַיֹּאמֶר

2.5. Fill out the verb analysis chart (1.3) for וַיֹּאמֶר :

root	stem	form	person, gender, number	function	basic root meaning

Translate וַיְדַבֵּר אֱלֹהִים אֶל־מֹשֶׁה וַיֹּאמֶר אֵלָיו :

Direct speech

2.6a. The third and last clause in our lesson is comprised of the two Hebrew words אֲנִי יהוה These two words are the direct speech which וַיֹּאמֶר introduces. Notice there are no quotation marks, other punctuation marks, or capital letters to mark the beginning of direct speech as there are in English. A speech introduction formula such as וַיֹּאמֶר and context are the best clues as to when direct speech begins or ends. It may seem redundant in our lesson sentence that the same bit of speech is introduced twice, first by וַיְדַבֵּר and then by וַיֹּאמֶר but this is common practice in Biblical Hebrew narrative. Often, וַיֹּאמֶר is preceded by a wayyiqtol verb form which relates the *manner* in which the speech was given and then וַיֹּאמֶר marks the beginning of the actual speech, similar to our quotation marks.

2.6b. Direct speech is a critical part of Hebrew narrative, carrying much of the action and detail of the accounts in the Hebrew Bible and very useful to the Hebrew writers for building suspense.

The verbless clause

2.7a. אֲנִי means *I.* יהוה means _____ (1.1b)

2.7b. The words אֲנִי יהוה are the third clause of our lesson verse even though they lack the *to be-* verb that would be necessary in English to make a complete sentence. Hebrew is very efficient!

> RULE: When two nouns or a noun and pronoun are put together so that one renames the other, we have a **noun sentence**, otherwise known as a **verbless clause**, requiring the English verb *to be* for translation.

The noun sentence or verbless clause is considerably more common in direct speech and poetry than narrative discourse because it labels or describes rather than moves forward the plot of a story. This book will usually use the term *verbless clause*.

> RULE: **The verbless clause gives scene-setting information in Historical Narrative.**

Translation: *I am the LORD* or *I am YHWH.*

2.7c. The **subject** of a clause is the *topic* about which a comment is made in the clause. The **predicate** is the *comment* about that topic. So the verbless clause in our lesson sentence has the word order S-P. This is important because the ancient Hebrew would switch the word order to change the nuance of meaning. [1]

> RULE: **Standard word order for a verbless clause is S-P.** Any deviation from this standard word order will move some element to the first position in the clause, thereby

---

[1] A long-standing thesis is presented by Anderson, *The Hebrew Verbless Clause in the Pentateuch* (Nashville: Abington, 1970), and followed largely by Waltke and O'Connor(1990), §8.4 in which S-P word order in verbless clauses has the function *identification* and P-S order has the function *description*. However, this text follows Buth, "Word Order in the Verbless Clause: A Generative-Functional Approach," *The Verbless Clause in Biblical Hebrew*, ed. Miller (Winona Lake: Eisenbrauns, 1999), 79-108.

creating a focus on the "fronted" element. [1]

2.7d.   Since the Hebrew writer would play with the word order in a verbless clause, it is occasionally difficult or impossible to know which half of a Hebrew verbless clause is the subject and which is the predicate. On the other hand, there are two helpful clues that will decide most cases:[2]

1.   **A subject pronoun is always the subject.** In the first fifty vocabulary words you learned אֲנִי Another couple of examples are אַתָּה meaning *you* (masculine, singular) and הֵם meaning *they* (masculine, plural), which are both in your next fifty vocabulary words.

2.   **The subject is what is already known by context.** The predicate is what is new. For example, look at some of 1 Samuel 1:1 in English: *There was a man... His name was Elkanah.* The existence of a man is made known by the first sentence. In the second sentence, the word *His* refers back to the man. It refers back to the known. The new information is the name *Elkanah.* In Hebrew the word order is the standard S-P: שְׁמוֹ אֶלְקָנָה If the word order had been אֶלְקָנָה שְׁמוֹ an oral reader would emphasize the name אֶלְקָנָה to reflect the focus put on the name by the shift in word order.[3]

Assignments

2.8a.   As you translate the following items, you may write the English on this page, but you should eventually wean yourself from this practice, leaving the Hebrew in Hebrew.

Hosea 1:4

1.   וַיֹּאמֶר יהוה אֵלָיו

Exodus 6:13   The word you do not know is a name.

2.   וַיְדַבֵּר יהוה אֶל־מֹשֶׁה וְאֶל אַהֲרֹן

Exodus 32: 21

3.   וַיֹּאמֶר מֹשֶׁה אֶל־אַהֲרֹן

Judges 11:13

4.   וַיֹּאמֶר מֶלֶךְ

Psalm 10:16   This is the first time you have seen the *tetragrammaton* with one of its customary sets of nikkud (see 1.1b).

5.   יְהוָה מֶלֶךְ

1 Samuel 21:12   Another name here.

6.   דָּוִד מֶלֶךְ

Joshua 22:34   You can see in this clause how difficult it can be to distinguish subject from predicate without a context.

7.   יהוה אֱלֹהִים

---

[1] In a sense, this rule suggests one of the guiding principles of a discourse analytical approach to a language. We do our best to determine what are the dominant structures in a language and consider them *unmarked.* Deviations from these unmarked structures are *marked.* That is, the deviant structures stand out from the regular flow of text and are useful for guiding a listener/reader through a text.

[2] A more rigorous rule for differentiating between the subject and the predicate of a verbless clause is by the criterion "relative definiteness." The subject will be the more relatively definite of the two. For a thorough treatment of this criterion see Lowery, "Relative Definiteness and the Verbless Clause," *The Verbless Clause in Biblical Hebrew*, ed. Miller (Winona Lake: Eisenbrauns, 1999), 251.

[3] Buth(1999), 103.

2.8b. Check (√) the **two** verbless clauses below that have special focus on a fronted predicate:

8.____ אֲנִי יוֹסֵף Genesis 45:3 (Yet another name.)

9.____ אֲנִי יְהוָה Leviticus 18:30

10.____ עֲמָלֵקִי אָנֹכִי 2 Samuel 1:8
(אָנֹכִי is long for אֲנִי and עֲמָלֵקִי means *an Amalekite*)

11.____ וַאֲנִי עַם Joshua 17:14

12.____ אִשָּׁה אָנֹכִי 1 Samuel 1:15 (אִשָּׁה means *a woman*)

Lesson 3

וַיֵּ֥לֶךְ מֹשֶׁ֑ה וַיְדַבֵּ֛ר אֶת־הַדְּבָרִ֥ים אֶל־כָּל־יִשְׂרָאֵֽל

Deuteronomy 31:1

Goals:

- Identify and read Qal wayyiqtol forms derived from first *yod* [י] roots and הלך
- Identify the sign of the DDO.
- Identify the definite article.
- Identify the masculine plural ending

What we already know

3.1a. Each lesson from this point forward will begin with a short section which scans our lesson verse for what we already know. This brief section has a two-fold purpose: (1) It serves as a review. (2) It helps to relate new topics to what you have learned before.

3.1b. When you scan our lesson verse you can now spot the [·וַ] at the beginning, knowing that it is the

sign of the _____ verb form (1.2c) and_____

discourse (1.2 rule). Is there another wayyiqtol in our lesson verse? _____ Why doesn't it have a

dagesh in the *yod*? _____ (2.2e)

3.1c. The first word of the lesson verse וַיֵּ֥לֶךְ ends with a final *khoph* [ך]. You may have wondered about the two dots inside the letter. They are a silent *shewa*, slightly raised just as we have seen a *qamets* is when it is with a *khoph*. One idiosyncrasy of Biblical Hebrew is that the final *khoph* almost never appears without a vowel even though other letters, when final in a word, more often than not appear a silent *shewa*.

First *yod* roots in wayyiqtol

3.2a. The י in וַיֵּ֥לֶךְ is the _____ (1.2c.2) Once we have removed the sign of the wayyiqtol verb form we are left with only two root letters: ל + ך Yet there is still a tri-consonantal root to be found.

> RULE: When one of the letters of a root is missing from a wayyiqtol (or yiqtol) verb
> form, **the nikkud under the prefix subject pronoun will indicate what the missing
> letter is.** In the case of a *tsere*, as is under our *yod* [יֵ], the missing letter will normally
> be the first letter of the root, and the missing letter is *yod* .

It just so happens that our lesson verse's first word, a very common word in the wayyiqtol form, is one exception to the above rule. The missing letter is ה so that the root is הלך which means *walk*. The root הלך acts just like a root with a *yod* as a first letter. Eventually you will learn a total of four

13

missing letter rules, all of which are shown in "Helpful Chart I" near the back of the book.

3.2b. Fill out the verb analysis chart for וַיֵּלֶךְ :

Root	Stem	form	person, gender, number	function	basic root meaning

No letters have been added to our word, only taken away, so the stem is Qal. Easy, right? The meaning is therefore the basic *go* or *walk*.

Translation: *And (then) he went (or walked).*

3.3. What is the relationship of מֹשֶׁה to וַיֵּלֶךְ ?_____ (1.4)

Translation: *And (then) Moses went*

Qamets-khatuf

3.4. The narrative which was begun with the wayyiqtol verb form וַיֵּלֶךְ continues in our lesson verse

with the next wayyiqtol, one which should look familiar to you. וַיְדַבֵּר means_____(2.2d)

3.5a. We can now skip one word to another word which also should look familiar to you אֶל־ which

means_____ As before this word introduces a prepositional phrase the rest of which is כָּל־יִשְׂרָאֵל

יִשְׂרָאֵל means_____

3.5b. That leaves us with כָּל which appears as כֹּל in your vocabulary list meaning *all*. To understand its spelling, we have to remember the significance of the *maqqefs*(2.4b) in the phrase. Recall that the *maqqefs* tie together several words into one pronunciation unit with one accented syllable. In the case of אֶל־כָּל־יִשְׂרָאֵל the last syllable of the entire unit, as usual, gets the emphasis. The *qamets* under the *koph* of כָּל therefore has a special pronunciation just as a *holem*.

> RULE: A *qamets* in a **closed and unaccented syllable** is called a **qamets-khatuf** and should be pronounced as a *holem* /o/.

By far, the most common occurrence of the *qamets-khatuf* is in the word כָּל which is invariably pronounced with an /o/ sound.

Translation: *to all Israel*

14

The sign of the DDO and the definite article

3.6a. In the sentences we have studied so far the slot after the wayyiqtol verb form and before the prepositional phrase has been filled by a subject word if there is one. In our lesson verse, however, there is no subject word. Remember that an independent subject word is optional in a Biblical Hebrew sentence. אֶת־הַדְּבָרִים is the direct object in the sentence.

A direct object answers the question ___(subject)___ ___(verb)___ *whom or what?* For instance, when analyzing the sentence "Herb studies Hebrew every night," the direct object answers the question *Herb studies whom or what?* The answer, of course, is *Hebrew.*

The direct object in our lesson verse is very easy to spot because of the particle אֵת which is the **sign of the definite direct object (DDO)**.

> RULE: **The DDO is not translated. It is an optional marker of *definite* direct objects.** Definiteness will be described fully in Lesson 6. Even when the direct object is definite, the DDO is not always used. It is used less in poetry than prose.[1]

3.6b. You may recall the masculine plural noun ending on אֱלֹהִים It is also used on הַדְּבָרִים Actually הַדְּבָרִים is made of three parts:

> הַ֫ = *the*
>
> דְבַר = *word*
>
> ֹים = *plural*
>
> RULE: הַ֫ meaning *the*, is always attached to the beginning of a word just like the particle וְ meaning *and*. Before letters that cannot take a *dagesh* (ר ע ח ה א) we will see *qamets* under the *heh* instead of *patakh*. E.g. הָאִישׁ meaning *the man.*

Notes:
1. The letters that cannot take a dagesh are called the **guttural letters**. Once again: ר ע ח ה א
2. Nouns without the definite article הַ֫ will often need *a/an* for a smooth translation. There is no article *a/an* in Hebrew.

Translation of the entire verse: *And (then) Moses went, and he spoke the words to all Israel.*

Assignments:
3.7a. Translate:

Genesis 12:4   וַיֵּלֶךְ אַבְרָם 1.

Genesis 26:1 Can you guess the two names?   וַיֵּלֶךְ יִצְחָק אֶל־אֲבִימֶלֶךְ 2.

---

[1] Actually, many Hebraists no longer accept the function of אֵת as being the marker of the definite direct object even though it does account for the vast majority of the uses of the particle. For more on this issue, see 42.4.

3. וַיֵּלֶךְ אֶל־אַרְצוֹ

Exodus 18:27 אַרְצוֹ = אֶרֶץ + וֹ (see 2.4c)

4. וַיֹּאמֶר הָאִישׁ נָסָעוּ וַיֵּלֶךְ יוֹסֵף

Genesis 37:17 נָסְעוּ means *They have left*. And יוֹסֵף = another name.

5. וַיֹּאמֶר יְהוָה אֶל־אַהֲרֹן לֵךְ וַיֵּלֶךְ

Exodus 4:27 לֵךְ = *Go!*

6. וַיֵּלֶךְ אֵלָיו וַיֹּאמֶר הֲלָנוּ אַתָּה

Joshua 5:13 הֲלָנוּ אַתָּה = *Are you for us?*

7. וַיֹּאמֶר אֵלָיו הַאַתָּה אִישׁ־הָאֱלֹהִים וַיֹּאמֶר אָנִי

1 Kings 13:14 The *heh* in הַאַתָּה is *not* the definite article. הַאַתָּה means *Are you...?* אִישׁ־הָאֱלֹהִים means *the man of God*. Note the affirmative answer in number 7. There is no word for *yes* in Biblical Hebrew.

8. וַיֵּצֵא מֹשֶׁה וְאַהֲרֹן

Exodus 8:8 Notice how a 3rd m. s. subject is used with a compound subject. In English we would use a plural verb. In Hebrew both singular and plural are found with a compound subject like this one.

9. וַיֵּצֵא דָוִד

1 Samuel 18:5

10. וַיֵּצֵא הֲתָךְ אֶל־מָרְדְּכָי

Esther 4:6 The second and forth words are names.

11. וַיֵּצֵא הַשָּׂטָן

Job 1:12 שָׂטָן means *adversary*, and we recognize it as a name of the devil.

12. וַיֵּצֵא אֵלָיו

1 Kings 20:33

13. וַיֵּשֶׁב מֹשֶׁה לִשְׁפֹּט

Exodus 18:13 לִשְׁפֹּט means *to judge*.

14. וַיֵּשֶׁב הָעָם

Exodus 32:6 We think of *people* as a plural noun, but here you see it can sometimes be used as a singular noun in Hebrew.

16

Lesson 4
וַיִּשְׁמַע יִתְרוֹ אֵת כָּל־אֲשֶׁר עָשָׂה אֱלֹהִים
Exodus 18:1

Goals:
- **Identify a dependent clause by a relative pronoun.**
- **Identify and read the relative past background given by a Qal qatal verb form in a dependent clause.**

What we already know

4.1a. Translate the wayyiqtol at the beginning of our lesson verse_____

What does the wayyiqtol tell us about the genre of discourse we are in? _____

4.1b. יִתְרוֹ is the name *Jethro*. Is it Jethro who heard, or is it Jethro who was heard. In other words, is Jethro the subject of וַיִּשְׁמַע or the direct object? Before you answer, consider the particle that follows

יִתְרוֹ _____

4.1c. אֵת is the DDO even though the nikkud is different than in our last lesson. (We will explain the difference in the nikkud in a later chapter.) In this case, the entire phrase that follows the DDO fills the direct object slot within the sentence. Since we have a DDO to mark the direct object in this sentence, יִתְרוֹ must be the subject of the sentence.

Translation: *And (then) Jethro heard [something]*

4.1d. We still know more: Is כָּל pronounced /kal/ or /kol/?_____ (3.5b rule)

And it means_____

Translation: *and (then) Jethro heard all (or every) [something]*

All-purpose relative pronoun

4.2a. אֲשֶׁר is the all-purpose relative pronoun in Biblical Hebrew. Relative pronouns are illustrated as the italicized words in the English sentences below.

> I like *what* you like.
> Can I taste the ice cream *that* you just ordered.
> I want to know *who* broke the window.
> The Bible, *which* he had purchased last year, was already worn.
> You can give the scholarship to *whomever* you have deemed worthy.

Essentially, אֲשֶׁר signals a **dependent clause**. A dependent clause is like the underlined sections above,

17

not a complete thought that can stand on its own as a sentence. It must be grammatically tied to an independent clause so that it does not "dangle." In Biblical Hebrew you may have to translate אֲשֶׁר using any of the italicized words above or others. It may serve you well to try *that, what,* or *who* first, reserving final judgment until you see what fits the context best.

4.2b. Two other Hebrew words also result in dependent clauses and are very commonly followed by the qatal verb form. They are אִם (meaning *if*) and כִּי (meaning *when, because*).

The Qatal

4.3a. You have been taught that the wayyiqtol verb form functions as the mainline of the Historical Narrative genre in Biblical Hebrew. Before we proceed to the specifics of another verb form, the qatal, it is important for you to understand a principle that holds true in any genre of Biblical discourse.

> RULE: Every genre of discourse has a mainline clause type constructed with a particular verb form. **All other clause types (constructed with other verb forms) within that genre are off-the-line. Off-the-line clauses are subordinate to, or serve the mainline.** Each off-the-line verb form has functions that are particular to it.

4.3b. The qatal verb form has two functions in Historical Narrative, one of which we will learn in this lesson and one of which we will learn in the next lesson. To reiterate, the qatal verb form, when it follows אֲשֶׁר (or אִם or כִּי) is in a **dependent clause,** that is, a clause that cannot stand on its own as a complete thought.

> RULE: A qatal form, when in a dependent clause, functions in Biblical Hebrew by giving **background in the relative past.** Relative past means *past as compared to the main clause of the sentence.* In Historical Narrative the main clause will most often be the wayyiqtol clause.

4.3c. Finding the root of the verb עָשָׂה is easy because there are only three letters. All the letters are part of the root, which means *make, do.* As for stem, there is no evidence of any augment to the root so we

can assume what stem?_____ (1.3c)

4.3d. Whereas, with the wayyiqtol verb form, the subject is a letter prefixed to the verb, with the qatal verb form the subject is a letter or letters affixed to the end of the verb. We will refer to the subject pronoun of the wayyiqtol as the **prefix** and the subject pronoun of the qatal as the **affix.**

4.3e. In the case of our lesson verb the affix is null[Ø]. This is always the affix for the third person, masculine, singular subject pronoun, our *he, it.* Just to clarify by comparison, the affix for second person, masculine, singular, our *you,* is תָ –

Qatal in the Qal stem

שָׁמַע
[Ø] affix meaning *he*

שָׁמַעְתָּ
[תָ] affix meaning *you*

18

4.3f. Fill out the verb analysis chart for עָשָׂה :

root	stem	form	person, gender, number	function	basic root meaning
				qatal in dep. clause = relative past background	

4.3g. Notice the vowel under the first root letters in each Hebrew word in the chart above. It is *qamets*.

RULE: A *qamets* under the **first root letter** is the sign of the **qatal verb form** in the **Qal stem**.

4.3h. To capture the *relative past background* meaning of a qatal which follows אֲשֶׁר we use the English verb form which performs the same function, the past or present perfect which uses the helping verb *had, have* or *has*. For now let your instincts guide you as to which of the helping verbs you use. You will learn a more technical method later.

Translation of the dependent clause: *which he had done*

Word order

4.4a. The word order in our lesson verse's dependent clause is the same as we have seen in main clauses with the wayyiqtol verb form, V-S. So what would the relationship of אֱלֹהִים be to the verb עָשָׂה ?

_____

Translation of the dependent clause complete with its subject: *which God had done*

4.4b. Translate the entire lesson verse_____

Assignments
4.5a. Translate:

1. וַיִּשְׁמַע אֶת כֹּל אֲשֶׁר אָמַר	9. וַיֵּצֵא מֹשֶׁה	17. וַיֵּדַע אֶת אֲשֶׁר עָשָׂה אַבְרָהָם
2. וַיִּשְׁמַע מֹשֶׁה אֶת כֹּל אֲשֶׁר שָׁלַח	10. וַיֵּלֶךְ מֹשֶׁה	18. וַיֵּדַע אֶת כָּל־אֲשֶׁר אָכַל
3. וַיִּשְׁמַע כֹּל אֲשֶׁר עָשָׂה אַבְרָהָם	11. וַיֵּשֶׁב	19. וַיֵּדַע אֶת אֲשֶׁר שָׁמַע
4. וַיִּשְׁמַע מֹשֶׁה אֲשֶׁר אָמַר	12. וַיֵּלֶךְ	20. וַיֵּדַע כֹּל אֲשֶׁר עָשָׂה אַבְרָהָם
5. וַיִּשְׁמַע אֶת כֹּל אֲשֶׁר אָכַל	13. וַיֵּשֶׁב מֹשֶׁה	21. וַיֵּדַע אֶת אֲשֶׁר נָתַן אַבְרָהָם
6. וַיִּשְׁמַע כָּל־אֲשֶׁר רָאָה אַבְרָהָם	14. וַיֵּדַע מֹשֶׁה	22. וַיֵּדַע מֹשֶׁה אֶת כָּל־אֲשֶׁר לָקַח
7. וַיִּשְׁמַע מֹשֶׁה אֶת כָּל־אֲשֶׁר אָמַר	15. וַיֵּדַע	23. וַיֵּדַע מֹשֶׁה אֶת אֲשֶׁר אָמַר
8. וַיִּשְׁמַע מֹשֶׁה אֲשֶׁר נָתַן אַבְרָהָם	16. וַיֵּצֵא	24. וַיֵּדַע אֶת כָּל־אֲשֶׁר רָאָה

19

4.5b. Translate:

Genesis 48:9 בָּנַי הֵם means *they are my sons...*

1. וַיֹּאמֶר יוֹסֵף בָּנַי הֵם אֲשֶׁר־נָתַן אֱלֹהִים

Exodus 18:24 Beware: missing ה on וַיַּעַשׂ

2. וַיִּשְׁמַע מֹשֶׁה וַיַּעַשׂ כֹּל אֲשֶׁר אָמָר

Genesis 24:66 סִפֵּר in the Piel stem means *recount (a story)* and דָּבָר can mean *thing* as well as *word*.

3. וַיְסַפֵּר אֵת כָּל־הַדְּבָרִים אֲשֶׁר עָשָׂה

Genesis 45:27 This time a missing ה on הָעֲגָלוֹת and וַיַּרְא means *the wagons*.

4. וַיַּרְא אֶת־הָעֲגָלוֹת אֲשֶׁר־שָׁלַח יוֹסֵף

Genesis 22:3 מָקוֹם means *place*.

5. וַיֵּלֶךְ אֶל־הַמָּקוֹם אֲשֶׁר־אָמַר הָאֱלֹהִים

Ezekiel 37:24 עֲלֵיהֶם means *over them*.

6. דָּוִד מֶלֶךְ עֲלֵיהֶם

Genesis 9:24 לוֹ is made of two parts, the preposition ל and the suffix וֹ

7. וַיֵּדַע אֵת אֲשֶׁר־עָשָׂה־לוֹ

4.5c. Fill out verb analysis charts for the two verbs in number 1, the three verbs in number 2, and the first verb in number 5.

Lesson 5

וּלְאָדָם אָמַר

Genesis 3:17

Goal:

• **Identify and read the X-qatal construction.**

What we already know

5.1a. The first word in our lesson verse is pronounced /ul-a-DAM/. The *shewa* under the *lamed* is a silent *shewa* because it closes or ends a syllable.[1]

5.1b. We have only two words in our lesson verse, and you should be able to find the verb. Fill out the verb analysis chart:

root	stem	form	person, gender, number	function	basic root meaning

We will have to save the function column of the chart until later in the lesson. This lesson verse does not have the qatal form in a dependent clause as we studied in Lesson 4. Since the qatal is part of a different construction in our lesson verse, the function is also changed. We do not have the function "relative past background" in this verse.

The significance of the qatal

5.2. It is time to begin further developing your understanding of the qatal verb form. **The qatal verb form gives an attribute to the subject of the verb.**[2] This is a difficult concept to capture consistently in the

---

[1] Some teachers maintain that a *shewa* that follows a long vowel (either shureq, holem or qamets) is a vocal *shewa,* resulting here in /ul-e-a-DAM/. We adhere more closely to common modern Israeli pronunciation.

[2] This description of the verbal semantics of the qatal verb form as an attribution represents one of a few decisions in this book to go down "the road less traveled." Most grammarians hold that the qatal is the simple past tense of Biblical Hebrew, equal in meaning to a wayyiqtol. See Gesenius, *Gesenius' Hebrew Grammar* (Oxford: Clarendon U. Press, 1910), §106; Jouon/Muraoka, *A Grammar of Biblical Hebrew* (Rome: Editris Pontifico Instituto Biblico, 1993), §112; Lambdin, *Introduction to Biblical Hebrew* (NY: Charles Scribner's and Sons, 1971), §44.1. Waltke and O'Connor(1990), §30 assign qatal an aspectual rather than time referent asserting that the qatal expresses a complete situation as one unanalyzable whole. This writer finds both positions untenable and holds to an interpretation of the qatal which is more reflective of its origin, described variously as nominal, stative, adjectival, attributive. This account of its origin is held by Brockelmann, *Hebräische Syntax* (Neukirchen: Neukirchen Verlag, 1956), §41; Bergsträsser, *Introduction to the Semitic languages*, trans. Daniels (Winona Lake: Eisenbrauns, 1983), §1.2.2.2; Hetzron, "Hebrew," *The World's Major Languages*, ed. Comrie (NY: Oxford, 1990) 661. Simply put then, I hold to a meaning for the qatal that views the meaning of the form at a more primitive stage of development than generally held. Cf. Turner, "The Tenses of the Hebrew Verb," *Studies Biblical and Oriental* (Edinburgh: Black, 1876), 384; Michel, *Tempora und Satzstellung in den Psalmen* (Bonn: Bouvier, 1960), 110 and quoted in Waltke and O'Connor(1990), 473; Hatav, *The Semantics of Aspect and Modality: Evidence from English and Biblical Hebrew* (Philadelphia: John Benjamins, 1997), 18, 177; and Eskhult, *Studies in Verbal Aspect and Narrative Technique in Biblical Hebrew Prose*(Uppsala: Uppsala

English language. Fortunately, our main concern in this course is *understanding* Biblical Hebrew, not *translating* it. Therefore, we can "talk our way to the concept." Translate many of the qatal verb forms which do not follow אֲשֶׁר (or אִם or כִּי) as "attributions." For your translation, use an *-er* word or a gerund (*-ing* noun) + possessive pronoun. In translation, you may need to add an extra word *of* if the verb is an action verb that takes a direct object.

Translation of אָמַר : *He was a sayER (of)*

or

His sayING (of)

Notes:

1. The word *of* is optional. Use *of* when the clause contains a direct object. In other words, if the action of the verb is done *to something or someone* you will need the word *of* in your translation.
2. The use of the *er*-word will be much more common.
3. The subject or doer of the verb אָמַר is not specified in our lesson verse, so it is translated according to the null affix ending which means 3rd m. s., our *he, it*. If you would read the verses before our lesson verse in your Bible, you would see that the subject of the verb is *YHWH* God.
4. The significance of the qatal as a verb form that pins an attribute on its subject may seem an overly abstract concept right now. Don't worry. We will be constantly developing this idea with numerous examples as the book progresses. Allow the course to unfold like a good movie in which each scene's contribution to the over-all theme of the movie is not instantly clear.

X-qatal

5.3a. The first word in our lesson verse is made of three parts as follows:

ו‍ = *And* (Note that the nikkud with the *vav* does not alter the meaning of it. A *vav* at the beginning of a word always means *and, but, or*.)

לְ = *to, for* (like אֶל)

אָדָם = *Adam, man*

Translate וּלְאָדָם :_____

5.3b. The word וּלְאָדָם is the indirect object in our lesson verse. An indirect object answers the question "To whom or what?" about a verb and its subject. Our verse is about some speaking that was going on to Adam.

> **RULE: In Historical Narrative a qatal verb form will almost never occur in the first position of a clause called the *clause-initial* position.**

The qatal verb form in Historical Narrative will be preceded by one or the other of two elements: (1) a word like אֲשֶׁר אִם or כִּי resulting in a *dependent clause* or (2) some other element resulting in an

---

U., 1990), §2.2.2. Lambdin, §44.4 admits an adjective-like habitual meaning for qatal in some cases whereas I am suggesting it for all.

independent clause. The element in number (2) that precedes the qatal we label as a **fronted X-element** or "**X**" for short. In our lesson verse, the "X" is the indirect object וּלְאָדָם

> RULE: **The fronted X-element of a Hebrew clause might be the clause's subject, direct object, indirect object, or a prepositional phrase.**

5.3c. Our lesson verse therefore has the generalized word-order formula [X, verb] or [X-V] for short. To be more specific, our lesson verse is an X-qatal construction. To reflect the departure from the normal V-S word order of Biblical Hebrew, we will translate in an appropriately unusual English word order.

> RULE: When we find X-V word order in a Biblical Hebrew clause use the following construction for translation: [1]

(And) It was ___(Fronted "X" element)___ who(that)___(Remainder of clause)___.

Translation of וּלְאָדָם אָמַר : *And it was to Adam that was a sayer*

5.3d. The X-Qatal construction has a number of functions in Historical Narrative discourse. Basically, we shall say that it represents a summary of what follows when at the beginning of a discourse and a change in focus when it is in the middle of a discourse. Often, in the middle of a discourse, we shall find that the X-qatal construction is used to clarify a switch in the time or participants of the story. The one word we use for all these functions is **topicalization**.[2]

> RULE: **In Historical Narrative, the X-Qatal has focus-shifting function, called topicalization.**

Now you can finally fill out the "function" column of the verb analysis chart in 5.1b with the words

X-qatal =
topicalization

---

[1] This formula for translation of the X-qatal is adapted from one suggested by a number of Hebraists, among them Talstra, "Text Grammar and Hebrew Bible I," *Bibliotheca Orientalis 35,* (May-July 1978), 171; and Niccacci, "On the Hebrew Verbal System," *Biblical Hebrew and Discourse* Linguistics, ed. Bergen (Dallas: Summer Institute of Linguistics, 1994), 117-137; although Niccacci, unlike Bandstra, advocates differentiating between two X-qatal clause types, only one of which qualifies as topicalization. See Niccacci, *Syntax of the Verb in Classical Hebrew Prose,* trans. Watson (Sheffield: Sheffield Academic Press, 1990), §§123-126.

[2] The concept topicalization is here simplified as a focus-shifting device. It will take some time and a number of examples to develop the concept more fully. I borrow the term topicalization from Bandstra, "Word Order and Emphasis in Biblical Hebrew Narrative," *Linguistics and Biblical Hebrew,* ed. Bodine (Winona Lake: Eisenbrauns, 1992), who describes "the discourse effect of placing new information [what we call *comment*] in the place where given information [what we call *topic*] is typically found" 120.

5.3e. Here is a summary in chart form:

QATAL IN HISTORICAL NARRATIVE:

DEPENDENT CLAUSES	INDEPENDENT CLAUSES
preceded by a relative:	preceded by any other word or phrase:
כִּי אִם אֲשֶׁר	**an "X"**
translate using *has, had, have*	translate *It was_____who(that)*

Concerning English Bibles

5.4a. The Revised Standard Version of the Bible translates our lesson verse this way:

And to Adam he said

5.4b. Most English translations generally ignore the difference between the qatal and the wayyiqtol verb forms. Genesis 1:1 is a qatal verb form, and translators generally use a simple past translation: "In the beginning God *created*." Genesis 1:3 is a wayyiqtol verb form, and translators use simple past once again: "And God *said...*" This book, on the other hand, suggests trying to capture the difference in meaning between the qatal and wayyiqtol verb forms: "It was in the beginning that God *was creator*...And then God *said...*"

The meaning of the verb forms has been debated for centuries. The debate has resulted in books like Leslie McFall's *The Enigma of the Hebrew Verbal System: Solutions from Ewald to the Present* (Sheffield: The Almond Press, 1982).[1] The difference between the wayyiqtol and the qatal makes for an interesting discussion, but we will save the discussion for later lessons and your own studies once you have finished this book. However, it is worth mentioning the much-debated nature of the Hebrew Verbal System at this point because this book will suggest a translation of the qatal verb form which will be somewhat different than the English translations you may be using to check your translations.

This book often suggests the most literal of translations. It often suggests the ugliest of circumlocutions which may be feeble attempts to capture the special character of the Biblical Hebrew Verbal System at the expense of good or smooth-flowing English. Do not be uncomfortable if your translations do not conform to your English Bibles. The reason we are learning Biblical Hebrew is not to once again translate the Hebrew Bible. Many excellent translations already exist. Rather, we are trying to better understand the nuance of the original language.

Assignments

5.5a. Translate the following (Note that some are not complete sentences):

1. וַיִּשְׁלַח דָּוִד	6. וַיֵּצֵא דָּוִד	11. וַיֵּדַע דָּוִד כָּל־אֲשֶׁר שָׁמַע
2. אֲשֶׁר שָׁלַח דָּוִד	7. וַיֵּצֵא דָּוִד וּלְחֶבְרוֹן הָלַךְ	12. וַיִּשְׁמַע וְדָוִד עָשָׂה
3. דָּוִד שָׁלַח	8. וַיֵּלֶךְ דָּוִד	13. וַיֹּאמֶר וְדָוִד שָׁמַע
4. דָּוִד יָצָא	9. וְאֶת חֶבְרוֹן רָאָה	14. וַיִּשְׁמַע וְדָוִד אָמַר
5. מִן חֶבְרוֹן יָצָא דָּוִד	10. מִן חֶבְרֹן אֲשֶׁר לָקַח	15. אֶל דָּוִד אָמַר וַיִּשְׁמַע

---

[1] See also Waltke and O'Connor(1990), §29 and Mettinger, "The Hebrew Verb System," *Annual of the Swedish Theological Institute* 9, 1974, 64-84.

22. וַיֵּדַע דָּוִד אֵת אֲשֶׁר נָתַן	19. וַיְדַבֵּר אֵת אֲשֶׁר עָשָׂה	16. וַיְדַבֵּר וְדָוִד שָׁמַע
23. מֹשֶׁה נָתַן וְדָוִד יָדַע	20. דָּוִד נָתַן	17. וַיְדַבֵּר וּלְדָוִד שָׁמַע
24. וּמִן דָּוִד לָקַח מֹשֶׁה	21. אֲשֶׁר נָתַן דָּוִד	18. וַיְדַבֵּר כָּל־אֲשֶׁר שָׁמַע

5.5b. Translate:

Genesis 43:5 נוּ-- is the suffix meaning *us, our* like וֹ or וּ is the suffix meaning *he, his*.

1.   הָאִישׁ אָמַר אֵלֵינוּ

Genesis 3:14, 16, 17   הַנָּחָשׁ means *the serpent.* If אִישׁ means *man,* what do you guess אִשָּׁה means?

2.   וַיֹּאמֶר יְהוָה אֱלֹהִים אֶל־הַנָּחָשׁ...
       אֶל־הָאִשָּׁה אָמַר...
       וּלְאָדָם אָמַר...

2 Samuel 19:12   The sentence mentions two servants of the king.

3.   דָּוִד שָׁלַח אֶל־צָדוֹק וְאֶל־אֶבְיָתָר

1 Kings 2:26

4.   וּלְאֶבְיָתָר אָמַר הַמֶּלֶךְ

2 Samuel 13:21   Do you remember how to pronounce כָּל ?(3.5b)

5.   דָּוִד שָׁמַע אֵת כָּל־הַדְּבָרִים

2 Kings 9:11   יֵהוּא means *Jehu.*

6.   וְיֵהוּא יָצָא וַיֹּאמֶר

1 Kings 11:18

7.   וְאֶרֶץ נָתַן לוֹ

5.5c. Fill out verb analysis charts for the verbs in numbers 2, 3, and 7.

25

Lesson 6

יְהוָה דִּבֶּר אֶת־הַדָּבָר
Isaiah 24:3

Goals:
- **Identify and read the Piel qatal.**
- **Learn the topicalization function of an X-qatal.**
- **Learn what makes a noun definite.**

What we already know

Translate the first word of our lesson verse, a proper noun. _____ (1.1b)

And translate the last two words. _____ (3.6)

The Piel qatal

6.2a. We will jump right to the verb of our lesson verse, דִּבֶּר   There are several familiar things about

this verb. What is the root?_____ And the root's meaning?_____ You may
have noticed that when we have studied this root in the past, it has always been in the Piel stem. Such is
the case here as well. In fact, the root דבר is used almost exclusively in the Piel stem. What

characteristic of the Piel stem is exhibited in our verb?_____ (2.2b) Our word
exhibits no prefix or affix subject pronouns. What is the only verb form we know so far that will have
neither a prefix nor affix showing?_____ This is indeed the verb form of דִּבֶּר To
be technical, the verb *does have* an affixed subject pronoun. What does the null affix pronoun mean in

English?_____ (4.3e) A verb's nikkud and construction signify two things: the verb's form
and the verb's stem.

6.2b.   RULE: **The sign of a Piel stem verb in the qatal form is a *hireq* [.] under the first
         root letter and a *dagesh forte* in the second root letter.**

Here is a summary of the identifying features or "signs" of the two stems and the two forms we have
learned so far:

The Identifying Features of the
WAYYIQTOL AND QATAL FORMS
in the
QAL AND PIEL STEMS

Note: This is your first exposure to some simple symbolism that is used throughout this course. The space held by a cirle $\bigcirc$ signifies a root letter. The space made by _____ signifies a pronoun, either prefixed or affixed.

Verb Form / Stem	QAL	PIEL
WAYYIQTOL	$\bigcirc\bigcirc\bigcirc\ \dot{}\ \text{וַ}$	$\bigcirc\odot\bigcirc\ \text{וַ}$
QATAL	$\underline{\ \ }\bigcirc\bigcirc\bigcirc_{\bar{}}$	$\underline{\ \ }\bigcirc\bigcirc\odot$

In case the matrix seems a bit abstract, below it is filled in with the appropriate specifics for the roots אמר and דבר for third person, masculine, singular subjects. אמר as a verb is used almost exclusively in the Qal stem, דבר as a verb, is used almost exclusively in the Piel stem.

Verb Form / Stem	QAL	PIEL
WAYYIQTOL	וַיֹּאמֶר	וַיְדַבֵּר
QATAL	(Ø)אָמַר	(Ø)דִּבֶּר

We now have the beginnings of the pronunciation system which Biblical Hebrew uses to express verbal aspect and nuance of meaning by tri-consonantal roots.

6.2c. Here are some critical principles to remember as we begin to piece together the Hebrew verbal system.

GUIDING PRINCIPLES OF THE HEBREW VERBAL SYSTEM:

1. *Verb forms, not verbal stems, have special discourse functions.*

2. *Verbal stems affect a root's meaning, not its function within a discourse.*

3. All the verbal <u>stems</u> you will learn are used in all the verb <u>forms</u> you will learn.

6.2d. In Lesson 5 there was no independent word specifying the subject of the qatal verb form, so we used the pronoun *he* in our English translation. In our lesson verse, however, there is a word that specifies the subject. Keeping in mind that the אֶת locates a direct object for us, what word specifies the subject or

doer of the verb?_____ which means?_____ Since this subject *fronts* or comes before the verb, what discourse function can we assign to the construction יְהוָה דִּבֶּר ?

_____ (5.3) Be reminded that a fronted X-element can be any one of the following: subject, direct object, indirect object, or prepositional "phrase." *Phrase* is in quotation marks because a prepositional phrase in English can often be compressed into one word in Hebrew.

Fill out the verb analysis chart for יְהוָה דִּבֶּר :

root	stem	form	person, gender, number	function	basic root meaning

Translation יְהוָה דִּבֶּר : *It was_____who was_____.*
REMINDER: We have a Piel stem verb here. Piel stem has nothing to do with the *function* of the construction, only the *meaning* of the verb. It is the verb *form*, together with its second position in the clause that gives the verb its "X-qatal = topicalization" discourse function.

Topicalization

6.3. You need some examples that will begin to clarify how the wayyiqtol and X-qatal relate to each other within the context of a discourse. The first example comes from the beginning of a narrative.

Genesis 22:1 אֱלֹהִים נִסָּה אֶת־אַבְרָהָם וַיֹּאמֶר אֵלָיו
It was God who was a tester of Abraham, and He said to him

If you realize that this verse begins a detailed account of Abraham being tested, you will see that the X-qatal presents God in an introductory manner.[1] The testing of the Piel qatal verb נִסָּה is not expressed as one in a string of events as a wayyiqtol would. Rather, it is labeling God's character. The wayyiqtol וַיֹּאמֶר is actually the first event in the story. The second example comes in the middle of a narrative, that is, in the middle of a string of wayyiqtols, which recounts the immigrations of Abram and Lot in Genesis 13:11-12. Immediately preceding the Hebrew shown below is a wayyiqtol clause that translates *And they separated themselves each from his kin...*

_____

[1] Bandstra(1992) says Gen. 22:1, because of its discourse-initial position establishes the theme for the following unit, 116.

אַבְרָם יָשַׁב בְּאֶֽרֶץ־כְּנָֽעַן

It was Abram that was a dweller in the Land of Canaan

וְלוֹט יָשַׁב בְּעָרֵי הַכִּכָּר

And it was Lot that was a dweller in the cities of the plain

As in the first example, these "mid-discourse" X-qatals do not present actions per se. Rather, they elaborate on the preceding wayyiqtol about the separation of the men.[1] In this example, the fronting of the names helps to contrast who is who so we can better keep straight where each man settled. These two examples by no means exhaust the many possible uses of the X-qatal. For instance, we will encounter X-qatals that do represent an event that is in series with the wayyiqtol plot line. But these two examples should begin to illustrate to you how the X-qatals value as a topicalizer and an attribution is utilized by the Biblical Hebrew writer to interrupt the wayyiqtol string.

Definiteness

6.4a. What function does אֵת have?_____ (3.6a) Translate אֶת־הַדָּבָר :

_____ Let us now establish a rule for **definiteness**.

RULE: A noun is **definite** or specific by three means:

1. It has the definite article הַ (or הָ before a letter that cannot take a *dagesh*.)
   הַדָּבָר
2. It is a proper noun, that is, a name.
   מֹשֶׁה or בֵּית־לֶחֶם (*Bethlehem*)
3. It has an attached possessive pronoun like *my, his, their,* etc.
   בֵּיתוֹ (*his house*) or אַרְצֵנוּ (*our land*)

By the way, notice the shortening of the vowels when the suffixes are added. This shortening of vowel sounds was also mentioned in 2.4d.

בֵּיתוֹ = וֹ + בַּיִת

אַרְצֵנוּ = נוּ + אֶרֶץ

6.4b. Translate the entire lesson verse:_____

Assignments

6.5a. Label each of the following words as definite or indefinite:

1. אֱלֹהִים	5. הָאָרֶץ	9. הַר	13. הַשֶּׂה	17. יָדוֹ	21. שֶׁמֶשׁ
2. אַבְרָם	6. שֵׁם	10. מָקוֹם	14. בְּצַלְמוֹ	18. אֶרֶץ	22. מֹשֶׁה
3. צֹאן	7. הַמִּדְבָּר	11. בְּאַפָּיו	15. נְעָרָיו	19. אִישׁ	23. הַדָּבָר
4. אֲנָשָׁיו	8. הַיּוֹם	12. יְרוּשָׁלַם	16. הַשָּׁמַיִם	20 מִזְבֵּחַ	24. שְׁמוֹ

---

[1] Niccacci(1990) distinguishes between the X-qatal in which the X is a conjunction or particle as giving information understood as being previous to the mainline of the narrative, §8 and an X-qatal where the X is a noun or adverbial element as giving peripheral information, §15. Our Abraham and Lot example is of the second type.

6.5b. Translate:

Exodus 6:28

2 Kings 1:9 רְדָה means *Go down!*

Numbers 10:29 טוֹב means *good.*

1 Kings 21:23 This time the לְ can be translated *of.*

1 Kings 22:13 The name is Micaiah.

Judges 7:8

1 Samuel 13:2 Taken out of context this can mean *It was the people who was a sender*, but you translate it differently.

Exodus 16:23 אֲלֵהֶם הוּא means *to them that.*

Deuteronomy 1:6 Notice how אֱלֹהִים shortens when the suffix is added.

Psalm 50:1 אֶרֶץ here is best translated *earth.*

1. בְּיוֹם דִּבֶּר יְהוָה אֶל־מֹשֶׁה

2. הַמֶּלֶךְ דִּבֶּר רֵדָה

3. יְהוָה דִּבֶּר־טוֹב עַל־יִשְׂרָאֵל

4. לְאִיזֶבֶל דִּבֶּר יְהוָה

5. מִיכָיְהוּ דִּבֶּר אֵלָיו

6. וְאֵת כָּל־אִישׁ שָׁלַח

7. הָעָם שָׁלַח

8. וַיֹּאמֶר אֲלֵהֶם הוּא אֲשֶׁר דִּבֶּר יְהוָה

9. אֱלֹהֵינוּ דִּבֶּר אֵלֵינוּ

10. יְהוָה דִּבֶּר וַיִּקְרָא־אָרֶץ

Lesson 7

וּמַלְאַ֤ךְ יְהוָה֙ דִּבֶּ֣ר אֶל־אֵלִיָּ֔ה

2 Kings 1:3

Goal:

• **Identify and read construct chains.**

What we already know

The first two words of our lesson verse are part of one construction that we will learn about later in this lesson. Together they make an "X" before the verb. As for the verb, what stem is identified by the

hireq under the first root letter and the *dagesh forte* in the second root letter?_____ (6.2b) And

what form?_____ (also 6.2b) And what is the function of the X-qatal construction?

_____ (5.3d)

Fill out the verb analysis chart for our lesson verse's verb:

root	stem	form	person, gender, number	function	basic root meaning

Translate   דִּבֶּ֣ר אֶל־אֵלִיָּ֔ה X-   (אֵלִיָּה   is the name Elijah): *It was X who* _____ .

Construct chains

7.2a.   וּמַלְאַךְ   is made of two parts:

וּ   =   *and*

(Remember that the nikkud with the vav does not change its meaning.)

מַלְאַךְ   =   *messenger* or *angel*

What does   יְהוָה   mean?_____

7.2b. If you are now recalling that two nouns, which we do have in   וּמַלְאַךְ יְהוָה   can make a clause called a verbless clause, that is good, but this time it is not the correct label for the construction. If we review the rule for noun sentences in 2.7b it says, "... two nouns or a noun and a pronoun are put together **so that one renames the other**..." In our lesson verse,   מַלְאַךְ   does not rename   יְהוָה

31

RULE: When two or more nouns are linked together so that the second or any succeeding noun has a modifying relationship to the noun before it, we have a **construct chain** requiring English *of* for translation.

Partial translation of מַלְאַךְ יְהוָה : *angel of YHWH*

7.2c. Definiteness has an application to construct chains. Which of the two nouns in our phrase is

definite?_____ Why?_____ (6.4a)

RULE: **When the last word of a construct chain (called the *absolute*) is definite, the entire chain is definite. In translation, add the word *the* to each of the other words (called *constructs*) in the chain.**

Translation of וּמַלְאַךְ יְהוָה : *and the angel of YHWH*

Note: If you are wondering if it is sometimes hard to distinguish between a verbless clause and a construct chain in Biblical Hebrew, yes! Context will be a big help.

7.2d. The construct chain in our lesson verse וּמַלְאַךְ יְהוָה should be taken together as one unit which performs as the subject of the clause.

RULE: **No matter how long a construct chain is, the entire chain can be thought of as a unit which can perform all the same functions as a single noun. A construct chain can be the subject of a sentence, a direct object, an indirect object, even the object of a preposition.**

Translate the entire lesson verse: *And it was* _____

7.2e. It was said in 7.2d above that a construct chain, no matter how long it is, can perform, as a unit, all the same functions that a single noun can. Let us take two fairly common construct chains from the Scriptures, אִישׁ־אֱלֹהִים meaning *the man of God* and אֶרֶץ כְּנַעַן meaning *the Land of Canaan*, and see them in several functions.

As the subject of a clause with V-S word order:
וַיָּבֹא אִישׁ־אֱלֹהִים 1 Samuel 2:27
And the man of God came

As the subject of a clause with S-V (which is also X-V= topicalization) word order:
אִישׁ אֱלֹהִים בָּא 1 Kings 13:1
It was the man of God who was an enterer

As part of a verbless clause:
אִישׁ־אֱלֹהִים בָּעִיר 1 Samuel 9:6
The man of God was in the city

32

As a definite direct object:

וְנָתַתִּי אֶת כָּל־אֶרֶץ כְּנַעַן Genesis 17:8

And I will be a giver of all the Land of Canaan

As the object of a preposition:

אֶל־אֶרֶץ כְּנַעַן Leviticus 14:34

to the Land of Canaan

Assignments

7.3a. Mark the following construct chains as definite or indefinite. Remember that if the *absolute* of the construct chain is definite by any of the three means you learned in 6.3a, then the entire chain is definite. You do not need to understand all the words in a chain to know if the chain is definite. No proper nouns (names) will be used which are not very familiar.

1.	בְּנֵי־יִשְׂרָאֵל	9.	יַד־דָּוִד	16.	יַד מַלְכּוֹ
2.	אֶרֶץ יִשְׂרָאֵל	10.	אַמַּת־אִישׁ	17.	מוּסַר אָב
3.	אִישׁ־אֱלֹהִים	11.	קוֹל אִישׁ	18.	דִּבְרֵי אָבִיו
4.	בֵּית אֱלֹהִים	12.	בְּפֶשַׁע אֶרֶץ	19.	צִבְאוֹת עַם
5.	בֵּית אָבִיו	13.	וּתְרוּעַת מֶלֶךְ	20.	נֹגְשֵׂי הָעָם
6.	שַׂר הַטַּבָּחִים	14.	בְּנֵי הַמֶּלֶךְ	21.	בְּנֵי־עַמּוֹ
7.	בֵּית דָּוִד	15.	חֲמַת־מֶלֶךְ	22.	עַם יִשְׂרָאֵל
8.	אֲבִי דָוִד				

7.3b. Translate:

Isaiah 1:20 פִּי means *mouth*.

1. פִּי יְהוָה דִּבֵּר

Genesis 13:12 The prefixed בְּ means *in*.

2. אַבְרָם יָשַׁב בְּאֶרֶץ־כְּנַעַן

Genesis 37:1

3. וַיֵּשֶׁב יַעֲקֹב בְּאֶרֶץ כְּנַעַן

Genesis 24:10 The name is *Nakhor*.

4. וַיֵּלֶךְ אֶל־עִיר נָחוֹר

Genesis 26:26

5. וַאֲבִימֶלֶךְ הָלַךְ אֵלָיו

Judges 9:1 Notice how בֵּן shortens to בֶּן when it is in construct. בֶּן־יְרֻבַּעַל simply renames the subject.

6. וַיֵּלֶךְ אֲבִימֶלֶךְ בֶּן־יְרֻבַּעַל

Numbers 11:10

7. וַיִּשְׁמַע מֹשֶׁה אֶת־הָעָם

1 Kings 20:21

8. וַיֵּצֵא מֶלֶךְ יִשְׂרָאֵל

33

9. וַיֵּלֶךְ מֶלֶךְ־יִשְׂרָאֵל עַל־בֵּיתוֹ

1 Kings 20:43

10. וַיֵּלֶךְ מֶלֶךְ יִשְׂרָאֵל וּמֶלֶךְ־יְהוּדָה

2 Kings 3:9

11. מֶלֶךְ־מִצְרַיִם עָלָה

1 Kings 9:16 מִצְרַיִם means *Egypt*.

12. וְאֶל־מֹשֶׁה אָמַר

Exodus 24:1

13. וְאֶל־יִרְמְיָהוּ הָיָה דְבַר־יְהוָה

Jeremiah 39:15 The root היה can have an active sense, *happen*.

14. וּלְשָׂרָה אָמַר הִנֵּה

Genesis 20:16

15. לְשָׁאוּל לָקַח אֶת־אִישׁ בֹּשֶׁת בֶּן־שָׁאוּל

2 Samuel 2:8 אִישׁ בֹּשֶׁת is a name meaning *man of shame*, and בֶּן־שָׁאוּל renames him like in 6.

Lesson 8

וַיֵּלְכוּ וַיַּעֲשׂוּ בְּנֵי יִשְׂרָאֵל כַּאֲשֶׁר צִוָּה יְהוָה אֶת־מֹשֶׁה וְאַהֲרֹן כֵּן עָשׂוּ

Exodus 12:28

Goals:

- Identify and read 3rd masculine plural wayyiqtol and qatal verbs.
- Identify and read Qal wayyiqtol forms derived from third *heh* [ה] roots.
- Identify and read masculine plural nouns in the construct state.

What we already know

This lesson's verse is your first entire Bible verse! Congratulations! A number of things should look

familiar in the verse. For instance, how many wayyiqtols are there in the verse?_____

Copy here a qatal form in the Piel stem _____ (6.2b) The subject of this Piel qatal

verb is in the normal Biblical Hebrew word order. What is it?_____ Who are the two

men who together make up the definite direct object in the verse? _____ (3.6a)

Third person, masculine plural

8.2a. In the two wayyiqtol verbs וַיַּעֲשׂוּ and וַיֵּלְכוּ what person and gender does the prefix subject

pronoun י represent?_____ (1.3e) But notice the ו that ends each word.
Because this ending complements the prefix subject pronoun, making the subject of the verb third person,
masculine, *plural* rather than third person, masculine, *singular*, it is called a **prefix complement**.

HE/IT	THEY
וַיֹּOOO	וַיֹּOOOוֹ
(Root) ↑	↑ (Root) ↑
prefix pronoun	complement prefix pronoun

8.2b. Fill out the verb analysis charts for וַיַּעֲשׂוּ and וַיֵּלְכוּ :

root	stem	form	person, gender, number	function	basic root meaning
			they (masculine)		

root	stem	form	person, gender, number	function	basic root meaning
			they (masculine)		

Third ה verbs

8.3a. Perhaps you guessed that the root in וַיַּעֲשׂוּ is עשה meaning *do, make*. Here is your second of four missing letter rules:

> RULE: **When a root letter is <u>completely</u> missing[1] and the nikkud under the prefix pronoun is anything other than *tsere* (ֵ) or *qamets* (ָ) the missing letter is a ה from the end of the root.**

Remember that a *tsere* means the missing letter is a *yod* [י] from the beginning of the root (3.2a rule). We will learn the *qamets* later.

Translation of first two words: _____

Masculine plural ending in a construct chain

8.4a. Notice the ֵי -- at the end of בְּנֵי This is the masculine plural construct (within a construct chain) ending. The special construct ending is often accompanied by the shortening of the vowel sound, something quite common in construct chains. Here are some examples:

PLURAL ABSOLUTE	PLURAL CONSTRUCT
בָּנִים	בְּנֵי
דְּבָרִים	דִּבְרֵי
אֱלֹהִים	אֱלֹהֵי (Translated *God* most of the time like אֱלֹהִים)

Note: Since the Hebrew word בֵּן particularly when plural in a construct chain, connotes males and females, it is traditionally translated *children* rather than *sons*.

Translation: *the children of Israel*

8.4b. What is the relationship of the construct chain to the wayyiqtol verbs?_____ (1.4)
Translation of the first section of our verse requires us to use the greater context of the Biblical account to choose between the following:

---

[1] We must specify *completely missing* here due to the rule that you will learn in 9.2b in which a first *nun* is represented by a *dagesh forte*. Both third *heh* and first *nun* may have *hireq* under the prefixed subject pronoun. The difference will be that a doubled root letter will still represent the first nun whereas the third *heh* will be gone without a trace.

36

And (then) they went and then the children of Israel did

or

And (then) the children of Israel went and did

It turns out that the latter is preferable.

8.4c. You need to learn a little more about the Hebrew noun here. The appearance of a Hebrew noun is controlled by four variables: definiteness, gender (masculine or feminine), number (singular or plural), and state. **State** is a distinction among Hebrew nouns that may be a bit foreign to you. Hebrew nouns have two **states** or forms, one with which one can build called the **construct state**. The construct state of a noun is used when building construct chains or when adding pronominal suffixes onto the end of a noun. The other state or form is the **absolute state**, the "regular" form of a noun which comes last in a construct chain or which stands without any pronominal suffix. In memorizing the nouns on your vocabulary list, you are memorizing the *singular absolute state* of a noun. The singular absolute state is the "dictionary form" that stands at the head of dictionary entries in Hebrew-English lexicons.

8.4d. We often refer in the course to vowel shortening, especially when words are put into their construct state, when pronominal suffixes are added, or in certain verb forms. Vowel shortening means that the customary vowel that is found in the lexical form of a word or as expected in the verb form, then has shifted to a shorter sound. We cannot entirely trust our ear to determine where on a gradient of vowel sounds the nikkud belong because we are learning Modern Israeli pronunciation instead of strictly Masoretic pronunciation. Here is a gradation of the vowel sounds **as the Masoretes understood them**:

LONG-TO-SHORT GRADATION OF NIKKUD

LONGEST	SHORTER	SHORTEST	SILENT
qamets [ָ]	*patakh* [ַ]	The compound *shewas*:	silent *shewa* [ְ]
sere [ֵ] or *sere-yod* [ֵי]	*seghol* [ֶ]	[ֱ]	
holem [וֹ or ֹ]		[ֲ]	
hireq [ִ] saying /i/ as in *machine* or *hireq-yod* [ִי]	*hireq* [ִ] saying /I/ as in *pin*	[ֳ]	
		shewa [ְ]	
shureq [וּ] or *kibbuts* [ֻ]	*qamets khatuph* [ָ]		

The dependent clause

8.5a. Like the אֲשֶׁר -clause in Lesson 4, כַּאֲשֶׁר signals a dependent clause. With the particle כְּ (*like, as*) attached to it כַּאֲשֶׁר means *like-that-which*, *according to*, or *when*.

8.5b. Fill out the verb analysis chart for צִוָּה If you do not know the stem or form check 6.2b. For the function, check 4.3b and 4.3f. The root צוה means *command*. It is part of your second group of fifty words to learn.

root	stem	form	person, gender, number	function	basic root meaning

8.5c. A note about pronunciation: at times ו is pronounced /v/ and at times /u/. It depends whether it is a consonant or a vowel. We can determine this by whether it is accompanied by a vowel. A vowel would not be accompanied by a vowel so the *vav* would then be a consonant. The *vav* in צִוָּה is accompanied by a *patakh*, so it is a consonant pronounced /v/.

8.5d. The double definite direct object אֶת־מֹשֶׁה וְאַהֲרֹן only uses the DDO once for both Moses and Aaron. This is common practice, but each member of such a compound direct object sometimes gets its own DDO. Then, of course, no DDO at all will be found at other times. The reasons for this may be unlocked by discourse analysis, but we do not know them yet.

With יהוה as the subject of the qatal verb, translate: כַּאֲשֶׁר צִוָּה יְהוָה אֶת־מֹשֶׁה וְאַהֲרֹן

8.5e. כֵּן means *thus*. Fill out the verb analysis chart for עָשׂוּ :

root	stem	form	person, gender, number	function	basic root meaning

What stem and form does the *qamets* under the ע signify? _____ (4.3g)

Notice that the *heh* has dropped from the end of the root without a trace. This is normal for roots with a *heh* for a third root letter in 3rd m. p. qatal forms.

The ו at the end of the word is the subject affix for third person, masculine *and* feminine, plural *they*, similar to the prefix complement on the wayyiqtol verb form except that it is genderless or **common**.

38

REVIEW OF QAL QATAL:

	WAYYIQTOL	QATAL
HE	וַיַּעֲשֶׂה	עָשָׂה
THEY	וַיַּעֲשׂוּ	עָשׂוּ
	(masculine)	(common)

Translation: *It was thus that they were doers*

Translation of the entire verse:_____

Assignments

8.6a. As mentioned in 8.4a., there is a typical shortening of a vowel sound in the construct(s). This is true for singular constructs as well as plural. Mark the following words according to the category to which they belong:

A. Absolute singular   B. Absolute plural   C. Construct singular   D. Construct plural

____1. דִּבְרֵי

____2. שְׁנֵי

____3. בַּיִת

____4. בֵּית

____5. נַעֲלֵי

____6. מַלְכֵי

____7. בֵּן

____8. בָּתִּים

____9. מְלכים

____10. בֵּן

____11. דָּבָר

____12. דְּבַר

8.6b. Translate:

Genesis 45:21

1. וַיַּעֲשׂוּ־כֵן בְּנֵי יִשְׂרָאֵל

Exodus 7:10

2. וַיַּעֲשׂוּ כֵן כַּאֲשֶׁר צִוָּה יְהוָה

Genesis 45:24 אֶחָיו means *his brothers.*

3. וַיְשַׁלַּח אֶת־אֶחָיו וַיֵּלְכוּ וַיֹּאמֶר

Exodus 3:15 We would need commas in English.

4. אֱלֹהֵי אַבְרָהָם אֱלֹהֵי יִצְחָק וֵאלֹהֵי יַעֲקֹב

Genesis 9:24 If you forgot what the *tsere* under the prefix pronoun means (3.2a rule).	5. וַיֵּדַע אֵת אֲשֶׁר־עָשָׂה
Genesis 43:17	6. וַיַּעַשׂ הָאִישׁ כַּאֲשֶׁר אָמַר יוֹסֵף
I Chronicles 16:26 We have here a construct chain as the subject of a verbless clause. אֱלִילִים means *idols*.	7. כִּי כָּל־אֱלֹהֵי הָעַמִּים אֱלִילִים
Exodus 15:3 Two verbless clauses here. מִלְחָמָה means *war*. שֵׁם = שְׁמוֹ + וֹ (2.4c)	8. יְהוָה אִישׁ מִלְחָמָה יְהוָה שְׁמוֹ
Genesis 12:4	9. וַיֵּלֶךְ אַבְרָם כַּאֲשֶׁר דִּבֶּר אֵלָיו יְהוָה
Genesis 13:4	10. וַיִּקְרָא שָׁם אַבְרָם
Joshua 17:14	11. וַיְדַבְּרוּ בְּנֵי יוֹסֵף
Exodus 5:1 Translate כֹּה־אָמַר *Thus was YHWH's speaking*. The subject is an expansion of *YHWH God*.	12. כֹּה־אָמַר יְהוָה אֱלֹהֵי יִשְׂרָאֵל
Deuteronomy 34:9	13. וַיִּשְׁמְעוּ אֵלָיו בְּנֵי־יִשְׂרָאֵל וַיַּעֲשׂוּ כַּאֲשֶׁר צִוָּה יְהוָה אֶת־מֹשֶׁה
1 Kings 20:40	14. וַיֹּאמֶר אֵלָיו מֶלֶךְ־יִשְׂרָאֵל
Exodus 10:7 עֶבֶד means *servant*.	15. וַיֹּאמְרוּ עַבְדֵי פַרְעֹה אֵלָיו

Lesson 9

וַיִּקַּח מֹשֶׁה מִדָּמוֹ וַיִּתֵּן עַל־תְּנוּךְ אֹזֶן־אַהֲרֹן

Leviticus 8:23

Goal:

• Identify and read Qal wayyiqtol forms derived from first *nun* [נ] roots and לקח .

What we already know

9.1. How many wayyiqtols can you spot?_____

What does a string of wayyiqtols indicate?_____

First **nun** *roots*

9.2a. Examining our two wayyiqtols you should notice some similarities:

Nikkud under the prefixed subject pronoun:_____

What kind of *dagesh* in the first root?_____which means?_____
So the letters in our wayyiqtols are as follows:

וַיִּקַּח = ו + י + י + ק + ק + ח

וַיִּתֵּן = ו + י + י + ת + ת + נ

9.2b. You may be thinking that these two wayyiqtols are Piel stems of a root that has dropped the first letter. Not bad thinking, but not right either. Remember that the Piel stem usually has a *shewa* under the prefixed subject pronoun and no *dagesh forte* in the pronoun as follows:

וַיְקַח   and   וַיְתֵן

Neither of these is an attested word in the Hebrew Bible.

> RULE: When the first root letter which appears in the wayyiqtol (or yiqtol) verb form is doubled by a dagesh forte, the first root letter is a missing first *nun* (נ) or the special case of the first *lamed* (ל) of the root לקח meaning *take*.

Our roots are therefore נתן and לקח

9.2c. We have now learned the third of four **missing letter rules**. We learned the first in Lesson 3.2 when we learned how to identify when a *yod* is missing from the beginning of a root. We will now begin to classify roots by their spellings. For instance, roots which have a *yod* as their first root letter tend to behave in the same peculiar way. We call them *first yod roots*. Then there are third *heh* roots. Roots that have a *nun* for their first letter also tend to behave in their own way, and we classify them as *first nun roots*. The rule is to identify the class of roots by the critical letter and its first, second, or third position in the root.

9.2d. The next challenge for understanding our lesson verse is to figure out the stem for our two verbs. Again, the Piel is calling to us because of the *dageshes* which we now know are in the second root letters. But the *dagesh* is the result of the assimilation of the nasal *nun* or *lamed* sounds into the second root letters, *not the Piel stem*. The dagesh is what is left of the assimilated first *nun* or *lamed* so we call it a **footprint dagesh**.

> **RULE: A dagesh cannot be both the sign of the Piel stem and a footprint dagesh at the same time. I.e., if we have a footprint dagesh, we have the Qal stem.** In the Piel stem, a first *nun* does *not* assimilate.

9.2e. Fill out the verb analysis charts for וַיִּקַּח and וַיִּתֵּן :

root	stem	form	person, gender, number	function	basic root meaning

root	stem	form	person, gender, number	function	basic root meaning

Translate: וַיִּקַּח מֹשֶׁה _____

וַיִּתֵּן _____

Prepositions

9.3a. You may have noticed from our work with ל meaning *to, of, for*, what is also true for many other Hebrew prepositions, that they are prefixed to their objects. Such is the case with our lesson's מִדָּמוֹ The word is actually three parts:

מִ	=	מִן	=	*from*
דָּם	=			*blood*
וֹ	=			*his* or *its*

The same as the first *nun* of וַיִּתֵּן assimilated into the *tav* as a *dagesh forte*, the *nun* at the end of מִן

assimilated into the *dalet* of כַּם as a *dagesh forte*.

9.3b. Another preposition that is commonly prefixed to its object besides מִן and לְ is בְּ which can mean *in, by, with, from, against, to*.

Translation of וַיִּקַּח מֹשֶׁה מִדָּמוֹ : _____

9.3c. Another preposition in Hebrew is עַל which means *on, upon, against, near*, but can also have the sense of *concerning, on account of*. עַל is different than מִן because it always stands as an independent word whereas מִן may stand independently or be fused to another word as it is in our lesson verse. Other prepositions from your vocabulary list so far which always stand alone are אֶל (*to, toward, into, at*) עַד (*as far as, until, while*) and עִם (*with, beside*)

The construct chain

9.4. There are three elements to the construct chain after עַל two constructs and an absolute. Even though you do not know what the first two words mean, can you determine whether the chain is definite or

indefinite? _____ (7.2c) What is the reason for your decision? _____

Translation of עַל־תְּנוּךְ אֹזֶן־אַהֲרֹן : *upon* **the lobe of the** *ear of Aaron*

Translation of the entire lesson verse (You may use the meaning *put, place* for the root נתן and you may insert an extra *it* after וַיִּתֵּן for a smooth English sentence):

_____

Assignments

9.5a. Memorize vocabulary words 51-100 for Lessons 9-16.

9.5b. There are times when looking at Hebrew may seem like looking at a confusion of *vav*'s. In this exercise mark the use of each word's *vav* as follows:

a. Part of the root   **b.** Subject affix   **c.** Plain conjunctive   **d.** Sign of the   **e.** Prefix complement   **f.** Pronoun suffix
    (1.3b)   (8.5e)   *and* (1.2a)   wayyiqtol (1.2c)   (8.2a)   (2.4c)

_____1. וֵאלֹהִים   _____6. יוֹם

_____2. יָדְעוּ   _____7. יהוה

_____3. וַיֹּאמֶר   _____8. נְעָרָיו

_____4. אַרְצוֹ   _____9. אֵלָיו

_____5. וַיִּשְׁמַע   _____10. וּבֶן

43

____ 11. דָּוִד   ____ 14. עֵשָׂו

____ 12. הוּא   ____ 15. בְּנוֹ

____ 13. צִוָּה   ____ 16. וְאַהֲרֹן

9.5c. Translate:

Genesis 20:14 צֹאן means *sheep*.

1. וַיִּקַּח אֲבִימֶלֶךְ צֹאן וַיִּתֵּן לְאַבְרָהָם

Genesis 6:2 Notice that when the *koph* of וַיִּקְחוּ closes a syllable, it does not take a *dagesh*. In other words, the root's *lamed* has disappeared without a trace. בחר means *choose*.

2. וַיִּרְאוּ בְנֵי־הָאֱלֹהִים וַיִּקְחוּ מִכֹּל אֲשֶׁר בָּחָרוּ

Genesis 14:12

3. וַיִּקְחוּ אֶת־לוֹט וַיֵּלֵכוּ

2 Kings 22:2

5. וַיֵּלֶךְ בְּכָל־דֶּרֶךְ דָּוִד אָבִיו

2 Chronicles 11:4

6. וַיִּשְׁמְעוּ אֶת־דִּבְרֵי יְהוָה

Genesis 31:1

7. וַיִּשְׁמַע אֶת־דִּבְרֵי בְנֵי־לָבָן

1 Samuel 12:6

8. וַיֹּאמֶר שְׁמוּאֵל אֶל־הָעָם יְהוָה אֲשֶׁר עָשָׂה אֶת־מֹשֶׁה וְאֶת־אַהֲרֹן

Deuteronomy 3:18 --כֶם = a suffix meaning *you* or *your* (masculine, plural).

9. יְהוָה אֱלֹהֵיכֶם נָתַן לָכֶם אֶת־הָאָרֶץ

Numbers 7:7 אַרְבַּעַת הַבָּקָר means *the four oxen*.

10. וְאֵת אַרְבַּעַת הַבָּקָר נָתַן לִבְנֵי גֵרְשׁוֹן

1 King 14:26 The first two DDOs follow a verb. The third DDO is a fronted X-element on the second sentence. אוֹצְרוֹת means *treasures*. הַכֹּל means *everything*. The point is that the X-qatal gives a summary and also lends emphasis to the wayyiqtol before it.

11. וַיִּקַּח אֶת־אֹצְרוֹת בֵּית־יְהוָה וְאֶת־אוֹצְרוֹת בֵּית הַמֶּלֶךְ וְאֶת־הַכֹּל לָקָח

1 Kings 8:12   אָז means *then*.

2 Chronicles 13:5   מַמְלָכָה is a word made from the root מלך It means *kingdom*.

Job 1:21

12.   אָז אָמַר שְׁלֹמֹה יְהוָה אָמַר

13.   יְהוָה אֱלֹהֵי יִשְׂרָאֵל נָתַן מַמְלָכָה לְדָוִיד עַל־יִשְׂרָאֵל

14.   יְהוָה נָתַן וַיהוָה לָקָח

45

Lesson 10

וַיָּבֹא עַד־הַיַּרְדֵּן וִיהוּדָה בָּא

2 Samuel 19:16

Goal:

- Identify and read Qal wayyiqtol and qatal forms derived from hollow roots.

Numbering of verses

10.1.   Occasionally, the numbering of verses in a Hebrew Bible and most English translations will not agree. Our lesson verse is one example. It is verse 16 in Hebrew but 15 in English. Different verse numbering is particularly common in Psalms.

What we already know

10.2.   What do you recognize in the first word of our lesson sentence?

Form:_____

Function:_____

Subject pronoun:_____

Wayyiqtol of hollow or second י ו וֹ verbs

10.3a.   You should be getting used to what is next: the challenge is now to determine what letter from the

tri-consonantal root is missing. Where do we look for the answer?_____(3.2a rule)

> **RULE: When we see a *qamets* (ָ) under the prefix pronoun the missing letter is the second or middle letter and will be a ו or וֹ or י . Any root with one of these letters as its middle letter has the nickname *hollow root*.**

10.3b.   In the case of our root the middle letter is a וֹ so בוא pronounced /bo/ and meaning

_____. Is there any augment to the root?_____ So the stem will be

_____ (1.3c)

Fill out the verb analysis chart for וַיָּבֹא :

root	stem	form	person, gender, number	function	basic root meaning

Translation of our lesson word:_____

10.3c. The next phrase is really just vocabulary.

עַד means_____

הַ means_____

יַרְדֵּן is the name of the famous river_____

Notice the root ירד meaning *go down* in the name of the river. Of course, all rivers go down, but the source of the Jordan is Mt. Hermon, a symbolic source of Israel's blessings in Psalm 133 and elsewhere. The Jordan was named so, probably long before Israel came into Canaan. Could it have received its name from the fact that it flows to the lowest place on earth, the Dead Sea? We are not sure. The point is that even common and proper nouns are more times than not made of one or more tri-consonantal roots.

Qatal of hollow roots

10.4a. The verb in the second of our two lesson clauses is also from the root בוא As with the wayyiqtol form, the *vav* is missing. If you have noticed the *qamets* under the first root letter of the verb and are anticipating a qatal verb form in the Qal stem, take a gold star! You are correct! Just realize that our lesson's word can also be a masculine singular participle. No need to learn this now. Just do not become cocky. Since there is no visible ending on this qatal form, what is the person, gender, number?

_____ (4.3e)

Fill out the verb analysis chart for בָּא :

root	stem	form	person, gender, number	function	basic root meaning

Translation of the verb: *he was the goer (or enterer)*

10.4b. The word before the verb is a name with a prefixed *vav*. Translate it_____

10.4c. The following will help you if you had trouble filling out the function box on the above verb analysis chart:

What is the relationship of וִיהוּדָה to בָּא ?_____ (5.3c)

So what is the word order in this clause?_____

Remembering that S-V word order translates into an X-qatal construction, what is the function of the

X-qatal construction in Historical Narrative_____ (5.3d) Is this

function a mainline or off-the-line function_____ (4.3a rule) It just so happens in this passage that David is the main participant on whom the wayyiqtol string focuses. However, our lesson's off-the-line topicalization momentarily changes the focus to the tribe of Judah. There is some suspense in the account as to whether Judah will come and receive their returning king David. The writer could choose no better verb form and clause construction to settle the issue.

Translation of the clause so far: *And it was_____who was_____*

Translation of the entire lesson verse:_____

10.4d. You need to begin becoming familiar with a few of the special qualities of hollow roots in the Qal qatal. Whereas the usual pattern for the 3rd m. s. Qal qatal is OOϘ only two roots letters are usually showing for hollow roots, eg. our lesson verse's בָּא Also, the root קוּם becomes קָם *he is (was) an ariser,* the root שׁוּב becomes שָׁב *he is (was) a returner,* and the root שִׂים becomes שָׂם *he is (was) a putter*. Some other hollow roots do not even have the *qamets* under the first root letter as all the above examples. These exceptions are usually verbal roots that have stative or adjective-like meanings which, by the way, *do not* require our eccentric *er*-word translation method. Examples from the vocabulary for this course include the root מוּת which has a 3rd m. s. Qal qatal מֵת *he is (was) dead* and the root בּוֹשׁ which, interestingly, has a 3rd m. s. Qal qatal בּוֹשׁ *he is (was) ashamed.* Hollow roots are the only verbal roots which do not usually use the 3rd m. s. Qal qatal as a lexical form. Instead they usually use their tri-consonantal form.

Assignments

10.5a.. In each of the following cases, what does the nikkud indicate is the missing letter?

1. וַ__OO _____ (3.2a)

2. וָ__OO _____ (10.3a)

3. וַ__OO _____ (8.3a)

4. וְ__⊙OO _____ (9.2b)

10.5b. Translate:

17. וַיִּשְׁמֹר	9. וַיִּשָּׂא	1. וַיַּעַשׂ יְהוָה
18. וַיֵּדְעוּ	10. וַיַּרְא	2. וַיִּקַּח
19. וַיַּעֲשׂוּ	11. וַיַּעַל	3. וַיִּתֵּן
20. וַיִּרְאוּ	12. וַיִּקְרָא אֱלֹהִים	4. וַיֹּאכְלוּ
21. וַיִּמְחוּ	13. וַיָּשִׂימוּ	5. וַיַּעֲבֹר אַבְרָם
22. וַיֹּאכַל	14. וַיִּקְרְאוּ	6. וַיָּשֶׂם
23. וַיֵּלֶךְ אִישׁ	15. וַיָּבֹאוּ	7. וַיָּקָם
24. וַיִּשְׁלַח אַבְרָהָם	16. וַיִּתְּנוּ	8. וַיִּשְׂאוּ

10.5c. Translate:

2 Samuel 19:16 This item is from the same Bible verse as our lesson.

1. וַיָּשָׁב הַמֶּלֶךְ

Genesis 7:15

2. וַיָּבֹאוּ אֶל־נֹחַ

Genesis 8:3 הַמַּיִם means *water*.

3. וַיָּשֻׁבוּ הַמַּיִם מֵעַל הָאָרֶץ

Judges 3:24 וְהוּא means *and he*, and וַעֲבָדָיו means *and his servants*. Here we have two X-qatals, which identify the participants in the story before the wayyiqtol string begins.

4. וְהוּא יָצָא וַעֲבָדָיו בָּאוּ וַיִּרְאוּ

2 Chronicles 32:1
אַחֲרֵי הַדְּבָרִים הָאֵלֶּה means *after these things*, so we have an X-qatal here. סַנְחֵרִיב means *Senacharib* and אַשּׁוּר means *Assyria*.)

5. אַחֲרֵי הַדְּבָרִים הָאֵלֶּה בָּא סַנְחֵרִיב מֶלֶךְ־אַשּׁוּר וַיָּבֹא בִיהוּדָה

49

Genesis 4:16	וַיֵּצֵא קַיִן וַיֵּשֶׁב בְּאֶרֶץ־נוֹד	6.
Genesis 19:30	וַיַּעַל לוֹט מִצּוֹעַר וַיֵּשֶׁב בָּהָר	7.
Genesis 22:19 נַעַר means *servant*. נְעָרָיו means *his servants*. נַעֲרוֹ would be *his servant*. Notice the different nikkud with the name Beer-Sheba.	וַיָּשָׁב אַבְרָהָם אֶל־נְעָרָיו וַיֵּלְכוּ אֶל־בְּאֵר שֶׁבַע וַיֵּשֶׁב אַבְרָהָם בִּבְאֵר שָׁבַע	8.
2 Samuel 1:1	וְדָוִד שָׁב וַיֵּשֶׁב דָּוִד בְּצִקְלָג	9.
2 Samuel 3:23 This is a very unusual case where a qatal begins a clause. Notice how בֵּן shortens to בֶּן־ when in a construct chain. Do you know what שָׁלוֹם means?	בָּא־אַבְנֵר בֶּן־נֵר אֶל־הַמֶּלֶךְ וַיֵּלֶךְ בְּשָׁלוֹם	10.
Genesis 33:18 This time the word שָׁלֵם is the name of a city of Shechem. עִיר שְׁכֶם is a construct chain renaming שָׁלֵם	וַיָּבֹא יַעֲקֹב שָׁלֵם עִיר שְׁכֶם אֲשֶׁר בְּאֶרֶץ כְּנַעַן	11.
1 Samuel 16:4 בֵּית לֶחֶם is the name of a famous little town.	וַיַּעַשׂ שְׁמוּאֵל אֵת אֲשֶׁר דִּבֶּר יְהוָה וַיָּבֹא בֵּית לֶחֶם	12.
Genesis 11:31 There are seven people or place names here. שָׁם means *there*. וֹ + בֵּן = בְּנוֹ	וַיִּקַּח תֶּרַח אֶת־אַבְרָם בְּנוֹ וְאֶת־לוֹט בֶּן־הָרָן וְאֵת שָׂרַי וַיֵּצְאוּ מֵאוּר וַיָּבֹאוּ עַד־חָרָן וַיֵּשְׁבוּ שָׁם	13.
Leviticus 9:5	וַיִּקְחוּ אֵת אֲשֶׁר צִוָּה מֹשֶׁה	14.
1 Kings 13:12 בָּנָיו means *his sons*. דֶּרֶךְ means *way*.	וַיִּרְאוּ בָנָיו אֶת־הַדֶּרֶךְ אֲשֶׁר הָלַךְ אִישׁ הָאֱלֹהִים אֲשֶׁר־בָּא מִיהוּדָה	15.

Lesson 11

וַיְהִי יְשַׁעְיָהוּ לֹא יָצָא וּדְבַר־יְהוָה הָיָה אֵלָיו

2 Kings 20:4

Goals:

- Identify and read the Historical Narrative transition marker וַיְהִי .
- Identify and read irrealis comments constructed with לֹא.
- Begin constructing a discourse profile scheme for Historical Narrative.
- Use an understanding of Hebrew clause construction to help identify clause boundaries.

What we already know

11.1. Although it's taking things somewhat out of order, let's focus on the last clause of our lesson verse. All the grammar in clause should look familiar.

Translate the construct chain וּדְבַר־יְהוָה _____

Fill out the verb analysis chart for הָיָה :

root	stem	form	person, gender, number	function	basic root meaning
				X-qatal = topicalization	

Although you should write *be, happen* in the box for basic root meaning, traditionally, the root הָיָה is translated into some form of *come* when the reference is to *the Word of YHWH*. For example, several English versions translate our verse *And the Word of YHWH came...* However, you can use a form of *happen* if you want to.

Translation of clause: *It was* _____ *that was* _____

Historical Narrative transition marker

11.2a.

> RULE: **The word** וַיְהִי **has a special function in Biblical Hebrew as a transition marker.**[1]

This wayyiqtol form of הָיָה is simultaneously a divider and joiner of text. It is a divider in the sense that it marks the onset of a new scene or a new episode or the entrance of a new participant in a story. At the same time it does indeed join the scene or episode it marks to a larger discourse. Since the nikkud in this verb are irregular, you should learn to recognize the word without analysis, i.e. as a sight word.

---

[1] See Gesenius(1910), §111f; Schneider (1982), 251-252; Niccacci(1990) §§12, 28, 36, 78; van der Merwe, "The Elusive Biblical Hebrew Term וַיְהִי . A Perspective in Terms of its Syntax, Semantics, and Pragmatics in 1 Samuel" (paper delivered at SBL, 1997).

Recognizing it will be no problem because the word is used over 700 times in the Hebrew Bible!
Translation: *And (then) it happened*

11.2b. The word is the wayyiqtol form of the root היה but it does not contain the customary *dagesh forte* in the prefix pronoun. In this respect, it looks like a Piel stem, but it is Qal. Many scholars believe the word has the nikkud it does because of the "triply weak" nature of the root. First ה roots are often irregular. So are second י and third ה roots. היה is all three of these combined!

11.2c. Fill out the verb analysis chart for וַיְהִי :

root	stem	form	person, gender, number	function	basic root meaning

When filling out the person, gender, number column, remember that Hebrew has no neuter gender translated *it*. Therefore both the masculine and feminine genders will at times be translated *it*. Such is the case with this word, so write "3rd m. s. *it*" in the space.

Even though וַיְהִי is a wayyiqtol verb form, since it is a special case for a special root, write in "transition marker" for the function. This word is an off-the-line verb form.

The root היה does not translate into English precisely. It is close to the English verb that expresses existence, *be*, but it has the added nuance of something happening. In Genesis 1:3, God said, "Let there be light" using the root היה and then we read וַיְהִי that is, light *was, it happened*. As above in 11.1, write *be, happen* in the basic root meaning space.

Irrealis

11.3a. In the clause יְשַׁעְיָהוּ לֹא יָצָא we have an X-qatal construction. What is the X-element?

_____ (5.3) יְשַׁעְיָהוּ is the name Isaiah. What is the

relationship of יְשַׁעְיָהוּ to the verb יָצָא ?_____

11.3b. לֹא means *no, not*. Though it is pronounced the same, it is not to be confused with לוֹ which means *to him* or *his*, depending on the context.

> RULE: The conversion of any verb to **irrealis**, that is, **a statement of what is not rather than what is**, by the word לֹא moves the verb form to the lowest place in the **discourse profile scheme** of a genre.[1]

---

[1] Longacre(1989), 82 notes that in some special cases of irrealis which he calls "momentous negation" in which the negation of a qatal is probably best considered equal to a second-rank construction(X-qatal). He gives the לֹא-qatal in Gen. 8:2 as an example where the dove does not return to the ark.

Discourse profile

11.4a. Let's look at what we have so far learned of the discourse profile scheme for the Historical Narrative genre. The idea is that the mainline verb form is like the skeleton from which hang all the tissue of detail, setting, summary, and elaboration. All off-the-line verb forms in a genre provide these details, settings, summaries, and elaborations as they retard the forward progress of the mainline. The lower a verb form is in the profile, the farther away it is from the mainline and the more it tends to retard the forward progress of the mainline.[1]

DISCOURSE PROFILE OF THE HISTORICAL NARRATIVE GENRE

1. Mainline: Wayyiqtol

Off-the-line:
  2. Topicalization: X-qatal
    3. Relative past background: אֲשֶׁר qatal
      4. Transition marker: Wayyiqtol of היה
        5. Scene setting: Verbless Clause
          6. Irrealis scene setting: Negation of any verb by לֹא

11.4b. We run the risk of a misunderstanding here. The profile scheme *does not suggest a relative importance* of the information presented by the different constructions. ***The ranking represents the degrees to which a construction slows the forward progress of the discourse.*** The profile scheme helps us to analyze the structure or shape of the narrative. We may think of a discourse as a video. The mainline forms keep the video playing. The off-the-line forms slow or even freeze the video for commentary, often at the points of greatest emphasis.

11.4c. Fill out the verb analysis chart for לֹא יָצָא :

root	stem	form	person, gender, number	function	basic root meaning
				w/ לֹא = Irrealis scene-setting	

Translation of יְשַׁעְיָהוּ לֹא יָצָא : *It was_____who was not_____.*
Stuck on יָצָא ? Try *a goer forth.*

Identifying where clauses begin and end

11.5a. In reading our lesson verse, it may seem difficult to know what to do with יְשַׁעְיָהוּ It seems as though it could be the subject of וַיְהִי as well as יָצָא This is an important matter because when we

---

[2]We have been proceeding all along through this module towards this introduction of the discourse profile scheme of Historical Narrative. The scheme itself is adapted from Longacre's verb ranking clines, *Joseph,* 81 and elsewhere. We prefer to call them discourse profile schemes because the ranks are characterized by syntax as well as verb form (see Joosten, "The Indicative System of the Biblical Hebrew Verb," *Narrative Syntax and the Hebrew Bible.* (Leiden: Brill, 1997), 56, 68). Longacre does not show dependent clauses on his scheme, nor is he clear on how clauses with qatal forms are to be differentiated from each other. The description of ranks as differing degrees of "slowing the forward progress of the genre" is our own, but Longacre has given his approval in private conversation.

analyze a discourse we will proceed in a clause-by-clause manner considering the clause to be the basic building block of a discourse.[1] You must therefore become secure in your ability to find clause boundaries. But to complicate matters, Hebrew does not use punctuation marks as we know them! It's not so hard after all. Chunking a verse into clauses is a two-step procedure as follows:

1. Locate the verbs around which a clause can be built. For instance, right now you are aware that each wayyiqtol and qatal represents a clause.
2. Between the verbs, decide which words go with the verb before them and which words go with the verb after them.

11.5b. For instance, how many verbs are in our lesson verse?_____ So there are three clauses. Let us stretch out our lesson verse to spatially isolate the verbs.

אֵלָיו   הָיָה   וּדְבַר־יְהוָה   לֹא יָצָא   יְשַׁעְיָהוּ   וַיְהִי
       verb   ←?→   verb   ←?→   verb

The question is with the material between the clauses. Does יְשַׁעְיָהוּ go with וַיְהִי or לֹא יָצָא ? The *maqqef* in וּדְבַר־יְהוָה helps us understand that the words belong together as one unit, but does the unit go with the verb before it or the verb after it? In the case of וּדְבַר־יְהוָה it does not make sense for it to go with יָצָא because of the *vav*. Even more significantly however, there is one understanding that will help us with both of the phrases in question. We know that in Historical Narrative, that the qatal almost never appears clause-initially. Rather, a qatal will appear either in a dependent clause or in an X-qatal construction. Since neither of the qatals in our lesson verse is in a dependent clause preceded by אֲשֶׁר or כִּי or another relative, we can therefore draw lines between the clauses in the following manner so that we divide the verse into one wayyiqtol-clause and two X-qatal clauses:

וַיְהִי / יְשַׁעְיָהוּ לֹא יָצָא / וּדְבַר־יְהוָה הָיָה אֵלָיו

11.5c. Compare the following two examples:

a. וַיְהִי דָוִד בָּא   2 Samuel 15:32
    verb ←?→ verb

b. וַיְהִי בַּיּוֹם הַהוּא וַיָּבֹאוּ   Genesis 26:32
    verb   ←?→   verb

In which example does the middle material go with the verb before it, and in which does it go with the verb after it? Example (a.) has the qatal בָּא that "needs" a fronted "X" element in Historical Narrative, so דָוִד goes with it. Example (b.) has a wayyiqtol in the same slot as (a.)'s qatal. A wayyiqtol *cannot* be preceded by anything within its clause, so בַּיּוֹם הַהוּא which means, by the way, *in that day*, must go with the verb before it, וַיְהִי

---

[1] Joosten(1997), 56, indicates that the sentence, not the paragraph, is the building block of Hebrew discourse, in contrast with Longacre. We will side with Joosten, however, preferring clause to sentence.

It is recommended, as your translation exercises become more challenging that you draw slashes between the clauses to help yourself. There are, of course, many situations which this little lesson on chunking clauses does not cover, verbless clauses for one, but the lesson is a start.

Translation of entire lesson verse:_____

_____

Assignments

11.6a. Translate:

17.	אֲשֶׁר רָאָה פַרְעֹה	9.	וּפַרְעֹה מֵת בָּאָרֶץ	1.	פַּרְעֹה אָמַר לוֹ
18.	כִּי רָאָה פַרְעֹה	10.	בָּאָרֶץ עָמַד	2.	וְלוֹ נָתַן פַּרְעֹה
19.	כְּפַרְעֹה רָאָה	11.	כִּי שָׁלַח פַּרְעֹה	3.	לְבֵית־לֶחֶם בָּא
20.	כִּי רָאָה כְּפַרְעֹה	12.	וּבָאָרֶץ הָלַךְ	4.	אֲשֶׁר בָּוֹ לְבֵית לֶחֶם
21.	כְּפַרְעֹה עָבַד	13.	וּפַרְעֹה הָלַךְ בָּאָרֶץ	5.	לְפַרְעֹה שָׁלַח
22.	וּפַרְעֹה אָכַל כְּדָוִד	14.	וּפַרְעֹה שָׁב בָּאָרֶץ	6.	לְפַרְעֹה עָשָׂה
23.	וְדָוִד מֵת כְּפַרְעֹה	15.	כִּי בְפַרְעֹה עָשָׂה	7.	וּפַרְעֹה קָם לוֹ
24.	אֲשֶׁר רָאָה כְּפַרְעֹה	16.	בְּפַרְעֹה נָתַן	8.	וְלוֹ שָׁב פַּרְעֹה

11.6b. Translate:

Genesis 26:1 רָעָב is not a verb.
It means *famine*.

1. וַיְהִי רָעָב בָּאָרֶץ

Genesis 26:32 הַהוּא means
that, an adjective describing יוֹם

2. וַיְהִי בַּיּוֹם הַהוּא וַיָּבֹאוּ עַבְדֵי יִצְחָק

Genesis 29:10

3. וַיְהִי כַּאֲשֶׁר רָאָה יַעֲקֹב אֶת־רָחֵל בַּת־לָבָן

Exodus 6:28

4. וַיְהִי בְּיוֹם דִּבֶּר יְהוָה אֶל־מֹשֶׁה בְּאֶרֶץ מִצְרָיִם

Exodus 16:27 הַשְּׁבִיעִי is an
adjective for בַּיּוֹם meaning
seventh.

5. וַיְהִי בַּיּוֹם הַשְּׁבִיעִי יָצְאוּ מִן־הָעָם

Numbers 22:41
בַּבֹּקֶר means *in the morning*.
Look for two names.

6. וַיְהִי בַבֹּקֶר וַיִּקַּח בָּלָק אֶת־בִּלְעָם

Joshua 6:27 Remember that אֵת
can mean *with*. There is no action
verb so there can be no direct
object.

7. וַיְהִי יְהוָה אֶת־יְהוֹשֻׁעַ

55

8. Joshua 24:29 אַחֲרֵי has the usual nikkud for the word *after*. הָאֵלֶּה means *these*.

וַיְהִי אַחֲרֵי הַדְּבָרִים הָאֵלֶּה וַיָּמָת יְהוֹשֻׁעַ

9. Exodus 34:28 לֶחֶם means *bread*, and the root שׁתה means *drink*.

וַיְהִי־שָׁם עִם־יְהוָה לֶחֶם לֹא אָכַל וּמַיִם לֹא שָׁתָה

10. 1 Kings 12:16

וַיַּרְא כָּל־יִשְׂרָאֵל כִּי לֹא־שָׁמַע הַמֶּלֶךְ

11. Joshua 8:35

לֹא־הָיָה דָבָר מִכֹּל אֲשֶׁר־צִוָּה מֹשֶׁה אֲשֶׁר לֹא־קָרָא יְהוֹשֻׁעַ

12. Judges 2:17

לֹא־עָשׂוּ כֵן

13. 2 Chronicles 35:18 כַּפֶּסַח means *as the Passover*.

וְכָל־מַלְכֵי יִשְׂרָאֵל לֹא־עָשׂוּ כַּפֶּסַח אֲשֶׁר־עָשָׂה יֹאשִׁיָּהוּ

14. Genesis 42:21,23 אִישׁ has the sense here of *each one*. אֲשֵׁמִים אֲנַחְנוּ means *We are guilty*, and שֹׁמֵעַ means *was listening*. Notice how the qatal with לֹא gives background for the speech event rather than advancing the narrative.

וַיֹּאמְרוּ אִישׁ אֶל־אָחִיו אֲשֵׁמִים אֲנַחְנוּ וְהֵם לֹא יָדְעוּ כִּי שֹׁמֵעַ יוֹסֵף

15. Psalm 54:5 לְנֶגְדָּם means *before them*. The two verbs are the same type as lesson 10.4's בָּא

כִּי קָמוּ לֹא שָׂמוּ אֱלֹהִים לְנֶגְדָּם

16. Genesis 22:1 Thus begins the very famous narrative of Abraham offering his son Isaac. Notice the typical scene-setting before the way-yiqtol string begins. A few pointers or notes:

וַיְהִי אַחַר הַדְּבָרִים הָאֵלֶּה וְהָאֱלֹהִים נִסָּה אֶת־אַבְרָהָם וַיֹּאמֶר אֵלָיו אַבְרָהָם וַיֹּאמֶר הִנֵּנִי

1. אַחַר הַדְּבָרִים הָאֵלֶּה see number 8 above. Notice the different nikkud.
2. Notice the definite article on הָאֱלֹהִים
3. The root נסה means *test*.
4. הִנֵּנִי means *Behold me!* Or *Here I am!*

56

Lesson 12

וַיִּרְאוּ הַשֹּׁמְרִים אִישׁ יוֹצֵא מִן־הָעִיר

Judges 1:24

Goals:

• **Identify and read masculine singular and masculine plural participles.**

What we already know

12.1. Fill out the verb analysis chart for וַיִּרְאוּ :

root	stem	form	person, gender, number	function	basic root meaning

The participle

12.2a. We have two examples of one new verb form in our lesson sentence, the participle.

> RULE: **The sign of the participle in the Qal stem is a holem** וֹ or O **after the first root letter.**

The same participle may appear at different places in the Hebrew Bible spelled either with the וֹ or with the O There is no difference in meaning as a result of the different spellings. The spelling that uses the וֹ is called **plene**, meaning *full*, versus O called **defectiva**.

plene
נוֹתֵן

defectiva
נֹתֵן

12.2b. With the Hebrew participle, the line between noun and verb is fuzzy. Therefore, it is not altogether surprising that we often find the definite article [הַ] on the participle. It is the only verb form on which we will find the definite article. Participles, also somewhat like nouns, may be singular or plural, masculine or feminine. We do not designate participles as 1st, 2nd, or 3rd person. In this lesson we will cover the masculine singular and masculine plural forms, by far the most common in the Bible.

Masculine singular→   no ending: יוֹצֵא

Masculine plural →masculine plural ending ים ִ : הַשֹּׁמְרִים

12.2c. As said above, a participle is a verb form that is closely associated with a noun, namely, **one doing an action.** For this reason we may have to translate the Biblical Hebrew participle with an *-er-word* like the

57

qatal. However, the qatal and the participle do mean a shade differently from each other. As you know, the qatal expresses an attribute of the subject. The participle on the other hand, expresses on-going or **durative** action.

12.2d. The participle may function as a verb, noun, or adjective.

> **As a verb:** use the English "progressive" tenses with the auxiliary form of *be*: *was, were* for past situations, and *is, am, are* for present situations, and *will be* for future situation. Allow context to be your guide. E.g.
>
> אִישׁ יוֹצֵא → *a man was (is, will be) going out*
>
> **As a noun:** use the English phrase *the one(s) who was (were)_____-ing__* E.g.
>
> וַיִּרְאוּ הַשֹּׁמְרִים → *And (then) **the ones who were watching** saw*
>
> **As an adjective:** use an English *-ing* participle. We have to go outside our lesson verse for an example.
>
> לֵב שֹׁמֵעַ (1 Kings 3:9) → *a hearing heart*   Note what will be the subject of a later lesson: adjectives come *after* the noun they modify.

12.2e. Let us take a brief departure from our lesson verse for a point about participles. Often, when the definite article is attached to the participle, the participle follows a noun and renames the noun. *When one noun follows and renames another noun, the second noun is said to be in **apposition** to the first.* Our definition of a verbless clause also requires that a second noun or pronoun rename the first. The difference is that when one noun is in apposition to another, the first noun, the one renamed, is already committed to the grammatical structure of a clause. For example, if the first noun is already functioning as the subject or direct object of a clause, it cannot very well be part of a verbless clause at the same time.

> RULE: **A participle in apposition is often best translated using the words *the one(s) who*.**

For example: וַתִּקְרָא שֵׁם־יְהוָה הַדֹּבֵר אֵלֶיהָ אַתָּה אֵל רֳאִי Genesis 16:13
And she called the name of YHWH, the one who was speaking to her, "You are God, the one seeing me"
(literally, *my one who is seeing*).

12.2f.

> RULE: **The function of the participle in Historical Narrative is to give backgrounded activities.[1]**

---

[1] This rule may be somewhat of an oversimplification. At times, when the participle functions as an adjective, and even more often when it functions as a noun, the function of the participle cannot really be considered as having a value in our discourse profile scheme.

58

12.2g. Fill out the verb analysis charts. Remember that we do not specify person for participles.

root	stem	form	person, gender, number	function	basic root meaning
שׁמר					

root	stem	form	person, gender, number	function	basic root meaning
יצא					

Translate וַיִּרְאוּ הַשֹּׁמְרִים _____

Translate אִישׁ יוֹצֵא מִן־הָעִיר _____

The second clause answers the question "What did they see?" about the first clause. The question that answers such a question is a direct object. The entire second clause is the direct object of the entire verse. Translate the entire verse (You may want to insert the word *that* into the middle of your translation for a

smoother flow.): _____

Discourse profile of Historical Narrative with participles added

12.3. Here is the participle's place in the discourse profile scheme for Historical Narrative:[1]

1. Mainline: Wayyiqtol

   Off-the-line:
   2. Topicalization: X-qatal
      3. Relative past background: אֲשֶׁר qatal
         4. **Backgrounded activities: Participle**
            5. Transition marker: Wayyiqtol of היה
               6. Scene setting: Verbless Clause
                  7. Irrealis scene setting: Negation of any verb by לֹא

---

[1] Once again, the rank of the participles is based on Longacre (1989), 81.

Assignments

12.4a. Match the following examples with their verb form functions in Historical Narrative:

_____1. וַיִּרְאוּ	_____8. שֵׁם אַחַת חַנָּה	A. Mainline
_____2. יוֹצֵא	_____9. אֲשֶׁר צִוָּה	B. Topicalization
_____3. לֹא־הָיָה דָבָר	_____10. יְהוָה אָמַר	C. Relative past background
_____4. אֲשֶׁר־עָשָׂה	_____11. וַיְהִי־שָׁם	D. Backgrounded activities
_____5. וַיְהִי בַּיּוֹם הַהוּא	_____12. הַנּוֹתֵן	E. Transition marker
_____6. וַיֹּאמְרוּ	_____13. לֹא לָקָחוּ	F. Scene-setting
_____7. וַעֲבָדָיו בָּאוּ	_____14. שֹׁמְרִים	G. Irrealis scene-setting

12.4b. Translate:

Genesis 18:16

1. וְאַבְרָהָם הֹלֵךְ

Genesis 42:23

2. לֹא יָדְעוּ כִּי שֹׁמֵעַ יוֹסֵף

1 Kings 5:24 אֲרָזִים
עֲצֵי means *trees of cedar*.

3. וַיְהִי חִירוֹם נֹתֵן לִשְׁלֹמֹה עֲצֵי אֲרָזִים

2 Samuel 8:15
מִשְׁפָּט means *judgment*.

4. וַיְהִי דָוִד עֹשֶׂה מִשְׁפָּט

Joshua 16:1 הַמִּדְבָּר
means *the wilderness*.
מִירִיחוֹ בָּהָר בֵּית־אֵל
means *from Jericho to Bethel*.

5. הַמִּדְבָּר עֹלֶה מִירִיחוֹ בָּהָר בֵּית־אֵל

Genesis 39:23 שַׂר
means *captain*.
כָּל־מְאוּמָה means
everything. אִתּוֹ =
אֵת + וֹ

6. שַׂר רֹאֶה אֶת־כָּל־מְאוּמָה בְּיָדוֹ בַּאֲשֶׁר יְהוָה אִתּוֹ

60

7.

וַיִּקַּח דָּוִד אֶת הַמַּיִם וַיֵּלְכוּ וְאֵין רֹאֶה וְאֵין יוֹדֵעַ

1 Samuel 26:12 וְאֵין translates *And there was not..*

8.

הַטּוֹבָה אֲשֶׁר יְהוָה אֱלֹהֶיךָ נָתַן לָךְ

Deuteronomy 4:21 הַטּוֹבָה means *the good*. ךָ- is the 3.m.s. objective or possessive suffix meaning *you* or *your*. אֱלֹהֶיךָ = אֱלֹהִים + ךָ- = *your God*. ךָ- + לְ = לָךְ = *to you*.

9.

וַיהוָה הֹלֵךְ לִפְנֵיהֶם

Exodus 13:21 לִפְנֵיהֶם means *before them*.

10.

וְהַפְּרִזִּי אָז יֹשֵׁב בָּאָרֶץ

Genesis 13:7 וְהַפְּרִזִי אָז means *the Perizite then...*

11.

וְלוֹט יֹשֵׁב בְּשַׁעַר־סְדֹם וַיַּרְא־לוֹט

Genesis 19:1 שַׁעַר means *gate*.

12.

כַּאֲשֶׁר עָשָׂה לִבְנֵי עֵשָׂו הַיֹּשְׁבִים בְּשֵׂעִיר

Deuteronomy 2:22

13.

וּבְנֵי יִשְׂרָאֵל הַיֹּשְׁבִים בְּעָרֵי יְהוּדָה וַיִּמְלֹךְ עֲלֵיהֶם רְחַבְעָם

1 Kings 12:17 Guess what the root מלך means. עֲלֵיהֶם means *over them*.

14.

וְכָל־עֲבָדָיו הַשֹּׁמְעִים אֵת כָּל־הַדְּבָרִים

Jeremiah 36:24

12.4c. Fill out verb analysis charts for numbers 1 through 3, and 12.

MODULE TWO—DIRECT SPEECH AND MORE ON THE SYSTEM OF VERB FORMS

OVERVIEW: We have thus far managed an introduction to the Historical Narrative genre of Biblical Hebrew, and we will continue to practice with this material. Learning Historical Narrative is the best place to begin when learning to read Biblical Hebrew prose because Historical Narrative accounts for the greatest single portion of Biblical prose. The Historical Narrative genre is also like the glue which holds a Biblical story together. So you may now be anxious to try your new understanding on a full text. However, we still need to build vocabulary and begin learning about **Direct Speech** before we can begin our first reading. In a sense, Direct Speech is the "other half" of Biblical prose. We can define Direct Speech in the following way:

> DEFINITION: **Direct Speech is communication in which the speaker refers to that which is in the immediate context of the speaker and/or listener. This type of communication includes dialogue, prayer, sermons, prophecy, etc.**[1]

Direct speech in Biblical Hebrew is commonly marked by one of the speech verbs like אמר or דבר Biblical Hebrew does not use quotation marks or any other kind of special punctuation mark to systematically separate narration from quoted speech; however, you may be aided here by a slightly over-simplified analogy: Module Two will begin to teach you about what would be *inside our quotation marks* whereas Module One taught you what would be *outside our quotation marks.* If we can imagine Biblical Hebrew as having quotation marks, we would realize that the language inside and outside the marks use somewhat different systems of verb forms. Some scholars do, in fact, divide all prose into only two genres, Narration and Direct Speech.[2] However, you will learn several genres within the larger classification of Direct Speech that are helpful, namely **Predictive Narrative, Instructional Discourse and Hortatory Discourse.**[3] Even Historical Narrative can be found in Direct Speech when one person, in a dialogue or other direct speech act, tells a story set in the past. Here is a chart representing the genres to which you will have been introduced by the end of the first two modules of this course.

---

[1] See Talstra(1978), 170.

[2] Niccacci(1990), §3 called *discourse* or *comment* and *narrative*; Talstra(1978), 170 called *discursive* and *narrative*, both after Schneider, *Grammatik des biblischen Hebräisch*(Munich: Claudius Verlag, 1974). The variety of terminology in this area as in Hebrew studies generally is unfortunate. The designation "inside" or "outside the quotation marks" does not coincide perfectly with the distinction between two genres of these Hebraists. For instance, they would also include Procedural Discourse(Module 4) in *discourse(discursive)*.

[3] These three genre names are based on Longacre's latest nomenclature in "Weqatal Forms in Biblical Hebrew Prose," *Biblical Hebrew and Discourse Linguistics*(ed. Bergen. Dallas: Summer Institute of Linguistics, 1994), 50-98 which distinguishes between a +projection Instructional Discourse and -projection Procedural Discourse(see this volume Module 4) and Dawson(1994), §2.2.

MODULE ONE:	MODULE TWO:
outside the "quotation marks"	*inside the "quotation marks"* *or* *Direct Speech*
Historical Narrative	***Predictive Narrative** ***Instructional Discourse** ***Hortatory Discourse** **Historical Narrative**

Remember, the genres you will spend most of your time on in this module are the three starred genres above which are used exclusively in Direct Speech. Historical Narrative, on the other hand, may be found either inside or outside our imagined Hebrew quotation marks. In this module, there is even one lesson to show how Historical Narrative acts just a bit differently when it is inside direct speech.

Certainly all is not new in this new module. In learning the particulars of the Direct Speech genres, you will learn that they have discourse profile schemes that are in many ways similar, especially in the lower-ranking constructions, to the one you learned for Historical Narrative in 12.3. You will learn how the mainline/off-the-line distinction that exists in Historical Narrative also exists in the Direct Speech genres except that the **weqatal** and the **volitional forms** are the mainlines and **X-yiqtol** is used for topicalization.

Lesson 13

וַיֹּאמֶר וְהָיָה כִּי־יִרְאוּ אֹתָךְ וְאָמְרוּ אִשְׁתּוֹ זֹאת

Genesis 12:11-12

Goals:

- **Identify and read the Qal weqatal verb form.**
- **Identify and read the yiqtol verb form in a dependent clause.**
- **Learn some basics of identifying pronominal suffixes on the DDO and nouns.**
- **Identify and read the demonstrative pronouns.**

What we already know

Translate וַיֹּאמֶר _____ What genre of discourse does the Hebrew word

וַיֹּאמֶר indicate we are in? _____

Weqatal and +projection

13.2a. In addition to indicating that we are in the Historical Narrative genre, the Hebrew word וַיֹּאמֶר also almost always signals that direct speech, that is, a quotation, will soon begin. The next word of our lesson verse וְהָיָה is indeed direct speech. Hopefully, the word does not look altogether unfamiliar. If

we remove the *vav* which once again means *and*, what verb form are we left with? _____

> RULE: **The addition of a *vav* to the qatal form results in another verb form called the weqatal, pronounced /ve-ka-TAL/.**

13.2b. The addition of the *vav* to the word has an important effect on the word. It must now be necessarily the first word in its clause. We identify this first position in the clause as the ***clause-initial*** position. The weqatal, therefore shares two qualities with the wayyiqtol, the *vav* and its clause-initial position. And like the wayyiqtol functions as the mainline of the Historical Narrative genre, the weqatal functions as the mainline of several direct speech genres. The following proverb is an over-generalization, but it is very helpful at this stage of your studies: "Wayyiqtol outside the quotation marks; weqatal inside."

> RULE: **The weqatal verb form is the mainline of several Direct Speech genres which are +projection** (defined below).

13.2c. Now we move on to translating the weqatal. The weqatal shares the same meaning as the qatal, pinning an attribute on the subject of the verb. For instance, how do we translate the qatal verb form

אָמַר ? _____ (5.2) We also usually use an *er*-word and an optional *of* to translate the weqatal. However, in its context within direct speech, the weqatal often translates as English future with our words *will be*. For example, וְאָמַר translates *And he will be a sayer*. You will also see, as we proceed, that to call these genres *future tense genres* would not be entirely accurate. Therefore, we call the direct speech genres in which weqatal is the mainline, the ***plus-projection genres***.

64

DEFINITION: *Plus projection* (usually written *+projection*) **genres are forward-looking.**[1] **They are genres in which the speaker is expressing the way things *will be* or the way he *wants them to be.***

The root הָיָה since it expresses a state of being rather than an action, is one root with which we do *not* use the customary *er*-word for translating a qatal or weqatal in an independent clause.

Translation of וְהָיָה : *And (then) it will be*

13.2d. Here is how to fill out the verb analysis chart:

root	stem	form	person, gender, number	function	basic root meaning
הָיָה	Qal	weqatal	3rd m. s. *it*	Predictive Narrative Mainline	*be, happen*

Since weqatal is the mainline verb form of the direct speech genres generally, you may wonder why Predictive Narrative was chosen for the function of וְהָיָה Context, much of which has not been given to you for our lesson verse, can be helpful for distinguishing Predictive Narrative from the other direct speech genres. Also, our lesson phrase וְהָיָה כִּי translated *And it will be when*, is typically found in Predictive Narrative. Relax, we still have a lot of time to learn the distinctions between the direct speech genres.

DEFINITION: *Predictive Narrative* **tells a story set in the speaker's future like Historical Narrative tells a story set in the speaker's past.**

13.2e. Looking ahead in our lesson verse, we see that there is another weqatal verb form וְאָמְרוּ

Fill out the verb analysis chart:

root	stem	form	person, gender, number	function	basic root meaning
				Predictive Narrative Mainline	

Translation: *And (then) they will be sayers*

13.2f. Here is an important qualification on the use of *vav* in the weqatal form: *The vav of the weqatal verb*

---

[1] See Dawson(1994), §3.2.2.1.4.

65

form is not always accompanied by shewa. For example, the *vav* may be accompanied by a *hireq* [ְ] or it may appear as a *shureq* [וּ]. The *vav-patakh-dagesh forte* unit of Historical Narrative's wayyiqtol is much more consistent than the *vav* of the weqatal.

13.2g. The material you have learned so far in this lesson can easily be summarized and related to what you already know about Historical Narrative:

MAINLINES
- have the *vav*
- are clause-initial

HISTORICAL NARRATIVE	+PROJECTION DIRECT SPEECH GENRES
WAYYIQTOL	WEQATAL

The yiqtol in a dependent clause

13.3a. We also meet with our first off-the-line verb form for the Predictive Narrative Discourse in our lesson verse's יִרְאוּ Again, we should be able to spot the familiar in this verb form. It is just like the wayyiqtol we have seen so often in Historical Narrative, only it is minus the *vav-patakh-dagesh forte* unit. Remember that it is also normal for a 3rd *heh* root to lose the *heh* in the wayyiqtol.

> RULE: **The verb form with a prefixed subject pronoun and no *vav-patakh-dagesh forte* is called the *yiqtol* /yik-TOL/ verb form.**

13.3b. The כִּי in our lesson verse, like the אֲשֶׁר of earlier lessons, results in a dependent clause. Remember that [אֲשֶׁר -qatal] in Historical Narrative gives *relative past background*.

> RULE: **The yiqtol verb form, when in a dependent clause <u>in any genre,</u> expresses action that is *relative non-past background*. Allowing context to be your guide, use English present or future tense translations.**

Relative non-past background here does not refer to what is non-past for the speaker and his audience. Relative non-past means what is in *non-past relative to the time of the main clause.*

13.3c. Fill out the verb analysis chart for יִרְאוּ :

root	stem	form	person, gender, number	function	basic root meaning
				dep. clause w/ yiqtol = relative non-past background	

Translation: *when they see*

13.3d. Once again, a simple summary that relates what you learn in this lesson to what you learned in Module One about Historical Narrative may be helpful:

DEPENDENT CLAUSES

(identified by אֲשֶׁר כִּי or אִם)

with QATAL	with YIQTOL
RELATIVE PAST BACKGROUND	RELATIVE NON-PAST BACKGROUND

Pronominal suffixes

13.4a. The next word אֹתָךְ is made of two parts:

אֹת + ךְ, --

the sign of a DDO   object pronoun

here with *holem*   suffix *you*

defectiva [·]

Hebrew has a full complement of object pronoun suffixes, covering every combination of person, gender, and number, that can be attached to the DDO. These suffixes can also be attached to nouns as either possessive or objective pronouns like a וֹ or וֹ which means *him* or *his*. At this point in your studies you are only responsible to learn two more of the most common:

ךְ, --meaning *you* (feminine, singular)

ךָ --meaning *you* (masculine, singular)

Translation of כִּי־יִרְאוּ אֹתָךְ : *when they see you* (feminine, singular)

13.4b. Adding pronominal suffixes to nouns results in some changes to the appearance of the noun.

RULE: **A noun is put into its shortened construct form before the suffix is added to it.**

The construct state of the noun is very clearly seen with the masculine plural forms. For example, אֱלֹהִים becomes אֱלֹהֵי before the pronominal suffix is added. You will notice that the nikkud under the *heh* can vary but the *yod* after the *heh* is reliable:

אֱלֹהָיו means *his God*

אֱלֹהֶיךָ means *your* (masculine, singular) *God*

אֱלֹהַיִךְ means *your* (feminine, singular) *God*

Below the suffixes are added to לִפְנֵי which itself is made of two parts, פָּנִים + לְ and means *before, in the presence of.* Again, the nikkud under the last letter of the noun, here the *nun*, may vary, but the *yod* is reliable.

לְפָנָיו means *before him*

לְפָנֶיךָ means *before you* (masculine, singular)

לְפָנַיִךְ meaning *before you* (feminine, singular)

13.4c אִשְׁתּוֹ of our lesson verse is made of two parts.

אִשָּׁה (*wife, woman*) + וֹ (*his*)

Notice two things:

1. Hebrew nouns have gender, either masculine or feminine. אִשָּׁה is a feminine noun. One helpful way to identify feminine nouns is that they end in ה or ת Parts of the body are also largely feminine, even if they are references to the body parts of a male. Most other nouns are masculine.

2. The final ה of אִשָּׁה became a ת This is normal practice for words ending in ה when they are put into their construct state before a possessive suffix is added.

We will come back to the issue of pronominal suffixes in our next lesson.

Demonstrative pronouns

13.5 זֹאת means *this*. זֹאת is the *feminine singular demonstrative pronoun*. There are three demonstrative pronouns that fill four slots.

DEMONSTRATIVE PRONOUNS

	MASCULINE	FEMININE
SINGULAR	זֶה (*this*)	זֹאת (*this*)
PLURAL	אֵלֶּה (*these*)	אֵלֶּה (*these*)

Translation of זֹאת אִשְׁתּוֹ ____*This (one) is his wife*____

Since the word order in this verbless clause is P-S, we may interpret the Egyptians as expressing surprise such as *This one is HIS WIFE (and NOT his sister)!*

Assignments

13.6a. Translate:

1. בְּיָדְךָ		9. עֵינָיו		17. דְּבָרֶיךָ
2. יָדוֹ		10. עֵינוֹ		18. דְּבָרָיו
3. יָדָיו		11. עֵינְךָ		19. דְּבָרוֹ
4. אֱלֹהָיו		12. עֵינֶךָ		20. הַדֶּרֶךְ
5. אֱלֹהֶיךָ		13. עֵינֶיךָ		21. מִדְּרָכֶיךָ
6. לְקֹלֶךָ		14. שְׁמֶךָ		22. לְדַרְכּוֹ
7. אֵלֶיךָ		15. שִׁמְךָ		23. בְּאַרְצוֹ
8. לְךָ		16. בְּשִׁמְךָ		24. מֵאַרְצְךָ

68

13.6b. By now you should discontinue the practice of writing the English translations in your book. Leave the Hebrew in Hebrew. If you are wondering how you will remember what the Hebrew says, merely translate it once again if you want to. Translate:

Deuteronomy 13:2

1. וְנָתַן אֵלֶיךָ

Deuteronomy 7:24

2. וְנָתַן בְּיָדֶךָ

Deuteronomy 13:18 רַחֲמִים means *mercies*.

3. וְנָתַן־לְךָ רַחֲמִים

Deuteronomy 19:8 You may add an *of*.

4. וְנָתַן אֶת־כָּל־הָאָרֶץ אֲשֶׁר דִּבֶּר

Genesis 3:22 הַחַיִּים is a noun is construct with מֵעֵץ and means *the life*.

5. וְלָקַח גַּם מֵעֵץ הַחַיִּים וְאָכַל

Exodus 7:4 כֶם - is the pronoun suffix for *you* masculine plural. A yiqtol can be made irrealis by לֹא as well as any other verb.

6. וְלֹא־יִשְׁמַע אֲלֵכֶם פַּרְעֹה

2 Samuel 14:16

7. כִּי יִשְׁמַע הַמֶּלֶךְ

Genesis 26:24 אֲבִי is the singular construct of אָב אָבִיךָ renames אַבְרָהָם

8. וַיֹּאמֶר אָנֹכִי אֱלֹהֵי אַבְרָהָם אָבִיךָ

Exodus 3:18

9. וְשָׁמְעוּ לְקֹלֶךָ

Exodus 23:33

10. לֹא יֵשְׁבוּ בְּאַרְצְךָ

Judges 21:22

11. וְהָיָה כִּי־יָבֹאוּ

Genesis 46:33 מַה־מַּעֲשֵׂיכֶם means *What are your (masculine plural) occupations?*

12. וְהָיָה כִּי־יִקְרָא לָכֶם פַּרְעֹה וְאָמַר מַה־מַּעֲשֵׂיכֶם

Exodus 4:16 הוּא is a subject pronoun meaning *he* put in here for emphasis.

13. וְדִבֶּר־הוּא לְךָ אֶל־הָעָם

Jeremiah 28:6 אָמֵן is Amen!

14. וַיֹּאמֶר יִרְמְיָה אָמֵן כֵּן יַעֲשֶׂה יְהוָה

Genesis 27:20

15. וַיֹּאמֶר יִצְחָק אֶל־בְּנוֹ מַה־זֶּה

Genesis 3:13

16. וַיֹּאמֶר יְהוָה אֱלֹהִים לָאִשָּׁה מַה־זֹּאת

69

13.6c. Fill out verb analysis charts for the verbs in numbers 4, 5, 10, 11, and 15.

Lesson 14
וְשָׁמְעוּ אֶת־דְּבָרֶיךָ וְאוֹתָם לֹא יַעֲשׂוּ

Ezekiel 33:31

Goals:
- **Identify and read nouns with pronominal suffixes attached.**
- **Identify and read the X-yiqtol construction.**

What we already know

14.1. This time our lesson verse does not contain the speech introduction formula which uses the root אמר because it precedes our lesson verse by several Biblical verses. Fill out the verb analysis chart for וְשָׁמְעוּ (13.2a):

root	stem	form	person, gender, number	function	basic root meaning

Make sure you have taken proper note of the third person, masculine *plural* subject pronoun affix.

Possessive suffixes on singular and plural nouns

14.2a. דְּבָרֶיךָ means *your words*. It is made by first putting the word into its construct form, and then adding the possessive suffix. Look at the variations that are attested for the masculine word דָּבָר when it is singular or plural, with and without a possessive suffix:

MASCULINE NOUNS

SINGULAR: *PLURAL:*

   Absolute: דָּבָר   Absolute: דְּבָרִים

   Construct: דְּבַר   Construct: דִּבְרֵי

   W/ possessive suffix: דְּבָרֶךָ דְּבָרְךָ דְּבָרֶךָ   W/ possessive suffix: דְּבָרֶיךָ דְּבָרֶיךָ דְּבָרֶיךָ

Notes:

1. This first may seem like a lot of picky nikkud, but it's not so bad if you focus on the right details. Notice that that none of the singular forms use a *yod* before the suffix, but all the plural forms do. This pattern, using the auxiliary *yod* to identify plural nouns is quite reliable *except* with irregular nouns. You will be exposed to two common but irregular nouns below in 14.2c. and then a fairly comprehensive list of irregular nouns in 18.4.

2. It also helps to notice that the construct forms have shortened or abbreviated vowel sounds and that the plural with a possessive suffix is really only the construct form with the suffix added. Be thankful you are now learning to read Biblical Hebrew and not yet compose it!

71

14.2b. Although our lesson verse does not have an example, it is time we learned more about what feminine nouns look like with pronominal suffixes since we are on the topic. As we saw in 13.4c, feminine nouns often end in *heh*, and the *heh* changes to *tav* before a pronominal suffix is added. This transformation of *heh* into *tav* must be clarified because it is easy to confuse the plural and construct forms. Let us look at the Hebrew word מִשְׁפָּחָה meaning *family*. Notice that it ends in *heh*. It is indeed a feminine noun. Compare the following forms:

מִשְׁפָּחֹת	מִשְׁפַּחְתּוֹ	מִשְׁפְּחֹתָיו
plural	singular w/ 3rd m. s. suffix	plural w/ 3rd m. s. suffix
families	*his family*	*his families*

Notice that, like the masculine plural noun with an attached pronominal suffix, the feminine plural, with its usual ת -- ending (here written defectiva), also uses the auxiliary *yod* (compare 8.4a).

14.2c. Even though it is a handy clue, you need to know that all nouns which are feminine do not necessarily end in *heh* or *tav*. Here is the synopsis for a feminine noun נֶפֶשׁ meaning *soul*.

FEMININE NOUNS

SINGULAR:	*PLURAL:*
Absolute: נֶפֶשׁ	Absolute: נְפָשׁוֹת
Construct: נֶפֶשׁ	Construct: נַפְשֹׁת
W/ possessive suffix: נַפְשְׁךָ	W/ possessive suffix: נַפְשֹׁתֵיכֶם

Note: The 2nd m. p. suffix is shown on the plural because the singular form is neither attested with נֶפֶשׁ nor would it make sense. Notice how the feminine plural with a suffix has both the feminine plural ending וֹת-- and the *yod* that we also see on the masculine plural construct just as we saw in 13.4b.

14.2d. As an additional note, many very common nouns are irregular, and we will study them more in Lesson 18. For now let us look at two: אָח is shown with the first person, singular, common suffix ִי --(*my*) and אָב is shown with the third person, masculine, singular suffix יו --(*his*).

TWO IRREGULAR NOUNS

SINGULAR:	*PLURAL:*
Absolute: אָח	Absolute: אַחִים
Construct: אֲחִי	Construct: אֲחֵי
W/ possessive suffix: אָחִי	W/ possessive suffix: אַחַי

Absolute: אָב	Absolute: אָבֹת אָבוֹת
Construct: אֲבִי	Construct: אֲבוֹת
W/ possessive suffix: אָבִיו	W/ possessive suffix: אֲבֹתָיו

Translation of the third clause   וְשָׁמְעוּ אֶת־דְּבָרֶיךָ   : _____

72

X-yiqtol

14.3a. וְאוֹתָם is made of three parts as follows:

$$וְ = \textit{and}$$

$$אוֹת = \text{sign of the DDO (plene spelling)}$$

$$ם\text{ָ} = 3^{rd} \text{ m. plural ending } \textit{(them)}$$

14.3b. לֹא יַעֲשׂוּ is easy enough. Translate it with the future tense that is appropriate to the predictive context that we are in.

14.3c. The important new thing to see in this second clause in our lesson verse is the word order. We can call this an X-yiqtol construction, similar to the X-qatal construction that we learned about in Lesson 5.3. The point is that the +projection genres have an analogous structure in them that performs the same topicalization as the X-qatal does in Historical Narrative.

> RULE: **The X-yiqtol construction in the +projection genres has the multi-faceted function** *topicalization*. **Translate X-yiqtol constructions in the +projection genres in future or present time as follows:**
> **Future:** *(And)It will be ___(Fronted X-element)___ who(that) will___ (Remainder of clause)*
> **Present:** *(And)It is ___(Fronted X-element___ who(that)___ (Remainder of present time clause)*

Allow context to guide you to a present or future tense translation. Fill out the verb analysis chart for יַעֲשׂוּ :

root	stem	form	person, gender, number	function	basic root meaning

Translation of the fourth clause: *It will be them (the words) that they will not do*

Translation of the entire lesson verse:_____

_____

14.3d. Notice how the constructions work together in our lesson verse:

Clause 1:	Weqatal **(Consequential) Mainline**	*And so they will be hearers of your words*
	2: X-yiqtol **Topicalization**	*But it will be the words that they will not do*

By using a variety of verb forms the prophet expresses his incitement of the uncooperative people in the most powerful way, putting the spotlight first on them as *hearers*. Then the writer surprises us by changing the focus to the *words*. It seems as though his audience was willing to do *anything but* the words of the prophet.

The four component Hebrew Verbal System

14.4a. We can pair the wayyiqtol yiqtol, weqatal, and qatal verb forms in three different ways, and in so doing, create a simple overview of the Hebrew Verbal system as we have learned it so far. You will want to refer to this page frequently through the course, and so it is also printed in the "Helpful Charts" section near the back of the book. First, the four verb forms may be paired according to their shared *meanings* as follows:

SHARED MEANINGS:

YIQTOL and WAYYIQTOL[1]	QATAL and WEQATAL
Describes emerging action. Focus on the process.	Pins an attribute on the subject. Focus on the whole adjectivally or statively.
These verb forms describe action as it emerges like a video with sound.	This verb form expresses facts like snap shots on which appear the qatal or weqatal "mini-sentences" as captions.
For instance, the word יִשְׁמַע could be used to describe *He hears, He is hearing, He will hear.*	For instance, the word שָׁמַע could be used as the caption on a snapshot: *He is a hearer, He was a hearer.*

14.4b. The same four verb forms may also be paired in a different way, this time according to their shared *discourse functions* as follows:

SHARED DISCOURSE FUNCTIONS:

WAYYIQTOL and WEQATAL	QATAL and YIQTOL
Mainline These mainline forms have the *vavs*, and they are necessarily clause-initial.[2]	Off-the-line The off-the-line forms are without the *vavs*, and they are generally not clause-initial in Predictive Narrative or Instructional Discourse.

---

[1] We risk oversimplification here by putting together all prefixed forms. There are actually two prefixed forms, one that sometimes appears shorter that is modal and has made its way into the wayyiqtol as the verb form dedicated to moving forward narrative time. The other prefixed form is usually identical in appearance with the first and is used for generic past as well as non-past. See Hetzron(1990), 697-698. Pairing these the prefixed forms is still justified because, taken together, they are indeed the only truly fientive form.

[2] Hatav(1997), § 2.2.

14.4c. A third pairing is necessary to complete the summary of what you have learned so far. The same four verb forms may be paired according to the *genres* they share as follows:

SHARED GENRES:

WAYYIQTOL and (X-)QATAL	WEQATAL and (X-)YIQTOL
-Projection: Historical Narrative	+Projection: Predictive Narrative and Instructional Discourse

Notice that the third pairing specifies X-qatal and X-yiqtol. Although the qatal and yiqtol are used in dependent clauses in all genres, the independent X-qatal and X-yiqtol clauses do not cross genre boundaries.

The third pairing is the one that comes closest to pairing the forms by the time or tense that they express. It is the pairing that previous introductory grammars stress the most while ignoring the first two pairings almost completely.[1] However, it is the third pairing that is actually the least consistent of the three because all four verb forms are known to cross time as well as genre boundaries. We tend, with our Indo-European language backgrounds, to think of times, for example past, present or future, as each being represented by their own dedicated verb forms. Not so in Biblical Hebrew in which time is a function of genre.

Assignments

14.5a. Translate:

1. דְּבַר־אֱלֹהִים
2. דִּבְרֵי אֱלֹהִים
3. כָּל־דִּבְרֵי יְהוָה
4. דְּבָרַי
5. דְּבָרִי
6. בְּנֵי־הָאֱלֹהִים
7. בְּנִי
8. לִבְנִי

9. בְּעַבְדְּךָ
10. בְּעַבְדִּי
11. עַבְדֵי אָבִיו
12. אֶל־אֲבֹתֶיךָ
13. אֲבֹתַי
14. אָבִיךָ
15. לְאָחִיךָ
16. מֵאָחִיךָ

17. אֲדֹנֶיךָ
18. לְפָנֶיךָ
19. לִפְנֵי הָאֱלֹהִים
20. לִפְנֵי בְּנֵי יִשְׂרָאֵל
21. לְפָנַי
22. שְׁנוֹתֶיךָ
23. שְׁנוֹתַי
24. מִכֹּל מַלְכֵי יִשְׂרָאֵל

14.5b. Translate:

1 Kings 3:12

1. וְאַחֲרֶיךָ לֹא־יָקוּם

2 Kings 6:31 אִם creates a dependent clause. הַיּוֹם means *today*.

2. וַיֹּאמֶר כֹּה־יַעֲשֶׂה־לִי אֱלֹהִים אִם־יַעֲמֹד רֹאשׁ אֱלִישָׁע עָלָיו הַיּוֹם

2 Samuel 19:37 כִּמְעַט means *just a little way*. Remember that אֵת can mean *with*.

3. כִּמְעַט יַעֲבֹר עַבְדְּךָ אֶת־הַיַּרְדֵּן אֶת־הַמֶּלֶךְ

---

[1] It was already mentioned in the note in 5.2 that the majority of grammarians hold to a tense-based model of the Biblical Hebrew verbal system. For a tense-based view that is particularly sensitive to syntax and discourse, see Revell, "The System of the Verb in Standard Biblical Prose," *Hebrew Union College Annual, LX*(1989), 1-37.

4. וַיֹּאמֶר הַמֶּלֶךְ אִתִּי יַעֲבֹר כִּמְהָם וַאֲנִי אֶעֱשֶׂה־לּוֹ אֶת־הַטּוֹב בְּעֵינֶיךָ

2 Samuel 19:39 אִתִּי means *with me*. כִּמְהָם is a name. In אֶעֱשֶׂה א is the prefix pronoun meaning *I*.

בְּ + עֵינֶי + ךָ = בְּעֵינֶיךָ

5. וְדָם יַעֲבָר־בָּךְ

Ezekiel 5:17 If you have forgotten דָּם see the Lesson 9 lesson verse.

6. וְשָׁמְעוּ לְקֹלֶךָ

Exodus 3:18

7. כִּי־יֵלֵךְ מַלְאָכִי לְפָנֶיךָ

Exodus 23:23 Do not forget to account for the suffix ִי -- (see 14.2d).

8. הִנֵּה מַלְאָכִי יֵלֵךְ לְפָנֶיךָ

Exodus 32:34

9. וַיֹּאמֶר מֹשֶׁה אֶל־יְהוָה וְשָׁמְעוּ מִצְרַיִם

Numbers 14:13

10. וְשָׂמוּ לָהֶם רֹאשׁ אֶחָד וְעָלוּ מִן־הָאָרֶץ כִּי גָדוֹל יוֹם יִזְרְעֶאל

Hosea 2:2 In 8.3e you learned that 3rd *heh* roots can lose the *heh* in 3rd m. p. Qal qatal, and in this lesson you learned that only two roots letters of a hollow root will appear in Qal qatal. In this verse, which verb is hollow and which is a 3rd *heh*? It pays to know your roots.

11. וְקָרְאוּ לְפָנָיו כָּכָה יֵעָשֶׂה לָאִישׁ

Esther 6:9 כָּכָה is made from the particle כְּ and a form of כֹּה

12. וְהָלְכוּ אֵלַיִךְ וְקָרְאוּ לָךְ עִיר יְהוָה

Isaiah 60:14

13. יְהוּדָה יַעֲמֹד עַל־גְּבוּלוֹ וּבֵית יוֹסֵף יַעַמְדוּ עַל־גְּבוּלָם

Joshua 18:5 גְּבוּל means *border*, and גְּבוּלָם means *their border*.

14. וְנָשְׂאוּ כְּלִמָּתָם אֲשֶׁר עָשׂוּ

Ezekiel 44:13 כְּלִמָּתָם means *their shame*.

15. וְצֹאנָם יִקָּחוּ
וּגְמַלֵּיהֶם יִשְׂאוּ לָהֶם
וְקָרְאוּ עֲלֵיהֶם מָגוֹר מִסָּבִיב

Jeremiah 49:29   There is a lot of vocabulary here that you do not know, but it is worth including the verse because of the series of verbs which you do know. ‏ָם‎ or ‏הֶם‎ used as a suffix four times in the verse, means *their* or *them*. ‏צֹאן‎ are *sheep*, and ‏גְמַלֵּי‎ are *camels*. You may translate ‏עֲלֵיהֶם מָגוֹר מִסָּבִיב‎ ...*concerning them, "Fear is all around."* Even though footprint *dagesh* in the ‏שׂ‎ is missing, ‏יִשְׂאוּ‎ is still made from the 1st ‏נ‎ root that the hireq under the prefix pronoun suggests. The *nun* tends to be com-pletely lost in this manner when the footprint *dagesh* precedes a guttural letter, here the *aleph*.

14.5c. Fill out verb analysis charts for the verbs in numbers 4, 6, 7, 13, and 14.

Lesson 15

וַיְהִי בַבֹּקֶר וַיֹּאמֶר אֶל־לָבָן מַה־זֹּאת עָשִׂיתָ לִּי הֲלֹא בְרָחֵל עָבַדְתִּי עִמָּךְ
וְלָמָּה רִמִּיתָנִי:

Genesis 29:25

Goals:

- Identify and read the nikkud of the definite article when used with a preposition.
- Identify and read the Qal and Piel qatal and weqatal verb forms in all persons, genders, and numbers.
- Identify and read questions.

What we already know

15.1. Fill out the verb analysis chart for וַיֹּאמֶר and וַיְהִי :

root	stem	form	person, gender, number	function	basic root meaning

root	stem	form	person, gender, number	function	basic root meaning

Preposition with the nikkud of the definite article

15.2. בַבֹּקֶר means *in the morning*. There is an important detail of note. The prefixed preposition בְּ is accompanied by the nikkud of the definite article, the *patakh* and the following *dagesh forte*. This is how we know the word means *in the morning*.

> RULE: When בְּ or the other prefixed prepositions precede the definite article
> [הַ] the ה is normally dropped, and the preposition receives the ה's nikkud
> [בַּ]. We translate with the word *the*, as in *in the.*

Translate וַיְהִי בַבֹּקֶר וַיֹּאמֶר אֶל־לָבָן : _____

_____

Verb charts for qatal

15.3a. The rest of our lesson verse contain the following three verbs:

עָשִׂ֫יתָ

עָבַ֫דְתִּי

רְמִיתָ֫נִי

The *qamets* under the first root letter of the first two verbs indicate what form and stem?

_____ (4.3g) The *hireq* under the *resh* of the third word together with the

dagesh in the *mem* indicate what stem for the third verb?_____ (6.2b)   Below are the appropriate verb charts for our three words, but first we will clarify some terminology.

15.3b. Note: **Strong roots** have three strong root letters. **Weak roots** have one or more weak letters which cause exceptional verb forms. Weak letters include the following:

WEAK LETTERS:
1st *nun* [נ]
1st *yod* [י]
1st guttural letters
2nd *yod* [יִ]
2nd *vav* [ו] or [וֹ]
3rd *heh* [ה]

Below we have charts for the weak verbs with *heh* in the third position and guttural letters (ע ח ה א ר) in the first position. We will encounter other weak verbs later in our studies.

Note: In the charts below and as a rule when you are given charts in this book, the qatal will be given but not the weqatal. The weqatal is conjugated the same as the qatal except that the weqatal has the prefixed *vav*. When you know how to conjugate the qatal you also know how to conjugate the weqatal. You will later see that the same comment, with a few exceptions, can be made about the yiqtol and wayyiqtol conjugations.

For complete conjugations of the many root types in their several verb forms you can refer to the verb charts near the back of this book. You will no doubt want to refer to the verb charts there often throughout the remainder of this course.

QAL QATAL

	STRONG ROOT	THIRD ה	FIRST GUTTURAL
SING. 3 M. (he, it)	קָטַל	עָשָׂה	עָמַד
3 F (she, it)	קָטְלָה	עָשְׂתָה	עָמְדָה
2 M (you)	קָטַלְתָּ	עָשִׂיתָ	עָמַדְתָּ
2 F (you)	קָטַלְתְּ	עָשִׂית	עָמַדְתְּ
1 C (I)	קָטַלְתִּי	עָשִׂיתִי	עָמַדְתִּי
PLUR. 3 C (they)	קָטְלוּ	עָשׂוּ	עָמְדוּ
2 M (you)	קְטַלְתֶּם	עֲשִׂיתֶם	עֲמַדְתֶּם
2 F (you)	קְטַלְתֶּן	עֲשִׂיתֶן	עֲמַדְתֶּן
1 C (we)	קָטַלְנוּ	עָשִׂינוּ	עָמַדְנוּ

A [֡] is used in the place of a regular *qamets* when the *qamets* should be pronounced normally even though it is in a closed, unaccented syllable (3.5b). The vertical slash next to the *qamets* is called a **meteg**. Essentially, the meteg tells us whether to pronounce the *qamets* regularly or to pronounce it as an /o/ as in *boat* because it is a *qamets khatuf* (see 3.5b for a review of *qamets khatuf*).

PIEL QATAL

	STRONG ROOTS		THIRD ה
SING. 3 M. (he, it)	קִטֵּל	קִטַּל	צִוָּה
3 F (she, it)		קִטְּלָה	צִוְּתָה
2 M (you)		קִטַּלְתָּ	צִוִּיתָ
2 F (you)		קִטַּלְתְּ	צִוִּית
1 C (I)		קִטַּלְתִּי	צִוִּיתִי צִוֵּיתִי
PLUR. 3 C (they)		קִטְּלוּ	צִוּוּ
2 M (you)		קִטַּלְתֶּם	צִוִּיתֶם
2 F (you)		קִטַּלְתֶּן	צִוִּיתֶן
1 C (we)		קִטַּלְנוּ	צִוִּינוּ

15.3c. Notice that the subject pronouns in all the charts are quite consistent as follows (The chart below is also available in the "Helpful Charts" section near the back of the book.):

QATAL SUBJECT AFFIXED PRONOUNS:

he (it)	Ø---	they	וּ---
she (it)	ה---		
you (sing. masc.)	תָ---	you (plur. masc.)	תֶּם---
you (sing. fem)	תְ---	you (plur. fem.)	תֶּן---
I	תִי---	we	נוּ---

Also notice how the signs of the Qal and Piel stems are quite consistent, the *qamets* under the first root letter for the Qal and the *hireq* under the first root letter plus *dagesh forte* in the middle root letter for Piel. The exceptions are with the Qal stem in the second person plurals. *To enjoy reading Biblical Hebrew, you must thoroughly memorize the affixed subject pronouns.*

The 3rd *heh* verbs can be tricky. The *heh* drops in all but the third person, masculine singular, but what takes its place is inconsistent. Most of the time the substitute is a *hireq-yod*, but not in third person feminine singular or third person common plural. Fortunately, there is a helpful generalization:

> *When only two root letters appear in the qatal verb forms, suspect either a 3rd heh root or a hollow root.*

Actually there is a third possibility, a geminate root which is much less common, and which we will cover later.

15.3d. Fill out the verb analysis charts for עָשִׂיתָ   עָבַדְתִּי and רִמִּיתָנִי :

The נִי at the end of רִמִּיתָנִי is an object suffix that means *me*. The root רמה is only used in the Piel stem and means *beguile*.

root	stem	form	person, gender, number	function	basic root meaning

root	stem	form	person, gender, number	function	basic root meaning

root	stem	form	person, gender, number	function	basic root meaning

Questions, questions

15.4a. For the function column in the charts above write *question.*[1] Our lesson verse has three questions asked in three different ways. Laban, Rachel's father, has just cheated Jacob by having him work seven years for Rachel's hand in marriage. Rather than give Rachel to Jacob, Laban gives Jacob another daughter Leah. No wonder Jacob asks Laban for an explanation in three different ways!

15.4b. Two of the questions use question words: In the first מַה זֹּאת is familiar to us from the Lesson 13 translation assignments, meaning *What's this?* In our lesson verse, the two Hebrew words are actually the X-element in an X-qatal construction. Therefore the translation is a variation of our X-qatal translation formula.

X-qatal:

> *It is _____(Fronted X-element)_____who(that)_____(Remainder of clause)*

מַה־זֹּאת עָשִׂיתָ לִּי

> *What is _____this_____that is_____your doing to me_____?*

15.4c. The third question in our lesson verse also uses a question word לָמָּה meaning *Why?* Most English versions translate וְלָמָּה רִמִּיתָנִי something like *And why have you deceived me?* (As stated in 15.3d, נִי is an object suffix meaning *me.*) Since we are not bothered in our work by very awkward translations, we will try to bring out the meaning of the qatal which, as a reminder, expresses an attribute of the subject.

Translation: *Why are you a deceiver of me?*

Notice that in one translation of a qatal עָשִׂיתָ we use the *-ing-word* (a verbal noun called a gerund) and a possessive pronoun, while in the other רִמִּיתָנִי we use an *-er-word.* Translation requires that you remember your options and use some flexibility.

15.4d. The middle question of our lesson verse is הֲלֹא בְרָחֵל עָבַדְתִּי עִמָּךְ

> RULE: A *heh* [הֲ] usually accompanied by a *khataf patakh* [הֲ] on the first word
> of a phrase means a question. It is called *interrogative heh.*

---

[1] For a catalogue of question types see Waltke and O'Connor §18.

We know that Jacob worked *for* Rachel so we may be surprised see a בְּ rather than a לְ prefixed to רָחֵל but בְּ as a preposition is often used in matters of cost or price in the sense of *for*. This is a good example of how leniently the Hebrew prepositions need to be translated.

Once again, we have a situation in this question where the verb is fronted, in this case, by the prepositional "phrase" בְרָחֵל Normally, the X-qatal formula begins *It is...* or *It was...* but in the case of a question we merely change it to *Is it...* or *Was it...*

> *Was it not ____for Rachel____ that____ I was a server(or servant) ____with you?*

Pausal forms

15.5a. If you are curious why the masculine Laban was referred to with what looks like a feminine object suffix on עִמָּךְ very good observation! Jacob was not trying to insult Laban! There are typically two places in a Biblical Hebrew verse where a ceremonial reader of the Scriptures is supposed to pause with his voice, about mid-way in the verse and at the end of each verse. The pause often causes a change in the nikkud or accent in the word located at the pause, and ךָ -- is the typical second person masculine singular suffix at a place of pause. We call it a **pausal form**.

15.5b. The mid-verse and end-of-verse pauses are marked in your Hebrew Bible. The mid-verse mark is called an *atnakh* and looks like a carat [∧] placed beneath the letters and beside the vowels. The *atnakh* is generally not written in this book. The end-of-verse mark is called a *sof-passuq* which literally means *end of verse*. It is the colon-like mark [׃] written on the end of our lesson verse for this lesson, and will only be written on lesson verses or translation exercises in this book when an entire verse is written without any "editions" to it for teaching purposes.

15.5c. There are many other marks in your Hebrew Bible besides the vowels. These marks are conjunctive and disjunctive accents that the Masoretes, the originators of the nikkud, put in to regulate pronunciation during oral reading of the Hebrew Bible. These marks are useful to learn even if one is not a canter, a synagogue reader, because they provide clues to the phrasing of some difficult passages. However, most of the Masoretic accentual system is not a top priority to a first year student of Biblical Hebrew, so we will not spend very much time on it in this course.[1] One thing that is worth noting, however, is that all the accentual marks do identify the accented syllable of the word to which they are attached.

Assignments

15.6a. Memorize all the qatal subject endings and the signs of the Qal and Piel stems for qatal. Review the exceptional forms of the third ה roots.

15.6b. Write out the Qal qatal conjugations for הלך אמר

Write out the Piel qatal conjugation for שלח

15.6c. From now on each lesson will be accompanied by a discourse translation and analysis. The first one begins in Genesis 22, and the discourse notes which accompany each reading begin after Lesson 50.

---

[1] For an account of the discourse functions of the Masoretic accents see Lode, "A Discourse Perspective on the Significance of the Masoretic Accents," *Biblical Hebrew and Discourse Linguistics*(Dallas: Summer Institute of Linguistics, 1994), 155-172.

15.6d. Translate:

Genesis 13:9

1.   הֲלֹא כָל־הָאָרֶץ לְפָנֶיךָ

Genesis 44:15   הַזֶּה
הַמַּעֲשֶׂה   means *this
deed*.

2.   וַיֹּאמֶר יוֹסֵף מָה־הַמַּעֲשֶׂה הַזֶּה אֲשֶׁר עֲשִׂיתֶם הֲלוֹא
יְדַעְתֶּם

Genesis 50:19

3.   הֲתַחַת אֱלֹהִים אָנִי

Exodus 4:11

4.   הֲלֹא אָנֹכִי יְהוָה

Exodus 14:12

5.   הֲלֹא־זֶה הַדָּבָר אֲשֶׁר דִּבַּרְנוּ אֵלֶיךָ בְמִצְרַיִם

Exodus 16:4   תּוֹרָה
means *instruction*.

6.   הֲיֵלֵךְ בְּתוֹרָתִי

2 Samuel 20:17   Notice
that the interrogative *heh*
may have other vowels
than the *khataf patakh*
before a guttural letter.

7.   וַתֹּאמֶר הָאִשָּׁה הַאַתָּה יוֹאָב

1 Samuel 9:21   בֶּן־יְמִינִי
means *Benjamite*.
כַּדָּבָר הַזֶּה   means
this way.

8.   וַיֹּאמֶר הֲלוֹא בֶן־יְמִינִי אָנֹכִי וְלָמָּה דִּבַּרְתָּ אֵלַי כַּדָּבָר
הַזֶּה

Genesis 4:9   אֵי הֶבֶל
means *Where is Abel...*
The root שׁמר   means
watch, keep.

9.   וַיֹּאמֶר יְהוָה אֶל־קַיִן אֵי הֶבֶל אָחִיךָ וַיֹּאמֶר לֹא
יָדַעְתִּי הֲשֹׁמֵר אָחִי אָנֹכִי

2 Kings 13:6   הָאֲשֵׁרָה
is the Asherah cult idol.
שֹׁמְרוֹן   means *Samaria*.

10.   וְגַם הָאֲשֵׁרָה עָמְדָה בְּשֹׁמְרוֹן

1 Samuel 1:22

11.   וְחַנָּה לֹא עָלָתָה

Ezekiel 38:16

12.   וְעָלִיתָ עַל־עַמִּי יִשְׂרָאֵל

Ezekiel 13:23   Here we
have an unusual but cor-
rect form of the vav-con-
secutive of the predictive

13.   וִידַעְתֶּן כִּי־אֲנִי יְהוָה

84

narrative mainline.

1 Chronicles 4:9

14. וְאִמּוֹ קָרְאָה שְׁמוֹ יַעְבֵּץ

1 Samuel 3:5 For הִנְנִי
see 11.6A, 16. You see
here a variant spelling of
what you saw there.

15. וַיֹּאמֶר הִנְנִי כִּי־קָרָאתָ לִּי וַיֹּאמֶר לֹא־קָרָאתִי

Lesson 16

וְעָשִׂיתָ כִּיּוֹר נְחֹשֶׁת לְרָחְצָה וְנָתַתָּ אֹתוֹ בֵּין־אֹהֶל מוֹעֵד וּבֵין הַמִּזְבֵּחַ

Exodus 30:18

Goals:

- Distinguish between Predictive Narrative and Instructional Discourse.
- Identify and read the Qal qatal of נתן in all persons, genders, and numbers.
- Identify and read the Qal infinitive construct.

What we already know

What verb forms are וְעָשִׂיתָ and וְנָתַתָּ ?_____ (13.2a)

Translate וְעָשִׂיתָ כִּיּוֹר נְחֹשֶׁת (כִּיּוֹר נְחֹשֶׁת means *basin of brass*)

_____

If you need help on the affix pronoun on וְעָשִׂיתָ see 15.3c, but do not move on. Stop now and memorize the qatal affixes.

Instructional Discourse

16.2a. What is this verb form's function in Predictive Narrative?_____ (13.2a, b)

This lesson's verse is another +projection genre, Instructional Discourse.[1] In Instructional Discourse the speaker/writer does not foretell the future in a story-like manner as in Predictive Narrative. Rather he expresses instructions. It is the genre we find in computer manuals or the directions that come in a box with a disassembled bicycle. The focus of the discourse is on the accomplishment of a goal. Weqatals, the mainline verb form of Instructional Discourse, translate into English future time the same way that they do in Predictive Narrative.

> RULE: **The speaker's task in Instructional Discourse is to tell someone how to do something.**

16.2b. Fill out the verb analysis chart for וְעָשִׂיתָ :

root	stem	form	person, gender, number	function	basic root meaning
				Instructional Discourse Mainline	

---

[1] See Longacre, "Building for the Worship of God: Exodus 25:1-30:10," *Discourse Analysis of Biblical Literature: What it is and What it Offers*(ed. Bodine. Atlanta: The Society of Biblical Literature, 1995), 21-50.

The special case of נתן

16.3a. The root of the second weqatal verb in our lesson verse (וְנָתַתָּ) is נתן one of the most common roots in the Hebrew Bible. It follows the regular pattern for 1st *nun* roots in the yiqtol form which we will learn in Lesson 17.4c., but it is irregular in the qatal and weqatal forms in which it often loses its final *nun* without a trace. It is time we learned this root's irregular behavior.

THE SPECIAL CASE OF THE QAL QATAL OF נתן:

SINGULAR 3 M.	נָתַן	PLURAL 3 C.	נָתְנוּ
3 F.	נָתְנָה		
2 M.	נָתַתָּ	2 M.	נְתַתֶּם
2 F.	נָתַתְּ	2 F.	-----
1 C.	נָתַתִּי	1 C.	נָתַנּוּ

Note: Look especially closely at the 3rd c. p. and the 1st c. p.

Fill out the verb analysis chart for וְנָתַתָּ :

root	stem	form	person, gender, number	function	basic root meaning
				Instructional Discourse Mainline	

16.3b. The instructions in this verse are directed toward the whole nation of Israel, yet the subject of these verbs is masculine *singular*. This is common, but plural subjects can also be found in similar constructions. The question is why the singular form was chosen. It may be that the speaker thought of Israel collectively, as a singular entity. It may also be a way of saying that each individual in Israel should follow the instructions.

Translation of the two weqatals:_____

The Qal infinitive construct

16.4a. For the time being, we will concentrate on the first clause of our lesson verse. כִּיּוֹר נְחֹשֶׁת is often translated *laver of brass*. A laver is a wash basin used for ceremonial washing during one's approach to *YHWH* in worship. The next word לְרָחְצָה is made of two parts, a prefixed preposition (the *lamed*) translated here *to* or *for* and an example of our sixth verb form, the infinitive. There are actually two kinds of infinitive, one with which a writer/speaker can build, called the *construct*, and one with a specialized function which we will learn later, called the *absolute*. Our lesson verse's infinitive does *not* exhibit the most commonly attested sign of the Qal infinitive which is fairly easy to identify using the following rule:

RULE: The Qal infinitive construct is the only verb form which can be prefixed by a preposition. Its sign is usually a *holem*, either plene or defectiva, after the second root letter. It can usually be translated by an English infinitive or *-ing*-noun called a gerund.

Although our lesson's word לְרָחְצָה does not follow this rule, it does in other attestations in which it appears according to the common rule: לִרְחֹץ The feminine ending on our lesson verse's infinitive is most often seen on stative verbs which are explained in Lesson 33.2.

16.4b. Begin filling out the verb analysis chart לְרָחְצָה (רצח means *wash*):

Root	stem	form	person, gender, number	function	basic root meaning

An infinitive does not have a person, gender, number or dedicated discourse function, so you may leave these spaces blank.

Translation of וְעָשִׂיתָ כִּיּוֹר נְחֹשֶׁת לְרָחְצָה : *And you will be a maker of a laver of brass for washing (or to wash)*

16.4c. Below the regular sign of the Qal infinitive construct is illustrated with strong roots and some common weak root types. A *lamed* is prefixed to each example to illustrate how the infinitive may be prefixed by a preposition. You need to memorize these four types of Qal infinitive constructs.

STRONG ROOTS	THIRD ה ROOTS	HOLLOW ROOTS	FIRST י ROOTS
קטל <--- לִקְטֹל	היה ---> לִהְיוֹת	בוא <--- לָבוֹא	ישב <--- לָשֶׁבֶת
	עשה ---> לַעֲשׂוֹת	שוב <--- לָשׁוּב	ידע <--- לָדַעַת
	ראה <--- לִרְאוֹת	מות <--- לָמוּת	יצא <--- לָצֵאת
	עלה <--- לַעֲלוֹת	קום <--- לָקוּם	

FIRST י ROOTS (continued):

Notice how the *yod* is dropped

and a *tav* is added to the end

הלך <--- לָלֶכֶת

As usual, הלך acts like a first י root.

88

Another common but irregular infinitive is תֵּת as in לָתֵת which is the infinitive of נתן meaning *to give* or *for giving*.

16.4d. We now have two verb forms, the qatal and the infinitive which may need to be translated by the English gerund. In Hebrew the line between verb and noun is fuzzy in both the qatal and the infinitive. However, you should think of them distinctly. The qatal expresses the attribute of the subject adjectivally. The attribute may be action, so we use an *er*-word or a gerund in our English translation. The focus is on the subject or doer of the verb. However, with the Hebrew infinitive, the focus is on the action itself, the *doing*, rather than the *doer*.

16.4e. On to the second clause of our lesson verse. אֹתוֹ should remind you of Lesson 13's אֹתְךָ or Lesson 14's אֹתָם It is indeed the DDO with a 3rd m. s. pronominal suffix attached, the whole unit meaning *him*. בֵּין־אֹהֶל מוֹעֵד וּבֵין הַמִּזְבֵּחַ means *between the tent of meeting and (between) the altar*. It is given in the lesson verse simply to retain some context for וְנָתַתָּ

Translate the entire lesson verse: _____

Assignments
16.5a. Memorize the infinitive forms in 16.4c's chart.
16.5b. Read Genesis 22:1-2.
16.5c. Translate:

1. אִם מְצָאתִי	9. יְהוּדָה דִּבֵּר	17. יְהוּדָה בָּא
2. כִּי־מָצָאתָ	10. וְדִבֵּר יְהוּדָה	18. אִם בָּא יְהוּדָה
3. אֲשֶׁר מְצָאָנוּ	11. וְדִבַּרְתָּ לִיהוּדָה	19. לִיהוּדָה בָּאָה
4. וּמָצָא	12. אֲשֶׁר דִּבֶּר לוֹ	20. וּבָאנוּ
5. רָחֵל מָצָאת	13. אֲשֶׁר יְדַבֵּר	21. אֲשֶׁר בָּאתֶם
6. אֲשֶׁר יִמְצָא	14. וְדִבַּרְתְּ רָחֵל	22. לָבוֹא
7. וּמְצָאתֶן רָחֵל וְלֵאָה	15. לוֹ דִּבַּרְנוּ	23. בְּדַבֵּר
8. וּמָצָא	16. וְדִבְּרוּ אֶל רָחֵל	

16.5d. Translate:

Deuteronomy 5:32 כֶם--
is the 2nd m. p. suffix
meaning *you, your*.

1. וּשְׁמַרְתֶּם לַעֲשׂוֹת כַּאֲשֶׁר צִוָּה יְהוָה אֱלֹהֵיכֶם אֶתְכֶם

Deuteronomy 26:16
אֹתָם means *them*.
לֵב = לֵבָב

2. וְשָׁמַרְתָּ וְעָשִׂיתָ אוֹתָם בְּכָל־לְבָבְךָ וּבְכָל־נַפְשֶׁךָ

Deuteronomy 31:12 Do
you remember תּוֹרָה
from 13.6b.15?

3. וְשָׁמְרוּ לַעֲשׂוֹת אֶת־כָּל־דִּבְרֵי הַתּוֹרָה

89

Deuteronomy 8:6 מִצְוֹת means *commandments*.	4. וְשָׁמַרְתָּ אֶת־מִצְוֹת יְהוָה אֱלֹהֶיךָ לָלֶכֶת בִּדְרָכָיו
2 Chronicles 34:31 וַיִּכְרֹת אֶת־הַבְּרִית means *And then he made the covenant.*	5. וַיַּעֲמֹד הַמֶּלֶךְ וַיִּכְרֹת אֶת־הַבְּרִית לִפְנֵי יְהוָה לָלֶכֶת אַחֲרֵי יְהוָה וְלִשְׁמוֹר אֶת־מִצְוֹתָיו
1 Chronicles 17:4 לֹא אַתָּה תִּבְנֶה־לִי means *It is not you who will build for Me...*	6. וְאָמַרְתָּ אֶל־דָּוִיד עַבְדִּי כֹּה אָמַר יְהוָה לֹא אַתָּה תִּבְנֶה־לִי הַבַּיִת לָשָׁבֶת:
Genesis 3:13	7. וַיֹּאמֶר יְהוָה אֱלֹהִים לָאִשָּׁה מַה־זֹּאת עָשִׂית
Genesis 24:4	8. וְלָקַחְתָּ אִשָּׁה לִבְנִי לְיִצְחָק
1 Kings 19:11	9. וְעָמַדְתָּ בָהָר לִפְנֵי יְהוָה וְהִנֵּה יְהוָה עֹבֵר
Leviticus 4:7 קַרְנוֹת מִזְבַּח means *the horns of the altar.*	10. וְנָתַן הַכֹּהֵן מִן־הַדָּם עַל־קַרְנוֹת מִזְבַּח
Leviticus 4:34 הַחַטָּאת means *sin offering.* קַרְנֹת מִזְבֵּחַ means...did you forget after only one exercise?	11. וְלָקַח הַכֹּהֵן מִדַּם הַחַטָּאת וְנָתַן עַל־קַרְנֹת מִזְבֵּחַ
Leviticus 16:18 פַּר means *bull*, and שָׂעִיר means *goat*.	12. וְיָצָא אֶל־הַמִּזְבֵּחַ אֲשֶׁר לִפְנֵי־יְהוָה וְלָקַח מִדַּם הַפָּר וּמִדַּם הַשָּׂעִיר וְנָתַן עַל־קַרְנוֹת הַמִּזְבֵּחַ
Deuteronomy 19:8	13. וְנָתַן לְךָ אֶת־כָּל־הָאָרֶץ אֲשֶׁר דִּבֶּר לָתֵת לַאֲבֹתֶיךָ
Deuteronomy 12:10 The first word is a correct nikkud for a 1st guttural of this form, stem, person, gender, and number.	14. וַעֲבַרְתֶּם אֶת־הַיַּרְדֵּן וִישַׁבְתֶּם בָּאָרֶץ

15. וְהָיָה לָכֶם לְמִשְׁמֶרֶת עַד אַרְבָּעָה עָשָׂר יוֹם
לַחֹדֶשׁ הַזֶּה וְשָׁחֲטוּ אֹתוֹ כֹּל קְהַל עֲדַת־יִשְׂרָאֵל
בֵּין הָעַרְבָּיִם:
וְלָקְחוּ מִן־הַדָּם וְנָתְנוּ עַל־שְׁתֵּי הַמְּזוּזֹת וְעַל־הַמַּשְׁקוֹף
עַל הַבָּתִּים אֲשֶׁר־יֹאכְלוּ אֹתוֹ בָּהֶם:
וְאָכְלוּ אֶת־הַבָּשָׂר בַּלַּיְלָה הַזֶּה צְלִי־אֵשׁ

Exodus 12:6-8 There is a great deal of material here that you may not know, and that is O.K. The verses have been arranged so that the main verb in each Hebrew sentence is at the right margin. In so doing, you can see a string of weqatals instructing Moses how Israel is to institute the Passover. You should be familiar with all the weqatals except for the one containing the root שׁחט which means *flay*. As for the rest of the material, spot what is familiar, and we will translate the rest another time.

16.5e. Fill out verb analysis charts for all the verbs in numbers 1, 4, and 9. Do not forget infinitives or participles.

Lesson 17

וּמֹשֶׁה עָלָה אֶל־הָאֱלֹהִים וַיִּקְרָא אֵלָיו יְהוָה מִן־הָהָר לֵאמֹר כֹּה תֹאמַר
לְבֵית יַעֲקֹב

Exodus 19:3

Goals:

- **Distinguish *vav*-consecutive from conjunctive (or disjunctive) *vav*.**
- **Identify and read the speech introduction formula with** לֵאמֹר
- **Identify and read the Qal yiqtol and wayyiqtol forms in all persons, genders, and numbers.**

What we already know

17.1. In this lesson verse we have a bit of two genres. The first two clauses are Historical Narrative that introduces some direct speech. The direct speech is Instructional Discourse. Fill out the verb analysis chart for the first two verbs in our lesson verse עָלָה and וַיִּקְרָא:

root	stem	form	person, gender, number	function	basic root meaning

root	stem	form	person, gender, number	function	basic root meaning

The function column for וַיִּקְרָא is easy to fill out because of the *vav-patakh-dagesh forte* unit that is prefixed to the verb (1.2).

As for the discourse function of עָלָה do not forget to take note of the word which precedes it before you decide. What is the relationship of וּמֹשֶׁה to the verb?_____ (5.3b)

Conjunctive vav versus vav-consecutive

17.2a. Both the clauses in עָלָה אֶל־הָאֱלֹהִים וַיִּקְרָא אֵלָיו יְהוָה מִן־הָהָר לֵאמֹר
וּמֹשֶׁה begin with *vav*'s, but the *vav* in וּמֹשֶׁה has a different function than the *vav* in וַיִּקְרָא The latter word has a *vav-consecutive*.

RULE: **The *vav*'s which are part of the mainline verb forms are called *vav-consecutive*. The *vav-consecutive* means *and, but* and also has the special discourse function of linking together the string of events which make up the mainline of a discourse. The *vav-consecutive* indicates that the action of the verb is the consequence of the preceding situation.**

In Historical Narrative, the *vav-consecutive* comes before the yiqtol verb form, usually in a *vav-patakh-dagesh forte* unit [֦ ֣ וַ]. In Predictive Narrative and Instructional Discourse the *vav-consecutive* comes before the qatal, commonly pointed with the *shewa* [וְ]. Here are the *vav-consecutives* illustrated in the paradigm root קטל :

וַיִּקְטֹל

וְקָטַל

17.2b. On the other hand, the *vav* on וּמֹשֶׁה is at the beginning of an 'X-element' on an X-qatal clause. It is called a **conjunctive (or disjunctive) *vav***.

> RULE: *Conjunctive (or disjunctive) vav* **may be attached to almost any word, including a verb form, and means *and, but* like the *vav-consecutive*, but it does not have the additional function of stringing together actions in a sequence.** We call this *vav* conjunctive when its clause adds depictive or explanatory material to the mainline and it is best translated *and*. We call it disjunctive when its clause is used for contrastive purposes, and it is best translated *but*.

We may think of the conjunctive *vav* as representing a lighter connection between words, but the major difference between the two is the discourse function of the *vav-consecutive*.[1] The discourse function of the *vav-consecutive* is the reason why we often translate it with the additional word *then* or *so*. You will see later that it may be appropriate to translate the *vav-consecutive* with the word *consequently*. As should be expected, there are exceptions to these "rules," but the rules do hold true for the vast majority of Biblical Hebrew prose.

17.2c. Remember that we only find *vav-consecutive* on mainline verb forms. Why do we care? The first clause of our lesson verse is *not* given as a consequence of the preceding situation which, in this case, depicts the children of Israel setting up camp in the wilderness. The first clause has the discourse function *topicalization*. וּמֹשֶׁה עָלָה אֶל־הָאֱלֹהִים shifts the focus from the action of setting up camp to the person Moses. Because of the contrast between the action and the person, we may translate the *vav* as a *but* as in ***But it was Moses who was a goer up to God.***

The *vav* in וַיִּקְרָא on the other hand, is a *vav-consecutive*, so this event is a consequence of the preceding situation, namely, Moses' going up to God. Use a *then* in your translation.

Translate the second clause of our lesson verse:_____

---

[1] See Jouon-Muraoka(1993), §115; Waltke and O'Connor(1990), §§ 8.3b, 39.2.

לֵאמֹר

17.3. You may get stuck on the last word of the clause לֵאמֹר because it is a somewhat new form to you. The root is quite familiar. What is it?_____ What verb form does the *holem* after the second root letter signify?_____ (16.4a rule) What does the לְ mean?_____ However, we do not generally translate לֵאמֹר *to say*.

> RULE: **When the Hebrew word** לֵאמֹר **is used to introduce direct speech we translate it** *saying*. לֵאמֹר is generally used together with another wayyiqtol or qatal verb which identifies the nature of the speech act (As in our lesson verse's וַיִּקְרָא).[1] It is usually found in contexts which are not a typical dialogic exchange between a speaker and an addressee, for instance, to introduce re-quoted quotes or messages for which no response is expected.[2]

Yiqtol charts

17.4a. Because of לֵאמֹר we expect direct speech for our third and final clause, and Instructional Discourse is a common genre for direct speech. What does כֹּה mean? _____ The next word תֹאמַר is the second person, masculine, singular (*you*) of the yiqtol form. כֹּה is therefore the X-element before a yiqtol verb form requiring the formula

> It will be ___*(Fronted X-element)*___ *that(who)*___*(Remainder of clause)*___.

Translation of כֹּה תֹאמַר לְבֵית יַעֲקֹב : *It will be thus that you will say to the house of Jacob.*

17.4b. Fill out the verb analysis chart for תֹאמַר :

root	stem	form	person, gender, number	function	basic root meaning

Translate the entire lesson verse: _____

_____

---

[1] See Miller, "Introducing Direct Speech in Biblical Hebrew Narrative," *Biblical Hebrew and Discourse Linguistics*(ed. Bergen. Dallas: Summer Institute of Linguistics, 1994), 199-241.
[2] We may translate לֵאמר "for saying." This may shed light on its pleonastic use with a finite form of אמר or דבר when it seems to mark words meant to be repeated. See Rocine "Quotable Quotes: The Pleonastic Use of לֵאמר"(mss.).

17.4c. It is now time to learn the full yiqtol conjugation for some root types. Once again, you are reminded that a full set of conjugations for all the major root types in the critical verb forms is near the end of this book.

QAL YIQTOL

		STRONG ROOT	FIRST *YOD*	FIRST *NUN*
SING.	3 M (he, it)	יִקְטֹל	יֵשֵׁב	יִפֹּל
	3 F(she, it)	תִּקְטֹל	תֵּשֵׁב	תִּפֹּל
	2 M (you)	תִּקְטֹל	תֵּשֵׁב	תִּפֹּל
	2 F (you)	תִּקְטְלִי	תֵּשְׁבִי	תִּפְּלִי
	1 C (I)	אֶקְטֹל	אֵשֵׁב	אֶפֹּל
PLUR.	3 M (they)	יִקְטְלוּ	יֵשְׁבוּ	יִפְּלוּ
	3 F (they)	תִּקְטֹלְנָה	תֵּשַׁבְנָה	תִּפֹּלְנָה
	2 M (you)	תִּקְטְלוּ	תֵּשְׁבוּ	תִּפְּלוּ
	2 F (you)	תִּקְטֹלְנָה	תֵּשַׁבְנָה	תִּפֹּלְנָה
	1 C (we)	נִקְטֹל	נֵשֵׁב	נִפֹּל

Notice that the subject pronoun and its complement, if there is one, are quite consistent as follows:

YIQTOL SUBJECT PREFIXES AND COMPLEMENTS:

he (it)	י־־־	they (masc.)	י־־־וּ
she (it)	ת־־־	they (fem.)	ת־־־נָה
you (sing. masc.)	ת־־־	you (plur. masc.)	ת־־־וּ
you (sing. fem.)	ת־־־ִי	you (plur. fem.)	ת־־־נָה
I	א־־־	we	נ־־־

17.4d. **The above set of prefixes and complements are the same prefixes and complements that are used to conjugate the wayyiqtol verb form.** It is very important, if you expect to enjoy reading Biblical Hebrew, that you now memorize these prefixes and complements. They are also shown in a chart in the "Helpful Charts" section near the back of the book. Although there are some differences in the nikkud of the yiqtol versus the nikkud of the wayyiqtol, basically speaking, when you learn to conjugate the yiqtol verb form you have learned to conjugate the wayyiqtol.

The occasional difference between the yiqtol proper and the "yiqtol" when it is embedded within the wayyiqtol is a shortening of the form in the wayyiqtol. This shorter "yiqtol" within a wayyiqtol is called the **apocopated** form and several are illustrated below.

Some differences between 3rd m. s. wayyiqtol and yiqtol forms:

	Wayyiqtol	Yiqtol
Hollow roots	וַיָּבֹא	יָבוֹא
	וַיָּשֶׂם	יָשִׂים
	וַיָּמָת	יָמוּת
	וַיֵּשֶׁב	יָשׁוּב
Third ה roots	וַיַּרְא	יִרְאֶה
	וַיַּעַשׂ	יַעֲשֶׂה
	וַיְהִי	יִהְיֶה

The prefix pronoun and the vowel under the prefix pronoun are the same in both forms. The difference is that the wayyiqtol contains within it an apocopated form of its yiqtol equivalent.

17.4e. Notice also that **the same missing letter rules we learned for the wayyiqtol verb form will apply to the yiqtol.** The qualifications to this principle are that hollow verbs will not always lose the middle consonant in yiqtol like they do in the wayyiqtol, and 3rd *heh* verbs will not lose the *heh* as often in the yiqtol.

17.4f. One important detail to notice about the wayyiqtol verb forms is in the 1st c. s. or *I* conjugation. Since the prefix pronoun *aleph*[א] cannot take a *dagesh*, this one person, gender, and number will not show the customary *vav-patakh-dagesh forte* unit of the wayyiqtol verb form. Here are a few examples:

1st C. S. WAYYIQTOL FORMS:

וָאֶקְרָא	*And I called*	וָאֶשְׁמַע	*And I heard*
וָאֹמַר	*And I said*	וָאֶקַּח	*And I took*
וָאֶשָּׂא	*And I lifted*	וָאֶתֵּן	*And I gave*
וָאֵרֶד	*And I went down*	וָאֵשֵׁב	*And I dwelt*

Assignments
17.5a. Memorize vocabulary words 101-150 for Lessons 17-22.
17.5b. Memorize the yiqtol conjugations for strong, first yod, and first nun roots.

17.5c. Translate:

17. אֲשֶׁר נָתַתָּ	9. וַתִּשְׁלַח	1. וָאֶעֱמֹד
18. שָׂרָה נָתְנָה־לִי	10. וְשָׁלְחוּ	2. עֹמְדִים
19. שָׂרָה תִּתֵּן	11. לִשְׁלֹחַ	3. שָׂרָה תַּעֲמֹד
20. לְשָׂרָה תִּתְּנִי	12. לְאַהֲרֹן שָׁלַחְתָּ	4. וַתַּעֲמֹד
21. אִם יִתְּנוּ	13. אֲנִי אֶשְׁלַח	5. עָמַדְתִּי
22. מִתֵּת	14. וַיִּשְׁלְחוּ	6. וְעָמַדְתָּ
23. נְתֻנִים	15. אֲשֶׁר תִּשְׁלַח	7. אֲשֶׁר נַעֲמֹד
24. וְנָתַנוּ	16. שָׁלֵחַ	8. וַתַּעֲמֹדְנָה

17.5d. Translate (Note that there is a mix of genres in the exercises):

Exodus 20:4 פֶּסֶל means *an idol*.

1. לֹא תַעֲשֶׂה־לְךָ פֶסֶל

Exodus 4:9
מִמֵּימֵי הַיְאֹר means *from the water of the Nile*. Notice how *water* takes a plural verb. Also, remem-ber how the root לקח behaves like a first *nun* root. Notice the difference in sense between the first וְהָיוּ and the second. The first has the same paragraph-marking function that we saw for the root היה in Histor-ical Narrative, but the second has the sense *And then they will become*.

2. וְלָקַחְתָּ מִמֵּימֵי הַיְאֹר וְהָיוּ הַמַּיִם אֲשֶׁר תִּקַּח מִן־הַיְאֹר וְהָיוּ לְדָם

Deuteronomy 7:3 בַּת is the construct singular for בַּת

3. בִּתְּךָ לֹא־תִתֵּן לִבְנוֹ וּבִתּוֹ לֹא־תִקַּח לִבְנֶךָ

1 Samuel 16:2
עֶגְלַת בָּקָר means *heifer*, and the root זבח means *sacrifice*.

4. וַיֹּאמֶר יְהוָה עֶגְלַת בָּקָר תִּקַּח בְּיָדֶךָ וְאָמַרְתָּ לִזְבֹּחַ לַיהוָה בָּאתִי

Jeremiah 16:2

5. לֹא־תִקַּח לְךָ אִשָּׁה וְלֹא־יִהְיוּ לְךָ בָּנִים

Numbers 8:8
פַּר בֶּן־בָּקָר means *young bullock*.. שֵׁנִי means *second*. לְחַטָּאת means *for a sin offering*. Notice how the first instruction is given with a Instructional Discourse mainline weqatal, but the second is given with an X-yiqtol. The *they* of the first instruction is given to the Levites.

6. וְלָקְחוּ פַּר בֶּן־בָּקָר וּפַר־שֵׁנִי בֶן־בָּקָר תִּקַּח לְחַטָּאת

They will be takers of *one bullock*. By fronting וּפַר־שֵׁנִי בֶּן־בָּקָר in the second clause, the fate of the second bullock is contras-ted to the fate of the first. The instructions thereby serve as a warning to the Levites not to take for themselves more than is their due.

Exodus 5:2

7.   לֹא יָדַעְתִּי אֶת־יְהוָה וְגַם אֶת־יִשְׂרָאֵל לֹא אֲשַׁלֵּחַ

Exodus 8:24   אֶתְכֶם means *you* (m. p.).

8.   וַיֹּאמֶר פַּרְעֹה אָנֹכִי אֲשַׁלַּח אֶתְכֶם

Exodus 12:11

9.   וְכָכָה תֹּאכְלוּ אֹתוֹ

Exodus 12:25   לָכֶם means *to you* (m. p). These clauses give conditions for the in-structions. Both אֲשֶׁר--qatal constructions refer to the relative past.

10.   וְהָיָה כִּי־תָבֹאוּ אֶל־הָאָרֶץ אֲשֶׁר יִתֵּן יְהוָה לָכֶם כַּאֲשֶׁר דִּבֵּר

Judges 6:23

11.   וַיֹּאמֶר לוֹ יְהוָה שָׁלוֹם לְךָ לֹא תָמוּת

Numbers 20:17

12.   דֶּרֶךְ הַמֶּלֶךְ נֵלֵךְ

Exodus 8:23
דֶּרֶךְ שְׁלֹשֶׁת יָמִים means *three day's journey*. זֶבַח means *sacrifice*.

13.   דֶּרֶךְ שְׁלֹשֶׁת יָמִים נֵלֵךְ וְזָבַחְנוּ לַיהוָה

2 Chronicles 20:12
וַאֲנַחְנוּ means *and (but) we*.

14.   וַאֲנַחְנוּ לֹא נֵדַע מַה־נַּעֲשֶׂה

Numbers 16:12

15.   וַיִּשְׁלַח מֹשֶׁה לִקְרֹא לְדָתָן וְלַאֲבִירָם בְּנֵי אֱלִיאָב וַיֹּאמְרוּ לֹא נַעֲלֶה

1 Samuel 14:9
תַּחְתֵּינוּ means *our place*. אֲלֵיהֶם means *to them*. The second clause paraphrases the first.

16.   וְעָמַדְנוּ תַחְתֵּינוּ וְלֹא נַעֲלֶה אֲלֵיהֶם

Joshua 24:15

17.   וְאָנֹכִי וּבֵיתִי נַעֲבֹד אֶת־יְהוָה

17.5e. Read Genesis 22:3-4.

Lesson 18

וַיֹּאמֶר חֹתֵן מֹשֶׁה אֵלָיו לֹא־טוֹב הַדָּבָר אֲשֶׁר אַתָּה עֹשֶׂה:

Exodus 18:17

Goals:
- **Identify and read adjectives.**
- **Identify and read the independent subject pronouns.**
- **Identify and read the most common irregular nouns.**

What you already know

Why don't you take a try at translating the entire lesson verse (חֹתֵן means *(father)in-law* and טוֹב

means *good*). _____

_____

Here are a couple of helpful hints.

1. One challenge is to decide where the direct speech begins.
2. לֹא־טוֹב הַדָּבָר is a verbless clause. Remember that דָּבָר can be translated in more ways than *word*.
3. The definiteness (see 6.4a) of הַדָּבָר indicates it is the subject of the clause, so the word order is P-S. Use normal English word order for a descriptive clause: *The thing is not good.* אֲשֶׁר אַתָּה עֹשֶׂה is a comment about הַדָּבָר If you need help with עֹשֶׂה see 12.2.

Adjectives

18.2a. In the second clause of our lesson verse we see that an adjective can fill the predicate slot of a verbless clause. There are two kinds of adjectives in Biblical Hebrew. One is the kind of adjective in our lesson verse, which fills the predicate slot of a verbless clause, and the other follows a noun and is attached to it, making a noun-adjective unit.

> RULE: **A *predicate adjective* is the adjective that fills the predicate slot of a verbless clause. This adjective often precedes the noun it modifies.**
> **E.g.** Numbers 11:18 כִּי־טוֹב לָנוּ בְּמִצְרָיִם
> *For in Egypt (it) was good for us*

An *attributive adjective* follows the noun it modifies and mostly agrees with it in gender, number, and definiteness.

> **E.g.** Deuteronomy 3:25 הָהָר הַטּוֹב הַזֶּה
> ...*this good mountain*...(masc. sing. definite)
> 1 Kings 12:7 דְּבָרִים טוֹבִים
> ...*good words*...(masc. plur. indefinite)
> Numbers 5:30 הַתּוֹרָה הַזֹּאת
> ...*this instruction*...(fem. sing. definite)
> 2 Kings 4:8 אִשָּׁה גְדוֹלָה
> ...*a great woman*...(fem. sing. indefinite)

99

18.2b. Notice how, when the noun being modified is in any way definite (see 6.4a), the adjective is then prefixed by the definite article (הַ). Also notice how the words זֶה and זֹאת which we have previously known as *demonstrative pronouns* can also be used as *demonstrative attributive adjectives*.

In order to make an attributive adjective match the noun it is modifying in gender and number regular noun endings are often added to the adjective as follows:

NOUN AND ADJECTIVE ENDINGS:

	MASCULINE	FEMININE
SINGULAR	NONE	ה---
PLURAL	--- יִם	וֹת--- or ת ---

18.2c. You must be warned, however, that adjectives in Biblical Hebrew are few as compared to our liberal use of them in English, and perfect grammatical matching of adjectives to the nouns they modify does not seem to be a high priority to the Ancient Hebrew. Here are some more examples:

MASCULINE SINGULAR
Indefinite:

בֵּן חָכָם *(a wise son)*

אִישׁ גָּדוֹל *(a great man)*

אִישׁ רָשָׁע *(a wicked man)*

Definite:

הָאָדָם הַגָּדוֹל *(the great man)*

MASCULINE PLURAL
Indefinite:

יָמִים רַבִּים *(many days)*

Singular אִישׁ רָשָׁע becomes

אֲנָשִׁים רְשָׁעִים *(wicked men)*. In this case the singular noun אִישׁ has an irregular plural form אֲנָשִׁים

Definite:

Singular הָאָדָם הַגָּדוֹל becomes plural הַגְּדֹלִים *(the great men)*. In this case the adjective itself has become the noun. An adjective used as a noun is called a *substantive*.

FEMININE SINGULAR
Indefinite:

אִשָּׁה גְּדוֹלָה *(a great woman)*

נֶפֶשׁ חַיָּה *(a living soul)*

חֲטָאָה גְדֹלָה *(a great sin)*

Definite:

הָעִיר הַגְּדֹלָה *(the great city)*

FEMININE PLURAL
Indefinite:

פָּרוֹת אֲחֵרוֹת *(other cows)*

צֹאן רַבּוֹת *(many sheep)* Notice that צֹאן is a collective noun, singular in form, but taking a plural adjective.

עָרִים גְּדֹלוֹת *(great cities)*. Notice that fem. עִיר takes the masculine plural ending.

Definite:

הַפָּרוֹת הָרַקּוֹת *(the lean cows)*

הַצֹּאן הַמְקֻשָּׁרוֹת *(the strong sheep)*

100

Independent subject pronouns

18.3a. Looking once again at our lesson verse's clause אֲשֶׁר אַתָּה עֹשֶׂה we can see that the independent subject pronoun אַתָּה is used as a subject with a participle as the clause's verb. Here is a synopsis of uses of the independent subject pronouns:

USES OF INDEPENDENT SUBJECT PRONOUNS:[1]

1. As the subject of a participle: As in our lesson verse.
2. To emphasize the subject of a V-S word order clause: וְדִבֶּר־הוּא לָךְ Exodus 4:16
3. To topicalize the subject in a S-V word order clause: אַתָּה יָדַעְתָּ אֶת־הָעָם Exodus 32:22
4. As the subject of a verbless clause: אַתָּה יְהוָה Numbers 14:14

18.3b. Here are all the independent subject pronouns, also shown near the back of the book in the "Helpful Charts" section (You will not be asked to memorize them here for the simple reason that memorizing them is already part of your vocabulary assignments:

SINGULAR 3. M.	הוּא	PLURAL 3. M.	הֵם הֵמָּה
3. F.	הִיא	3. F.	הֵן הֵנָּה
2. M.	אַתָּה	2. M.	אַתֶּם
2. F.	אַתְּ	2. F.	אַתֵּן אַתֵּנָה
1. C.	אֲנִי אָנֹכִי	1. C.	אֲנַחְנוּ נַחְנוּ אָנוּ

Irregular nouns

One of the tricky points in Hebrew is the irregularity of some of the most common nouns. In case you may think it is not so in English remember that the plural of *man* is not *mans*, and the plural of *child* is not *childs*. Memorize the following forms, some of which you saw earlier in 14.2, because they are extremely common.

---

[1] For thorough treatment of the discourse significance of independent subject pronouns, see Muraoka(1985), §§2-3.

	אָב	אָח	אָחוֹת sister	אִישׁ	אִשָּׁה	בַּיִת	בֵּן	בַּת	יוֹם	עִיר	שֵׁם
singular absolute	אָב	אָח	אָחוֹת	אִישׁ	אִשָּׁה	בַּיִת	בֵּן	בַּת	יוֹם	עִיר	שֵׁם
singular construct	אֲבִי	אֲחִי	אֲחוֹת	אִישׁ	אֵשֶׁת	בֵּית	בֵּן	בַּת	יוֹם	עִיר	שֵׁם or שֶׁם
sing. with 2nd m. s. suffix	אָבִיךָ	אָחִיךָ	אֲחוֹתְךָ	אִישְׁךָ	אִשְׁתְּךָ	בֵּיתְךָ	בִּנְךָ	בִּתְּךָ	יוֹמְךָ	עִירְךָ	שִׁמְךָ
plural absolute	אָבוֹת	אַחִים	----	אֲנָשִׁים	נָשִׁים	בָּתִּים	בָּנִים	בָּנוֹת	יָמִים	עָרִים	שֵׁמוֹת
plural construct	אֲבוֹת	אֲחֵי	----	אַנְשֵׁי	נְשֵׁי	בָּתֵּי	בְּנֵי	בְּנוֹת	יְמֵי	עָרֵי	שְׁמוֹת
plural with 2nd m.s. suffix	אֲבֹתֶיךָ	אַחֶיךָ	אַחְיֹתֶיךָ	אֲנָשֶׁיךָ	נָשֶׁיךָ	בָּתֶּיךָ	בָּנֶיךָ	בְּנֹתֶיךָ	יָמֶיךָ	עָרֶיךָ	----

Notes:

1. An auxiliary *yod* is used before adding a suffix to the plural nouns as expected, but it is also used in some places where we would not have expected it, namely, in the singular constructs אֲבִי and אֲחִי

2. Look for irregular plural forms.

3. The forms with the 1st c. s. suffix are not shown but they are generally ִי -- for singular nouns and ַי -- for plural nouns. In other words, none of the nouns, singular or plural would have *both* the auxiliary *yod* and the 1st c. s. suffix. For example בְּנִי *my son*, בָּנַי *my sons*, אָחִי *my brother*, אַחַי *my brethren*.

Discourse profiles for Predictive Narrative and Instructional Discourse

18.5a. Our lesson verse records the words of Moses' father-in-law Jethro as he advises Moses how to appoint additional judges from the children of Israel to help Moses judge the people. Jethro's instructions follow our lesson verse in the form of a relatively lengthy string of weqatal verb forms as we would expect for Instructional Discourse. Our lesson verse serves as the introduction to the instructions by describing the scene that is calling for help. The introductory material is also given in the expected constructions, namely, a verbless clause and a participle.

18.5b. Fortunately for the student of Biblical Hebrew the discourse profile schemes for the different genres are different only at and near the mainline. The lower ranked constructions like dependent clauses, verbless clause, the participle, the הָיָה forms, and irrealis have the same functions in almost all genres. We can therefore sketch what we have learned about the discourse profile schemes in three different genres as follows:[1]

---

[1] See Longacre(1989), 107; Dawson(1994), 115.

Historical Narrative	Predictive Narrative	Instructional Discourse

1. Mainline: Wayyiqtol   Weqatal   Weqatal

Off-the-line:
2. Topicalization   X-qatal   X-yiqtol   X-yiqtol

CONSTRUCTIONS SHARED IN ALL THREE GENRES:

3. **Relative past background:** Qatal in dependent clause
4. **Non-past background:** Yiqtol in a dependent clause
5. **Backgrounded activities:** participle
6. **Transition marker:** Mainline form of היה
7. **Scene-setting:** Verbless clause
8. **Irrealis:** Negation of any verb

Note: As you can see by the similarities in the discourse profiles, distinguishing between Predictive Narrative and Instructional Discourse can be difficult. One key difference is that Predictive Narrative follows people or other agents through a series of events, story-like. On the other hand, Instructional Discourse follows the accomplishment of a goal. Any people or other agents are simply treated as qualified individuals for accomplishing the goal. You will also learn that another distinction between Predictive Narrative and Instructional Discourse is that the latter uses an occasional imperative, a verb form you will learn about in Lesson 19.

18.5c. Your Lesson 16 reading assignment in Genesis 22, shows that Direct Speech, which is often embedded within Historical Narrative, may itself be comprised of any of the above genres as well as at least one more which you will learn shortly. The Direct Speech genres then have a place in the discourse profile scheme of Historical Narrative as follows:[1]

1. Mainline: Wayyiqtol

Off-the-line:
2. Topicalization: X-qatal
3. **Embedded Direct Speech**
4. Relative past background: Qatal in a dependent clause
5. Relative non-past background: Yiqtol in a dependent clause
6. Backgrounded activities: Participle
7. Transition marker: Wayyiqtol of היה
8. Scene setting: Verbless Clause
9. Irrealis scene setting: Negation of any verb by לאֹ

---

[1] See the note on Lesson 16 reading in Gen. 22.

Assignments

18.6a. Memorize the irregular nouns in their different forms as shown in 18.4B.

18.6b. Match the following prefixed and affixed subject pronouns with their English counterparts.

1. he, it	9. he, it = a ___-er	___ a. Ø _____	___ i. _____ א
2. she, it / you (m. s.)	10. she, it = a ___-er	___ b. _____ ת	___ j. וֹ _____ י
3. you (f. s.)	11. you(m. s.) = a ___-er	c. ו _____ ת	___ k. _____ נ
4. I	12. you(f. s.) = a ___-er	___ d. וֹ _____	___ l. תִי _____
5. they (m. p.)	13. I = a ___-er	___ e. תָ _____	___ m. י _____ ת
6. they(f. p.) /you(f. p.)	14. they = ___-ers	___ f. נָה _____ ת	___ n. תָ _____
7. you (m. p.)	15. you(m. p.) = ___-ers	___ g. נוּ _____	___ o. תֶם _____
8. we	16. you(f. p.) = ___-ers	___ h. ה _____	___ p. תֶן _____
	17. we = ___-ers		___ q. _____ י

18.6c. Translate:

25. אִישׁ חַי	17. אֲדָמָה רַבָּה	9. אֵלֶּה הָאֲנָשִׁים	1. הָאִישׁ הַטּוֹב
26. נֶפֶשׁ חַיָּה	18. הָאֲדָמָה הָרַבָּה	10. הָאֲנָשִׁים הָאֵלֶּה	2. אֲנִי טוֹב
27. הַנֶּפֶשׁ הַחַיָּה	19. רַבָּה הָאֲדָמָה	11. הָאֲנָשִׁים הָהֵם	3. טוֹבָה הִיא
28. נְפָשׁוֹת חַיּוֹת	20. הָאֲדָמָה הַזֹּאת	12. הָאִישׁ הַזֶּה	4. הֵם טֹבִים
29. חַיּוֹת הַנְּפָשׁוֹת	21. הִיא הָאֲדָמָה	13. אֲנָשִׁים גְּדֹלִים	5. טֹבוֹת הֵן
30. אֲנָשִׁים חַיִּים	22. אֵלֶּה אֲדָמוֹת	14. גְּדֹלִים הָאֲנָשִׁים	6. הַדְּבָרִים הַטּוֹבִים
31. הָאֲנָשִׁים הַחַיִּים	23. אֲדָמוֹת רַבּוֹת	15. הוּא הָאִישׁ הַגָּדֹל	7. אַתְּ טֹבָה
32. חַיִּים הָאֲנָשִׁים	24. רַבַּת הָאֲדָמוֹת	16. הָאִישׁ הָהוּא	8. טוֹב אַתָּה

18.6d. Translate the excerpts from Jethro's instructions written clause-by-clause. You may be surprised how little help you need translating them. They are taken from Exodus 18:21-23.

עֲלֵהֶם means *over them*. The rest of the clause translates *captains of thousands, captains of hundreds, captains of fifties, and captains of tens.*

1. וְשַׂמְתָּ עֲלֵהֶם שָׂרֵי אֲלָפִים שָׂרֵי מֵאוֹת שָׂרֵי חֲמִשִּׁים וְשָׂרֵי עֲשָׂרֹת:

The root שׁפט means *judge.* בְּכָל־עֵת means *at all times.*

2. וְשָׁפְטוּ אֶת־הָעָם בְּכָל־עֵת

3. וְהָיָה

יָבִיאוּ is the root בוא in the yiqtol form in the Hiphil stem in which it means *bring.*

4. כָּל־הַדָּבָר הַגָּדֹל יָבִיאוּ אֵלֶיךָ

5. וְכָל־הַדָּבָר הַקָּטֹן יִשְׁפְּטוּ־הֵם

קָטֹן is the opposite of גָּדֹל   הֵם means *they*.

6. וְנָשְׂאוּ אִתָּךְ

7. אִם אֶת־הַדָּבָר הַזֶּה תַּעֲשֶׂה

This dependent clause marks the beginning of another subset of instruc-tions.

8. וְצִוְּךָ אֱלֹהִים

The ending on the verb form is a direct object suffix meaning *you* (masculine, singular).

9. וְיָכָלְתָּ עֲמֹד

The root יכל means *be able*. Since *be able* is al-ready attributive as trans-lations of qatal require, you do not need an *-er-word*. Translate the infin-itive as if it has a לְ attached.

10. וְגַם כָּל־הָעָם הַזֶּה עַל־מְקֹמוֹ יָבֹא בְשָׁלוֹם:

מָקוֹם means *place*. The singular verb form with the subject עָם is very com-mon, in fact, more frequent than a plural form. עָם is called a *collective noun*. The X-yiqtol construction here culminates the instruc-tions by putting the focus on the people and by using the vivid yiqtol which describes action which will emerge from the recipe for success.

18.6e.   Fill out verb analysis charts for the verbs in numbers 1, 2, 4, and 7.
18.6f.   Read Genesis 22:5-6.

Lesson 19

שְׁמַע יִשְׂרָאֵל יְהוָה אֱלֹהֵינוּ יְהוָה אֶחָד׃ וְאָהַבְתָּ אֵת יְהוָה אֱלֹהֶיךָ בְּכָל־לְבָבְךָ

Deuteronomy 6:4-5

Goals:

- **Identify and read the Qal masculine singular imperative.**
- **Distinguish Hortatory Discourse from the other direct speech genres.**
- **Identify and read the pronominal suffixes.**
- **Learn the mitigative function weqatal in Hortatory Discourse.**

What we already know

Scan ahead to the final clause of our lesson verse. With the understanding that the root אהב

means *love*, and לֵבָב is a noun meaning *heart*, you can translate it. _____

_____

If you do not know the meaning of the affix on וְאָהַבְתָּ stop all other progress and memorize all the qatal/weqatal endings now. You may want to translate the *bet* on בְּכָל as *with* rather than *in*.

The imperative

19.2a. Is the first word, שְׁמַע of our lesson verse, a yiqtol form?_____Does it have the sign of

either a Qal or Piel qatal form? _____ What are the signs of the Qal and Piel qatal forms?

_____ and_____(6.2b) What is the sign of the Qal participle?_____(12.2a)

What letter would very likely be prefixed to our word if it were an infinitive?_____ (16.4a) So we are now introduced to our next verb form, the **imperative**.

> RULE: **The sign of the Qal masculine singular imperative is a *shewa* under the first root letter: ○○○̩ Translate this direct order with the English imperative.**

The Qal imperative is often the 2nd person yiqtol forms minus the prefixed pronoun, in somewhat the same way that English imperatives leave the subject unwritten or unsaid.

English Imperative	**Biblical Hebrew Imperative**
(You) Listen to the voice of the people!	(תָּ)שְׁמַע בְּקוֹל הָעָם
unwritten	unwritten
subject	subject

Translation of שְׁמַע : *Listen!* or *Hear!*

19.2b. Consistent with the idea mentioned above, that the Qal imperative is often the 2nd person yiqtol form minus the prefixed pronoun, 1st *nun* and 1st *yod* roots, which are normally missing their first root letters in the yiqtol form, will also be missing the first root letter in the imperative forms of these roots.

QAL IMPERATIVES of 1st *NUN* and 1st *YOD* ROOTS

	Yiqtol 2nd person, masculine, singular	Imperative masculine, singular
First *nun* (נתן)	תִּתֵּן	תֵּן
First *yod* (יצא)	תֵּצֵא	צֵא

Notes:

1. Do you remember that הלך looks like a 1st yod root in the yiqtol form (3.2a)? It does in the imperative, too. Its masculine singular form is לֵךְ

2. Do you remember that לקח looks like a 1st nun root in the yiqtol form (9.2b)? Likewise in the imperative. Its masculine singular form is קַח

19.2c. Our lesson verse serves as our introduction to another of the Direct Speech genres, Hortatory Discourse.

> RULE: *Hortatory Discourse is the +projection genre in which the speaker/writer is persuading his audience, or trying to alter its behavior.*[1] **One of its mainline verb forms is the** *imperative.* **Like Predictive Narrative and Instructional Discourse, Hortatory Discourse is found only in direct speech.**[2]

Hortatory Discourse, like Instructional Discourse, does not foretell the future per se. Rather, it expresses the speaker's desire for the future. Here is a summary of the genres of Biblical Hebrew to which we have been exposed and the respective task performed in each:

GENRES AND THE TASKS THEY PERFORM

GENRE:	*TASK*:
Historical Narrative	Tell a story about the past.
Predictive Narrative	Tell a story set in the future.
Instructional Discourse	Tell how to do something.
Hortatory Discourse	Influence the behavior of someone.

Fill out the verb analysis chart for שְׁמַע:

root	stem	form	person, gender, number	function	basic root meaning
				Hortatory Discourse Mainline	

---

[1] See Dawson(1994), § 2.2.1.5.
[2] Niccacci(1990), §135.

All imperatives are second person verb forms, and שְׁמַע as stated above, is the masculine singular form, so you can now fill in the person, gender, number column. In the function column put "hortatory mainline."

Vocative

19.3. Since the subject of an imperative is unwritten, יִשְׂרָאֵל cannot be the subject of the sentence even though it does name the one being spoken to. Rather it names the addressee.   We may think of this word as the subject of the verb but it is better thought of as a **vocative**.

> DEFINITION: When the one to whom direct speech is addressed (the *addressee*) is named in the address, the word of direct address is called a **vocative**. The only way to distinguish between a vocative and the regular subject of the sentence is by context, and it is not always a clear distinction.

You can translate vocatives with *O*, as in *O, Israel* in our lesson verse.

Translate שְׁמַע יִשְׂרָאֵל using *O* with *Israel* if you like:_____

Pronominal suffixes in two verbless clauses

19.4a. The next four words of our lesson verse are probably the most famous in the Hebrew Bible, but they are also somewhat of an enigma. They are very important in Jewish tradition, being written on the

doorposts of many traditional Jewish homes. What does יְהוָה mean?_____The next two words יְהוָה אֱלֹהֵינוּ may be a verbless clause. What form of אֱלֹהִים is אֱלֹהֵי ?

_____ (8.4a) נוּ is the third person common pronominal suffix meaning *our*.

Translate יְהוָה אֱלֹהֵינוּ :_____

19.4b. It is time we learned a full contingency of these pronominal suffixes. Remember that they can be either objective suffixes or possessive suffixes.   Realize that the pronominal suffixes may be found objectively on the DDO, prepositions, and verbs. The suffixes may be found possessively on nouns and the preposition לְ   In the chart below the suffixes are used objectively with the DDO אֵת   And they are used possessively with the word אֱלֹהִים   Notice how the nikkud of the DDO changes to *holem* when the suffix is added.   Notice how אֱלֹהִים is put into its construct form אֱלֹהֵי before the suffix is added.

PRONOMINAL SUFFIXES

Used Objectively:		**Used Possessively:**	
אֹתִי me	אֹתָנוּ us	אֱלֹהַי my God	אֱלֹהֵינוּ our God
אֹתְךָ you (m.s.)	אֶתְכֶם you (m.p.)	אֱלֹהֶיךָ your (m.s.) God	אֱלֹהֵיכֶם your (m.p.) God
אֹתָךְ you (f.s.)	אֶתְכֶן you (f.p.)	אֱלֹהַיִךְ your (f.s.) God	אֱלֹהֵיכֶן your (f.p.) God
אֹתוֹ him, it	אֶתְהֶם or אֹתָם them (m.p.)	אֱלֹהָיו his God	אֱלֹהֵיהֶם their (m.p.) God
אֹתָהּ her, it	אֶתְהֶן them (f.p.)	אֱלֹהֶיהָ her God	אֱלֹהֵיהֶן their (f.p.) God

Here are the suffixes themselves, not attached to any other word or sign. This chart is also in the "Helpful Charts" section near the back of the book.

PRONOMINAL SUFFIXES (unattatched):

י ָ me, my		נוּ ָ us, our	
ךָ ָ you, your (m.s.)		כֶם ָ you, your (m.p.)	
ךְ ָ you, your (f.s.)		כֶן ָ you, your (f.p.)	
ו ָ him, it, his, its		ם ָ or הֶם ָ them, their (m.p.)	
ה ָ or הָ ָ her, it, hers, its		הֶן ָ them, their (f.p.)	

Notes:

1. The chart above shows the most consistent parts of the pronominal suffixes. Several of them are found with a variety nikkud in a variety of situations. For instance, אָחִי *my brother* versus אַחַי *my brothers*. The consistent part is the *yod* meaning *my*.

2. Notice the dot in the *heh* of the 3rd f. s. suffix meaning *her, it*. It is not a *dagesh*.

> DEFINITION: **A mappiq** is a special mark in the 3rd f. s. ending. It will help you distinguish this pronominal use of *heh* from its many other uses at the ends of words. It is pronounced as a release of breath during pronunciation of the preceding vowel, usually a *qamets*.

19.4c. The second possibility for a verbless clause, יְהוָה אֶחָד should not pose a problem for you. If indeed these two words are a verbless clause, what kind of adjective would the masculine form of אֶחָד

the number *one*, be?_____ (18.2a)

Translate יְהוָה אֶחָד : _____

19.4d. If indeed we are looking at two verbless clauses, is the word order in them S-P or P-S?_____

So does the word order put put special focus on a fronted element? _____ (2.7c)

19.4e. As this section has been suggesting all along, יְהוָה אֱלֹהֵינוּ יְהוָה אֶחָד may not be two verbless clauses. It may be only one. We may also think of אֶחָד as an *attributive* adjective. In this case two words, יְהוָה אֱלֹהֵינוּ serve as the subject of the clause and two words, יְהוָה אֶחָד serve as the predicate.

Translate the four words according to this one-clause interpretation:_____

_____

19.4f. You may be thinking that אֶחָד would have the definite article [הַ] on it if it is an attributive adjective because יהוה is a name and hence, definite. Very good! Gold star! This puts a one-clause interpretation in some doubt. On the other hand, there are other places in the Hebrew Bible where אֶחָד *is* used as a definite adjective even though it does not have the definite article. We are not sure if a one or a two-clause interpretation is better. The fact is, scholars have suggested several other possibilities as well for these four words.[1] You might try to think of one or more. Hint: one or more of the words may be in apposition; that is, a noun which renames one of the other nouns.

Mitigation in Hortatory Discourse

19.5a. Even though we have already translated it, let us return to the last clause of our lesson verse. Fill out the verb analysis chart for וְאָהַבְתָּ :

root	stem	form	person, gender, number	function	basic root meaning

Perhaps you need a bit of help with the function box. Remember the proverb, "Wayyiqtol outside the quotation marks; weqatal inside"? Weqatal is not only the mainline verb form in the other two direct speech genres Predictive Narrative and Instructional Discourse, it also has a key role in the third direct speech discourse Hortatory Discourse. The weqatal can "stand in" as the mainline of Hortatory Discourse to give commands in the *style* of Instructional Discourse or even Predictive Narrative.

---

[1] Waltke and O'Connor(1990), §8.4.2g.

110

RULE: **In Hortatory Discourse the weqatal is a continuation form. It generally continues the string of commands which was begun by one or more imperatives. The weqatal gives commands in a softened or mitigated style as compared to the direct order of the imperative.[1] Translate them as you would in Instructional Discourse and Predictive Narrative.**

In the verb analysis chart above, write "Hortatory--mitigated mainline" in the "function" box.

19.5b. Predictive Narrative is at one end of a continuum and Hortatory Discourse is at the other end.

Concentration of **imperatives**

increases

-->

Predictive Narrative |----------------------------|----------------------------------| Unmitigated

Mitigated Hortatory   **Hortatory Discourse**

and Instructional Discourses

At one extreme, the end with Predictive Narrative no use of imperatives. At the other end, the Hortatory end, there is a heavy concentration of imperatives. In the middle of the continuum, the genres are harder to distinguish based on the use of verb forms alone. The basic idea is when the concentration of imperatives increases we are approaching unmitigated Hortatory Discourse.

> **A word about mitigation:** *Mitigation* of Hortatory Discourse by replacing imperatives with weqatals (or yiqtols) does not necessarily reflect that the speaker is any less serious or earnest in his intentions. Mitigation merely reflects a gentler *style*.

Translate the entire lesson verse: _____

_____

Assignments

19.6a. Memorize the pronominal suffixes.

19.6b. Translate (שָׂדֶה is odd in that it is a masculine noun that sometimes appears feminine.):

1. דְּבָרָיו	9. שָׂדוֹת	17. מְקוֹמָהּ	25. עֵינָהּ
2. דִּבְרֵיהֶם	10. שָׂדְךָ	18. מְקוֹמוֹ	26. עֵינֶיךָ
3. דְּבָרֵנוּ	11. שְׂדֹתֵיהֶם	19. מְקוֹמִי	27. עֵינוֹ
4. דְּבָרַי	12. שְׂדֹתֵינוּ	20. מְקוֹמְךָ	28. עֵינֵיכֶם
5. דְּבָרֵינוּ	13. שָׂדֵינוּ	21. מְקוֹמֹתֵיכֶם	29. עֵינִי
6. דְּבָרֶיהָ	14. שְׂדֵי־מוֹאָב	22. מְקוֹמָם	30. עֵינֶיהָ
7. דַּבְּרֶךָ	15. שְׂדוֹתֵיכֶם	23. מְקוֹמֹתָם	31. עֵינֵיהֶם
8. דְּבָרֶיךָ	16. שָׂדֶיךָ	24. מְקוֹמֹתַי	32. עֵינָיו

---

[1] Longacre(1989), §5; Revell(1989), 22, 24, 26.

19.6c. Here, divided clause by clause, are some parts of Deuteronomy 6:6-12 following our lesson verse. Much of the unlearned material has been edited out. Translate the clauses, and notice how the discourse ranges from Hortatory to Instructional Discourse.

The weqatal of the root היה almost always refers to the future.

1. וְהָיוּ הַדְּבָרִים הָאֵלֶּה עַל־לְבָבֶךָ:

Look for the infinitive of the root הלך with several "appendages."

2. וְדִבַּרְתָּ בָּם וּבְלֶכְתְּךָ בַדֶּרֶךְ

The root כתב means *write*. מְזוּזֹת means *doorposts*.

3. וּכְתַבְתָּם עַל־מְזוּזֹת בֵּיתֶךָ

4. וְהָיָה

יְבִיאֲךָ is the third person, masc. sing. yiqtol of the Hiphil stem for the root בוא meaning *he will bring you*.

5. כִּי יְבִיאֲךָ יְהוָה אֱלֹהֶיךָ אֶל־הָאָרֶץ

נִשְׁבַּע means *He had sworn*. Masc. sing. אָב has the irregular plural form אֲבֹת

6. אֲשֶׁר נִשְׁבַּע לַאֲבֹתֶיךָ לְאַבְרָהָם לְיִצְחָק וּלְיַעֲקֹב לָתֶת לָךְ עָרִים גְּדֹלֹת וְטֹבֹת

The root בנה means *build*.

7. אֲשֶׁר לֹא־בָנִיתָ:

8. וְאָכַלְתָּ

The root שבע means *be satisfied*.

9. וְשָׂבָעְתָּ:

הִשָּׁמֶר is a Niphal stem masc. sing. imperative meaning *Take heed!*

10. הִשָּׁמֶר לְךָ

פֶּן means *lest*. The root שכח means *forget*.

11. פֶּן־תִּשְׁכַּח אֶת־יְהוָה

19.6d. Translate the following verses with imperatives. Remember that if you are missing a root letter think of first yod roots (and הלך) or first nun roots (and לקח).

Genesis 12:19

12. הִנֵּה אִשְׁתְּךָ קַח וָלֵךְ

Genesis 13:14 Translate נָא *please*.

13. שָׂא נָא עֵינֶיךָ וּרְאֵה

Exodus 4:18

14. וַיֹּאמֶר יִתְרוֹ לְמֹשֶׁה לֵךְ לְשָׁלוֹם:

Exodus 11:8

15. צֵא אַתָּה וְכָל־הָעָם

112

Exodus 19:21

16.   וַיֹּאמֶר יְהוָה אֶל־מֹשֶׁה רֵד

Exodus 31:2   This verse has a clause-initial
qatal which is common in direct speech.

17.   רְאֵה קָרָאתִי בְשֵׁם בְּצַלְאֵל

2 Kings 4:42

18.   תֵּן לָעָם

19.6e.   Read Genesis 22:7-8.

Lesson 20

וַיֹּאמֶר עֵלִי לִשְׁמוּאֵל לֵךְ שְׁכָב וְהָיָה אִם־יִקְרָא אֵלֶיךָ וְאָמַרְתָּ דַּבֵּר יְהוָה כִּי
שֹׁמֵעַ עַבְדֶּךָ וַיֵּלֶךְ שְׁמוּאֵל וַיִּשְׁכַּב בִּמְקוֹמוֹ׃

1 Samuel 3:9

Goals:

- Identify and read Qal and Piel imperatives in all genders and numbers.
- Use verb forms to locate the boundaries between discourses.

What we already know

20.1a. How many wayyiqtols does our lesson verse contain? _____ Translate each of them:

וַיֹּאמֶר עֵלִי לִשְׁמוּאֵל _____

וַיֵּלֶךְ שְׁמוּאֵל _____

שָׁכַב (שכב) means *lie down*. As an interesting point of note, is it Qal or Piel stem? וַיִּשְׁכַּב בִּמְקוֹמוֹ

Hint: Is the *dagesh* in the *khoph forte* or *lene*?) _____

20.1b. You still know quite a bit more. Locate the beginning of the direct speech, and translate the two

imperatives there (19.2b). _____ and _____

20.1c. Next, notice how the weqatal forms continue where the imperatives leave off. Translate וְהָיָה

_____ and וְאָמַרְתָּ _____

20.1d. Finally, translate the yiqtol in a dependent clause (13.3), which is subordinated to וְהָיָה

_____

Furtive patakh

20.2. It has been a long time since we have dealt with any issues of pronunciation, but we must learn a pronunciation rule here. In our lesson word שֹׁמֵעַ we have a *furtive patakh* at the end of the word.

> RULE: When a word ends with *khet* [ח] or *ayin* [ע] and has a *patakh* as its vowel, the *patakh* will be written slightly to the right of normal in your Bible and is called *furtive patakh*. The *furtive patakh* is to be pronounced before its accompanying consonant, rather than after, as normal. The *furtive patakh* also usually shifts the emphasis in a word from its last syllable to the second to the last.

The only noticeable pronunciation change a *furtive patakh* makes when it is with *ayin* is the shifting of the emphasis. שֹׁמֵעַ is pronounced /sho-MEH-ah/. Also, we either have seen or will see in our next section of vocabulary words, a *furtive patakh* in the following:

רוּחַ /RU-akh/ not /ru-KHAH/

מִזְבֵּחַ /miz-BEH-akh/ not /miz-beh-KHAH/

יְהוֹשֻׁעַ /yᵉho-SHU-ah/ not /yᵉho-shu-AH/

When to use the English word then

20.3. The three wayyiqtols in our lesson verse give us the outline of a story. Eli spoke, and then Samuel went and lied down. When the wayyiqtol string switches from Eli doing the action to Samuel, it is a good time to use the word *then* in the translation of the *vav*.

> RULE: **When the subject of a string of wayyiqtols or weqatals switches, it is usually a good time to translate the vav on the wayyiqtol *and then* or simply *then*.**[1] When a string of wayyiqtols or weqatals proceeds uninterrupted with the same subject, translate the *vav* with the usual *and*.

Determining a genre of direct speech

20.4a. As a matter of good training, and to help us build a foundation for examining the switch from one genre to another, let us backtrack, and fill out some verb analysis charts, first for לֵךְ and שְׁכַב (19.2c):

root	stem	form	person, gender, number	function	basic root meaning

root	stem	form	person, gender, number	function	basic root meaning

20.4b. Now consider וְהָיָה and וְאָמַרְתָּ We know, as weqatals, that they are mainline verb forms in the direct speech genres. The question is whether we are in Predictive Narrative, Instructional Discourse, or Hortatory Discourse. We noted in the rule at 19.5a that the weqatal is a continuation form.

---

[1] In essence, the shift in pronoun referent divides or breaks a text. For an excellent account of participant reference tracking and its pertinence to text segmentation see Exter Blokland, *In Search of Syntax: Towards a Syntactic Segmentation Model for Biblical Hebrew*(Amsterdam: VU University Press, 1995).

That is, it continues the sense of the verb which precedes it. If an imperative precedes weqatal, the weqatal most often continues a line of exhortations. This would seem the case in our lesson verse, but we must add another condition.

> RULE: **The weqatal which continues a line of exhortations in a Hortatory Discourse must be of the same person, gender, and number as the command form which precedes it.**

This is exactly the case in the lesson verse of Lesson 19, shown here once again only slightly edited to help you focus on the series of 2nd m. s. references (Remember that even though we do not write it in the verb analysis chart, all imperatives are second person verbs):

וְאָהַבְתָּ ... שְׁמַע יִשְׂרָאֵל   *Hear, O Israel ... and you will be a lover ...*
↑   ↑
2nd m. s.   2nd m. s.
reference   reference

The weqatal וְהָיָה in our current lesson verse breaks the chain of 2nd m. s. reference begun by the imperatives. Observe:

וְהָיָה   שְׁכָב   לֵךְ   *Go! Lie down! And it will be...*
↑   ↑   ↑
3rd m. s.   2nd m. s.   2nd m.s.

In fact וְהָיָה often signals the start of a new discourse, very often a switch to Predictive Narrative. In our lesson verse there are two details which recommend Instructional Discourse:

1. The next weqatal וְאָמַרְתָּ once again refers directly to the addressee with a second person subject as is often the case with Instructional Discourse.
2. Predictive Narrative tells of people doing things in the future. It is focused on the people.[1] Instructional Discourse, on the other hand, focuses on the accomplishing of a goal as in our lesson verse.

Fill out the verb analysis charts for וְהָיָה and וְאָמַרְתָּ

root	stem	form	person, gender, number	function	basic root meaning

---

[1] Longacre, "Discourse Perspective on the Hebrew Verb: Affirmation and Restatement"(1987), *Linguistics and Biblical Hebrew*(ed. Bodine. Winona Lake: Eisenbrauns, 1992), 183.

root	stem	form	person, gender, number	function	basic root meaning

Translate   לֵךְ שְׁכָב וְהָיָה אִם־יִקְרָא אֵלֶיךָ וְאָמַרְתָּ

_____

_____

Piel imperative

20.5a. Eli instructs Samuel to say דַּבֵּר יְהוָה כִּי שֹׁמֵעַ עַבְדֶּךָ What kind of *dagesh* is in the בּ

of דַּבֵּר ?_____ So the middle letter of the word is doubled. What stem is

indicated by this doubled letter?_____ (2.2b)

> RULE: A *patakh* under the first root letter and a doubled middle root letter are the
> signs of Piel imperative: ⃝ ⊙ ⃝̱

Notice, as with the Qal, the Piel stem imperative is like the Piel 2nd person yiqtol minus the prefixed
pronoun:

Piel yiqtol   Piel imperative

תְּדַבֵּר   דַּבֵּר

The *dagesh lene* in the first root letter of the imperative is a minor difference that will sometimes affect the
pronunciation of the word.

Fill out the verb analysis chart for דַּבֵּר :

root	stem	Form	person, gender, number	function	basic root meaning

A reminder: all imperatives are 2nd person forms. The gender, and number of the imperative that has no ending is the masculine, singular.

Translate דַּבֵּר :_____

20.5b. Here is a chart showing the Piel and Qal imperatives of strong roots in all persons, genders, and numbers:

Qal Imperatives		Piel Imperatives	
masc. sing.	פְּקֹד	masc. sing.	דַּבֵּר
fem. sing. ←	פִּקְדִי	fem. sing.	דַּבְּרִי
masc. plur. ←	פִּקְדוּ	masc. plur.	דַּבְּרוּ
fem. plur.	פְּקֹדְנָה	fem. plur.	דַּבֵּרְנָה

Some notes:
1. You may want to lightly circle the endings. They are very regular for the imperatives of all roots in all stems.
2. The arrows mark locations where the imperative forms do not result from a simple removal of the 2nd person yiqtol's prefix pronoun.
3. To distinguish between the imperative and qatal forms of Qal and Piel stems, remember to focus on the *vowel under the first root letter*. What is the vowel under the first root letter of the Qal qatal?

_____ And the Piel qatal?_____ (6.2b)
4. There are only twelve or so attestations of feminine plural imperatives in the Hebrew Bible. They are often missing the *heh* in which case, they end with final *nun* (ן) or final *nun* with a *qamets* (ָן) as in שְׁמַעַן or קְרֶאןָ

20.5c. What is the relationship of יְהוָה to the rest of the clause?_____ (19.3)

20.5d. Fill out the verb analysis chart for שְׁמַע :

root	stem	form	person, gender, number	function	basic root meaning

20.5e. In the word עַבְדֶּךָ עֶבֶד means _____ and its suffix ךָ-- means

_____ (19.4b) You may realize that the normal form for *your servant* is עַבְדְּךָ However, our word is located at a major disjunctive accent which is near the middle of most verses, called an *atnakh*.

Therefore, the nikkud of the word is altered, and the accent within the word is shifted forward

from the last syllable. What is the name for a special form of this sort? _____ (15.5)

Translate דַּבֵּר יְהוָה כִּי שֹׁמֵעַ עַבְדֶּךָ: _____

Shifting from genre to genre

20.6. Our lesson verse is a good example of how Biblical Hebrew prose quickly and fluently shifts from one discourse genre to another and embeds one genre within another. It is just as we would expect from someone fluent in the language with which he has grown up. Let us review the genre shifts and embedding in the lesson verse.

1.

The over-all context of the verse is
Historical Narrative, as evidenced by the
three wayyiqtol verb forms,

וַיִּשְׁכַּב   וַיֵּלֶךְ   וַיֹּאמֶר

2.

Embedded within the Historical Narrative
is Eli's direct speech which is itself
two genres as follows:

2a.	**2b.**
Hortatory Discourse as	Instructional Discourse as
evidenced by the two imperatives	as evidenced by the string of weqatals
שְׁכַב לֵךְ	וְהָיָה וְאָמַרְתָּ

3.

Embedded within Eli's Instructional
Discourse is the Hortatory Discourse that
Eli recommends Samuel should use with *YHWH*:

דַּבֵּר יְהוָה

Speak, O YHWH

Note: Discourse 2b. above may also be considered *mitigated Hortatory Discourse* following the rule in 19.5, but, as is true in all languages, the boundaries between genres is sometimes fuzzy. We might refer to the fuzzy boundaries between some genres as a language's elasticity.

Assignments

20.7a. Learn words 101 through 150 for the lessons 20 through 22.

20.7b. Translate:

13.	שִׁמְעַן	7.	דִּבְרִי	1.	שָׁמָר
14.	שָׁמַע	8.	וְדִבֶּר	2.	שִׁמְרוּ
15.	תִּשְׁמַע	9.	דַּבֵּר	3.	וְשָׁמְרוּ
16.	וַיִּשְׁמַע	10.	לְדַבֵּר	4.	וְשִׁמְרִי
17.	שִׁמְעִי	11.	דַּבְּרוּ	5.	תִּשְׁמֹרְנָה
18.	שִׁמְעוּ	12.	וְדִבְּרוּ	6.	לִשְׁמֹר

20.7c. Translate:

Exodus 4:23 If the first verb throws you, see 17.4f.

1.   וָאֹמַר אֵלֶיךָ שַׁלַּח אֶת־בְּנִי

Exodus 5:1

2.   וְאַחַר בָּאוּ מֹשֶׁה וְאַהֲרֹן וַיֹּאמְרוּ אֶל־פַּרְעֹה כֹּה־אָמַר יְהוָה אֱלֹהֵי יִשְׂרָאֵל שַׁלַּח אֶת־עַמִּי

Exodus 6:29 Notice the participle דֹּבֵר is in Qal stem!

3.   וַיְדַבֵּר יְהוָה אֶל־מֹשֶׁה לֵּאמֹר אֲנִי יְהוָה דַּבֵּר אֶל־פַּרְעֹה מֶלֶךְ מִצְרַיִם אֵת כָּל־אֲשֶׁר אֲנִי דֹבֵר אֵלֶיךָ:

Leviticus 11:2 הַחַיָּה means *the animal*. Is זֹאת הַחַיָּה standard word order?(2.7c).

4.   דַּבְּרוּ אֶל־בְּנֵי יִשְׂרָאֵל לֵאמֹר זֹאת הַחַיָּה אֲשֶׁר תֹּאכְלוּ

Joshua 4:3 Imperatives can be prefixed by a vav, too.

שְׁתֵּים־עֶשְׂרֵה אֲבָנִים means *twelve stones*.

5.   וְצַוּוּ אוֹתָם לֵאמֹר שְׂאוּ־לָכֶם מִזֶּה מִתּוֹךְ הַיַּרְדֵּן שְׁתֵּים־עֶשְׂרֵה אֲבָנִים

Genesis 21:18 הַנַּעַר means *the boy*. Are the commands given to the boy or his mother?

6.   קוּמִי שְׂאִי אֶת־הַנַּעַר

Judges 9:10 לַתְּאֵנָה means *to the fig tree*. אַתְּ means *you* (fem. sing. subject).

7.   וַיֹּאמְרוּ הָעֵצִים לַתְּאֵנָה לְכִי־אַתְּ מָלְכִי עָלֵינוּ

Ruth 1:15 Context must tell you whether וַתֹּאמֶר has *you*(m.s.) or *she* as the subject, but *she* is the more common in the way-yiqtol form. שָׁבָה is the regular 3 f. s. qatal for a hollow root, meaning *she is a returner*. יְבִמְתֵּךְ means *your sister-in-law*.

8.   וַתֹּאמֶר הִנֵּה שָׁבָה יְבִמְתֵּךְ אֶל־עַמָּהּ וְאֶל־אֱלֹהֶיהָ שׁוּבִי אַחֲרֵי יְבִמְתֵּךְ:

1 Samuel 25:17 The root ראה can mean *consider* as well as *see*.

9.   וְעַתָּה דְּעִי וּרְאִי מַה־תַּעֲשִׂי

2 Samuel 13:7

10.   וַיִּשְׁלַח דָּוִד אֶל־תָּמָר לֵאמֹר לְכִי נָא בֵּית אַמְנוֹן אָחִיךְ

Song of Solomon 3:11 בַּת has an irregular plural בָּנוֹת

11.   צְאֶינָה וּרְאֶינָה בְּנוֹת צִיּוֹן

Observe in the following verses how statements that may seem like instructions in English translations, are more clearly direct orders in Hebrew:

Genesis 19:15 These are the commands of the messengers of *YHWH* to Lot when Lot was in Sodom. שְׁתֵּי Is the construct form for שְׁתַּיִם

12.   קוּם קַח אֶת־אִשְׁתְּךָ וְאֶת־שְׁתֵּי בְנֹתֶיךָ

Genesis 27:9 These are commands of Rebekah to Jacob as she planned a deception of her husband.

13.   לֶךְ־נָא אֶל־הַצֹּאן וְקַח־לִי מִשָּׁם

1 Kings 21:15 These are the commands of Jezebel for her husband Ahab. The root ירשׁ means *take possession of*. נָבוֹת כֶּרֶם means *vineyard of Naboth*.

14.   וַתֹּאמֶר אִיזֶבֶל אֶל־אַחְאָב קוּם רֵשׁ אֶת־כֶּרֶם נָבוֹת

20.7d. Read Genesis 22:9-11.

121

Lesson 21

וַיֹּאמֶר אֵלֶיהָ אֵלִיָּהוּ אַל־תִּירְאִי בֹּאִי עֲשִׂי כִדְבָרֵךְ

1 Kings 17:13

Goals:

- Identify and read second class first *yod* roots.
- Identify and read prohibitive commands.
- Identify and read imperatives of first guttural and hollow roots.

What we already know

21.1. Translate וַיֹּאמֶר אֵלֶיהָ אֵלִיָּהוּ _____

אֵלֶיהָ is a preposition with a pronominal suffix (19.4b) and אֵלִיָּהוּ is the name *Elijah*.

Second class 1st yod roots

21.2a. We know from our translation of the first clause, that Elijah is speaking to a woman. So we may guess that the *tav* on תִּירְאִי is a prefix pronoun meaning, together with the final yod as a complement,

you (f.s.). This is correct! So the root is one of your newer vocabulary words_____. What may be surprising is that the nikkud for this first *yod* root is not typical of the 1st *yod* roots we have learned so far. What is the typical vowel under the yiqtol's prefix pronoun for the Qal stem of a 1st *yod* root?

_____ (3.2a)

21.2b. There are a few 1st *yod* roots that do not have the *sere* under the prefix pronoun. We call them **second class 1st *yod* roots**. The only other roots on our vocabulary list for this course which are second class 1st *yod* roots besides יָרֵא are יָטַב meaning *be good* and יָשַׁר meaning *be right*. Most often these second class 1st *yod* roots are descriptive of *a state of being* rather than action. You will learn more about this distinction in Lesson 33.

21.2c. Fortunately, the different nikkud for this class of roots does help us differentiate between the yiqtols, and even more so, the wayyiqtols for the Qal of יָרֵא the Qal of רָאָה and the Niphal of רָאָה which means *appear*. Compare them below, concentrating most on the 3rd person masculine, singular and plural which are the most common. There is no need to concentrate very hard on the Niphal stem of רָאָה at this time; it is only shown at this point to impress you with the value of a solid understanding of certain details of nikkud. We won't study the Niphal stem in earnest until Lesson 38. The reason the wayyiqtols look more alike than the yiqtols is because the wayyiqtols of רָאָה lose the 3rd *heh*. Also notice how some conjugations of רָאָה have a *sere* under the prefix pronoun like *first class* 1st *yod* roots.

It is easy to derive the yiqtol forms for יָרֵא or other second class 1st *yod* roots by taking the *vav-patakh* off the forms in the chart. Unattested forms are not given in the chart.

WAYYIQTOLS OF ירא and ראה

	QAL of ירא	QAL of ראה	NIPHAL of ראה Given for comparison only
SING. 3 M (he, it)	וַיִּירָא	וַיַּרְא	וַיֵּרָא
3 F (she, it)	וַתִּירָא	וַתֵּרֶא	-----
2 M (you)	וַתִּירָא	וַתֵּרֶא	-----
2 F (you)	וַתִּירְאִי	-----	-----
1 C (I)	וָאִירָא	וָאֵרֶא	וָאֵרָא
PLUR. 3 M (they)	וַיִּירְאוּ	וַיִּרְאוּ	וַיֵּרָאוּ
3 F (they)	וַתִּירֶ֫אןָ	וַתִּרְאֶ֫ינָה	-----
2 M (you)	וַתִּירְאוּ	וַתִּרְאוּ	-----
2 F (you)	וַתִּירֶ֫אןָ	וַתִּרְאֶ֫ינָה	-----
1 C (we)	וַנִּירָא	וַנִּרְאֶה	-----

Prohibitive commands

21.3a. We have studied some ways the ancient Hebrew told someone what to do, as a direct order with the imperative, and as mitigated commands or instructions with the weqatal and yiqtol. The word אַל joined to תִּירָאִי by the *maqqef* (2.4b) is the way the ancient Hebrew told someone what *not to do*, or a command in the form of a prohibition. *The imperative is never negated in Hebrew.*

> RULE: **The *do-not*'s of Hebrew are given with the yiqtol form preceded by the word אַל or לֹא This construction is a high-ranking off-the-line verb form in Hortatory Discourse. Translate as a prohibition with *not, do not,* or *shall not.***[1]

21.3b. Fill out the verb analysis chart for אַל־תִּירָאִי:

root	stem	form	person, gender, number	function	basic root meaning
				w/ אַל = prohibitive command	

Translate אַל־תִּירָאִי as unmitigated: *Fear not!*

---

[1] Gesenius(1910) §107o-p; Jouon-Muraoka(1993) §114I; Revell,(1989), 27.

Imperatives of hollow and 1st guttural roots

21.4a. The next two words of our lesson verse are both imperatives, the first one from the root בוא and the second one from the root עשה Fill out the verb analysis charts for them both:

root	stem	form	person, gender, number	function	basic root meaning

root	stem	form	person, gender, number	function	basic root meaning

21.4b. Here are the Qal imperative conjugations of בוא given as an example of hollow roots and עשה given as an example of 1st guttural roots. Remember that the guttural letters are ר ע ח ה א Since עשה is not only a 1st guttural but it is also a 3rd *heh* root, עמד is also shown.

	Hollow roots	עשה	1st guttural roots
Masculine singular	בּוֹא	עֲשֵׂה	עֲמֹד
Feminine singular	בּוֹאִי	עֲשִׂי	עִמְדִי
Masculine plural	בּוֹאוּ	עֲשׂוּ	עִמְדוּ
Feminine plural	בֹּאנָה	עֲשֶׂינָה	עֲמֹדְנָה

Notes:
1. The vowels within imperatives are the most variable of any of the verb forms. Use context and your understanding that the imperative is a shortened yiqtol to help you identify imperatives.
2. Hollow verbs with *holem* or *shureq* may be spelled plene or defectiva.
3. There are no feminine plural attestations of imperatives for the roots בוא עשה or עמד but they are given in the chart because there are attestations of other roots of their types.

21.4c. The final word in our lesson verse is made of three parts:

$$ ֵךְ \quad + \quad דְּבָר \quad + \quad כְּ $$
$$ your\ (f.s.) \qquad word \qquad as $$

124

Translate אַל־תִּירְאִי בֹּאִי עֲשִׂי כִדְבָרֵךְ _____

More on mitigation

21.5a. As we learned in Lesson 19, as the concentration of weqatals in Hortatory Discourse increases, the mitigation of the commands increases (19.5b). In other words, less imperatives means a gentler (not less earnest) discourse. You may well have noticed that a string of commands often begins with one or more imperatives that command immediate action. Then the string continues with the weqatal forms which give commands that are more like instructions.[1] Such is the case with the earlier lesson verses, Deuteronomy 6:4-5

שְׁמַע ...וְאָהַבְתָּ אֵת יְהוָה אֱלֹהֶיךָ

and 1 Samuel 3:9

לֵךְ שְׁכָב וְהָיָה אִם־יִקְרָא אֵלֶיךָ וְאָמַרְתָּ

21.5b. Such is *not* the case in our lesson verse for this lesson. In essence, Elijah the prophet is telling his listener, a destitute widow, what to do (or not to do) in the most direct and commanding style available to him. Perhaps this was customary treatment of a widow by a prophet in those days. Let us prefer, though, that the woman was afraid, and needed an authoritative exhortation.[2]

21.5c. We find in the Hebrew Bible that the verb forms a speaker chooses to influence the behavior of others are somewhat affected by how the speaker perceives his relationship to his audience. When a speaker wants to assert his authority or the urgency of a situation, he will tend to use more imperatives. Prayer to *YHWH*, which often falls under the heading Hortatory Discourse, often uses imperatives to reflect the urgency of the supplicant's cry. On the other hand, when the speaker is trying to influence the behavior of a social superior, his verb forms will range closer to those of Instructional Discourse, or in the extreme, Predictive Narrative with third person subjects. The relationship between mitigation of Hortatory Discourse and social situation is summarized in the graphic below.

speaker asserting authority ⟶ speaker outranked by
or urgency   addressee
↓   ↓

Unmitigated Hortatory Discourse → **Instructional Discourse** → **Predictive Narrative**

Assignments

21.6a. Translate:

1. עֲשֵׂה	9. לָבוֹא	17. תִּחְיֶין
2. וַעֲשׂוּ	10. וּבֹאוּ	18. חֲיִי
3. וְעָשׂוּ	11. וּבָאוּ	19. וְהָיוּ
4. עֲשִׂי	12. וּבָאנוּ	20. עֲלֵה
5. וּבֹאִי	13. חֲיוּ	21. עֲלוּ
6. וּבָא	14. וְהָיְיָה	22. וְעָלוּ
7. בֹּאִי	15. וְהָיָה	23. עֲלִי
8. בֹּא	16. לִהְיוֹת	24. וְעָלֵה

---

[1] Revell,(1989), 22.

[2] For a thorough account of social ranking of individuals and its effect on discourse see Revell, *The Designation of the Individual: Expressive Usage in Biblical* Narrative(The Netherlands: Kok Pharos, 1996).

21.6b. Translate the following Hortatory Discourses. The passages reflect a variety of social settings which will illustrate varying degrees of mitigation. Each is written so that there is a "command" per line so that you can better get a feel for the pattern of the verb forms used to give the commands or requests.

Unmitigated Hortatory Discourse. Genesis 43:11-13 In this passage the patriarch Israel commands arrangements for the return of eleven of his sons to a high official of Egypt whom he does not yet realize is his twelfth son Joseph. Israel's place as commander of his tribe is threatened by the famine at home in Canaan and the imperious official in Egypt. It is the perfect setting in which to find the imperatives of unmitigated Hortatory Discourse. Some unlearned material has been removed including only one unfamiliar yiqtol form.

1. וַיֹּאמֶר אֲלֵהֶם יִשְׂרָאֵל אֲבִיהֶם

2. זֹאת עֲשׂוּ

3. קְחוּ מִזִּמְרַת   מִזִּמְרַת means *from the best fruits*.

4. וְכֶסֶף מִשְׁנֶה קְחוּ   וְכֶסֶף מִשְׁנֶה means *and double silver*.
Notice the X-imperative topical-ization structure.

5. וְאֶת־אֲחִיכֶם קָחוּ

6. וְקוּמוּ

7. שׁוּבוּ אֶל־הָאִישׁ:

Partially Mitigated Hortatory Discourse. Genesis 45:9-13 This passage has Joseph speaking to his brothers during their second visit, *after* he has made his identity known to his brothers. In his brothers' first visit, Joseph gave them several commands, with a concentration of imperatives and no weqatals. Notice, in the passage below, how Joseph "tones down" his commands using several weqatal forms.

8. מַהֲרוּ   This root מהר is used twice in the passage, once here as a Piel imperative and once at the end as a Piel weqatal, and it means *hurry*.

9. וַעֲלוּ אֶל־אָבִי

10. וַאֲמַרְתֶּם אֵלָיו כֹּה אָמַר בִּנְךָ יוֹסֵף

11. רְדָה אֵלַי   We will learn about the *heh* on the end of רְדָה in the next lesson. It does not change the essential mean-ing of this imperative.

12. אַל־תַּעֲמֹד

13. וְיָשַׁבְתָּ בְאֶרֶץ־גֹּשֶׁן

126

קָרוֹב means *near*.	וְהָיִיתָ קָרוֹב אֵלַי אַתָּה וּבָנֶיךָ וּבְנֵי בָנֶיךָ	14.
The unusual root כלכל means *nourish*.	וְכִלְכַּלְתִּי אֹתְךָ שָׁם	15.
This is a Hiphil weqatal meaning *and you will be tellers*.	וְהִגַּדְתֶּם לְאָבִי	16.
See number 8 above.	וּמִהַרְתֶּם	17.
This is another Hiphil weqatal, this one meaning *and you will be bringers down of*.	וְהוֹרַדְתֶּם אֶת־אָבִי	18.

"Totally" Mitigated Discourse. 2 Chronicles 6:16-25 Is prayer Hortatory Discourse? Very often, yes, it is. Prayer does, after all, try to influence *YHWH*. This passage is from King Solomon's prayer at the public dedication of the Temple of *YHWH*. Since the passage is long and complicated, including many dependent clauses, only those parts which contain the actual prayer requests are included. Notice how the carefully worded prayer is almost totally mitigated as Solomon addresses his Sovereign.

This section contains the only imperative. It clarifies that the prayer is indeed hortatory.	וְעַתָּה יְהוָה אֱלֹהֵי יִשְׂרָאֵל שְׁמֹר לְעַבְדְּךָ דָוִיד אָבִי אֵת אֲשֶׁר דִּבַּרְתָּ לּוֹ	19.
יֵאָמֵן is a Niphal yiqtol that means *may it be con-firmed*.	וְעַתָּה יְהוָה אֱלֹהֵי יִשְׂרָאֵל יֵאָמֵן דְּבָרְךָ	20.
The root פנה means *turn*. תְּפִלַּת is the feminine construct form of תְּפִלָּה meaning *prayer*.	וּפָנִיתָ אֶל־תְּפִלַּת עַבְדְּךָ	21.
תַּחֲנוּנֵי is the masculine plural construct of תַּחֲנוּן meaning *supplication for grace*.	וְשָׁמַעְתָּ אֶל־תַּחֲנוּנֵי עַבְדְּךָ וְעַמְּךָ יִשְׂרָאֵל	22.
	וְאַתָּה תִּשְׁמַע מִן־הַשָּׁמַיִם	23.
	וְשָׁמַעְתָּ	24.
The root סלח means *forgive*.	וְסָלַחְתָּ	25.
	וְאַתָּה תִּשְׁמַע מִן־הַשָּׁמַיִם	26.
	וְעָשִׂיתָ	27.
The root שפט means *judge*.	וְשָׁפַטְתָּ אֶת־עֲבָדֶיךָ	28.

21.6c. Read Genesis 22:12-15

Lesson 22

וַיֹּאמְרוּ לְיִפְתָּח לְכָה וְהָיִיתָה לָנוּ לְקָצִין

Judges 11:6

Goal:
- Identify and read weqatals which are off-the-line in Hortatory Discourse.

What we already know

Translate לְיִפְתָּח וַיֹּאמְרוּ (יִפְתָּח is a name.): _____

In what genre of discourse does the verb form indicate we are? _____

And what class of genres do we expect to follow? _____ (13.2a)

Paragogoic heh on the imperative

In exercise 21.6b.11 we saw an imperative with a הָ on the end of it, and we see it once again in our lesson verse's לְכָה which is normally written לֵךְ The addition of the *heh* happens occasionally, and it may be like the *heh* on the cohortative which you will learn about in Lesson 24, a way to express intention and further evidence of the imperative's original connection to the yiqtol. Or it may be a way to make the imperative more emphatic. A third possibility, one supported by another extra *heh*-ending later in our lesson verse, is that the *heh* is evidence of a regional dialect of Biblical Hebrew. An extra *heh* added on to the end of a word is called a *paragogic heh*, *paragogic* meaning "added to the end."

Translate לְכָה : _____

Weqatal as an off-the-line verb form in Hortatory Discourse

22.3a. We have already seen how the weqatal can stand in for the mainline of Hortatory Discourse, the imperative, in order to mitigate the discourse. The weqatal can also function as an off-the-line verb form in Hortatory discourse as it does in our lesson verse's וְהָיִיתָה

> RULE: **A weqatal or series of weqatals that are subordinate to or serve the mainline of a Hortatory Discourse are off-the-line verb forms used to give consequence or purpose. Translate the weqatal using English *so* for the *vav* and *may be* instead of *will be*.**

Fill out the verb analysis chart for וְהָיִיתָ :

root	stem	form	person, gender, number	function	basic root meaning
				Hortatory purpose or consequence	

Translation: *So you may be*

Notice, by the way, the paragogic *heh* on the end of the weqatal form which would normally be written וְהָיִ֫תָ Translation of the entire lesson verse:

_____

(קָצִין means *chief, ruler*.)

22.3b. The challenge is to interpret weqatals in a Hortatory context. They may be a surrogate mainline in a mitigated Hortatory or they may be off-the-line forms that provide motivation for obedience. For instance, in our lesson verse, the question would be whether Jephthah is being exhorted to *go and be chief* or *go so that you may become chief*. There is a cause and effect relationship between the events in the latter interpretation that does not exist in the former. The second interpretation expresses a command and motivation for obedience to it. The key to the interpretation is to remember the mainline/off-the-line distinction. Weqatals that are on the mainline of Mitigated Hortatory are like instructions that the listener is being exhorted to carry out. On the other hand, weqatals that are off-the-line are not instructions that can be directly carried out by the listener. Rather, they are the reasons why to carry out the mainline.

22.3c. One sign of a switch from the mainline of a Hortatory Discourse to a weqatal that is off-the-line may be a change in the person of the subject, for instance from a 2nd person subject to a 1st.[1] An example would be Deuteronomy 5:27

קְרַב אַתָּה וּשֲׁמָע אֵת כָּל־אֲשֶׁר יֹאמַר יְהוָה אֱלֹהֵינוּ וְשָׁמַ֫עְנוּ וְעָשִׂ֫ינוּ

\   /   \   /

1st person weqatals   2nd person imperatives

You approach, and hear all that YHWH our God speaks, so we may hear and do.

In this verse the switch from the imperative forms which are in the 2nd person to the weqatals which are 1st person help to signal that the weqatals are off-the-line in regular Hortatory Discourse rather than the start of Mitigated Hortatory.

22.3d. Below is a summary of the discourse profile scheme for Hortatory Discourse as it shapes up so far. Notice that the imperative shares the mainline with some weqatals that give commands. Also, notice that the weqatals which give consequences are off-the-line as you have learned in this lesson and that participles and verbless clauses are included in much the same roles as in the other genres.

_____

[1] The study of pronoun reference as related to discourse is referred to as "participant reference tracking," already mentioned in the note for 20.2a.

Mainline: 1a. Imperative

        1b. Weqatal (for Mitigated Hortatory Discourse)

Off-the-line:

2. Topicalization: X-Imperative

3. Prohibitive commands: אַל or לֹא + yiqtol

4. Consequence, purpose: Weqatal

5. Backgrounded activities: Participle

6. Scene setting: Verbless Clause

Assignments

22.4a. Often, an imperative and a weqatal work as a pair, the first giving the command and the second giving the consequence. Translate the following pairs:

1 Chronicles 14:10

וּנְתַתִּים is a weqatal + pronominal suffix, not a participle.

1.   עֲלֵה וּנְתַתִּים בְּיָדֶךָ

Numbers 4:19

2.   וְזֹאת עֲשׂוּ לָהֶם וְחָיוּ

1 Samuel 9:19 הַבָּמָה means *to the high place.*

3.   עֲלֵה לְפָנַי הַבָּמָה וַאֲכַלְתֶּם עִמִּי הַיּוֹם

1 Samuel 12:24 בֶּאֱמֶת means *in truth.*

4.   יְראוּ אֶת־יְהוָה וַעֲבַדְתֶּם אֹתוֹ בֶּאֱמֶת בְּכָל־לְבַבְכֶם

Genesis 12:13 אָחוֹת means *sister.*

5.   אִמְרִי־נָא אֲחֹתִי אָתְּ וְחָיְתָה נַפְשִׁי

Exodus 4:21 רָאֵה can mean *understand.* מֹפְתִים means *wonder.*

6.   רְאֵה כָּל־הַמֹּפְתִים אֲשֶׁר־שַׂמְתִּי בְיָדֶךָ וַעֲשִׂיתָם לִפְנֵי פַרְעֹה

Exodus 34:1 פְּסָל means *carve.* פְּסָל־לְךָ שְׁנֵי־לֻחֹת אֲבָנִים כָּרִאשֹׁנִים means *Carve for yourself two stone tablets as at first.*

7.   וַיֹּאמֶר יְהוָה אֶל־מֹשֶׁה פְּסָל־לְךָ שְׁנֵי־לֻחֹת אֲבָנִים כָּרִאשֹׁנִים וְכָתַבְתִּי עַל־הַלֻּחֹת

2 Samuel 24:2 מִסְפַּר means *number.*

8.   וּפִקְדוּ אֶת־הָעָם וְיָדַעְתִּי אֵת מִסְפַּר הָעָם

1 Kings 2:36

9.   בְּנֵה־לְךָ בַיִת בִּירוּשָׁלַם וְיָשַׁבְתָּ שָׁם

130

1 Kings 22:15

10.   וַיֹּאמֶר אֵלָיו עֲלֵה וְנָתַן יְהוָה בְּיַד הַמֶּלֶךְ

Jeremiah 7:23

11.   שִׁמְעוּ בְקוֹלִי וְהָיִיתִי לָכֶם לֵאלֹהִים

Jeremiah 11:4

12.   שִׁמְעוּ בְקוֹלִי וִהְיִיתֶם לִי לְעָם

22.4b.   Read Genesis 22:16-19.

Lesson 23

וַיֹּאמֶר עֵשָׂו יֶשׁ־לִי רָב אָחִי יְהִי לְךָ אֲשֶׁר־לָךְ:

Genesis 33:9

Goals:
- Identify and read expressions of possession.
- Identify and read jussives.

What we already know

23.1a. Translate וַיֹּאמֶר _____

23.1b. Look closely at the nikkud in עֵשָׂו Is it an imperative?_____ (21.4b) Taking the same three consonants, add the nikkud which would make it an imperative

עשו

The word, as marked in our lesson verse is the name *Esau*. How important are the nikkud! God bless the Masoretes, the Jewish scholars who figured out the proper nikkud to add to what was originally a purely consonantal text!

Translate וַיֹּאמֶר עֵשָׂו _____

Possession

23.2a. The next two words are one of two ways that possession is expressed in our lesson verse. The two words can be thought of as follows:

יִ   +   לְ   +   יֶשׁ

me   to   there is

We translate this idiom *I have*. Also attested in the Hebrew Bible is יֶשׁ לוֹ *he has*.

Translate יֶשׁ־לִי רָב אָחִי _____ (For help with אָחִי see 18.4.)

23.2b. Another way possession is expressed in the Hebrew Bible is with the preposition לְ with a pronominal suffix or noun attached. This method is used twice in our lesson verse and can be translated *yours*, meaning *that which is yours*, both times. Below are a few more examples of this type of possessive construction. By the way, do you know why לָךְ has the nikkud it does rather than the nikkud of לְךָ ?

_____ (15.5)

הֲשָׁלוֹם לוֹ Genesis 29:6

(lit. *How is his wholeness?*) *Is he well?*

132

לַיהוָה הָאָרֶץ Psalm 24:1
The earth is YHWH's

וְכֹל אֲשֶׁר־אַתָּה רֹאֶה לִי־הוּא Genesis 31:43
And all that you are seeing, it is mine

מִי־לִי בַשָּׁמָיִם Psalm 73:25
Whom do I have in heaven?

וַיְהִי־לָהּ לְבֵן Exodus 2:10
And (then) he became her son

בְּאֶרֶץ לֹא לָהֶם Genesis 15:13
In a land not theirs

Jussives

23.3a. The word יְהִי is a shortened or apocopated yiqtol form of the root הָיָה The regular yiqtol form would have been יִהְיֶה To be perfectly correct we would not call the word in our lesson verse a yiqtol because it is apocopated. However, for simplicity's sake we will continue to call this form a yiqtol, but a special variety of the yiqtol called the **jussive**. Unlike our lesson's word, the jussive is, more times than not, identical in appearance to a yiqtol.

> RULE: **The jussive is the third person singular or plural yiqtol form which is used to give a "command" concerning a third person. The jussive, sometimes a shortened version of the yiqtol, shares the mainline of Hortatory Discourse with the imperative.**

Fill out the verb analysis chart for יְהִי :

root	stem	form	person, gender, number	function	basic root meaning
		yiqtol (juss)		Hortatory Mainline	

23.3b. In the rule, *command* is in quotation marks because it is literally quite difficult to command someone who is a third person, that is, a person other than the speaker or listener. The jussive actually expresses the speaker's will or desire for the third person. Here is how we do it in English:

May he ...
Let him ...
May they...
Let them...

133

23.3c. One of the big differences between English and Biblical Hebrew is the lack, in Biblical Hebrew, of modals, words like *let, may, should, would, shall*. To a large degree, genre and other context clues must determine when Hebrew verb forms have these nuances of meaning. Shortening or, we will see later, lengthening of the yiqtol form is one way the ancient Hebrew expressed these nuances. Another clue for determining when the yiqtol is on the Hortatory mainline is when the word נָא meaning *"please"* follows the yiqtol or the word אַל which we learned in Lesson 19 is used to make a prohibitive command, precedes it.

23.3d. To repeat a key point, the jussive is more often than not identical in appearance with any other yiqtol. However, we have one more good way to help us distinguish between the jussive and other yiqtols. Is the yiqtol a mainline or off-the-line verb in Predictive Narrative and Instructional Discourse?

_____ (18.5b) Is the yiqtol typically the first word of a Predictive

Narrative or an Instructional Discourse clause? _____ (14.4b)

> RULE: **In all genres of Biblical Hebrew prose, clauses on the mainline of the discourse tend to have clause-initial verbs.** Clauses that are off-the-line tend to have their verbs in something other than the initial position. We can represent mainline clause word order as V1 (verb-initial) or V-X.

Therefore, a 3rd person yiqtol in the clause-initial position, especially in direct speech, is almost always a jussive.

Translation of יְהִי לְךָ אֲשֶׁר־לָךְ *May yours be what is yours*

23.3e. Here's an important definition:

> DEFINITION: *Clause-initial* **means the first independent word in a clause. A clause-initial word may have a prefixed "word" on it such as a** *vav*, **but it may not have another, independent word before it like** אֲשֶׁר כִּי לֹא or עַתָּה

Assignments
23.4a. Memorize words 151-190 for Lessons 23-26.
23.4b. Translate:
Genesis 24:51

1. הִנֵּה־רִבְקָה לְפָנֶיךָ קַח וָלֵךְ וּתְהִי אִשָּׁה לְבֶן־אֲדֹנֶיךָ

Genesis 24:55 Remember, clause-initial equals main-line. הַנַּעֲרָ; is the feminine version. אִתָּנוּ means *with us* as opposed to אֹתָנוּ which means *us*.

2. וַיֹּאמֶר אָחִיהָ וְאִמָּהּ תֵּשֵׁב הַנַּעֲרָ אִתָּנוּ יָמִים

134

Genesis 27:31 צַיִד means *game, meat*.	3. וַיֹּאמֶר לְאָבִיו יָקֻם אָבִי וְיֹאכַל מִצֵּיד
Genesis 33:14	4. יַעֲבָר־נָא אֲדֹנִי לִפְנֵי עַבְדּוֹ
Genesis 38:23 פֶּן means *lest*. לָבוּז means *be shamed*.	5. וַיֹּאמֶר יְהוּדָה תִּקַּח־לָהּ פֶּן נִהְיֶה לָבוּז
Exodus 16:29 אִישׁ has the sense *each one of you*. הַשְּׁבִיעִי means *seventh*.	6. שְׁבוּ אִישׁ תַּחְתָּיו אַל־יֵצֵא אִישׁ מִמְּקֹמוֹ בַּיּוֹם הַשְּׁבִיעִי:
Exodus 20:19	7. וַיֹּאמְרוּ אֶל־מֹשֶׁה דַּבֵּר־אַתָּה עִמָּנוּ וְאַל־יְדַבֵּר עִמָּנוּ אֱלֹהִים פֶּן־נָמוּת:
Numbers 12:12	8. אַל־נָא תְהִי כַּמֵּת
Deuteronomy 33:6 The regular yiqtol יָמוּת has been shortened to the jussive.	9. יְחִי רְאוּבֵן וְאַל־יָמֹת
Joshua 9:21 חֹטְבֵי means *hewers of*.	10. וַיֹּאמְרוּ אֲלֵיהֶם יִחְיוּ וַיִּהְיוּ חֹטְבֵי עֵצִים
Judges 13:8 בִּי is an often untranslated word used as a particle of entreaty to a superior. You may translate it *please*.	11. וַיֹּאמַר בִּי אֲדוֹנָי אִישׁ הָאֱלֹהִים אֲשֶׁר שָׁלַחְתָּ יָבוֹא־נָא עוֹד אֵלֵינוּ
Ruth 4:12	12. וִיהִי בֵיתְךָ כְּבֵית פֶּרֶץ אֲשֶׁר־יָלְדָה תָמָר לִיהוּדָה
1 Samuel 27:5	13. יִתְּנוּ־לִי מָקוֹם בְּאַחַת עָרֵי הַשָּׂדֶה
2 Samuel 2:14	14. וַיֹּאמֶר אַבְנֵר אֶל־יוֹאָב יָקוּמוּ נָא הַנְּעָרִים וַיֹּאמֶר יוֹאָב יָקֻמוּ:
1 Kings 18:23	15. וְיִתְּנוּ־לָנוּ שְׁנַיִם פָּרִים
1 Kings 22:17	16. יָשׁוּבוּ אִישׁ־לְבֵיתוֹ בְּשָׁלוֹם

23.4c. Read the introduction to Reading 2 and Genesis 17:1-2.

Lesson 24

וַיֹּאמֶר דָּוִד אֶל־גָּד נֵצַר־לָנוּ נִפְּלָה־נָא בְיַד־יְהוָה כִּי־רַבִּים רַחֲמָיו וּבְיַד־אָדָם אַל־אֶפֹּלָה:

2 Samuel 24:14

Goal:

• Identify and read cohortatives.

What we already know

24.1. Translate   וַיֹּאמֶר דָּוִד אֶל־גָּד _____

The cohortative

24.2a. The word   נָא   means _____ It is a clue that we are in what genre?

_____(23.3c) This information will help us analyze the verb   נִפְּלָה

24.2b. Let us remove the letter *heh* from the end of   נִפְּלָה   momentarily. Can you now begin to fill out the verb analysis chart? If you need help, you may need to be reminded about the meaning of the *footprint dagesh*. For more help turn to 9.2c and/or 17.4c.

root	stem	form	person, gender, number	function	basic root meaning
		yiqtol (co-hort)			

24.2c. Now for the *heh* on the end of the verb. This particular word-ending *heh* is *not* a paragogic *heh* such as we learned about in 22.2.

> RULE: When we see an additional *heh* on the end of the first person yiqtol forms, the yiqtol form has been transformed into a *cohortative*. The cohortative is a type of command concerning oneself and, perhaps, one's partner(s). It is the third and final yiqtol variation that makes up the mainline of Hortatory Discourse.

Here is how we do it in English:

> Singular: *Let me...*
> *May I...*
> *I shall...*(as an intention, not a prediction)
> Plural: *Let us...*
> *May we...*
> *The boy and I shall...*(again, intention)

24.2d. The imperative, jussive, and cohortative, together make up the mainline of Hortatory Discourse.

136

Together, the three are called the *volitional forms* because they all express the speaker's will or *volition*. All three are either yiqtol forms or based on the yiqtol form. Here is a summary of them:

VOLITIONAL FORMS:

	Cohorative	Imperative	Jussive
Person	1st person	2nd person	3rd person
Yiqtol change	usually adds הַ	loses prefix pronoun may add הַ (see 22.2)	may shorten
Translation	Let me/us... May I/we...	Do!	Let him/her/them... May he/she/they...

Note: As we become more acquainted with the other verb stems of Hebrew, we will find that the imperative is not always a mere removal of the prefixed pronoun of the yiqtol form. However, at this point in our studies, it is best to stress the area of common ground between all the volitional forms and the yiqtol.

Translate: נִפְּלָה־נָּא בְיַד־יְהוָה _____

24.2e. What does אַל means?_____ (21.3a) The *aleph* on the

beginning of אֶפְּלָה ?_____ (17.4c) And the *heh* on the end of the same

word?_____ (24.2c) Finish filling out the verb analysis chart:

root	stem	form	person, gender, number	function	basic root meaning

More of what we already know

24.3. What type of clause is כִּי־רַבִּים רַחֲמָיו ?_____ (18.2a)

Is the clause identifying or describing?_____ (2.7c) Is the word רַחֲמָיו

singular or plural?_____ (If you cannot tell by looking at it, you can use the predicate adjective as a clue, or see 14.2) רַחֲמִים means in this case, *mercies*. Although it is plural in form, it is often translated in the singular in other contexts.

Translate the verbless clause:_____

Another cohortative

24.4a. Notice the word order in the last clause of our lesson verse: וּבְיַד־אָדָם אַל־אֶפֹּלָה What is the "X" element in the clause?_____ (14.3c) Just as we have X-qatal constructions in Historical Narrative and X-yiqtol constructions in Predictive Narrative and Instructional Discourse, we can have X-cohortative (and X-jussive or X-imperative) constructions in Hortatory Discourse which have the same function as its counterparts in the other genres.. What is the function of

this type of construction? _____ (again, 14.3c)

Translate the X-element:_____

Fill out the verb analysis chart for אֶפֹּלָה :

root	stem	form	person, gender, number	function	basic root meaning
		yiqtol (co-hort)		X-cohort. = topicalization and w/ אַל = prohib. Command	

Translation of וּבְיַד־אָדָם אַל־אֶפֹּלָה : *And into the hand of man let me not fall.*

Notes:

1. In the above translation, the formula we have previously used for topicalization (*It is ___X___that_ (remainder of clause)___.*) has been abandoned because it does not result in a proper English sentence. However, the Hebrew word order is still somewhat respected.

2. Our lesson sentence is a good example of how the topicalization construction can be used to contrast the topic of one clause with corresponding information in a preceding clause or clauses. In our lesson verse, *the hand of man* is contrasted with *His mercies* and *the hand of YHWH.*

24.4b. In Lesson 23 you learned that the clause-initial yiqtol is generally a mainline verb form that is volitional, an expression of the speaker's desire or will. (In Lesson 48, you will learn another closely-related use of the clause-initial yiqtol.) This clause-initial position of the yiqtol is a great help in identifying volitional yiqtols.[1] The problem, then, is with the X-yiqtol. It is ambiguous. It may express a number of senses: the speaker's knowledge about the future as it has from Lesson 14 until this lesson, the speaker's desire as it does in this lesson, or a couple more senses which you will learn in Lessons 36 and 48.

---

[1] Niccacci(1990), §64; a more extreme position is held by Revell(1989), 32, who asserts that if a clause-medial prefix form is *not* accompanied by אַל or נָא it is indicative.

138

Discourse profile of Hortatory Discourse

24.5. Here is the discourse profile scheme for Hortatory Discourse:

Mainline: 1a. Imperative
        1b. Jussive   Note: These four are equally ranked
        1c. Cohortative
        1d. Weqatal (for Mitigated Hortatory Discourse)

  Off-the-line:
  2. Topicalization: X-Imperative (or Jussive or Cohortative)
     3. Prohibitive commands: אַל or לֹא + yiqtol
       4. Consequence, purpose: Weqatal
         5. Backgrounded activities: Participle
           6. Scene setting: Verbless Clause

Assignments

24.6a. Match the following examples with their forms (you may want to refer to the verb charts near the back of the book for help with some items):

_____1. וַיֹּאמֶר	_____15. אֵלְכָה	A. Wayyiqtol		
_____2. נָתַן	_____16. וְנֹחַ מָצָא	B. X-yiqtol		
_____3. בַּמִּלְחָמָה יֵרֵד	_____17. יוֹמוֹ יָבוֹא	C. Weqatal		
_____4. וּמָלַךְ	_____18. לֵאמֹר	D. X-qatal		
_____5. עֲשׂוֹת	_____19. וְאָשׁוּבָה	E. Participle		
_____6. וַיִּשְׁלַח	_____20. בֶּאֱכֹל	F. Infinitive		
_____7. וְאַבְרָהָם שָׁב	_____21. שָׁב	G. Imperative		
_____8. שֵׁב	_____22. יְהִי	H. Jussive		
_____9. וַיְהִי	_____23. וִיהִי	I. Cohortative		
_____10. לָכֶם יִהְיֶה	_____24. וְהָיָה			
_____11. וְאֶתְּנָה	_____25. דַּע	_____29. עַתָּה תִרְאֶה		
_____12. דְּעוּ	_____26. וּדְעוּ	_____30. וַתֵּרֶא		
_____13. וְדָוִד יָדְעוּ	_____27. וַיֵּדְעוּ	_____31. רְאֵה		
_____14. וְיָדְעוּ	_____28. יָדַע	_____32. תֵּרֶא		

24.6b. Match the following forms with their functions:

_____1. Wayyiqtol		A. Historical Narrative Mainline
_____2. Weqatal		B. Historical Narrative Topicalization
_____3. X-qatal		C. Relative past background
_____4. Irrealis		D. Historical Narrative transitional device
_____5. Volitional forms		E. Mainline of Predictive Narrative, Instructional Discourse, and Mitigated Hortatory Discourse
_____6. Participle		F. Mainline of all genres
_____7. X-yiqtol		G. Mainline of Unmitigated Hortatory Discourse
_____8. אֲשֶׁר yiqtol		H. Topicalization in +Projection genres
_____9. וַיְהִי		I. Non-past background
_____10. Clause-initial forms		J. Prohibitive commands in Hortatory Discourse
_____11. אֲשֶׁר qatal		K. Negative scene-setting in any genre
_____12. אַל + yiqtol		L. Positive scene-setting in any genre
_____13. Verbless clause		M. Backgrounded activities in any genre

24.6c. Translate:

Genesis 18:21

1. אֵרֲדָה־נָּא וְאֶרְאֶה

Exodus 4:18

2. אֵלְכָה נָּא וְאָשׁוּבָה אֶל־אַחַי אֲשֶׁר־בְּמִצְרַיִם

Exodus 20:19 פֶּן means *lest*.

3. וַיֹּאמְרוּ אֶל־מֹשֶׁה דַּבֵּר־אַתָּה עִמָּנוּ וְנִשְׁמָעָה וְאַל־יְדַבֵּר עִמָּנוּ אֱלֹהִים פֶּן־נָמוּת:

Numbers 9:8

4. וַיֹּאמֶר אֲלֵהֶם מֹשֶׁה עִמְדוּ וְאֶשְׁמְעָה מַה־יְצַוֶּה יְהוָה לָכֶם:

Numbers 11:13 בָּשָׂר means *flesh*.

5. תְּנָה־לָּנוּ בָשָׂר וְנֹאכֵלָה

140

Numbers 14:4 The root נתן can mean *place, put, ordain*. A ה on the end of a noun naming a place is called a ה-*directive*. It indicates movement towards or simply *to*.	6. וַיֹּאמְרוּ אִישׁ אֶל־אָחִיו נִתְּנָה רֹאשׁ וְנָשׁוּבָה מִצְרָיְמָה:
Numbers 20:17 Notice the contrasting word orders in the clauses. By the way, the King's Way is a road in present-day Jordan that is as old as civilization.	7. נַעְבְּרָה־נָּא בְאַרְצֶךָ לֹא נַעֲבֹר בְּשָׂדֶה דֶּרֶךְ הַמֶּלֶךְ נֵלֵךְ
2 Chronicles 20:9	8. נַעַמְדָה לִפְנֵי הַבַּיִת הַזֶּה וּלְפָנֶיךָ כִּי שִׁמְךָ בַּבַּיִת הַזֶּה
2 Chronicles 1:10	9. תֶּן־לִי וְאֵצְאָה לִפְנֵי הָעָם־הַזֶּה וְאָבוֹאָה
2 Kings 6:2 אִישׁ קוֹרָה אֶחָת means *each man one beam*.	8. נֵלְכָה־נָּא עַד־הַיַּרְדֵּן וְנִקְחָה מִשָּׁם אִישׁ קוֹרָה אֶחָת וְנַעֲשֶׂה־לָּנוּ שָׁם מָקוֹם לָשֶׁבֶת שָׁם וַיֹּאמֶר לֵכוּ:
2 Samuel 17:5 בְּפִתוֹ means literally *in his mouth*, an idiom for *according to his words*.	9. וַיֹּאמֶר אַבְשָׁלוֹם קְרָא נָא גַם לְחוּשַׁי הָאַרְכִּי וְנִשְׁמְעָה מַה־בְּפִיו
Genesis 19:20	10. וּתְחִי נַפְשִׁי
Genesis 24:51	11. הִנֵּה־רִבְקָה לְפָנֶיךָ קַח וָלֵךְ וּתְהִי אִשָּׁה לְבֶן־אֲדֹנֶיךָ כַּאֲשֶׁר דִּבֶּר יְהוָה:
Genesis 27:28 טַל means *dew*.	12. וְיִתֶּן־לְךָ הָאֱלֹהִים מִטַּל הַשָּׁמַיִם
Genesis 27:31 בַּעֲבוּר means *so that*. נִי-- is a pronominal suffix meaning *me*.	13. וַיֹּאמֶר לְאָבִיו יָקֻם אָבִי וְיֹאכַל בַּעֲבוּר תְּבָרֲכַנִּי נַפְשֶׁךָ:
Genesis 34:2 1See 18.4 if you have trouble with נָשִׁים	14. וַיֵּשְׁבוּ בָאָרֶץ אֵת־בְּנֹתָם נִקַּח־לָנוּ לְנָשִׁים וְאֶת־בְּנֹתֵינוּ נִתֵּן לָהֶם:

15. וַיִּתֵּן יְהוָה גַּם אֶת־יִשְׂרָאֵל עִמְּךָ בְּיַד־פְּלִשְׁתִּים

1 Samuel 28:19

24.6d. Read Genesis 17:3-6.

Lesson 25

וַתֹּאמֶר לִנְעָרֶיהָ עִבְרוּ לְפָנַי הִנְנִי אַחֲרֵיכֶם בָּאָה

1 Samuel 25:19

Goals:
- **Distinguish Qal qatal and Qal participles of hollow roots.**
- **Identify and read participles referring to the imminent future.**

What we already know

25.1a. What two meanings can the *tav* prefix on the word וַתֹּאמֶר have?_____ or_____

(17.4c.) What does the suffix on the end of לִנְעָרֶיהָ mean?_____ (19.4b) The meaning of the suffix should help you determine the correct meaning for the *tav*. The word נַעַר means *boy* or *servant*.

Translate וַתֹּאמֶר לִנְעָרֶיהָ : _____

25.1b. How can you tell that עִבְרוּ is *not* a Qal qatal? _____
(4.3g)

Fill out the verb analysis chart for עִבְרוּ (21.4b or the verb charts at the back of the book):

root	stem	form	person, gender, number	function	basic root meaning

25.1c. What does the *yod* on the end of לְפָנַי mean?_____ (19.4b)

Translate עברו לְפָנַי _____

הִנֵּה and הֵן

25.2. The word הִנְנִי is made of two parts, הִנֵּה or הֵן and the first person singular suffix נִי The word הִנְנִי may be akin to הִנֵּה אֲנִי used in 2 Kings 10:9 and meaning *Behold me!* or *Here I am!* The word is more often than not found הִנֶּנִּי or הִנֵּנִי the latter being its pausal form. Often the word can be thought of as an interjection, a word expressing exclamation which is not part of the grammatical structure of the clause. However, as we shall see in the case our lesson verse, the pronominal suffix may represent the subject of a clause.

Qatals and participles of hollow roots contrasted

25.3a. Before we can deal adequately with הִנְנִי or the next word of our lesson verse, אַחֲרֵיכֶם we

143

need to jump ahead to the word בָּאָה Many lessons ago, back in 10.4a to be exact, you were forewarned of the manner in which hollow verbs look alike in the qatal and participle forms. It is time to develop this idea fully. Below are the four participle forms and the nine qatal forms for hollow roots.

בּוֹא

PARTICIPLE		QATAL	
Masculine Singular	בָּא	SINGULAR 3 M. (he, it)	בָּא
Feminine Singular	בָּאָה	3 F. (she, it)	בָּאָה
Masculine Plural	בָּאִים	2 M. (you)	בָּאתָ
Feminine Plural	בָּאוֹת	2 F. (you)	בָּאת or קַמְתְּ for most other hollow roots
		1 C. (I)	בָּאתִי
		PLURAL 3 C. (they)	בָּאוּ
		2 M. (you)	בָּאתֶם
		2 F. (you)	----
		1 C. (we)	בָּאנוּ

Notice that the ambiguity between the feminine singular participle and the 3rd feminine singular qatal is cleared up by accent.

25.3b. Think back for a moment to the masculine plural imperative עִבְרוּ It has alerted us to the genre we are in for our lesson verse.

What genre is it?_____ (19.2c) Is this genre + or - *projection*?

_____? (also 19.2c) The +projection context of our lesson verse is the best indicator for whether בָּאָה is a participle or qatal. The qatal would not be used for expressing projection unless it was in the weqatal form. The participle, on the other hand, is sometimes used in a special way in +projection genres.

RULE: The participle is sometimes used to express imminent future in +projection genres.[1]

We do the same thing in English when we yell into the kitchen at dinner time, "I'm coming!" and we actually mean "I will come in a minute."

25.3c. Fill out the verb analysis chart for בָּאָה :

---

[1] Waltke and O'Connor(1990), §37.6f.

144

root	stem	form	person, gender, number	function	basic root meaning
		part.		Backgrounded activities	

The usual way to make a clause with a participle uses S-V word order. In a manner of speaking, we have this word order in our lesson verse's הִנְנִי בָאָה However, we also have the אַחֲרֵיכֶם fronting the participle in a kind of *topicalization*. We will try to account for this topicalization in our translation.

Translation of הִנְנִי אַחֲרֵיכֶם בָאָה : *Behold, it is after you that I am coming.*

It is not surprising that the wealthy woman speaker needed to clarify for her servants that she would proceed after them using the appropriate topicalization construction. The servants would have been used to conducting their mistress wherever she needed to go.

More on participles

25.4a. There are several classes of hollow roots, but all display the same ambiguities, 3rd m. s. qatal with m. s. participle and 3rd f. s. qatal with f. s. participle.

3rd m. s. qatal and m. s. participle	קָם	בָּא	שָׂם	מֵת	בּוֹשׁ
3rd f. s. qatal and f. s. participle	קָמָה	בָּאָה	שָׂמָה	מֵתָה	בּוֹשָׁה

25.4b. The Qal qatal of the root מות is worth conjugating completely at this point because it shows some idiosyncrasies.

SINGULAR 3. M.	מֵת	PLURAL 3. C.	מֵתוּ
3. F.	מֵתָה		
2. M.	מַתָּה	2. M.	מַתֶּם
2. F.	מַתְּ*	2. F.	מַתֶּן*
1. C.	מַתִּי	1. C.	מַתְנוּ

*Unattested in the Hebrew Bible

25.4c. The Qal participle of almost every root except for the hollow roots is quite regular and can usually

145

be identified by a *holem* after the first root letter plus the appropriate noun ending. Defectiva spelling outnumbers plene spelling about 4 to 1. Below all four forms are shown for one root. You fill in the forms for the other two.

QAL PARTICIPLES

Masculine Singular	הֹלֵךְ	אֹמֵר	נֹפֵל
Feminine Singular	* הֹלֶכֶת		
Masculine Plural	הֹלְכִים		
Feminine Plural	הֹלְכוֹת		

*The feminine singular can also be written with a הָ ending as with רֹאָה This is particularly the case with hollow verbs and 3rd *heh* verbs.

Assignments

25.5a. We have learned many functions for a *heh* on the end of a word including the following:

A. שָׁנָה Feminine noun ending (18.2b)

B. טוֹבָה Feminine adjective ending (18.2b)

C. אֵלְכָה Cohortative ending (24.2c)

D. יָשְׁבָה 3rd f. s. subject pronoun for qatal (15.3c)

E. לֵכְנָה Feminine plural imperative (20.5b)

F. יְרוּשָׁלַיְמָה ה-directive (24.6c.6)

G. נַעֲרֶיהָ 3rd f. s. pronominal suffix (19.4b)

or בֵּיתָה (Remember what a *mappiq* is? (19.4b, n.2))

H. רְדָה Extra imperative ending (22.2)

I. תִּשְׁמַעְנָה 2nd and 3rd f. p. yiqtol complements (17.4c)

J. בָּאָה F. s. participle ending (25.3a)

K. רָאָה 3rd *heh* root

L. אַתָּה A vocabulary item that happens to end in ה

For each of the following words, identify the use of the final *heh* by writing a letter from the above list.

ـــــ1. נִלְקָחָה	ـــــ8. אָשִׂימָה	ـــــ15. לְכָה	ـــــ22. אָמְרָה
ـــــ2. נָתְנָה	ـــــ9. יוֹשְׁבֶיהָ	ـــــ16. רַבָּה	ـــــ23. עָלָה
ـــــ3. לְאִשָּׁה	ـــــ10. שָׂדֶה	ـــــ17. וְהָיָה	ـــــ24. רְאֵה
ـــــ4. וְהִנֵּה	ـــــ11. קָמָה	ـــــ18. יְרוּשָׁלָמָה	ـــــ25. עַתָּה
ـــــ5. תִּפָּקַחְנָה	ـــــ12. יִהְיֶה	ـــــ19. לֵכְנָה	ـــــ26. גְּדוֹלָה
ـــــ6. הָיְתָה	ـــــ13. תִּקְרֶאנָה	ـــــ20. דִּבְּרָה	ـــــ27. שְׁמַעְנָה
ـــــ7. מִצְרַיְמָה	ـــــ14. הָאֲדָמָה	ـــــ21. שָׁמָה	ـــــ28. וְנֵדְעָה

25.5b. Translate:

Exodus 3:5 הֲלֹם is an adverb meaning *hither*.

1. וַיֹּאמֶר אַל־תִּקְרַב הֲלֹם כִּי הַמָּקוֹם אֲשֶׁר אַתָּה עוֹמֵד עָלָיו אַדְמַת־קֹדֶשׁ הוּא:

Exodus 3:13 שְׁלָחַנִי is made of שָׁלַח and the suffix נִי-- which means *me*. Remember that the vowels in a word are shorteened by the addition of a suffix.

2. הִנֵּה אָנֹכִי בָא אֶל־בְּנֵי יִשְׂרָאֵל וְאָמַרְתִּי לָהֶם אֱלֹהֵי אֲבוֹתֵיכֶם שְׁלָחַנִי אֲלֵיכֶם

Genesis 29:6

3. וַיֹּאמֶר לָהֶם הֲשָׁלוֹם לוֹ וַיֹּאמְרוּ שָׁלוֹם וְהִנֵּה רָחֵל בִּתּוֹ בָּאָה עִם־הַצֹּאן:

1 Kings 14:5 The root דרשׁ means *seek*. The *dagesh* in the *heh* in בְּנָהּ helps us identify the *heh* as a 3. f. s. pronominal suffix.

4. וַיהוָה אָמַר אֶל־אֲחִיָּהוּ הִנֵּה אֵשֶׁת יָרָבְעָם בָּאָה לִדְרשׁ דָּבָר מֵעִמְּךָ אֶל־בְּנָהּ

Ezekiel 7:5 אַחַת is the feminine version of אֶחָד

5. כֹּה אָמַר אֲדֹנָי יהוִה רָעָה אַחַת רָעָה הִנֵּה בָאָה:

Ezekiel 7:6 קֵץ is a masculine noun that means *end*. Why the feminine participle בָּאָה? It may well refer back to the רָעָה of the prior verse.

6. קֵץ בָּא בָּא הַקֵּץ הֵנֵּה בָּאָה

Exodus 7:15 בֹּקֶר means *morning*.

7. לֵךְ אֶל־פַּרְעֹה בַּבֹּקֶר הִנֵּה יֹצֵא הַמַּיְמָה

Exodus 10:8

8. וַיֹּאמֶר אֲלֵהֶם לְכוּ עִבְדוּ אֶת־יְהוָה אֱלֹהֵיכֶם מִי וָמִי הַהֹלְכִים:

Exodus 11:4

9. וַיֹּאמֶר מֹשֶׁה כֹּה אָמַר יְהוָה אֲנִי יוֹצֵא בְּתוֹךְ מִצְרָיִם:

Deuteronomy 2:18 הַיּוֹם means *today*.

10. אַתָּה עֹבֵר הַיּוֹם

Deuteronomy 3:21
עֵינֶיךָ הָרֹאֹת has nearly the same sense as רָאִיתָ עֵינֶיךָ would have except Moses stresses the continuous nature of the seeing by using the participle.

11. וְאֶת־יְהוֹשׁוּעַ צִוֵּיתִי לֵאמֹר עֵינֶיךָ הָרֹאֹת אֵת כָּל־אֲשֶׁר עָשָׂה יְהוָה אֱלֹהֵיכֶם

Deuteronomy 4:12   There are two clauses. The trick is to draw the dividing line between them.

12. וַיְדַבֵּר יְהוָה אֲלֵיכֶם מִתּוֹךְ הָאֵשׁ קוֹל דְּבָרִים אַתֶּם שֹׁמְעִים

Deuteronomy 4:22   אֵינֶנִּי = אֵין + ־נִי

13. כִּי אָנֹכִי מֵת בָּאָרֶץ הַזֹּאת אֵינֶנִּי עֹבֵר אֶת־הַיַּרְדֵּן וְאַתֶּם עֹבְרִים

1 Sam 3:11

14. וַיֹּאמֶר יְהוָה אֶל־שְׁמוּאֵל הִנֵּה אָנֹכִי עֹשֶׂה דָבָר בְּיִשְׂרָאֵל

1 Samuel 21:3 מְאוּמָה translates *anything of...*

15. אַל־יֵדַע מְאוּמָה אֶת־הַדָּבָר אֲשֶׁר־אָנֹכִי שֹׁלֵחֲךָ וַאֲשֶׁר צִוִּיתִךָ

25.6c. Read Genesis 17:7-8.

Lesson 26

וַיֹּאמְרוּ בָּאנוּ אֶל־הָאָרֶץ אֲשֶׁר שְׁלַחְתָּנוּ

Numbers 13:27

Goals:

- Identify and read the qatal that starts an oral Historical Narrative.
- Identify and read pronominal suffixes on verbs.

What we already know

Translate וַיֹּאמְרוּ : _____

What genre of discourse does the verb form indicate? _____

And a wayyiqtol of the root אמר typically indicates a switch to what class of discourse genres?

_____

Opening oral Historical Narratives with a qatal

26.2a. It has already been mentioned that the Historical Narrative genre can appear in direct speech when a speaker orally tells a story. Often the "narrative" within direct speech can only loosely be considered a narrative because, being one of the brief exchanges that so often occur in dialogue, the "narrative" is only one or two clauses long. We may reasonably argue that a narrative would have to be a minimum of two clauses long because it takes at least two statements to make a story. A one-clause discourse is really just a statement of fact. Of course, fairly long, well-developed narratives can also be found in direct speech.

And something else you have already learned: A qatal is not a clause-initial verb form the way weqatal, wayyiqtol, or the volitive forms are. Qatal is always preceded by either an "X" resulting in a topicalization structure or a relative like אֲשֶׁר or כִּי resulting in a dependent clause. Look closely, however, at our lesson verse.

26.2b. Fill out the verb analysis chart for בָּאנוּ except for the function column:

root	stem	form	person, gender, number	function	basic root meaning
				open an oral Historical Narrative	

Notice that the qatal form is preceded by neither an "X" nor a relative.

149

RULE: **A clause-initial qatal often opens Historical Narrative that is within direct speech. A wayyiqtol never does.** After the opening clause of an oral Historical Narrative, it proceeds just like any non-oral Historical Narrative.[1]

As was mentioned above, a "narrative" in direct speech is often only one clause long. Often, this one clause will have a qatal as its first word, sometimes the only word, stating a fact. However, all narratives within direct speech do not begin with clause-initial qatals. They may also begin with an X-qatal, a verbless clause, or a clause with a participle. Once again, unlike regular Historical Narrative, oral Historical Narratives may not begin with a wayyiqtol.

Note: Verb-subject word order is still a common occurrence with the clause-initial qatals of oral Historical Narrative.

Translation of בָּאנוּ : *We were enterers*

Translate בָּאנוּ אֶל־הָאָרֶץ : _____

Pronominal suffixes on verbs

26.3a. Let us stretch out the word שְׁלַחְתָּנוּ so we can better identify its component parts.

נוּ	תָּ	שָׁלַח
us	you (m. s.)	were a sender of

As was mentioned in passing in Lesson 19.4b, you can see in this word how the same pronominal suffix that we so often see on nouns, prepositions, and the DDO can also be used as a direct object attached directly to a qatal form. They may also be attached to all the other verb forms except for the infinitive absolute which you have not learned yet.

26.3b. The vocalization rules for adding pronominal suffixes are extremely complicated and technical, but we can reduce the subtleties to the following generalizations:

1. The nikkud in the verb is likely to change, as it did in our lesson verse which appears שָׁלַחְתָּ without the suffix. In the Qal stem, the qatal and weqatal which usually have *qamets* under the first root letter have a *shewa* instead when a suffix is added. In a mirror image to this change, the imperative, which often has a *shewa* under the first root letter, may have a *qamets* when a suffix is added.

2. Some of the suffixes are a bit different than what we are accustomed to seeing on nouns, prepositions, and the DDO. Below is a summary of the differences only.

	With nouns, prepositions, and the DDO	With verbs
1st c. s.	יִ -- or יַ --	נִי--
3rd m. s.	וֹ-- or וֹ	הוּ --נ or וֹ or נוּ--
3rd m. p.	הֶם-- or ם--	possibly מוֹ --(mostly in poetry)

---

[1] Niccacci(1990), §§22-23, although Niccacci is obviously mistaken to say that qatal *always* comes first in a direct speech narrative. It *may* come first in the discourse-initial clause of an oral Historical Narrative.

Note: The 3rd m. s. וּ-- is not to be confused with the 1st c. p. נוּ-- , the difference being the *dagesh* in the *nun*. The *nun* with the *dagesh* in the pronominal suffix is called an **energic nun**.

1. Watch out for the defectiva spelling of a verb affix or prefix complement *shureq*[וּ] as [◌ֻ] as in וַאֲכָלֻהוּ *And they will be eaters of it,* יַעַבְדֻנִי *May they serve me,* or עִבְדֻהוּ *Serve* (m. p.) *him!*

2. Watch out for the combination 1st c. s. qatal or weqatal plus 3rd m. p. suffix as in יְדַעְתִּים *I am the knower of them* or נְתַתִּים *I am the giver of them*, which masquerades as the masculine plural noun ending.

Translation of qatals in dependent clauses

26.4. As we translate the אֲשֶׁר-qatal clause in our lesson verse, let us refine our ability. In your lessons on the אֲשֶׁר-qatal clause you were taught to translate using English *had, has,* or *have*. You can just choose the one of these that feels right, and you will probably be right most of the time, but there is a more precise way that is not too difficult to learn.

Had is the English auxiliary verb we use for the *past perfect tense*. This is the English tense we use to specify that a situation is completely in the past. The situation is described as a whole, without reference to its beginning, middle or any part of it. On the other hand, *has* (for singular subjects) and *have* (for plural subjects) are the auxiliaries we use in English to make the *present perfect tense*. Present perfect verbs also describe situations as a whole which began in the past. The difference from past perfect is that present perfect does not put the situation entirely in the past. With present perfect, some residual of the past situation is specified as remaining in the speaker/writer's present, either the action itself or the effects of the action. Here are a couple verses to illustrate:

וַיַּרְא אֱלֹהִים אֶת־כָּל־אֲשֶׁר עָשָׂה   Genesis 1:31
And God saw all that He had made.

The English past perfect is used because the making is entirely past relative to the main verb וַיַּרְא

וַיֹּאמֶר יְהוָה אֶמְחֶה אֶת־הָאָדָם אֲשֶׁר־בָּרָאתִי   Genesis 6:7
And YHWH said, "Let me wipe out the race of man which I have created."

This time the Speaker also refers to something He did entirely in the past relative to the main verb אֶמְחֶה but which is clearly a part of His present as well. The English present perfect is therefore the appropriate choice.

Since the speakers of our lesson verse are clearly back from the mission on which they were sent (else how could they now be speaking to their sender about it), we can consider the sending as entirely in the past. No part of the actual trip remains into the present. The past perfect's auxiliary verb *had* is the best choice for translation.

Translation of the entire lesson verse: _____

151

Assignments

26.5a. Translate:

17.	מְצָאָהּ	9.	יֹאכְלֵהוּ	1.	שְׁמָעוּנִי
18.	דִּבְּרוֹ	10.	וַנֹּאכְלֵהוּ	2.	שָׁמְרֵנִי
19.	וַיְדַבְּרֵם	11.	אֲכָלָיו	3.	דָּעֵהוּ
20.	וּבֵרַכְתִּיהָ	12.	אוֹכְלֶיהָ	4.	יְדַעְתִּיו
21.	בָּרְכֵנִי	13.	זִכְרֵנִי	5.	יְדָעָהּ
22.	נְשָׂאוֹ	14.	זְכַרְתַּנִי	6.	שְׁמַעְתִּיךָ
23.	שָׂאֵהוּ	15.	תִּמְצָאֵהוּ	7.	יִשְׁמָעֵנִי
24.	וַיִּשָּׂאֵם	16.	תִּמְצָאֵךָ	8.	צִוִּיתִיךָ

26.5b. Translate:

Genesis 27:35

1. וַיֹּאמֶר בָּא אָחִיךָ

Genesis 29:5

2. וַיֹּאמֶר לָהֶם הַיְדַעְתֶּם אֶת־לָבָן

Genesis 48:19

3. וַיֹּאמֶר יָדַעְתִּי בְנִי יָדַעְתִּי גַּם־הוּא יִהְיֶה־לְּעָם וְגַם־הוּא יִגְדָּל

Exodus 10:16   מהר means *hurry*.

4. וַיְמַהֵר פַּרְעֹה לִקְרֹא לְמֹשֶׁה וּלְאַהֲרֹן וַיֹּאמֶר חָטָאתִי לַיהוָה אֱלֹהֵיכֶם וְלָכֶם:

Numbers 21:7   Here ב means *against*, called an *adversative bet*.

5. וַיָּבֹא הָעָם אֶל־מֹשֶׁה וַיֹּאמְרוּ חָטָאנוּ כִּי־דִבַּרְנוּ בַיהוָה וָבָךְ

Judges 16:23

6. וַיֹּאמְרוּ נָתַן אֱלֹהֵינוּ בְּיָדֵנוּ אֵת שִׁמְשׁוֹן

2 Samuel 12:19

7. וַיֹּאמֶר דָּוִד אֶל־עֲבָדָיו הֲמֵת הַיֶּלֶד וַיֹּאמְרוּ מֵת

2 Kings 9:13

8. וַיֹּאמְרוּ מָלַךְ יֵהוּא

Isaiah 21:9

9. וַיֹּאמֶר נָפְלָה נָפְלָה בָּבֶל

26.5c. Read the introduction to Reading 3 and Judges 16:4-5.

152

MODULE THREE—COMPARING THE PIEL AND HIPHIL STEMS

<u>OVERVIEW</u>: In this module your understanding of the Historical Narrative, Predictive Narrative, Instructional Discourse, and Hortatory Discourse will be refined, especially in your readings. As for the regular lesson material, the major thrust will not be new information on discourse analysis. Rather, you will gain a more thorough understanding of the Biblical Hebrew **System of Verbal Stems**. The system of verbal stems of Semitic languages is like nothing we have in English or other Indo-European languages. In Biblical Hebrew, one tri-consonantal root (e.g. עלה) in one form (e.g. qatal) *can have two different meanings if it is conjugated into two different stems.* For example, view two verbs which are both 3rd m. s. qatal forms of עלה :

TWO 3RD M. S. QATALS:

Qal stem עָלָה means *He was (is) a goer up.*

But **Hiphil** stem הֶעֱלָה means *He was (is) an offerer up.*

Notice how the addition of a *heh* and altered nikkud changed the meaning of עלה from *goer* to *offerer*. The principle behind the system of verbal stems is *"changed pronunciation (spelling) means changed meaning."* Fortunately, the pronunciation changes from stem to stem are reliably patterned, and the alterations of meaning from stem to stem are somewhat reliably patterned.

You have so far dealt primarily with the Qal stem and a very few verbs in the Piel stem. Remember from Lesson 1.3c that the Qal stem is the basic or unaugmented stem. In this module you will begin to see how all the major stems relate with each other as a system for altering the meanings of verbal roots. To do so, we will compare and contrast the Qal, Piel, and Hiphil stems which together account for almost 91% of Biblical Hebrew verbs.

Lesson 27
וְאוֹתָנוּ הוֹצִיא מִשָּׁם
Deuteronomy 6:23

Goals:
- **Identify and read the Hiphil qatal verb forms.**
- **Identify and read the Piel qatal.**

What we already know

27.1. The word וְאוֹתָנוּ is made of three parts as follows:

וְ = _____

אוֹת = plene spelling of אֵת the _____ (19.4b)

נוּ = object suffix meaning _____

Since the DDO is part of this word, we know right away that the word is an *X-element* at the beginning of a

clause. What function does a clause with a fronted X-element have?_____

Translate וְאוֹתָנוּ _____

The Hiphil qatal

27.2a. If you remember all the way back to lesson 1.3c, when a root is augmented, the augment is a sign of
a change from the root's basic meaning or Qal stem meaning. For example, what is the augment which

signals the Piel stem?_____ (2.2b) Do you
remember how the Piel stem changes the root's basic meaning? Very likely you do not since we have
hardly stressed this point since Lesson 2! To review, the Piel stem refers to the *causing of something to be
in a state or condition*. For example:

PIEL STEM
יהוה דִּבֶּר *It was YHWH who was causer of something to be verbalized.*

What a mouthful! And the translation is potentially misleading, because it obscures that *YHWH* did the
speaking. We will therefore stick with *It was YHWH who was speaker*.

27.2b. Our lesson word הוֹצִיא is made from the root יצא meaning _____

Two augments and one transformation have been made to the root. We will examine them in order from
right to left with (+/=) as a symbol for an augment, and (→) as a symbol for a transformation.

154

1. A preformative has been *added* to the beginning of the word:
$$\text{הִיצֵא} = \text{ה} + \text{יצֵא}$$

2. The *yod* has been *transformed* into a *holem*:
$$\text{הוֹצֵא} \leftarrow \text{הִיצֵא}$$

3. A *hireq-yod* has been *added* after the second root letter:
$$\text{הוֹצִיא} = \text{ִי} \text{ (after 2nd root letter)} + \text{הוֹצֵא}$$

The two augments to the root **יצֵא** are the signs of yet another stem, the *Hiphil stem*.

> RULE: **The most common signs of the *Hiphil stem* of the qatal and weqatal verb forms are a *heh* added to the beginning of the root and a *dot vowel* added between the 2nd and 3rd root letters:** __הֹ◯ֹ◯ִיֹ◯__ The *dot* vowels include ◯ִי ◯ֹ ◯ֻ ◯ֻ

27.2c. In any stem, including the Hiphil stem, any one of the verb forms may be used including the wayyiqtol, qatal, weqatal, yiqtol, participle, imperative, and infinitives. The same prefixed and affixed subject pronouns which we have learned for the Qal and Piel stems are also used in the Hiphil. Here is the root **יצֵא** fully conjugated as the Hiphil stem in the qatal form.

HIPHIL QATAL of 1st *YOD* ROOT יצֵא :

SINGULAR 3. M.	הוֹצִיא	PLURAL 3. C.	הוֹצִיאוּ
3. F.	הוֹצִיאָה		
2. M.	הוֹצֵאתָ	2. M.	הוֹצֵאתֶם
2. F.	הוֹצֵאת	2. F.	הוֹצֵאתֶן
1. C.	הוֹצֵאתִי	1. C.	הוֹצֵאנוּ

Notice the variability of the vowel after the 2nd root letter, yet also notice that the variations are all *dot vowels*.

27.2d. The root **יצֵא** is not typical of first *yod* roots in every way because it ends in the weak letter *aleph*. A more typical example would be the root **ישׁב** shown below. Notice that the "dot" vowel is missing in a number of cases, but the preformed *heh* is quite consistent.

155

HIPHIL QATAL OF A TYPICAL 1ST *YOD* ROOT:

SINGULAR 3. M.	הוֹשִׁיב	PLURAL 3. C.	הוֹשִׁיבוּ
3. F.	הוֹשִׁיבָה		
2. M.	הוֹשַׁבְתָּ	2. M.	הוֹשַׁבְתֶּם
2. F.	הוֹשַׁבְתְּ	2. F.	הוֹשַׁבְתֶּן
1. C.	הוֹשַׁבְתִּי	1. C.	הוֹשַׁבְנוּ

The meaning of the Hiphil and Piel stems

27.3a. Like the Piel stem, the Hiphil stem changes a root's basic meaning. It is best to place the Hiphil alongside the Qal and Piel stems to get a clearer idea of their respective nuances.

> RULE: Whereas the Qal stem expresses simple action, and the Piel stem expresses the causing of something or someone to be in a state, **the Hiphil stem expresses the causing of something or someone to act or be active.**

27.3b. To further clarify the differences between the Piel and Hiphil stems, we may cite the following English sentences borrowed with slight modifications from the Hebrew grammarians Waltke and O'Connor:[1]

QAL STEM	PIEL STEM	HIPHIL STEM
1. John cooked the cabbage.	John caused the cabbage to be cooked.	John caused the cabbage to cook.
2. Sarah is flying.	Sarah is flying the airplane in spite of the dust storm.	Sarah is flying the airplane higher.

In neither trio of sentences is the difference primarily with the action of the sentences' subjects. The subjects are all active. The difference is with the degree of activity or passivity of the object. In the Piel representations, the objects are caused to be in states. In number 1, the cabbage is in a cooked state, and in number 2, the airplane is in a flown state in spite of the adversity. In the Hiphil representations, the objects are active. In number 1, the cabbage is doing what cabbage does when you drop it in a pot of boiling water, and in number 2, the airplane is doing what good airplanes do.

27.3c. In the Qal stem, יצא means *come out*. In the Hiphil stem, it means *cause to come out* or better, *bring out*. When we think of a subject *causing* someone or something to act, we must be careful. In so doing, we may often be suggesting a forcing or coercing that is *not* present in Hebrew. To avoid the notion of coercion, it is often best to avoid using the English words *cause* or *make*.

---

[1] Waltke and O'Connor (1990), 355-356.

Fill out the verb analysis chart for הוֹצִיא :

root	stem	form	person, gender, number	function	basic root meaning

Translation of וְאוֹתָ֫נוּ הוֹצִיא מִשָּׁם : *And it was we that he was the bringer-out-of from there.*

If it bothers you that the translation seems particularly awkward, perhaps not even acceptable English, please remember that it is not the objective of this course to translate per se. There are already many very good English translations. Rather our objective is to discuss and understand the meaning of the Hebrew. Our sometimes ugly translations are merely a tool to facilitate discussion.

Piel qatal

27.4. Although there is no example of a Piel qatal or weqatal in our lesson verse, now is a good time to clarify the conjugation of the Piel qatal and weqatal. You learned way back in lesson 6.2b that the sign of the Piel qatal is a *hireq* under the first root letter and a *dagesh forte* in the second root letter. This rule has sufficed very well for the roots צוה דבר and שׁלח which have accounted for the vast majority of instances of the Piel qatal and weqatal so far. However, you now need to learn some of the peculiarities of

another root type, namely 2nd guttural roots. What are the guttural letters? _____
(3.6b) If you remember, the guttural letters cannot take a *dagesh*. Although it may not be a technically accurate explanation, perhaps this thought will help you to remember the conjugation below: Imagine that the *dagesh* bounced off the guttural second root letter and fell beneath the first root letter where we see the vowel *sere*.

PIEL QATAL of 2nd GUTTURAL ROOTS:

SINGULAR 3. M.	בֵּרַךְ	PLURAL 3. C.	בֵּרְכוּ
3. F.	בֵּרְכָה		
2. M.	בֵּרַ֫כְתָּ	2. M.	בֵּרַכְתֶּם
2. F.	בֵּרַכְתְּ	2. F.	בֵּרַכְתֶּן
1. C.	בֵּרַ֫כְתִּי	1. C.	בֵּרַ֫כְנוּ

Assignments

27.5a. Memorize vocabulary words 191-230 for Lessons 27-30.
27.5b. Memorize the conjugation of Hiphil qatal for 1st *yod* roots and Piel qatal for 2nd guttural roots.

27.5c. Write the root, stem, form, and where applicable, the person, gender, and number of the following verbs.

15. וָאֶפְקֹד	8. הוֹצֵאתִי	1. שָׁמְעוּ			
16. נִבְרְכָה	9. יֵצֵא	2. הִשְׁמִיעוּ			
17. וּבֵרַכְתִּי	10. וְדִבַּרְתָּ	3. וְהִשְׁמַעְתִּי			
18. בֵּרַכְתִּי	11. וַתְּדַבֵּר	4. הוֹצִיא			
19. בֵּרַכְנוּ	12. וּפָקַדְתִּי	5. וַיֵּצֵא			
20. וּבֵרַכְתֶּם	13. וְהִפְקִיד	6. צְאוּ			
	14. וַיִּפְקֹד	7. הוֹצִיא			

27.5d. Translate:

Genesis 11:27 תּוֹלְדֹת is a word made from the root ילד meaning *generations*.

וְאֵלֶּה תּוֹלְדֹת תֶּרַח תֶּרַח הוֹלִיד אֶת־אַבְרָם אֶת־נָחוֹר וְאֶת־הָרָן וְהָרָן הוֹלִיד אֶת־לוֹט: 1.

Genesis 25:19

וְאֵלֶּה תּוֹלְדֹת יִצְחָק בֶּן־אַבְרָהָם אַבְרָהָם הוֹלִיד אֶת־יִצְחָק: 2.

Genesis 14:18 מַלְכִּי־צֶדֶק is actually a proper name.

וּמַלְכִּי־צֶדֶק מֶלֶךְ שָׁלֵם הוֹצִיא לֶחֶם   3.

Genesis 43:22 אַחֵר is an adjective meaning *other*.

וְכֶסֶף אַחֵר הוֹרַדְנוּ בְיָדֵנוּ   4.

Genesis 45:13 We have seen this verse before in 21.6.b.18 as an example of Mitigated Hortatory Discourse.

וְהוֹרַדְתֶּם אֶת־אָבִי   5.

Exodus 7:4 If you need help with צָבָא think צִבְאֹתַי + fem. pl. ending ת -- + 1st c. pronom-inal suffix י--

וְלֹא־יִשְׁמַע אֲלֵכֶם פַּרְעֹה וְנָתַתִּי אֶת־יָדִי בְּמִצְרָיִם וְהוֹצֵאתִי אֶת־צִבְאֹתַי   6.

Exodus 7:5

וְיָדְעוּ מִצְרַיִם כִּי־אֲנִי יְהוָה וְהוֹצֵאתִי אֶת־בְּנֵי־יִשְׂרָאֵל מִתּוֹכָם: 7.

Exodus 12:17 Here X-qatal refers to the present.

הַיּוֹם הַזֶּה הוֹצֵאתִי אֶת־צִבְאוֹתֵיכֶם מֵאֶרֶץ   8.

158

Leviticus 23:43 בַּסֻּכּוֹת means *in booths*.

9. בַּסֻּכּוֹת הוֹשַׁבְתִּי אֶת־בְּנֵי יִשְׂרָאֵל

Leviticus 25:45 The root קנה means *purchase*. לַאֲחֻזָּה means *for a possession*.

10. מֵהֶם תִּקְנוּ וּמִמִּשְׁפַּחְתָּם אֲשֶׁר עִמָּכֶם אֲשֶׁר הוֹלִידוּ בְּאַרְצְכֶם וְהָיוּ לָכֶם לַאֲחֻזָּה:

Numbers 33:52

11. וְהוֹרַשְׁתֶּם אֶת־כָּל־יֹשְׁבֵי הָאָרֶץ מִפְּנֵיכֶם

Numbers 33:53 If you need help with לָרֶשֶׁת see 16.4c.

12. וְהוֹרַשְׁתֶּם אֶת־הָאָרֶץ וִישַׁבְתֶּם־בָּהּ כִּי לָכֶם נָתַתִּי אֶת־הָאָרֶץ לָרֶשֶׁת אֹתָהּ:

Deuteronomy 11:23 Which of the two יֹרֵשׁ forms is Qal stem and which is Hiphil stem? גּוֹיִם גְּדֹלִים וַעֲצֻמִים מִכֶּם means *nations greater and mightier than you.*

13. וְהוֹרִישׁ יְהוָה אֶת־כָּל־הַגּוֹיִם הָאֵלֶּה מִלִּפְנֵיכֶם וִירִשְׁתֶּם גּוֹיִם גְּדֹלִים וַעֲצֻמִים מִכֶּם:

Joshua 16:10

14. וְלֹא הוֹרִישׁוּ אֶת־הַכְּנַעֲנִי הַיּוֹשֵׁב בְּגָזֶר

2 Kings 21:2 כְּתוֹעֲבֹת הַגּוֹיִם means *as the abominations of the nations.*

15. וַיַּעַשׂ הָרַע בְּעֵינֵי יְהוָה כְּתוֹעֲבֹת הַגּוֹיִם אֲשֶׁר הוֹרִישׁ יְהוָה מִפְּנֵי בְּנֵי יִשְׂרָאֵל:

2 Chronicles 20:7

16. הֲלֹא אַתָּה אֱלֹהֵינוּ הוֹרַשְׁתָּ אֶת־יֹשְׁבֵי הָאָרֶץ הַזֹּאת מִלִּפְנֵי עַמְּךָ יִשְׂרָאֵל

Exodus 18:20 Even though there is no *dot vowel*, the first verb is Hiphil stem.

17. וְהוֹדַעְתָּ לָהֶם אֶת־הַדֶּרֶךְ יֵלְכוּ בָהּ

1 Samuel 10:8

18. וְהוֹדַעְתִּי לְךָ אֵת אֲשֶׁר תַּעֲשֶׂה:

Nehemiah 8:12 הֵבִינוּ is the Hiphil qatal 3 c. p. of the root בִּין

19. וַיֵּלְכוּ כָל־הָעָם כִּי הֵבִינוּ בַּדְּבָרִים אֲשֶׁר הוֹדִיעוּ לָהֶם:

27.5e. Read Judges 16:6-9.

Lesson 28

וַיֹּאמֶר יִשְׂרָאֵל אֶל־יוֹסֵף הִנֵּה אָנֹכִי מֵת וְהָיָה אֱלֹהִים עִמָּכֶם וְהֵשִׁיב אֶתְכֶם
אֶל־אֶרֶץ אֲבֹתֵיכֶם׃

Genesis 48:21

Goals:
- Identify and read several classes of hollow roots.
- Identify and read Hiphil qatal of hollow roots.

What we already know

28.1a. Translate וַיֹּאמֶר יִשְׂרָאֵל אֶל־יוֹסֵף _____

28.1b. The second clause is הִנֵּה אָנֹכִי מֵת The verb מֵת may be two forms, either a 3rd m. s. qatal or a m.s. participle of the hollow root מוּת Which must it be to agree with the subject אָנֹכִי ?

_____

Several classes of hollow roots

28.2a. There are several classes of hollow roots. In all the classes, there is an ambiguity between the 3rd m. s. qatal and the m. s. participle as follows:

QAL QATALS and PARTICIPLES of HOLLOW VERBS

	Class 1 שִׂים בּוֹא קוּם	"E" Class מוּת	"O" Class בּוֹשׁ
3rd m. s.(he, it) qatal or m. s. participle	קָם בָּא שָׂם	מֵת	בּוֹשׁ
3rd f. s.(she, it) qatal or f. s. participle	קָמָה בָּאָה שָׂמָה	מֵתָה	בּוֹשָׁה

Note: The 3rd feminine singular qatals have their accents on the first syllable, and the feminine singular participles have their accents on the last syllable.

Fill out the verb analysis chart for מֵת :

root	stem	form	person, gender, number	Function	basic root meaning

160

Translate הִנֵּה אָנֹכִי מֵת _____

28.2b. Let us examine the third clause of out lesson verse: וְהָיָה אֱלֹהִים עִמָּכֶם Fill out the verb analysis chart for וְהָיָה (13.2a):

root	stem	form	person, gender, number	function	basic root meaning

Translate the clause: _____

28.2c. Since we can now see that we are in a +projection genre, namely Predictive Narrative, what nuance

might we apply to the participle מֵת which we studied in 25.3b?_____

Hiphil qatals of hollow roots

28.3a. Our next clause begins with the verb וְהֵשִׁיב Hopefully you can see the two augments which normally accompany the Hiphil stem which are:

1._____

2._____ (27.2b)

Only notice that, as we have often seen, the middle root letter of the hollow root שׁוב is missing, so that the dot vowel of the Hiphil stem follows the first root letter. The root שׁוב is completely conjugated below in the qatal form of the Hiphil stem as an example of Hollow roots.

HIPHIL QATAL of HOLLOW ROOTS:

SINGULAR	3 M.	הֵשִׁיב	PLURAL	3 C.	הֵשִׁיבוּ
	3 F.	הֵשִׁיבָה			
	2 M.	הֲשִׁיבֹותָ		2 M.	הֲשִׁיבֹותֶם
	2 F.	הֲשִׁיבֹות		2 F.	הֲשִׁיבֹותֶן
	1 C.	הֲשִׁיבֹותִי		1 C.	הֲשִׁיבֹונוּ

Notes:
1. Notice that many of the forms have an additional *holem* before the customary subject pronoun affix that we have not seen before. This *holem* may be spelled plene as in the chart or defectiva.
2. The vowel under the preformative *heh* is somewhat variable from root to root.

28.3b. וְהֵשִׁיב is part of the mainline string of a Predictive Narrative. It is a weqatal verb form, and you are correct to conclude that even though the stem is new to you, the discourse function of the verb form is not.

RULE: It is the verb *forms* that have various functions within discourse, not verb *stems*.

Fill out the verb analysis chart for וְהֵשִׁיב :

root	stem	form	person, gender, number	function	basic root meaning

Whereas the meaning of the root שׁוב is *return*, the meaning of the root in the Hiphil stem is *cause to return* or better, *bring back*.

Translate וְהֵשִׁיב _____

28.3c. In case you need help with אֲבֹתֵיכֶם it is made of three parts as follows:
1. the normally irregular plural of אָב _____ (14.2d)

2. יֵ which normally comes between plural nouns ending in וֹת-- and a suffix

3. כֶם-- the pronominal suffix

Translate וְהֵשִׁיב אֶתְכֶם אֶל־אֶרֶץ אֲבֹתֵיכֶם _____

Translate the entire lesson verse: _____

_____

Hiphils of motion verbs

28.4.   There are many verbs of motion with which we are quite familiar that can be translated using *brought* and a particle of direction. Often the direction is lost in the commonly used English versions, so it is nice to know the Hebrew.

ROOT	QAL MEANING	HIPHIL MEANING
ירד	descend	bring down
עלה	ascend	bring up

162

בּוֹא	come, enter	bring in
יָצָא	exit, leave	bring out
שׁוֹב	return	bring back
קרב	approach	bring near
הלך	go, walk	bring

A note on verbal stems

28.5. All roots are not used in all stems. There is no one stem, not even the Qal stem, in which all roots are used. Some roots are only used in one, two or three stems, and not necessarily the Qal stem.

Assignments

28.6a. Memorize the conjugation of hollow roots in the qatal and participle forms of the Qal stem and the qatal form of the Hiphil stem.

28.6b. Translate:

25. הוּא יָצָא	17. אָחִיו מֵת	9. קָם	1. וּבָא
26. וְהוּא יָצָא	18. אֲשֶׁר־יָמוּת	10. הַקָּמִים	2. וְהֵבִיא
27. וְהוּא הוֹצִיא	19. וָמֵתוּ	11. וְהֵקִים	3. בָּאָה
28. וְהוֹצֵאתִי	20. לֹא הֵמִיתוּ	12. וַהֲקֵמֹתָ	4. כִּי־הֲבֵאתָ
29. וְהוֹצֵאת	21. וְהֵמַתָּה	13. וַהֲקֵמֹתוֹ	5. וַהֲבֵאתֶם
30. הוֹצֵאתִים	22. הֱמִתְהוּ	14. וְהֵקִימוּ	6. וַאֲנַחְנוּ הֲבִיאָנָם
31. הַיּוֹצְאִים	23. וְהֵמַתִּי	15. הֲקֵמֹתִי	7. אֲשֶׁר הֵבִיאוּ
32. וְהוֹצֵאתַנִי	24. וַהֲמִתִיהָ	16. קָמָה	8. וְהֵבִיאָם

28.6c. Translate:

Genesis 6:18

וַהֲקִמֹתִי אֶת־בְּרִיתִי אִתָּךְ 1.

Genesis 17:7

וַהֲקִמֹתִי אֶת־בְּרִיתִי בֵּינִי וּבֵינֶךָ 2.

Numbers 20:4 קָהָל a noun in singular construct meaning *congregation*.

וְלָמָה הֲבֵאתֶם אֶת־קְהַל יְהוָה אֶל־הַמִּדְבָּר הַזֶּה לָמוּת שָׁם 3.

Numbers 22:8
לִינוּ פֹה הַלַּיְלָה means *lodge here tonight*. אֶתְכֶם here means the same as לָכֶם

וַיֹּאמֶר אֲלֵיהֶם לִינוּ פֹה הַלַּיְלָה וַהֲשִׁבֹתִי אֶתְכֶם דָּבָר כַּאֲשֶׁר יְדַבֵּר יְהוָה אֵלָי 4.

Deuteronomy 4:39 Remember that כִּי may include the senses *for, that, because, when,* or *but.* Keep them all in mind when translating this item, 9, and 12.	5. וְיָדַעְתָּ הַיּוֹם וַהֲשֵׁבֹתָ אֶל־לְבָבֶךָ כִּי יְהוָה הוּא הָאֱלֹהִים בַּשָּׁמַיִם
Joshua 11:15	6. לֹא־הֵסִיר דָּבָר מִכֹּל אֲשֶׁר־צִוָּה יְהוָה אֶת־מֹשֶׁה
1 Samuel 15:13	7. הֲקִימֹתִי אֶת־דְּבַר יְהוָה:
Exodus 33:1 This verse contains a Hiphil qatal of a 3rd *heh* root.	8. וַיְדַבֵּר יְהוָה אֶל־מֹשֶׁה לֵךְ עֲלֵה מִזֶּה אַתָּה וְהָעָם אֲשֶׁר הֶעֱלִיתָ מֵאֶרֶץ מִצְרָיִם
Exodus 32:7 The root שחת means *ruin, destroy.*	9. וַיְדַבֵּר יְהוָה אֶל־מֹשֶׁה לֶךְ־רֵד כִּי שִׁחֵת עַמְּךָ אֲשֶׁר הֶעֱלִיתָ מֵאֶרֶץ מִצְרָיִם:
Exodus 18:19 מוּל הָאֱלֹהִים means *in front of God.*	10. עַתָּה שְׁמַע בְּקֹלִי וִיהִי אֱלֹהִים עִמָּךְ הֱיֵה אַתָּה לָעָם מוּל הָאֱלֹהִים וְהֵבֵאתָ אַתָּה אֶת־הַדְּבָרִים אֶל־הָאֱלֹהִים:
1 Samuel 8:22 Even though וְהִמְלַכְתָּ does not have the dot vowel, it is Hiphil stem.	11. וַיֹּאמֶר יְהוָה אֶל־שְׁמוּאֵל שְׁמַע בְּקוֹלָם וְהִמְלַכְתָּ לָהֶם מֶלֶךְ
1 Samuel 12:24 Which imperative is the root ראה and which is ירא? The root גדל in Hiphil means to *make great* or *do great things.*	12. אַךְ יְראוּ אֶת־יְהוָה כִּי רְאוּ אֵת אֲשֶׁר־הִגְדִּל עִמָּכֶם
1 Samuel 16:17	13. וַיֹּאמֶר שָׁאוּל אֶל־עֲבָדָיו רְאוּ־נָא לִי אִישׁ וַהֲבִיאוֹתֶם אֵלָי
Exodus 40:12	14. וְהִקְרַבְתָּ אֶת־אַהֲרֹן וְאֶת־בָּנָיו אֶל־פֶּתַח אֹהֶל מוֹעֵד

15. וְהִקְרִיב אֹתָהּ הַכֹּהֵן וְהֶעֱמִדָהּ לִפְנֵי יְהוָה׃

Numbers 5:16 Do you remember the significance of the *mappiq* in the *heh* in אֹתָהּ ? See 19.4b if not.

28.6d. Which verses in the exercise above are Hortatory Discourse or Instructional Discourse?

28.6e. Read Judges 16:10-12.

Lesson 29

וְהִכִּיתֶם כָּל־עִיר מִבְצָר וְכָל־עִיר מִבְחוֹר וְכָל־עֵץ טוֹב תַּפִּילוּ
2 Kings 3:19

Goals:
- **Identify and read the Hiphil qatal of** נכה **and other third** *heh* **roots.**
- **Identify and read the Hiphil yiqtol of first** *nun* **roots.**

What we already know

29.1. Looking at the verb וְהִכִּיתֶם what form does the *vav* together with the תֶם-- affixed

pronoun indicate? _____ And what stem do the pre-formed *heh* and the dot vowel

indicate? _____ (27.2b)

The special case of נכה and other 3rd heh roots

29.2a. Notice that once we remove all these accounted-for letters on וְהִכִּיתֶם we are left with only one
root letter כ Uh, oh! The good news is that at least the root letter has what kind of *dagesh* in it?

_____ We must then, if we are to find a tri-consonantal root in this verb,
suspect a "doubly weak" root. So it is.

> HINT: When only one root letter appears, suspect the common but doubly weak root
> נכה which appears 462 times in the Bible, about 96% of which are in the Hiphil stem.
> נכה in the Hiphil stem means *strike, kill*.

With נכה and other 1st *nun* roots, the preformative *heh* of the Hiphil stems pushes the *nun* out of the
word. The *nun* remains only as a *footprint dagesh* (9. 2d). Then there is the matter of נכה also being a
3rd *heh* root. As with other 3rd *heh* roots in the qatal form of many stems, the *heh* is often dropped without
a trace.

29.2b. Here is the root נכה fully conjugated in the Hiphil stem and qatal form. All the forms shown
may appear in the weqatal form as well. Notice that many persons, genders, and numbers are not attested.

QATAL of נכה **in the HIPHIL STEM** *Forms unattested in the Bible.

SINGULAR 3. M.	הִכָּה	PLURAL 3. C.		הִכּוּ
3. F.	* הִכְּתָה			
2. M.	הִכִּיתָ	2. M.		הִכִּיתֶם
2. F.	* הִכִּית	2. F.		הִכִּיתֶן *
1. C.	הִכֵּיתִי	1. C.		הִכִּינוּ *

166

Fill out the verb analysis chart for וְהִכִּיתֶם :

root	stem	form	person, gender, number	function	basic root meaning

Translate וְהִכִּיתֶם : _____

29.2c. Third *heh* roots often do not have the Hiphil stem's customary dot vowel after the second root letter. Here is the full conjugation of the root רֶאה as an example.

HIPHIL QATAL of 3rd HEH ROOTS:

SINGULAR 3. M.	הִרְאָה	**PLURAL 3. C.**	הִרְאוּ
3. F.	הִרְאָתָה		
2. M.	הִרְאִיתָ	2. M.	הִרְאִיתֶם
2. F.	הִרְאֵית	2. F.	*הִרְאִיתֶן
1. C.	הִרְאִיתִי	1. C.	הִרְאִינוּ

Translating כָּל

29.3. In the phrases כָּל־עִיר מִבְצָר and וְכָל־עִיר מִבְחוֹר we have two examples of exactly the same construction. In both cases, כֹּל is followed by two singular nouns. The words you may not know are מִבְצָר meaning *a fortress* and מִבְחוֹר meaning *a fine choice*. Supply the word *of* in the

middle of each pair of nouns. What are these *noun-noun* constructions called? _____
(7.2b) As for the translation of כָּל :

> RULE: When כָּל **is followed by a singular noun or singular construct chain**
> **translate it** *every*. **When it is followed by a plural noun or plural construct chains or**
> **collective nouns (e.g.** עַם **), translate it** *all*.

Hiphil yiqtol

29.4a. Translate וְכָל־עֵץ טוֹב _____ It is difficult to tell whether this phrase ends the previous clause or begins the next. Since we are in a +projection genre and the last word in our lesson verse is a yiqtol, we should look for an "X" in front of the yiqtol unless the yiqtol can be construed as volitive. וְכָל־עֵץ טוֹב is therefore an "X" for the clause that follows it.

167

What is the function of the X-V construction? _____ (5.3d and 6.3)   In this case the construction helps to make a transition from the topic עִיר to the topic עֵץ

29.4b. The partnership between the weqatal mainline וְהִכִּיתֶם and the X-yiqtol off-the-line form is perhaps the best context clue for labeling the form of תַּפִּילוּ Hopefully you can recognize the root here as נפל You surely recognize the nikkud does not match the nikkud of the Qal stem as we learned it. The 2nd m. p. Qal yiqtol of נפל is תִּפְּלוּ

> RULE: **The signs of the yiqtol and wayyiqtol of the Hiphil stem are a *patakh* under the prefixed pronoun and a dot vowel after the second root letter: ─○ ִ○ ○─**

The prefixed pronoun and the preformed *heh* of the Hiphil qatal cannot both appear before the root. The prefixed pronoun takes precedence in that it appears in the yiqtol form of the Hiphil stem, but the Hiphil's *heh* does not. The *dagesh* you see in the *peh* of the word תַּפִּילוּ is the *footprint dagesh* left by the missing 1st *nun*. Fill out the verb analysis chart for תַּפִּילוּ :

root	stem	form	person, gender, number	Function	basic root meaning

Translate וְכָל־עֵץ טוֹב תַּפִּילוּ : _____
נפל in the Hiphil stem means *cause to fall* or *fell* (as in *We will fell the tree.*)

29.4c. Using תַּפִּילוּ as your pattern, write in the correct forms in the chart below of the very common 1st *nun* root נגד which appears almost exclusively in the Hiphil stem:

YIQTOL of נגד in the HIPHIL STEM

SINGULAR 3. M.	_____	**PLURAL 3. M.**	_____
3. F.	_____	3. F.	_____
2. M.	_____	2. M.	_____
2. F.	_____	2. F.	_____
1. C.	_____	1. C.	_____

29.4d. Below are the attested persons, genders and numbers for the wayyiqtol of the root נכה in the Hiphil stem. You are being shown the wayyiqtol instead of the yiqtol because it is apocopated. If you remember, the *heh* is more often missing in the wayyiqtol of 3rd *heh* roots in the Qal stem. The 3rd *heh* is also missing in the Hiphil wayyiqtol, thus making a root just a bit tougher to identify in Hiphil wayyiqtol

168

than Hiphil yiqtol. In other words, if you can identify the wayyiqtol forms, you should be able to identify the yiqtol forms which usually appear with the *heh*.

WAYYIQTOL of נכה in the HIPHIL STEM:

SINGULAR 3. M.	וַיַּךְ	PLURAL 3. M.	וַיַּכּוּ
3. F.	וַתַּךְ	3. F.	* וַתַּכֶּינָה
2. M.	וַתַּךְ	2. M.	* וַתַּכּוּ
2. F.	* וַתַּכִּי	2. F.	* וַתַּכֶּינָה
1. C.	וָאַכֶּה	1. C.	וַנַּכֶּה

*The form is unattested in the Bible in either wayyiqtol or yiqtol.

Verbs used exclusively or almost exclusively in the Hiphil stem

29.5. In Lesson 2 we first encountered the root דבר which is used almost exclusively in the Piel stem. In this lesson we have learned about two verbs that are used almost exclusively in the Hiphil stem, נכה and נגד With words such as these, either the Qal had been lost at the time the Bible was written, or it is not attested in the Bible, or it simply never existed. These words seem to have developed their own meanings apart from the causative sense that other Hiphil's have. For instance, does נכה mean *cause to hurt*? Perhaps, but we do not know, so we will simply say it means *strike, kill*.

Assignments

29.6a. Memorize the conjugation of Hiphil qatal of 3rd *heh* roots and Hiphil yiqtol of 1st *nun* roots.

29.6b. Translate:

1. וַיַּךְ	9. נָפַל	19. וַיַּגֵּד			
2. וַיַּכּוּ	10. אַפִּילָה־נָא	20. וַיַּגִּידוּ			
3. וָאַכֶּה	11. וּנְפַלְתֶּם	21. וָאַגֵּד			
4. וַיַּכּוּהָ	12. וַיִּפְּלוּ	22. אֲשֶׁר לֹא־תַגִּיד			
5. וְהִכִּיתָ	13. וְהִפִּילוּ	23. אֲשֶׁר יַגִּידוּ			
6. לָמָה הִכִּיתָנוּ	14. וְרָחֵל תַּפִּיל	24. אַבְרָם הִגִּידָה			
7. וְהֵם הִכּוּ	15. וַיַּפִּילוּ	25. וְהִגַּדְתֶּם			
8. וְהִכּוּנִי	16. וַיַּפִּילֵם	26. לֹא־הִגַּדְתָּ			

29.6c. Translate:

Exodus 3:20

וְשָׁלַחְתִּי אֶת־יָדִי וְהִכֵּיתִי אֶת־מִצְרַיִם 1.

Leviticus 26:24 Here a
casus pendens is "hanging"
inside a clause rather than
at the beginning.

וְהִכֵּיתִי אֶתְכֶם גַּם־אָנִי שֶׁבַע עַל־חַטֹּאתֵיכֶם 2.

3. | Exodus 17:6 צוּר means *boulder.* | הִנְנִי עֹמֵד לְפָנֶיךָ שָּׁם עַל־הַצּוּר בְּחֹרֵב וְהִכִּיתָ בַצּוּר וְיָצְאוּ מִמֶּנּוּ מַיִם

4. Deuteronomy 7:2 The *mems* at the ends of the verbs are object pronominal suffixes(19.4b).

וּנְתָנָם יְהוָה אֱלֹהֶיךָ לְפָנֶיךָ וְהִכִּיתָם

5. Genesis 14:7 Here is the first time we have looked at the word עֵין meaning *spring.*

וַיָּשֻׁבוּ וַיָּבֹאוּ אֶל־עֵין מִשְׁפָּט וַיַּכּוּ אֶת־כָּל־שְׂדֵה הָעֲמָלֵקִי

6. Joshua 10:26

וַיַּכֵּם יְהוֹשֻׁעַ אַחֲרֵי־כֵן

7. Joshua 10:40 The *heh* on the end of the verb is not a pronominal suffix because it does not have a mappiq in it. It is a case where, for an unknown reason, the *heh* did not drop off.

וַיַּכֶּה יְהוֹשֻׁעַ אֶת־כָּל־הָאָרֶץ הָהָר

8. Joshua 11:8

וַיִּתְּנֵם יְהוָה בְּיַד־יִשְׂרָאֵל וַיַּכּוּם

9. Judges 3:31

וְאַחֲרָיו הָיָה שַׁמְגַּר בֶּן־עֲנָת וַיַּךְ אֶת־פְּלִשְׁתִּים

10. Deuteronomy 17:10 The idiom עַל־פִּי means *according to.*

וְעָשִׂיתָ עַל־פִּי הַדָּבָר אֲשֶׁר יַגִּידוּ לְךָ מִן־הַמָּקוֹם הַהוּא

11. Joshua 2:14

אִם לֹא תַגִּידוּ אֶת־דְּבָרֵנוּ זֶה

12. 1 Samuel 9:19 Start: *It is all which...*

וְכֹל אֲשֶׁר בִּלְבָבְךָ אַגִּיד לָךְ

13. 1 Samuel 20:10

מִי יַגִּיד לִי

14. Genesis 46:31 Notice how it is no problem to use the cohortative in the Hiphil stem.

אֶעֱלֶה וְאַגִּידָה לְפַרְעֹה וְאֹמְרָה אֵלָיו אַחַי בָּאוּ אֵלַי

Genesis 29:12 If you have trouble with אָחִי turn to 14.2d.

15.   וַיַּגֵּד יַעֲקֹב לְרָחֵל כִּי אֲחִי אָבִיהָ הוּא

Genesis 44:24 Is the *nun* in וַנַּגֶּד a root letter?

16.   וַיְהִי כִּי עָלִינוּ אֶל־עַבְדְּךָ אָבִי וַנַּגֶּד־לוֹ אֵת דִּבְרֵי אֲדֹנִי:

Genesis 45:26

17.   וַיַּגִּדוּ לוֹ לֵאמֹר עוֹד יוֹסֵף חַי

Exodus 33:19 טוּבִי means *My goodness*.

18.   וַיֹּאמֶר אֲנִי אַעֲבִיר כָּל־טוּבִי עַל־פָּנֶיךָ

Exodus 40:14

19.   וְאֶת־בָּנָיו תַּקְרִיב

Genesis 2:21 תַּרְדֵּמָה means *deep sleep*.

20.   וַיַּפֵּל יְהוָה אֱלֹהִים תַּרְדֵּמָה עַל־הָאָדָם

Nehemiah 12:42 הַמְשֹׁרְרִים means *the singers*.

21.   וַיַּשְׁמִיעוּ הַמְשֹׁרְרִים

29.6d. Read Judges 16:13-14.

171

Lesson 30

אֲשֶׁר־יֵצֵא לִפְנֵיהֶם וַאֲשֶׁר יָבֹא לִפְנֵיהֶם וַאֲשֶׁר יוֹצִיאֵם וַאֲשֶׁר יְבִיאֵם

Numbers 27:17

Note: For the first time, our lesson verse does not contain a main or independent clause. That is, the verse cannot stand alone as a complete thought. Yet, the verse contains several dependent clauses that make for a good study.

Goals:
- Identify Hiphil yiqtols of first *yod* roots.
- Identify Hiphil yiqtols of hollow roots.

What we already know

30.1. Fill out the verb analysis charts for יֵצֵא and יָבֹא   Do not forget to take note of the vowels under the prefixed subject pronouns (3.2a and 10.3a) and the use of the אֲשֶׁר (13.3b).

root	stem	form	person, gender, number	function	basic root meaning

root	stem	form	person, gender, number	function	basic root meaning

The lack of context makes אֲשֶׁר difficult to translate exactly. Use *he who*, and translate the two

clauses:_____

Hiphil yiqtols of 1st yod roots

30.2a. Let us analyze יוֹצִיאֵם   Using the [ִי] in the middle of this word as a sign of the verb's stem,

what stem is this word?_____ (29.4b) The root of the verb has undergone the same

transformation as 1st *yod* roots in qatal verbs of the Hiphil stem (27.2b.2), so what is the root?_____
The verb is formed as follows:

172

1. The *yod* has been transformed into a *holem*.

יָצָא ← וֹצָא

2. A *hireq-yod* has been added after the second root letter.

וֹצָא + ִי (after the 2nd root letter) = וֹצִיא

3. The 3rd m. s. prefixed subject pronoun is added.

וֹצִיא + י = יוֹצִיא

4. The 3rd m. p. object suffix is added.

יוֹצִיא + ָ ם = יוֹצִיאֵם

RULE: A *holem* after the prefixed subject pronoun and a dot vowel after the second root letter are the signs of the yiqtol form of the Hiphil stem of 1st *yod* roots and the special case root הלך : וֹ__יֹ֗O

30.2b. Fill out the verb analysis chart for יוֹצִיאֵם :

root	stem	form	person, gender, number	function	basic root meaning

Translate וָאֲשֶׁר יוֹצִיאֵם : _____

30.2c. Here is the complete conjugation:

YIQTOL in the HIPHIL STEM of 1st YOD ROOTS:

SINGULAR 3. M.	יוֹצִיא	**PLURAL 3. M.**		יוֹצִיאוּ
3. F.	תּוֹצִיא	3. F.		תּוֹצֵאנָה
2. M.	תּוֹצִיא	2. M.		תּוֹצִיאוּ
2. F.	תּוֹצִיאִי	2. F.		*תּוֹצֵאנָה
1. C.	אוֹצִיא	1. C.		נוֹצִיא

Notes:

1. The number, person, and gender marked with * is not attested in any 1st *yod* roots in either the yiqtol or wayyiqtol forms.
2. The wayyiqtol forms look the same as the yiqtol forms except that they may have a different dot vowel and of course, they will have the added *vav-patakh-dagesh forte unit*.

173

30.2d. Using the 3rd m. s. form as your cue, fill out the full yiqtol Hiphil conjugation for the root יָשַׁב
You may use the verb charts near the back of the book to check your answers.

YIQTOL in the HIPHIL STEM of יָשַׁב

SINGULAR	3. M.	יוֹשִׁיב	PLURAL	3. M.	_____
	3. F.	_____		3. F.	_____
	2. M.	_____		2. M.	_____
	2. F.	_____		2. F.	_____
	1. C.	_____		1. C.	_____

Hiphil yiqtol of hollows roots

30.3a. When analyzing וַאֲשֶׁר יְבִיאֵם all that has come before it in our lesson verse becomes a great context clue as to what is going on with this verb form. Our verse contains a pair of roots, used first in the Qal stem and then in the Hiphil stem. So יְבִיאֵם is a conjugation of the root בוא and our first look at a hollow verb in the yiqtol form and the Hiphil stem.

Fill out the verb analysis chart for יְבִיאֵם :

root	stem	form	person, gender, number	function	basic root meaning

Translate וַאֲשֶׁר יְבִיאֵם : _____

30.3b. Our lesson word is in a way not a particularly good word from which to learn the Hiphil yiqtol of a hollow root because it has a pronominal suffix on it that has altered the nikkud. Below, then, is the complete Hiphil yiqtol conjugation of בוא

174

HIPHIL YIQTOL of HOLLOW ROOTS:

SINGULAR 3. M.	יָבִיא	PLURAL 3. M.	יָבִ֫יאוּ
3. F.	תָּבִיא	3. F.	תָּבִיאֶ֫ינָה
2. M.	תָּבִיא	2. M.	תָּבִ֫יאוּ
2. F.	תָּבִ֫יאִי	2. F.	תָּבִיאֶ֫ינָה
1. C.	אָבִיא	1. C.	נָבִיא

Notes:

1. Notice that with hollow roots, the customary *patakh* under the prefixed pronoun is a *qamets* instead.

2. The wayyiqtol forms look the same as the yiqtol forms except that they may have a different dot vowel and of course, they will have the added *vav-patakh-dagesh forte unit*.

3. Our lesson verse's יְבִיאֵם has a *shewa* rather than the hollow root's customary *qamets* under the prefixed subject pronoun because of the addition of the object suffix.

30.3c. Translate the entire lesson verse: _____

_____

Assignments

30.4a. Memorize the 1st *yod* and hollow verb conjugations for the Hiphil yiqtol.

30.4b. Translate:

1. יוֹצֵא	9. דַּע	17. בּוֹא
2. בַּבַּיִת יוֹצִיו	10. אֲשֶׁר יָדַע	18. לָבוֹא
3. הַיּוֹצֵא	11. וַיֵּדַע	19. וַיָּבֵא
4. וְדָוִד הוֹצִיו	12. וַיֵּדַע	20. וַיְבִיאֵ֫נִי
5. וַיּוֹצֵא	13. הַיּוֹדֵעַ	21. וְהֵבִיאָה
6. וַתּוֹצִיאָ֫נוּ	14. וְדָוִד הוֹדִיעַ	22. אֲשֶׁר־יָבִיאוּ
7. וָאוֹצִיאֵם	15. תּוֹדִיעֵ֫נִי	23. תְּבִיאֶ֫ינָה
8. וְאֶת הָאָדָם תּוֹצִיאוּ	16. אֶת דָּוִד אוֹדִיעַ	24. תְּבִיאֵ֫נוּ

30.4c. Translate:

1 Samuel 3:12

1. בַּיּוֹם הַהוּא אָקִים אֶל־עֵלִי אֵת כָּל־אֲשֶׁר דִּבַּ֫רְתִּי
אֶל־בֵּיתוֹ

1 Samuel 5:11 Notice the shift in subject between the (2nd) m. p. imperative and the 3rd m. s. yiqtol. This shift in subjects marks the

2. וַיֹּאמְרוּ שַׁלְּחוּ אֶת־אֲרוֹן אֱלֹהֵי יִשְׂרָאֵל וְיָשֹׁב לִמְקֹמוֹ
וְלֹא־יָמִית אֹתִי וְאֶת־עַמִּי

yiqtol as giving the purpose
for the imperative in a
manner similar to that
noted in 22.3c.

Genesis 19:8   A Hiphil
cohortative.

3. אוֹצִיאָה־נָּא אֶתְהֶן אֲלֵיכֶם

Exodus 3:11

4. מִי אָנֹכִי כִּי אֵלֵךְ אֶל־פַּרְעֹה וְכִי אוֹצִיא אֶת־בְּנֵי
יִשְׂרָאֵל מִמִּצְרָיִם:

Exodus 34:24   The root
יָרַשׁ   in the Hiphil stem
can mean *dispossess*.

5. כִּי־אוֹרִישׁ גּוֹיִם מִפָּנֶיךָ

Genesis 11:24

6. וַיּוֹלֶד אֶת־תָּרַח

Exodus 19:17

7. וַיּוֹצֵא מֹשֶׁה אֶת־הָעָם

Deuteronomy 1:25   פְּרִי
means *fruit*.

8. וַיִּקְחוּ בְיָדָם מִפְּרִי הָאָרֶץ וַיּוֹרִדוּ אֵלֵינוּ וַיָּשִׁבוּ אֹתָנוּ
דָבָר

Deuteronomy 4:20

9. וְאֶתְכֶם לָקַח יְהוָה וַיּוֹצִא אֶתְכֶם מִמִּצְרָיִם

Joshua 10:27   The 3rd m.
p. object suffix is on both
verbs. Notice the defectiva
spelling of the subject
complement in וַיַּשְׁלִכֵם
A מְעָרָה   is a *cave*.

10. וַיּוֹרִדוּם מֵעַל הָעֵצִים וַיַּשְׁלִכֵם אֶל־הַמְּעָרָה

Genesis 17:21

11. וְאֶת־בְּרִיתִי אָקִים אֶת־יִצְחָק אֲשֶׁר תֵּלֵד לְךָ שָׂרָה

Exodus 13:11

12. וְהָיָה כִּי־יְבִאֲךָ יְהוָה אֶל־אֶרֶץ הַכְּנַעֲנִי

1 Kings 2:4

13. לְמַעַן יָקִים יְהוָה אֶת־דְּבָרוֹ

2 Kings 23:27

14. וַיֹּאמֶר יְהוָה גַּם אֶת־יְהוּדָה אָסִיר מֵעַל פָּנַי

1 Chronicles 17:13   חֶסֶד
means *covenant love*.

15. אֲנִי אֶהְיֶה־לּוֹ לְאָב וְהוּא יִהְיֶה־לִּי לְבֵן וְחַסְדִּי
לֹא־אָסִיר מֵעִמּוֹ

Genesis 19:10 Do you remember what a *heh* on the end of a noun can mean?(24.6c.6).

16. וַיִּשְׁלְחוּ הָאֲנָשִׁים אֶת־יָדָם וַיָּבִיאוּ אֶת־לוֹט אֲלֵיהֶם הַבָּיְתָה

Genesis 20:14

17. וַיִּקַּח אֲבִימֶלֶךְ צֹאן וַיִּתֵּן לְאַבְרָהָם וַיָּשֶׁב לוֹ אֵת שָׂרָה אִשְׁתּוֹ:

Genesis 24:67

18. וַיְבִאֶהָ יִצְחָק הָאֹהֱלָה שָׂרָה אִמּוֹ

Genesis 27:14

19. וַיֵּלֶךְ וַיִּקַּח וַיָּבֵא לְאִמּוֹ

Exodus 4:7 חֵיק means *bosom*. בָּשָׂר means *flesh*. For help with שָׁבָה see 25.3a.

20. וַיָּשֶׁב יָדוֹ אֶל־חֵיקוֹ וַיּוֹצִאָהּ מֵחֵיקוֹ וְהִנֵּה־שָׁבָה כִּבְשָׂרוֹ:

Joshua 14:7 Can the verb be a wayyiqtol? See 17.4f.

21. וָאָשֵׁב אֹתוֹ דָּבָר

30.4d. Fill out verb analysis charts for the verbs in numbers 1, 2, and 10.
30.4e. Read Judges 16:15-17.

Lesson 31

אִם־אֵינְךָ מְשַׁלֵּחַ אֶת־עַמִּי הִנְנִי מַשְׁלִיחַ בְּךָ אֶת־הֶעָרֹב

Exodus 8:17

Goals:

- Identify and read the particles of existence with participles.
- Identify and read Hiphil participles.
- Identify and read Piel participles.

What we already know

31.1. Do you remember how to pronounce מְשַׁלֵּחַ and מַשְׁלִיחַ ? (20.2a)

Particles of existence with participles

31.2. Our lesson word אֵינְךָ is made of two parts, the construct of אַיִן which means

_____ and the pronominal suffix. Try translating אִם־אֵינְךָ literally:

_____ In Hebrew there are two verb-like words sometimes referred to as *particles* for expressing the idea of existence. The positive is יֵשׁ meaning something like *there is*. The negative is אַיִן meaning something like *there is not*.

הֲיֵשׁ יְהוָה בְּקִרְבֵּנוּ אִם־אָיִן   Exodus 17:7
Is YHWH in our midst or not?

Either of these words can precede a participle and have a pronominal suffix attached to mean someone is or is not doing something. The construction is over ten times more common with אַיִן than יֵשׁ In the discourse profile schemes of the discourses we are studying, all these constructions are low-ranking.

אַיִן and יֵשׁ with PARTICIPLES:

אֵין רֹאֶה   Exodus 22:9
No one sees

אֵינְכֶם רֹאִים   Deuteronomy 4:12
You (m. p.) are not seeing

אֵינֶנִּי נֹתֵן לָכֶם תֶּבֶן   Exodus 5:10
I am not giving you straw.

אִם־יֶשְׁכֶם עֹשִׂים חֶסֶד   Genesis 24:49
If you (m. p.) are doers of grace

178

Hiphil and Piel participles

31.3a. The construction we have just learned above, the *particle of existence plus participle*, is exactly the construction we have in our lesson sentence, only the participles look unfamiliar. What is the sign of a

participle in the Qal stem?_____ (12.2a)

> RULE: **In all stems except for Qal and Niphal stems, one of the signs of the participle form is a *mem* attached to the beginning of the participle.**

This rule helps us to identify both מַשְׁלִיחַ and מְשַׁלֵּחַ as participles, but notice the nikkud with each. We need more rules to help us differentiate between the participles of the Hiphil and Piel stems which are used in our lesson verse. The signs are really not new to you.

31.3b. RULE: **The signs of the Piel stem of the participle form are a pre-formed *mem* and a *dagesh forte* in the second root letter (a doubled second root letter):** מְֹO⊙O

Which of our two lesson participles is therefore the Piel participle?_____

The genre is Predictive Narrative. What function does the participle often have in Predictive Narrative?

_____ (25.3b)

Fill out the verb analysis chart for the Piel participle:

root	stem	form	person, gender, number	function	basic root meaning

The root שׁלח in the Piel stem means *send away, dismiss*. Translate אִם־אֵינְךָ מְשַׁלֵּחַ אֶת־עַמִּי

_____

31.3c. RULE: **For strong roots, the sign of the Hiphil stem of the participle form are a pre-formed *mem*, a *patakh* under the *mem*, and a dot vowel after the second root letter:** מַֹOֹO⊙Oי

Notice that the vowel under the *mem* is the same as we expect under the prefixed subject pronoun of the yiqtol form in the Hiphil stem.

Fill out the verb analysis chart for the Hiphil participle in our lesson verse:

root	stem	form	person, gender, number	function	basic root meaning

The root שׁלח in the Hiphil stem means *send (to do)*. עָרֹב means *swarm*, probably of flies in this case.

Translate הִנְנִי מַשְׁלִיחַ בְּךָ אֶת־הֶעָרֹב : _____

31.3d. Here is the root שׁלח fully conjugated as the Piel and Hiphil participles:

PIEL PARTICIPLE:		HIPHIL PARTICIPLE:	
Masculine Singular	מְשַׁלֵּחַ	Masculine Singular	מַשְׁלִיחַ
Feminine Singular	מְשַׁלַּחַת	Feminine Singular	מַשְׁלַחַת
Masculine Plural	מְשַׁלְּחִים	Masculine Plural	מַשְׁלִיחִים
Feminine Plural	מְשַׁלְּחוֹת	Feminine Plural	מַשְׁלִיחוֹת

Assignments

31.4a. Weak roots do not always have the same nikkud under the Hiphil participle's pre-formed *mem* that strong roots do. Conjugate the following 1st *yod*, 1st *nun*, and hollow roots as Hiphil participles using the given forms as your cues. Do not fill in the dashed slots because they are not attested in the Hebrew Bible. If you need help, use the appropriate verb charts near the back of the book.

ישׁב		נגד		קום	
M. S.	מוֹשִׁיב	M. S.	מַגִּיד	M. S.	מֵקִים
F. S.	_____	F. S.	_____	F. S.	מְ_____
M. P.	_____	M. P.	_____	M. P.	מְ_____
F. P.	-----	F. P.	-----	F. P.	מְ_____

31.4b. Memorize words 231-270 for Lessons 31-34.

31.4c. Translate:

Genesis 41:24

הַחַרְטֻמִּים means *the magicians*.

1. וָאֹמַר אֶל־הַחַרְטֻמִּים וְאֵין מַגִּיד לִי:

180

Genesis 43:5	וְאִם־אֵינְךָ מְשַׁלֵּחַ לֹא נֵרֵד	2.
Deuteronomy 4:22 See 25.3.	כִּי אָנֹכִי מֵת בָּאָרֶץ הַזֹּאת אֵינֶנִּי עֹבֵר אֶת־הַיַּרְדֵּן	3.
Joshua 6:1	אֵין יוֹצֵא וְאֵין בָּא	4.
1 Kings 21:5 סָרָה is an f. s. adjective from סוּר	מַה־זֶּה רוּחֲךָ סָרָה וְאֵינְךָ אֹכֵל לָחֶם	5.
2 Kings 12:8 מַדּוּעַ means *why?* בֶּדֶק means *breaches, broken walls*.	מַדּוּעַ אֵינְכֶם מְחַזְּקִים אֶת־בֶּדֶק הַבָּיִת	6.
2 Kings 17:26	אֵינָם יֹדְעִים אֶת־מִשְׁפַּט אֱלֹהֵי הָאָרֶץ	7.
Genesis 43:4	אִם־יֶשְׁךָ מְשַׁלֵּחַ אֶת־אָחִינוּ אִתָּנוּ נֵרְדָה	8.
Deuteronomy 13:4 Do you remember the use of a *heh* at the beginning of a clause?(15.4d)	הֲיִשְׁכֶם אֹהֲבִים אֶת־יְהוָה אֱלֹהֵיכֶם בְּכָל־לְבַבְכֶם וּבְכָל־נַפְשְׁכֶם	9.
Deuteronomy 32:39 עִמָּדִי means *with Me.* Do not forget to account for the *dagesh* in וַאֲחַיֶּה	רְאוּ עַתָּה כִּי אֲנִי אֲנִי הוּא וְאֵין אֱלֹהִים עִמָּדִי אֲנִי אָמִית וַאֲחַיֶּה וְאֵין מִיָּדִי מַצִּיל:	10.
Judges 8:34	וְלֹא זָכְרוּ בְּנֵי יִשְׂרָאֵל אֶת־יְהוָה אֱלֹהֵיהֶם הַמַּצִּיל אוֹתָם מִיַּד כָּל־אֹיְבֵיהֶם	11.
Judges 3:9	וַיָּקֶם יְהוָה מוֹשִׁיעַ לִבְנֵי יִשְׂרָאֵל וַיּוֹשִׁיעֵם אֵת עָתְנִיאֵל	12.
Judges 6:36	וַיֹּאמֶר גִּדְעוֹן אֶל־הָאֱלֹהִים אִם־יֶשְׁךָ מוֹשִׁיעַ בְּיָדִי אֶת־יִשְׂרָאֵל כַּאֲשֶׁר דִּבַּרְתָּ:	13.
Genesis 37:16	וַיֹּאמֶר אֶת־אַחַי אָנֹכִי מְבַקֵּשׁ	14.

Exodus 4:19 We have only some complicated suspicions why the *dageshes* are left out of the *mem* and *qoph* of the Piel
הַמְבַקְשִׁים

15. וַיֹּאמֶר יְהוָה אֶל־מֹשֶׁה בְּמִדְיָן לֵךְ שֻׁב מִצְרָיִם כִּי־מֵתוּ כָּל־הָאֲנָשִׁים הַמְבַקְשִׁים אֶת־נַפְשֶׁךָ:

Judges 18:1 For help with הָהֵם see Reading 1, verse 14. שֵׁבֶט הַדָּנִי means *the tribe of the Danites.*

16. וּבַיָּמִים הָהֵם שֵׁבֶט הַדָּנִי מְבַקֶּשׁ־לוֹ נַחֲלָה לָשֶׁבֶת

Exodus 14:30 In the first word notice how the Hiphil wayyiqtol does not have the customary "dot" vowel. This is standard for Hiphil wayyiqtol of a 3rd guttural. שְׂפַת הַיָּם means *lip of the sea, coast.*

17. וַיּוֹשַׁע יְהוָה בַּיּוֹם הַהוּא אֶת־יִשְׂרָאֵל מִיַּד מִצְרָיִם וַיַּרְא יִשְׂרָאֵל אֶת־מִצְרַיִם מֵת עַל־שְׂפַת הַיָּם:

Exodus 7:5 בִּנְטֹתִי = ב + נְטֹת → נטה י ֹ -- See 16.4.

18. וְיָדְעוּ מִצְרַיִם כִּי־אֲנִי יְהוָה בִּנְטֹתִי אֶת־יָדִי עַל־מִצְרָיִם וְהוֹצֵאתִי אֶת־בְּנֵי־יִשְׂרָאֵל מִתּוֹכָם:

Joshua 8:26

19. וִיהוֹשֻׁעַ לֹא־הֵשִׁיב יָדוֹ אֲשֶׁר נָטָה בַּכִּידוֹן

Deuteronomy 27:19 אָרוּר means *cursed.*

20. אָרוּר מַטֵּה מִשְׁפַּט

1 Samuel 8:3 One root letter in the verbs should remind us of נכה 1st *nun* and 3rd *heh.* Then the challenge is to figure out the stems of each. Key in on the vowel under the prefix pronoun. See 29.4b and 9.2b. בֶּצַע means *unjust gain.*

21. וַיִּטּוּ אַחֲרֵי הַבָּצַע וַיַּטּוּ מִשְׁפָּט

Ezra 7:28

22. וְעָלַי הִטָּה־חֶסֶד לִפְנֵי הַמֶּלֶךְ

31.4d. Read Judges 16:18-20.

Lesson 32

וַיִּשְׁלַח שָׁאוּל אֶת־הַמַּלְאָכִים לִרְאוֹת אֶת־דָּוִד לֵאמֹר הַעֲלוּ אֹתוֹ בַמִּטָּה אֵלַי לַהֲמִתוֹ:

1 Samuel 19:15

Goals:
- Identify and read the Hiphil imperative.
- Identify and read the Hiphil infinitive.
- Identify and read the Piel infinitive.

What we already know

32.1a. Translate וַיִּשְׁלַח שָׁאוּל אֶת־הַמַּלְאָכִים : _____

32.1b. Fill out the verb analysis chart for לִרְאוֹת If you need help see 16.4a.

root	stem	form	person, gender, number	function	basic root meaning

Translate לִרְאוֹת אֶת־דָּוִד : _____

32.1c. What is the special function of the infinitive לֵאמֹר ?_____ (17.3)

Translate it:_____ (also 17.3) So we can now expect a transition from

what genre of discourse_____ to one of the Direct Speech genres.

What are the Direct Speech genres? 1. _____

                        2. _____

                        3. _____ (Module Two Overview)

Of course, you remember that oral Historical Narrative is also a possibility.

Hiphil imperative

32.2a. The next word of our lesson sentence, הַעֲלוּ is a Hiphil imperative.

183

RULE: **The sign of the Hiphil imperative is a pre-formed *heh* with a *patakh* under it [-- הַ].** The Hiphil imperative has the same function as the imperative in the Qal or Piel stems, mainline of Hortatory Discourse. The endings on the Hiphil imperatives are the same as on the other imperative forms we learned.

32.2b. Fill out the verb analysis chart for הַעֲלוּ :

root	stem	form	person, gender, number	function	basic root meaning

Whereas the Qal עֲלוּ means *Go up*, הַעֲלוּ אֹתוֹ means *Bring him up*.

Translate הַעֲלוּ אֹתוֹ בַּמִּטָּה אֵלָי (מִטָּה means *bed*.):_____

32.2c. Here are a variety of roots fully conjugated as Hiphil imperatives:

HIPHIL IMPERATIVES:

	Strong root פקד	3rd heh עלה	1st nun נגד	Hollow שוב	1st yod יצא
M. S.	הַפְקֵד	הַעַל	הַגִּידָה or הַגֵּד	הָשֵׁב	הוֹצֵא
F. S.	הַפְקִידִי	הַעֲלִי	הַגִּידִי	הָשִׁיבִי	הוֹצִיאִי
M. P.	הַפְקִידוּ	הַעֲלוּ	הַגִּידוּ	הָשִׁיבוּ	הוֹצִיאוּ
F. P.	הַפְקֵדְנָה	-----	-----	-----	-----

Notes:
1. The dashed forms are unattested in that root type.
2. There is one potentially ambiguous form above, the masculine plural imperative of 1st *yod* roots. Using the root יצא as a model, the masculine plural Hiphil imperative is הוֹצִיאוּ Except for an emphasis shift, this would be identical with the 3rd person, masculine plural Hiphil qatal meaning *They were bringers up*. Fortunately, however, there is not one single attestation of a 1st *yod* root in the 3rd m. p. Hiphil qatal!

Hiphil infinitive

32.3a. What is the one verb form that may be preceded by a preposition?_____ (16.4a)

184

לַהֲמִתוֹ is made of three parts as follows:

וֹ   הֲמִת   לַ

suffix   infinitive   preposition

The attached preposition is the best clue that this word is an infinitive. As for determining the Hiphil stem, we have the old faithfuls, the pre-formed *heh* and a dot vowel after the 2nd root letter (or, as in the case of our lesson's hollow root, the 1st root letter).

32.3b. Fill out the verb analysis chart for לַהֲמִתוֹ :

root	stem	form	person, gender, number	function	basic root meaning

Whereas the Qal לָמוּת means *to die*, the Hiphil לַהֲמִתוֹ means *to cause him to die* or *to kill him*.

32.3c. Here are the Hiphil infinitives with attached *lamed* in a variety of stem types:

HIPHIL INFINITIVES:

Strong root פקד	3rd *heh* עלה	1st *nun* נגד	Hollow שוב	1st *yod* יצא

Infinitives: לְהַפְקִיד   לְהַעֲלֹת   לְהַגִּיד   לְהָשִׁיב   לְהוֹצִיא

Piel infinitives

32.4. Since it is the object of this module to compare and contrast the Hiphil and Piel stems, let us look at the Piel infinitive in the same roots. There is no great mystery to the Piel infinitive. Once again, it is the only form which may be preceded by a preposition, and it has the Piel's characteristic doubling of the second root letter.

PIEL INFINITIVES:

Strong root דבר	3rd *heh* חיה	1st *nun* נצח (*excel*)	Hollow קום	1st *yod* יסד (*lay foundation*)

Infinitives: לְדַבֵּר   לְחַיּוֹת   לְנַצֵּחַ   לְקַיֵּם   לְיַסֵּד

Comparing the same roots across three stems

32.5. A couple of the roots used above are used in the Qal, Piel, and Hiphil stems. Remember: the Piel signifies causing something or someone to be in a state, and the Hiphil signifies causing something or someone to act. Let us compare the roots חיה and קום :

185

QAL		PIEL	HIPHIL
חיה	לִחְיוֹת	לְחַיּוֹת	לְהַחֲיוֹת
	to live	*to cause to be alive, revive*	*to cause to keep living*
קום	לָקוּם	לְקַיֵּם	לְהָקִים
	to arise, stand up	*to cause to remain standing, confirm*	*to cause to stand up, establish*

Assignments

32.6a. Memorize the signs of the Hiphil imperative and infinitive and the Piel infinitive.

32.6b. Write the root, stem, form, and where applicable the person, gender, and number of the following verbs.

1. יָרַדְנוּ	9. רְדוּ	17. הָקֵם	וְהֶחֱזִיק 2
2. וַיִּרְדוּ	10. קָמָה	18. וַיֶּחֱזַק	וַיְחַזְּקוּ 2
3. וַיֵּרֶד	11. קַמְתֶּם	19. חֲזַק	הַחֲזִיקִי 2
4. וַיִּרְדוּ	12. הֲקֵמֹת	20. מְחַזֵּק	הֶחֱזִק 2
5. וַיּוֹרִדוּ	13. וַהֲקִמֹתִי	21. וַיְחַזֵּק	
6. וְהוֹרַדְתֶּם	14. מֵקִים	22. וְחִזַּקְתִּי	
7. מוֹרִיד	15. לְהָקִים	23. חִזְּקוּ	
8. יֹרְדִים	16. לָקוּם	24. מַחֲזִיק	

32.6c. Translate:

Genesis 19:12

1. וְכֹל אֲשֶׁר־לְךָ בָּעִיר הוֹצֵא מִן־הַמָּקוֹם:

Genesis 20:7

2. וְעַתָּה הָשֵׁב אֵשֶׁת־הָאִישׁ כִּי־נָבִיא הוּא

Genesis 21:18

3. קוּמִי שְׂאִי אֶת־הַנַּעַר וְהַחֲזִיקִי אֶת־יָדֵךְ בּוֹ

2 Chronicles 29:5 נִדָּה means *filth*.

4. וַיֹּאמֶר לָהֶם שְׁמָעוּנִי הַלְוִיִּם וְקַדְּשׁוּ אֶת־בֵּית יְהוָה אֱלֹהֵי אֲבֹתֵיכֶם וְהוֹצִיאוּ אֶת־הַנִּדָּה מִן־הַקֹּדֶשׁ:

Jeremiah 51:27 עָלֶיהָ can be translated *concerning her(it)*. In the preceding verse of Jeremiah 51, the *it* is identified as *the land*.

5. קַדְּשׁוּ עָלֶיהָ גּוֹיִם הַשְׁמִיעוּ עָלֶיהָ

186

6. נְטֵה אֶת־מַטְּךָ וְהַךְ אֶת־עֲפַר הָאָרֶץ

Exodus 8:12 מַטֶּה has lost its *heh* before the suffix. The second imperative only shows one root letter (29.2a).

7. וְאָמַרְתִּי אֲלֵיכֶם הַכּוּ אֶת־אַמְנוֹן וַהֲמִתֶּם אֹתוֹ אַל־תִּירָאוּ

2 Samuel 13:28

8. וַיֹּאמֶר קַח הַחִצִּים וַיִּקָּח וַיֹּאמֶר לְמֶלֶךְ־יִשְׂרָאֵל הַךְ־אַרְצָה וַיַּךְ

2 Kings 13:18 חֵץ means *arrow*.

9. וַיֹּאמְרוּ לוֹ שָׂרֵי פְלִשְׁתִּים הָשֵׁב אֶת־הָאִישׁ וְיָשֹׁב אֶל־מְקוֹמוֹ אֲשֶׁר הִפְקַדְתּוֹ שָׁם וְלֹא־יֵרֵד עִמָּנוּ

1 Samuel 29:4 Notice in הִפְקַדְתּוֹ how the addition of the suffix has caused the affixed subject pronoun to lose its customary *qamets*.

10. וַיֹּאמֶר מֹשֶׁה אֶל־יְהוָה רְאֵה אַתָּה אֹמֵר אֵלַי הַעַל אֶת־הָעָם הַזֶּה וְאַתָּה לֹא הוֹדַעְתַּנִי אֵת אֲשֶׁר־תִּשְׁלַח עִמִּי

Exodus 33:12 Do not be tripped up by עִמִּי as opposed to עַמִּי

11. הַקְרֵב אֶת־מַטֵּה לֵוִי וְהַעֲמַדְתָּ אֹתוֹ לִפְנֵי אַהֲרֹן הַכֹּהֵן

Numbers 3:6

12. קַח אֶת־הַמַּטֶּה אַתָּה וְאַהֲרֹן אָחִיךָ וְדִבַּרְתֶּם אֶל־הַסֶּלַע לְעֵינֵיהֶם וְנָתַן מֵימָיו וְהוֹצֵאתָ לָהֶם מַיִם

Numbers 20:8 סֶלַע means *boulder*.

13. כָּל־אֵלֶּה אַנְשֵׁי מִלְחָמָה בָּאוּ חֶבְרוֹנָה לְהַמְלִיךְ אֶת־דָּוִיד עַל־כָּל־יִשְׂרָאֵל

1 Chronicles 12:39

14. וַיְהִי בְּהַעֲלוֹת יְהוָה אֶת־אֵלִיָּהוּ בַּסְעָרָה הַשָּׁמָיִם וַיֵּלֶךְ אֵלִיָּהוּ וֶאֱלִישָׁע מִן־הַגִּלְגָּל׃

2 Kings 2:1 סְעָרָה means *whirlwind*.

15. וַיֹּאמֶר הַאֱלֹהִים אָנִי לְהָמִית וּלְהַחֲיוֹת

2 Kings 5:7

16. וַיָּמָת הַיֶּלֶד וַיִּרְאוּ עַבְדֵי דָוִד לְהַגִּיד לוֹ כִּי־מֵת הַיֶּלֶד כִּי אָמְרוּ הִנֵּה בִּהְיוֹת הַיֶּלֶד חַי דִּבַּרְנוּ אֵלָיו וְלֹא־שָׁמַע בְּקוֹלֵנוּ

2 Samuel 12:18 יֶלֶד means *boy*.

Exodus 6:13	וַיְדַבֵּר יְהוָה אֶל־מֹשֶׁה וְאֶל־אַהֲרֹן לְהוֹצִיא אֶת־בְּנֵי־יִשְׂרָאֵל מֵאֶרֶץ מִצְרָיִם	17.
Joshua 23:13	תֵּדְעוּ כִּי לֹא יוֹסִיף יְהוָה אֱלֹהֵיכֶם לְהוֹרִישׁ אֶת־הַגּוֹיִם הָאֵלֶּה מִלִּפְנֵיכֶם	18.
Numbers 8:19	וָאֶתְּנָה אֶת־הַלְוִיִּם לַעֲבֹד אֶת־עֲבֹדַת בְּנֵי־יִשְׂרָאֵל בְּאֹהֶל מוֹעֵד	19.

Genesis 17:22 וַיְכַל
is the Piel wayyiqtol of
כלה It has the
customary *shewa* under the
prefixed pronoun and the
missing third *heh*. The
lamed is prone to losing its
dagesh.

	וַיְכַל לְדַבֵּר אִתּוֹ	20.
Genesis 18:33	וַיֵּלֶךְ יְהוָה כַּאֲשֶׁר כִּלָּה לְדַבֵּר אֶל־אַבְרָהָם	21.
Genesis 43:2 שֶׁבֶר means *wheat*.	וַיְהִי כַּאֲשֶׁר כִּלּוּ לֶאֱכֹל אֶת־הַשֶּׁבֶר אֲשֶׁר הֵבִיאוּ מִמִּצְרָיִם	22.
Deuteronomy 31:24	וַיְהִי כְּכַלּוֹת מֹשֶׁה לִכְתֹּב אֶת־דִּבְרֵי הַתּוֹרָה־הַזֹּאת	23.

32.6d. Read the introductory material to Reading 4 and Deuteronomy 6:1-3.

Lesson 33

וְקִדַּשְׁתָּ אֹתוֹ וְהָיָה הַמִּזְבֵּחַ קֹדֶשׁ קָדָשִׁים כָּל־הַנֹּגֵעַ בַּמִּזְבֵּחַ יִקְדָּשׁ

Exodus 29:37

Goal:

• Identify and read the change in meaning from Qal stative roots to Piel transitive roots.

What we already know

33.1. Fill out the verb analysis chart for וְקִדַּשְׁתָּ :

root	stem	form	person, gender, number	function	basic root meaning

Qal stative versus Piel transitive

33.2a. In the Qal stem קדשׁ means *be holy*. In the Piel stem it means *cause to be holy* or simply *sanctify*.

Translate וְקִדַּשְׁתָּ אֹתוֹ : _____

(If you have trouble with אֹתוֹ see 19.4b, and then memorize the chart there.)

33.2b. To elucidate the main point of this lesson, let us now jump ahead to the last clause of our lesson verse. Fill out the verb analysis chart for יִקְדָּשׁ :

root	stem	form	person, gender, number	function	basic root meaning

The key to figuring out the stem is to decide what kind of *dagesh* is in the *dalet*. Also be careful about identifying the function. A quick look at the rest of the verse will identify a weqatal mainline. So we expect a yiqtol to either be in a dependent clause or have an "X" in front of it. Which is the case in our

lesson verse? What is the "X"? _____

Translate כָּל־הַנֹּגֵעַ בַּמִּזְבֵּחַ יִקְדָּשׁ : _____

(The root נגע means *touch*, and the meaning of קדשׁ in the Qal stem is noted above in 33.2a.)

189

33.2c. Our lesson verse's uses of one root in two stems teaches a lesson.

STATIVE MEANING

There is a group of roots which have stative rather than active meanings in the Qal stem. This group of roots often have *sere* [ּ] or *holem* [ ] after the second root letter in the Qal qatal as in כָּבֵד meaning *he (it) is heavy* or קָטֹן meaning *he (it) is small.* Some of the other Qal stative roots are the second class 1ˢᵗ *yod* roots you learned about in Lesson 21. The stative Qals are easy to identify in your vocabulary list because their English glosses use the word *be* as in כבד *be heavy* or מלא *be full.* It just so happens that the root קדשׁ in the Qal qatal does *not* have either *sere* or *holem* after the second root letter, but it is a stative Qal. The special nikkud of the stative Qal qatal cannot be considered a hard and fast rule.

33.2d. The translation of stative roots in the Qal qatal and weqatal do not use the customary *er*-word or *ing*-word that you have been taught for translation. If you recall, the purpose of these idiosyncratic translation methods is to try to express that the qatal and weqatal give an attribute, almost adjectivally, to the subject of the verb. By being stative, the Qal stative roots describe the subject of the verb adjectivally as a function of the root itself rather than the verb form. Notice how all the following Hebrew words describe their subjects adjectivally:

מָלֵא   *he is (was) filled*

וּמָלְאוּ   *and they will be (were) filled*

יִמְלְאוּ   *they will be filled*

וַיִּמְלְאוּ   *and they were filled*

Also notice how the distinct meanings of the qatal and weqatal versus the yiqtol and wayyiqtol that we are used to with Qal active roots is blurred with Qal stative roots.

33.2e. Here are the roots that are in the vocabulary list for this course and their Qal stative senses:

ROOTS that are STATIVE in the QAL:

ירא	*be afraid*	חזק	*be strong, firm*
מלא	*be full*	כלא	*be complete, finished*
רום	*be high, exalted*	יכל	*be able*
אבד	*be lost*	קדשׁ	*be holy*
טמא	*be unclean*	כבד	*be heavy, honored*
בושׁ	*be ashamed*	שלם	*be complete, sound*
יטב	*be well, pleasing*		

33.2f. The Piel stem very often changes the meaning of these stative Qal roots into active verbs that are transitive.

190

DEFINITION: **Transitive verbs are those which take direct objects to complete their sense.**

An English example of a transitive verb is *kill*. One generally does not refer just to *killing*, but *killing something*. Intransitive verbs, on the other hand, cannot take direct objects. An English example is *die*. One does not *die something* (unless, of course, one spells it *dye*). As you can probably readily imagine, there are many verbs which can be transitive or intransitive. An English example is *perform*. Transitively one can perform a dance, or intransitively, one can simply perform as in *He performed well*. Stative verbs, including all the Hebrew examples in the list above, are intransitive. For many of these same Hebrew roots the Piel is transitive as you can see in the list below.

PIEL'S TRANSITIVE SENSE:

מלא	*fill*	חזק	*strengthen*
רום	*exalt*	אבד	*destroy*
קדש	*sanctify*	טמא	*defile*
כבד	*honor*	בוש	*delay (in shame)*
שלם	*requite, restore*		

33.2g. Just as with English, some Hebrew roots can be either transitive or intransitive in one stem. For instance, the root ירא in the Qal stem means statively and intransitively *be afraid* and transitively *fear (something)*. For instance:

Intransitive:

וָאִירָא כִּי־עֵירֹם אָנֹכִי   Genesis 3:10

And I was afraid because I was naked

Transitive:

כִּי יָרֵאתִי אֶת־הָעָם   1 Samuel 15:24

...because I have feared the people

33.2h. When a root is made transitive by virtue of its being in the Piel stem, the qatal in an independent clause and weqatal will be translated with the customary *-er* word or *-ing* word plus possessive pronoun. In other words, the distinction qatal and weqatal versus yiqtol and wayyiqtol once again becomes apparent. Compare the following verbs in the Piel stem of מלא with their Qal counterparts in 33.2d.

מִלֵּא	*he is (was) a filler of*
וּמִלְאוּ	*and they will be fillers of*
יְמַלְּאוּ	*they (will) fill*
וַיְמַלְּאוּ	*and they filled*

191

Leitwort

33.3a. Let us now return to the middle clause of our lesson verse that we earlier skipped. Fill out the verb analysis chart for וְהָיָה :

root	stem	form	person, gender, number	function	basic root meaning

You must decide what to do with הַמִּזְבֵּחַ   Is the verse reading *And it will be the altar...* or *And the altar will be...(something)*? If you see a "something" it will help you decide.

33.3b. What does קֹדֶשׁ mean? _____ קָדָשִׁים is the plural form. Is the construct chain definite or not? _____ It is therefore to be distinguished from הַקֳּדָשִׁים קֹדֶשׁ which refers to the inner sanctuary of the Tabernacle (מִקְדָּשׁ) and the Temple. Translate וְהָיָה הַמִּזְבֵּחַ קֹדֶשׁ קָדָשִׁים:

_____

Translate the entire lesson verse: _____

_____

33.3c. In our lesson verse you can see the fondness of the ancient Hebrew writer for repeating a key root in a number of different stems or other variations in order to explore the root's range of meanings and point toward a theme. Some Hebraists refer to the key words which are repeated throughout a discourse with the German term *Leitwort*.[1] Often times, this type of Hebrew root-motif is not evident in English translations, so that one of the great benefits of reading the Hebrew Bible in Hebrew is that it enhances the ability to see this word play.

---

[1] Alter, *The Art of Biblical Narrative*(NY: Basic Books, 1981), 93.

Assignments

33.4a. Translate:

וְהַבַּיִת מָלֵא	1.	אָבְדוּ	9.	כִּי־כָלָה	17.
כִּי־מָלְאָה	2.	אָבַדְתָּ	10.	כִּי־כָלְתָה	18.
לֹא יִמָּלְאוּ	3.	וַיֹּאבְדוּ	11.	אֲשֶׁר כָּלוּ	19.
וּמָלֵאתָ	4.	אִבַּדְתִּי	12.	וְעַד־כַּלֹּתוֹ	20.
מָלֵא	5.	וּלְאַבֵּד	13.	וָאֲכַלֶּה	21.
כֵּן יִמָּלְאוּ	6.	וַתְּאַבֵּד	14.	וָאֲכַלֵּם	22.
וַתִּמָּלֵא	7.	וַיְאַבְּדוּם	15.	וַיְכַלּוּ	23.
וַיְמַלֵּא	8.	וַיְאַבְּדֵם	16.	כַּאֲשֶׁר כִּלָּה	24.

33.4b. Translate:

Genesis 41:56
רָעָב means *famine*.

וַיֶּחֱזַק הָרָעָב בְּאֶרֶץ מִצְרָיִם 1.

Genesis 41:57

כִּי־חָזַק הָרָעָב בְּכָל־הָאָרֶץ 2.

Genesis 47:20

כִּי־חָזַק עֲלֵהֶם הָרָעָב 3.

Exodus 4:21

וַאֲנִי אֲחַזֵּק אֶת־לִבּוֹ 4.

Exodus 9:12

וַיְחַזֵּק יְהוָה אֶת־לֵב פַּרְעֹה 5.

Exodus 14:4

וְחִזַּקְתִּי אֶת־לֵב־פַּרְעֹה 6.

Genesis 20:8

וַיִּירְאוּ הָאֲנָשִׁים מְאֹד 7.

Genesis 28:17 נוֹרָא is
the Niphal adjective made
from ירא meaning
fearful.

וַיִּירָא וַיֹּאמַר מַה־נּוֹרָא הַמָּקוֹם הַזֶּה 8.

Exodus 14:31

וַיַּרְא יִשְׂרָאֵל אֶת־הַיָּד הַגְּדֹלָה אֲשֶׁר עָשָׂה יְהוָה 9.
בְּמִצְרַיִם וַיִּירְאוּ הָעָם אֶת־יְהוָה

Joshua 4:14

וַיִּרְאוּ אֹתוֹ כַּאֲשֶׁר יָרְאוּ אֶת־מֹשֶׁה כָּל־יְמֵי חַיָּיו 10.

Deuteronomy 34:9
חָכְמָה means *wisdom*.

וִיהוֹשֻׁעַ בִּן־נוּן מָלֵא רוּחַ חָכְמָה 11.

Genesis 25:24

וַיִּמְלְאוּ יָמֶיהָ לָלֶדֶת 12.

193

<table>
<tr><td>Genesis 1:28 פרה is a stative Qal that means *be fruitful*.</td><td align="right">וַיְבָרֶךְ אֹתָם אֱלֹהִים וַיֹּאמֶר לָהֶם אֱלֹהִים פְּרוּ וּמִלְאוּ אֶת־הָאָרֶץ</td><td>13.</td></tr>
<tr><td>Numbers 3:3 לְכַהֵן is a Piel infinitive, and you can probably guess what it means if you know the corresponding noun.</td><td align="right">אֵלֶּה שְׁמוֹת בְּנֵי אַהֲרֹן הַכֹּהֲנִים אֲשֶׁר־מִלֵּא יָדָם לְכַהֵן:</td><td>14.</td></tr>
<tr><td>Exodus 31:3 See 11 above for בְּחָכְמָה</td><td align="right">וָאֲמַלֵּא אֹתוֹ רוּחַ אֱלֹהִים בְּחָכְמָה</td><td>15.</td></tr>
<tr><td>Exodus 23:26 מִסְפַּר means *number*.</td><td align="right">אֶת־מִסְפַּר יָמֶיךָ אֲמַלֵּא</td><td>16.</td></tr>
</table>

33.4c. Read Deuteronomy 6:4-9.

Lesson 34

נָתוֹן תִּתֵּן לוֹ וְלֹא־יֵרַע לְבָבְךָ בְּתִתְּךָ לוֹ

Deuteronomy 15:10

Goals:

- Identify and read the infinitive absolute.
- Identify and read the temporal adverb made with the infinitive construct.

What we already know

Skip the first word of our lesson verse, and translate the clause   תִּתֵּן לוֹ   _____

_____

Infinitive absolute

34.2a. When you examine the first two words of our lesson verse   נָתוֹן תִּתֵּן   you can see that we have two forms of one root. This is a construction that we have met before in our readings, but have never examined in the regular lesson material. The second verb should look familiar. The first one is called an **infinitive absolute**.

Even though all the verbs in the lesson verse are in the Qal stem and this module has been a comparison of the Hiphil and Piel stems, we will now depart from this theme and look at a couple of special uses of the infinitive in this lesson. There is no really better spot within the outline of this book to stick an important lesson on the infinitive absolute.

34.2b. When we think of the infinitive absolute, we must compare it with the infinitive construct which we first studied in Lesson 16.4a. The infinitive construct's name reminds us that a Hebrew writer could build with it, by adding to it prepositions and pronominal suffixes. Unlike the infinitive construct, the absolute almost always stands without any appendages. (By the way, remember that infinitive constructs *may* also appear without any preposition or suffix.) Like the infinitive construct, the absolute does not have separate conjugations for person, gender, or number.

> RULE: **The infinitive absolute appears before a regularly conjugated yiqtol or qatal verb form and intensifies its partner verb. Literally, the infinitive absolute is like an English gerund meaning _a   (root meaning) -ing_. However, when translating into English, we usually translate the yiqtol or qatal normally and add an English _surely_ or _indeed_ to capture the doubly-intense meaning of the phrase.**

Translation of   נָתוֹן תִּתֵּן   : Literally: *A giving you will give*
                                        Or: *You will surely give...*

Fill out the verb analysis charts for תִּתֵּן and נָתוֹן :

root	stem	form	person, gender, number	function	basic root meaning

For the function of תִּתֵּן write Hortatory mainline. The verb is a somewhat unusual 2nd person jussive. How do we know it's a mainline verb form? You really cannot unless you would be given the greater context of the verse.

root	stem	form	person, gender, number	function	basic root meaning
		infinitive absolute		intensification	

34.2c. Formally, or with respect to its nikkud, the infinitive absolute looks only minimally different from the infinitive construct. Here are some examples:

INFINITVE CONSTRUCTS VS. ABSOLUTES:

	Qal Strong root	Hiphil Strong root	Qal 1st yod	Hiphil 1st yod	Qal 1st nun	Hiphil 1st nun	Qal Hollow	Hiphil Hollow
Infin. Const.	*פְּקֹד	הַפְקִיד	שֶׁבֶת	*הוֹשִׁיב	נְפֹל	*הַגִּיד	*קוּם	הָקִים
Infin. Absol.	פָּקֹד	*הַפְקֵד	יָשֹׁב	*הוֹשֵׁב	נָפֹל	*הַגֵּד	קוֹם	הָקֵם

* These forms are ambiguous. הוֹשִׁיב is identical to the Hiphil qatal 3rd m. s., and all the other ambiguous forms are exactly like the m. s. imperative forms. The good news is that context will readily clear up the ambiguity.

Infinitive absolutes seem painfully like their infinitive construct counter-parts. Once again, context is a big help for identifying most infinitive absolutes. Most of them are in the type of construction that is in our lesson verse wherein the root is repeated by a regularly conjugated yiqtol or qatal.

196

34.2d. Infinitive absolutes are sometimes used in a way that is not exhibited in our lesson verse.

RULE: **An infinitive absolute may substitute for an imperative.**

Here are examples:

וַיֹּאמֶר מֹשֶׁה אֶל־הָעָם זָכוֹר אֶת־הַיּוֹם הַזֶּה   Exodus 13:3
And Moses said to the people, "Remember this day..."

וַיְצַו מֹשֶׁה אֶת־הָעָם לֵאמֹר שָׁמֹר אֶת־כָּל־הַמִּצְוָה   Deuteronomy 27:1
And Moses commanded the people saying, "Keep every commandment..."

A rebellious root

34.3. A rebellious root is one which does not conjugate according to normal patterns. Such is the case with the verb in the second clause of our lesson sentence, וְלֹא־יֵרַע לְבָבְךָ   Judging by the *sere* under the *yod* what would we expect is the root of this yiqtol verb form?_____ Rather the root is disputed, being either רעע or רעה In either case, it is a Qal yiqtol meaning *He (it) will grieve* or *May he (it) grieve*. It is included in the lesson to expose you to a rebellious root, and for the context it provides for the rest of the verse.

Translate וְלֹא־ יֵרַע לְבָבְךָ :_____

Infinitive construct preceded by בְּ

34.4a. The last two words of our lesson verse, בְּתִתְּךָ לוֹ contain a Qal infinitive construct with a prefixed preposition and a pronominal suffix. If you have any trouble discerning the root, look back at Lesson 16 , and when you are done with this lesson, go back and memorize the infinitive forms there before you proceed.

We may translate the phrase literally, *in your giving to him.* If you care to leave the translation like this, it is fine, but you need to become aware of a special use of the preposition בְּ when it is used with an infinitive in any stem.

RULE: **An infinitive construct used with the preposition בְּ or כְּ functions as a** *temporal adverb* **that may be translated using the English** *when...*[1]

Translation: *When you give to him.*

34.4b. This *temporal adverb* use of an infinitive construct with the preposition בְּ or כְּ is often seen near the beginning of a narrative, and often with the transition marker וַיְהִי to set a time reference for the narrative. Here are a few examples:

---

[1] Late explanations on the use of this construction in narrative are found in Niccacci(1990), §§ 30, 36, 112, 127; Isaksson, "'Abberant' Usages of Introductory *wehaya* in the Light of Text Linguistics," *Proceedings of IOSOT*(ed. Lang, forthcoming); and van der Merwe(1997).

בְּלֶדֶת־הָגָר אֶת־יִשְׁמָעֵאל לְאַבְרָם Genesis 16:16
When Hagar bore Ishmael for Abraham

וְרִבְקָה שֹׁמַעַת בְּדַבֵּר יִצְחָק אֶל־עֵשָׂו Genesis 27:5
And Rebekah was listening when Isaac was speaking to Esau

וַיְהִי בְּשַׁלַּח פַּרְעֹה אֶת־הָעָם Exodus 13:17
And it happened when Pharaoh let the people go

כִּשְׁמֹעַ עֵשָׂו אֶת־דִּבְרֵי אָבִיו Genesis 27:34
When Esau heard the words of his father

וַיְהִי כֶּאֱמֹר יְהוֹשֻׁעַ אֶל־הָעָם Joshua 6:8
And it happened when Joshua spoke to the people

Assignments

34.5a.   Translate:

17.	כְּכַלֹּתוֹ לְדַבֵּר	9.	הַרְבָּה אַרְבֶּה	1.	מוֹת יָמוּת
18.	כְּכַלּוֹת מֹשֶׁה לִכְתֹּב	10.	הֵאָסֹף יֵאָסֵף	2.	בְּמֹתָם
19.	כְּכַלּוֹת יִשְׂרָאֵל לַהֲרֹג	11.	אָסֹף אֶאֱסֹף	3.	בַּהֲרֹג דָּוִד
20.	בְּכַלּוֹתִי	12.	בְּאָסְפְּךָ	4.	בְּהִגָּלוֹת יְהוָה
21.	וּבְקָרְבָתָם	13.	בְּאָסְפְּכֶם	5.	לִשְׁאוֹל
22.	בְּהַקְרִיבָם	14.	בְּעָזְבָם אֶת־יְהוָה	6.	שָׁאוּל שָׁאַל־הָאִישׁ
23.	בְּהַקְרִיבְכֶם	15.	בַּעֲזָבְכֶם אֶת־מִצְוֹת יְהוָה	7.	כִּשְׂמֹחַ כָּל־הָאָרֶץ
24.	בִּקְרֹב־אִישׁ	16.	עָזֹב תַּעֲזֹב	8.	בִּזְבְּחוֹ אֶת־הַזְּבָחִים

34.5b.   Translate:

Genesis 37:8

1. וַיֹּאמְרוּ לוֹ אֶחָיו הֲמָלֹךְ תִּמְלֹךְ עָלֵינוּ

Genesis 50:25

2. פָּקֹד יִפְקֹד אֱלֹהִים אֶתְכֶם

Deuteronomy 15:5 To
help you analyze מְצַוְּךָ
notice the *mem* and *dagesh
forte* in the *vav*(31.3b).

3. אִם־שָׁמוֹעַ תִּשְׁמַע בְּקוֹל יְהוָה אֱלֹהֶיךָ לִשְׁמֹר לַעֲשׂוֹת
אֶת־כָּל־הַמִּצְוָה הַזֹּאת אֲשֶׁר אָנֹכִי מְצַוְּךָ הַיּוֹם:

Deuteronomy 24:9 מִרְיָם
is a name.

4. זָכוֹר אֵת אֲשֶׁר־עָשָׂה יְהוָה אֱלֹהֶיךָ לְמִרְיָם בַּדֶּרֶךְ
בְּצֵאתְכֶם מִמִּצְרָיִם:

Genesis 35:18

5. וַיְהִי בְּצֵאת נַפְשָׁהּ כִּי מֵתָה וַתִּקְרָא שְׁמוֹ בֶּן־אוֹנִי

Exodus 16:8 עֶרֶב means *evening*, and בָּשָׂר means *flesh*.

6. וַיֹּאמֶר מֹשֶׁה בְּתֵת יְהוָה לָכֶם בָּעֶרֶב בָּשָׂר לֶאֱכֹל

Exodus 34:29

7. וַיְהִי בְּרֶדֶת מֹשֶׁה מֵהַר סִינַי

Numbers 7:89 The כַּפֹּרֶת is traditionally called the *Mercy Seat*, although it literally means *covering, atonement*. It refers to the lid which was on top of the ark of the covenant.

8. וּבְבֹא מֹשֶׁה אֶל־אֹהֶל מוֹעֵד לְדַבֵּר אִתּוֹ וַיִּשְׁמַע אֶת־הַקּוֹל מִדַּבֵּר אֵלָיו מֵעַל הַכַּפֹּרֶת

Deuteronomy 9:23

9. וּבִשְׁלֹחַ יְהוָה אֶתְכֶם מִקָּדֵשׁ בַּרְנֵעַ לֵאמֹר עֲלוּ וּרְשׁוּ אֶת־הָאָרֶץ אֲשֶׁר נָתַתִּי לָכֶם וְלֹא שְׁמַעְתֶּם בְּקֹלוֹ:

Genesis 4:8 This is an unusual case of the verb וַיֹּאמֶר does not mark the beginning of quoted speech. The הוּ-- ending on וַיַּהַרְגֵהוּ is yet another pronominal suffix meaning *him*.

10. וַיֹּאמֶר קַיִן אֶל־הֶבֶל אָחִיו וַיְהִי בִּהְיוֹתָם בַּשָּׂדֶה וַיָּקָם קַיִן אֶל־הֶבֶל אָחִיו וַיַּהַרְגֵהוּ:

Genesis 2:16 גָּן means *garden*.

11. וַיְצַו יְהוָה אֱלֹהִים עַל־הָאָדָם לֵאמֹר מִכֹּל עֵץ־הַגָּן אָכֹל תֹּאכֵל:

Genesis 3:4 נָחָשׁ means *serpent*. The *nun* on the end of תְּמֻתוּן is not uncommon, but it is not understood either. It may lend emphasis to the word or be for pure sound value.

12. וַיֹּאמֶר הַנָּחָשׁ אֶל־הָאִשָּׁה לֹא־מוֹת תְּמֻתוּן:

Genesis 8:3 Perhaps the infinitive absolute can be translated *continually* although it literally means *a going*.

13. וַיָּשֻׁבוּ הַמַּיִם מֵעַל הָאָרֶץ הָלוֹךְ

14. וַיְשַׁלַּח אֶת־הָעֹרֵב וַיֵּצֵא יָצוֹא וָשׁוֹב

Genesis 8:7 עֹרֵב means *a raven*. The two infinitive absolutes mean *a going out and a returning*.

15. כֹּל אֲשֶׁר־יְדַבֵּר בֹּא יָבוֹא

1 Samuel 9:6

16. וַיֹּאמֶר יָדֹעַ יָדַע אָבִיךָ כִּי־מָצָאתִי חֵן בְּעֵינֶיךָ

1 Samuel 20:3

17. וַיֹּאמֶר הַמֶּלֶךְ מוֹת תָּמוּת אֲחִימֶלֶךְ אַתָּה וְכָל־בֵּית אָבִיךָ:

1 Samuel 22:16   This is King Saul talking to Abimelech.

18. וַיֹּאמֶר דָּוִד יְהוָה אֱלֹהֵי יִשְׂרָאֵל שָׁמֹעַ שָׁמַע עַבְדְּךָ כִּי־מְבַקֵּשׁ שָׁאוּל לָבוֹא אֶל־קְעִילָה

1 Samuel 23:10

19. וַיֹּאמְרוּ רָאוֹ רָאִינוּ כִּי־הָיָה יְהוָה עִמָּךְ

Genesis 26:28

20. וַיֹּאמֶר עָלֹה נַעֲלֶה וְיָרַשְׁנוּ אֹתָהּ

Numbers 13:30

34.5c. Read Deuteronomy 6:10-13.

MODULE FOUR—SPECIAL USES OF WEQATAL

OVERVIEW: We have so far learned that the weqatal verb form is the mainline of the Predictive, Instructional, and Mitigated Hortatory Discourses. In so doing, you may have concluded that weqatal means future tense; however, in this module you will learn that weqatal can be used to refer to past time as well. You will learn that in **Procedural Discourse**, a genre that is usually embedded in Historical Narrative, the weqatal is used as the mainline verb form to tell how something was repeatedly done in the past. In this module you will also learn of another weqatal that refers to the past, the **isolated weqatal within a wayyiqtol string** which is used by the Biblical Hebrew writer to·mark a climactic or pivotal event.[1]

---

[1] The functions of the weqatal in this module are based on Longacre(1994); see also Isaksson(forthcoming).

Lesson 35

וַיְהִי הַיּוֹם וַיִּזְבַּח אֶלְקָנָה וְנָתַן לִפְנִנָּה אִשְׁתּוֹ וּלְכָל־בָּנֶיהָ וּבְנוֹתֶיהָ מָנוֹת:

1 Samuel 1:4

Goal:
- Identify and read the weqatal of Procedural Discourse.

What we already know

35.1a. Fill out the verb analysis chart for וַיְהִי :

root	stem	form	person, gender, number	function	basic root meaning

The word הַיּוֹם in the first clause, as the word יוֹם does throughout the first chapter of 1 Samuel, means *time* rather than the customary *today*.

Translation of וַיְהִי הַיּוֹם : _____

35.1b. Translate וַיִּזְבַּח אֶלְקָנָה : _____
What genre do the first two verb forms of our lesson verse indicate we are reading?

_____

Procedural Discourse

35.2a. There is nothing difficult about determining the verb form of וְנָתַן However, figuring out how to express it in English is another matter. You have already learned that the weqatal verb form is the mainline form in Predictive, Instructional, and Mitigated Hortatory Discourses. In all three of these

+projection genres, how would we translate the weqatal וְנָתַן ? _____

However, this translation does not make sense:

*And the time came (when) Elkanah sacrificed, **and he will be a giver***

One of the problems here is that we have not switched from Historical Narrative to Direct Speech. If you recall, Predictive, Instructional, and Hortatory (mitigated or not) Discourses are exclusively Direct Speech Discourses (see 13.2a and 19.2c).

35.2b.

> **RULE: A series of weqatals within a Historical Narrative represent the mainline of an embedded Procedural Discourse that tells how something was done repeatedly in the past. Translate with the customary *er-word* for the weqatal, but use the English word *would* instead of *will* as we use in the Direct Speech genres.**

Fill out the verb analysis chart for וְנָתַן :

root	stem	form	person, gender, number	function	basic root meaning

Translation: *And he would be a giver*

Note: The rule above speaks of a *series* of weqatals, and our lesson sentence's one weqatal can hardly be a series. The next weqatal in the series is not until 1 Samuel 1:6, so you are only seeing the first weqatal in the series in this lesson.

A long indirect object

35.3a. Which of these two English sentences do you think utilizes better writing style?

    a. *Elkanah gave to Pennina his wife and to her sons and to her daughters a portion.*
    b. *Elkanah gave a portion to Pennina his wife and to her sons and to her daughters.*

Probably neither one presents a problem for you because you are a very practiced reader of English. However, the large interruption in *a* between the verb *gave* and what was given, *a portion*, may seem unhandy. Now if you add to the situation the kind of halting reading ability that you have in Hebrew, the word order in *a* can cause more than a moment of hesitation. The point is, though you may prefer one, both are acceptable English. Both word orders are also found in Biblical Hebrew.

Translate וְנָתַן לִפְנִנָּה אִשְׁתּוֹ וּלְכָל־בָּנֶּיהָ וּבְנוֹתֶיהָ מָנוֹת (מָנָה means *portion*):

_____

35.3b. Let us compare a variety of forms using the nouns בֵּן and בַּת to refresh and elaborate upon what you learned in Lesson 18.4.

singular absolute	plural absolute	singular construct	plural construct	singular with 3rd f. s. suffix ה--	plural with 3rd f. s. suffix הָ--
בֵּן	בָּנִים	בֶּן	בְּנֵי	בְּנָהּ	בָּנֶּיהָ
בַּת	בָּנוֹת	בַּת	בְּנוֹת	בִּתָּהּ	בְּנוֹתֶיהָ

Notes:

1. The plural absolute of בַּת is not בַּתוֹת The feminine noun בַּת is said to be irregular.
2. The construct forms, both alone and with a suffix, have shortened vowels in the noun; however, to what the vowel shortens is inconsistent. Just be thankful you are learning to read Biblical Hebrew, not compose it.
3. You can distinguish between the singular with a suffix and the plural with a suffix by the *yod* that precedes the suffix on the plural form.
4. Notice the alternate nikkud with the 3rd f. s. pronominal suffix.

Assignments

35.4a. Memorize vocabulary words 271-310 for Lessons 35-38.

35.4b. Translate:

17. בִּתְּךָ	9. וְלְבָנֵינוּ	1. בְּנוֹ
18. בְּנֹתַי	10. בְּנֵנוּ	2. וּבָנֶיךָ
19. וְלִבְנֹתַי	11. בֵּיתוֹ	3. בָּנָיו
20. בִּתִּי	12. בִּתּוֹ	4. וְאֶת־בְּנָהּ
21. בֵּיתִי	13. בָּתֵּיכֶם	5. בִּנְךָ
22. וּמִבָּתֶּיךָ	14. בָּתֵּינוּ	6. בְּנִי
23. בֵּיתָהּ	15. בְּנֹתָיו	7. לִבְנִי
24. בָּתֶּהָ	16. וּבְנֹתֶיךָ	8. לְבָנַי

35.4c. Translate these clauses which have been borrowed from Exodus 33:7-12

The verb is a Hitpael wayyiqtol that means *And they stripped themselves.* עֲדִי means *ornament.* The verse is given to show you the wayyiqtol context of the following clauses.

1. וַיִּתְנַצְּלוּ בְנֵי־יִשְׂרָאֵל אֶת־עֶדְיָם

The yiqtol in a past time context also represents repeated action in the past.

2. וּמֹשֶׁה יִקַּח אֶת־הָאֹהֶל

3. וְנָטָה־לוֹ מִחוּץ לַמַּחֲנֶה

4. וְקָרָא לוֹ אֹהֶל מוֹעֵד

The verb is a Niphal qatal of נצב and means *they will be standers of them-selves.*

5. וְהָיָה כְּצֵאת מֹשֶׁה אֶל־הָאֹהֶל

6. וְנִצְּבוּ אִישׁ פֶּתַח אָהֳלוֹ

עַמּוּד הֶעָנָן means *the pillar of the cloud.*

7. וְרָאָה כָל־הָעָם אֶת־עַמּוּד הֶעָנָן עֹמֵד פֶּתַח הָאֹהֶל

8. וְקָ֥ם כָּל־הָעָ֖ם

רֵעַ means *friend, com-panion*.

9. וְדִבֶּ֨ר יְהוָ֤ה אֶל־מֹשֶׁה֙ פָּנִ֣ים אֶל־פָּנִ֔ים
    כַּאֲשֶׁ֛ר יְדַבֵּ֥ר אִ֖ישׁ אֶל־רֵעֵ֑הוּ

10. וְשָׁ֖ב אֶל־הַֽמַּחֲנֶ֑ה

We take this wayyiqtol as referring to a particular occasion when Moses was doing his regular practice as described above. The wayyiqtol brings us back to the mainline of the narrative.

11. וַיֹּ֥אמֶר מֹשֶׁ֖ה אֶל־יְהוָֽה

35.4d. Read Deuteronomy 6:14-19.

205

Lesson 36

וּמְעִיל קָטֹן תַּעֲשֶׂה־לּוֹ אִמּוֹ וְהַעַלְתָה לוֹ מִיָּמִים יָמִימָה

1 Samuel 2:19

Goal:

- Identify and read the X-yiqtol construction in Procedural Discourse.
- Identify and read עלה in the Qal and Hiphil qatal and yiqtol.
- Identify and read Discourse Switch Cues (DSCs).

X-Yiqtol and Procedural Discourse

36.1a. Although there is not a single wayyiqtol in our lesson verse, the context of this verse is indeed Historical Narrative. There is no shortage of wayyiqtols either before or after the verse. The story being recounted is the birth and childhood of Samuel the prophet in which his mother Hannah and father Elkanah are key players.

36.1b. וּמְעִיל קָטֹן means *And a small cloak*. Is the *vav* a conjunctive *vav* or a *vav*-consecutive?

_____(17.2) You should recognize an X-yiqtol construction.

36.1c. What is the function of an X-yiqtol in the +projection genres we have learned in which weqatal is

the mainline?_____ (14.3c)   As we might expect in Procedural Discourse wherein the mainline is also weqatal, the X-yiqtol construction performs the same *function* as it does in the +projection genres. However, in the +projection genres, the yiqtol describes an event in the future, perhaps a singular event, an event that may be repeated, or the beginning of a process. In Procedural Discourse's past context, the meaning of the yiqtol is more specific.

> RULE: A yiqtol verb form, when used in a main clause rather than a dependent clause in Procedural Discourse, refers to repeated or habitual action in the past. Translate using the English word *would*.

Fill out the verb analysis chart for תַּעֲשֶׂה :

root	stem	form	person, gender, number	function	basic root meaning
		X-yiqtol		Proc. Discourse topicalization	

Translation of וּמְעִיל קָטֹן תַּעֲשֶׂה : *And it was a small cloak that she would make*

206

Conjugating עלה in Qal and Hiphil

36.2. Keeping in mind that the larger context of our lesson verse is Historical Narrative, fill out the verb analysis chart for וְהַעֲלִתָ :

root	stem	form	person, gender, number	function	basic root meaning

Translation of וְהַעֲלִתָה לוֹ : _____

Because it is 1st guttural and 3rd *heh*, the root is a tricky root to conjugate, and it has numerous ambiguous forms. Here it is in the four most common conjugations, Qal qatal, Hiphil qatal, Qal yiqtol, and Hiphil yiqtol:

	QATAL FORMS			YIQTOL FORMS	
	QAL	HIPHIL		QAL	HIPHIL
SING. 3. M.	עָלָה	הֶעֱלָה	SING. 3. M.	יַעֲלֶה	יַעֲלֶה
3. F.	עָלְתָה	הֶעֶלְתָה	3. F.	תַּעֲלֶה	תַּעֲלֶה
2. M.	עָלִיתָ	הֶעֱלִיתָ	2. M.	תַּעֲלֶה	תַּעֲלֶה
2. F.	עָלִית	הֶעֱלִית	2. F.	תַּעֲלִי	*תַּעֲלִי
1. C.	עָלִיתִי	*הֶעֱלִיתִי	1. C.	אֶעֱלֶה	אַעֲלֶה
PLUR. 3. C.	עָלוּ	הֶעֱלוּ	PLUR. 3. M.	יַעֲלוּ	יַעֲלוּ
			3. F.	תַּעֲלֶינָה	*תַּעֲלֶינָה
2. M.	עֲלִיתֶם	הַעֲלִתֶם	2. M.	תַּעֲלוּ	תַּעֲלוּ
2. F.	*עֲלִיתֶן	*הַעֲלִתֶן	2. F.	*תַּעֲלֶינָה	*תַּעֲלֶינָה
1. C.	עָלִינוּ	*הֶעֱלִינוּ	1. C.	נַעֲלֶה	נַעֲלֶה

Notes:
1. * means the form is not attested in the Hebrew Bible.
2. Every person, gender and number in the Hiphil qatal does *not* have a dot vowel after the second root letter.
3. The Qal yiqtol and Hiphil yiqtol form are nearly indistinguishable. You will have to lean on context for distinguishing most of these cases.
4. Many of the *hehs* on the ends of the yiqtol forms drop off in the wayyiqtol forms.

Expressions using יוֹם

36.3a. You have already seen the word יוֹם used many times to mean *day* in a number of contexts, but it is used twice in our lesson verse in two of its other senses. The first time, the idiom מִיָּמִים יָמִימָה means *from year to year*. It is also used in 1 Samuel 1:3 to describe Elkanah's yearly habit of bringing his family to Shiloh to do sacrifice to *YHWH*. It is also used with this meaning in Exodus 13:10, Judges 11:40,

207

and 21:19. Translate the entire lesson verse:

וּמְעִיל קָטֹן תַּעֲשֶׂה־לּוֹ אִמּוֹ וְהַעַלְתָה לוֹ מִיָּמִים יָמִֽימָה

36.3b. Other expressions using יוֹם are below. Try translating them literally.

זֶבַח הַיָּמִים   1 Samuel 2:19
the yearly sacrifice

וַיְהִי כִּי אָרְכוּ־לוֹ שָׁם הַיָּמִים   Genesis 26:8
And when he had been there a long time

וַיִּרְבּוּ הַיָּמִים   Genesis 38:12
And in the course of time

כָּל־הַיָּמִים   Genesis 43:9
forever

כְּיוֹם בְּיוֹם   1 Samuel 18:10
day by day

דְּבַר־יוֹם בְּיוֹמוֹ   Exodus 5:13
the daily task

וַיְהִי לִשְׁנָתַיִם יָמִים   2 Samuel 13:23
And after two years

יָמִים אַרְבָּעָה חֳדָשִׁים   Judges 19:2
a time of four months

The point of these examples is not to memorize the idiomatic uses of the word יוֹם although you may. It is more to create the impression that you may need to translate this Hebrew word as a broader reference to time than our common conception of English *day*.

Discourse switch cues

36.4a. Procedural Discourse is the only type of discourse we have learned about so far other than Historical Narrative that does not begin with the onset of direct speech. Direct speech, so often introduced by וַיֹּאמֶר cues the reader as to the shift from Historical Narrative to another embedded discourse. Although Procedural Discourse is *not* marked by a switch to direct speech, there are other cues used by the Hebrew writer to notify his reader that he is switching to an embedded Procedural Discourse.

> **A Biblical Hebrew writer uses a *Discourse Switch Cue (DSC)* to aid his reader in realizing that the genre has changed.**

Some examples of DSC's include:[1]

Any speech introduction.

A shift from a string of one mainline type (e.g. wayyiqtol) to another (e.g. weqatal or
imperative).

An X-yiqtol within a string of wayyiqtols.

Expressions of time duration.

Which two DSCs are used in our lesson verse? _____

_____

36.4b. The X-yiqtol, in a sense, does not belong in Historical Narrative, and in this way, it helps to mark
the onset of Procedural Discourse. There are even X-yiqtols that appear in isolation in Historical Narrative.
That is, they are not followed by any string of weqatals that characterizes the mainline of a Procedural
Discourse. As such, an isolated X-yiqtol in a Historical Narrative may be considered a mini Procedural
Discourse. 1 Kings 17:6 is an example:

וְהָעֹרְבִים מְבִיאִים לוֹ לֶחֶם וּבָשָׂר בַּבֹּקֶר וְלֶחֶם וּבָשָׂר בָּעָרֶב וּמִן־הַנַּחַל יִשְׁתֶּה׃

And the ravens were bringing him bread and meat in the morning and bread and meat in the evening,
and it was from the brook that he would drink.

You can see from this example, that the X-yiqtol is teamed with a participle. A participle, you surely
remember, gives backgrounded activities in Historical Narrative. So does the X-yiqtol, and so, in fact, does
Procedural Discourse. In other words, Procedural Discourse is a "dependent" genre devoted to giving
backgrounded activity in a host Historical Narrative.

36.4c. The words מִיָּמִים יָמִימָה function as a second DSC in our lesson verse. They are a
convenient reference to the time-quality to which the X-yiqtol and weqatal of our lesson verse refer. They
clarify for us that Hannah's making of a cloak for her son and bringing it to him was not a one-time
occasion. In a sense, they explain for the reader the presence of an X-yiqtol and a weqatal which would
otherwise be unexpected in Historical Narrative.

Procedural Discourse added to the Historical Narrative discourse profile scheme

36.5. It is not necessary to display a discourse profile scheme for Procedural Discourse. It really only has
the weqatal mainline and the X-yiqtol topicalization structures. What is more important is to display how
Procedural Discourse relates to Historical Narrative. Procedural Discourse gives background for a
Historical Narrative. The background is not of exactly the same nature as that given by the participle which
is on-going during the narrative. Procedural Discourse, on the other hand, gives habitual activity that
precedes and explains the narrative. Seeing that they both give background to a narrative the participle and
embedded Procedural Discourse are ranked very closely in the profile scheme of Historical narrative as
follows:[2]

---

[1] Longacre(1994), 58ff.
[2] As mentioned previously, Longacre has put forth both the discourse profile scheme which he calls a verb-ranking
cline(1989) and the outline of Procedural Discourse(1994), but he has not related the two genres to each other in a
scheme like the one shown here.

Mainline: 1. Wayyiqtol

Off-the-line:
2. Topicalization: X-qatal
3. Embedded Direct Speech
4. Relative past background: Qatal in a dependent clause
5. Relative non-past background: Yiqtol in a dependent clause
6. Backgrounded activities: Participle
7. **Embedded Procedural Discourse**
8. Transition marker: Wayyiqtol of היה
9. Scene setting: Verbless Clause
10. Irrealis scene setting: Negation of any verb by לֹא

Assignments

36.6a. Translate the following. Pay attention to the chapters and verses so you can use and appreciate the verb form sequences. Even if you see no verb form evidence of it in the material you are given in the exercises, you may assume all the following verses are in a Historical Narrative context.

1. Judges 2:18

וְכִי־הֵקִים יְהוָה לָהֶם שֹׁפְטִים וְהָיָה יְהוָה עִם־הַשֹּׁפֵט וְהוֹשִׁיעָם מִיַּד אֹיְבֵיהֶם כֹּל יְמֵי הַשּׁוֹפֵט

2. Judges 2:19

וְהָיָה בְּמוֹת הַשּׁוֹפֵט יָשֻׁבוּ

3. Genesis 2:6 אֵד means *mist*. The root שׁקה in Hiphil stem means *quaff, water*.

וְאֵד יַעֲלֶה מִן־הָאָרֶץ וְהִשְׁקָה אֶת־כָּל־פְּנֵי־הָאֲדָמָה׃

4. Exodus 34:34 הַמַּסְוֶה means *veil*.

וּבְבֹא מֹשֶׁה לִפְנֵי יְהוָה לְדַבֵּר אִתּוֹ יָסִיר אֶת־הַמַּסְוֶה עַד־צֵאתוֹ וְיָצָא וְדִבֶּר אֶל־בְּנֵי יִשְׂרָאֵל

5. Exodus 34:35 הַמַּסְוֶה see number 4.

וְרָאוּ בְנֵי־יִשְׂרָאֵל אֶת־פְּנֵי מֹשֶׁה וְהֵשִׁיב מֹשֶׁה אֶת־הַמַּסְוֶה עַל־פָּנָיו עַד־בֹּאוֹ לְדַבֵּר אִתּוֹ

6. Exodus 35:1 This verse *is* the verse which directly follows number 5 which you just translated.

וַיֹּאמֶר אֲלֵהֶם אֵלֶּה הַדְּבָרִים אֲשֶׁר־צִוָּה לַעֲשֹׂת אֹתָם

7. 2 Kings 25:28 כִּסֵּא means *seat, throne.* מֵעַל means *above.* בְּבָבֶל means *in Babylon.*

וַיְדַבֵּר אִתּוֹ טֹבוֹת וַיִּתֵּן אֶת־כִּסְאוֹ מֵעַל כִּסֵּא הַמְּלָכִים אֲשֶׁר אִתּוֹ בְּבָבֶל׃

8. 2 Kings 25:29 תָּמִיד

וְאָכַל לֶחֶם תָּמִיד לְפָנָיו כָּל־יְמֵי חַיָּיו

210

means *continually*, and functions as a DSC.

1 Samuel 2 :13 There is no clause here. It is more like a heading that acts as a DSC. זֹבֵחַ means *sacrifice*, here used as both a participle and a noun. זֹבֵחַ is *not* an infinitive absolute which would have the nikkud זָבוֹחַ

9.   וּמִשְׁפַּט הַכֹּהֲנִים אֶת־הָעָם כָּל־אִישׁ זֹבֵחַ זֶבַח

1 Samuel 2:13 You will see that *an intruder* might be a good word for the priest's servant.

10.   וּבָא נַעַר הַכֹּהֵן

1 Samuel 2:14 בַּכִּיּוֹר אוֹ בַדּוּד means *in the pot* or *in the kettle*.

11.   וְהִכָּה בַכִּיּוֹר אוֹ בַדּוּד

1 Samuel 2:14 A מַזְלֵג is a *fork*, like a trident. The first four words together are an "X" before יִקַּח.

12.   כֹּל אֲשֶׁר יַעֲלֶה הַמַּזְלֵג יִקַּח הַכֹּהֵן בּוֹ

1 Samuel 2:14

13.   כָּכָה יַעֲשׂוּ לְכָל־יִשְׂרָאֵל הַבָּאִים שָׁם בְּשִׁלֹה

1 Samuel 2:20 This verse is the continuation of the Procedural Discourse begun in our lesson verse. What stem is בֵּרַךְ ? Remember that *resh* cannot take a *dagesh*.

14.   וּבֵרַךְ עֵלִי אֶת־אֶלְקָנָה וְאֶת־אִשְׁתּוֹ וְאָמַר יָשֵׂם יְהוָה לְךָ זֶרַע מִן־הָאִשָּׁה הַזֹּאת וְהָלְכוּ לִמְקֹמוֹ

2 Samuel 12:16 בְּעַד means *on behalf*. The root לִין means *stay the night*.

15.   וַיְבַקֵּשׁ דָּוִד אֶת־הָאֱלֹהִים בְּעַד הַנָּעַר וּבָא וְלָן וְשָׁכַב אָרְצָה

36.6b. Read Deuteronomy 6:20-25.

211

Lesson 37

וַיֵּצֵא מֶלֶךְ יִשְׂרָאֵל וַיַּךְ אֶת־הַסּוּס וְאֶת־הָרָכֶב וְהִכָּה בַאֲרָם מַכָּה גְדוֹלָה:
1 Kings 20:21

Goal:
- Identify and read the isolated weqatal within a wayyiqtol string.

What we already know

37.1a. Translate וַיֵּצֵא מֶלֶךְ יִשְׂרָאֵל : _____

37.1b. In the second verb of our lesson verse, there is only one root letter showing, but this is quite

common in the yiqtol and wayyiqtol of this root. What is the root? _____ (29.2a) The
vocabulary to which you have not yet been introduced is סוּס meaning *horse* and רָכֶב meaning
chariot. Notice how the singular form is used to refer to the set. In other words, *the horse* is used to refer
to *horses*. This is quite common in both Biblical Hebrew and English.

Translate וַיַּךְ אֶת־הַסּוּס וְאֶת־הָרָכֶב : _____

The isolated weqatal in a wayyiqtol string

37.2a. Looking ahead to the lesson verse's next verb, וְהִכָּה the root, stem, and form are not too
difficult to figure out if you remember Lesson 29.2b. What is surprising is that the form seems to be out
of place. The previous two verb forms in our lesson verse were wayyiqtols. Perhaps the weqatal marks the
onset of another, embedded discourse. What are four DSC's?

_____   _____

_____   _____(36.4a)

Do you see any DSC? _____ The weqatal here is therefore an interruption in the narrative
framework that we have thus far learned.

> **RULE: An isolated weqatal *that stands in for a wayyiqtol* within a wayyiqtol string
> marks a climactic or pivotal event in a narrative. The isolated weqatal is a
> surrogate mainline in Historical Narrative.**

37.2b. Fill out the verb analysis chart for וְהִכָּה :

root	stem	form	person, gender, number	function	basic root meaning
				pivotal/climactic event	

212

Translation of וְהִכָּה : *And he was a smiter (of)*

In the twenty or so verses before our lesson verse a conflict arises between the king of Israel and the king of Syria. The tension builds until our lesson verse when it finally becomes clear that the king of Israel will win the conflict: the perfect location for this type of weqatal.

Translation synopsis for weqatal

37.3a. Here is a synopsis of our translation formulas for weqatal in the different genres using וְהִכָּה as a model.

GENRE	TRANSLATION
Predictive Narrative:	and he will be a smiter (of)
Instructional Discourse:	and he will be a smiter (of)
Hortatory Discourse (as an off-the-line form):	so he may be a smiter (of)
Mitigated Hortatory (as a mainline form):	and he will be a smiter (of)
Procedural Discourse:	and he would be a smiter (of)
Historical Narrative:	and he was a smiter (of)

37.3b. And here is a revised discourse profile scheme for Historical Narrative with the isolated weqatal added.

1a. **Mainline:** Wayyiqtol
1b. Pivotal/ climactic event on the mainline: Isolated Weqatal[1]

  Off-the-line:
   2. Topicalization: X-qatal
    3. Embedded Direct Speech
     4. Relative past background: Qatal in a dependent clause
      5. Relative non-past background: Yiqtol in a dependent clause
       6. Backgrounded activities: Participle
        7. Embedded Procedural Discourse
         8. Transition marker: Wayyiqtol of הִיה
          9. Scene setting: Verbless Clause
           10. Irrealis scene setting: Negation of any verb by לֹא

Assignments

37.4a. Translate each of the following, and read in your English Bible the verses before and after each exercise so you can think about how the weqatal marks a climactic or pivotal event.

Genesis 37:3

כְּתֹנֶת פַּסִּים means literally *coat of palms/soles (of hands and feet).* We are not sure of the nature of this special coat,

1. וְיִשְׂרָאֵל אָהַב אֶת־יוֹסֵף וְעָשָׂה לוֹ כְּתֹנֶת פַּסִּים:

---

[1] As mentioned previously, Longacre has put forth both the discourse profile scheme which he calls a verb-ranking cline(1989) and this pivot-marking function of the weqatal(1994), but he has not shown the "isolated weqatal" in the profile. I put it as a surrogate mainline because it does represent a single completed event in the past and thereby moves forward the narrative as a mainline verb form should.

but it may have been a long, luxurious coat.

Judges 3:23
בַּעֲדוֹ וַיִּסְגֹּר דַּלְתוֹת הָעֲלִיָּה
means *And he closed the door of the upper room upon himself.* The root נעל in Qal means *lock.*

2 Samuel 13:18 מְשָׁרֵת is a Piel participle meaning *servant.* וְנָעַל has dif-ferent nikkud than numbers 2's word because 2's word is in pause.

1 Samuel 25:19-20 נָבָל is a name. רכב means *ride.* A חֲמוֹר is a *donkey.*

2 Kings 18:6-7 שׂכל means *act prudently, prosper.*

2 Kings 14:13 פרץ means *break through.* A חוֹמָה is a *wall.* שֹׁמְרוֹן means *Samaria.*

2 Kings 24:13-15 אוֹצָרוֹת means *treasures.* The last line contains the name of a man and the name of a place with a *heh*-directive on it.

1 Samuel 10:9 כְּהַפְנֹתוֹ שִׁכְמוֹ means *when he turned his shoulder.* הפך means *turn about, turn over.*

2 Samuel 6:16

2. וַיֵּצֵא אֵהוּד וַיִּסְגֹּר דַּלְתוֹת הָעֲלִיָּה בַּעֲדוֹ וְנָעָל:

3. וַיֵּצֵא אוֹתָהּ מְשָׁרְתוֹ הַחוּץ וְנָעַל הַדֶּלֶת אַחֲרֶיהָ:

4. וַתֹּאמֶר לִנְעָרֶיהָ עִבְרוּ וּלְאִישָׁהּ נָבָל לֹא הִגִּידָה: וְהָיָה הִיא רֹכֶבֶת עַל־הַחֲמוֹר

5. וַיִּשְׁמֹר מִצְוֹתָיו אֲשֶׁר־צִוָּה יְהוָה אֶת־מֹשֶׁה: וְהָיָה יְהוָה עִמּוֹ בְּכֹל אֲשֶׁר־יֵצֵא יַשְׂכִּיל

6. וַיִּפְרֹץ בְּחוֹמַת יְרוּשָׁלַ͏ִם וְלָקַח אֶת־כָּל־הַזָּהָב־וְהַכֶּסֶף וַיָּשָׁב שֹׁמְרוֹנָה:

7. וַיּוֹצֵא מִשָּׁם אֶת־כָּל־אוֹצְרוֹת בֵּית יְהוָה וְהִגְלָה אֶת־כָּל־יְרוּשָׁלַ͏ִם וַיֶּגֶל אֶת־יְהוֹיָכִין בָּבֶלָה

8. וְהָיָה כְּהַפְנֹתוֹ שִׁכְמוֹ לָלֶכֶת מֵעִם שְׁמוּאֵל וַיַּהֲפָךְ־לוֹ אֱלֹהִים לֵב אַחֵר

9. וְהָיָה אֲרוֹן יְהוָה בָּא עִיר דָּוִד

37.4b. Read the introductory material to Reading 5 and 1 Samuel 17:32-33.

214

MODULE FIVE—THE PASSIVE/REFLEXIVE STEMS

<u>Overview</u>: Although some grammarians believe there may be as many as nineteen verbal stems in Biblical Hebrew, most agree that there are seven major stems. In this introductory course you will only be required to learn the seven major stems plus one special stem that is only used with one root. In Module Three we compared three of the major stems which account for over 90% of the verbs in the Hebrew Bible, the Qal, Piel, and Hiphil stems. In this module you will learn the stems which account for almost all of the remaining verbs, called the **passive/reflexive stems**. You will learn what **active**, **passive**, and **reflexive** verbs are and how they are communicated in Biblical Hebrew. The passive stems include the Qal's passive counterpart **Niphal**, the Piel's passive counterparts **Pual** and **Hitpael**, the Hiphil's passive counterpart **Hophal**. Here is an outline of the system in chart form:

ACTIVE STEMS	PASSIVE/REFLEXIVE STEMS
QAL	*NIPHAL*
PIEL	*PUAL* *and* *HITPAEL*
HIPHIL	*HOPHAL*

In this module you will also learn about the **Qal passive participle** which is passive even though it is not in a special passive stem.

Lesson 38

בְּלֶכְתְּךָ הַיּוֹם מֵעִמָּדִי וּמָצָאתָ שְׁנֵי אֲנָשִׁים וְאָמְרוּ אֵלֶיךָ נִמְצְאוּ הָאֲתֹנוֹת

1 Samuel 10:2

Goals:
- Identify and read pronominal suffixes attached to prepositions.
- Identify and read the cardinal numbers one through ten.
- Identify and read the Niphal qatal.

What we already know

38.1a. Our lesson verse is part of a direct speech. Looking ahead to the verbs וּמָצָאתָ and וְאָמְרוּ we can see a series of weqatals. Direct speech + a series of weqatals = what three possibilities for discourse genre?

_____

_____

_____

Now translate וְאָמְרוּ :_____ The word would

almost certainly point to which of the above genres? _____ In other words, is *And they will be sayers* most likely prediction, instruction, or exhortation?

38.1b. Translate בְּלֶכְתְּךָ הַיּוֹם :_____ If you need help review 34.4a.

Conjugating the prepositions with pronominal suffixes

38.2a. The word in our lesson verse מֵעִמָּדִי is made of four parts as follows:

מֵ	=	preposition
עִם	=	preposition
ד	=	?
ִי	=	pronominal suffix

You are familiar with all the parts except perhaps for the *dalet* which is a point of disagreement among Hebrew grammarians. Jouon[1] suggests the form is a derivative of עִם + יְדִי meaning *next to me, near me, with me*. Gesenius[2] says it is probably a derivative of the Arabic עִנְדִי meaning *beside, with*.

The conjugation of עִם with the pronominal suffixes is predictable except for the 1st c. s. form. Basically, the chart below can be used as a paradigm for one of two ways to attach pronominal suffixes to

---

[1] Jouon-Muraoka (1993), 395.
[2] Gesenius(1910) 301.

216

prepositions. The paradigm also applies for בֵּין and (the preposition) אֵת לְ בְּ

1ST PARADIGM FOR ATTACHING PRONOMINAL SUFFIXES:

with him	עִמּוֹ		with them (m. p.)	עִמָּם / עִמָּהֶם	
with her	עִמָּהּ		with them (f. p.)	*עִמָּהֵנָה / *עִמָּן	
with you (m. s.)	עִמְּךָ		with you (m. p.)	עִמָּכֶם	
with you (f. s.)	עִמָּךְ		with you (f. p.)	*עִמָּכֶן	
with me	עִמִּי / עִמָּדִי		with us	עִמָּנוּ	

with several of the prepo-sition in this 1st para-digm, -נִי is used as the 1st c. s. suffix.

*unattested in the Hebrew Bible

38.2b. The second paradigm for attaching pronominal suffixes uses the helping *yod*, reminiscent of the masculine plural construct ending for nouns. We have seen this *yod* many times already, and it is used with the independent prepositions עַל עַד אֶל Let us use עַל as an example.

2ND PARADIGM FOR ATTACHING PRONOMINAL SUFFIXES

upon him	עָלָיו		upon them (m. p.)	עֲלֵיהֶם	
upon her	עָלֶיהָ		upon them (f. p.)	עֲלֵיהֶן	
upon you (m. s.)	עָלֶיךָ		upon you (m. p.)	עֲלֵיכֶם	
upon you (f. s.)	עָלַיִךְ		upon you (f. p.)	*עֲלֵיכֶן	
upon me	עָלַי		upon us	עָלֵינוּ	

*unattested in the Hebrew Bible

The cardinal numbers 1-10

38.3a. Translate וּמְצָאתָ :_____

38.3b. The next expression שְׁנֵי אֲנָשִׁים is technically a construct chain made of the masculine construct form of שְׁנַיִם and the masculine plural of אִישׁ which, you will remember, has this irregular form. The forms of numbers in Hebrew are rather technical, but once again, you are somewhat unburdened by the necessity only to read Hebrew and not compose it. Here is a listing of the absolute and construct forms of the masculine and feminine cardinal numbers 1 through 10.

	MASCULINE		FEMININE	
	Absolute	Construct	Absolute	Construct
one	אֶחָד	אַחַד	אַחַת	אַחַת
two	שְׁנַ֫יִם	שְׁנֵי	שְׁתַּ֫יִם	שְׁתֵּי
three	שְׁלֹשָׁה	שְׁלֹ֫שֶׁת	שָׁלֹשׁ	שְׁלֹשׁ
four	אַרְבָּעָה	אַרְבַּ֫עַת	אַרְבַּע	אַרְבַּע
five	חֲמִשָּׁה	חֲמֵ֫שֶׁת	חָמֵשׁ	חֲמֵשׁ
six	שִׁשָּׁה	שֵׁ֫שֶׁת	שֵׁשׁ	שֵׁשׁ
seven	שִׁבְעָה	שִׁבְעַת	שֶׁ֫בַע	שְׁבַע
eight	שְׁמֹנָה	שְׁמֹנַת	שְׁמֹנֶה	שְׁמֹנֶה
nine	תִּשְׁעָה	תִּשְׁעַת	תֵּ֫שַׁע	תְּשַׁע
ten	עֲשָׂרָה	עֲשֶׂ֫רֶת	עֶ֫שֶׂר	עֶ֫שֶׂר

Notes:

1. In case you did not notice when you were memorizing your vocabulary, the masculine forms have the *feminine* ending heh.

2. The *heh* on the masculine absolute form changes to *tav* in the construct form just as with feminine nouns.

38.3c. The use of the cardinal numbers displays a considerable degree of variability.

1. The construct form can be used as an adjective and come before the object that is numbered as it is in our lesson sentence.

2. In its construct form a number can function substantively, that is, like a noun.

וְאִם־יִתְקְפוֹ הָאֶחָד הַשְּׁנַ֫יִם יַעַמְדוּ נֶגְדּוֹ   Qohelet 4:12
And if the one overcomes him, the two will stand before him.

3. The absolute form can be used as an adjective and come before the object that is numbered.

וַיִּשְׁלַח יְהוֹשֻׁעַ־בִּן־נוּן מִן־הַשִּׁטִּים שְׁנַ֫יִם־אֲנָשִׁים   Joshua 2:1
And Joshua the son of Nun sent two men from Shittim.

4. The absolute form can be used as an adjective and come *after* the object that is numbered.

לְקַח פַּר אֶחָד בֶּן־בָּקָר וְאֵילִם שְׁנַ֫יִם תְּמִימִם   Exodus 29:1
Take one young bull and two sound rams.

218

38.3d. Translate וּמְצָאתָ שְׁנֵי אֲנָשִׁים : _____

38.4. Translate וְאָמְרוּ אֵלֶיךָ : _____

Niphal qatal

38.5a. The word נִמְצְאוּ may at first look like a 1st c. p. Qal yiqtol with another in a seemingly never-ending variety of pronominal suffixes. Good thinking, but not quite!

> RULE: **A pre-formed *nun* is the sign of the Niphal qatal and weqatal. The Niphal stem gives a passive or reflexive sense to a root. We *do not* translate the Niphal qatal with the *er*-word or *ing*-word plus possessive pronoun that we have used with all the active qatals and weqatals in independent clauses so far.**

The use of an *er*-word or gerund plus possessive pronoun for translating qatals is done in an attempt to capture the qatal sense of pinning an attribute on the subject of the verb. The qatal form is adjective-like. On the other hand, the Niphal and other passive stems have this adjective-like quality as a function of verbal stem. The passive stems do not require our eccentric translation technique of using an *er*-word or *ing*-word plus possessive pronoun.

38.5b.

> DEFINITION: ***Passivity* is when the subject of the verb is the recipient of the action of the verb rather than the doer of the action. We can speak of the voice of a sentence as being either *active* or *passive*.**

Here are a couple of English sentences to illustrate:

> 1. Active voice: *I ate the bear.*
> 2. Passive voice: *I was eaten by the bear.*

We can also express the same thought with either the active or passive voice. Compare the following passive sentence with the active number 1 above:

> 3. Passive voice: *The bear was eaten by me.*

In the two passive sentences above the passive construction pins an attribute on the subject of verb like an adjective. In number 2, it is the *I* that has the attribute of having been eaten. In number 3, it is the *bear* that has the same attribute. When we translate Hebrew passives our translations will sound very much like the English examples 2 and 3 above.

Fill out the verb analysis chart for נִמְצְאוּ :

root	stem	form	person, gender, number	function	basic root meaning

The form is a clause-initial qatal in a Historical Narrative. What then is the likely context of the qatal?

answer will help you to know what to write in the function column.

Translation of נִמְצְאוּ הָאֲתֹנוֹת : *The she-asses were found.*

Do not be uncomfortable that the *doer* of the finding is not specified. The doer will often be left a mystery just as in English.

38.5c. As we did in 38.5b when we examined the same English verb used in an active and passive sense, we can do the same thing with our lesson verse wherein active is *being a finder* and passive is *being found.*

QAL (ACTIVE):   וּמָצָאתָ שְׁנֵי אֲנָשִׁים

And you will be finders of two men

NIPHAL (PASSIVE):   נִמְצְאוּ הָאֲתֹנוֹת

The she-asses were found

38.5d. Here is the full conjugation of a strong root in the Niphal qatal:

NIPHAL QATAL of a STRONG ROOT

SINGULAR 3. M.	נִקְטַל	PLURAL 3. C.		נִקְטְלוּ
3. F.	נִקְטְלָה			
2. M.	נִקְטַּלְתָּ	2. M.		נִקְטַלְתֶּם
2. F.	נִקְטַלְתְּ	2. F.		נִקְטַלְתֶּן
1. C.	נִקְטַּלְתִּי	1. C.		נִקְטַּלְנוּ

38.5e. In the Niphal stem, the *yod* of 1st *yod* verbs becomes a *holem* as it does in the Hiphil stem. Fill out the conjugation using the paradigm above and the forms provided for you as aids.

NIPHAL QATAL of 1st YOD ROOTS

SINGULAR 3. M.	נוֹדַע	PLURAL 3. C.	_____
3. F.	נוֹדְעָה		
2. M.	_____	2. M.	_____
2. F.	_____	2. F.	_____
1. C.	_____	1. C.	_____

38.5f. The *nun* of 1st *nun* roots assimilates into a footprint *dagesh* in the second letter of the root so that we do not see both the preformative *nun* of the Niphal stem and the *nun* of the root. There are two features that will help us differentiate between the Qal qatal of a 1st *nun* root and the Niphal qatal of the same root.

220

Whereas the pre-formed *nun* of the Niphal stem has a *hireq* under it, what vowel is under the first root letter of a Qal qatal? _____ The other distinctive feature of the Niphal qatal of a 1st *nun* root is the *dagesh*. Conjugate נתן in the Niphal qatal.

NIPHAL QATAL of 1st NUN ROOTS

SINGULAR 3. M.	נִתַּן		PLURAL 3. C.	_____	
3. F.	נִתְּנָה				
2. M.	_____		2. M.	_____	
2. F.	_____		2. F.	_____	
1. C.	_____		1. C.	_____	

Assignments

38.6a. Memorize the conjugations of the Niphal qatal for strong, 1st *yod*, and 1st *nun* roots.

38.6b. Translate:

1. בַּיּוֹם הַהוּא כָּרַת
2. אֲשֶׁר כָּרַת יְהוָה
3. הַדְּבָרִים הָאֵלֶּה כָּרַתִּי
4. אֲשֶׁר־כָּרְתוּ
5. וְנִכְרְתָה
6. וְנִכְרַת
7. וְנִכְרְתוּ הַנְּפָשׁוֹת
8. וְנִכְרַתָּ

9. וְהָאָדָם יָדַע
10. יָדַעְתִּי
11. וִידַעְתֶּם
12. וְנוֹדְעָה
13. וְלֹא נוֹדַע
14. וְהַדָּבָר נוֹדַע
15. לֹא נוֹדַעְתִּי
16. אִם־נוֹעֲדוּ

17. וְנָתְנוּ
18. וְנִתְּנוּ
19. וְנוֹתַן
20. נִתְּנוּ
21. לֹא־נִתְּנָה
22. נִתְּנוּ
23. לֹא נִתַּן־לָהּ
24. וְנִתַּתֶּם

38.6c. Translate:

Genesis 9:2

1. בְּיֶדְכֶם נִתָּנוּ

Genesis 38:14

2. לֹא־נִתְּנָה לוֹ לְאִשָּׁה

Leviticus 26:25 דֶּבֶר means *pestilence*.

3. וְנֶאֱסַפְתֶּם אֶל־עָרֵיכֶם וְשִׁלַּחְתִּי דֶבֶר בְּתוֹכְכֶם וְנִתַּתֶּם בְּיַד־אוֹיֵב:

2 Chronicles 28:5

4. וְגַם בְּיַד־מֶלֶךְ יִשְׂרָאֵל נִתָּן וַיַּךְ־בּוֹ מַכָּה גְדוֹלָה

Exodus 2:14 אָכֵן means *surely*.

5. וַיִּירָא מֹשֶׁה וַיֹּאמַר אָכֵן נוֹדַע הַדָּבָר

Exodus 6:3

6. וּשְׁמִי יְהוָה לֹא נוֹדַעְתִּי לָהֶם

Leviticus 4:14

7. וְנוֹדְעָה הַחַטָּאת אֲשֶׁר חָטְאוּ עָלֶיהָ

221

8. וְנוֹדַע לָכֶם לָמָּה לֹא־תָסוּר יָדוֹ מִכֶּם

1 Samuel 6:3

9. וְנִזְכַּרְתֶּם לִפְנֵי יְהוָה אֱלֹהֵיכֶם וְנוֹשַׁעְתֶּם מֵאֹיְבֵיכֶם

Numbers 10:9

10. וַיֹּאמֶר פַּרְעֹה אֶל־עֲבָדָיו הֲנִמְצָא כָזֶה אִישׁ אֲשֶׁר רוּחַ אֱלֹהִים בּוֹ:

Genesis 41:38

11. וַיֹּאמֶר שָׁאוּל אֶל־דּוֹדוֹ הַגֵּד הִגִּיד לָנוּ כִּי נִמְצְאוּ הָאֲתֹנוֹת

1 Samuel 10:16 דּוֹד means *uncle*. If הָאֲתֹנוֹת stumps you, look back at the lesson verse.

12. וַיְבַקְשֻׁהוּ וְלֹא נִמְצָא

1 Samuel 10:21 Even though the *dagesh* is missing from the *qoph* in וַיְבַקְשֻׁהוּ it is a Piel.

13. וְנִקְדַּשְׁתִּי בְּתוֹךְ בְּנֵי יִשְׂרָאֵל אֲנִי יְהוָה מְקַדִּשְׁכֶם

Leviticus 22:32

14. בְּהוֹצִיאִי אֶתְכֶם מִן־הָעַמִּים וְנִקְדַּשְׁתִּי בָכֶם לְעֵינֵי הַגּוֹיִם

Ezekiel 20:41

15. שֹׁמֵר כָּל־עַצְמוֹתָיו אַחַת מֵהֵנָּה לֹא נִשְׁבָּרָה:

Psalm 34:21

16. וְהָיָה כְּצֵאת מֹשֶׁה אֶל־הָאֹהֶל יָקוּמוּ כָּל־הָעָם וְנִצְּבוּ אִישׁ פֶּתַח אָהֳלוֹ

Exodus 33:8

38.6d.   Read 1 Samuel 17:34-38.

Lesson 39

וַיֹּאמֶר אַבְרָהָם אָנֹכִי אִשָּׁבֵעַ
Genesis 21:24

Goal:

• **Identify and read the Niphal yiqtol.**

What we already know

39.1. Translate וַיֹּאמֶר אַבְרָהָם : _____

Niphal yiqtol

39.2a. Our lesson verse is two clauses, and you have already translated the first. Examine the verb and word order in the second, and start to fill out the verb analysis chart:

root	stem	form	person, gender, number	function	basic root meaning

We will save translation for the end of the lesson.

In determining the stem of the verb, you need to look for any evidence of an augment to the verb. The augment is the *dagesh forte* in the *shin* just like the *dagesh forte* in a middle root letter is the sign of the Piel stem.

> RULE: **The sign of the Niphal yiqtol and wayyiqtol is a *dagesh forte* in the first root letter:** ◯◯◯⊙___ **or** ◯◯◯⊙___וַ

39.2b. You remember that in 1st *nun* roots, the *nun* also assimilates into the *footprint dagesh* in the Qal stem. For instance:

יִתֵּן

You may wonder why the *footprint dagesh* is not considered an augment to the root in a case like this but it is in אִשָּׁבֵעַ A letter has not been added to יִתֵּן Rather, one letter *nun* has been transformed into one *tav*. Remember that the *dagesh forte* represents a doubling of the letter in which it is placed. One of the *tavs* is original to the root, and one of the *tavs* is the transformed 1st *nun*.

Now look again at אִשָּׁבֵעַ No root letter has been transformed into a *dagesh forte* here. Instead, the preformative *nun* of the Niphal stem has been transformed into a *dagesh forte* in the root letter *shin* [שׁ].

39.2c. Let us work on our Niphal yiqtol conjugations.

NIPHAL YIQTOL of a STRONG VERB:

SINGULAR 3. M.	יִקָּטֵל	PLURAL 3. M.	יִקָּטְלוּ
3. F.	תִּקָּטֵל	3. F.	תִּקָּטַ֫לְנָה
2. M.	תִּקָּטֵל	2. M.	תִּקָּטְלוּ
2. F.	תִּקָּטְלִי	2. F.	תִּקָּטַ֫לְנָה
1. C.	אֶקָּטֵל	1. C.	נִקָּטֵל

39.2d. As we have often seen now in the augmented stems, 1st *yod* transforms to *vav*, only in the case of Niphal yiqtol, the *vav* is consonantal rather than a *holem*. Fill in the missing forms in the chart below.

NIPHAL YIQTOL of 1st YOD ROOTS:

SINGULAR 3. M.	יִוָּשֵׁב	PLURAL 3. M.	יִוָּשְׁבוּ
3. F.	_____	3. F.	תִּוָּשַׁ֫בְנָה
2. M.	_____	2. M.	_____
2. F.	_____	2. F.	_____
1. C.	_____	1. C.	_____

39.2e. If you understand the system of nikkud for marking stem in Biblical Hebrew you may well be anticipating some challenges. For instance, you may be wondering how Niphal yiqtol and wayyiqtol look with 1st *nun* roots because the *nun* has assimilated into a *footprint dagesh* in all the other stems we have studied. The answer is simple. The *nun* does not assimilate in the Niphal stem, for instance, יִנָּתֵן

39.2f. You may also be wondering what happens if the first root letter is guttural, that is, it cannot take a *dagesh*. If you have forgotten any of these letters you can review them in 3.6b. The sign of the Niphal yiqtol or wayyiqtol of a 1st guttural root is a *sere* under the prefixed pronoun. Though the explanation may not be technically accurate you may be aided by this thought: the Niphal's pre-formed *nun* turned into a *dagesh* but bounced off the guttural letter, landing under the prefixed pronoun. Fill in the missing forms in the chart below.

NIPHAL YIQTOL of 1ST GUTTURAL ROOTS:

SINGULAR 3. M.	יֵעָמֵד	**PLURAL 3. M.**		יֵעָמְדוּ
3. F.	_____	3. F.		תֵּעָמַ֫דְנָה
2. M.	_____	2. M.		_____
2. F.	_____	2. F.		_____
1. C.	_____	1. C.		_____

The Niphal's reflexive sense

39.3a. There is a special kind of passive called *reflexive*, which the Niphal stem sometimes expresses.

> DEFINITION: **When a verb is *reflexive* the subject of the verb receives the action of the verb as with other passive verbs. However, the subject of a reflexive verb is *also the doer of the action*. Reflexive action is therefore action done to oneself or in one's own interests.**

Let us compare several root in their Qal and Niphal reflexive senses:[1]

	QAL	NIPHAL
שׁמר	*watch*	*take heed to oneself*
שׁפט	*judge*	*enter into controversy*
שׁאל	*ask*	*ask for oneself*
קדשׁ	*set apart*	*show oneself sacred*
ברך	*kneel, bless*	*bless oneself*

39.3b. The Niphal yiqtol אִשָּׁבֵעַ in our lesson verse has this reflexive sense, and we can finally translate it. Notice that it is from the same root as the number for *seven*. The word means literally to *seven oneself*, that is, to bind oneself by seven things or to completely bind oneself. It is difficult sometimes to carry the reflexive sense in Hebrew across to English so most English translators say, "I swear" for Genesis 21:24's אָנֹכִי אִשָּׁבֵעַ

Our version: *As for me, I bind myself with an oath*

Assignments

39.4a. Memorize vocabulary words 311-340 for Lessons 39-42.

39.4b. Memorize the signs of the Niphal yiqtol for strong, 1st *yod*, and 1st guttural roots.

39.4c. Write the root, stem, form, and where applicable the person, gender, and number of the following verbs.

---

[1] Waltke and O'Connor(1990), §23.4.

21. הַמְצִיאוּ	11. יִזָּכֵר	1. וַיִּזָּכֵר
22. רָאִיתִי	12. הַזְכִּירוּ	2. וְזָכַרְתִּי
23. הֶרְאֵיתִי	13. זֻכַּר	3. לִזְכֹּר
24. יֵרָאֶה	14. זְכֹרוּ	4. וָאֶזְכֹּר
25. לְהֵרָאוֹת	15. מְצָאוּ	5. מַזְכִּיר
26. תֵּרָאֶה	16. מְצָא	6. אַזְכִּיר
27. נִרְאוּ	17. יִמָּצֵא	7. תַּזְכִּירוּ
28. וַיֵּרָא	18. וַיִּמָּצֵא	8. מֻזְכֶּרֶת
	19. נִמְצָא	9. נִזְכַּרְתֶּם
	20. וַיִּמָּצְאוּ	10. תִּזָּכֵר

39.4d. Translate:

Exodus 23:13

1. וּבְכֹל אֲשֶׁר־אָמַרְתִּי אֲלֵיכֶם תִּשָּׁמֵרוּ וְשֵׁם אֱלֹהִים אֲחֵרִים לֹא תַזְכִּירוּ

Judges 13:13

2. וַיֹּאמֶר מַלְאַךְ יְהוָה אֶל־מָנוֹחַ מִכֹּל אֲשֶׁר־אָמַרְתִּי אֶל־הָאִשָּׁה תִּשָּׁמֵר:

Genesis 12:3

3. וְנִבְרְכוּ בְךָ כֹּל מִשְׁפְּחֹת הָאֲדָמָה

1 Samuel 12:7

4. וְאִשָּׁפְטָה אִתְּכֶם לִפְנֵי יְהוָה

Isaiah 43:26   יַחַד means *together*.

5. הַזְכִּירֵנִי נִשָּׁפְטָה יָחַד

Ezekiel 20:36   נְאֻם meaning *oracle* is a difficult word to translate. It marks the start of a divine speech and is traditionally translated "says."

6. כַּאֲשֶׁר נִשְׁפַּטְתִּי אֶת־אֲבוֹתֵיכֶם בְּמִדְבַּר אֶרֶץ מִצְרָיִם כֵּן אִשָּׁפֵט אִתְּכֶם נְאֻם אֲדֹנָי יְהוִה:

Leviticus 10:3

7. וַיֹּאמֶר מֹשֶׁה אֶל־אַהֲרֹן הוּא אֲשֶׁר־דִּבֶּר יְהוָה לֵאמֹר בִּקְרֹבַי אֶקָּדֵשׁ וְעַל־פְּנֵי כָל־הָעָם אֶכָּבֵד

Exodus 33:21   A צוּר is a *rock*.

8. וַיֹּאמֶר יְהוָה הִנֵּה מָקוֹם אִתִּי וְנִצַּבְתָּ עַל־הַצּוּר:

Genesis 29:26

9. וַיֹּאמֶר לָבָן לֹא־יֵעָשֶׂה כֵן בִּמְקוֹמֵנוּ

Leviticus 23:3

10. שֵׁשֶׁת יָמִים תֵּעָשֶׂה מְלָאכָה

Judges 11:37	וַתֹּאמֶר אֶל־אָבִיהָ יֵעָשֶׂה לִּי הַדָּבָר הַזֶּה וְאֵלְכָה וְיָרַדְתִּי	11.
Genesis 6:21 מַאֲכָל means *food*.	וְאַתָּה קַח־לְךָ מִכָּל־מַאֲכָל אֲשֶׁר יֵאָכֵל	12.
Isaiah 61:6 מְשָׁרְתֵי means *ministers of*.	וְאַתֶּם כֹּהֲנֵי יְהוָה תִּקָּרֵאוּ מְשָׁרְתֵי אֱלֹהֵינוּ יֵאָמֵר	13.
Ruth 3:3	אַל־תִּוָּדְעִי לָאִישׁ עַד כַּלֹּתוֹ לֶאֱכֹל וְלִשְׁתּוֹת	14.
Ruth 3:14 גֹּרֶן means *threshing floor*.	וַיֹּאמֶר אַל־יִוָּדַע כִּי־בָאָה הָאִשָּׁה הַגֹּרֶן	15.
2 Samuel 22:4	וּמֵאֹיְבַי אִוָּשֵׁעַ	16.
Isaiah 66:8	מִי־שָׁמַע כָּזֹאת מִי רָאָה כָּאֵלֶּה אִם־יִוָּלֵד גּוֹי פַּעַם אֶחָת	17.
Exodus 13:17	כִּי אָמַר אֱלֹהִים פֶּן־יִנָּחֵם הָעָם בִּרְאֹתָם מִלְחָמָה וְשָׁבוּ מִצְרָיְמָה	18.
2 Kings 18:30 אַשּׁוּר means *Assyria*.	וְלֹא תִנָּתֵן אֶת־הָעִיר הַזֹּאת בְּיַד מֶלֶךְ אַשּׁוּר	19.
Esther 2:13	אֵת כָּל־אֲשֶׁר תֹּאמַר יִנָּתֵן לָהּ	20.

39.4e. Read the Reading Six Introductory material and Genesis 29:1-3.

Lesson 40

וַיֵּרָא יְהוָה אֶל־אַבְרָם וַיִּבֶן שָׁם מִזְבֵּחַ לַיהוָה הַנִּרְאֶה אֵלָיו
Genesis 12:7

Goal:

- **Identify and read the Niphal participle.**

What we already know

40.1a. Name the root and stem of each of the following:

	root	stem	
וַיֵּרָא	_____	_____	(39.2f)
וַיֵּרְא	_____	_____	(21.2c)
וַיֵּרְא	_____	_____	(21.2c)

40.1b. Translate   וַיֵּרָא יְהוָה אֶל־אַבְרָם   (Note that *was seen* does not quite work for the verb.
Sometimes we have to express Niphals as active verbs in English to avoid the ungrammatical. In this case

ראה in the Niphal stem means *appear*.) _____

40.1c. Typically, when only two root letters show and the vowel under the prefixed subject pronoun is a

hireq, what is the missing root letter? _____ (8.3a)

Translate   וַיִּבֶן שָׁם מִזְבֵּחַ לַיהוָה : _____

Niphal participle in apposition

40.2a. What is the one verb form which can have the definite article attached to it like our lesson word

הַנִּרְאֶה ? _____ (12.2b)   And recall that when the participle is in
apposition to a noun that it may be best to translate using the phrase *...the one who...* See 12.2e.

40.2b. The participle in our lesson verse, הַנִּרְאֶה contains what root? _____

> **RULE: As with the Niphal qatal and weqatal, the sign of the Niphal participle is a
> pre-formed *nun*. Remember that the Qal and Niphal participles are the only stems that
> do not use pre-formed *mems*.**

You may now be anticipating that the Niphal 3rd m. s. qatal and the Niphal m. s. participle look the same if
the participle *does not* have the definite article. Very good! Here they are:

Niphal 3rd m. s. qatal: נִרְאָה

Niphal m. s. participle: נִרְאָה

In some roots, the difference is only a *qamets* under the second root letter for the qatal, and a *patakh* for the participle. Furthermore, some roots have identical forms in these two situations. Fortunately, the participle often has a definite article on it, and the similarities are limited to only this one combination of person, gender, and number. Context, as always, is helpful.

40.2c. Fill out the verb analysis chart for הַנִּרְאֶה :

root	stem	form	person, gender, number	function	basic root meaning

Translate הַנִּרְאֶה אֵלָיו : _the one who_ _____.

Translate the entire lesson verse: _____

Niphal participle conjugations

40.3. The particulars of the Niphal participle are largely predictable.

NIPHAL PARTICIPLES:

	Strong root	1st *yod*	Hollow	1st *nun*	
Masculine Singular	נִקְטָל	נוֹשָׁב	נָכוֹן	נִתָּן
Feminine Singular	נִקְטֶּלֶת	נוֹשֶּׁבֶת	נְכוֹנָה	נִתֶּנֶת
Masculine Plural	נִקְטָלִים	נוֹשָׁבִים	נְכוֹנִים	נִתָּנִים
Feminine Plural	נִקְטָלוֹת	נוֹשָׁבוֹת	-----	נִתָּנוֹת

Notes:
1. The 1st *yods* change to *vavs* as we have seen before, but a *holem* rather than a consonantal *vav* as with Niphal yiqtol.
2. The nikkud, especially with the feminine singular is quite variable.

Assignments

40.4a. Write the root, stem, form, and when applicable, the person, gender, and number of the following verbs. If the form is ambiguous, write all the possibilities.

1. וְהָיָה	9. הַבָּאִים	17. הַנִּתָּן	יִפָּקֵד
2. הָיְתָה	10. לָבוֹא	18. וּפָקַדְתָּ	נִפְקָד
3. הָיִינוּ	11. הֵבֵאתָ	19. תִּפָּקֵד	וַיִּפְקְדוּ
4. וִהְיִיתֶם	12. וַיָּבִיאוּ	20. וַתִּתְפַּקְדִי	תֻּפְקַד
5. וַתִּהְיוּ	13. נָתְנוּ	21. הִפְקִיד	
6. וִיהִי	14. וְנָתְנוּ	22. יָפְקֵד	
7. בָּא	15. יִנָּתֵן	23. וְהִפְקַדְתִּי	
8. וַיָּבֹאוּ	16. יִתֵּן	24. מְפַקֵּד	

40.4b. Translate:

Exodus 16:35

1. וּבְנֵי יִשְׂרָאֵל אָכְלוּ אֶת־הַמָּן אַרְבָּעִים שָׁנָה עַד־בֹּאָם אֶל־אֶרֶץ נוֹשָׁבֶת

Exodus 18:14 מַדּוּעַ means why? עָרֶב means evening. It has a qamets because it is in pause.

2. מַדּוּעַ אַתָּה יוֹשֵׁב לְבַדֶּךָ וְכָל־הָעָם נִצָּב עָלֶיךָ מִן־בֹּקֶר עַד־עָרֶב

Exodus 19:15

3. וַיֹּאמֶר אֶל־הָעָם הֱיוּ נְכֹנִים לִשְׁלֹשֶׁת יָמִים

Exodus 34:2

4. וֶהְיֵה נָכוֹן לַבֹּקֶר וְעָלִיתָ בַבֹּקֶר אֶל־הַר סִינַי וְנִצַּבְתָּ לִי שָׁם עַל־רֹאשׁ הָהָר:

Exodus 34:10

5. כִּי־נוֹרָא הוּא אֲשֶׁר אֲנִי עֹשֶׂה עִמָּךְ

Leviticus 19:6 Is זִבְחֲכֶם a noun or verb?

6. בְּיוֹם זִבְחֲכֶם יֵאָכֵל

Deuteronomy 1:19 The first word's nikkud is rather eccentric, but it is a Qal wayyiqtol.

7. וַנִּסַּע מֵחֹרֵב וַנֵּלֶךְ אֵת כָּל־הַמִּדְבָּר הַגָּדוֹל וְהַנּוֹרָא הַהוּא

Genesis 47:14 לקט in Piel means gather.

8. וַיְלַקֵּט יוֹסֵף אֶת־כָּל־הַכֶּסֶף הַנִּמְצָא בְאֶרֶץ־מִצְרַיִם וּבְאֶרֶץ כְּנַעַן

Deuteronomy 3:22

9. לֹא תִּירָאוּם כִּי יְהוָה אֱלֹהֵיכֶם הוּא הַנִּלְחָם לָכֶם:

Deuteronomy 8:15
10.   הַמּוֹלִיכֲךָ בַּמִּדְבָּר הַגָּדֹל וְהַנּוֹרָא

Deuteronomy 20:11 מַס means *body of forced laborers.*

11.   וְהָיָה כָּל־הָעָם הַנִּמְצָא־בָהּ יִהְיוּ לְךָ לָמַס וַעֲבָדוּךָ:

Deuteronomy 29:28 סתר means *hide, conceal.*

12.   הַנִּסְתָּרֹת לַיהוָה אֱלֹהֵינוּ וְהַנִּגְלֹת לָנוּ וּלְבָנֵינוּ עַד־עוֹלָם

Joshua 23:10 רדף means *pursue.* אֶלֶף has a *patakh* in it because it is at the mid-verse pause.

13.   אִישׁ־אֶחָד מִכֶּם יִרְדָּף־אָלֶף כִּי יְהוָה אֱלֹהֵיכֶם הוּא הַנִּלְחָם לָכֶם

Exodus 12:10 שרף means *burn.*

14.   וְלֹא־תוֹתִירוּ מִמֶּנּוּ עַד־בֹּקֶר וְהַנֹּתָר מִמֶּנּוּ עַד־בֹּקֶר בָּאֵשׁ תִּשְׂרֹפוּ:

1 Samuel 30:9

15.   וַיֵּלֶךְ דָּוִד הוּא וְשֵׁשׁ־מֵאוֹת אִישׁ אֲשֶׁר אִתּוֹ וְהַנּוֹתָרִים עָמָדוּ:

1 Kings 20:30

16.   וַיָּנֻסוּ הַנּוֹתָרִים אֲפֵקָה אֶל־הָעִיר

2 Chronicles 31:10 בֵּרַךְ is a Piel qatal. הָמוֹן means *abundance.* Translate the participle *And He is the one who...*

17.   יְהוָה בֵּרַךְ אֶת־עַמּוֹ וְהַנּוֹתָר אֶת־הֶהָמוֹן הַזֶּה

40.4c. Read Genesis 29:4-12.

Lesson 41

הִשָּׁמֶר לְךָ אַחֲרֵי הִשָּׁמְדָם מִפָּנֶיךָ
Deuteronomy 12:30

Goals:
- Identify and read the Niphal imperative.
- Identify and read the Niphal infinitive.

What we already know

What kind of *dagesh* is in הִשָּׁמֶר ? _____ (1.2b) What Hebrew letter very

commonly assimilates into a *dagesh*? _____ (9.2b, 9.3a, 39.2e)

Niphal imperative

41.2a. The first word of our lesson verse, הִשָּׁמֶר will launch us into our last lesson devoted to the Niphal stem.

> RULE: **The sign of the Niphal imperative is a pre-formed *heh-hireq-dagesh forte* [הִּ].**

As you can see in our lesson word, the *nun* which we normally associate with the Niphal stem has assimilated into the *dagesh forte* in the *shin*. Be careful not to confuse the sign of the Niphal imperative with the sign of the Hiphil imperative which, once again, is *heh-patakh* [הַ].

41.2b. Fill out the verb analysis chart for הִשָּׁמֶר :

root	stem	form	person, gender, number	function	basic root meaning

Recall that the discourse function of a verb is not changed by the verb's stem.

The translation of הִשָּׁמֶר לְךָ is interesting because we have both the reflexive nature of the stem and the reflexive nature of the preposition לְ for which to account: *Guard yourself for yourself!*[1]

Niphal infinitive

41.3a. Our lesson word הִשָּׁמְדָם looks very much like the Niphal imperative you just learned about earlier in the lesson except it is a different root, and it has the pronominal suffix ם -- attached to it. The problem is trying to translate a passive/reflexive verb with a pronoun as the direct object. It cannot be done because the subject of the verb is already receiving the action of the verb.

---

[1] Waltke and O'Connor(1990), §23.4c.

232

RULE: The sign of the Niphal infinitive is the same as the sign of the Niphal imperative, a *heh-hireq-dagesh forte* [הִּ]. As you learned in 16.4a, you can often translate Hebrew infinitives using an English gerund, only in the case of the passive stem, the gerund is always *being*.

By the way, the root שׁמד in Niphal means *be exterminated*. Translation of הִשָּׁמְדָם : *their being exterminated*. Do you think *their extermination* means the same thing?

Translate the entire lesson verse: _____

Note: The changes that we have previously seen take place with roots in the Niphal stem also take place in both the imperative and the infinitive. First *yods* change to (consonantal) *vav*, and when the first root letter is a guttural, that is, it cannot take a *dagesh*, the *dagesh* "bounces off and becomes a *sere*" under the *heh*.

41.3b. There are a few things that will help you distinguish between the Niphal imperative and the Niphal infinitive. Of the two, only the infinitive can be preceded by a preposition, as it often is.

וַיַּעַשׂ יְהוֹשֻׁעַ כַּאֲשֶׁר אָמַר־לוֹ מֹשֶׁה לְהִלָּחֵם   Exodus 17:10
And Joshua did as Moses had said to him to fight.

Of the two, only the infinitive takes a pronominal suffix as in our lesson verse. And, as you now expect to be told, context is often your best indicator.

Assignments
41.4a. Translate:

17. שָׂא נָא	9. עֲשֵׂה לְךָ	1. לִשְׁבֹּר
18. הִנָּשֵׂא	10. אֵת־כָּל־אֲשֶׁר עָשָׂה	2. לְהִשָּׁבֵר
19. וַיִּשְׂאוּ	11. וַיַּעַשׂ אֱלֹהִים	3. וַיִּשְׁבֹּר
20. וְלֹא־נִשָּׂא	12. לֹא־יֵעָשׂוּ	4. אֲשֶׁר יִשָּׁבֵר
21. עַתָּה אֶנָּשֵׂא	13. לֹא־יֵעָשֶׂה	5. וְנִשְׁבַּר
22. וּבְהִנָּשְׂאָם	14. וְכָל־נַעֲשָׂה	6. וַתִּשָּׁבֵר
23. וְנִשָּׂא־בָם	15. אֲשֶׁר נַעֲשׂוּ	7. כִּי נִשְׁבְּרָה
24. כִּי־נִשֵּׂאת	16. לְהֵעָשׂוֹת	8. לְנִשְׁבְּרֵי־לֵב

41.4b. Translate:

Genesis 47:31

1. וַיֹּאמֶר הִשָּׁבְעָה לִי וַיִּשָּׁבַע לוֹ

Genesis 21:23 The *heh* on the end of the imperative, if you will remember, is common.

2. וְעַתָּה הִשָּׁבְעָה לִי בֵאלֹהִים

Exodus 23:21

3. הִשָּׁמֶר מִפָּנָיו וּשְׁמַע בְּקֹלוֹ

233

Genesis 24:6 שָׁמָּה is שָׁם with a *heh*-directive on it meaning *thither*.	וַיֹּאמֶר אֵלָיו אַבְרָהָם הִשָּׁמֶר לְךָ פֶּן־תָּשִׁיב אֶת־בְּנִי שָׁמָּה:	4.
Genesis 25:33	וַיֹּאמֶר יַעֲקֹב הִשָּׁבְעָה לִּי כַּיּוֹם וַיִּשָּׁבַע לוֹ	5.
Genesis 31:24	וַיָּבֹא אֱלֹהִים אֶל־לָבָן הָאֲרַמִּי וַיֹּאמֶר לוֹ הִשָּׁמֶר לְךָ פֶּן־תְּדַבֵּר עִם־יַעֲקֹב מִטּוֹב עַד־רָע:	6.
Genesis 49:1	וַיִּקְרָא יַעֲקֹב אֶל־בָּנָיו וַיֹּאמֶר הֵאָסְפוּ וְאַגִּידָה לָכֶם	7.
Deuteronomy 32:50	וּמֻת בָּהָר אֲשֶׁר אַתָּה עֹלֶה שָׁמָּה וְהֵאָסֵף אֶל־עַמֶּיךָ	8.
Jeremiah 4:5 This is Hortatory embedded in Hortatory. מִבְצָר means *fortification*.	קִרְאוּ מַלְאוּ וְאִמְרוּ הֵאָסְפוּ וְנָבוֹאָה אֶל־עָרֵי הַמִּבְצָר	9.
Exodus 10:28 The textual variants section of the *BHS* indicates a good possibility אַל should be אֶל	וַיֹּאמֶר־לוֹ פַרְעֹה לֵךְ מֵעָלָי הִשָּׁמֶר לְךָ אַל־תֹּסֶף רְאוֹת פָּנַי כִּי בְּיוֹם רְאֹתְךָ פָנַי תָּמוּת:	10.
Exodus 17:9	וַיֹּאמֶר מֹשֶׁה אֶל־יְהוֹשֻׁעַ בְּחַר־לָנוּ אֲנָשִׁים וְצֵא הִלָּחֵם בַּעֲמָלֵק	11.
Exodus 34:12	הִשָּׁמֶר לְךָ פֶּן־תִּכְרֹת בְּרִית לְיוֹשֵׁב הָאָרֶץ אֲשֶׁר אַתָּה בָּא עָלֶיהָ	12.
Numbers 16:24 מִשְׁכַּן means *dwelling place*.	דַּבֵּר אֶל־הָעֵדָה לֵאמֹר הֵעָלוּ מִסָּבִיב לְמִשְׁכַּן־קֹרַח דָּתָן וַאֲבִירָם	13.
Numbers 17:10(Eng. 16:45) רֶגַע means *a moment*.	הֵרֹמּוּ מִתּוֹךְ הָעֵדָה הַזֹּאת וַאֲכַלֶּה אֹתָם כְּרָגַע וַיִּפְּלוּ עַל־פְּנֵיהֶם	14.
Deuteronomy 20:4	כִּי יְהוָה אֱלֹהֵיכֶם הַהֹלֵךְ עִמָּכֶם לְהִלָּחֵם לָכֶם עִם־אֹיְבֵיכֶם לְהוֹשִׁיעַ אֶתְכֶם:	15.
Deuteronomy 20:10	כִּי־תִקְרַב אֶל־עִיר לְהִלָּחֵם עָלֶיהָ וְקָרָאתָ אֵלֶיהָ לְשָׁלוֹם:	16.
Judges 10:9	וַיַּעַבְרוּ בְנֵי־עַמּוֹן אֶת־הַיַּרְדֵּן לְהִלָּחֵם	17.

Esther 2:8	וַיְהִי בְּהִשָּׁמַע דְּבַר־הַמֶּלֶךְ	18.
Psalm 37:33	יְהוָה לֹא־יַעַזְבֶנּוּ בְיָדוֹ בְּהִשָּׁפְטוֹ	19.
Psalm 109:7	בְּהִשָּׁפְטוֹ יֵצֵא רָשָׁע	20.
Isaiah 55:6	דִּרְשׁוּ יְהוָה בְּהִמָּצְאוֹ	21.

41.4c. Read Genesis 29:13-22.

235

Lesson 42

וָאֶתְנַפַּל לִפְנֵי יְהוָה אֵת אַרְבָּעִים הַיּוֹם וְאֶת־אַרְבָּעִים הַלַּיְלָה אֲשֶׁר הִתְנַפָּלְתִּי

Deuteronomy 9:25

Goal:

• Identify and read verbs in the Hitpael stem.

What we already know

There are a wayyiqtol and a qatal in our lesson sentence. What are they? _____

and _____ (In case you have trouble finding the 1st c. s. form, see 17.4f.)

The signs of the Hitpael stem

42.2a. You will probably find the Hitpael stem one of the easiest to identify because of its clearly defined signs as shown in our lesson words הִתְנַפָּלְתִּי and וָאֶתְנַפַּל   This stem has the same signature augment to the root in all verb forms.

> RULE: **The signs of the Hitpael stem are a pre-formed *something-tav* unit [ת_] and a *dagesh forte* in the middle root letter:** ○⊙○תִה or ○⊙○תַ__ or
> ○⊙○תְמ

Here are the ways in which the pre-formed unit is constructed:

1. In the qatal, weqatal, imperative, and infinitive the pre-formed unit is הִת as in our lesson word הִתְנַפָּלְתִּי

2. In the yiqtol and wayyiqtol, the pre-formed unit is made with the prefixed subject pronoun and *tav* as in our lesson word וָאֶתְנַפַּל

3. In the participle, the pre-formed unit is תְמ as in
   קוֹל יְהוָה אֱלֹהִים מִתְהַלֵּךְ בַּגָּן   Genesis 3:8
   The voice of YHWH God walking to and fro in the garden

42.2b. Fill out the verb analysis charts for הִתְנַפָּלְתִּי and וָאֶתְנַפַּל :

root	stem	form	person, gender, number	function	basic root meaning

root	stem	form	person, gender, number	function	basic root meaning

Remember that form and context give discourse function, not stem.

The meaning of the Hitpael stem

42.3a. What is the meaning of the root נפל in the Qal stem? _____ In the Hitpael stem it means *prostrate oneself, throw oneself upon.*

42.3b. The Hitpael stem, like the Niphal at times, gives a root a reflexive meaning. Remember that the reflexive meaning gives double-duty to the subject of the verb, that is, the subject is both doer and receiver of the action. Hence we get the Hitpael *prostrate oneself* from the Qal *fall.* Often, the reflexive sense of the root has a frequentive or repetitive meaning. Below are several examples of roots that are used in the Qal and Hitpael stems to show you the Hitpael's alteration of a root's basic meaning.

	QAL	**HITPAEL**
ראה	see	look at one another
הלך	walk, go	go to and fro
לקח	take	take hold of oneself, flash about (said of lightning)
חזק	strengthen	strengthen oneself
נשׂא	lift	exalt oneself
קדשׁ	set apart	display or celebrate one's holiness

The particle אֵת as a marker of the accusative case

42.4. Thus far we have seen אֵת used as a preposition meaning *with,* and as the marker of a definite direct object. Our lesson verse uses the word in another way that is related to its use as a DDO. If you recall, a direct object answers the question ___(subject)___ ___(verb)___ *whom or what?* Do you remember "Herb studies Hebrew every night"? The direct object answers the question *Herb studies whom or what?* However, the אֵת in our lesson verse sets apart the words which tell for *how long* the speaker prostrated himself. So the words אֵת אַרְבָּעִים הַיּוֹם וְאֶת־אַרְבָּעִים הַלַּיְלָה function basically like an adverb. (By the way, אַרְבָּעִים means *forty,* and לַיְלָה means *night.*) An adverb and a direct object are both in the **accusative case**. The accusative case is *that which modifies the verb,* something that both direct objects and adverbs do.   In Biblical Hebrew, both definite direct object and adverb may be marked by the particle אֵת [1] Interestingly, in our lesson verse, הַיּוֹם and הַלַּיְלָה both have the definite article on them which is difficult to carry over to English. It may be that the frequent use of the DDO with definite direct objects generalized to make these two words definite however awkwardly.

---

[1] Gesenius(1910), §117a-m; Waltke and O'Connor(1990), §10.3.

The particle אֵת is even occasionally used to mark nouns used as subjects in verbal and verbless clauses. This use with subjects does not fall under the umbrella of the accusative case. Actually, the erratic use of the particle is still somewhat of a mystery of Biblical Hebrew. Some modern scholars believe that the particle is used to mark emphasis rather than accusative case. Perhaps אֵת does mark emphasis, but we must be careful not to assign the function *emphasis* to every idiosyncrasy of the ancient language that we do not yet understand. Perhaps the particle may simply have several uses which developed over a long history. A thorough study of the particle אֵת may be one subject you would like to tackle in your future studies of Hebrew.

Translate the entire lesson verse, and as you do, give careful consideration to whether the adverbial phrase goes with the verb before it or after it.

Assignments

42.5a. Tell the root, stem, form, and where applicable, the person, gender, and number of the following verbs. If there are ambiguous forms, note all the possibilities for that form.

1. הָלְכוּ	11. וַיִּתְהַלֵּךְ	21. וְנִקְדַּשְׁתִּי
2. הִתְהַלֵּךְ	12. וְקִדַּשְׁתָּ	22. וְקִדַּשׁ
3. וַתֵּלֶךְ	13. וְקִדַּשְׁתִּי	23. וַיְקַדְּשׁוּ
4. הַהֹלֵךְ	14. אֲקַדֵּשׁ	24. חָזַק
5. הוֹלִיךְ	15. וְהִתְקַדִּשְׁתֶּם	25. וְחִזַּקְתִּי
6. יוֹלֵךְ	16. הִתְקַדְּשׁוּ	26. וְהֶחֱזַקְתָּ
7. נֶהֱלַכְתִּי	17. וַיִּתְקַדְּשׁוּ	27. הִתְחַזַּק
8. מִתְהַלֵּךְ	18. הַמִּתְקַדְּשִׁים	28. וַיִּתְחַזַּק
9. הִתְהַלַּכְתִּי	19. אֲקַדֵּשׁ	
10. יִתְהַלְּכוּ	20. וְנִקְדַּשׁ	

42.5b. Translate:

Genesis 6:9
1. אֶת־הָאֱלֹהִים הִתְהַלֶּךְ־נֹחַ

Genesis 5:22
2. וַיִּתְהַלֵּךְ חֲנוֹךְ אֶת־הָאֱלֹהִים אַחֲרֵי הוֹלִידוֹ אֶת־מְתוּשֶׁלַח

Genesis 13:17
3. קוּם הִתְהַלֵּךְ בָּאָרֶץ

Deuteronomy 23:15
4. כִּי יְהוָה אֱלֹהֶיךָ מִתְהַלֵּךְ בְּקֶרֶב מַחֲנֶךָ

Genesis 9:21 שָׁכַר
means *be drunk*. ה --
means *his*.
5. וַיֵּשְׁתְּ מִן־הַיַּיִן וַיִּשְׁכָּר וַיִּתְגַּל בְּתוֹךְ אָהֳלֹה:

238

6.

Genesis 48:2

וַיֻּגַּד לְיַעֲקֹב וַיֹּאמֶר הִנֵּה בִּנְךָ יוֹסֵף בָּא אֵלֶיךָ וַיִּתְחַזֵּק יִשְׂרָאֵל

7.

Numbers 13:20

וְהִתְחַזַּקְתֶּם וּלְקַחְתֶּם מִפְּרִי הָאָרֶץ

8.

1 Chronicles 11:10

וְאֵלֶּה רָאשֵׁי הַגִּבּוֹרִים אֲשֶׁר לְדָוִיד הַמִּתְחַזְּקִים עִמּוֹ

9.

2 Chronicles 13:7   רַךְ
means *tender*.

וּרְחַבְעָם הָיָה נַעַר וְרַךְ־לֵבָב וְלֹא הִתְחַזַּק לִפְנֵיהֶם

10.

Exodus 34:5   עָנָן means
cloud.   יצב   in Hitpael
stem means *station oneself,
present oneself.*

וַיֵּרֶד יְהוָה בֶּעָנָן וַיִּתְיַצֵּב עִמּוֹ שָׁם וַיִּקְרָא בְשֵׁם יְהוָה:

11.

Numbers 11:16

וְלָקַחְתָּ אֹתָם אֶל־אֹהֶל מוֹעֵד וְהִתְיַצְּבוּ שָׁם עִמָּךְ:

12.

Exodus 14:13

וַיֹּאמֶר מֹשֶׁה אֶל־הָעָם אַל־תִּירָאוּ הִתְיַצְּבוּ וּרְאוּ אֶת־יְשׁוּעַת יְהוָה

13.

Deuteronomy 31:14

וַיֵּלֶךְ מֹשֶׁה וִיהוֹשֻׁעַ וַיִּתְיַצְּבוּ בְּאֹהֶל מוֹעֵד

14.

Deuteronomy 3:26   עבר
in the Hitpael stem means
infuriate oneself.

וַיִּתְעַבֵּר יְהוָה בִּי לְמַעַנְכֶם

15.

Genesis 22:18

וְהִתְבָּרֲכוּ בְזַרְעֲךָ כֹּל גּוֹיֵי הָאָרֶץ

16.

Genesis 24:40
יְהוָה אֲשֶׁר־הִתְהַלַּכְתִּי
לְפָנָיו   is an "X" for
יִשְׁלַח

וַיֹּאמֶר אֵלַי יְהוָה אֲשֶׁר־הִתְהַלַּכְתִּי לְפָנָיו יִשְׁלַח מַלְאָכוֹ אִתָּךְ

17.

Leviticus 11:44

כִּי אֲנִי יְהוָה אֱלֹהֵיכֶם וְהִתְקַדִּשְׁתֶּם וִהְיִיתֶם קְדֹשִׁים כִּי קָדוֹשׁ אָנִי

18.

Numbers 11:18

וְאֶל־הָעָם תֹּאמַר הִתְקַדְּשׁוּ

19.

Leviticus 26:12

וְהִתְהַלַּכְתִּי בְּתוֹכְכֶם וְהָיִיתִי לָכֶם לֵאלֹהִים וְאַתֶּם תִּהְיוּ־לִי לְעָם:

20.

Numbers 2:33   פקד   in
Hitpael(technically Hotpael
here) means *be mustered.*

וְהַלְוִיִּם לֹא הָתְפָּקְדוּ בְּתוֹךְ בְּנֵי יִשְׂרָאֵל כַּאֲשֶׁר צִוָּה יְהוָה אֶת־מֹשֶׁה:

Judges 20:15　21. וַיִּתְפָּקְדוּ בְנֵי בִנְיָמִן בַּיּוֹם הַהוּא מֵהֶעָרִים עֶשְׂרִים
וְשִׁשָּׁה אֶלֶף אִישׁ

42.5c. Read Genesis 29:23-30.

Lesson 43

וְשׁוּב עַמִּי וְהִשְׁתַּחֲוֵיתִי לַיהוָה אֱלֹהֶיךָ:
1 Samuel 15:30

Goals:
* Identify and read verbs in the Hishtaphel stem.
* Identify spelling peculiarities in the Hitpael stem.

What we already know

43.1. The first word in our lesson verse וְשׁוּב might be either of two different forms. What are they?

_____ (16.4a) and _____ (21.4b) Seeing the word is a parallel to a weqatal later in the verse, which of the two is more likely? As for עַמִּי is it a

vocative as we often see with an imperative? _____ What would be the nikkud that would mean *my*

people? _____

Translate וְשׁוּב עַמִּי : _____

The Hishtaphel stem

43.2a. We have seen forms of the next verb once or twice before, but you are not here expected to remember its meaning. On the other hand, the word's beginning and ending and place within the general word order of the verse should indicate both that it is a verb and a weqatal. It means literally *And I will be a bower down.*

43.2b. The switch to a first person subject in this verb form helps us realize that the weqatal is not a mitigation of the mainline of a Hortatory Discourse. What must its discourse function therefore be?

_____

43.2c. The third word of our lesson verse contains a singularly disputed but fairly common stem and form. Some scholars believe the root is חוה and the stem's pre-formed sign is -תּ[הְשַׁ]. Another view is that the root is חוו from Biblical Hebrew's cousin language Ugaritic and the stem is a version of the Hiphil stem.[1] Others including Brown, Driver, and Briggs, believe the root is שׁחה and the stem is Hitpael.[2] This would require a transposition or switching of the root's *shin* and the Hitpael's pre-formed *tav*, but as you will see later in this lesson such a transposition is found in the Hitpael conjugations of a number of other roots which begin with *samekh*, *tsadeh*, *shin*, or *sin*. In any case, the word, whatever its root and stem, can be recognized easily by its distinctive appearance. It is definitely worth learning since it is used 178 times!

---

[1] Jouon-Muraoka(1991), §§59g, 79t; van der Merwe, et. al.(1999), p. 139.
[2] Waltke and O'Connor(1990), §21.2.3d.

RULE: **The Hebrew word that means** *bow down* **(worshipfully) can be recognized in all its forms by the sequence** שׁתחו[___]

As with the Hitpael stem, the blank is filled by *heh* in the qatal, weqatal, imperative, and infinitive forms; the prefixed subject pronoun in the yiqtol and wayyiqtol forms; and *mem* in the participle form.

43.2d. Fill out the verb analysis chart for וְהִשְׁתַּחֲוֵיתִי Be sure to account for its relationship to the 2nd person imperative before it (22.3a).

root	stem	form	person, gender, number	function	basic root meaning

Translation of the entire lesson verse:

_____

43.2e. Keep in mind that the *vav* which ends the four letter sequence is not an affix or a prefix complement. An affix or complement would be added to the sequence, sometimes resulting in two *vavs* in a row. Here is a complete Hishtaphel qatal conjugation which shows many of the signs of a 3rd *heh* root in its attested forms.

HISHTAPHEL QATAL:

SINGULAR 3. M.	הִשְׁתַּחֲוָה	PLURAL 3. C.	הִשְׁתַּחֲווּ
3. F.	----		
2. M.	הִשְׁתַּחֲוִיתָ	2. M.	הִשְׁתַּחֲוִיתֶם
2. F.	----	2. F.	----
1. C.	הִשְׁתַּחֲוֵיתִי	1. C.	----

Spelling peculiarities in the Hitpael stem

43.3a. As was mentioned earlier, roots with *samekh, tsadeh, shin,* or *sin* often have a transposition of the first root letter and the stem preformative's *tav* in the Hitpael stem. Some Hebrew grammarians refer to this phenomenon as **metathesis.** Here are some examples:[1]

שׁמר	becomes	אֶשְׁתַּמְּרָה
שׁפך (pour)	becomes	תִּשְׁתַּפֵּךְ

---

[1] Waltke and O'Connor(1990), §26.1.1b-c.

שׁכח (forget)	becomes	וַיִּשְׁתַּכְּחוּ
סתר (hide)	becomes	מִסְתַּתֵּר
צדק	becomes	נִצְטַדָּק

(Notice the transformation of *tav* into *tet*.)

43.3b. Another spelling peculiarity of the Hitpael stem occurs when a root begins with *dalet, tet,* or *tav*. In such a case, the *tav* of the stem preformative assimilates into the root's first letter.

דבר	becomes	מִדַּבֵּר
דמה (resemble)	becomes	אֶדַּמֶּה
טהר (purify)	becomes	הִטַּהֲרוּ
טמא	becomes	תִּטַּמָּאוּ
תמם (be upright)	becomes	תִּתַּמָּם

Assignments

43.4a. Memorize vocabulary words 341-377 to finish your vocabulary for this course.

43.4b. Write the root, stem, form, and where applicable, the person, gender, and number of the following verbs. If a form is ambiguous write all the possible interpretations.

1. יִטְמָא	10. שָׁמַר	19. וְשָׁמְרוּ	28. גָּלָה
2. וְטָמֵא	11. שֹׁמְרִים	20. וְגָלִיתִי	29. תִּגָּלֶה
3. תִּטַּמָּאוּ	12. הִשָּׁמֵר	21. גָּלוֹת	30. לְגַלּוֹת
4. נִטְמְאִים	13. וָאֶשְׁתַּמֵּר	22. אַגְלֶה	31. הִגְלוּ
5. טִמֵּא	14. יִשְׁתַּמֵּר	23. גָּלָה	32. וַיִּשְׁתַּחֲווּ
6. תִּטַּמָּאוּ	15. תִּשָּׁמְרוּ	24. נִגְלוּ	33. הִגְלִיתָ
7. תִּטַּמָּאוּ	16. וְנִשְׁמַרְתֶּם	25. תִּגְלֶה	34. וַיִּגֶל
8. יִטַּמָּא	17. לִשְׁמֹר	26. נִגְלֵיתִי	(you would expect *patakh* under the prefix)
9. לִטְמֹא	18. תִּשְׁמֹר	27. הִגְלָה	35. מִשְׁתַּחֲוִים
			36. וַיִּשְׁתַּחוּ

43.4c. Some imperative and qatal forms in the Hitpael and Hishtaphel stems are identical. Watch out for this ambiguity in the translation exercises below:

Exodus 11:8	1.	וְיָרְדוּ כָל־עֲבָדֶיךָ אֵלֶּה אֵלַי וְהִשְׁתַּחֲווּ־לִי לֵאמֹר צֵא אַתָּה וְכָל־הָעָם
Exodus 33:10	2.	וְקָם כָּל־הָעָם וְהִשְׁתַּחֲווּ אִישׁ פֶּתַח אָהֳלוֹ
Genesis 13:17	3.	קוּם הִתְהַלֵּךְ בָּאָרֶץ
1 Chronicles 16:29 הֲדָרָה means *holy adornment, glory.*	4.	שְׂאוּ מִנְחָה וּבֹאוּ לְפָנָיו הִשְׁתַּחֲווּ לַיהוָה בְּהַדְרַת־קֹדֶשׁ

243

Isaiah 27:13	וְהִשְׁתַּחֲווּ לַיהוָה בְּהַר הַקֹּדֶשׁ בִּירוּשָׁלָ͏ִם	5.
Psalm 45:11	כִּי־הוּא אֲדֹנַיִךְ וְהִשְׁתַּחֲוִי־לוֹ	6.
Ezekiel 46:2 מִפְתָּן means *threshold*.	וְעָשׂוּ הַכֹּהֲנִים אֶת־עוֹלָתוֹ וְהִשְׁתַּחֲוָה עַל־מִפְתַּן הַשַּׁעַר וְיָצָא וְהַשַּׁעַר לֹא־יִסָּגֵר	7.
Numbers 11:18	וְאֶל־הָעָם תֹּאמַר הִתְקַדְּשׁוּ	8.
Joshua 7:13	קֻם קַדֵּשׁ אֶת־הָעָם וְאָמַרְתָּ הִתְקַדְּשׁוּ	9.
Joshua 18:8	לְכוּ וְהִתְהַלְּכוּ בָאָרֶץ וְשׁוּבוּ אֵלַי	10.
2 Chronicles 5:11	כָּל־הַכֹּהֲנִים הַנִּמְצְאִים הִתְקַדָּשׁוּ	11.
Genesis 48:15-16	וַיֹּאמַר הָאֱלֹהִים אֲשֶׁר הִתְהַלְּכוּ אֲבֹתַי לְפָנָיו אַבְרָהָם וְיִצְחָק יְבָרֵךְ אֶת־הַנְּעָרִים	12.
Genesis 37:10	הֲבוֹא נָבוֹא אֲנִי וְאִמְּךָ וְאַחֶיךָ לְהִשְׁתַּחֲוֺת לְךָ אָרְצָה	13.
Genesis 45:1 יָדַע in Hitpael means *make oneself known*.	וְלֹא־עָמַד אִישׁ אִתּוֹ בְּהִתְוַדַּע יוֹסֵף אֶל־אֶחָיו	14.
1 Samuel 1:12 פָּלַל in Piel means *mediate, judge*, and in Hitpael means *pray*.	וְהָיָה כִּי הִרְבְּתָה לְהִתְפַּלֵּל לִפְנֵי יְהוָה וְעֵלִי שֹׁמֵר אֶת־פִּיהָ׃	15.
1 Samuel 1:27 The preposition here means *for*, not *to*.	אֶל־הַנַּעַר הַזֶּה הִתְפַּלָּלְתִּי	16.
1 Kings 8:42	וּבָא וְהִתְפַּלֵּל אֶל־הַבַּיִת הַזֶּה	17.
Deuteronomy 9:20	וָאֶתְפַּלֵּל גַּם־בְּעַד אַהֲרֹן בָּעֵת הַהִוא	18.

43.4d. Read the introduction to Reading Seven and Ezekiel 37:1-6.

Lesson 44

כִּי־אִישׁ אִישׁ אֲשֶׁר יְקַלֵּל אֶת־אָבִיו וְאֶת־אִמּוֹ מוֹת יוּמָת

Leviticus 20:9

Goals:

- **Identify and read Juridical Discourse.**
- **Identify and read verbs in the Hophal stem.**

What we already know

44.1. Translate the middle part of our lesson verse אִישׁ אֲשֶׁר יְקַלֵּל אֶת־אָבִיו וְאֶת־אִמּוֹ
(קָלַל means *curse, slight* in the Piel stem.):

_____

Juridical Discourse

44.2a. Juridical Discourse is the genre of Biblical Hebrew which gives the legal codes of the Bible.[1] These codes are located largely in Exodus through Deuteronomy, but they can be found elsewhere as well. We will only attempt a brief introduction to Juridical Discourse in this course.

The grammar of Juridical Discourse makes use of the same verb forms you have already learned in some specialized ways. The most common construction in Juridical Discourse is *protasis-apodosis*. The protasis is the "when" or "if"-part of a "when (if)-then" construction and the apodosis is the "then"-part.

RULE: The **protasis** of Biblical Hebrew Juridical Discourse is often constructed with the word כִּי or אִם and one of the following:

1. **A subject-yiqtol.** (As in our lesson verse.)
2. **A yiqtol-subject.**

וְכִי־יִגַּח שׁוֹר אֶת־אִישׁ Exodus 21:28

And if an ox gore a man…

3. **If the protasis is complicated, the yiqtol may be followed by either weqatals and/or X-yiqtols.**

כִּי־יָמוּךְ אָחִיךָ וּמָכַר מֵאֲחֻזָּתוֹ Leviticus 25:25

If your brother becomes poor and so is a seller from his possessions…

The **apodosis** usually contains one of the following:

1. **An infinitive absolute plus yiqtol.** (As in our lesson verse.)
2. **A לֹא plus yiqtol.**

אִם־יוֹם אוֹ יוֹמַיִם יַעֲמֹד לֹא יֻקַּם Exodus 21:21

*If he (a slave) continues a day or two, **then he (an assailant) will not be punished**.*

---

[1] Longacre(1987), 189; Ben Zvi, Hancock, Beinert, *Readings in Biblical Hebrew*(New Haven: Yale University Press, 1993), 55-98; Waltke and O'Connor(1990), §§32.2.1b-c, 32.2.3b.

3. An X-yiqtol.

אִם־בְּגַפּוֹ יָבֹא בְּגַפּוֹ יֵצֵא   Exodus 21:3

*If by himself he comes in, **then it is by himself that he goes out**.*

4. <u>**Most often the apodosis is one or more weqatals.**</u>

וְכִי־יָרֹק הַזָּב בַּטָּהוֹר וְכִבֶּס בְּגָדָיו וְרָחַץ בַּמַּיִם וְטָמֵא עַד־הָעָרֶב: Leviticus 15:8

*And if the one with a discharge spit upon one who is clean, **then he will be a washer of his garments and a rinser in water and be unclean until the evening**.*

Note: If the protasis ends with a weqatal clause and the apodosis begins with a weqatal clause the boundary between the protasis and apodosis can be challenging to find. For instance, the translators of the King James Version and the Revised Standard Version had a difference of opinion about the protasis/apodosis boundary in Leviticus 25:25, shown here in its entirety:

כִּי־יָמוּךְ אָחִיךָ וּמָכַר מֵאֲחֻזָּתוֹ וּבָא גֹאֲלוֹ הַקָּרֹב אֵלָיו וְגָאַל אֵת מִמְכַּר אָחִיו:

The King James translates, *If thy brother be waxen poor, and hath sold away some of his possession, and if any of his kin come to redeem it, **then** shall he redeem that which his brother sold.*

But the Revised Standard translates, *If your brother becomes poor, and sells part of his property, **then** his next of kin shall come and redeem what his brother has sold.*

Which do you think makes better sense?

44.2b. You may translate כִּי־אִישׁ אִישׁ אֲשֶׁר יְקַלֵּל literally, using *when* for כִּי however, when the word אִישׁ is used to specify the subject of a verb, something very often seen in Juridical Discourse, it has the sense *each one, anyone.* אִישׁ is also seen with this sense in the other genres as well. Our lesson verse's double use of אִישׁ is an interesting variation.

Translation of כִּי־אִישׁ אִישׁ אֲשֶׁר יְקַלֵּל אֶת־אָבִיו וְאֶת־אִמּוֹ:

_____

Hophal stem

44.3a. The last two words of our lesson verse are a fairly common apodosis in Juridical Discourse.

Which of the apodosis constructions in 44.2a is מוֹת יוּמָת ? _____

In case you are not sure, compare the following forms of the root מות :

מָוֶת = masculine noun

מוּת = Qal infinitive construct

מוֹת = Qal infinitive absolute, or masculine noun

44.3b. Let us also compare the same root in the same yiqtol form in several different stems:

יָמוּת = Qal: *he will die, he dies*

יָמִית = Hiphil: *he will kill, he kills*

יוּמָת = Hophal: *he will be killed*

246

RULE: **The Hophal stem is the passive version of the Hiphil stem. Its sign in all forms is a *qamets* [ָ] , *shureq*[וּ], or *qibbuts* [ֻ] under the pre-formed letters that correspond to the Hiphil stem or the yiqtol form's prefixed subject pronoun.**

We will examine examples shortly, but first fill out the verb analysis chart for יוּמָת :

root	stem	form	person, gender, number	function	basic root meaning
				apodosis	

Translation of מוֹת יוּמָת : *he will surely be killed*

Notice, by the way, that a Qal infinitive absolute is used to emphasize a verb in a non-Qal stem. For all non-Qal yiqtols and qatals used with infinitive absolutes, about 70% of the infinitive absolutes are Qal.

Translation of the entire lesson verse: _____

_____

44.3c. Here is the root מוּת shown in the Hiphil and Hophal stems in all forms:

SYNOPSIS of מוּת in HIPHIL and HOPHAL:

	HIPHIL	HOPHAL
Qatal 3rd m. s.	הֵמִית	הוּמָת
Yiqtol 3rd m. s.	יָמִית	יוּמָת
Wayyiqtol 3rd m. s.	וַיָּמֶת	וַיּוּמַת
Imperative m. s.	הָמֵת	*הוּ---
Participle m. s.	מֵמִית	מוּמָת
Infinitive	הָמִית	**הוּמַת

*Hophal imperative is attested only twice in the Hebrew Bible. **Not attested in the Hebrew Bible

Assignments

44.4a. Write the root, stem, form, and where applicable, the person, gender, number of the following verbs. If a form is ambiguous, write all the possibilities.

34. יוּמָת	23. וּרְאִיתֶן	12. נִרְאוּ	1. וַיִּפְקְדוּ
35. יוּמְתוּ	24. וַיָּמֹת	13. נִרְאָה	2. פֻּקְדוּ
36. וְהוּמַת	25. וַיָּמָת	14. וַיִּרְאוּ	3. פֻּקַד
37. וְהִכָּהוּ	26. לָמוּת	15. וַנֵּרָאֶה	4. הִפְקִיד
38. וַיַּךְ	27. מֵת	16. וַיֵּרָא	5. הֻפְקַד
39. הַמֻּכֶּה	28. לְהָמִית	17. הֵרָאָה	6. וַיַּפְקֵד
40. הֻכּוֹת	29. וַיָּמֶת	18. מַרְאֶה	7. מֻפְקָד
41. יֻכֶּה	30. תָּמִית	19. הַרְאֵה	8. יֻפְקַד
42. וְהֻכָּה	31. מֵתוּ	20. מָרְאֶה	9. לְהִפָּקֵד
43. וַיֻּכּוּ	32. וְהֵמִית	21. הָרְאֵיתָ	10. הַמֻּפְקָדִים
44. מֻכִּים	33. מֵמִית	22. וְהָרְאָה	11. הָפְקַד

44.4b. Translate

Exodus 21:12

1. ‏מַכֵּה אִישׁ וָמֵת מוֹת יוּמָת:

Exodus 21:15

2. ‏וּמַכֵּה אָבִיו וְאִמּוֹ מוֹת יוּמָת:

Exodus 21:18-19 רִיב
means *quarrel.* נקה
means in Piel means *leave unpunished.*

3. ‏וְכִי־יְרִיבֻן אֲנָשִׁים וְהִכָּה־אִישׁ אֶת־רֵעֵהוּ בְּאֶבֶן וְלֹא יָמוּת אִם־יָקוּם וְהִתְהַלֵּךְ וְנִקָּה הַמַּכֶּה

Exodus 21:20 נקם in Hophal means *be avenged.*

4. ‏וְכִי־יַכֶּה אִישׁ אֶת־עַבְדּוֹ בַּשֵּׁבֶט וּמֵת תַּחַת יָדוֹ נָקֹם יִנָּקֵם:

Exodus 21:26 שחה in Piel means *ruin,* and חָפְשִׁי is a substantive meaning *freedom.*

5. ‏וְכִי־יַכֶּה אִישׁ אֶת־עֵין עַבְדּוֹ וְשִׁחֲתָהּ לַחָפְשִׁי יְשַׁלְּחֶנּוּ תַּחַת עֵינוֹ

Exodus 26:30

6. ‏וַהֲקֵמֹתָ אֶת־הַמִּשְׁכָּן כְּמִשְׁפָּטוֹ אֲשֶׁר הָרְאֵיתָ בָּהָר:

1 Samuel 15:12 נגד is one of the most common roots seen used in the Hophal stem.

7. ‏וַיֻּגַּד לִשְׁמוּאֵל לֵאמֹר בָּא־שָׁאוּל

248

8. אִם־אֵינְךָ מְמַלֵּט אֶת־נַפְשְׁךָ הַלַּיְלָה מָחָר אַתָּה מוּמָת

1 Samuel 19:11 מלט in Piel means *deliver*. מָחָר means *tomorrow*.

9. וְהֵם הֻמְתוּ בִּימֵי קָצִיר

2 Samuel 21:9 קָצִיר means *harvest*.

10. וְהִנֵּה לֹא־הֻגַּד־לִי הַחֵצִי

1 Kings 10:7 חֵצִי means *half*.

11. וַיֵּלֶךְ וַיִּמְצָאֵהוּ אַרְיֵה בַּדֶּרֶךְ וַיְמִיתֵהוּ וַתְּהִי נִבְלָתוֹ מֻשְׁלֶכֶת בַּדָּרֶךְ

1 Kings 13:24 אַרְיֵה means *lion*, and נְבֵלָה means *carcass*.

12. וְאֶת־בְּנֵי הַמַּכִּים לֹא הֵמִית כַּכָּתוּב בְּסֵפֶר תּוֹרַת־מֹשֶׁה אֲשֶׁר־צִוָּה יְהוָה לֵאמֹר לֹא־יוּמְתוּ אָבוֹת עַל־בָּנִים וּבָנִים לֹא־יוּמְתוּ עַל־אָבוֹת

2 Kings 14:6 כַּכָּתוּב בְּסֵפֶר תּוֹרַת־מֹשֶׁה means *as it is written in the Instruction of Moses.*

13. וְהַבָּא אֶל־הַבַּיִת יוּמָת וִהְיוּ אֶת־הַמֶּלֶךְ בְּבֹאוֹ וּבְצֵאתוֹ

2 Chronicles 23:7

14. בָּבֶלָה יוּבָאוּ וְשָׁמָּה יִהְיוּ עַד יוֹם פָּקְדִי אֹתָם נְאֻם־יְהוָה וְהַעֲלִיתִים וַהֲשִׁיבֹתִים אֶל־הַמָּקוֹם הַזֶּה׃

Jeremiah 27:22

44.4c. Read Ezekiel 37:7-14.

Lesson 45

אֵלֶּה פְקוּדֵי הַמִּשְׁכָּן מִשְׁכַּן הָעֵדֻת אֲשֶׁר פֻּקַּד עַל־פִּי מֹשֶׁה

Exodus 38:21

Goals:

- **Identify and read the Qal passive participle.**
- **Identify and read verbs in the Pual stem.**

What we already know

Translate אֵלֶּה _____ What is the gender and number of פְּקוּדֵי ?

_____ (8.4) What is the word's basic root meaning?

_____

Qal passive participle

45.2a. פְקוּדֵי is a participle form being used as the construct in a construct chain.

> **RULE: A *shureq*, either plene or defectiva, after the second root letter is the sign of the Qal passive participle: O ֹ O O** We will not assign a discourse function to the Qal passive participle because it is more often used adjectivally (or substantively) than verbally. **Translate with an English *-ed*-word.**

Translation of אֵלֶּה פְקוּדֵי הַמִּשְׁכָּן : *these are the observed (things) of the tabernacle*

45.2b. One of the roots most commonly used as a Qal passive participle is בר ך shown here:

יְהִי יְהוָה אֱלֹהֶיךָ בָּרוּךְ 1 Kings 10:9
May YHWH your God be blessed!

or

וַיֹּאמֶר בּוֹא בְּרוּךְ יְהוָה Genesis 24:31
And he said, "Come in, O blessed of YHWH!"

45.2c. What is the relationship of the next construct chain in our lesson verse, מִשְׁכַּן הָעֵדֻת with

פְקוּדֵי הַמִּשְׁכָּן ? _____ (40.2a) It may appear that we have another Qal passive participle in the word הָעֵדֻת from the root עדה but if you check your dictionary you will find that עדה is not a root after all. The word עֵדֹות meaning *testimonies* and the singular form עֵדוּת meaning *testimony* come from the root עוד Be careful not to over-generalize.

Translation of אֵלֶּה פְקוּדֵי הַמִּשְׁכָּן מִשְׁכַּן הָעֵדֻת : _____

_____

45.2d. Third *heh* roots display one special characteristic as Qal Passive participles. A *yod* is added after the *shureq* and before the final *heh* as in נְטוּיָה *stretched out* or הָעֲשׂוּיָה *the performed*. Occasionally the final *heh* drops off as in עָשׂוּי *performed, made*.

Pual stem

45.3a. The last clause of our lesson verse is indeed an אֲשֶׁר-qatal clause which has what discourse

function? _____ What kind of *dagesh* is in the *peh* of

פֻּקַּד ? _____ So only the letter's pronunciation is affected; it is

not doubled. What kind of *dagesh* is in the *qoph*? _____ What stem

does a doubled middle root letter point to? _____ The word פֻּקַּד is in
the Piel stem's passive counterpart, the Pual.

> **RULE: The sign of the Pual stem is a *qibbuts*[ֻ] or *holem*[ֹ] after the first root letter and a doubled middle root letter.**

Fill out the verb analysis chart for פֻּקַּד :

root	stem	form	person, gender, number	Function	basic root meaning

Translation of אֲשֶׁר פֻּקַּד : *which had been called into account*

45.3b. Our introduction to the seven most common verb stems, accounting for about 99% of all verbs in the Hebrew Bible, is now almost complete. Let us review these seven stems as they work together as a system. To do so, let us consider a verb's **agent** the doer of the verb. We shy away from the word subject here because of the passive stems in which the concept "subject" becomes elusive. Let us consider the one who is acted upon to be the verb's **patient**. *Both the agent and the patient can alternate between active and passive to give us the basic outline of the Biblical Hebrew system of verbal stems.* The following matrix is adapted from Waltke and O'Connor[1].

---

[1] Waltke and O'Connor(1990), 358.

Patient: Agent:	NULL	PASSIVE	ACTIVE
ACTIVE	QAL: to act	PIEL: to cause to be in a state	HIFIL: to cause to act
PASSIVE	NIFAL: to be acted upon	PUAL: to be caused to be in a state	HOFAL: to be caused to act
REFLEXIVE (DOUBLE STATUS)	NIFAL: to act and consequently, be acted upon	HITPAEL: to cause oneself to act	

The root פקד is one of the few roots that is used in the seven stems we have studied. It is worth reviewing the different nuances of the word in those stems in which it does appear. To do so, let us examine the same matrix as above with the senses of פקד plugged into the slots.

Patient: Agent:	NULL	PASSIVE	ACTIVE
ACTIVE	*observe*	*gather for observation*	*appoint as overseer*
PASSIVE	*be observed*	*be gathered for observation*	*be delivered for oversight*
REFLEXIVE (DOUBLE STATUS)		*account for oneself*	

45.3c. A word of caution: Although it is very helpful to view the Biblical Hebrew language as a system, it is easily possible to over-generalize. Languages develop over a very long time, and they develop on the street, in the market, in the courts, etc. of living people who do not ask anyone's permission before they use their language in a certain way. As a result of the way languages develop, they often defy systematic description. Words in their certain contexts simply mean what they do. We cannot always force a root's several senses in several stems into a neat chart as above or a quaint etymology. As you come across exceptions to the system view you are learning, view the exceptions as only natural. On the other hand, to try and learn a language as isolated pieces and parts that do not in any way fit into patterns is not only misleading. It would make learning a language an unnecessarily difficult challenge.

The construct form and meaning of פֶּה

45.4. The word פֶּה meaning *mouth* conjugates irregularly, but easily. Its singular construct form is פִּי Whenever suffixes are added to the word, they are added to this construct form. The noun plus 1st c. s. suffix, our *my*, is written the same as the singular construct without any suffix, again פִּי You will have to use context to tell the difference. In our lesson verse, do you think פִּי means *my mouth* or *mouth of*? Actually, the expression עַל פִּי means *according to the word of* or simply, *according to*.

Translation of the entire lesson verse: _____

_____

252

Assignments

45.5a.   Write the root, stem, form, and where applicable, the person, gender, number of the following verbs. If a form is ambiguous, write all the possibilities.

1.	וַתֵּלֶד	11.	הֻלֶּדֶת	21.	וְנִבְרְכוּ	31.	מִצְוָה
2.	וַיֵּלְדוּ	12.	הַיִּלּוֹד	22.	וַיַּבְרֵךְ	32.	מִצְוָה
3.	יָלַד	13.	הַמְיַלֶּדֶת	23.	וְהִתְבָּרְכוּ	33.	וַיְצַו
4.	וַיִּוָּלֵד	14.	לָלֶדֶת	24.	יִתְבָּרֵךְ	34.	וַיְצַוּוּ
5.	יָלְדָה	15.	נִבְרְכָה	25.	מְבָרֵךְ	35.	לְצַוּוֹת
6.	נוֹלַד	16.	וַיְבָרֶךְ	26.	תְּבָרֵךְ	36.	צִוִּיתָה
7.	נוֹלְדוּ	17.	בָּרוּךְ	27.	יְבָרֵךְ	37.	יְצַוֶּה
8.	הַנּוֹלַד	18.	וַיְבָרֵךְ	28.	צִוִּיתִי	38.	צִוִּיתִי
9.	הַנּוֹלָדִים	19.	וּבֵרַכְתִּי	29.	צַו	39.	צִוָּה
10.	יֻלַּד	20.	בֵּרֵךְ	30.	צִוָּה	40.	צַוּוּ

45.5b.   Translate:

Genesis 44:3 חֲמוֹר means *donkey*.

1. וְהָאֲנָשִׁים שֻׁלְּחוּ הֵמָּה וַחֲמֹרֵיהֶם:

Genesis 45:19

2. וְאַתָּה צֻוֵּיתָה זֹאת עֲשׂוּ

Exodus 34:34   This is from a stretch of Procedural Discourse.

3. וְיָצָא וְדִבֶּר אֶל־בְּנֵי יִשְׂרָאֵל אֵת אֲשֶׁר יְצֻוֶּה

Numbers 3:16

4. וַיִּפְקֹד אֹתָם מֹשֶׁה עַל־פִּי יְהוָה כַּאֲשֶׁר צֻוָּה:

Numbers 36:2

5. וַאדֹנִי צֻוָּה בַיהוָה לָתֵת אֶת־נַחֲלַת צְלָפְחָד אָחִינוּ לִבְנֹתָיו

Judges 5:15

6. בָּעֵמֶק שֻׁלַּח בְּרַגְלָיו

2 Samuel 7:29 בְּרָכָה is the noun form.

7. וּמִבִּרְכָתְךָ יְבֹרַךְ בֵּית־עַבְדְּךָ לְעוֹלָם

1 Kings 21:14 סֻקַּל means *throw stones to execute*. מוּת appears וַיָּמֹת when in pause and וַיָּמָת otherwise.

8. וַיִּשְׁלְחוּ אֶל־אִיזֶבֶל לֵאמֹר סֻקַּל נָבוֹת וַיָּמֹת:

9.	אַתָּה יְהֹוָה בֵּרַכְתָּ וּמְבֹרָךְ לְעוֹלָם	1 Chronicles 17:27

1 Chronicles 17:27

9.   אַתָּה יְהֹוָה בֵּרַכְתָּ וּמְבֹרָךְ לְעוֹלָם

1 Chronicles 17:27

10.   אֹרְרֶיךָ אָרוּר וּמְבָרְכֶיךָ בָּרוּךְ

Genesis 27:29 One of the most common Qal passive participle is בָּרוּךְ *blessed*, and another is אָרוּר *its opposite.*

11.   וַיַּרְא יְהֹוָה כִּי־שְׂנוּאָה לֵאָה וַיִּפְתַּח אֶת־רַחְמָהּ

Genesis 29:31 פתח in Qal means *open*. רֶחֶם means *womb* from which comes רַחוּם *compassion*.

12.   מִנְחָה הִוא שְׁלוּחָה לַאדֹנִי לְעֵשָׂו

Genesis 32:19

13.   וּצְבָאוֹ וּפְקֻדֵיהֶם תִּשְׁעָה וַחֲמִשִּׁים אֶלֶף וּשְׁלֹשׁ מֵאוֹת:

Numbers 2:13 תִּשְׁעָה means *nine*.

14.   נְתֻנִים נְתֻנִים הֵמָּה לִי מִתּוֹךְ בְּנֵי יִשְׂרָאֵל

Numbers 8:16

15.   וַיֹּצִאֲךָ יְהֹוָה אֱלֹהֶיךָ מִשָּׁם בְּיָד חֲזָקָה וּבִזְרֹעַ נְטוּיָה

Deuteronomy 5:15 זְרוֹעַ means *arm*.

16.   וַיְצַו הַמֶּלֶךְ אֶת־חִלְקִיָּהוּ הַכֹּהֵן הַגָּדוֹל לְהוֹצִיא אֵת כָּל־הַכֵּלִים הָעֲשׂוּיִם

2 Kings 23:4 הַכֹּהֵן הַגָּדוֹל means *High Priest*. כֵּלִים is the plural of כְּלִי

17.   וַיִּחַר־אַף יְהֹוָה בָּאָרֶץ הַהִוא לְהָבִיא עָלֶיהָ אֶת־כָּל־הַקְּלָלָה הַכְּתוּבָה בַּסֵּפֶר הַזֶּה:

Deuteronomy 29:26 חרה means *kindle*. With אַף it means to become very angry. קְלָלָה means *a curse*.

18.   וַיַּעַזְבוּ אֶת־הָעִיר פְּתוּחָה וַיִּרְדְּפוּ אַחֲרֵי יִשְׂרָאֵל

Joshua 8:17

19.   וַיַּעַל גִּדְעוֹן דֶּרֶךְ הַשְּׁכוּנֵי בָאֳהָלִים

Judges 8:11

20.   וַיִּקַּח שָׁאוּל שְׁלֹשֶׁת אֲלָפִים אִישׁ בָּחוּר מִכָּל־יִשְׂרָאֵל וַיֵּלֶךְ לְבַקֵּשׁ אֶת־דָּוִד

1 Samuel 24:3

45.5c. Read the introductory material to Reading 8 and Genesis 43:1-5, 8-10.

MODULE SIX—GEMINATE ROOTS AND MORE ON NUMBERS

<u>Overview</u>: You are on the way home! Congratulations! The last five lessons of the course are fairly easy ones. You will be learning about a kind of root which we have not encountered much, the geminate root. There are only three geminate roots on your vocabulary list, סבב   חלל and הלל but there are many other geminate roots in the Hebrew Bible, and it is important that you know how to analyze these promiscuous roots. You will also be filling out your understanding of numbers which began in your earlier readings and Lesson 38.3. Finally, this module will cover some important discourse issues such as **using a qatal to set the time of a scene, modal yiqtol**, and **marking peak in a discourse** as we finish the very exciting eighth reading which began in Lesson 45. Hopefully you are saddened by the news that there is no new Hebrew vocabulary added during this module.

Lesson 46

וַיָּסֹבּוּ אֶת־הָעִיר כַּמִּשְׁפָּט הַזֶּה שֶׁבַע פְּעָמִים רַק בַּיּוֹם הַהוּא סָבְבוּ אֶת־הָעִיר שֶׁבַע פְּעָמִים

Joshua 6:15

Goal:

• Identify and read verbs made from geminate roots.

What we already know

Copy the Qal wayyiqtol and Qal qatal verb forms here. _____ and _____

Judging by the nikkud, what do you expect is the root of וַיָּסֹבּוּ ? _____ (10.3)

Qal yiqtol and wayyiqtol of geminates

46.2a. You might make a few guesses, either a root that you have learned as part of your vocabulary, סבב or a root that is indicated by the *qamets* under the prefixed pronoun, either סִיב סוֹב or probably סוֹב It turns out that the "hollow roots" are unattested, and that סבב is correct.

> DEFINITION: Roots whose 2nd and 3rd letters are the same are called *geminates*.
> They conjugate erratically, often losing one of the twin root letters and showing the nikkud of a hollow verb.

Translate וַיָּסֹבּוּ אֶת־הָעִיר : _____

46.2b. Below is the chart for the yiqtol of סבב as an example of geminate roots. Two conjugations are listed because they are both attested. Even so, some other patterns of nikkud are also attested. Keep in mind that you are again somewhat unburdened from having to remember every detail for conjugating every geminate root because you are interested in reading Biblical Hebrew rather than composing it. The best strategy for dealing with geminates is to know the commonly used roots and keep them in mind when you only see two root letters of a verb.

QAL YIQTOL of GEMINATES:

	A	B			A	B
SINGULAR 3. M.	יָסֹב	יִסֹּב	PLURAL 3. M.	יָסֹבּוּ	יִסְבוּ
3. F.	תָּסֹב	תִּסֹּב	3. F.	תְּסֻבֶּינָה*	תִּסֹּבְנָה*
2. M.	תָּסֹב	תִּסֹּב	2. M.	תְּסֹבּוּ	תִּסְבוּ
2. F.	תָּסֹבִּי	תִּסְבִי	2. F.	תְּסֻבֶּינָה*	תִּסֹּבְנָה*
1. C.	אָסֹב	אֶסֹּב	1. C.	נָסֹב	נִסֹּב

256

46.2c. The word מִשְׁפָּט can mean *manner, custom* as well as *judgment*. Translate

וַיָּסֹבּוּ אֶת־הָעִיר כַּמִּשְׁפָּט הַזֶּה שֶׁבַע פְּעָמִים :

Qal qatal and weqatal of geminates

46.3a. Translate רַק בַּיּוֹם הַהוּא : _____

Do you think this phrase belongs with the preceding or the following clause and why? _____

_____ (11.5)

46.3b. Fill out the verb analysis chart for סָבְבוּ making sure to note the construction of the clause when you fill in the function column.

root	stem	form	person, gender, number	function	basic root meaning

Translate רַק בַּיּוֹם הַהוּא סָבְבוּ אֶת־הָעִיר שֶׁבַע פְּעָמִים : _____

_____

46.3c. The Qal qatal (and weqatal) of geminate roots has its own set of peculiarities as you can see below. The roots סבב and תמם are displayed.

QAL QATAL OF GEMINATES:

	SINGULAR			PLURAL	
3. M.	תַּם	סָבַב	3. C.	תַּמּוּ סָבְבוּ	
3. F.	תַּמָּה סָבְבָה				
2. M.	סַבֹּותָ		2. M.	סַבֹּותֶם	
2. F.	סַבֹּות		2. F.	סַבֹּותֶן	
1. C.	סַבֹּותִי		1. C.	סַבֹּונוּ	

Other Qal forms of geminate roots

46.4a. Masculine Qal imperatives of geminate roots follow the *A* pattern in the chart in 46.2b, and feminine singular imperatives follow the *B* pattern, so fill in three imperative forms accordingly for the root סבב :

257

s. _____

s. _____

p. _____

46.4b. Qal participles of geminate roots are regular, so fill in the following participle forms for סבב :

s. _____

f. s. _____

p. _____

s. passive _____ (45.2)

46.4c. Qal infinitives of geminate roots follow the pattern for סבב : סֹב or סְבֹב for the construct and סֹב or סָבוֹב for the absolute.

Other geminate roots

46.5. The only other geminate roots on your vocabulary list for this course besides סבב are הלל meaning *praise* and חלל meaning *profane* or *begin*. Here are other fairly common geminate roots most of which are seen in the Hebrew Bible fifty times or more. They are arranged by their frequency.

רעע	be evil	צרר	be hostile	רבב	become great
שמם	be desolate	ארר	curse	חמם	become warm
חנן	show favor	רנן	give a piercing cry	המם	make a noise
פלל	pray	מדד	measure		
תמם	be complete	שדד	lay waste		

Assignments

46.6a. Translate:

Joshua 6:3

1. וְסַבֹּתֶם אֶת־הָעִיר כֹּל אַנְשֵׁי הַמִּלְחָמָה

Joshua 6:4 הַשְּׁבִיעִי means *seventh*.

2. וּבַיּוֹם הַשְּׁבִיעִי תָּסֹבּוּ אֶת־הָעִיר שֶׁבַע פְּעָמִים

Joshua 6:14 הַשֵּׁנִי means *second*.

3. וַיָּסֹבּוּ אֶת־הָעִיר בַּיּוֹם הַשֵּׁנִי פַּעַם אַחַת

1 Samuel 7:16

4. וְהָלַךְ מִדֵּי שָׁנָה בְּשָׁנָה וְסָבַב בֵּית־אֵל

258

5.

1 Kings 5:17 מִפְּנֵי here means *because of*. Notice that singular הַמִּלְחָמָה is the antecedent for the plural subject pronoun of סְבָבֻהוּ

אַתָּה יָדַעְתָּ אֶת־דָּוִד אָבִי כִּי לֹא יָכֹל לִבְנוֹת בַּיִת לְשֵׁם יְהוָה אֱלֹהָיו מִפְּנֵי הַמִּלְחָמָה אֲשֶׁר סְבָבֻהוּ

6. Psalm 88:17

סַבּוּנִי כַמַּיִם כָּל־הַיּוֹם

7. Psalm 118:10

כָּל־גּוֹיִם סְבָבוּנִי

8. Qohelet 7:25

סַבּוֹתִי אֲנִי וְלִבִּי לָדַעַת חָכְמָה

9. Genesis 37:7 אֲלֻמָּה means *sheaf*.

וְהִנֵּה תְסֻבֶּינָה אֲלֻמֹּתֵיכֶם וַתִּשְׁתַּחֲוֶיןָ לַאֲלֻמָּתִי

10. 2 Samuel 14:24

וַיֹּאמֶר הַמֶּלֶךְ יִסֹּב אֶל־בֵּיתוֹ

11. 1 Samuel 5:8 גַּת either refers to the city which spoke or the city towards which the ark would be turned.

וַיֹּאמְרוּ גַּת יִסֹּב אֲרוֹן אֱלֹהֵי יִשְׂרָאֵל

12. Genesis 42:24

וַיִּסֹּב מֵעֲלֵיהֶם וַיֵּבְךְּ וַיָּשָׁב אֲלֵהֶם

13. Deuteronomy 2:1

וַנָּסָב אֶת־הַר־שֵׂעִיר יָמִים רַבִּים

14. Judges 11:18

וַיֵּלֶךְ בַּמִּדְבָּר וַיָּסָב אֶת־אֶרֶץ אֱדוֹם

15. Judges 20:5

וַיָּקֻמוּ עָלַי בַּעֲלֵי הַגִּבְעָה וַיָּסֹבּוּ עָלַי אֶת־הַבַּיִת

16. 2 Samuel 18:15

וַיָּסֹבּוּ עֲשָׂרָה נְעָרִים נֹשְׂאֵי כְּלֵי יוֹאָב וַיַּכּוּ אֶת־אַבְשָׁלוֹם וַיְמִיתֻהוּ׃

17. 2 Samuel 18:30

וַיֹּאמֶר הַמֶּלֶךְ סֹב הִתְיַצֵּב כֹּה וַיִּסֹּב וַיַּעֲמֹד׃

46.6b.   Read the discourse analysis for Genesis 44:18-25.

Lesson 47

וַיַּסֵּבוּ אֶת־אֲרוֹן אֱלֹהֵי יִשְׂרָאֵל וַיְהִי אַחֲרֵי הֵסַבוּ אֹתוֹ וַתְּהִי יַד־יְהוָה בָּעִיר מְהוּמָה גְדוֹלָה מְאֹד

1 Samuel 5:8-9

Goals:
- **Identify and read Hiphil yiqtol and wayyiqtol of geminate roots.**
- **Identify and read a qatal form being used to set the time of a scene.**

What we already know

47.1. Fill out the verb analysis chart for וַיַּסֵּבוּ   (See 46.2, but you may want to delay filling in the stem.):

root	stem	form	person, gender, number	function	basic root meaning

Hiphil yiqtol and wayyiqtol of geminates

47.2a. As for the stem of וַיַּסֵּבוּ   the customary sign is in place, the *patakh* under the prefixed subject

pronoun. This sign is common in the wayyiqtol of what stem? _____ (29.4b) In the Hiphil stem סבב follows the pattern of other verbs of motion in Hiphil, meaning *bring* or in the case of סבב *bring, carry around*. Translate וַיַּסֵּבוּ אֶת־אֲרוֹן אֱלֹהֵי יִשְׂרָאֵל :

_____

47.2b.   The Hiphil wayyiqtols of geminate roots that have *patakh* under the prefixed pronoun far out number the wayyiqtols and yiqtols which do not.   However, there are a few Hiphil wayyiqtols and yiqtols of geminate roots which you are here warned may have *qamets* under the prefixed subject pronoun rather than the Hiphil's customary *patakh* as in 1 Chronicles 13:3's 1st c. p. cohortative:

וְנָסֵבָּה אֶת־אֲרוֹן אֱלֹהֵינוּ אֵלֵינוּ

Setting the time of a scene with וַיְהִי plus preposition plus qatal

47.3a. Translate וַיְהִי אַחֲרֵי : _____

What is the discourse function of וַיְהִי ? _____

260

47.3b. Let us work on the verb analysis chart for הֵסַבּוּ :

root	stem	form	person, gender, number	function	basic root meaning
				temporal scene-setting	

The root is the now familiar סבב We have to divine Hiphil qatal from the combination pre-formed *heh* of the Hiphil stem and the affixed subject pronoun *shureq* [וּ].

47.3c. The function of the qatal in this case is tricky although you have seen it before in Judges 16:16. The construction is not simply an X-qatal, with אַחֲרֵי as the "X." The phrase וַיְהִי אַחֲרֵי together with the following qatal הֵסַבּוּ create a temporal clause much like the temporal adverbial phrases you learned about in (34.4a) which are constructed with the prefixed preposition בְּ or כְּ plus the infinitive. Only this time the prefixed preposition plus infinitive is replaced by the independent preposition אַחֲרֵי plus the qatal. In this case the qatal does identify another clause, but the clause is really part and parcel with the transition marker וַיְהִי A qatal in this case is relegated to a scene-setting function.[1]

> RULE: **When a preposition plus qatal follows וַיְהִי in Historical Narrative, the entire construction has a scene-setting function, usually identifying the time of the scene. This construction places the qatal in a low-ranking function in Historical Narrative like the participle.**

A clarification here: Because we are studying primarily geminate roots in this lesson, you may get the idea that there is a connection between the root type and the discourse function. Not so. A qatal of any root type or, in fact, any stem may function as a temporal adverbial clause when it follows וַיְהִי

Translation of וַיְהִי אַחֲרֵי הֵסַבּוּ אֹתוֹ : *And it happened after they were carriers around of it*

In a construction of this type, the frequently used כִּי means *when* as it does when it is between וַיְהִי and an infinitive.

---

[1] van der Merwe(1997).

Hiphil qatal, weqatal, and other forms of geminate roots

47.4a. Here is the pattern for Hiphil qatal and weqatal of geminate roots.

HIPHIL QATAL OF GEMINATE ROOTS:

SINGULAR 3. M.	הֵסֵב הֵסַב	PLURAL 3. C.	הֵסַּבּוּ הֵחֵלּוּ
3. F.	הֵסֵּבָּה		
2. M.	הֲסִבֹּתָ	2. M.	הֲסִבוֹתֶם
2. F.	הֲסִבּוֹת	2. F.	הֲסִבּוֹתֶן
1. C.	הֲסִבֹּתִי	1. C.	הֲסִבֹּונוּ

47.4b. Hiphil imperatives looks a lot like hollow roots:

s. הָסֵב

f. s. הָסֵבִּי

p. הָסֵּבּוּ

47.4c. Hiphil participles of geminate roots also resemble hollow roots and are only attested in the masculine forms:

s. מֵסַב or מַסְבִיב

m. p. מְסִבִּים

47.4d. Hiphil infinitives of geminates resemble the masculine singular imperative as do hollow roots:

construct: הָסֵב

absolute: הָסֵב or הַסְבֵב

Wayyiqtol of היה on the mainline

47.5a. Fill out the verb analysis chart for וַתְּהִי :

root	stem	form	person, gender, number	function	basic root meaning

What is the discourse function of the verb? Though it is a wayyiqtol of היה it does not have either the common scene-setting function of this root in this form.   Most English translations use the *to be* verb for וַתְּהִי as in *And the hand of YHWH was...* which reflects the state of things at the start of this paragraph, a scene-setting function. However, an X-qatal would be better suited for expressing a state. Remember that the root הָיָה is not an exact equivalent for our English *to be*. It often has the sense of *happen*. The wayyiqtol is therefore a mainline verb form. With a bit of license we may translate וַתְּהִי יַד־יְהֹוָה this way: *And the hand of YHWH came...*

47.5b. The rest of the clause requires a bit of flexibility for translation. A prefixed בְּ is often used with verbs which express hostility to mean *against*. It seems that this is the sense in בָּעִיר   The word מְהוּמָה means *tumult*, and the sense of the verse seems to require an added English *with*.

Translation of וַתְּהִי יַד־יְהֹוָה בָּעִיר מְהוּמָה גְּדוֹלָה מְאֹד :

Assignments

47.6a.   Identify the stem and form of the following geminates.

1. חָנַן	11. הֻשַׁמּוּ	21. וַיָּרֵעוּ
2. וְחַנֹּתִי	12. יָשִׂים	22. הָרֵעַ תָּרֵעוּ
3. חַנֻּנוּ	13. מַשְׁמִים	23. וַתָּרַע
4. יָחְנְךָ	14. הֻשַּׁמֵּם	24. וַיַּסֵּב
5. אָחֹן	15. תָּרֵעוּ	25. מֵסֵב
6. חוֹנֵן	16. נָרַע	26. יָסֹב
7. וְשָׁמְמוּ	17. לְהָרַע	27. הֵסַבּוּ
8. הַשְׁמוֹת	18. הֲרֵעֹתֶם	28. הָסֵב
9. וַהֲשִׁמּוֹתִי	19. הֲרֵעֹתָה	29. הָסֵבִּי
10. וְהָשַׁמּוּ	20. הָרַע	30. לְהָסֵב

47.6b. The root חָלַל has two entirely different meanings. In the Hiphil stem, it usually means *begin*. In the Piel stem, which conjugates regularly for this root, it usually means *pollute, defile*. It is therefore especially important that you discern the stem of the verbs in translation exercises 1-11 below.

Genesis 6:1   1. וַיְהִי כִּי־הֵחֵל הָאָדָם לָרֹב עַל־פְּנֵי הָאֲדָמָה וּבָנוֹת יֻלְּדוּ לָהֶם:

Genesis 41:54   2. וַתְּחִלֶּינָה שֶׁבַע שְׁנֵי הָרָעָב לָבוֹא

Deuteronomy 2:25 פַּחַד means *dread,* and יִרְאָה means *fear.*   3. הַיּוֹם הַזֶּה אָחֵל תֵּת פַּחְדְּךָ וְיִרְאָתְךָ עַל־פְּנֵי הָעַמִּים תַּחַת כָּל־הַשָּׁמָיִם

47.6c. Read the discourse analysis of Genesis 44:26-34.

4. אֲדֹנָי יְהוִה אַתָּה הַחִלּוֹתָ לְהַרְאוֹת אֶת־עַבְדְּךָ אֶת־גָּדְלְךָ

Deuteronomy 3:24 Notice how one אֵת marks a direct object, and one marks an indirect object. Both are accusative case (42.4)

5. וְלֹא תְחַלֵּל אֶת־שֵׁם אֱלֹהֶיךָ

Leviticus 18:21

6. וְלֹא־תִשָּׁבְעוּ בִשְׁמִי לַשָּׁקֶר וְחִלַּלְתָּ אֶת־שֵׁם אֱלֹהֶיךָ אֲנִי יְהוָה:

Leviticus 19:12

7. מִזַּרְעוֹ נָתַן לַמֹּלֶךְ לְמַעַן טַמֵּא אֶת־מִקְדָּשִׁי וּלְחַלֵּל אֶת־שֵׁם קָדְשִׁי

Leviticus 20:3

8. וַהֲסִבּוֹתִי פָנַי מֵהֶם וְחִלְּלוּ אֶת־צְפוּנִי

Ezekiel 7:22 צפן means hide.

9. וְאֶת־שַׁבְּתֹתַי חִלָּלְתְּ

Ezekiel 22:8

10. וְהוּא יָחֵל לְהוֹשִׁיעַ אֶת־יִשְׂרָאֵל מִיַּד פְּלִשְׁתִּים

Judges 13:5

11. וַיָּחֶל שְׁלֹמֹה לִבְנוֹת אֶת־בֵּית־יְהוָה בִּירוּשָׁלִַם בְּהַר הַמּוֹרִיָּה אֲשֶׁר נִרְאָה לְדָוִיד אָבִיהוּ

2 Chronicles 3:1

12. וַיְהִי כִּי עָלִינוּ אֶל־עַבְדְּךָ אָבִי וַנַּגֶּד־לוֹ אֵת דִּבְרֵי אֲדֹנִי:

Genesis 44:24

13. וַיְהִי כִּי חָזְקוּ בְּנֵי יִשְׂרָאֵל וַיִּתְּנוּ אֶת־הַכְּנַעֲנִי לָמַס

Joshua 17:13 מַס means forced labor, tribute.

14. וַיְהִי כִּי־חָזַק יִשְׂרָאֵל וַיָּשֶׂם אֶת־הַכְּנַעֲנִי לָמַס

Judges 1:28

15. וַיְהִי עַד דִּבֶּר שָׁאוּל אֶל־הַכֹּהֵן

1 Samuel 14:19

16. וַיְהִי כִּי־חָטְאוּ בְנֵי־יִשְׂרָאֵל לַיהוָה אֱלֹהֵיהֶם הַמַּעֲלֶה מֵאֶרֶץ מִצְרַיִם אֹתָם מִתַּחַת יַד פַּרְעֹה מֶלֶךְ־מִצְרָיִם וַיִּירְאוּ אֱלֹהִים אֲחֵרִים:

2 Kings 17:7

Lesson 48

וְיִשְׁמְעוּ הַכְּנַעֲנִי וְכֹל יֹשְׁבֵי הָאָרֶץ וְנָסַבּוּ עָלֵינוּ

Joshua 7:9

Goals:

- **Identify and read a subjunctive yiqtol.**
- **Identify and read geminate roots in the Niphal stem.**

What we already know

48.1.   What verb form is   וְיִשְׁמְעוּ   ? _____ Be careful to pay close attention to the nikkud accompanying the *vav* and the prefixed subject pronoun. How have you learned to interpret

this verb form, when it is clause-initial? _____ (23.3d)

Other subjunctive yiqtols besides volitives

48.2a.   Although the yiqtol in our lesson verse is part of a Hortatory Discourse, the clause-initial yiqtol is *not* a volitive (jussive) which gives a command or expresses the speaker's desire for a third party. In fact, the greater context of our lesson verse shows us that the speaker, Joshua, dreaded that the Canaanites might hear of Israel's setback in Canaan. Our lesson verse's clause-initial yiqtol is part of a larger class that also includes volitional yiqtol. It expresses possibility rather than desire, the concept we express with the English word *might*. Both the yiqtol which expresses desire and the yiqtol which expresses possibility fall under the general heading *subjunctive mood*.

> DEFINITION: *Subjunctive mood* is the speaker's expression of desire (which we know as the volitive forms) or possibility. The subjunctive mood contrasts with the *indicative mood* which is the speaker's expression of reality or knowledge.

By the way, the wayyiqtol of Historical Narrative and the weqatal of Predictive Narrative are both indicative mood. To explore the subjunctive mood, look at a few English expressions, all +projection:

Subjunctive Mood:
Expressing desire (volitional): *May he...*
Expressing possibility: *He may... He might...*

Indicative Mood:
Expressing knowledge: *He will...*

48.2b.   As mentioned in 23.3c and the reading on 1 Samuel 17:37F, one of the difficult challenges of understanding Biblical Hebrew is due to its lack of modals, words like *may, might, could, will*, etc. The combination of verb-form and genre picks up most of the slack, but not all of it. You will be largely dependent on other context clues for these two situations:

Ambiguities in the use of the yiqtol:

When a yiqtol is *not* clause-initial it may be either subjunctive or indicative.

Subjunctive: גַּם אֶת־הַכֹּל יִקָּח   2 Samuel 19:31
Even the all, **may** *he take (it)*

Indicative: וְאָנֹכִי אַעַלְךָ גַם־עָלֹה   Genesis 46:4
And I, **I will** *bring you up, even a going up*

וַיהוָה יִרְאֶה לַלֵּבָב   1 Samuel 16:7
And it is YHWH that looks for the heart.

The same ambiguity between indicative and subjunctive also exists in English from time to time. We have the indicative *will* which expresses knowledge of the future as in *The sun* will *come up tomorrow* and the subjunctive *will* which expresses an intention as in the *I will*'s of a marriage ceremony.

Once you have determined a yiqtol is subjunctive, it may be expressing either desire or possibility.

Possibility: Our lesson verse or

אֶת־שְׁנֵי בָנַי תָּמִית אִם־לֹא אֲבִיאֶנּוּ אֵלֶיךָ   Genesis 42:37
It is my two sons that you **may** *kill if I do not bring him to you*

Desire: See Lessons 23 and 24 on the volitives or

כֹּל אֲשֶׁר־דִּבֶּר יְהוָה נַעֲשֶׂה וְנִשְׁמָע   Exodus 24:7
All that YHWH has commanded, **may** *we do and obey (it)*

48.2c. Fill out the verb analysis chart for וְיִשְׁמְעוּ except for the function:

root	stem	form	person, gender, number	function	basic root meaning
				express possibility	

Like the volitive forms you learned about in Module Two, this new subjunctive yiqtol is also found in Hortatory Discourse. It is an off-line verb form in that it lends logical motivation for the mainline exhortations. In Joshua 7 from which our lesson sentence comes, Joshua is trying to convince *YHWH* to respond to help Israel overcome its first defeat in the Promised Land.

Translate וְיִשְׁמְעוּ הַכְּנַעֲנִי וְכֹל יֹשְׁבֵי הָאָרֶץ (If you need help with הַכְּנַעֲנִי see the *adjective of nationality* in the reading on 1 Samuel 17:32D.):

Discourse profile scheme of Hortatory Discourse with modal yiqtol added

48.3. Here is an outline of the discourse profile scheme for Hortatory Discourse with the modal yiqtol added:[1]

Mainline: 1a. Imperative
    1b. Jussive   Note: These four are equally ranked
    1c. Cohortative
    1d. Weqatal (for Mitigated Hortatory Discourse)

  Off-the-line:
  2. Topicalization: X-Imperative (or Jussive or Cohortative)
    3. Prohibitive commands: אַל or לֹא + yiqtol
      4. Express possibility: yiqtol
        5. Consequence, purpose: Weqatal
          6. Consequence, purpose: לֹא or פֶּן + yiqtol
            7. Consequence, purpose: Embedded Predictive Narrative
              8. Identification of problem: Embedded Historical Narrative
                9. Backgrounded activities: Participle
                  10. Scene setting: Verbless Clause

Niphal of geminate roots

48.4a. When we analyze our lesson verse's וְנָסַבּוּ we may first be challenged by the thought that this is a 1st c. p. yiqtol with a conjunctive *vav* because the preceding clause contained a yiqtol with a pre-formed *vav*. The affix on the end of the word should deflect that idea. The next alternative is a weqatal since we know that a weqatal often continues a series begun by a yiqtol. Indeed וְנָסַבּוּ is an off-the-line Niphal weqatal in our little excerpt from Joshua's Hortatory Discourse. The word's *nun* is the sign of the Niphal qatal.

Fill out the verb analysis chart for וְנָסַבּוּ reviewing 22.3 on the off-the-line weqatal if you need to:

root	stem	form	person, gender, number	function	basic root meaning

---

[1] Longacre(1989), 121.

267

48.4b. The Niphal forms of geminate roots follow this pattern:

NIPHAL OF GEMINATES:	
3rd m. s. qatal:	נָסַב
2nd m. s. qatal:	נְסַבּוֹתָ
3rd m. s. yiqtol:	יִסַּב
m. s. imperative:	הִסַּב
m. s. participle:	נָסָב
f. s. participle:	נְסַבָּה
infinitive construct:	הִסַּב
infinitive absolute:	הִסּוֹב

Notes:

1. The qatal (weqatal) and participle forms have the customary pre-formed *nun* that we are used to for these forms in the Niphal stem.
2. The yiqtol (and wayyiqtol) have the customary *dagesh forte* in the first root letter. Things get tricky with first guttural geminates like חלל The *dagesh* "bounces off" the guttural letter, and you should know where it lands (41.3a).
3. The imperative and the infinitives have the customary pre-formed *heh-hireq* [הִ].

Polel, and Pilpel

48.5a. Geminate roots have regular conjugations in the Piel stem as you can see in the translation exercises in Lesson 47. The only irregularity that is attested in the Piel stem is the frequent lack of *dagesh forte,* as in the masculine plural participle מְהַלְלִים However, geminates are also attested in two other vocalizations patterns that are equivalent to the Piel, namely the Polel and Pilpel stems. Although the Polel and Pilpel stems are important, they represent only a very small percentage of the verb forms attested in the Hebrew Bible, so we will not belabor them with a separate lesson. Another good reason to deal with them quickly is that they are fairly easy to identify. The Polel stem has a very regular pattern סוֹבֵב in all forms. For instance:

POLEL STEM:	
3rd m. s. qatal:	סוֹבֵב
2nd m. s. qatal:	סוֹבַּבְתָּ
3rd m. s. yiqtol:	יְסוֹבֵב
3rd m. p. yiqtol:	יְסוֹבֲבוּ
m. s. imperative:	סוֹבֵב
m. s. participle:	מְסוֹבֵב
infinitive construct:	סוֹבֵב

Notes:

1. Notice the identical forms.
2. Remember that the Qal participle is סֹבֵב

48.5b. The Pilpel stem is a result of doubling the essential two letters of a root. An example of a geminate root in the Pilpel stem is the root גלל which has a 3rd m. s. qatal גִּלְגֵּל and means *he is a roller* Other root types also show up in the Pilpel stem, namely second *ayin* roots and some second *vav* roots. For instance, the root כול has a 3rd m. s. qatal כִּלְכֵּל and means *he is a sustainer, nourisher*

Assignments

48.6a. Tell the root, stem, person, gender, and number of the following. Watch out for pronominal suffixes:

1.	הַלְלוּ	13.	וַאֲסוֹבְבָה	25.	וְנָשַׁמּוּ
2.	וַיְהַלְלוּ	14.	הַסּוֹבֵב	26.	יְמַדּוּ
3.	יִתְהַלֵּל	15.	וְגָלְלוּ	27.	יָמַד
4.	וְהַלֵּל	16.	וַיִּגֶל	28.	תָּחֶל
5.	בְּהַלֵּל	17.	וְגִלְגַּלְתִּיךָ	29.	יָחֶל
6.	מְהַלְלִים	18.	וְכִלְכַּלְתִּי	30.	וָאָחֶל
7.	מְהַלֵּל	19.	וַיְכַלְכֵּל	31.	לְהָחֵלוּ
8.	תְּסוֹבֵב	20.	אֲכַלְכֵּל	32.	וְנָחֵלוּ
9.	תְּסוֹבְבֵךְ	21.	נָסַבּוּ	33.	נָחֵל
10.	יְסוֹבְבֶנּוּ	22.	וְנָסַב	34.	וַיְחַלְלוּ
11.	יְסוֹבְבֶהָ	23.	יָסֹבּוּ	35.	יָחֵל
12.	וִיסוֹבְבוּ	24.	נָסֵבָּה	36.	וַיְּחֶל

48.6b. Translate:

Genesis 19:4

1. וְאַנְשֵׁי הָעִיר אַנְשֵׁי סְדֹם נָסַבּוּ עַל־הַבַּיִת מִנַּעַר וְעַד־זָקֵן

Jeremiah 6:12

2. וְנָסַבּוּ בָתֵּיהֶם לַאֲחֵרִים שָׂדוֹת וְנָשִׁים יַחְדָּו

Ezekiel 1:9

3. לֹא־יִסַּבּוּ בְּלֶכְתָּן

Ezekiel 10:11

4. כִּי הַמָּקוֹם אֲשֶׁר־יִפְנֶה הָרֹאשׁ אַחֲרָיו יֵלֵכוּ לֹא יִסַּבּוּ בְּלֶכְתָּם

Ezekiel 7:24 מִקְדָּשׁ means *sanctuary*.

5. וְנָחֲלוּ מִקַּדְשֵׁיהֶם

Genesis 19:7 see 46.5 if you do not know what רעע means.

6. וַיֹּאמַר אַל־נָא אַחַי תָּרֵעוּ׃

Genesis 31:7

7. וְלֹא־נְתָנוֹ אֱלֹהִים לְהָרַע עִמָּדִי

269

8. וַיֵּרַע בְּעֵינֵי יְהוָה אֲשֶׁר עָשָׂה וַיָּמֶת גַּם־אֹתוֹ:

Genesis 38:10 וַיֵּרַע is Qal stem. If you look back at 46.2b, you will see in conjugation "A" that the first root letter takes a *dagesh*. A *resh* does not usually take a *dagesh*, and hence, the *sere* in וַיֵּרַע

9. וַיֹּאמֶר יִשְׂרָאֵל לָמָה הֲרֵעֹתֶם לִי

Genesis 43:6

10. וַיַּרְא יוֹסֵף כִּי־יָשִׁית אָבִיו יַד־יְמִינוֹ עַל־רֹאשׁ אֶפְרַיִם וַיֵּרַע בְּעֵינָיו

Genesis 48:17

11. וַיָּשָׁב מֹשֶׁה אֶל־יְהוָה וַיֹּאמַר אֲדֹנָי לָמָה הֲרֵעֹתָה לָעָם הַזֶּה לָמָה זֶּה שְׁלַחְתָּנִי:

Exodus 5:22

12. וַיְצַו יְהוָה אֱלֹהִים עַל־הָאָדָם לֵאמֹר מִכֹּל עֵץ־הַגָּן אָכֹל תֹּאכֵל:

Genesis 2:16

13. וַתֹּאמֶר הָאִשָּׁה אֶל־הַנָּחָשׁ מִפְּרִי עֵץ־הַגָּן נֹאכֵל:

Genesis 3:2 נָחָשׁ means *serpent*, and גָּן means *garden*.

14. וְלַאֲחֹתוֹ אֲשֶׁר לֹא־הָיְתָה לְאִישׁ לָהּ יִטַּמָּא

Leviticus 21:3

15. וַאֲנִי בְּרֹב חַסְדְּךָ אָבוֹא בֵיתֶךָ

Psalm 5:8

16. אִם־אֹתָהּ תִּקַּח־לְךָ קָח כִּי אֵין אַחֶרֶת

1 Samuel 21:10

17. הֲיָדוֹעַ נֵדַע כִּי יֹאמַר הוֹרִידוּ אֶת־אֲחִיכֶם

Genesis 43:7

18. וַיֹּאמֶר מֹשֶׁה אֶל־הָאֱלֹהִים מִי אָנֹכִי כִּי אֵלֵךְ אֶל־פַּרְעֹה וְכִי אוֹצִיא אֶת־בְּנֵי יִשְׂרָאֵל מִמִּצְרָיִם:

Exodus 3:11 Here you see that a yiqtol in a dependent clause can be subjunctive.

48.6c. Read the discourse analysis of Genesis 45:1-8.

Lesson 49

בְּנֵי־פַחַת מוֹאָב לִבְנֵי יֵשׁוּעַ וְיוֹאָב אֲלָפִּים וּשְׁמֹנֶה מֵאוֹת שְׁמֹנָה עָשָׂר׃

Nehemiah 7:11

Goals:

- **Read and identify dual numbers.**
- **Read and identify cardinal numbers in addition to one through ten (see Lesson 38.3).**

What we already know

49.1a. Translate בְּנֵי־פַחַת מוֹאָב thinking of פַחַת מוֹאָב as a proper noun:

_____

Be advised, however, that פַחַת can be interpreted as the construct form of the word פֶּחָה meaning *governor*.

49.1b. The next phrase further pinpoints the identity of the people being talked about in the lesson verse.

Translate לִבְנֵי יֵשׁוּעַ וְיוֹאָב : _____

Dual numbers

49.2a. You should know the word אֶלֶף from your vocabulary studies, but look carefully at its nikkud in our lesson verse. Note that it is *not* אֲלָפִים which means *thousands*.

> RULE: The ◌ַיִם -- ending on a noun rather than the customary ◌ִים – plural ending is called the *dual* ending and denotes *two* of a thing which typically occurs in pairs. The dual ending can be found on the masculine אֶלֶף as in אֲלָפִּים meaning *2000* or on the feminine מֵאָה as in מָאתַיִם meaning *200* as well as many other nouns.

Translate אֲלָפִּים : _____

49.2b. Here are some other words in their dual forms:

יָדַיִם	*both hands*
יוֹמַיִם	*two days*
שְׂפָתַיִם	*both lips* (from שָׂפָה)
כְּנָפַיִם	*both wings* (from כָּנָף)
רַגְלַיִם	*both feet*
קַרְנַיִם	*both horns* (from קֶרֶן)

Tens, hundreds, and thousands

49.3a. The words וּשְׁמֹנֶה מֵאוֹת should not be a problem to translate since you know the vocabulary. What is worth noting is the gender. Unlike the cardinal numbers from 1 to 10 which usually agree in

271

gender with the thing numbered (Lesson 38.3), the Hebrew word מֵאָה has only a feminine (besides dual) form regardless of what is numbered. The word וּשְׁמֹנֶה in our lesson verse has the correct feminine form to agree with the feminine מֵאוֹת Recall, also from Lesson 38.3, that the feminine numbers 1 through 10 look like a masculine form, and the masculine look like a feminine.

49.3b. Words which express tens beginning with 20 (20, 30, 60, etc.) and thousands (1000, 5000, 8000, etc.), like מֵאָה have only one gender, except that the form is masculine. Observe:

twenty	עֶשְׂרִים	two thousand	אַלְפַּֽיִם
thirty	שְׁלֹשִׁים	three thousand	שְׁלֹשֶׁת אֲלָפִים
forty	אַרְבָּעִים	four thousand	אַרְבַּעַת אֲלָפִים
fifty	חֲמִשִּׁים	five thousand	חֲמֵשֶׁת־אֲלָפִים
sixty	שִׁשִּׁים	six thousand	שֵׁשֶׁת אֲלָפִים
seventy	שִׁבְעִים	seven thousand	שִׁבְעַת אֲלָפִים
eighty	שְׁמֹנִים	eight thousand	שְׁמֹנַת אֲלָפִים
ninety	תִּשְׁעִים	nine thousand	unattested

Notes:
1. The word for 20 is based on the word for 10.
2. The word for 2000 has the dual ending.
3. The word which specifies the number of thousands is in the masculine construct form for numbers.

Fill in the translations in the following couple of examples. Note that the numbered noun is in the singular form even though the sense is plural. Numbered nouns are only put into the plural form with the numbers 2-10.

וַיְחִי אֱנוֹשׁ תִּשְׁעִים שָׁנָה Genesis 5:9

And Enosh lived _____

וַיְהִי־שָׁם עִם־יְהוָה אַרְבָּעִים יוֹם וְאַרְבָּעִים לַֽיְלָה Exodus 34:28

And he was there with YHWH _____

Numbers from 11 to 19

49.4. The last two words of our lesson verse, שְׁמֹנָה עָשָׂר are a good example of how the numbers 11 through 19 are formed. There are both masculine and feminine forms and there is no *vav* used between the units number and the form for 10.

Translate שְׁמֹנָה עָשָׂר : _____

Here is a complete list of the forms:

	MASCULINE	FEMININE
eleven	אַחַד־עָשָׂר	אַחַת־עֶשְׂרֵה
twelve	שְׁנֵים־עָשָׂר	שְׁתֵּים עֶשְׂרֵה
thirteen	שְׁלֹשָׁה עָשָׂר	שְׁלֹשׁ עֶשְׂרֵה
fourteen	אַרְבָּעָה עָשָׂר	אַרְבַּע־עֶשְׂרֵה
fifteen	חֲמִשָּׁה עָשָׂר	חֲמֵשׁ עֶשְׂרֵה
sixteen	שִׁשָּׁה עָשָׂר	שֵׁשׁ עֶשְׂרֵה
seventeen	שִׁבְעָה־עָשָׂר	שְׁבַע עֶשְׂרֵה
eighteen	שְׁמוֹנָה עָשָׂר	שְׁמֹנֶה עֶשְׂרֵה
nineteen	תִּשְׁעָה־עָשָׂר	תְּשַׁע־עֶשְׂרֵה

Numbers with tens and units

49.5. For numbers between 21 and 99 that include tens and units (21, 47, 99, etc.), the tens and units may be in either order, they will be joined by a *vav*[וֹ], and the gender of the units-word will match the gender of the thing numbered. Fill in the translations of the following representative examples. Once again, note how the numbered noun is plural only when it accompanies 2-10.

וַיְחִי מַהֲלַלְאֵל חָמֵשׁ שָׁנִים וְשִׁשִּׁים שָׁנָה   Genesis 5:15

And Mahalalel lived _____

וַיִּהְיוּ כָּל־יְמֵי־יֶרֶד שְׁתַּיִם וְשִׁשִּׁים שָׁנָה וּתְשַׁע מֵאוֹת שָׁנָה   Genesis 5:20

And all the days of Jered were _____

וַיִּהְיוּ חַיֵּי שָׂרָה מֵאָה שָׁנָה וְעֶשְׂרִים שָׁנָה וְשֶׁבַע שָׁנִים   Genesis 23:1

And the lifetime of Sarah was _____

Translate the entire lesson verse: _____

_____

Assignments

49.6a. Translate:

Joshua 8:20   1.   וְלֹא־הָיָה בָהֶם יָדַיִם לָנוּס

2 Kings 11:16   2.   וַיָּשִׂמוּ לָהּ יָדַיִם

Numbers 11:19   3.   לֹא יוֹם אֶחָד תֹּאכְלוּן וְלֹא יוֹמָיִם וְלֹא חֲמִשָּׁה יָמִים
וְלֹא עֲשָׂרָה יָמִים וְלֹא עֶשְׂרִים יוֹם׃

273

4. וַיֹּאמֶר מֹשֶׁה לִפְנֵי יְהוָה הֵן אֲנִי עֲרַל שְׂפָתַיִם וְאֵיךְ יִשְׁמַע אֵלַי פַּרְעֹה:

Exodus 6:30 עֲרַל means *uncircumcised*, and אֵיךְ means *how?*

5. כִּי אִישׁ טְמֵא־שְׂפָתַיִם אָנֹכִי וּבְתוֹךְ עַם־טְמֵא שְׂפָתַיִם

Isaiah 6:5

6. וַיְחִי אָדָם שְׁלֹשִׁים וּמְאַת שָׁנָה

Genesis 5:3

7. וַיִּהְיוּ כָּל־יְמֵי אָדָם אֲשֶׁר־חַי תְּשַׁע מֵאוֹת שָׁנָה וּשְׁלֹשִׁים שָׁנָה

Genesis 5:5

8. וְאֵלֶּה יְמֵי שְׁנֵי־חַיֵּי אַבְרָהָם אֲשֶׁר־חָי מְאַת שָׁנָה וְשִׁבְעִים שָׁנָה וְחָמֵשׁ שָׁנִים:

Genesis 25:7

9. וְאֵלֶּה שְׁנֵי חַיֵּי יִשְׁמָעֵאל מְאַת שָׁנָה וּשְׁלֹשִׁים שָׁנָה וְשֶׁבַע שָׁנִים

Genesis 25:17

10. וַיִּרְדֹּף דָּוִד הוּא וְאַרְבַּע־מֵאוֹת אִישׁ וַיַּעַמְדוּ מָאתַיִם אִישׁ

1 Samuel 30:10

11. וְאֶת־אַבְשָׁלוֹם הָלְכוּ מָאתַיִם אִישׁ מִירוּשָׁלַם

2 Samuel 15:11

12. בְּנֵי פַרְעֹשׁ אַלְפַּיִם מֵאָה שִׁבְעִים וּשְׁנָיִם:

Ezra 2:3

13. וּצְבָאוֹ וּפְקֻדֵיהֶם אַרְבָּעָה וְשִׁבְעִים אֶלֶף וְשֵׁשׁ מֵאוֹת:

Numbers 2:4

14. בֶּן־אַרְבָּעִים שָׁנָה אִישׁ־בֹּשֶׁת בֶּן־שָׁאוּל בְּמָלְכוֹ עַל־יִשְׂרָאֵל וּשְׁתַּיִם שָׁנִים מָלָךְ

2 Samuel 2:10   If you do not remember the formula for giving age in Hebrew, see the reading on Gen. 17.

15. בְּחֶבְרוֹן מָלַךְ עַל־יְהוּדָה שֶׁבַע שָׁנִים וְשִׁשָּׁה חֳדָשִׁים וּבִירוּשָׁלַם מָלַךְ שְׁלֹשִׁים וְשָׁלֹשׁ שָׁנָה עַל כָּל־יִשְׂרָאֵל וִיהוּדָה:

2 Samuel 5:5

16. וְהַיָּמִים אֲשֶׁר מָלַךְ יָרָבְעָם עֶשְׂרִים וּשְׁתַּיִם שָׁנָה וַיִּשְׁכַּב וַיִּמְלֹךְ נָדָב בְּנוֹ

1 Kings 14:20

17. בֶּן־שֵׁשׁ עֶשְׂרֵה שָׁנָה הָיָה בְמָלְכוֹ וַחֲמִשִּׁים וּשְׁתַּיִם שָׁנָה מָלַךְ בִּירוּשָׁלָם

2 Kings 15:2

49.6b. Read the discourse analysis of Genesis 45:9-15.

Lesson 50

וּבַחֹדֶשׁ הַשֵּׁנִי בְּשִׁבְעָה וְעֶשְׂרִים יוֹם לַחֹדֶשׁ יָבְשָׁה הָאָרֶץ:

Genesis 8:14

Goal:

• **Identify and read ordinal numbers.**

What we already know

50.1a. Fill out the verb analysis chart for the only verb in our lesson verse (You will have to look up the meaning of the root in your dictionary):

root	stem	form	person, gender, number	function	basic root meaning

Recall from Lesson 33 that Qal stative roots do not require the customary -er-word or gerund plus possessive pronoun that other Qal qatals do. The gender of the verb matches the gender of what noun in

the clause? _____

Translate יָבְשָׁה הָאָרֶץ : _____

50.1b. Now that we have identified a qatal verb form that is not clause-initial we can assign the label "X" to the series of prepositional constructions which precede it. Together, the prepositional constructions behave as a temporal adverb. In Historical Narrative, prepositions, numbers and time words like יוֹם שָׁנָה or חֹדֶשׁ are used to construct a temporal "X". Or וַיְהִי plus the same preposition, number, and time word is used to create a temporal wayyiqtol clause. Both constructions can be used early in an episode or paragraph to set the time of a scene.

Ordinal numbers

50.2a. Let us spend our last lesson in this course refining your understanding of numbers by concentrating primarily on ordinal numbers.

Translate וּבַחֹדֶשׁ _____

The next word הַשֵּׁנִי is an adjective for וּבַחֹדֶשׁ What kind of adjective is it?

_____ (18.2a) The word הַשֵּׁנִי means *second*.

Translate וּבַחֹדֶשׁ הַשֵּׁנִי : _____

The ordinal numbers, that is, those expressing order, from *first* through *tenth* will most likely follow the noun they number. They will also gender-match the noun they modify as follows:

	MASCULINE	FEMININE
first	רִאשׁוֹן	רִאשׁוֹנָה
second	שֵׁנִי	שֵׁנִית
third	שְׁלִישִׁי	שְׁלִישִׁיָּה שְׁלִישִׁית
forth	רְבִיעִי	רְבִיעִית
fifth	חֲמִשִּׁי חֲמִישִׁי	חֲמִישִׁית
sixth	שִׁשִּׁי	שִׁשִּׁית
seventh	שְׁבִיעִי	שְׁבִיעִית
eighth	שְׁמִינִי	שְׁמִינִית
ninth	תְּשִׁיעִי	תְּשִׁיעִית
tenth	עֲשִׂירִי	עֲשִׂירִיָּה עֲשִׂירִית

50.2b. You can probably translate the phrase בְּשִׁבְעָה וְעֶשְׂרִים יוֹם without much of a problem because you know the vocabulary. Numbers above 10 have no special ordinal and cardinal forms. Context must tell you the difference between ordinal and cardinal numbers above 10.

Translate בְּשִׁבְעָה וְעֶשְׂרִים יוֹם : _____

The *lamed* of לַחֹדֶשׁ is used to express a relationship of possession which translates into English *of*.

Translate בְּשִׁבְעָה וְעֶשְׂרִים יוֹם לַחֹדֶשׁ : _____

_____

50.2c. The same rule which calls for no special forms for ordinal numbers above 10 is in play with very large numbers in the hundreds which use מֵאָה   Fill in the translations of the examples given below. There simply are no ordinal numbers attested which use any form of אֶלֶף

וַיְהִי בְּאַחַת וְשֵׁשׁ־מֵאוֹת שָׁנָה Genesis 8:13

And it happened in _____

וַיְהִי בִשְׁמוֹנִים שָׁנָה וְאַרְבַּע מֵאוֹת שָׁנָה 1 Kings 6:1

And it happened in _____

Note in the above examples the plural form of the feminine word מֵאָה which is also a cardinal number as you saw in Lesson 49.

50.2d. The concept of an ordinal number can also be expressed by an alternate word order which uses the construct form of the thing which is numbered. Fill in the translations of the following examples:

בִּשְׁנַת שְׁמוֹנֶה עֶשְׂרֵה Jeremiah 52:29

_____

וְקִדַּשְׁתֶּם אֵת שְׁנַת הַחֲמִשִּׁים שָׁנָה Leviticus 25:10

And you will be sanctifiers of _____

וַיָּמָת שָׁם בִּשְׁנַת הָאַרְבָּעִים לְצֵאת בְּנֵי־יִשְׂרָאֵל מֵאֶרֶץ מִצְרַיִם Numbers 33:38

And he died there in _____ *of coming out of the children of Israel from the land of Egypt*

בִּשְׁנַת שְׁתַּיִם 1 Kings 15:25

_____

Note in the final example how even numbers 1 through 10 do not use an ordinal form in this type of construction even though the notion is ordinal.

Translate the entire lesson verse: _____

_____

Assignments
50.3a. Translate:
Exodus 16:29

1. הוּא נָתַן לָכֶם בַּיּוֹם הַשִּׁשִּׁי לֶחֶם יוֹמָיִם שְׁבוּ אִישׁ תַּחְתָּיו אַל־יֵצֵא אִישׁ מִמְּקֹמוֹ בַּיּוֹם הַשְּׁבִיעִי

Genesis 1:23

2. וַיְהִי־בֹקֶר יוֹם חֲמִישִׁי

Genesis 32:20 עֵדֶר
means *flock*.

3. וַיְצַו גַּם אֶת־הַשֵּׁנִי גַּם אֶת־הַשְּׁלִישִׁי גַּם אֶת־כָּל־הַהֹלְכִים אַחֲרֵי הָעֲדָרִים

2 Kings 17:6

4. בִּשְׁנַת הַתְּשִׁיעִית לְהוֹשֵׁעַ לָכַד מֶלֶךְ־אַשּׁוּר אֶת־שֹׁמְרוֹן

Numbers 10:11 עָנָן
means *cloud*.

5. וַיְהִי בַּשָּׁנָה הַשֵּׁנִית בַּחֹדֶשׁ הַשֵּׁנִי בְּעֶשְׂרִים בַּחֹדֶשׁ נַעֲלָה הֶעָנָן

1 Kings 15:9

6. וּבִשְׁנַת עֶשְׂרִים לְיָרָבְעָם מֶלֶךְ יִשְׂרָאֵל מָלַךְ אָסָא מֶלֶךְ יְהוּדָה:

7. 2 Kings 13:1

בִּשְׁנַת עֶשְׂרִים וְשָׁלֹשׁ שָׁנָה לְיוֹאָשׁ בֶּן־אֲחַזְיָהוּ מֶלֶךְ
יְהוּדָה מָלַךְ יְהוֹאָחָז בֶּן־יֵהוּא עַל־יִשְׂרָאֵל בְּשֹׁמְרוֹן
שְׁבַע עֶשְׂרֵה שָׁנָה:

8. 2 Kings 15:23

בִּשְׁנַת חֲמִשִּׁים שָׁנָה לַעֲזַרְיָה מֶלֶךְ יְהוּדָה מָלַךְ
פְּקַחְיָה בֶן־מְנַחֵם עַל־יִשְׂרָאֵל בְּשֹׁמְרוֹן שְׁנָתָיִם:

9. Genesis 8:13 חָרֵב
means *dry up*.

וַיְהִי בְּאַחַת וְשֵׁשׁ־מֵאוֹת שָׁנָה בָּרִאשׁוֹן בְּאֶחָד לַחֹדֶשׁ
חָרְבוּ הַמַּיִם מֵעַל הָאָרֶץ

10. Genesis 1:5

וַיִּקְרָא אֱלֹהִים לָאוֹר יוֹם וְלַחֹשֶׁךְ קָרָא לָיְלָה
וַיְהִי־עֶרֶב וַיְהִי־בֹקֶר יוֹם אֶחָד:

11. Exodus 40:2 Here אֶחָד
is used in the sense of *first*.

בְּיוֹם־הַחֹדֶשׁ הָרִאשׁוֹן בְּאֶחָד לַחֹדֶשׁ תָּקִים אֶת־מִשְׁכַּן
אֹהֶל מוֹעֵד:

12. Numbers 2: 9

כָּל־הַפְּקֻדִים לְמַחֲנֵה יְהוּדָה מְאַת אֶלֶף וּשְׁמֹנִים אֶלֶף
וְשֵׁשֶׁת־אֲלָפִים וְאַרְבַּע־מֵאוֹת לְצִבְאֹתָם רִאשֹׁנָה יִסָּעוּ:

50.3b. Read the discourse analysis of Genesis 45:21-28.

READINGS

How the Readings work:

As mentioned in the assignments section of Lesson 15, each lesson, from now on will be accompanied by a reading assignment. The readings are from extended passages of the Bible, anywhere from ten to thirty or more verses in length, and you will be asked to read at a pace of a few verses per lesson. We must do larger readings to see how the discourse principles that you learn in the lessons are utilized within a full-blown discourse. In addition, you cannot even be exposed to some discourse analysis principles without exposure to larger passages of text. For these reasons, it is essential that you complete these readings in order to learn all the material in this course.

You or your instructor may prefer completing an entire reading without interruption by any lesson material instead of reading a few verses per lesson. There is really no problem in doing so, and, in fact, these readings are grouped together in a dedicated section of the book to facilitate doing so. On the other hand, you should understand that the readings are designed to run concurrently with the lessons. Because they run together, earlier readings give a great deal of help to the student, and as the readings progress it will be assumed that the student is familiar with more and more of the lesson material. In case you do not follow the lesson-by-lesson pace, here is a list of the lessons at which each reading is designed to begin so you can still keep the readings more or less in sync with the lessons.

READING	BEGINS AT LESSON:
1 *Abraham is Tested*	15
2 *Abram Gets a New Name*	23
3 *Samson Reveals the Secret of his Strength*	26
4 *Thou shalt love* YHWH *thy God*	32
5 *David becomes Israel's Champion*	37
6 *Jacob Falls in Love*	39
7 *Ezekiel's Valley of Dry Bones*	43
8 *Joseph Reveals Himself to his Brothers*	45

READING 1--Genesis 22:1-19   Abraham is Tested

Lesson 15--Gaining an overview of the discourse

Marking the boundaries of a discourse

We will now proceed to do our first full-blown discourse analysis. As a reminder, a discourse is a group of expressions linked together from a beginning to an ending so that they develop an idea in some orderly fashion.

The first step in analyzing a discourse is to determine the outer limits of the discourse you wish to analyze. Discourses are often arranged in a hierarchy in which one large discourse is made of several smaller, embedded discourses.[1] For our first discourse analysis, we need to deal with something small, and relatively self-contained. Perhaps we can use an English Bible to help us at this point because we can

---

[1] Exter Blokland, *In Search of Syntax: Towards a Syntactic Segmentation Model for Biblical Hebrew*(Amsterdam: VU University Press, 1995). Exter Blokland criticizes Longacre's text segmentation model, primarily at the level of paragraph, a level that we disregard in this course. He also proposes a model for text segmentation which is objective as it is anchored to morpho-syntax.

process more text so much more efficiently in English. Genesis 22:1 begins, in the Revised Standard Version of the Bible, "After these things God tested Abraham..." We may use the phrase "after these things" as a marker or signal of the beginning of a small, distinct discourse in the larger Historical Narrative discourse of Abraham's life.

Verse 22:1 also suggests to us that we may limit ourselves at the other end of our discourse by the end of God's testing of Abraham. Scanning ahead in English, when does it seem that the testing story is fully resolved? Is it in verse 12 when the angel of *YHWH* stops Abraham and proclaims, "Do not lay your hand on the lad or do anything to him; for now I know that you fear God, seeing you have not withheld your son, your only son, from me"? It is true that the test itself is finished at this point of the account. The suspense is largely over.

However, an important part of many stories takes place immediately after the story's climax, after the tension within a story is released, in the section of the story we refer to as the *resolution*. In verses 16-18, the angel of *YHWH* speaks to Abraham, informing Abraham of the promises that belong to him as a result of passing the test. In verse 19, Abraham returns to his servants and his home. Verse 19 brings the resolution and hence, the story to a close.

Verse 20 reads just like Genesis 22:1: וַיְהִי אַחֲרֵי הַדְּבָרִים הָאֵלֶּה *And then it happened after these things...* Here we have, once again, a faithful marker of another episode in the story of Abraham's life, confirming that verse 19 is indeed the end of the "Abraham is Tested" story.

Tracing the mainline

Find and translate the forty-six wayyiqtol verb forms that make up the mainline of the discourse we are analyzing. By isolating the wayyiqtols in this manner we are sketching the "skeleton" of the story from which all of the details will hang. Notice how many of the wayyiqtol forms are וַיֹּאמֶר This is evidence of what you have been taught already in the lessons, that much of the detail in Biblical Hebrew narrative is carried by dialogue. Of course, you only need to translate identical forms once, but you may want to include them in your work so you can better get an idea of how the "skeleton" of a Biblical Hebrew narrative looks. The meaning of roots or stems that you have not learned yet are given to you.

Vs. 3   וַיַּשְׁכֵּם (שׁכם in the Hiphil stem = *rise early*) _____

וַיַּחֲבֹשׁ (חבשׁ in the Qal stem = *gird, bind*) _____

וַיְבַקַּע (בקע in the Piel stem = *break, cleave*) _____

Vs. 9   וַיִּבֶן   (בנה in the Qal stem = *build*) _____

וַיַּעֲרֹךְ (ערך in the Qal stem = *arrange*) _____

וַיַּעֲקֹד (עקד in the Qal stem = *bind*) _____

Vs. 13   וַיַּעֲלֵהוּ (This is the familiar root עלה in the so far unfamiliar Hiphil stem in which the root means *offer up*. This is a 3rd m. *singular* wayyiqtol form. The heh dropped from the root as usual, but then a 3 m. s. pronominal suffix הוּ-- which in this case means *it* was added. The addition of this suffix is why the word appears like a 3rd m. *plural* wayyiqtol which for some reason did not lose its heh. Translate the word *And he offered it up*.)

280

Lesson 16--The narrative begins and an embedded Hortatory Discourse

Verse 1

In our verse-by-verse analysis, we will proceed, with a few exceptions, in a clause-by-clause manner. We will consider the clause as the basic building block of the discourse.

וַיְהִי אַחַר הַדְּבָרִים הָאֵלֶּה   Many narratives begin with the expression   וַיְהִי   and some expression of time. What is the "time-word" used in this narrative?_____

We have seen the common (both masculine and plural gender), plural demonstrative pronoun אֵלֶּה meaning *these* in Lesson 13.5. The word here also means *these*, but it is an demonstrative adjective which modifies הַדְּבָרִים rather than a pronoun. In Hebrew, attributive adjectives follow the nouns they modify and must agree with them in gender, number, and definiteness. To agree with הַדְּבָרִים in definiteness, אֵלֶּה must have the definite article attached to it.

וְהָאֱלֹהִים נִסָּה אֶת־אַבְרָהָם   It is very common for אֱלֹהִים to have the definite article on it in Hebrew, but English translations generally do not translate it. The natives of Canaan worshipped other gods besides Abraham's God. Some of these Canaanite gods required the sacrifice of children. The use of the definite article in this and succeeding verses may be to clarify that this test did not originate with any of the Canaanite gods.

The root נסה means *test*, and it is only attested in the one stem exhibited here. Noting the vowel under the first root letter and the *dagesh* in the second root letter, what stem is it?

So we have here an X-qatal construction. What is the function of this type of construction? _____ (5.3d) In fact, we can specify the function of the X-qatal further seeing that this particular X-qatal precedes the beginning of the episode's wayyiqtol string. In such a case the X-qatal often summarizes, like a headline, what is to follow.[1] Remember that the qatal labels its subject with an attribute. In this case, God is labeled as *a tester*. The narrator herein presents us readers with a special viewpoint. We know all through the account that it is God who is testing Abraham, but Abraham does not know it until it is over.

וַיֹּאמֶר אֵלָיו אַבְרָהָם   Each וַיֹּאמֶר labels the beginning of a new quotation and therefore, the beginning of a new Direct Speech Discourse, some of which are so short we will not stop to specify their type. We see a full-blown example in Genesis 22:1-19 how many small Direct Speech Discourses are embedded within and give detail to the **host discourse**, in this case, a Historical Narrative. Direct Speech therefore has its own niche in the discourse profile scheme of Historical Narrative as follows:[2]

---

[1] See the note on 6.3.

[2] Although the discourse profile schemes are based on Longacre, the representation of discourse embedding within the scheme itself is my own doing. I have placed it very high in the ranking scheme because embedded direct speech is used, in a sense indirectly, to move Biblical narrative forward. See Alter, *The Art of Biblical Narrative*(NY: Basic Books, 1981), §4. I say indirectly because the direct speech itself *is* an event whose connection to the plotline is made by the speech introduction formula typically given by a wayyiqtol.

1. Mainline: Wayyiqtol

Off-the-line:
2. Topicalization: X-qatal
  3. Embedded Direct Speech
    4. Relative past background: Qatal in a dependent clause
      5. Relative non-past background: Yiqtol in a dependent clause
        6. Backgrounded activities: Participle
          7. Transition marker: Wayyiqtol of הָיָה
            8. Scene setting: Verbless Clause
              9. Irrealis scene setting: Negation of any verb by לֹא

One challenge is in determining how much of what follows each וַיֹּאמֶר is actually "within the quotation marks." The subject of the first וַיֹּאמֶר would be attributed to the last referred-to participant, in this case, the *tester Elohim*. The אֵלָיו would then mean *to him (Abraham)*, and the word אַבְרָהָם would be the actual quote.

וַיֹּאמֶר הִנֵּנִי: Here is Abraham's response, one word made of two parts: הִנֵּ (shortened from הִנֵּה) + נִי-- a suffixed pronoun meaning *me*.

The colon-like mark at the end of the verse is called a *sof passuq*. This mark was added by the Jewish scholars, called Masoretes, who added the nikkud to the previously unvocalized text long after the original text was written. Every Hebrew Bible verse ends with a *sof passuq* which means, appropriately enough, *end of verse*. In your translation exercises in this book, the *sof passuq* will only be written when you are given a complete verse, completely unedited.

Verse 2
וַיֹּאמֶר The next וַיֹּאמֶר indicates another switch in speakers, back to the *tester, Elohim*.

קַח־נָא אֶת־בִּנְךָ אֶת־יְחִידְךָ   קַח is the masculine singular command form of לקח and means *Take!*

נָא is a *particle of entreaty* or exhortation meaning *I pray,* or in this case, *now*. We call a command form an *imperative*, and the imperative is the mainline of another of the Direct Speech genres called **Hortatory Discourse**. In Hortatory Discourse, the speaker commands or exhorts his audience (see 19.2c).

בִּנְךָ is a noun plus possessive suffix (13.4). When figuring out the noun, do not forget that the vowels are shortened to their construct form before the suffix is added (also 13.4).

יְחִידְךָ uses the adjective יָחִיד meaning *only* as a noun, as in *only one*. An adjective used as a noun is called a *substantive*. Like בִּנְךָ a vowel in the word has shortened due to the addition of the suffix. In יְחִיד it is the *patakh* that has shortened to a *shewa*. Notice that *your only one* does not name a second direct object but renames it. The lack of a *vav* helps us make this distinction.

282

אֲשֶׁר־אָהַבְתָּ   Here we have an אֲשֶׁר-qatal construction which has the function *relative past background*. The entire clause functions like an adjective modifying יְחִידְךָ This clause is a good example of how the qatal in a dependent clause can be used the same way in a Hortatory Discourse as it is in a Historical Narrative.

The root אהב which means *love*, does not take the usual translation recommended in 4.3h using the English helping verb *had*. It would give the sense that Abraham was no longer loving his son. Roots like אהב that refer to emotional and mental activity usually require present tense translations. Remember, the meanings of the Biblical Hebrew verb forms are not locked-on for time the way our English verb forms are. More important than the time of the qatal verb form in this clause is that it pins the attribute of *lover* onto Abraham. We now have the makings for a drama: a *tester* and a *lover*.

אֶת־יִצְחָק   should technically have been above as a third DDO following the command קַח־נָא But it is here because of the conspicuous interruption that אֲשֶׁר־אָהַבְתָּ makes in the series of DDO's. Rhythmically, אֶת־יִצְחָק seems to come as a surprise unveiling of the third key participant in the account because it follows the dependent clause which would typically have ended the thought.

וְלֶךְ־לְךָ אֶל־אֶרֶץ הַמֹּרִיָּה   Here is the second command from the *tester Elohim* in the continuing Hortatory Discourse. לֶךְ is the masculine singular command form made from the root הלך Notice how it lost its first root letter the same way as קַח did. With לְךָ the command suggests doing the command to or for oneself. Perhaps *Get yourself!* would be a good rendering. הַמֹּרִיָּה is the name of a place used as the *absolute* or last element in a construct chain (7.2c).

וְהַעֲלֵהוּ שָׁם לְעֹלָה עַל אַחַד הֶהָרִים   This is the third clause in the string of commands that make up this Hortatory Discourse. The imperative form וְהַעֲלֵהוּ is made of three parts:

The m. s. Hiphil stem imperative form of the root עלה	הַעֲלֵה
The 3rd m. s. object suffix (*him*): הוּ-- The root's final *heh* is dropped before the suffix *heh* is added.	הַעֲלֵהוּ
Then, of course, the *vav*.	וְהַעֲלֵהוּ

The Hiphil stem gives a causative sense to a root, so when עלה in Qal means *go up*, in Hiphil, it means *cause to go up* (in smoke) or *sacrifice*. With its suffixed pronoun and prefixed *vav* our word means *And sacrifice him*.

עֹלָה is another word from the root עלה It is a noun meaning *sacrifice*.

283

אֶחָד is the masculine word for *one*. אַחַד together with הֶהָרִים makes a construct chain. To find the noun in הֶהָרִים take off the definite article and m. p. ending, יִם --

אֲשֶׁר אֹמַר אֵלֶיךָ: If this construction were a dependent clause with a qatal form as we saw earlier in this verse, what would be the vowel under the *aleph*? _____ (4.3g) Rather it is a dependent clause with a yiqtol verb form which is used to give relative non-past background. It can be either *I will show* or *I show*.

The yiqtol is made with prefixed subject pronouns (some of which also need complements affixed to the ends of the root). In אֹמַר the root is אמר and the prefixed pronoun is א so one of the *alephs* had to go, and without a trace left behind. אמר is one of the most common roots in the Hebrew Bible, and it has a few tricky forms. The only difference in the following are the vowels:

אָמַר	Qal qatal 3rd m. s.
אֹמֵר	Qal participle m. s.
אֱמֹר	Qal imperative m. s.
אֹמַר	Qal yiqtol 1st c. s.

It is worth memorizing these four forms.

Lesson 17--The mainline of the Historical Narrative resumes

Verse 3

וַיַּשְׁכֵּם אַבְרָהָם בַּבֹּקֶר The root שכם is used only in the Hiphil stem as it is here, and it means *rise early*.

בֹּקֶר with the emphasis on the first syllable means *morning*. The *bet* prefixed to the word has the nikkud of the definite article, a *patakh* and a *dagesh forte* in the following letter [בַּ], so it is translated *in the...*

וַיַּחֲבֹשׁ אֶת־חֲמֹרוֹ The root חבשׁ here shown in the Qal stem means *gird, bind*.

A חֲמֹר is a *donkey*. You should know what the *holem* on the end means (2.4c).

וַיִּקַּח אֶת־שְׁנֵי נְעָרָיו אִתּוֹ וְאֵת יִצְחָק בְּנוֹ שְׁנֵי means *two* or *two of*. Notice the m. p. construct ending on it. The ending shows the word's connection to נְעָרָיו נַעַר means *boy, servant*, and you should know, as in the clause above, what the *vav* means (2.4c). The question is whether you can discern the plural form of נְעָרָיו We know it is plural because there are two specified, but in other contexts, you will need to recognize the *yod* as making the noun plural. Here are *his servant* and *his servants* contrasted:

his servants	נְעָרָיו
his servant	נַעֲרוֹ

284

אֹתוֹ should not be confused with אֹתוֹ The *dagesh* in the former indicates a preposition as opposed to the latter in which אֵת is a DDO. The former means *with him*, and the latter means simply *him*.

וַיְבַקַּע עֲצֵי עֹלָה Fill out the verb analysis chart for the verb form paying attention to the nikkud (2.2e):

root	stem	form	person, gender, number	function	basic root meaning
					break, cleave

עֵץ means *wood* which is in construct with עֹלָה which we learned in Genesis 22:2.

וַיָּקָם

וַיֵּלֶךְ אֶל־הַמָּקוֹם   מָקוֹם means *place*.

אֲשֶׁר־אָמַר־לוֹ הָאֱלֹהִים Remember that this construction represents relative past background (4.3b). In other words, when we use the mainline as a reference point in time--here, it is Abraham's getting up and going--we know that *Elohim **had** spoken to him* at an earlier point in time.

Verse 4

בַּיּוֹם הַשְּׁלִישִׁי Remember from above the significance of the nikkud with the preposition בְּ This significance is confirmed by the definite article on the attributive adjective הַשְּׁלִישִׁי which means *third*.

This phrase is not a clause. It has neither a verb, nor is it an equating of a predicate and a subject as we see in the Hebrew verbless clause. In this respect, it is somewhat of a "hanging fragment." It interrupts the flow of the wayyiqtol string, and thereby creates suspense. We might translate it *It was on the third day*.

וַיִּשָּׂא אַבְרָהָם אֶת־עֵינָיו What do the *hireq* under the prefix pronoun and the dagesh forte in the *shin* indicate is the missing root letter?_____ (9.2b) You should know the root.

You should know the root of עֵינָיו and the meaning of the suffix is covered above in the discussion of נְעָרָיו

וַיַּרְא אֶת־הַמָּקוֹם מֵרָחֹק: The word מֵרָחֹק is made of two parts, the preposition and the adjective רָחוֹק meaning *afar*.

Lesson 18--Another embedded Hortatory Discourse

Verse 5

וַיֹּאמֶר אַבְרָהָם אֶל־נְעָרָיו   Here comes another Direct Speech Discourse. What will it be--Predictive Narrative, Instructional Discourse, or perhaps more Hortatory Discourse?

שְׁבוּ־לָכֶם פֹּה עִם־הַחֲמוֹר   More Hortatory Discourse it is! שְׁבוּ is the m. p. imperative made from the root יָשַׁב Notice, for the third time in our reading, how an imperative has lost its first root letter. Loss of the first root letter is not a rule for imperatives, but it is quite common. We will begin learning about imperatives in earnest in Lesson 19.

פֹּה means *here*. Hopefully, you remember חֲמוֹר from verse 3.

וַאֲנִי וְהַנַּעַר נֵלְכָה עַד־כֹּה   The verb נֵלְכָה should look to you very much like the 1 c. p. yiqtol of הלך only with an additional *heh* on the end because this is exactly what it is. This form of the yiqtol is partners with the imperative and one other verb form as the mainline of Hortatory Discourse. It is called the **cohortative**, and it is translated *Let us...* in the plural and *Let me...* in the singular (see 24.2c).

With the fronting of the words וַאֲנִי וְהַנַּעַר in the clause, used by Abraham to shift the focus to himself and his son from the two servants, we can translate *As for me and the boy, let us go...*

עַד־כֹּה means literally *until there* (imagine Abraham pointing) or *yonder*.

וְנִשְׁתַּחֲוֶה   Notice, after removing the *vav*, the *nun* at the beginning of the word and the *heh* at the end like the cohortative we just saw. This word is indeed another cohortative on the mainline of Abraham's Hortatory Discourse. This is a disputed root in a disputed stem which we will discuss further later in the course. It is the only word in the Hebrew Bible which exhibits the four letters שתחו in sequence, and it is best to be able to identify the sequence on sight meaning *prostrate oneself, worship*.

וְנָשׁוּבָה אֲלֵיכֶם   The third in the series of cohortatives. Abraham intends that both he *and his son* will return. In other words, he believes in the power of the *tester Elohim* to raise his son from the dead!

Verse 6

וַיִּקַּח אַבְרָהָם אֶת־עֲצֵי הָעֹלָה   We are back on the mainline of the Narrative.

Notice now that עֲצֵי הָעֹלָה has become a "prop" in the account, it has become definite (6.3a) as opposed to verse 3's indefinite version.

וַיָּשֶׂם עַל־יִצְחָק בְּנוֹ   What does the vowel under the prefixed subject pronoun indicate here?_____ (10.3a) There has been a lot of debate over the years about how old Isaac was. How young could Isaac have been and still be able to carry the wood from one mountain top to another?

וַיִּקַּח בְּיָדוֹ אֶת־הָאֵשׁ וְאֶת־הַמַּאֲכֶלֶת אֵשׁ means *fire,* and מַאֲכֶלֶת means *knife.* We are aided in identifying מַאֲכֶלֶת as a feminine noun because most nouns ending in *tav* are feminine. It is constructed, as are many nouns, by the addition of a *mem* before a root, in this case, the root אכל which means *eat.*

וַיֵּלְכוּ שְׁנֵיהֶם יַחְדָּו: We saw שְׁנֵי in verse 3. The suffix הֶם-- means *them* (m. p.). יַחְדָּו is an adverb meaning *together.* There is a conspicuous similarity between this word and Verse 2's יְחִידְךָ

Lesson 19--A stretch of dialogue

Verse 7

וַיֹּאמֶר יִצְחָק אֶל־אַבְרָהָם אָבִיו Often in a situation like this, when there is a shift in the actor or subject of the narrative, the writer will use an X-qatal topicalization construction to clarify the shift in subject. However, we see here that the X-qatal is not mandatory, especially when the shift in subject is clear without it, as it is in this clause.

וַיֹּאמֶר אָבִי The repetition of the וַיֹּאמֶר is further evidence that the previous clause functioned more as a device for clarifying the shift in subject than as an actual advance in the narrative. We are seeing therefore, evidence of a larger issue, that the "rules" of discourse construction on which the ancient Hebrew based his linguistic decisions were not rules at all in the strict sense of the word. We would be better off referring to them as conventions which were elastic enough to allow creative tampering.

וַיֹּאמֶר הִנֶּנִּי בְנִי We see a bit of custom here. Abraham responds to his son's inquiry the same way he had earlier responded to his God's. The use of *my* with *father* by Isaac and with *son* by Abraham may sound a bit formal to us, but it probably did not sound so to them. Even in today's Israel, Hebrews use the pronominal suffix י with family-relationship words very affectionately.

וַיֹּאמֶר הִנֵּה הָאֵשׁ וְהָעֵצִים Here Isaac demonstrates to us that he had participated in this type of worship before. He knew the props and probably the protocol. With the word הִנֵּה Isaac asks his father to look.

וְאַיֵּה הַשֶּׂה לְעֹלָה: The first word means *And where...* We have here a verbless clause that needs an *is.* A שֶׂה is a *lamb.* There is a constant tension in this account between what can be seen and what cannot be seen. For instance, they see the fire and the wood but they do not see the lamb for the offering. We readers see that God is testing Abraham, but Abraham can only lift up his eyes and see the dreaded mountaintop.

Verse 8
וַיֹּאמֶר אַבְרָהָם

אֱלֹהִים יִרְאֶה־לּוֹ הַשֶּׂה לְעֹלָה בְּנִי Here we have our first X-yiqtol construction of the reading. What is the function of such a construction?_____ (14.3c)

287

Translation of יִרְאֶה might be either English present or future. In answer to Isaac's question Abraham uses the grammatical construction which puts the focus on *Elohim*. Abraham here assures his son that God does see even though they cannot.

לוֹ is an ambiguous reference. Does it mean *it* as a reference to the acquisition of a lamb or does it mean *for Him(self)* as a reference to *Elohim*?

The word בְּנִי is a vocative (19.3), a word in direct speech that names the addressee.

Thus ends the somewhat lengthy (by Hebrew Bible standards) dialogue. Aside from the string of וַיֹּאמֶר s, the stretch of dialogue is a stretch of Direct Speech. Relative to the larger, host discourse, this stretch of Direct Speech represents a departure from the mainline of the host discourse. So did the earlier Hortatory Discourse. The departure from the mainline of Historical Narrative into a variety of Direct Speech genres retards the forward movement of the narrative. In so doing, it creates suspense while the reader wonders whether Isaac is about to jump ship because he does not understand what he and his father are doing. We wonder how Abraham can respond to Isaac's questions or just how much he will tell Isaac.

There are two critical principles to learn here:

1. Departure from the mainline of any discourse slows the forward progress of the discourse. This "slowing" allows the writer to redirect the attention of his audience away from the main storyline so he can clarify, elaborate, build background. In so doing, the writer can often create tension or suspense.

2. A departure from the mainline of one discourse can often be accomplished by a shift to another embedded genre with its own different mainline. For instance, in this Historical Narrative, the writer departs from the mainline of his story when he shifts to one of the Direct Speech genres.

וַיֵּלְכוּ שְׁנֵיהֶם יַחְדָּו׃ As is often the case, the return to the mainline proper releases the tension build-up. Here, our doubts about the successful continuation of the expedition are erased by the conspicuous repetition of the clause from Verse 6. We see that in Biblical narrative, unlike modern English narrative, stories are extremely compact, with sudden build-ups of tension and releases just as sudden. On the other hand, it seems as though the techniques of good story-telling, whether compact or drawn out, are universal.

Lesson 20--Uninterrupted Mainline

Verse 9

וַיָּבֹאוּ אֶל־הַמָּקוֹם Continuation of the mainline.

אֲשֶׁר אָמַר־לוֹ הָאֱלֹהִים What is the function of this construction?_____ (4.3b)

וַיִּבֶן שָׁם אַבְרָהָם אֶת־הַמִּזְבֵּחַ The vowel under the prefixed subject pronoun tells you what letter is missing from the root?_____ (8.3a) בנה means *build*.

288

The word מִזְבֵּחַ is another noun like מַאֲכֶלֶת made from a root with a preformative *mem* that turns the root into a noun. In this case the root is זבח meaning *slaughter*, and the noun means *altar*.

וַיַּעֲרֹךְ אֶת־הָעֵצִים The root ערך in the Qal stem means *arrange*.

וַיַּעֲקֹד אֶת־יִצְחָק בְּנוֹ The root עקד in the Qal stem means *bind*. Note how the nikkud is exactly the same as the 1st guttural verb which precedes it.

וַיָּשֶׂם אֹתוֹ עַל־הַמִּזְבֵּחַ מִמַּעַל לָעֵצִים: Is it ironic that first Abraham placed the wood on Isaac, and then placed Isaac on the wood?

Remember from Verse 3 to contrast אֹתוֹ and אִתּוֹ

מִמַּעַל לָעֵצִים means *above the wood*.

Verse 10
וַיִּשְׁלַח אַבְרָהָם אֶת־יָדוֹ The narrative is moving forward very quickly now as we approach the climax.

וַיִּקַּח אֶת־הַמַּאֲכֶלֶת לִשְׁחֹט אֶת־בְּנוֹ: What verb form is לִשְׁחֹט?_____
(16.4a) The root שׁחט means *kill*, but the root is worth a closer look. Check it in your Hebrew-English dictionary. There are several, more general words for kill than this one. Notice how an infinitive can have its own DDO.

Verse 11
וַיִּקְרָא אֵלָיו מַלְאַךְ יְהוָה מִן־הַשָּׁמַיִם Perhaps you remember מַלְאַךְ from Lesson 7.

וַיֹּאמֶר אַבְרָהָם אַבְרָהָם As is often the case in Biblical Hebrew, וַיֹּאמֶר works in conjunction with another verb of speech. The first verb tells how the speech was said and the וַיֹּאמֶר marks the beginning of the quotation. In this case we have *cried* first in the clause above and *said* here.

וַיֹּאמֶר הִנֵּנִי: This is the many-times repeated response of Abraham in this account. His own ability to see may be limited all through the account, but he is willing, himself, to be seen.

Lesson 21--The third embedded Hortatory Discourse

Verse 12
וַיֹּאמֶר

אַל־תִּשְׁלַח יָדְךָ אֶל־הַנַּעַר We just learned the use of אַל in Lesson 21.

וְאַל־תַּעַשׂ לוֹ מְאוּמָה Notice how the root עשׂה has lost its final *heh*. This is typical of the yiqtol form of 3rd *heh* verbs in Hortatory Discourse.

מְאוּמָה means *anything, something*.

כִּי עַתָּה יָדַעְתִּי Do not confuse עַתָּה with אַתָּה As for the time of the English verb you use in translation, do you remember from Verse 2 what to do with qatals of roots that pertain to mental and emotional activity?

Here the dependent clause with a qatal is used to give background. In Hortatory Discourse, background often gives the reasons behind the commands and exhortations.

כִּי־יְרֵא אֱלֹהִים אַתָּה The word יְרֵא is an adjective from the root ירא meaning *fear*. It is used in construct here with אֱלֹהִים a sure give away that it is being used substantively or as a noun. Does the clause have S-P or P-S word order? (2.7c) It is the word order we would expect for the messenger's description of Abraham. It is like saying, *One who fears God (and not something else) are you.*

This time we see a verbless clause being used in a Hortatory Discourse to further explain the reason for the command *Do not send forth your hand to the boy.*

וְלֹא חָשַׂכְתָּ אֶת־בִּנְךָ אֶת־יְחִידְךָ מִמֶּנִּי: The root חשׂכ means *withhold*. מִמֶּנִּי is the preposition מִן in a lengthened form with the pronominal suffix ־נִי meaning *me*.

Here we have a negated qatal. Remember that negated verb forms, except for the אַל-yiqtol construction mentioned earlier in this verse, are considered irrealis (11.2b). So we have our third clause here with a low-ranking construction. Together the three give a rather complete elaboration of the reasons behind the original prohibitive command. Also be reminded of the caution in 11.4b: Low ranking in the discourse profile scheme *does not mean* low in importance. The reasons for the messenger's visit and commands reflect the very crux of the test around which this account is centered.

Notice in this clause the third use of a יחד-word, made all the more conspicuous because it is not a particularly common word in the Hebrew Bible.

Verse 13

וַיִּשָּׂא אַבְרָהָם אֶת־עֵינָיו Notice the parallelism with verse 4.

וַיַּרְא The parallelism continues.

וְהִנֵּה־אַיִל אַחַר נֶאֱחַז בַּסְּבַךְ בְּקַרְנָיו This is an X-qatal construction.

The X: אַיִל אַחַר means *a ram behind*. *Behind* what? Probably Abraham, but we do not know.

The qatal: נֶאֱחַז The *nun* on the beginning of the root could be a prefixed subject pronoun of a yiqtol form, but that does not make sense in the context and the nikkud is incorrect. It is the preformative that identifies the Niphal stem. אחז in the Niphal stem means *be seized*. Translate *It was a ram behind (him) that was seized.*

290

סְבַךְ בַּסְּבַךְ means *thicket*.

קֶרֶן means *horn*. The preposition בְּ this time indicates as it often does in Hebrew *means*, and we translate it *by*. For an explanation of the suffix, see verse 2's נְעָרָיו

Of great interest here is the use of the word הִנֵּה   Although the word has been used many times in this account, this is the first time in the account that the word is used in the regular narration, that is, *not within direct speech*. In such a case, a Biblical narrator signals the switch within the narrative from the detached perspective of a third person narrator to the perspective of one of the participants within the narrative.[1] With הִנֵּה the narrator signals us to see as Abraham saw. The most effective translation of this clause is therefore English present tense. Thematically, we can say that when he sees the ram, Abraham's eyes have finally opened to what we knew all along, that God was testing him.

וַיֵּלֶךְ אַבְרָהָם

וַיִּקַּח אֶת־הָאַיִל

וַיַּעֲלֵהוּ לְעֹלָה תַּחַת בְּנוֹ:   The first word is clearly a wayyiqtol. It is constructed exactly like the imperative of the same root in verse 2, including the pronominal suffix הו-- except for the *vav-patakh-dagesh forte* unit added and a *yod* in the place of the preformative *heh*. Like the imperative in verse 2, this wayyiqtol form is Hiphil stem.

תַּחַת means *in place of*

Verse 14

וַיִּקְרָא אַבְרָהָם שֵׁם־הַמָּקוֹם הַהוּא   In this clause הַהוּא means *that*. The words הוּא הִיא הֵם and הֵן like זֶה זֹאת and אֵלֶּה can be used as demonstrative adjectives (18.2b). When used in this way they will follow the noun they modify and agree with the noun in number, gender, and definiteness. Here is a complete review:

THE DEMONSTRATIVES:

English Gender	THIS	THESE	THAT	THOSE
MASCULINE	זֶה	אֵלֶּה	הוּא	הֵם
FEMININE	זֹאת	אֵלֶּה	הִיא	הֵן

יְהֹוָה יִרְאֶה   Most Hebrew names are sentences. This is a particularly good example. Notice, throughout the episode, how the letter sequence יר־א appears in different contexts, drawing together the meanings *see* and *fear*. This kind of root-play is common in Biblical Hebrew and is

[1] Berlin, *Poetics and Interpretation of Biblical* Narrative(Sheffield: The Almond Press, 1983).

called paronomasia. You may want to look ahead now to Lesson 33.3's explanation of *Leitwort*.

אֲשֶׁר יֵאָמֵר הַיּוֹם   The verb is a yiqtol form in the Niphal stem. Translate *which is said today*.

בְּהַר יְהוָה יֵרָאֶה   We treat this as a mini Direct Speech discourse. The clause is a good example of how the Hebrew Bible can still be a mystery. There are several possible meanings.

1. The verb with a *sere* under the *yod* is the Niphal stem and means *It (or he) is (or shall be) seen*.
   a. *In a mountain, it is YHWH who is (or shall be) seen*.
   b. with the mountain and *YHWH* as a construct chain: *It is in the mountain of YHWH that it shall be seen*.
2. The nikkud with verb may be a misinterpretation by the Masoretes who inserted the nikkud into the consonantal text around 1000 CE. Remove one dot from beneath the *yod*, and we would have *In a mountain, it is YHWH who sees (or will see)*.

Which explanation do you find most likely? In any case, this chapter is a good example of how the Biblical Hebrew writer will explore the range of meanings for one root in one account.

Verse 15

וַיִּקְרָא מַלְאַךְ יְהוָה אֶל־אַבְרָהָם שֵׁנִית מִן־הַשָּׁמָיִם: שֵׁנִית   means *a second time, again*.

Lesson 22--An embedded Predictive Narrative

Verse 16

וַיֹּאמֶר   See the explanation in vs. 11.

בִּי נִשְׁבַּעְתִּי נְאֻם־יְהוָה   The preposition בְּ once again indicates means, so it can be translated *by*, with its suffix, in this case, *by Myself*.

נִשְׁבַּעְתִּי   is a qatal form. The preformative נ identifies the stem as Niphal, and you should know what the affixed subject pronoun means. The root שׁבע in the Niphal stem means *be sworn*. We will learn how to translate Niphal stem verbs later in the course. For now, translate this verb *I am sworn*.

The qatal here does not refer to time or tense in and of itself like some English verb forms. Rather, the qatal expresses the pinning of an attribute on the subject. During this narrative, *YHWH* has gone from *tester* to *one sworn*. Translating this qatal, the English present probably makes best sense in the context seeing that *YHWH* is swearing at the same moment that He is speaking.

נְאֻם   labels an utterance of *YHWH*. We can translate it *says YHWH*. This word is often a signal that a +projection discourse is to follow, very often Predictive Narrative. Since *YHWH* is swearing Himself in this clause, the likelihood of a Predictive Narrative discourse is even greater.

כִּי יַעַן אֲשֶׁר עָשִׂיתָ אֶת־הַדָּבָר הַזֶּה   The combination יַעַן אֲשֶׁר introduces a dependent clause and means *because*.

עָשִׂיתָ   Again, we must be flexible with the time or tense of our translation. What is the function of a qatal in a dependent clause?_____ This function still holds in this verse, but the usual past time translation does not. Here, instead of the helping word *had*, which is usually recommended and would give us a *past perfect* translation, the helping word *have* would be more appropriate, giving us the English *present perfect* construction. The English *present perfect* refers to something which was done in the past and still affects the present. It is the best English translation here because it maintains the function **relative past background** of the qatal in the dependent clause and also the **present time context**.

Remember that it is *not* the goal of this book to once again translate the Hebrew Bible. It *is* the goal to understand the Hebrew. The qatal in this clause labels Abraham as a *doer*. That the qatal is here expressing this attribute of Abraham is much more important than the time of the English verb form we use in translation.

וְלֹא חָשַׂכְתָּ אֶת־בִּנְךָ אֶת־יְחִידֶךָ:   Another repetition of this clause from above further emphasizes Abraham's passing of the test.

Verse 17

כִּי־בָרֵךְ אֲבָרֶכְךָ   Notice the same root בּרך meaning in the Piel *bless* is used twice here. The first time it is in a form we have not learned yet called the **infinitive absolute** and the second time as a Piel 1st c. s. yiqtol. The double use of the root using the infinitive absolute and a regularly conjugated form is a way of emphasizing the verity of the statement. We often translate with a *surely, truly* or *indeed*.

וְהַרְבָּה אַרְבֶּה אֶת־זַרְעֲךָ כְּכוֹכְבֵי הַשָּׁמַיִם וְכַחוֹל   Again, a root, this time רבה in the Hiphil stem meaning *multiply,* is used twice, first in the infinitive absolute form and then in the regularly conjugated yiqtol form. Be careful not to over-generalize and think that every occurrence of a repeated root is another example of this construction. We will learn to identify infinitive absolutes in Lesson 34.2.

This is now the second in a series of yiqtol forms. *Ordinarily, it is the weqatal form that takes the mainline of a Predictive Narrative like this one.* However, the writer here is using the infinitive absolute + yiqtol instead. He cannot use the infinitive absolutes with the weqatal verb form because the infinitive absolute bumps the conjugated verb out of the first position in the clause, the only place a weqatal can be found. Even the emphasizing power of the infinitive absolutes is therefore increased because they are a break from the ordinary conventions of Predictive Narrative. *Breaks with convention are themselves part of a larger convention which says that such breaks create emphasis.*

Vocabulary for the rest of the clause:

זֶרַע   *seed*
כּוֹכָב   *star*
שָׁמַיִם   *heavens*
חוֹל   *sand*

293

אֲשֶׁר עַל־שְׂפַת־הַיָּם   This is a verbless dependent clause. The אֲשֶׁר does the job of English *which*, and we must supply the *be*-verb.

שְׂפַת־הַיָּם   means *lip of the sea* or *sea shore*.

וְיִרַשׁ זַרְעֲךָ אֵת שַׁעַר אֹיְבָיו: Do not be fooled into thinking that the verb is a weqatal. What would be the vowel under the first root letter of a weqatal? Rather this form is a clause-initial yiqtol which we will later learn expresses a possibility or the speaker's desire. We express these concepts in English with the words *may, might*. The root ירשׁ in Qal means *possess*, so we can translate *And may your seed possess...* The nikkud of וְיִרַשׁ is a bit strange because it follows neither the pattern of the first or second class first *yod* roots as you have learned them. We may call ירשׁ a rebellious root (see 34.3).

שַׁעַר אֹיְבָיו: either means *the gate of his enemies* or *gate of his enemies*. Which is it? (7.2c)

Verse 18

וְהִתְבָּרְכוּ בְזַרְעֲךָ כֹּל גּוֹיֵי הָאָרֶץ   The first word is a weqatal form, this time the 3rd m. p. Hitpael stem of the root בּרך meaning *bless oneself*. It continues, from the previous clause, the possibility opened by Abraham's obedience. See זֶרַע in Verse 17 above.

עֵקֶב אֲשֶׁר שָׁמַעְתָּ בְּקֹלִי: The combination עֵקֶב אֲשֶׁר means *because* or *as a consequence of*. We might expect a *lamed* before קֹלִי for a more literal correspondence between the Hebrew and the English *to My voice*, but the Hebrew usually uses the *bet* in this case. Although you may not use the expression in your translation, you might think of the English expression *to listen in*.

Verse 18 ends an artistic and nuanced unit which began with כִּי יַעַן אֲשֶׁר in Verse 16. The unit is bracketed by two expressions of Abraham's obedience which provide the condition on which the promises depend. The opening expression of condition begins כִּי יַעַן אֲשֶׁר and the closing expression of condition begins in Verse 18 with עֵקֶב אֲשֶׁר The first half of the promises belong to Abraham, and they are expressed in the most vivid and sure way using the infinitive absolute plus yiqtol. The second half of the unit is the promises for Abraham's seed. These promises are expressed as possibilities rather than sure things. This nuance is created by the clause initial yiqtol of Verse 17, וְיִרַשׁ A weqatal at this point would have acted conjunctively, continuing, in series, the sure promises which began with the infinitive absolute plus yiqtol constructions. A clause-initial yiqtol, by contrast, acts disjunctively, dividing the *sure* nature of the promises to Abraham versus the *possible* nature of the promises to Abraham's seed. As is often the case, the weqatal וְהִתְבָּרְכוּ continues, in series-fashion, the mood of the form which precedes it, here the clause-initial yiqtol's expression of possibility. The translation of וְהִתְבָּרְכוּ would be something like *And so may be blessers of themselves*. Here is the whole unit represented schematically:

294

CONDITION: כִּי יַּעַן אֲשֶׁר + qatals
And because you were a doer and not a withholder

SURE PROMISE: infinitive absolutes + yiqtols
I will surely bless...and I will surely multiply

BREAK: A break in mood from sure promises to possible is created by clause-initial yiqtol rather than a conjunctive weqatal.

POSSIBLE PROMISE: וְיִרַשׁ זַרְעֲךָ
And may your seed possess
וְהִתְבָּרֲכוּ
And so may they be blessers of themselves
CONDITION: עֵקֶב אֲשֶׁר + qatal
As a consequence of your hearing...

Verse 19

This verse returns to the mainline of the account for the remainder in a string of four wayyiqtols that should be no problem for you. The return to a string of wayyiqtols at the end of a discourse or perhaps an X-qatal is a common way for a Historical Narrative to resolve to finality.

Charting the discourse

At the beginning of this discourse analysis, we examined the forty-six wayyiqtol verb forms which represent the backbone of this account. We can now examine the profile of the entire discourse in chart form.

Notes:
1. Every וַיֹּאמֶר should theoretically mark a transition from Historical Narrative to one of the Direct Speech genres. However, because many of the quotations are very short and difficult to label, short, isolated Direct Speech is left on the same line of the chart with its וַיֹּאמֶר
2. It is the "discourse turbulence" created by the writer's shifting of verb forms from one rank to another that interests us and which we will study more as we progress.

Symbols:

W	wayyiqtol clause
M	mainline of another genre
========	boundaries of an embedded genre
-----------	boundaries of extended dialogue
indentations	lower ranking, i.e., the construction slows the forward progress of the narrative(11.4b).

Abraham is Tested

HISTORICAL NARRATIVE

Vs. 1   W of הִיה: *And then it happened after these things,*

        X-qatal: *and it was God who was tester of Abraham.*

W: *And he said to him, "Abraham."*

W: *And he said, "Behold me."*

295

Vs. 2   W: *And he said,*

===

EMBEDDED HORTATORY

      M: *Take now your son, your only one, Isaac*

            Dep. Clause w/ qatal: *of which you are a lover*

      M: *And get yourself to the land of Moriah*

      M: *And offer him there for a burnt offering upon one of the mountains*

            Dep. Clause w/ yiqtol *that I will show to you*

===

Vs. 3   W: *And then Abraham rose up early in the morning*

       W: *And he girded his donkey*

       W: *And he took his two servants with him and Isaac his son*

       W: *And he broke wood of offering*

       W: *And he arose*

       W: *And he went to the place*

            Dep. Clause w/ qatal: *of which to him God had spoken*

Vs. 4   Verbless Phrase: *It was on the third day*

       W: *And then Abraham lifted his eyes*

       W: *And he saw the place from afar*

Vs. 5   W: *And Abraham said to his servants*

===

EMBEDDED HORTATORY

      M: *Sit yourselves here with the donkey*

      M: *As for me and the boy, let us go yonder*

      M: *And let us worship*

      M: *And let us return to you*

===

Vs. 6   W: *And then Abraham took the wood of offering*

       W: *And he put (it) upon Isaac his son*

       W: *And he took in his hand the fire and the knife*

       W: *And the two of them went together*

Vs. 7   W: *And Isaac said to Abraham his father*

EXTENDED DIALOGUE

      W: *And he said, "My father."*

      W: *And he said, "Behold me, my son."*

      W: *And he said, "Behold the fire and the wood. But where is the lamb for an offering?"*

Vs. 8   W: *And Abraham said, "It is God who sees to it (Himself) for an offering, my son."*

      W: *And then the two of them went together.*

Vs. 9   W: *And they came to the place*

            Dep. Clause w/ qatal: *of which to him God was speaker.*

      W: *And Abraham built there the altar*

      W: *And he arranged the wood*

      W: *And he bound Isaac his son*

      W: *And he placed him upon the altar above the wood*

Vs. 10   W: *And Abraham sent forth his hand*
         W: *And he took the knife to flay his son*
Vs. 11   W: *And the messenger of YHWH called from heaven*
         W: *And he said, "Abraham! Abraham!"*
         W: *And he said, "Behold me."*
Vs. 12   W: *And he said*

==

EMBEDDED HORTATORY

Prohib. Command: *Do not send forth your hand to the boy*
Prohib. Command: *Do not do anything to him*
          Dep. Clause w/ qatal: *For now I am a knower*
                    Dep. Verbless: *that you are a God-fearer*
                     Irrealis: *And you are not a with-*
                     holder of your son, your only one,

===*from me*

Vs. 13   W: *And then Abraham lifted his eyes*
        X-qatal: *And behold, it was a ram behind (him) that was caught in a thicket by its horns*
         W: *And Abraham went*
         W: *And he took the ram*
         W: *And he offered it up for an offering in place of his son*
Vs. 14   W: *And Abraham called the name of that place* YHWH sees
           Dep. Clause w/ yiqtol: *which is said today,*

==

EMBEDDED UNLABELED DIRECT SPEECH

X-yiqtol: *It is in the mountain of YHWH that it is (will be) seen*

==

Vs. 15   W: *And then the messenger of YHWH called to Abraham a second time from heaven*
Vs. 16   W: *And he said,*

==

EMBEDDED PREDICTIVE NARRATIVE

          X-qatal: *It is by Myself that I am sworn, says YHWH*
Dep. clause w/ qatal: *because you are a doer of this thing*
                    Dep. clause w/ irrealis: *And you are*
                    not a withholder of your son, your
                    only one

Vs. 17   "M": *For I will surely bless you*
         "M": *And I will surely multiply your seed as the stars of heaven and as the sand*
                    Dep. clause w/ v-less: *which is on the*
                    seashore

          ------------BREAK IN MOOD-----------
          Clause-initial yiqtol: *And may your seed possess the gate of his enemies*
Vs. 18   Weqatal: *And may all the nations of the earth shall be blessers of themselves in*
    your seed
          Dep.clause w/qatal: *because you have heard my voice*

==

Vs. 19   W: *And then Abraham returned to his servants*
           W: *And they arose*
           W: *And they went together to Beer-Sheva.*
           W: *And Abraham dwelt in Beer-Sheva*

Observations:

1. An X-qatal in verse 1 is used in an introductory manner.

2. The test is initiated by Elohim's direct speech in Verse 2. In this sense, Elohim's speech shapes human destiny as a continuation of the theme which began in Genesis 1:3 when Elohim says, "Let there be light."

3. The wayyiqtol skeleton is "fleshed out" by off-the-line material, particularly by embedded direct speech sections. For instance, in Verses 5 and 7-8, embedded direct speech is used to give glimpses of Abraham's faith during the test. The off-the-line material, including the embedded direct speeches halt the forward movement of the narrative and give the reader depictive material. The most poignant example is when the messenger of YHWH speaks in Verse 12 and not only halts the forward progress of the story, the sacrifice of Isaac!

4. A motif in the episode is sight or vision. The motif is explored in the writer's play with several Hebrew roots. Elohim is tester (נסה), while Abraham lifts (נשא) his eyes, first to see the dreaded place of testing (Verse 4) and then the sacrifice which Elohim provides (Verse 13). Tension builds as Abraham first tells Elohim and then Isaac, and finally the messenger of YHWH to "behold" him (הִנֵּנִי) and then he finally "beholds" (הִנֵּה) the ram. The writer also plays with the Hebrew letter sequence *yod-resh-aleph (-heh)* as Abraham trusts that Elohim will see (אלהים יראה) the sacrifice; Elohim proves that Abraham fears (ירא אלהים); Abraham names the place יהוה יראה ; and we hear the enigmatic proverb, "In the mount of YHWH, it (or He?) shall be seen (יהוה יראה)".

READING 2--Genesis 17:1-9 Abram Gets a New Name

Lesson 23--Gaining an overview of the discourse

Marking the boundaries of a discourse

For this reading we will actually do two discourse analyses, both of the Direct Speech type. The first one is a Hortatory Discourse spoken by God to Abraham, and the second is a Predictive Narrative, also spoken by God to Abraham. Our goal is to learn the manner in which the writer slips into and out of these genres and to contrast these +projection genres. They are short discourses, and we will identify their boundaries as we work with them.

Verse 1

וַיְהִי   We see here that the verse begins with the word וַיְהִי   In what discourse type is this verb form and root usually found? _____ (11.2a)
What function does it have in the genre in which it appears? _____
(11.2a)   Therefore, the two Direct Speech genres on which we will focus are embedded in a Historical Narrative.

In our last discourse analysis we saw that the discourse was bounded by וַיְהִי plus a specification of time on both its extremities. This verse is another example of the same type. The specification of time is the verbless clause which follows.

אַבְרָם בֶּן־תִּשְׁעִים שָׁנָה וְתֵשַׁע שָׁנִים   The formula [בֶּן + a number] is the Hebrew way to say a male's age. [בַּת + a number] is the expression for a female. In this clause, the number is תִּשְׁעִים שָׁנָה meaning *90 years* (Notice שָׁנָה is in its singular form.) and וְתֵשַׁע שָׁנִים meaning *and 9 years* (Notice שָׁנִים is in its plural form.) The combination of plural and singular endings may seem incomprehensible at first glance, but this example follows the most commonly attested pattern in Biblical Hebrew. For the *ten's* 20 and above the number word has the plural ending and the noun which is modified has the singular ending. For numbers 19 and below, the number word has the singular ending and the noun which is modified has the plural form.

וַיֵּרָא יְהוָה אֶל־אַבְרָם   What is the nikkud for this root when it means *And then he saw?* _____ (8.3a) The verb here is *not* a 1st *yod* root which might be your first impulse based on the *sere* under the *yod*. However, the root יָרֵא meaning *fear* is a second class 1st *yod* that has the wayyiqtol form וַיִּירָא   Looking back at Lesson 21.2c you can see that וַיֵּרָא contains a Niphal stem verb meaning *appear*. Memorize the following:

וַיֵּרָא	*And he appeared*
וַיַּרְא	*And he saw*
וַיִּירָא	*And he feared*

וַיֹּאמֶר אֵלָיו   No problem here!

אֵל אֲנִי-אֵל שַׁדַּי is short for אֱלֹהִים and means *Mighty One, God*. שַׁדַּי may be related to the Hebrew word for *breast*, here as an substantive meaning *breasted-one*. This name of God would then be a construct chain that speaks of His ability to nurture and give life. Can you tell from the word order in the verbless clause whether God expects Abram to know of Him already? (2.7c)

הִתְהַלֵּךְ לְפָנַי Here we have a familiar root הלך in an unfamiliar stem, the Hitpael stem. The Hitpael stem gives a reflexive meaning to a root. That is, the verb speaks of *doing something to oneself.* הִתְהַלֵּךְ with its characteristic הִת preformative of the Hitpael imperative means more than *Walk!* which would be לֵךְ Rather, this imperative means *Walk to and fro!* implying that Abram must exert control over his own life. Previously, Abram had allowed his wife Sarai to convince him to have a son by her handmaid Hagar. Now *YHWH* is about to tell Abram that the son born according to his wife's plan is not to be "son of the covenant." It is time for Abram to exert himself in following *YHWH*'s plan.

לְפָנַי We have often seen לְפָנַי which uses the m. p. construct form of פֵּן לְפָנַי has the 1st c. s. pronominal suffix on it. It can be translated *before Me* or *before My presence.*

וֶהְיֵה תָמִים: Take off the *vav*, and what verb form do we have? _____ (19.2a) This form makes it clear that we are in Hortatory Discourse. That we are in Hortatory Discourse and gives perspective to the verbless clause with which *YHWH* opened the discourse. In Hortatory, the off-the-line verb forms are used to give motivation for the exhortations.

Verse 2

וְאֶתְּנָה בְרִיתִי בֵּינִי וּבֵינֶךָ On the mainline of Hortatory Discourse we have three verb forms, the **imperative**, the **jussive** which you just learned in Lesson 23, and the **cohortative** which we see in this verse you will learn about in Lesson 24. The cohortative is easy enough to spot if you know your yiqtol. It is the 1st s. or p. with an added *heh* at the end. Like the jussive, the cohortative is translated *Let...*, *May...*, or *...shall...* as an expression of the speaker's will. If you need more help with the verb see 17.4c. Vocabulary:

בְּרִית means *a covenant.*
בֵּין means *between* and usually precedes both objects of the preposition
תָמִים means *upright, complete.*

וְאַרְבֶּה אוֹתְךָ בִּמְאֹד מְאֹד This is another cohortative in a series. The root רבה here shown in the Hiphil stem, means *multiply.*

If one מְאֹד means *very* or *a lot*, and it does, then how much is מְאֹד מְאֹד ?

In this short Hortatory discourse we have had one verbless clause giving motivation for the exhortations, then one mainline imperative in which *YHWH* expresses His desire for Abram, and finally, two mainline cohortatives in which *YHWH* expresses His desire for Himself. We are seeing what we may loosely construe as a rule.

300

RULE: Cohortatives in a series often follow one or more imperatives giving the purpose(s) of the imperatives. In this case the *vavs* have the sense of *so,* as in *...so I may give My covenant...*

Lesson 24—The casus pendens used to shift focus, and a new genre

Verse 3

וַיִּפֹּל אַבְרָם עַל־פָּנָיו   The Hortatory Discourse is clearly bounded on either side by the Narrative which hosts it.

וַיְדַבֵּר אִתּוֹ אֱלֹהִים לֵאמֹר: And likewise, the Narrative marks the beginning of another Direct Speech discourse.

Verse 4

אֲנִי   The subject pronoun אֲנִי is called a *casus pendens,* which in Latin means *hanging case,* because it "hangs outside" the regular grammatical structure of the clause. It is an extra element that precedes the clause.

The purpose of the *casus pendens* is to shift the topic or focus of the audience's attention. It is the topicalization structure in the extreme. The word אֲנִי therefore confirms the idea that the previous Hortatory focused primarily on Abram as recipient of *YHWH*'s command. Now the Speaker, has switched from Abram to Himself. A *casus pendens* is a very likely location for a change in genre, and we expect Predictive Narrative.[1]

הִנֵּה בְרִיתִי אִתָּךְ   Notice the *dagesh* in the *tav,* and you will see the verbless clause (see the reading on Gen. 22:3).

וְהָיִיתָ לְאַב הֲמוֹן גּוֹיִם: The Hortatory we anticipated is confirmed in the weqatal.   הֲמוֹן means *crowd.*

Verse 5

וְלֹא־יִקָּרֵא עוֹד אֶת־שִׁמְךָ אַבְרָם   The dagesh in the *qoph* is the sign of the Niphal yiqtol. Niphal stem often makes the Qal meaning passive. קָרָא in Qal means *call,* and קָרָא in Niphal means *be called.* The subject is *Abram.* The negated yiqtol in a Predictive Narrative generally refers to future time like an X-yiqtol.

וְהָיָה שִׁמְךָ אַבְרָהָם   Here we have the weqatal that we expect in a Predictive Narrative. As was mentioned in our last reading, Hebrew names are often self-contained expressions. For instance, here is a possible interpretation of *Abram* and *Abraham:*

אַבְרָם	אַבְרָהָם
אַב + רָם	אַבִּיר + הָם(וֹן)
exalted father	*multitude (of) chief*

---

[1] The definition and interpretation of casus pendens, also known as nominate absolute, varies considerably from one Hebraist to another. See Muraoka(1985) §6; Niccacci(1990) §§119-122; Waltke and O'Connor(1990), §§4.7, 8.3, 16.3.3b-d.

Look above in Verse 4 for הֲמוֹן

כִּי אַב־הֲמוֹן גּוֹיִם נְתַתִּיךָ: If you did your Lesson 24 homework, you will be able to decipher the verb. Notice how a pronominal suffix can be added to verbs as well as prepositions and nouns. Remember that the root נתן has the senses *put, place, make* as well as *give*. Also notice that the verb is a qatal in a dependent clause, or a form expressing relative past background. We have now seen this construction giving relative past background in Historical Narrative, Hortatory Discourse, and Predictive Narrative. It is used in the same way in other genres as well. As in earlier cases, this qatal is probably best translated in the English present perfect using the helping verb *have*.

Verse 6

וְהִפְרֵתִי אֹתְךָ בִּמְאֹד מְאֹד This root פרה in the Hiphil stem means *make fruitful*. The double use of מְאֹד is difficult to translate without sacrificing style, but that's O.K. You can read it in Hebrew now and can appreciate the double strength promise.

וּנְתַתִּיךָ לְגוֹיִם Even though the *vav* has been made the vowel *shureq*, it still means *and*, and with the qatal form still signifies the mainline form of Predictive Narrative. The sense of the clause is elusive, but most likely speaks of Abraham and his descendants being put into places of authority and beneficence to the nations. You will see this sense confirmed in the next clause.

וּמְלָכִים מִמְּךָ יֵצֵאוּ: Here we have an X-yiqtol that uses a euphonious repetition of the sounds in the preceding verse. Not only are there repeated sounds, but if we were not clear on the meaning of the previous clause this one spells it out. Clarification, paraphrase, and elaboration of an idea are common uses of a topicalization structure.

Here is the full paradigm for the preposition מִן with pronominal suffixes attached:

SINGULAR 3. M.	מִמֶּנּוּ	PLURAL 3. C.	מֵהֶם
3. F.	מִמֶּנָּה		
2. M.	מִמְּךָ	2. M.	מִכֶּם
2. F.	מִמֵּךְ	2. F.	-----
1. C.	מִמֶּנִּי	1. C.	מִמֶּנּוּ

Note: Pay special attention to the 3rd m. s. and 1st c. p. which are identical.

Lesson 25--More Predictive Narrative
Verse 7

וַהֲקִמֹתִי אֶת־בְּרִיתִי It would have been best if this verse had come along a bit later in the course because it features a Hiphil qatal of a hollow verb, the subject of Lesson 27. The root is קוּם and the form is part of the Predictive Narrative's weqatal string. The root in Qal means *stand, arise*, and in Hiphil it means *establish*.

302

בֵּינִי וּבֵינֶךָ וּבֵין זַרְעֲךָ אַחֲרֶיךָ לְדֹרֹתָם   Although we do not have a clause here, we do have a good study on pronominal suffixes. There are five of them. Do not be fooled by בֵּין It is close to בֵּן meaning *son*. If it were *son*, it would not have the *yod*, and the nikkud would have shortened to בְּנִי and וּבִנְךָ

לְדֹרֹתָם is made as follows:

> לְ   = preposition
> דֹרֹת = feminine plural noun meaning *generations*
> ם ָ -- = 3rd m. p. suffix *them*

לְדֹרֹתָם לִבְרִית עוֹלָם לִהְיוֹת לְךָ לֵאלֹהִים וּלְזַרְעֲךָ אַחֲרֶיךָ:   Beware! The last word of our last phrase לְדֹרֹתָם has been recopied again here. This has not been done to confuse you, only to include it here in our mini study of the preposition לְ Substitute the following meanings of לְ as appropriate:[1]

A. for (indicating *becoming something*)   B. for (indicating *purpose*)
B. to (the one that goes with the   D. to (as in *towards a recipient*)
  the infinitive)

לְדֹרֹתָם	____1.	לְךָ	____4.
לִבְרִית	____2.	לֵאלֹהִים	____5.
לִהְיוֹת	____3.	וּלְזַרְעֲךָ	____6.

Verse 8

וְנָתַתִּי לְךָ וּלְזַרְעֲךָ אַחֲרֶיךָ אֵת אֶרֶץ מְגֻרֶיךָ אֵת כָּל־אֶרֶץ כְּנַעַן לַאֲחֻזַּת עוֹלָם
This seems like a real mouthful, but it is not an awfully difficult clause thanks to the DDO's, *vavs*, and *lameds*. The first thing to identify is that it is another weqatal in the mainline string of the Predictive Narrative.

To whom is the *giving*? The answer to this question is called the indirect object, which in Hebrew, is most often identified by the preposition *lamed*. It is most often found in the same position that an English indirect object is found, right after the verb as it is here. Biblical Hebrew is not so exotic after all, is it? This clause has two indirect objects, neither of which is too difficult if you remember the word זרע means *seed*. אַחֲרֶיךָ is made from the word אַחַר

The next question is *What will be given?* The answer is the direct object, and the two-fold direct object is easily identifiable by the DDO's. Each DDO is a construct chain, but the chains are definite for two different reasons. Can you name the reason for each? (6.3a) By the way, מְגֻרֶיךָ means *your sojourning*.

לַאֲחֻזַּת עוֹלָם   means *for a possession forever.*

וְהָיִיתִי לָהֶם לֵאלֹהִים:

---

[1] Waltke and O'Connor(1990), §11.2.10.

Observations:

1. The wayyiqtols are outnumbered by other forms in this reading; nevertheless, the wayyiqtols in Verses 1 and 3 frame the direct speeches.

2. In Verse 1, a וַיְהִי and a verbless clause, both off-the-line constructions, set the scene.

3. The verbs (two imperatives and two cohortatives) in the Hortatory Discourse of Verses 1 and 2 are all forms which are based on the yiqtol and are all clause-initial.

4. In contrast to the verbs of the Hortatory Discourse, none of the yiqtols in the Predictive Narrative of Verses 4-8 are clause-initial.

5. The weqatal verb form plays a leading role in the Predicitve Narrative, but it is not used in the Hortatory Discourse. (Of course, weqatal *can* be used in Hortatory Discourse to give either mitigated commands (20.3b, 21.5) or supportive material (22.3).)

READING 3-- Judges 16:4-20 Samson Reveals the Secret of His Strength

Lesson 26--Considering the Larger Context: Macrostructure

Macrostructure

Good story-tellers--and the story-tellers of the Bible are among the best--choose which details from an event to recount and which to leave out. They also choose the most advantageous way to relate these details. On what do they base their decisions? The rules of good story-telling require that only those details which contribute toward the over-all meaning and plan of the story be included. All the details given by a good story-teller are necessary, and none of the necessary details are left out. This principle has far-reaching significance. We are about to study the *Samson and Delilah* story. It has a meaning and a plan. But the rule of good story-telling indicates that the *Samson and Delilah* story itself would be meaningful as a part of the larger *Samson's Life* story. The *Samson's Life* story, in turn would be meaningful as a part of the story of the book of Judges.

We are about to consider the place of the Samson and Delilah story within its larger context.

> DEFINITION: **The over-all meaning and plan of a discourse, called its** *macrostructure*, **has effects on how a story is told all the way down to the level of word choices and grammar.**[1]

To appreciate better the Hebrew of the Samson and Delilah story, we will indeed consider its macrostructure including the whole Life of Samson story and the whole book of Judges story. You should consider a story's macrostructure any time you plan a full-blown discourse analysis.

The book of Judges as a whole recounts the history of the tribes of Israel from the time of the conquest of the Promised Land under the leadership of Joshua until the last of the judges, Samuel, in the book of 1 Samuel. 1 Samuel thus begins the account of the transformation of Israel from a theocratically governed band of tribes into a unified monarchy. During the book of Judges the tribes of Israel go through periods of obedience to *YHWH* during which He prospers and protects them. When Israel compromises its devotion to *YHWH,* and follows and serves the gods of their neighbors, *YHWH* is provoked. He then gives them into oppression at the hands of the neighbors whose gods they have chosen to serve. Invariably, *YHWH* raises up a charismatic judge to deliver Israel from bondage to their oppressors, and thus the cycle begins anew only to be repeated many times. The book of Judges is therefore a story about the tribes of Israel trying to establish and maintain a holy identity in the midst of the attractions of their neighbors' gods. Let us tag this recurring theme **maintaining a holy identity**.

If maintaining a holy identity is indeed the controlling theme of the Judges story, then the book's parts and plan should also serve this theme. The next level of macrostructure which we will examine is the "Life of Samson" narrative recounted in Judges 13:1-16:31. Samson's life was to be lived under a sacred vow of devotion to *YHWH* as a נְזִיר אֱלֹהִים meaning *Nazarite of God*. The Nazarite could drink no alcohol,

---

[1] Longacre(1989), 42; Niccacci(1994), 118.

touch no carcass of a dead animal or man, and he could not shave off his hair. Most who took the Nazarite vow did so for a specified period in their lives, but Samson was called by *YHWH* to be a Nazarite for his whole life. He was also called to be Israel's next deliverer and judge. However, Samson's personal life was a constant battle to maintain a holy identity just as was the life of his nation.

Samson once revisits the carcass of a lion he earlier killed and secretly takes honey out of the carcass. What is honey doing in a lion's carcass? Samson is as surprised by it as anyone, but it seems the perfect trap for getting a Nazarite to forsake his vow. He even gives some of the honey to his parents who would most likely have been shocked if they had known the origin of it. But this breech of his Nazarite devotion pales compared to Samson's weakness for women. Delilah is the third embarrassment. The first was a Philistine woman that Samson insisted upon marrying. The marriage ends not only in embarrassment, but conflict and death.

The brief account in Judges 16:1-3 of Samson and the second woman, a harlot of Gaza. The Hebrew reads וַיָּבֹא אֵלֶיהָ It seems clear enough that at least one of the themes of the Samson's Life story is the same as the theme of the whole book of Judges: maintaining a holy identity. It seems that the struggle of the tribes of Israel can in large measure be traced to the struggle of its great and God-ordained men. No wonder that in Judges 2:7 the Bible specifies "And the people served the Lord all the days of Joshua, and all the days of the elders who outlived Joshua." The verse seems like a reminder that "as the head goes, so goes the body."

The graphic below represents the place of the Samson and Delilah narrative as an embedded Historical Narrative within the larger "Life of Samson" narrative which in turn is embedded in the book of Judges. Each layer of embedding serves the theme **maintaining a holy identity**.

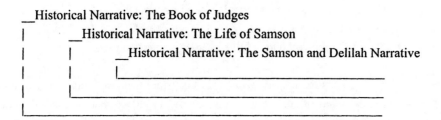

And so now we will proceed with a discourse analysis of the Samson and Delilah narrative which we will from now on refer to as *Samson Reveals the Secret of His Strength*. We will attempt to see how the Hebrew language is used to greatest advantage to promote the theme **maintaining a holy identity**.

Marking the boundaries of the text

We have already mentioned how Judges 16:1-3 tells the account of Samson and the harlot of Gaza. Verse 4 is a natural place for a new episode to begin, and our suspicions are confirmed by the presence there of the now familiar words וַיְהִי אַחֲרֵי At the other end of the episode we find verse 21 in which Samson is brought to a new scene where he is imprisoned by the Philistines. Let us use the change in scene to mark the other end of a conveniently-sized discourse for our analysis, a small grouping of episodes in the life of Samson that are unified by their shared participants, location, and conflict. We will therefore end with verse 20.

306

Dictionary use

Beginning with this reading, you will be given less and less information about unstudied roots. Rather, you will be guided through the word analysis process necessary for you to gain independence in using a Hebrew-English lexicon (a dictionary). No matter how long you study Biblical Hebrew you will have to have a (Biblical)Hebrew-English lexicon at hand. This is not because there are just too many words in the Hebrew Bible to learn. There are only 8000 or 9000 lexical items. The problem is that about 25% of these items are used only once each in the Bible. After going to the trouble to learn them all, you will likely not encounter them for such a long time that you will have forgotten them. The same is certainly also true for items used twice or three times. Advanced study of the Hebrew Bible recommends learning all the items that are used ten times and more, nearly 2000 items, and even so, the likelihood is high that one would forget some of these items because he does not encounter them very often.

You must have a *Biblical* Hebrew-English lexicon rather than a modern Hebrew-English dictionary. The most-used lexicon and the one this course will refer to frequently is *The New Brown-Driver-Briggs-Gesenius Hebrew-English Lexicon* published in Peabody, Massachusetts by Hendrikson in 1979. This work will be abbreviated *BDB*. You can see where to get a *BDB* in the introduction to this text.

Verse 4

וַיְהִי אַחֲרֵי־כֵן   We have earlier seen וַיְהִי אַחַר הַדְּבָרִים הָאֵלֶּה   to mark the onset of an episode.

וַיֶּאֱהַב אִשָּׁה בְּנַחַל שֹׂרֵק   The verb form here is a conspicuous choice. We are rather expecting an X-qatal construction here like we saw in Genesis 22:1 וְהָאֱלֹהִים נִסָּה אֶת־אַבְרָהָם We have two good reasons for our expectation. (1) It is the common structure for participant, time, or scene identification near the onset of a discourse as in Genesis 22:1 *And it was God who was tester of Abraham* or Genesis 1:1

בְּרֵאשִׁית בָּרָא אֱלֹהִים אֵת הַשָּׁמַיִם וְאֵת הָאָרֶץ
It was in the beginning that God was creator of the heavens and the earth.

(2) The root אהב would lend itself to a qatal form. Remember that roots which express emotional states or mental activities favor the qatal form. So we are a little put off balance because the writer has not chosen

אִשָּׁה בְּנַחַל שֹׂרֵק אָהַב שִׁמְשׁוֹן
It was a woman in the Wadi of Soreq who Samson was a lover of.

or

שִׁמְשׁוֹן אָהַב אִשָּׁה בְּנַחַל שֹׂרֵק
It was Samson who was a lover of a woman in the Wadi of Soreq.

The latter would be the same construction as we see in Genesis 37:3 at the beginning of the Joseph story:

וְיִשְׂרָאֵל אָהַב אֶת־יוֹסֵף
It was Israel who was a lover of Joseph.

307

Be reminded here of the meanings of the yiqtol and wayyiqtol versus the qatal and weqatal. You may refer back to the charts in Lesson 14.4a for a review. We may also say that the qatal verb form would have been used here to *tell* us something about Samson whereas the wayyiqtol is used to *show* us something about him. Perhaps a good translation would be *And then Samson fell in love.*

וְשָׁמָהּ דְּלִילָה   The dot in the *heh* is not a *dagesh*. Do you remember what it marks?
_____ It is called a *mappiq* (19.4b, n.2). Here we have the verbless clause we expect in the stage-setting section of a story.

Verse 5

וַיַּעֲלוּ אֵלֶיהָ סַרְנֵי פְלִשְׁתִּים   סֶרֶן   means *lord*. Is it singular or plural in this verse?_____(8.4a)

וַיֹּאמְרוּ לָהּ   Here is another example of a *mappiq*. Compare the 3rd f. s. pronominal suffix meaning *her* in this clause with the 3rd f. s. pronominal suffix in verse 4 which we should also translate *her*. We are looking at two versions of the same suffix.

פַּתִּי אוֹתוֹ   We anticipate here, because of the preceding context, a Hortatory Discourse, and perhaps the imperative form. The ending on   פַּתִּי   confirms our suspicions because we know the lords of the Philistines were speaking to a female. We must therefore figure out the root and stem of the imperative. Since we only have two root letters showing, one of the following would be likely candidates for a root:

פתה   from which dropped the 3rd *heh*, a common occurrence. If this is the root, the verb would be in the Piel stem because of the *dagesh forte* in the *tav*. The *patakh* under the *peh* confirms this possibility.

יפת   from which dropped a 1st *yod*, also a common occurrence, but unlikely here because we would most likely find a *sere* under the *peh* rather than a *patakh* and no *dageshes*. By the way, Piel imperatives do not lose 1st *yod*.

נפת   in which the 1st *nun* has assimilated into the *peh*'s *dagesh*. Once more, the dropping of a 1st *nun* is common enough in the imperative, but the *dagesh* in the *tav* would still be unaccounted for.

If you check your *BDB* you will see that only one of these educated guesses is ever attested as a root. What is its gloss?_____

וּרְאִי   The second in a pair of imperatives.

בַּמֶּה כֹּחוֹ גָדוֹל   The first word is made of two parts: מֶה   +   בַּ   The spelling of   מֶה   as opposed to   מַה   is a common variation that may be a spelling peculiar to writings which have more northerly origin. The entire verbless clause function as the direct object for the previous imperative.

The *furtive patakh* which we normally see in   כֹּחַ   is absent from   כֹחוֹ   because the suffix is added.

וּבַמֶּה נוּכַל לוֹ   This second clause compounds the direct object. The root יכל meaning *be able, overcome,* does not conjugate regularly in the Qal yiqtol. Here it is fully conjugated:

SINGULAR 3. M.	יוּכַל	PLURAL 3. M.	יוּכְלוּ
3. F.	תּוּכַל	3. F.	*תּוּכַלְנָה
2. M.	תּוּכַל	2. M.	תּוּכְלוּ
2. F.	*תּוּכְלִי	2. F.	*תּוּכַלְנָה
1. C.	אוּכַל	1. C.	נוּכַל

*These forms are not attested in the Hebrew Bible.

וַאֲסַרְנֻהוּ לְעַנֹּתוֹ   The first word, a familiar form, is made of four parts, the conjunction, the root, the affixed subject pronoun (defectiva spelling), and the suffixed object pronoun הוּ -- which means *him,* just like וֹ and וֹ   As you can see by comparing the suffixes in this verse or the feminine suffixes in verse 5, there is a considerable amount of variability in the pronominal suffixes in Biblical Hebrew.

לְעַנֹּתוֹ is made of three parts, the first of which is a preposition. As for the next part, which verb form has a *holem* after the second root letter_____ (16.4a) Remember also that this is the only verb form that can be followed by a preposition. What root letter has been transformed to a *tav* in לְעַנֹּתוֹ ?_____ (16.4a) You know the suffix. So the root is ענה   There are actually two different roots ענה which have their own meanings. In this verse, the sense is *to afflict, to humble.*

וַאֲנַחְנוּ נִתַּן־לָךְ אִישׁ אֶלֶף וּמֵאָה כָּסֶף: It seems that the speakers may be using this X-yiqtol to contrast themselves with Samson. It is not being used to identify a change in participants because the subject of this clause is the same as the subject of the preceding clause. אִישׁ does mean *man* as at any other time, but it may seem out of place within the structure of the clause. It is the Hebrew way for saying *each one.* אֶלֶף means *1000.*

The first two clauses of this direct speech section are clearly Hortatory Discourse with two mainline verb forms. The next two are interesting. וַאֲסַרְנֻהוּ and וַאֲנַחְנוּ נִתַּן may be considered an off-the-line weqatal as you learned of it in Lesson 22.3 and an off-the-line X-yiqtol. In a sense, though, they are together a short Predictive Narrative that gives the purposes for the imperatives. וַאֲסַרְנֻהוּ is both a mainline verb in a tiny embedded Predictive Narrative and an off-the-line verb form in the larger host Hortatory. This is a common occurrence in any language. One verb is, at the same time, a mainline verb form within one small discourse and an off-the-line verb form in the larger host discourse. We may represent hosting and embedding of discourses of the same and different types as follows:

309

```
__Historical Narrative: the book of Judges
|   __Historical Narrative: the Life of Samson
|   |   __Historical Narrative: Samson Reveals the Secret of His Strength
|   |   |   __Hortatory Discourse: פַּתִּי
|   |   |   |        וּרְאִי
|   |   |   |   __Predictive Narrative: וַאֲסַרְנֻהוּ
|   |   |   |_____|_____וַאֲנַחְנוּ נִתַּן
|   |   |_____
|   |_____
|_____
```

Lesson 27--Speech Introduction Formulas and Low-Ranking Verb Forms

Verse 6

וַתֹּאמֶר דְּלִילָה אֶל־שִׁמְשׁוֹן   This is the formula for dialogue initiation. Both the speaker and the addressee are named.[1]

הַגִּידָה־נָּא לִי   This is the Hiphil imperative which you will learn in Lesson 32. The *heh* with its *patakh* is your best clue to the root and form. The *dagesh* in the *gimel* is a footprint *dagesh* representing an assimilated *nun*.

בַּמֶּה כֹּחֲךָ גָדוֹל   Does her use of the exact words of the Philistine lords make her seem more the puppet?

וּבַמֶּה תֵּאָסֵר לְעַנּוֹתֶךָ   In the Qal stem we would see a *holem* with the prefixed subject pronoun. The *sere* is the result of the assimilated *nun* of the Niphal stem, giving the word a passive sense, as in ...*you may be bound*... The Qal would be ...*you may bind*...

לְעַנּוֹתֶךָ   See Verse 5 above.

Verse 7

וַיֹּאמֶר אֵלֶיהָ שִׁמְשׁוֹן   In contrast to the speech introduction formula used above wherein both the speaker and addressee are named to initiate the dialogue, we now see the speaker is named, but the addressee is not. This speech introduction formula is used when the speaker is ending or trying to end the dialogue. That is, he is trying to control the dialogue, and he does not expect a response.

אִם־יַאַסְרֻנִי בְּשִׁבְעָה יְתָרִים לַחִים   Here is a Qal version of the root we saw in verse 6 in the Niphal stem. There is a *patakh* with the prefix instead of a *holem* because the pronominal suffix, as usual, causes a shortening of the vowel sound in the word to which it is attached. Is it *If he will bind* or *If they will bind*? In other words, watch out for defectiva spellings.

---

[1] Longacre(1989), §7.

יְתָרִים לַחִים means *green, fresh leftovers*. It probably refers to tough, fibrous plant material that could be used like rope. Which word is the noun, and which is the adjective? _____ (18.2a)

אֲשֶׁר לֹא־חֹרָבוּ If the verb in this dependent clause were a Qal qatal, what vowel would we expect under the first root letter?_____ Rather, we have a Pual qatal. The Pual stem, like the Niphal we encountered above, is passive. The root חרב in the Qal stem means *dry up, make desolate*. In the Pual stem, it means *be dried up*. Translation: *which have not been dried up*.

וְחָלִיתִי You should be able to figure out this one and look it up in your *BDB*. If not, the next clause contains a very familiar root of the same type which can help you. There is no need to use an *-er*-word for this qatal because the root itself is what we call a *stative verb*, and translates adjectivally.

וְהָיִיתִי כְּאַחַד הָאָדָם היה is also a stative verb that does not require an *er*-word. It is simply *I will be...*

The idiom כְּאַחַד הַ-- means *as any*. By the way, an *idiom*, is an untranslatable phrase that develops its own meaning as a unit. In other words, you can know what all the parts mean, but not understand the phrase.

Verse 8

וַיַּעֲלוּ־לָהּ סַרְנֵי פְלִשְׁתִּים שִׁבְעָה יְתָרִים לַחִים Compare the first word here with the first one in Verse 5. They are formally identical but this one is Hiphil stem and Verse 5's is Qal stem. How can we tell the difference? Right! Context! Although this is a common root in a common form, the yiqtol form, and you need to be aware of it, there are not very many other cases like it. It is caused by עלה being a 1st guttural, 3rd *heh* root. Does it also happen with עשה? No. עשה is never used in the Hiphil stem. All the vocabulary in this clause is used earlier in the reading.

אֲשֶׁר לֹא־חֹרָבוּ

וַתַּאַסְרֵהוּ בָּהֶם The *bet* is used in its sense of *instrumentality* expressing the means by which something is done. Translate with *with* in this situation.

Verse 9

וְהָאֹרֵב יֹשֵׁב לָהּ בַּחֶדֶר What are the number and gender of the two participles? _____ (12.2b) Notice there are two of these in this clause, one functioning as the subject of the clause and one as the verb. The root ארב in the first participle means *lie in wait (to ambush)* and may here refer to *the ambush*, that is, a group of men. Most English translations use a plural translation.

וַתֹּאמֶר אֵלָיו We may have trouble figuring out what the ו refers to, the ambush or Samson, until we see what she says. Another clue is the formula used here to introduce the speech. Notice that neither speaker nor addressee are specifically named. This is the typical formula for dialogue continuation. It indicates that the *vav* refers to Samson.

פְּלִשְׁתִּים עָלֶיךָ שִׁמְשׁוֹן   Now we know. It is a verbless clause with שִׁמְשׁוֹן   being used as a vocative.

וַיְנַתֵּק אֶת־הַיְתָרִים   This should be no problem for determining root, stem, and form, etc.

כַּאֲשֶׁר יִנָּתֵק פְּתִיל־הַנְּעֹרֶת בַּהֲרִיחוֹ אֵשׁ   In the preceding clause, the location of the *dagesh* makes the stem Piel. In this clause the location of the *dagesh* makes the stem Niphal. Remember that Niphal stem gives a passive sense to a root. Translate the verb *it is torn away*.

Here is a parsing of פְּתִיל־הַנְּעֹרֶת בַּהֲרִיחוֹ אֵשׁ
פְּתִיל   m. s. construct noun meaning *thread*
הַנְּעֹרֶת   f. s. absolute noun meaning *tow (of flax)*
בַּהֲרִיחוֹ   Hiphil infinitive construct with a prefixed preposition and suffixed pronoun meaning *in its smelling* or *when it smells*. You will see that the sense is *when it gets near*.
אֵשׁ   s. (attested as both masculine and feminine) absolute noun

Translation: _____

וְלֹא נוֹדַע כֹּחוֹ   The verb is Niphal qatal meaning *he (it) was known*. What is the relationship of כֹּחוֹ   to the verb?_____ Keeping in mind the word וְלֹא   what is the function of this clause? _____ (11.3b) This clause is a good example of how a low-ranking construction within a genre's discourse profile scheme (11.4b) can be used for critical explanations. Low-ranking does not mean unimportant. Why do we call it low-ranking at all? The lower a verb is in the discourse profile scheme of a genre, the more it retards the forward progress of the task being performed by the discourse. In Historical Narrative, the task is to tell a story from the past. The wayyiqtol string is therefore like a videotape that is playing. As the tape rolls, the audience watches the action emerge. In the case of our clause here, the irrealis function completely stops the tape, like a freeze-frame, for the narrator's commentary.

Lesson 28--The Use of Repetition

Verse 10
וַתֹּאמֶר דְּלִילָה אֶל־שִׁמְשׁוֹן   Here we have the same dialogue initiation formula that is used in Verse 6.

הִנֵּה הֵתַלְתָּ בִּי   If you are thinking the verb is a Hiphil qatal, correct. The root is a difficult type called a geminate, having second and third root letters that are the same. The root is חלל   and means *mock* in the Hiphil stem.

The preposition בְּ   means *at, against*.

וַתְּדַבֵּר אֵלַי כְּזָבִים   Notice how this Historical Narrative mainline verb form is in Delilah's direct speech. We can consider it and the הִנֵּה   qatal which precedes it a miniature embedded Historical Narrative being used in support of the Hortatory which is to follow.

עַתָּה הַגִּידָה־נָּא לִי   The verb is the same Hiphil imperative that we saw in Verse 6. This is the crux of Delilah's direct speech, the point she is working towards with her little embedded Narrative. Notice her eloquent switch from בִּי in the preceding clause to לִי in this clause.

בַּמֶּה תֵּאָסֵר   See Verse 6.

Verse 11

וַיֹּאמֶר אֵלֶיהָ   This is the typical dialogue continuation formula again.

אִם־אָסוֹר יַאַסְרוּנִי בַּעֲבֹתִים חֲדָשִׁים   If you need help with אָסוֹר see our reading on Genesis 22:17. We saw יַאַסְרוּנִי in Verse 7 of this reading only with defectiva spelling.

בַּעֲבֹתִים חֲדָשִׁים   means *with new ropes*.

אֲשֶׁר לֹא־נַעֲשָׂה בָהֶם מְלָאכָה   If נַעֲשָׂה were Qal yiqtol 1st c. it would be נַעֲשֶׂה The verb in this clause is a Niphal qatal 3rd m. s. giving it the passive sense *be used* rather than the active sense *use*.

The preposition בְּ is used in its sense of *instrumentality*. So do you remember how to translate it? (see Verse 8 above)

וְחָלִיתִי   See Verse 7 for help.

וְהָיִיתִי כְּאַחַד הָאָדָם

Verse 12

וַתִּקַּח דְּלִילָה עֲבֹתִים חֲדָשִׁים

וַתַּאַסְרֵהוּ בָהֶם   We are left to imagine how this woman was able to bind the strong man.

וַתֹּאמֶר אֵלָיו פְּלִשְׁתִּים עָלֶיךָ שִׁמְשׁוֹן   See Verse 9.

וְהָאֹרֵב יֹשֵׁב בֶּחָדֶר

וַיְנַתְּקֵם מֵעַל זְרֹעֹתָיו כַּחוּט   Here the *mem* on the end of the verb performs the same function as in אֶת־הַיְתָרִים of Verse 9.

זְרֹעֹתָיו is made of three parts, the noun זרע , the feminine plural ending ת --, and the suffix.

חוט is another word for *thread*.

The plentiful repetition in this reading makes for easier reading. Furthermore, it makes us wonder if Samson is all brawn and no brains. Perhaps he is simply cocky. That is, he may understand that Delilah is an enemy, but he does not feel threatened.

Lesson 29--Textual Variations

Verse 13

וַתֹּאמֶר דְּלִילָה אֶל־שִׁמְשׁוֹן   What is one function of a speech introduction that names both the
speaker and addressee? _____ (see Verse 6 above)

עַד־הֵנָּה הֵתַלְתָּ בִּי   Translate the first two words literally and you will get the idea. For help with
the rest see Verse 10.

וַתְּדַבֵּר אֵלַי כְּזָבִים

הַגִּידָה לִּי

בַּמֶּה תֵּאָסֵר

וַיֹּאמֶר אֵלֶיהָ

אִם־תַּאַרְגִי אֶת־שֶׁבַע מַחְלְפוֹת רֹאשִׁי עִם־הַמַּסָּכֶת: Here we have evidence that Samson
knew Delilah was up to no good. The other two times he told her ineffective methods to nullify
his strength he suggested what the Philistines could do with the 3rd m. p. yiqtol form. This time he
uses the 2nd f. s. form that refers directly to her.

מַחְלְפוֹת רֹאשִׁי עִם־הַמַּסָּכֶת   means *plaits (braids) of my head with the web.* The
reference to the   הַמַּסָּכֶת   or *web* is probably to a section of unfinished material still in the
loom. Samson's hair would be inter-woven into the fabric, thus making him inseparable from the
weaver's beam, the lumber from which threads were stretched during weaving. From 1 Samuel
17:7 we get the idea that the weaver's beam was a sizable piece of lumber indeed.

Notice the clauses   וְחָלִיתִי וְהָיִיתִי כְּאַחַד הָאָדָם   are missing from Samson's words in
this third intrigue. What we do see is that Samson is getting tantalizingly close to the truth with
the woman he seems to know is out to uncover the secret of his strength.

Textual Variations

If you look at the end of the verse in the *Biblia Hebraica Stuttgartensia (BHS)* you will see the letter *b*.
The letter refers to a note at the bottom of the page in a section of editor's notes which we refer to as the
textual variants. Let us look at the textual variant for Verse 13, note *b*. We see the following:

Nonn vb exc, G +καὶ ἐγκρούσῃς τῷ πασσάλῳ εἰς τὸν τοῖχον καὶ ἔσομαι ὡς
εἷς τῶν ἀνθρώπων = וְתָקַעַתְּ בִּיתֵד אֶל־הַקִּיר וְחָלִיתִי וְהָיִיתִי כְּאַחַד
הָאָדָם

If you have a key to the Latin and other abbreviations used in the textual variations section of the *BHS* you
can read the note. Translated, it says, *several words have dropped out; the Septuagint adds...* Then comes
the Greek which in turn is translated into Hebrew for you. The Greek reads, *And fasten them (with) a peg*

314

into the wall and I will be as any weak man.

The *BHS* is the based upon the oldest known manuscript of the entire Hebrew Bible called the Leningrad Codex B 19a which was penned by the Masoretes in about 1008 or 1009 CE. Since this authoritative manuscript is part of a genealogy of copies, we expect that there will be some differences between it and other ancient manuscripts. The rigors of the scribal tradition are unbelievably strict, but then again, the most disciplined scribe is still only human.

Some of the sources of textual variations are mentioned here. There are some Masoretic manuscripts of similar age to the Leningrad Codex, also thought to be of excellent quality, which exhibit some significant textual variations to the Leningrad Codex. We also have the manuscripts discovered in the Judean wilderness, the Dead Sea Scrolls, which sometimes exhibit significant differences with the Leningrad Codex and far pre-date it. In addition, we have four immediate translations of the Hebrew Bible which pre-date the Masoretic texts like the Leningrad Codex:

> the Septuagint (LXX)
> the Targums of Onkelos and Jonathan ben Uzziel
> the Syriac Peshito
> the Latin Vulgate

The Dead Sea Scrolls or these translations may be based on older, purer Hebrew manuscripts than the Masoretes had in their possession in the 10th and 11th Centuries CE. It is possible in the few places where the Masoretic text (MT) diverges from the Dead Sea Scrolls or the above four translations, that the latter are more faithful to the original Hebrew manuscripts than the Leningrad Codex.

The question remains then, what is the most reliable manuscript? There is no easy answer. On the one hand, the Dead Sea Scrolls sometimes exhibit even closer agreement to the LXX than the MT. On the other hand, the Dead Sea Scrolls have done more to confirm the validity of the MT than erode it. The MT has a long, rigorous, continuous tradition behind it. As for the credibility of ancient translations of Hebrew manuscripts such as the LXX, we must ask ourselves whose job is more prone to error, the translator's or the copyist's?

We also have bits and pieces of very old copies of the Pentateuch in Hebrew from the Samaritans, a divergent tradition. These are copies, not translations, and it is sometimes interesting to compare them to the MT.

As for the LXX in particular:
The LXX was made in the time of Ptolemy Philadelphus (285-247 BCE) in Alexandria, Egypt for the benefit of Hellenistic Jews with little understanding of Hebrew. Clement of Alexandria (150 CE-250) and Eusebius (c.260 BCE-c.340) both mention that Aristobulus, a noteworthy Jewish priest who lived from 181 BCE until 146 refers to the LXX. Josephus the Jewish historian also refers to a Greek translation of the Hebrew Bible made during the reign of Ptolemy Philadelphus.

It is thought that the original translation included only the Pentateuch and that the other books of the Hebrew Bible were added until the translation was complete by about 150 BCE The LXX seems to be of a variety of qualities and styles ranging from expert Greek style in the poetic books to what may be the inferior translation of Isaiah and Daniel.

Three later editions of the LXX were made between 236 CE and 311. The Vatican possesses what is probably the oldest, purest manuscript of the LXX, one which predates any of the editions and probably was the basis of the first in 237. We do not possess an original manuscript of the LXX. It is most likely that the Qumran texts predate the oldest LXX texts we have.

As for our reading of Judges 16:13, does it seem to you that the *BHS* most likely has an error because it does not repeat for a third time the expression וְחָלִ֫יתִי וְהָיִ֫יתִי כְּאַחַ֖ד הָאָדָ֑ם ?

Verse 14

וַתִּתְקַ֖ע בַּיָּתֵ֑ד   Let us split duties. יָתֵ֑ד means *peg, nail*. You look up the other root for yourself. The idea is that Delilah somehow made fast Samson's hair in the weaving. She may have driven down the slat of wood used to pack tight the fibers of a weaving.

וַתֹּ֫אמֶר אֵלָ֔יו

פְּלִשְׁתִּ֥ים עָלֶ֖יךָ שִׁמְשׁ֑וֹן

וַיִּיקַ֖ץ מִשְּׁנָת֑וֹ   Remember that we have two types of 1ˢᵗ *yod* roots, regular (3.2a) and 2nd class (21.2b). מִשְּׁנָת֑וֹ is made of three parts, preposition, noun and suffix. The noun has undergone the normal transformation for a feminine noun that ends in *heh* when it is put in its construct state (13.4d) so it is שֵׁנָה meaning *sleep*.

וַיִּסַּ֧ע אֶת־הַיְתַ֛ד הָאֶ֖רֶג וְאֶת־הַמַּסָּֽכֶת   The root of the verb is in your next group of vocabulary words and means *journey* in Qal.

Notice how in Verse 13 the root אֶרֶג was used as a verb meaning *weave*, but here it is used as a noun meaning the machine with which one weaves, *a loom*. Nouns of this type with two syllables and the emphasis on the first syllable are called *segolate nouns*. They most often have *segol* as their vowels as in אֶ֫רֶג דֶּ֫רֶךְ מֶ֫לֶךְ אֶ֫רֶץ but we have also seen or learned בֹּ֫קֶר נַ֫עַר

Lesson 30--The Ancient Hebrew Writer's Alternatives

Verse 15

וַתֹּ֫אמֶר אֵלָ֔יו   Now the narrator has abandoned the speech initiation formula that he has used in Verses 6, 10, and 13 at beginning of each scene. The narrator uses the continuation formula here. Perhaps it has simply become so clear by this point in the narrative who the speaker and addressee are that he does not feel the need to use the full blown dialogue initiation formula. On the other hand, we may feel that the faster-paced rhythm of the continuation formula is appropriate as we near the climax of the narrative.

אֵ֣יךְ תֹּאמַ֗ר   אֵ֣יךְ means *How?* The yiqtol form, when used in a past time context as it is here, usually expresses repetitive, habitual action. This clause can therefore be translated *How do you*

316

keep saying?

אֲהַבְתִּיךְ   This is what Samson keeps saying. Notice how the use of Qal qatal with this root is so like the Qal qatal of the same root in Genesis 22:2 but different than the wayyiqtol of the same root in Verse 4 above. Remember that the qatal expresses a fact, pinning an attribute on its subject. It is the form the ancient Hebrew would often use to express the verity of his statement. In other words, Samson could express his love for Delilah in no stronger way than to use the qatal. In contrast, the yiqtol (or wayyiqtol) expresses action as it emerges. The narrator of this account does not pin the attribute *lover* on Samson in Verse 4. Rather, he expresses the relationship between Samson and Delilah as a thing that "happened."

וְלִבְּךָ אֵין אִתִּי   A *vav* can have several functions, two of which you learned in Lesson 17.2. Sometimes a *vav* is *disjunctive*. A disjunctive *vav* separates units that do not belong together, and many times these disjunctive *vavs* should be translated *but*. Other times, *vav* is *conjunctive*. A conjunctive *vav* draws two units together and should be translated *and*.

זֶה שָׁלֹשׁ פְּעָמִים הֵתַלְתָּ בִּי   See Verse 10 if you need to. פַּעַם means *time*.

וְלֹא־הִגַּדְתָּ לִי

בַּמֶּה כֹּחֲךָ גָדוֹל   The trick here is to figure out where to put the *to be* verb *is*. Since כֹּחַ is definite because of the pronominal suffix on it. Therefore, if גָדוֹל is an attributive adjective we would expect it to match כֹּחֲךָ in definiteness. With this reasoning we would expect a definite article [הַ] on גָדֹל The fact is, however, that attributive adjectives often do not have the definite article on them when they follow nouns made definite by a pronominal suffix as they "should."

Let us chart Delilah's little speech to Samson:

1. תֹאמַר   (yiqtol = repetitive action in the past)
2. אֲהַבְתִּיךְ   (qatal = attribution)
3. וְלִבְּךָ אֵין אִתִּי   (negative particle of existence)
4. הֵתַלְתָּ   (X-qatal)
5. וְלֹא־הִגַּדְתָּ   (Irrealis w/ qatal)
6. בַּמֶּה כֹּחֲךָ   (verbless clause)

As a native speaker of Hebrew Delilah had a number of styles available to her for putting the pressure on Samson. She could have voiced her complaint as a story, that is, as a series of events as follows:

AS A HISTORICAL NARRATIVE:

1. Then you told me
2. And you loved me
3. But your heart forsook me
4. And you mocked me
5. And you kept secrets
   The sixth clause does not translate as an event very well

317

If Delilah would have chosen to complain in this manner she would have chosen the series of wayyiqtols that has become so familiar to us, and we would have labeled the little discourse Historical Narrative. Then again, there is another kind of discourse that you will learn about in Module Four which Delilah could have used which may have been a more appropriate choice than the Historical Narrative.

Procedural Discourse tells how something used to be done in the past. It is usually the discourse of choice when the writer wanted to describe repeated, habitual action in the past. It would have been a very appropriate choice for Delilah to stress that Samson kept mocking her and so forth. In fact, the first form Delilah uses, the yiqtol, very often initiates a Procedural Discourse. Here is how a Procedural Discourse would have sounded:

AS A PROCEDURAL DISCOURSE:

1. You kept telling me
2. I am a lover of you
3. But you would be a mocker of me
4. And your heart would be a forsaker of me
5. And you would be a keeper of secrets
   Again, we will leave the sixth clause out.

However, the mainline verb form of Procedural Discourse is the weqatal, and Delilah does not use a single weqatal in her speech. Rather, she chooses 5 out of 6 (clauses 2-6) verb forms or clause types that are stative or adjectival in nature. Her little tirade is more about the *kind* of person Samson is than it is about anything he has done once or repeatedly. Do you remember the initial wayyiqtol of this entire reading? It is וַיֹּאמֶר with which the narrator of the account seems unwilling to do the very thing that Delilah is doing during this speech—criticize Samson's character.

EXPOSITORY DISCOURSE:

The question therefore remains: If Delilah did not use Historical Narrative or Procedural Discourse, what kind of discourse *did* she use. The answer is Expository Discourse. Expository Discourse is one of the least studied genres because passages of Expository Discourse in the prose sections of the Hebrew Bible are fairly infrequent and usually quite short.[1] This writer believes that Expository Discourse is critical to the subject of Biblical Hebrew poetry, but since this course is devoted only to prose, we won't spend much time studying Expository Discourse.

Recall that a genre is defined by the task it performs and the constructions which characterize it (see the introduction to Module One). The task in Expository Discourse is to explain and/or argue a thesis. Most of this book is Expository Discourse! The mainline construction in Biblical Hebrew Expository Discourse is that one which is best suited to making a statement: the verbless clause. Other nominal-type clauses like X-qatal and clauses formed with verbal participles are probably high-ranking. The lowest ranking clause-types are probably yiqtol and wayyiqtol constructions. In some ways, the discourse profile scheme for Expository Discourse is the

---

[1] Longacre(1989), §4.3.

318

Historical Narrative scheme flipped up-side-down. Below is a tentative discourse profile scheme for Expository Discourse.[1]

TENTATIVE EXPOSITORY DISCOURSE PROFILE SCHEME:

1. **Mainline:** Verbless clause

Off-the-line:
2. Clauses with qatal of הָיָה
   3. X-qatal of other roots
      4. Clauses with a participle as predicate, yiqtol with a present time reference, irrealis
         5. Qatal and yiqtol in dependent clauses
           6. Embedded discourse

Verse 16

וַיְהִי   The transition marker sets-off what is before it and what follows.

כִּי־הֵצִיקָה לּוֹ בִדְבָרֶיהָ כָּל־הַיָּמִים   Here the כִּי is best translated *when*. You most likely remember what the preformed *heh* and the dot vowel signify, but do you remember what the *sere* under the *heh* means? A 1ˢᵗ *yod* root? No, try again, or look at 28.3a.

כָּל־הַיָּמִים   can be translated literally. Remember: with a singular noun כָּל means *every*.

וַתְּאַלְצֵהוּ   Again the Hebrew writer has alternatives. He can use the pronominal suffix, as here, or he can use an independent object pronoun אֹתוֹ Is there a difference in meaning? Longacre suggests that the pronominal suffix is used to express dominance of the object so-named by the subject, as opposed to the more neutral independent object pronoun.[2] Using Longacre's thesis, we can look back at Verse 5 in which the Philistines say פַּתִּי אוֹתוֹ *Entice him!* using the independent subject pronoun when Samson's being dominated remains to be seen and וַאֲסַרְנֻהוּ *We will be binders of him* when their dominance of him will have been accomplished. Looking back through our reading (vv. 2, 5, 8, 9, 12), you can see that the pronominal suffix has been the preferred form right along.

וַתִּקְצַר נַפְשׁוֹ לָמוּת   You should be able to translate this clause with only the aid of a dictionary for the basic root meaning of the verb.

Verse 17

וַיַּגֶּד־לָהּ אֶת־כָּל־לִבּוֹ   The critical signals in the verb are the *patakh* under the prefixed subject pronoun and the *dagesh* in the *gimel*. If you need help see 29.4b.

וַיֹּאמֶר לָהּ   As we have seen before, one wayyiqtol is used to describe the speech act, and a וַיֹּאמֶר is used to mark the beginning of the actual speech.

---

[1] Dawson(1994), 116.
[2] Longacre(1989), 155.

מוֹרָה לֹא־עָלָה עַל־רֹאשִׁי   Samson is going to use the same type of emphasis on state rather than activity that Delilah used in her previous speech. He starts with this X-qatal.   מוֹרָה   means *razor*.

כִּי־נְזִיר אֱלֹהִים אֲנִי מִבֶּטֶן אִמִּי   You can see here that a dependent clause can be a verbless clause. The formula for this particular clause is as follows:

Construct chain predicate + pronoun subject + preposition   מִ   + construct chain

Here is the vocabulary you need:

> נְזִיר = *one consecrated* (Remember the vowels shorten when the noun is put into its construct state
> בֶּטֶן = *belly, womb*
> אִמִּי is not *with me* or *if me* or *my people*; it is *my*_____
>
> (you fill in the blank)

Does the verbless clause have standard S-P order?_____ So Samson is choosing to put the focus on   נְזִיר אֱלֹהִים   Try to reflect this focus in the intonation of your reading.

אִם־גֻּלַּחְתִּי   Of course, Samson is finally telling the truth here. In his first three responses to Delilah's inquiries his responses were   אִם-yiqtols: *if they bind* (vs. 7), *if they bind* (V. 11), and *if you weave* (V. 13). In contrast, we have here an   אִם-qatal. Samson is making it clear that the secret to conquering him does not lie in what others do to him. Rather he can only be bound if he will in some way be a changed man. Remember that the qatal is the form used to pin an attribute on its subject. In this particular instance, the root is   גלח   which means in the Piel stem, shave. However, notice the *shureq* under the *gimel*. It is the signature of the Piel's passive counterpart, the Pual stem. It is translated *If I am shaved*.

Our understanding is that *shaved* becomes the attribute of Samson. He is then weak, not because he has lost some mystical power in his hair. He has lost his holy identity. The hair is one of the marks of his consecration to *YHWH*. Whereas the narrator earlier avoided the qatal form when describing Samson's love for Delilah, here Samson himself uses the qatal form in revealing the secret of his strength, his holy identity.

וְסָר מִמֶּנִּי כֹחִי   Here we have a weqatal verb form. It was mentioned above that this form is the mainline of Procedural Discourse. Of what other two genres is it the mainline? _____ and _____ Which of the three genres is it here?_____ If you need help you can read ahead.

You can get the full conjugation of the preposition   מִן   in the reading on Genesis 17:6. If you do need this help, you should memorize the chart now.

וְחָלִיתִי   This should look familiar, from the earlier responses of Samson, only this time he is telling the truth.

320

וְהָיִ֫יתִי כְּכָל־הָאָדָם   Likewise as the above clause. Observe Samson's emphasis on himself and this string of five clauses.

Lesson 31--An isolated weqatal

Verse 18

וַתֵּ֫רֶא דְלִילָה   You should by now know the tricky behavior of this 3rd *heh* root.

כִּי־הִגִּיד לָהּ אֶת־כָּל־לִבּוֹ   Remember that a qatal in a dependent clause is *relative past background* no matter what the stem of the verb is. Verb forms have discourse function, not verb stems.

וַתִּשְׁלַח

וַתִּקְרָא לְסַרְנֵי פְלִשְׁתִּים לֵאמֹר

פַּ֫עַם עֲלוּ הַפָּ֫עַם   פַּ֫עַם you may recall means *time*. Words that that refer to time, when used with the definite article most often refer to the time at hand. Here are some example:

הַיּוֹם   =   *today*
הַשָּׁנָה   =   *this year*
הַפָּ֫עַם   =   *this time, at once*

כִּי־הִגִּיד לָהּ אֶת־כָּל־לִבּוֹ   The form לָהּ appears to be an incorrect form. If Delilah is saying *he has declared to me*, then the "correct" form would be לִי On the other hand, if the narrator is making a comment, he would write *for he had declared to her*,[1] and the "correct" form would be לָהּ We have neither "correct" form. In the left hand margin of the *BHS* you can see a *qoph* with a dot above it , and above the dot, לִי The *qoph* and dot means קְרֵי typically written *Qere* with our English alphabet. It means *to be read*, and marks several passages where the spelling of a word is inconsistent or incorrect. Now if we refer to the textual variations section at the bottom of the *BHS* page we can see that several Medieval manuscripts, that is, those dating to about the same time as the Leningrad Codex, have the Qere לִי as the written form.

The כְּתִיב meaning *to be written* is usually written with the English alphabet *Ketiv* or *Ketib* and represents another tradition, that of the written (as opposed to the spoken). In other words, when the spelling of a word is interpreted as dubious because of the context in which it appears, the Ketiv is the spelling which the context indicates would be correct.

וְעָלוּ אֵלֶ֫יהָ סַרְנֵי פְלִשְׁתִּים   What verb form is indicated by the *vav*, the *qamets* under the *ayin*, and the affixed subject pronoun?_____ (13.2a) But the use of a weqatal in this situation is something we have not seen before. We are in a string of past time events as represented by the wayyiqtols. For what three genres is the weqatal used as mainline? (Do not forget the genre to which you were introduced in Verse 15 above.)

---

[1] Thanks to Rodney Duke for this suggestion, given in private communication.

_____

_____

_____

RULE: An isolated weqatal _that stands in for a wayyiqtol_ within a wayyiqtol string marks a climactic or pivotal event in a narrative.

We will spend a lesson on this rule in Module Four. The point is for this reading that the lords of the Philistines had not earlier come up to bind Samson. But Delilah had control of Samson for sure this time, so she was calling in the "big guns." The Hebrew writer marks the lords' coming up as a pivotal event in Samson's life, and so it is.

וַיַּעֲלוּ הַכֶּסֶף בְּיָדָם   The verb is one of the ambiguous forms in Biblical Hebrew. The stem could be either Qal or Hiphil. Which stem does the context tell us is correct?

Notice the definite article on   כֶּסֶף   It makes the word refer to the "blood money" the lords offered Delilah in Verse 5.

בְּיָדָם   is made of three parts, preposition, noun and pronominal suffix.

Verse 19
וַתְּיַשְּׁנֵהוּ עַל־בִּרְכֶּיהָ   Try to tackle the verb with only your dictionary to help. Do not forget to account for the _dagesh_ in the _shin_.

You know the root   ברך   which means bless in the Piel stem. It also means _kneel_ in the Qal stem, and _knee_ as a segolate noun,   בֶּרֶךְ   Is   בֶּרֶךְ   in   בִּרְכֶּיהָ   singular or plural? _____ (14.2)

וַתִּקְרָא לָאִישׁ

וַתְּגַלַּח אֶת־שֶׁבַע מַחְלְפוֹת רֹאשׁוֹ   You can get the meanings of the verb root, here Piel instead of Pual stem from Verse 17, and the other words from Verse 13. Notice the subject pronoun with the verb. It refers to Delilah rather than the man that was called to do the shaving. One does not need to have a razor in hand to be able to _cause someone to be in a shaven state_ as the Piel indicates.

וַתָּחֶל לְעַנּוֹתוֹ   What type of root does the _qamets_ under the prefixed pronoun indicate? If you say hollow, gold star; however, there is another kind of root that is rather unpredictable, which often imitates the hollow verb called a geminate (see Lessons 46-48). It has 2nd and 3rd root letters that are the same. The root   חלל   has two meanings in the Hiphil stem and you can consider them both: _begin_ and _defile, pollute._

ענה   has four possible meanings because there are actually four roots which happen to be spelled ענה   If you check your dictionary, you will see that   ענה   I means _answer, respond,_   II

322

means *be occupied, busy with,* III means *humble afflict,* and IV means *sing.* Whereas both senses of the one root חלל merited consideration above, it seems only one meaning of one of the quadruplet roots fits the context of לְעַנּוֹתוֹ

וַיָּסַר כֹּחוֹ מֵעָלָיו   Here is another verb acting like a hollow root , and guess what? It is a hollow root. The word מֵעָלָיו (*from upon him*) may seem like a strange way to express the location of Samson's strength before it departs until one notices the phrase that is oft repeated in the larger Samson's life story: וַתִּצְלַח עָלָיו רוּחַ יְהוָה   *And the Spirit of YHWH came mightily upon him.*

Verse 20

וַתֹּאמֶר פְּלִשְׁתִּים עָלֶיךָ שִׁמְשׁוֹן   Do you think the repetition of this clause here adds irony to the account? The words were previously vain. It does not seem quite right that they should now be so tragic.

וַיִּקַץ מִשְּׁנָתוֹ   See Verse 14.

וַיֹּאמֶר   The speaker would be Samson since he was the subject of the last verb.

אֵצֵא כְּפַעַם בְּפַעַם   We have a clause-initial yiqtol here, so we interpret it as a mainline form. Is the Discourse therefore Predictive or Hortatory? Yiqtols are basically only clause-initial in Hortatory, so even though this word does not have a *heh* on the end of it, we will view it as cohortative. For yiqtols without a *heh* on the end to be cohortative is a fairly common occurrence. Their frequently clause-initial position is a big help in finding many of them.

If we translate כְּפַעַם בְּפַעַם literally, *as time in time,* is it a good clue to the idiom's sense, *as at other times, as always*?

וְאִנָּעֵר   The second clause-initial yiqtol.

וְהוּא לֹא יָדַע   Notice how the irrealis function is used to make a critical comment on Samson's condition.

כִּי יְהוָה סָר מֵעָלָיו   Here we have not only the qatal in a dependent clause but an X-qatal. This construction and the preceding irrealis are used to summarize the "state-of-things" at the end of the episode.

Conclusion: The "Samson Reveals the Secret of His Strength" account is one episode in the larger story, the "Life of Samson." The "Life of Samson" is, in turn, one part of the account given by the book of Judges. If indeed the theme of the book of Judges is "maintaining a holy identity," the account of Samson and Delilah serves the theme well. Moreover, even the verb forms applied by the writer both in the narration and direct speech serve the theme well. In the reading we have seen yiqtol and wayyiqtol verb forms which express emerging action are played off against those constructions which are of a stative or adjectival nature, namely the X-qatal, weqatal, verbless clause, אֵין clause, and irrealis. These verb forms are strategically placed by the writer as follows:

A wayyiqtol	Vs. 4 as an episode "opener" where an X-qatal is expected
Three yiqtols	Vss. 7, 11, 13 in which Samson lies about what others may do to him to take his strength away
A series of five stative clauses	Vs. 15 in which Delilah criticizes Samson's character
A series of six stative clauses	Vs. 17 in which Samson reveals his holy identity and the secret of his strength
An irrealis and X-qatal	Vs. 20 as a summary of Samson's state after he had lost his an identity

READING 4-- Deuteronomy 6:1-25   Thou shalt love YHWH thy God.

Lesson 32—A massive collection of Hortatory Discourses

Macrostructure

The book of Deuteronomy begins with the words

אֵלֶּה הַדְּבָרִים אֲשֶׁר דִּבֶּר מֹשֶׁה אֶל־כָּל־יִשְׂרָאֵל

This stately announcement makes clear that the message to follow will be a momentous direct speech of Moses. In fact, several times throughout the book we are reminded of the direct speech nature of the whole book by expressions such as the following. Translate them.

אֵלֶּה הָעֵדֹת וְהַחֻקִּים וְהַמִּשְׁפָּטִים אֲשֶׁר דִּבֶּר מֹשֶׁה אֶל־בְּנֵי יִשְׂרָאֵל

4:45

(הָעֵדֹת וְהַחֻקִּים means *the testimonies, and the statutes*.)

וַיִּקְרָא מֹשֶׁה אֶל־כָּל־יִשְׂרָאֵל וַיֹּאמֶר אֲלֵהֶם

5:1

וַיְדַבֵּר מֹשֶׁה וְהַכֹּהֲנִים הַלְוִיִּם אֶל כָּל־יִשְׂרָאֵל לֵאמֹר

27:9

וַיִּקְרָא מֹשֶׁה אֶל־כָּל־יִשְׂרָאֵל וַיֹּאמֶר אֲלֵהֶם

29:1

וַיִּקְרָא מֹשֶׁה לִיהוֹשֻׁעַ וַיֹּאמֶר אֵלָיו

31:7

וְזֹאת הַבְּרָכָה אֲשֶׁר בֵּרַךְ מֹשֶׁה אִישׁ הָאֱלֹהִים אֶת־בְּנֵי יִשְׂרָאֵל לִפְנֵי מוֹתוֹ: וַיֹּאמַר

33:1-2

(הַבְּרָכָה means *the blessing*.)

In much of his direct speech, Moses focuses on events from the past. In other words, he frequently speaks in the Historical Narrative genre. There is, however, a noticeable difference from most of the Historical Narrative we have studied so far in which the 3rd person forms predominate, our *he, she, they*. In much of Moses' narrative, he uses the 1st person forms, our *I, we*, and the 2nd person forms, our *you*, which are not only a reminder that Moses is the one speaking, but a reminder that he and his audience have been participants in the narratives.[1] One of Moses' messages to young Israel is that they should never forget their shared past.

The other great portion of the book of Deuteronomy is Hortatory Discourse in which Moses gives a

---

[1] Talstra(1978), 170.

collection of commandments and exhortations to the budding nation of Israel. In these sections of the book we see several key words repeated again and again that specify the commandments of *YHWH*.   You have learned one of the words already, but three others should be memorized before you begin the reading. They are below, and as you look over them, pay special attention to the roots from which each noun is derived.

מִצְוָה   *commandment*, from a root with which you are very familiar.

עֵדָה   used only in the plural עֵדֹת meaning *testimonies* from עוּד which means *return, go about, repeat, do again*

חֹק or חֻקָּה *statute* from חקק which means *engrave, inscribe*

מִשְׁפָּט   Ah! One that you know well!

So in the book of Deuteronomy as a whole, Moses, the man of God, speaks to the children of Israel as the mediator between their shared past and their future potential. He speaks of a past that the children of Israel are never to forget. Their shared past is to give force to the commandments of *YHWH* which will bring upon them a blessing in the future.

Marking the boundaries of the discourse

The seven or so phrases quoted above, and other like phrases in the book of Deuteronomy not only remind us that Moses is the speaker; they also serve to segment the book.   Our reading begins with just such a phrase in Deuteronomy 6:1,

וְזֹאת הַמִּצְוָה הַחֻקִּים וְהַמִּשְׁפָּטִים אֲשֶׁר צִוָּה יְהוָה אֱלֹהֵיכֶם

Each segment has a topic or theme which gives the segment unity while, at the same time, the segment itself supports the book's over-all goal of drawing together shared experiences of the past and exhortations that will secure *YHWH's* future blessing of the nation. Our segment is no different. As you read Deuteronomy 6:1-25, try to determine the chapter's theme.

As for the end of our analysis, we would expect a phrase something like the one which begins at the beginning of the next segment. The next and best candidate is in Deuteronomy 8:1,

כָּל־הַמִּצְוָה אֲשֶׁר אָנֹכִי מְצַוְּךָ הַיּוֹם

which does indeed begin a new segment. However, we are also going to consider Chapter Seven an independent segment.   Chapter Seven does not have the majestic and clear introductory clause that Chapters Six and Eight have, and especially in the first part of the chapter, it does seem to exhibit some degree of thematic overlap with our Chapter Six. However, it is distinct from Chapter Six which we will analyze as an independent unit. The theme of Chapter Seven is how Israel is to relate to the people of the Promised Land, introduced by 7:1,

כִּי יְבִיאֲךָ יְהוָה אֱלֹהֶיךָ אֶל־הָאָרֶץ אֲשֶׁר־אַתָּה בָא־שָׁמָּה לְרִשְׁתָּה
When YHWH your God brings you into the land which you are entering there to possess it...

Hopefully, you will see that this theme is distinct from that of Chapter Six. We are therefore left with twenty-five verses, Deuteronomy 6:1-25 for our discourse analysis. By the way, this discourse analysis ends with a chart that may also be helpful to preview now and at several points during the analysis.

Verse 1

In the previous readings, this book divided the readings into clauses for you. From now on, you are asked to divide the verses into their component clauses for yourself. The number of clauses in each verse will be indicated to you by the number of spaces that are allotted under each verse heading in which to copy the clauses in Hebrew if you choose to do so. It is suggested that you copy only the consonants of the Hebrew, including only the nikkud that you need as an learning aid.

Clause A. _____

In translating the part of Verse 1 that precedes אֲשֶׁר the lack of a verb there leads you to suspect what type of clause? _____ The word order, gender, and number of וְזֹאת and הַמִּצְוָה confirm the suspicion. The question is what to do with the next two words, הַחֻקִּים and וְהַמִּשְׁפָּטִים They may be two more nouns in a series with הַמִּצְוָה or they may rename and specify הַמִּצְוָה which refers to the whole body of commandments in the book of Deuteronomy.

Clause B. _____

Fill out the verb analysis chart for לְלַמֵּד :

root	stem	form	person, gender, number	function	basic root meaning

The root fits nicely what you have learned about the meaning of the Piel stem. In the Qal stem it means *learn*, and in the Piel stem it means *cause to be in a learned state* or simply, *teach*.

Fill out the verb analysis chart for לַעֲשׂוֹת If you need help see16.4c.

root	stem	form	person, gender, number	function	basic root meaning

Clause C. _____

Fill out the verb analysis chart for עֹבְרִים :

Root	stem	form	person, gender, number	function	basic root meaning

We have not seen a participle in Hortatory Discourse before. Notice here how the participle is used to express the imminent future as it often does in Predictive Narrative. It makes sense that the participle behaves the same way in both Hortatory and Predictive seeing both genres are +projection.

שָׁמָּה is made of two parts, שָׁם meaning _____ and ה-directive. It is often translated *thither*.

לְרִשְׁתָּהּ The mappiq is the clue to the meaning of the *heh* on the end of the word. As with לַעֲשׂוֹת above, if you need help with the rest see 16.4c.

Verse 2

Clause A. _____

You have learned that a clause-initial yiqtol is volitive, that is, it expresses the speaker's desire, but in תִּירָא we see that a yiqtol which is not clause-initial may also be volitive. The לְמַעַן and the many infinitives we have seen thus far are used to express the purposes for the מִצְוָה

Compare the gender of חֻקֹּתָיו in this clause with הַחֻקִּים in Clause 1.A. above.

Clause B. _____

Fill out the verb analysis chart for מְצַוְּךָ If you need help, see 31.3c, d

root	stem	form	person, gender, number	function	basic root meaning

This time, the participle is not referring to the imminent future as the last one did. Rather, it refers to the on-going activity of the discourse we are analyzing. So you must be fluent in the possibilities for some verb forms and allow context to be your guide.

What is type of construction is יְמֵי חַיֶּיךָ ? _____ If you need help, perhaps the ending on יְמֵי can trigger the answer. Is the construction definite or not? _____ חַיֶּיךָ is formed from the noun חַיִּים The noun's masculine plural ending has been changed to the construct form before the suffix is added. The pronominal suffix makes it definite, so it functions as the absolute in (but, of course, you have already written this above) a definite construct chain.

Notice in this verse and elsewhere as our reading progresses the repetition of the pronominal suffix ךָ --. It adds a euphony and a driving momentum to many passages in our reading. Be sure and read these passages aloud a few times for pleasure. Also, you may find it interesting how Moses speaks to all of Israel, but often resorts to masculine *singular* participant references, as if to stress either the personal responsibility to the commandment or the oneness of the nation.

Clause C. _____

328

Fill out the verb analysis chart for יַאֲרִכֻן

root	stem	form	person, gender, number	function	basic root meaning

Use the combination of the *patakh* under the prefixed pronoun and the *hireq* under the second root letter to determine the stem. When you determine the person, gender, and number, pay attention to the defectiva spelling of the prefix complement. Use your dictionary to determine the basic root meaning. The word has one feature that you have not seen before, the *nun* at the end. It is an auxiliary ending often seen on the end of yiqtols that end in vowels in the book of Deuteronomy but elsewhere also. It is called a *paragogic nun* which means simply "added to the end," and may be for sound value or, as we often say for details that are difficult to classify, for emphasis.

יָמֶיךָ and the earlier יְמֵי have the expected nikkud for the plural suffixed and plural construct of the irregular noun יוֹם In Hebrew, as with most languages including English, some of the most common nouns are irregular. Since the irregular forms of יוֹם are extremely common, they should be memorized. For a list of the irregular forms of some of the most common nouns see 18.4. If you are having trouble seeing the relationship of the noun to the clause's verb, let us make it a 50/50 proposition: subject or direct object?

Verse 3

Clause A. _____

Clause B. _____
It may seem odd that the first actual exhortations of this Hortatory Discourse are given by weqatal forms. It is indeed customary for even Mitigated Hortatory Discourse to open up with at least one imperative. One advantage gained by the use of the weqatal form here is the strength of the *vav*-consecutive. By using the *vav*-consecutive of the weqatal the speaker puts the exhortations in a consequential relationship to the motivations given in the preceding two verses. We will come back to these issues shortly.

Clause C. The construction or syntax of אֲשֶׁר יִיטַב לְךָ and the next clause is difficult. The clause may be considered subordinate to the infinitive before it, with אֲשֶׁר functioning as the subject of the verb in which case it translates, with the infinitive from the preceding clause, *to do what will be good for you.* In the Qal stem the root יטב means *be good, well,* and in the Hiphil stem *do good.* You can use *it* for a subject. Do you think the textual variation the *BHS* identifies as being in the Qumran scrolls changes the sense of the clause?

Clause D. The problem is that with our above interpretation of Clause C, Clause D, וַאֲשֶׁר תִּרְבּוּן מְאֹד does not translate into the parallel English clause that the parallel Hebrew clauses suggest, the reason being the different person, gender, and number of Clause D's verb. The root

רבה means *be many, become many.*

Clause E. _____

Although it is technically part of Clause E, leave off אֶ֫רֶץ זָבַת חָלָב וּדְבָשׁ   Translating וּדְבָשׁ חָלָב is no problem because we are simply looking at two nouns.   זָבַת is a bit more complicated. Its derivation goes as follows:

זוּב   →   זָבָה   →   זָבַת
root   f. s. participle   construct form

Remember that the participle can function as an adjective, but it still denotes on-going action. In our reading we have already seen the participle express three things: the imminent future, action in the present tense, and the quality of a noun. The common ground between the three is the on-going nature of action which characterizes the participle.

Lesson 33—One imperative in a crowd of weqatals

Verse 4

The verse can be divided into clauses in numerous ways if you remember from Lesson 19 in which this verse and some of verse five are the focus of the lesson. What we may notice in this reading that was not apparent in Lesson 19 is the way the first imperative of this discourse stands apart. Earlier, it was pointed out that it is a bit uncustomary for a Hortatory Discourse to begin with weqatals, even when mitigated. In a sense, therefore, we are put in suspense by the weqatals until this first imperative is sprung on the reader after the delay. To help you visualize how the imperative stands out within the discourse you may want to preview the chart at the end of this discourse analysis.

Verse 5

Notice in Verse 5 how the verb form reverts back to the series of weqatals that was begun before the lone imperative of Verse 4.

Verse 6

Clause A. _____

Beware when you write Clause A because it is interrupted by Clause B. It is not as hard as it might seem. We do it all the time in English with very nearly the same word order as is in this verse. The only difference between the word order in this verse and regular English word order is the initial verb-subject order in the Hebrew. Notice that the subject of this clause shifts away from the 2nd person subject that is typical of Hortatory mainline. Can a weqatal be off-the-line? _____ (22.3)

Clause B. _____

All of Clause B functions as an adjective that modifies the subject of Clause A. See how Clause B is embedded in the middle of Clause A just the way we do it in English. To what specific words do you think הַדְּבָרִים הָאֵ֫לֶּה is referring?

Verse 7

Clause A. _____

The weqatal string continues. Fill out the verb analysis chart for וְשִׁנַּנְתָּם   and as you do, notice

330

carefully the nikkud on the ending. Which ending is it?

2nd m. p. affixed subject pronoun: תֶּם

or

2nd m. s. affixed subject pronoun with a 3rd m. p. pronominal suffix: ם-- + תָ

For a clue you can look back to the last weqatal and ahead to the next.

root	stem	form	person, gender, number	function	basic root meaning

שנן in the Qal stem means *sharpen*. Our formula for the Piel nuance gives a nice touch to the word: *cause to be in a sharpened state.*

Clause B. _____

Here we have more of the beauty of Moses' oratory: the parallelism and the repetition of the pronominal suffix ך-- once again. בְּשִׁבְתְּךָ וּבְלֶכְתְּךָ וּבְשָׁכְבְּךָ וּבְקוּמֶךָ are four of something in a series, constructed exactly the same except for that the second, third, and fourth have the conjunction *vav*. If you can figure out one you can figure out all of them. If you need help, turn to 16.4.

Verse 8

Clause A. _____

לְאוֹת is not preposition plus DDO. אוֹת is a masculine noun meaning *sign* derived from the root אוה

Is יָדֶךָ Speaking of a singular or plural hand? What would be the regular nikkud for *your hand*? _____ For *your hands*? _____ (19.4b) The form you see in Verse 8 is altered because the word is in pause. The plural would have a *yod* before the pronominal suffix.

Clause B. _____

The word טֹטָפֹת is only used here, in Deuteronomy 11:18 and Exodus 13:16. It is often difficult to know for certain the derivation or original sense of such a seldom used or technical term. In their lexicon, Brown, Driver, and Briggs cite a possible connection between the word and an Assyrian word *tatapu* meaning *surround, encircle*. They also lean toward an originally figurative interpretation for dedication of the firstborn or "perpetual remembrance" which later turned into the Jewish custom of wearing phylacteries.

As in Verse 6A, notice how the shift of the subject from the customary 2nd person of the Hortatory mainline to the 3rd person shifts this clause off-the-line.

331

Verse 9

There is only one clause. The nikkud in בֵּיתֶךָ may remind you of Verse 8's יָדֶךָ because it is also in pause. The regular nikkud would be בֵּיתְךָ not to be confused with בָּתֶּיךָ *your houses* or בִּתְּךָ *your daughter*.

Lesson 34—Parallelism of many sorts

Verse 10

Clause A. _____

The clause, only one word long, really marks a break here, introducing the next massive clause and a shift to Predictive Narrative which sets a stage for the next exhortations. If you are cloudy on the earlier lesson on וְהָיָה כִּי see 13.2d and 20.3b.

Clause B (part one). _____

This is the beginning of a very long clause that goes well into Verse 11 and has several other clauses embedded within it. Only copy however much is part of Verse 10. Leave off from the line above the dependent clauses C and D which are embedded within B. If you have trouble knowing which parts of the verse are part of this main clause and which are not, identify the dependent clauses first, and come back to this clause with everything that remains. Fill out the verb analysis chart for יְבִיאֲךָ :

root	stem	form	person, gender, number	function	basic root meaning

The normal nikkud for the verb in this stem is יָבִיא It is altered in this verse by the addition of the pronominal suffix.

Clause C. _____

The *dagesh* in the verb is a *dagesh lene* because it is preceded by a *shewa*, so it does not double the letter as the Piel stem requires. שׁבע is here a Niphal qatal meaning *swear oneself*, and you saw it several times in your Genesis 17 reading. The אֲשֶׁר-qatal construction here has the same relative past background function as usual. The verb's stem does not affect the verb form's function. What word from the main B clause does this C clause modify?

Notice how the second, third, and forth words prefixed by *lameds* elaborate and specify the first. The series of words with *lamed* has a similar rhythm to the other series that have characterized this reading.

Clause D. _____

This is another אֲשֶׁר-qatal clause. What word in the main B clause does this clause modify? In your lessons on the אֲשֶׁר-qatal clause you were taught to translate using English *had, has,* or *have*. You can just choose the one of these that feels right, and you will probably be right most of the time, but there is a better way to choose that is not too difficult to learn.

Had is the English auxiliary verb we use for the *past perfect tense*. This is the English tense we use to specify that a situation is completely in the past. With the past perfect an English speaker describes a situation as a whole, without reference to its beginning, middle or any part of it. On the other hand, *has* and *have* are the auxiliaries we use in English to make the *present perfect tense*. Present perfect verbs also describe situations as a whole which began in the past. The difference from past perfect is that present perfect does not put the situation entirely in the past. With present perfect, some residual of the past situation is specified as remaining in the speaker/writer's present, either the action itself or the effects of the action. In Clause D, Moses is speaking about possessing cities that exist in their present situation. Therefore the present perfect *have* is the best choice for translating בָּנִיתָ

Verse 11

Clause A. _____

What we refer to here is actually not a clause. It is the latter half of Clause B from the previous verse, beginning here with a continuation of a direct object for Verse 10's לָתֵת It continues to specify what will be given. As you did in Verse 10, do not copy the dependent clauses which are embedded in this latter half of Verse 10's Clause B.

We can see, between Verse's 10 and 11, four parallel constructions hanging off of Verse 10's לָתֵת as follows:

	direct object	adjective	dependent adjective clause
1.	עָרִים	גְּדֹלֹת וְטֹבֹת	אֲשֶׁר לֹא־בָנִיתָ

2.	וּבָתִּים	מְלֵאִים כָּל־טוּב	Clause B. _____

3.	וּבֹרֹת	חֲצוּבִים	Clause C. _____

4.	כְּרָמִים וְזֵיתִים		Clause D. _____

This parallelism is worth noting, not only because of the heightened style of oratory that it represents but because the parallelism provides interesting points of grammar.

The root טוֹב is used as an adjective in section 1, but a noun in section 2.
The root מלא is used as an adjective in section 2, and a verb also in section 2 in Clause B. Fill out the verb analysis chart for Clause B:

root	stem	form	person, gender, number	function	Basic root meaning

Notice how וּבֹרֹת has a feminine ending, but its adjective has a masculine ending. It turns out the adjective is a better indicator of the noun's gender than the noun. בּוֹר (also written בֹּאר) is masculine.

In section 3, the root חצב is used as a Qal passive participle and a qatal.

> **RULE: The sign of the Qal passive participle is a *shureq* [וּ] between the second and third root letters. Translate most of them with an *-ed*-adjective.**

Translation of חֲצוּבִים : *hewn* (proper English for *hewed*!)

עֲנָבִים grow *in* a כֶּרֶם and זֵיתִים grow *on* זֵיתִים

You can probably make a good guess as to what the root נטע means.

Clause E. _____

We have two weqatals at the end of this verse. You must decide if they are mainline forms giving commands or off-the-line forms in a series with כִּי יְבִיאֲךָ of Verse 10.

Clause F. _____

Be very careful to distinguish between the roots שָׂבַע of Verse 10 and שָׁבַע here. Not only does the placement of the dot result in different meanings but it puts the two roots in different sections of many lexicons including the *BDB*.

Verse 12

הִשָּׁמֶר לְךָ   This is Clause A. The first word is a Niphal imperative. The Niphal gives a reflexive sense to a root so the command here is *Guard yourself*. The לְךָ is then added to the sense of the imperative like it was in Genesis 22:2. So the whole expression is translated *Guard yourself for yourself* (See 41.2b). We will study the Niphal in earnest in Lessons 38-41. What is important to notice here is that the string of mitigated commands in the form of weqatals has again been broken by the unmitigated command form, the imperative.

Clause B. _____

What kind of *dagesh* is in the *koph*? _____ Fill out the verb analysis chart:

334

root	stem	form	person, gender, number	function	basic root meaning

Clause C. _____

House of slaves works for בֵּית עֲבָדִים but it is usually thought of in a more abstract way, *house of bondage.*

Verse 13

Clause A. _____

Clause B. _____

Clause C. _____

וּבִשְׁמוֹ is four parts translatable by four English words.

Verse 10 used the same root and stem as this verb only in the qatal form with its characteristic pre-formed *nun* of the Niphal stem. Here we have the yiqtol form of the Niphal stem. Where did the pre-formed *nun* go? It assimilated into the *dagesh* of the first root letter. Look over the three forms of Niphal that we have encountered in this reading:

נִשְׁבַּע   qatal 3rd m. s.

הִשָּׁמֶר   imperative m. s.

תִּשָּׁבֵעַ   yiqtol 2nd m. s.

Three X-yiqtols in a row is a rather unusual occurrence in Biblical Hebrew. What is the discourse function of an X-yiqtol? _____ So it is generally used to shift the focus of a mainline or create a contrast. We cannot really assign one of these duties to these three X-yiqtols in a row. We are left to consider the parallelism as a particularly concerted effort to pinpoint the audience's focus. Although the use of parallelism throughout the discourse is persistent, the variety of types of parallelism is rich.

Lesson 35—Commands and the reasons for them

Verse 14

Clause A. _____

The *nun* at the end of תֵּלְכוּן is explained in Verse 2.C.

Of אַחֲרֵי and אֲחֵרִים which is the preposition, and which is the adjective? How can both words come from the same root? *Another*, in Hebrew, means literally *one coming behind.* אַחֵר conjugates as follows:

masculine singular	אַחֵר
feminine singular	אַחֶרֶת
masculine plural	אֲחֵרִים
feminine plural	אֲחֵרוֹת

Clause B. _____

This is a verbless clause in which the אֲשֶׁר functions as the subject. סָבִיב As you can tell from the feminine plural ending on it is being used as a substantive, that is, an adjective functioning as a noun. The clause can be translated *which surround you*.

Verse 15

Clause A. _____

אֵל is a title used for God, which we also saw in our Genesis 17 reading, that may or may not be related to אֱלֹהִים The word speaks of *might*, and as you read the rest of the verse you will see a graphic picture of the might of אֵל The trick with this verbless clause is two-fold. Figure out where to put the *to be* verb and decide whether the clause is S-P or P-S order (see 2.7).

Clause B. _____

Although the nikkud is unusual יֶחֱרֶה is indeed a Qal yiqtol. אַף means *nostril, nose, face, anger*. *Anger* apparently because of the way the nostrils flare, and breath becomes heavy during anger. *YHWH* describes Himself in Exodus 34:6 as אֶרֶךְ אַפַּיִם literally *long of nostrils* or *long-tempered*, but His potential is described here, particularly in the next clause.

Clause C. _____

The weqatal verb here is *not* giving a command. The context indicates it is predictive. Grammatically, it is in series with the previous yiqtol and part of the פֶּן or *lest* construction.

Verse 16

Clause A. _____

Notice how, in this reading, the speaker freely switches between 3rd m. s. to 3rd m. p. forms.

The same root is used three times in this verse, twice as verbs and once as the name of a place. If you cannot figure out the missing letter from the verbs, the noun in the next clause should help.

In Historical Narrative, a yiqtol with לֹא is a low-ranking construction, but in Hortatory Discourse, it is a high-ranking substitute for אַל-yiqtol which gives prohibitive commands. We translate the אַל-constructions with English *do not...*, and we translate לֹא-constructions with English *you will not*.

Clause B. _____

As alluded to above, the last word in this verse is a preposition plus proper noun.

Verse 17

Clause A. _____

Notice how the root is repeated in the first two words of the clause. We have seen this construction before if you recall, and the construction adds intensity to the yiqtol תִּשְׁמְרוּן The first word is called an infinitive absolute, and we will study the construction in earnest in Lesson 34. In any case you should be able to gather the heightened style of the oratory from the combination infinitive absolute and the paragogic *nun* on the yiqtol. You may remember that the infinitive absolute is often translated *surely, indeed.* Perhaps *diligently* would be a good translation here.

The double use of the root שׁמר in this construction beautifully echoes back to the imperative which began the section הִשָּׁמֶר Verse 17A thereby closes the section, in a sense, where it began, creating what we might refer to as an inclusio, helping us to see that the theme of clauses 12A-17A is "be careful." Once again, you may want to now preview the chart at the end of this discourse analysis.

Clause B. _____

Do you now why צִוְּךָ appears as it does rather than as צִוְּךָ ? _____ (15.5)
Notice once again the switch back to a singular *you*.

Verse 18

Clause A. _____

Clause B. _____
See Verse 3 if you need help with יִיטַב

Clause C. _____
You can consider this and the next weqatal clause as subordinate to the לְמַעַן All the clauses under the לְמַעַן a yiqtol, two weqatals, and an אֲשֶׁר-qatal, plus the entire next verse are off-the-line in the Hortatory Discourse. But we also have a string of weqatals that are mainline verbs, including וְעָשִׂיתָ in Clause A of this verse. It is probably best to consider the group of clauses that goes with לְמַעַן an embedded Predictive Narrative that gives motivation for the mainline exhortations. In the larger picture of the discourse therefore, we have some weqatals that are mainline and some that are off-the-line in the same discourse. The לְמַעַן serves as a cue for the discourse switch.

Clause D. _____

Clause E. _____
If you need help with the verb see Verse 10.

Verse 19

This entire verse is subordinate to Verse 18. The infinitive לַהֲדֹף ties the verse back to וִירִשְׁתָּ of the preceding verse. The only proper clause in the verse is the dependent clause.

Dependent Clause. _____

Lesson 36—An embedded Historical Narrative

Verse 20

Clause A. _____

Only go as far as the לֵאמֹר The כִּי begins a "when-then" construction. The "then" will be a command, but we will have to wait until Verse 21 to see it. מָחָר literally *tomorrow*, can be taken to mean *in the future* as we use *tomorrow* sometimes in English.

Clause B. _____

מָה when it begins a question, is often followed by one or more nouns, creating a verbless clause.

Clause C. _____

Notice the son says צִוָּה יְהוָה אֱלֹהֵינוּ אֶתְכֶם He includes himself in naming *YHWH, our God*, but he does not include himself as having received the command: *YHWH, our God is commander of you* (m. p.).

Verse 21

Clause A. _____

Here is the "then" of the "when-then" construction that was begun in Verse 20. The trick is to know where to put the quotation marks.

Clause B. _____

An X-qatal wherein the subject is the "X" and the root is היה is as grammatically bold-faced as a statement of fact can get. Remember that in oral Historical Narrative, as this is, a speaker has other options: opening the narrative with a clause-initial qatal or using a verbless clause would have also sufficed.

Clause C. _____

The oral Historical Narrative continues as expected, with a wayyiqtol. Do not be confused that the וּ‎-- ending is used as a suffix this time, not an affix.

In the phrase בְּיָד חֲזָקָה the *bet* is used as the *bet of instrumentality* (see reading of Judges 16:8, 11). חֲזָקָה is a f. s. adjective.[1]

Verse 22

_____

There is only one clause in this verse.

What are the genders and numbers of אוֹתֹת ? _____ And וּמֹפְתִים ? _____

What are the genders and numbers of the adjectives גְּדֹלִים וְרָעִים ? _____

The combination illustrates the usual practice of using masculine adjectives to modify a pair of nouns of mixed gender.

We studied אוֹת in Verse 8 above. In order to look up וּמֹפְתִים in the *BDB* you will, of course, have to remove the *vav* and the plural ending first. Another warning, however: If you do not find a word

---

[1] Waltke and O'Connor(1990) §11.2.5.

338

spelled defectiva, check plene and vice versa. Under מוֹפֵת the *BDB* will then send you to the verb root אפת

רַע is an adjective with a wide variety of applications such as *bad, evil, disagreeable, malignant.*

Verse 23

Clause A. _____

Some Hebrew scholars deny that an X-qatal construction is in any way emphatic. In pondering this issue we may consider that the message of Verse 23's first clause may have been written in any of the following ways:

וַיּוֹצֵא אוֹתָ֫נוּ

וַיּוֹצֵא אוֹתָ֫נוּ יהוה

וַיּוֹצֵא יהוה אוֹתָ֫נוּ

וְיהוה הוֹצִיא אוֹתָ֫נוּ

It is difficult to imagine after comparing it with these options, that the version which *is* extant in Verse 23 is not the prescribed option for a parent to tell his child that *It is us that He brought out from there.* It may be surprising that the focus in the parent-to-child teaching is not even on *YHWH.*

Clause B. _____

Clause C. _____

This is the third time in our reading that this אֲשֶׁר-clause is repeated.

Verse 24

_____

_____

There is only one clause in this verse, made long by a series of infinitive and prepositional phrases. As for לְיִרְאָה remember that a 3rd *heh* root such as ראה changes its *heh* to וֹת in the infinitive. This infinitive is made from the root ירא   and the "extra" *heh* may well have been added to avoid ירא's *aleph* from being next to another *aleph* in the next word, the DDO.

The *lameds* in the phrase לְטוֹב לָנוּ are not to be translated with the word *to.*

Pay close attention to the nikkud of לְחַיֹּתֵ֫נוּ to determine its stem. חיה in the Qal stem means *live,* but in the Piel stem, it means *cause to be alive, preserve alive.*

Verse 25

Clause A. _____

צְדָקָה means *righteousness.*

Clause B. _____

We saw the root שׁמר with the infinitive of עשׂה in Verse 3. Do you think the repetition gives a roundness to the discourse? The time of this clause and the preceding one is hard to ascertain. Together, they may be taken as either present or future.

Clause C. _____

The Piel qatal 1st c. p. of this root, which is never attested in the Hebrew Bible, would have been written צִוִּינוּ so the נוּ-- must be a suffix.

Charting the discourse

You should have noticed reading the discourse that the weqatal form predominates for giving commands, a sign of Mitigated Hortatory Discourse, given actually, in the style of Instructional Discourse. Perhaps this is one reason why the Law of Moses became known as the תּוֹרָה meaning *instruction* rather than the often-translated *law*. The word תּוֹרָה comes from the root ירה meaning *throw, shoot*. On other hand, there are two imperatives in the discourse which not only share the mainline of the discourse with the weqatals, but stand above it because they are unmitigated commands. Using the verb forms (other than infinitives and אֲשֶׁר-clauses) as reference points and proceeding in a clause-by-clause manner, we can analyze the discourse in chart form in order to help us locate the areas of peak emphasis within the discourse. The top line of the chart is more or less ordered by the discourse profile scheme of Hortatory Discourse. You will see that a few alterations have been made to better suit analysis of the present reading.

To simplify the chart, it does not include אֲשֶׁר-clauses which are used primarily as adjectival clauses in the discourse. On the other hand, even though they are also dependent clauses, clauses made with פֶּן and לְמַעַן כִּי are included because they often give the conditions or motivations for the commands.

	Imper-ative	main-line weqatal	X-yiqtol or infin. abs. + ylq.	negated yiqtol	off-line weqatal	פֶּן or לְמַעַן yiqtol	כִּי-yiqtol	וְהָיָה	embedded Hist. Narr.	Parti-ciple	verbless clause
1. A.											X
2. A						X					
2. C.						X					
3. A.		X									
3. B.		X									
4.	X										
5		X									
6. A.					X						
7. A.		X									
7. B.		X									
8. A.		X									
8. B.					X						
9		X									
10. A.								X			
10. B.							X				
11. E.					X						
11. F.					X						
12. A.	X										
12. B.						X					
13. A.			X								
13. B.			X								
13. C.			X								
14. A.				X							
15. A.											X
15. B.						X					
15. C.					X						
16. A.				X							
17. A.			X								
18. A.		X									
18. B.						X					
18. C.					X						
18. D.					X						
20. A.							X				
21. A.		X									

the embedded direct speech Historical Narrative of the parent begins

									wayyiqtol	X-qatal	לְמַעַן-qatal
21. B.										X	
21. C.									X		
22									X		
23. A.										X	
23. B.											X
24									X		

embedded Historical Narrative over

25. A.			X								

Observations:

1. There is really one principle at work in the following observations. A higher ranking mainline verb form is emphasized when the discourse around it shifts away from the mainline. Off-the-line verb forms retard the forward progress of the discourse and thereby call for the audience's attention.

2. The variety of verb forms in the discourse makes prominent the two lonely imperatives in 4 and 12A.

3. Compare the verbal regularity of the weqatals in Verses 3A through 9 and the verbal turbulence in the rest of the discourse.

4. The verbal turbulence which surrounds the commands in 12A, 17A, 18A, and 21A makes these commands prominent.

5. The repetition of the root שׁמר in 12A and 17A frame a section which elaborates on and gives motivations for "being careful."

6. The embedded Historical Narrative makes prominent the command in 21A.

7. A great deal of off-the-line material is given in this discourse, including several פֶּן and לְמַעַן clauses which support the command forms by giving motivation for obeying them.

8. There are two major breaks in the discourse, one created by the transition marker in 10A and one created when the direct speech portions which begin in 20B.

9. Almost all of the command forms in the discourse have to do with the communication of *YHWH*'s commands. The controlling idea of the Hortatory seems to be for parents to speak pointedly to their children about both their heritage and the commands which will result in the children's future well-being.

READING 5-- 1 Samuel 17:32-38 David Becomes Israel's Champion

Lesson 37—The Hebrew Verbal System

Introduction: By now you have been introduced to several genres of Biblical Hebrew discourse and how the verb forms function within these genres. In your study you have hopefully learned that the Biblical Hebrew verbal system is a loose, flexible one. For instance, you have seen that a limited number of verb forms is used in a number of different combinations, sometimes with slight modifications to express the many concepts represented in English by words like *then, so, so that, consequently, when, will, would, may, might*, and others. This very short reading is meant as a reinforcement of an over-guiding principle of the Biblical Hebrew verbal system.

> **A Biblical Hebrew writer is not often bound by any grammatical necessity to use a particular verb form. Rather, he chooses his forms within a system of linguistic conventions, choosing to the best advantage of his message and intention.**

You will see in this short reading several creative uses of the forms and verbal system which you have learned so far.

Macrostructure

The book of 1 Samuel was originally not separate from 2 Samuel. Taken together the books tell of Israel's transformation from a theocracy under the guidance of *YHWH*'s judges to its golden age as a monarchy during the reigns of David and Solomon. The beginning of this history is the birth of Samuel, both the last judge and the anointer of David. Perhaps we can consider the high point of the history to be Solomon's prayer of dedication of the Temple on Mount Zion and the glory of *YHWH* filling the Temple. However, between Samuel's life and *YHWH*'s filling of the Temple are the many trials of David, including his stormy relationship with his predecessor as king, Saul. Through these several "David and Saul" episodes we see the idea developed, "*YHWH*'s preference for David over Saul."

Marking the boundaries of the discourse

The discourse on which we will focus is another direct speech, this time David's direct speech as he convinces King Saul to let him represent Israel against the Philistine's champion Goliath. As you have often seen in direct speech discourses, this direct speech is hosted by a much larger Historical Narrative. We will more or less let the Historical Narrative go without analysis. We will, however, indulge, without proper attention to the boundaries of discourse, in a brief probe into the Historical Narrative before and after the direct speech proper that is the main focus of this reading.

Once again you may copy the Hebrew clause by clause, including the consonants and only the nikkud that you need.

Verse 32
Clause A. _____

What is the function of this speech introduction formula which names both speaker and addressee? _____ (see the reading on Judges 16:6)

Clause B. _____

Do you think the pronominal suffix on עָלָיו refers to אָדָם or Goliath?

Clause C. _____

The trick is whether עַבְדְּךָ goes with the clause before or after it. If יֵלֵךְ is Predictive Narrative, עַבְדְּךָ would be an "X," a very likely grammatical possibility, but one which the context does not exactly bear out. Since David is trying to convince Saul to let him fight Goliath, we must label the speech hortatory, not predictive. We will therefore say that the intention is hortatory, but the style is predictive. This is the most mitigated style of Hortatory Discourse, one appropriate for a young shepherd talking to his king (see 21.5).

Clause D. _____

Here we have the X-yiqtol's verb form partner, the weqatal. The root לחם meaning *fight* is used almost exclusively in the Niphal stem as it is in this verse. You may wonder what is passive about fighting. The Niphal stem often has a reflexive or reciprocal sense in which an action performed by the subject returns to him in kind. In this reflexive or reciprocal sense, the subject has double-duty as both the agent or the one who acts and patient or the one who is acted upon.

יְ -- is a common ending for an **adjective of nationality** as it is in Clause D. Here the adjective is used as a substantive. As mentioned in 18.2c. and elsewhere, a substantive is an adjective used as a noun.

Verse 33

Clause A. _____

Notice once again, that the speaker and addressee are named. This clause is no longer dialogue initiation as in Verse 32. According to Longacre, speech introductions which name both speaker and addressee *after a dialogue has already been initiated* mark one of two things, either a fresh beginning or "an important interview of two important people."[1] What is the function of the formula this time?_____

Clause B. _____

If you need a review of the irregular conjugation of יכל see the reading on Judges 16:5.

As per the note in the preceding verse, לְהִלָּחֵם is indeed a Niphal infinitive. Although a Hiphil infinitive of this root is not attested, in theory, it would be written לְהַלְחֵם

Clause C. _____

Why is the word order important?_____ (2.7c)

Clause D. _____

If you have trouble with מִנְּעֻרָיו start by removing the prefix and suffix, and then look for a familiar root. When looking for the word in the *BDB*, keep in mind whether מִנְּעֻרָיו is singular or plural and alternative plene and defectiva spellings.

---

[1] Longacre(1989), 184.

344

Lesson 38—Unusual uses of weqatal

Verse 34

Clause A. _____

Notice that for the third time we see the speech introduction formula that is used either dialogue-initially to identify the participants in a dialogue or thereafter to mark "an important interview of two important people."

Clause B. _____

You have learned רָעָה as a noun to mean *evil, distress*. It comes from the root רעע and is not to be confused with words derived from the root רעה which has such a different meaning. This clause has a participle form that is generally used as a noun for the one who continuously tends or pastures the flock.

We have used the following translations for בְּ: *in, on, with, against*. Here it seems to mean *among*.

Clause C. _____

Here we are surprised by a weqatal. We have so far seen the weqatal used in +projection genres, but that does not fit the context here. You have also learned that it may be used for procedures in the past, and we may yet conclude that the repeated, habitual action of the past is the sense in this reading.[1] However, David is speaking of a lion that was *a comer* (or *an intruder*), and it may not sit well with us that a lion's coming be considered a procedure.

Notice וְאֶת־הַדּוֹב   For the first time in this course a word marked by אֵת is more like the subject of a clause than a direct object. Although אֵת marking a subject or subject-like word is not nearly so common as its use with definite direct objects, we cannot consider it rare either. Some grammarians judge this use of אֵת with a subject to be a special marker of emphasis. Others believe that all uses of the particle אֵת are emphatic, and that the particle's use really has no special connection to definite direct objects after all. In any case we will take the details in the following direct speech to apply directly to the lion and to apply to the bear by parallel. The verb forms in the speech are all singular forms, and you will see that at least one of the details can only apply to a lion.

Clause D. _____

Here we have another weqatal in series with the first, again like Procedural Discourse. Aside from the earlier mentioned objection to interpreting the discourse as procedural, we may also note the absence of a DSC which usually accompanies and helps to identify a Procedural Discourse. What are the DSC's that you have learned?

_____
_____
_____
_____
(36.4a)

_____

[1] By far the most commonly held interpretation(e.g., Niccacci in private communication) of these weqatals is that they represent repeated or habitual action in the past. Under this interpretation David must have killed several lions and several bears. See Lambdin(1971), 281 although Lambdin does put the passage in a class with questionable interpretations.

עֵדֶר is a noun meaning *flock*. Notice that it is prefixed by a preposition *and* the definite article. We have heretofore seen the definite article assimilated into the preposition by giving the preposition the definite article's nikkud as in בַּבֹּקֶר meaning *in the morning* rather than בְּהַבֹּקֶר The construction we see in the latter and our reading's מֵהָעֵדֶר is used a virtual handful of times compared to hundreds where the definite article is assimilated into a prefixed preposition.

Verse 35

Clause A. _____

Clause B. _____
You will see a suffixed *vav* on many of the weqatal forms in this reading. Remember that a suffix can be used either possessively or objectively. These *vavs* function as the direct objects of the weqatal verbs to which they are attached.

Clause C. _____
Do not forget to account for the *dagesh* in the *tsadeh*. It represents a root letter. The direct object of the verb is not written. The direct object would be the lamb, probably best represented by the word *it* in our translation.

Clause D. _____
Why the switch to a wayyiqtol? There are only a handful of places in the Hebrew Bible that have a wayyiqtol interrupting a string of weqatals. We may interpret them as meaning *And when...*, but it is doubtful whether it has the sense of repeated action in the past like the weqatals of Procedural Discourse. On the other hand, the content of David's speech is sounding more and more like a Historical Narrative. The problem is that weqatals are seeming to carry the mainline in an unprecedented way. The wayyiqtol of this clause, though unusual in this narrative, is, of course, the common form for the mainline of a Historical Narrative.

Clause E. _____
The verb is a Hiphil weqatal.

זָקָן means *beard*, and זָקֵן means *old*. This clause gives the detail that applies only to lions since only lions have seizable beards. Although we may not need to worry about someone seizing a bear's beard because it is non-existent, the severest of warnings must be extended to all those who venture to seize lions by theirs!

Clause F. _____

Clause G. _____
Is this the end of the string of weqatals that refers to the past?

Verse 36

Clause A. _____
Here we have an X-qatal that is further evidence that the above string of weqatal verb forms is not a Procedural Discourse. The X-qatal is like the wayyiqtol in that we have only seen it in Historical

346

Narrative. The weqatal's partner in Procedural Discourse is X-yiqtol rather than X-qatal.

The repetition of the word גַּם gives the sense *both...and.*

We are reading David's account of his exploits as a shepherd protecting his father's flock. If the analogy between the intruding beasts of prey and the intruding Philistine Goliath is not clear enough, David will make the comparison entirely explicit in the next clause using the common Hebrew rhetorical device of word motif or Leitwort (see Lesson 33.3).

Clause 36A ends the direct speech discourse that begins in 34B which is the primary focus of this reading. We can see that the weqatal form predominates in the discourse, but the discourse is certainly not one of the +projection genres in which weqatal is the mainline verb form because it is about the past. The discourse is most likely not Procedural Discourse, a past time discourse in which weqatal is also the mainline because the discourse lacks any DSC like a yiqtol or an explicit reference to time duration. In addition, Procedural Discourse is typically oriented toward the goal of the procedure. David's little speech, on the other hand, is oriented towards the participants in the scene, himself and the animals. This "participant-orientation" is typical of Historical Narrative. David's discourse does indeed have some other qualities of Historical Narrative, namely a wayyiqtol and an X-qatal. It seems most reasonable to this writer that the account is about an exploit with one lion that is like an exploit with one bear. The question remains then, why would David express his Historical Narrative in an unprecedented string of weqatal verb forms?

There is no grammatical necessity in the Hebrew verbal system that prohibits him from doing so. Although it is an unconventional choice, David prefers the weqatal as the mainline of his little Historical Narrative. It is the form which expresses action as the attribute of the subject as opposed to the wayyiqtol which describes action as it emerges. The weqatal is the verb form that is best-suited for David's purpose. To convince Saul to appoint him as Israel's champion, he does not tell a story as much as he gives his resume. *I was a goer-forth, I was a rescuer, I was a smiter, I was a killer.* It is his promise to be Israel's victorious champion.

Clause B. _____
Is this weqatal part of the same string that we saw in the previous two verses which speak of past events, or does it have the more usual +projection?

Clause C. _____
What stem is חֵרֵף ? _____ Would *has* or *have* be the better English word to include in the translation? _____ (26.4)

When looking for מַעֲרֹכֺת in the dictionary start on the ends of the word and remove "appendages" until you have a good idea of the root. For instance, the ת -- ending is the feminine plural ending. The *mem* at the beginning is a common preformative on nouns. Now that you have the root, be prepared to look for the singular form of the noun under the main root heading rather than the plural as is seen in the verse.

Many English translations have *living God* for אֱלֹהִים חַיִּים but חַיִּים is often a noun rather than an adjective. If it is a noun in this case, אֱלֹהִים would be in the construct state, so it must be an adjective after all.

Verse 37

Clause A. _____

For speech introduction such as וַיֹּאמֶר to interrupt the speech of a single speaker may be noteworthy. The writer does not need to use this speech introduction to help the audience track who is speaking. It may therefore be considered supplementary and signaling something. It may signal a sense like *furthermore* as in *And then he continued saying*. Another possibility is that the supplementary speech introduction formula signals a new paragraph in David's speech. Perhaps you can think of other possibilities.

Clause B. _____

We saw the root in Verse 35 and will see it again later in this verse.

We know lions and bears have feet and paws to which יָד may be analogous, but the word more likely refers to the strength of the animals.

Clause C. _____

This clause is an X-yiqtol proper to the Predictive Narrative that began with Verse 36.B's וְהָיָה. הוּא functions as the "X," but it has double-duty. It also represents the entire previous clause. If you cannot see it, ask yourself, "Who is the הוּא ?" The entire previous clause answers the question. A pronoun which refers back to an earlier, usually fairly large portion of a sentence is called a **resumptive pronoun**.[1] Not only do independent pronouns function as resumptive pronouns; pronominal suffixes can also as in this verse:

$$\text{הָאָרֶץ אֲשֶׁר אַתָּה שֹׁכֵב עָלֶיהָ}$$ Genesis 28:13
The land which you are dwelling on it

The translation is terrible English, but is it understandable? How would we say the same thing in better English?

Clause D. _____

Clause E. _____

Clause F. _____

One of the frustrating mysteries of Biblical Hebrew is an X-yiqtol like this one. A clause-initial yiqtol is almost always a volitive form, either jussive or cohortative. But an X-yiqtol may be either volitive, indicating the speaker's will or indicative, indicating the speaker's knowledge. It is the difference between desire and prediction. The X-yiqtol in Clause F follows an imperative which is, of course, a mainline form in Hortatory Discourse. It is then very natural for us to view the yiqtol in the X-yiqtol as a jussive. If so, how would you translate it? _____

On the other hand, we may be looking at a switch to Predictive Narrative. If so, how would you translate Clause F? _____ There is as much difference between the two translations as there is between *may* and *will*, between desire and prediction.

---

[1] Waltke and O'Connor(1990), §§19.3b, 32.2.1e; Jouon-Muraoka(1993), §§146c, 156a; Muraoka(1985), §6.

Verse 38

Clause A. _____

Fill out the verb analysis chart for וַיַּלְבֵּשׁ :

root	stem	form	person, gender, number	function	basic root meaning

In this clause we have returned to the big Historical Narrative to which all the וַיֹּאמֶר s belong and in which all the direct speeches are embedded.

Saul probably had David armed by servants, as the stem of the verb probably suggests. מַדָּיו means *his armor*.

Clause B. _____

This isolated weqatal is not nearly so unusual as the string of weqatals discussed above. Hopefully, Lesson 37 prepared you for it. Fill out the verb analysis chart for וְנָתַן :

root	stem	form	person, gender, number	function	basic root meaning

Saul is presented as the *giver of his helmet*. What is it that makes Saul's giving his קוֹבַע *a helmet*, a climactic or pivotal event? Ought not Saul be Israel's champion and thereby solidify his position as king? Instead, it is like he is crowning David. Saul's giving of his helmet may well foreshadow the giving of his crown.

The adjective נְחֹשֶׁת is under the third root in the *BDB* spelled נחשׁ

Clause C. _____

The duplication of Clause A's verb here sandwiches the weqatal of Clause B and seems to bring even more attention to it.

שִׁרְיוֹן means *body-armor*.

Lesson 39—A new setting

Macrostructure

This is our second reading from the book of Genesis, but we did not yet learn about the concept of macrostructure when we read Genesis 22 about Abraham offering Isaac, so we did not consider the macrostructure of Genesis at that time. We will do so here.

The book of Genesis can be divided into ten sections, each one devoted to *the generations of...* or in Hebrew the תוֹלְדוֹת   The division of the book in this manner helps to identify the book as a chronicle of the nation of Israel's origins. The ten divisions begin at the following points:

2:4   אֵלֶּה תוֹלְדוֹת הַשָּׁמַיִם וְהָאָרֶץ

5:1   זֶה סֵפֶר תּוֹלְדֹת אָדָם

6:9   אֵלֶּה תוֹלְדֹת נֹחַ

10:1   וְאֵלֶּה תוֹלְדֹת בְּנֵי־נֹחַ

11:10 אֵלֶּה תוֹלְדֹת שֵׁם

11:27 וְאֵלֶּה תוֹלְדֹת תֶּרַח

25:12 וְאֵלֶּה תֹּלְדֹת יִשְׁמָעֵאל בֶּן־אַבְרָהָם

25:19 וְאֵלֶּה תוֹלְדֹת יִצְחָק בֶּן־אַבְרָהָם

36:1   וְאֵלֶּה תֹּלְדוֹת עֵשָׂו הוּא אֱדוֹם

37:2   אֵלֶּה תֹּלְדוֹת יַעֲקֹב

Some of the sections are as short as a genealogy, and others include detailed accounts wherein the children of the man named in the title of the section are often the key participants.[1] Abraham is the protagonist of the section named for his father Terah ; Joseph and Judah are the key participants in the Jacob section; etc. Our reading is in the section entitled וְאֵלֶּה תוֹלְדֹת יִצְחָק בֶּן־אַבְרָהָם and true to form, the attention is primarily on Jacob rather than his father Isaac for whom the section is named. The common theme in all the sections is *YHWH*'s providential relationship with his creation generally and His chosen ones specifically.

---

[1] Longacre(1989), 20-23.

Marking the boundaries of the discourse

In our earlier readings in the Historical Narrative genre you learned that an episode in a host narrative can also be analyzed as an independent narrative discourse. We will do so once again in this reading because episode-sized texts are useful teaching tools and because they fit our definition of a discourse: a group of expressions linked together from a beginning to an ending so that they develop an idea in some orderly fashion. In the case of the present reading, to have תּוֹלְדוֹת one obviously first needs marriage, and the subject of our reading is Jacob's falling in love with and marrying of Leah and Rachel.

The boundaries of an **episode** may be identified by one or more of the following characteristics:

A change in participants

A change in the protagonist (sometimes within the same set of participants)

A change in setting (time, place, or both)

A change in the challenge faced by the protagonist

The words of Genesis 29:1 specify in a unique manner the change in setting that marks the beginning of the episode we will analyze: וַיִּשָּׂא יַעֲקֹב רַגְלָיו In fact, you will see that the new setting is described in considerable detail. At the other end of the discourse is a change in protagonist. Jacob has finally acquired his beloved Rachel, and Verse 31 begins to unfold the troubles and consolation of Leah.

Indeed these boundary markers may seem more like the topic of a high school literature class than a course in Biblical Hebrew. However, we do need to use such measures to identify episode boundaries so we can analyze how the Hebrew works within the context of an episode.

Verse 1
Clause A. _____

Clause B. _____

Verse 2
Clause A. _____

Clause B. _____
What is the discourse function of a verbless clause?

Clause C. _____
What is the discourse function of a participle?

To what does the pronominal suffix on עָלֶיהָ refer?

Clause D. _____
The word הוּא should probably be written הִיא even though there is no note of an alternative spelling in the textual variations at the bottom of the page in your *BHS*. This is such a common spelling that it is not noted. Following the Qere tradition (see the reading notes on Judges 16:18), the word is always pronounced as הִיא even if it is spelled with a *vav*. Another word frequently "misspelled" but

always pronounced the same way according to the Qere tradition is יְרוּשָׁלַם which has the Ketiv form יְרוּשָׁלֵם but a Qere יְרוּשָׁלַיִם

Fill out the verb analysis chart for יַשְׁקוּ (see 29.4d for help):

root	stem	form	person, gender, number	function	basic root meaning
		yiqtol in dep. clause			

Keep in mind that it is very unusual for a yiqtol verb form to appear in a narrative text outside of direct speech. What embedded discourse might you suspect? _____ (36.2)

Clause E. _____
Take care how you translate וְהָאֶבֶן גְדֹלָה Is *And a great stone* or *And great was the stone* better? (18.2a)

פִּי is the singular construct of פֶּה

Verse 3
Clause A. _____
The *nun* on the verb should make you think either 1st c. p. yiqtol or Niphal qatal, but the ending on the word will not work with a yiqtol form. Fill out the verb analysis chart:

root	stem	form	person, gender, number	function	basic root meaning

You may want to wait on discourse function until some pattern emerges in the verb forms.

Clause B. _____
Fill out the verb analysis chart for וְנָגְלֲלוּ :

root	stem	form	person, gender, number	function	Basic root meaning

Perhaps two weqatals is enough of a pattern to hazard a guess as to discourse function. In addition, the two weqatals are in series with the yiqtol of Verse 2. The pattern yiqtol, weqatal, weqatal in a past time context should identify a genre for you.

מֵעַל is made of two prepositions. The *sere* under the *mem* rather than a *hireq* occurs when the word to which the preposition מִן begins with a guttural letter.

Clause C. _____

Fill out the verb analysis chart for וְהִשְׁקוּ :

root	stem	form	person, gender, number	function	Basic root meaning

Notice the repetition of the root from Verse 2, albeit in a different form.

Clause D. _____

Fill out the verb analysis chart for וְהֵשִׁיבוּ :

root	stem	form	person, gender, number	function	Basic root meaning

What does the *heh* with a *mappiq* within it[ה] at the end of לִמְקֹמָהּ ? אֶבֶן is indeed a feminine noun.

Notice in these first three verses of our reading the large amount (by Hebrew Bible standards) of scene-setting detail: 3 verbless clauses, 1 participle clause, an embedded Procedural Discourse with a yiqtol and 4 weqatals in a series. The role of the Procedural Discourse, embedded in a host Historical Narrative to give scene-setting detail, is a common use of Procedural Discourse. Notice how the entire Procedural Discourse is subordinated to the mainline of the Historical Narrative by the כִּי of Verse 2. The question remains--why all the scene-setting detail? We will see shortly that the gathering of the flocks by this well and the carefully depicted procedure for use of the well may help to establish the power of Laban within the region. Jacob has managed, in his life up to this point, to make gain through his conniving. We will see, however, that we he meets Laban, he meets a very powerful character indeed, one who is equipped to take advantage of even Jacob!

Lesson 40—Speech introduction formulas and close reading of the nikkud

Verse 4
Clause A. _____

Clause B. _____

אַחַי is part of the direct speech and speaks directly to the addressee. What is such a word called?

_____ (19.3) If you have forgotten whether אַחַי is singular or plural, you should re-memorize the chart in 18.4.

מֵאַיִן is constructed like מֵעַל The interrogative adverb אַיִן spelled just like the negative particle of existence, means *Where?*

Clause C. _____

Clause D. _____

Verse 5
Clause A. _____

This speech introduction formula in which the speaker is not named within the formula and the addressee is named by a pronoun is the formula used for continuation of a dialogue between peers. It seems that the basis for the all the mid-dialogue speech introduction formulas is that a dialogue has its own dynamic of social balance in which the speaker and addressee have their respective weight of influence. The Biblical writer elevates the status of the speaker or addressee within the dialogue when the writer specifies the speaker or addressee.

The table below, adapted from Longacre,[1] shows the commonly used speech introduction formulas and their uses to mark mid-dialogue dynamics. Keep in mind that these are formulas which introduce single utterances within an already running dialogue. Dialogue-initiation and re-direction are also performed by some of the same formulas. An example of every formula is given from our present reading in Genesis 29.

SPEECH INTRODUCTION FORMULAS WHICH MARK MID-DIALOGUE DYNAMICS:

Formula: (speaker specification) + (addressee specification)	Functions as a marker of:
Noun + Noun Example (Gen. 29:21): וַיֹּאמֶר יַעֲקֹב אֶל־לָבָן	Balance, tension, and confrontation, "an important interview between two important people."
Unspecified + Unspecified Example (Gen. 29:5): וַיֹּאמְרוּ	Civilities. A large social gap between speaker and addressee may eliminate tension between them.
Unspecified + Pronoun Example (Gen. 29:5): וַיֹּאמֶר לָהֶם	Dialogue between peers.
Noun + Pronoun Example (Gen. 29:14): וַיֹּאמֶר לוֹ לָבָן	Speaker dominance or his attempt to be dominant and gain control of the dialogue.
Noun + Unspecified Example (Gen. 29:19): וַיֹּאמֶר לָבָן	Speaker-centered outburst of emotion or point of view, often an attempt to close the dialogue.
Unspecified + Noun Example (Gen. 29:25): וַיֹּאמֶר אֶל־לָבָן	Addressee dominance.

---

[1] Longacre(1989), 184.

Clause B. _____

Do not confuse the verb with a Hiphil qatal. What happens to a 1st *yod* root in the Hiphil qatal? The *heh* on the verb is an interrogative *heh*. What time would you use for an English translation of this qatal?

Clause C. _____

Clause D. _____

The qatal is used without a direct object to state the affirmative simply and directly like our English *yes*.

Verse 6

Clause A. _____

Clause B. _____

שָׁלוֹם means *wholeness* as well as *peace*. See 23.2b if you need help with the translation.

Clause C. _____

Clause D. _____

Clause E. _____

If you remember from 25.3a, בָּאָה is an ambiguous form. Do you take it as a qatal or a participle in this verse? Does this reminder help: an X-qatal is a construction almost entirely limited in prose to Historical Narrative? The word הִנֵּה seems to indicate Rachel is in sight, and it is commonly used in Historical Narrative with a participle to shift the narrative viewpoint towards that of a character within the narrative (See the Reading notes on Gen 22:13). And if you do decide upon the participle, is the sense of it present time or the imminent future? By the way, the Masoretic accent, placed on the last syllable confirms the word as being a participle.

Verse 7

Clause A. _____

Clause B. _____

You may remember that הֵן is a form of הִנֵּה

Keep in mind what kind of adjective גָּדוֹל is, and begin your translation *The day is still...* expressing that it was only midday.

Clause C. : לֹא־עֵת הֵאָסֵף הַמִּקְנֶה

If you need help with the verb form see 41.3a. You can think of an "understood" subject *it* for this clause as in *It is not...* Then the remaining three words are a construct chain.

Clause D. _____

If you need help with the verb form, its being in a series with the next two verbs should help you., and you should review 32.2. In this reading, we have also seen this root used in the yiqtol in Verse 2, the qatal in Verse 3.

Clause E. _____

That imperatives can be put in series by *vav*'s is nothing new to you.

Clause F. _____

You know the root, and saw it in our previous reading. Think missing 3rd root letter. This imperative seems awkward in English without a direct object.

Verse 8

Clause A. _____

Clause B. _____

Clause C. _____

The word עַד goes with אֲשֶׁר somewhat like the particle כְּ can be attached to אֲשֶׁר The expression עַד אֲשֶׁר means *until*.

Clause D. _____

Notice how a yiqtol and a weqatal are used here as an embedded +projection discourse like a similar series is used in Verses 2 and 3 as a -projection Procedural Discourse. Just as the entire Procedural Discourse in Verses 2 and 3 was subordinated by the word כִּי this embedded discourse is subordinated by אֲשֶׁר עַד

Clause E. _____

This is another +projection clause. The indication seems to be that the *someone else* will be rollers of the stone, and then the *speakers* will be waterers of the sheep. Wells have always been precious in the Near East, the subjects of conflicts which frequently escalated into war. The speakers seem unwilling to uncover the well until Rachel arrives, so we may deduce that the well belongs to her father Laban.

Verse 9

Clause A. : עוֹדֶנּוּ מְדַבֵּר עִמָּם

עוֹדֶנּוּ translates literally *while he*. Remember that the majority of the time the 3rd m. s. suffix has a *dagesh* in the *nun* whereas the 1st c. p. does not. This seems like a dependent clause, especially after translation into English, but it does not connect with the next clause very well because of the way the next clause begins. The Biblical Hebrew writer was not opposed from time to time to leave a "dependent clause" unattatched. We may, in translation, add *It was...*

Clause B. _____

Here, as in Verse 6, we have the ambiguous בָּאָה except this time we have the X-V word order that suggests a qatal and Historical Narrative. Once again, our judgment is confirmed by the Masoretic accent, this time on the first syllable.

Clause C. _____

See 23.2 if you need help.

Clause D. _____

See the reading on 1 Samuel 17:34 for comparison.

Notice that the spelling הוּא for the usual הִיא is used with some consistency in this reading. How ever some might interpret הוּא as a mistake, it may well not be a slip-of-the-pen-type of mistake.

Verse 10

Clause A. _____

The use of the transition marker is not necessary. It is a good example of how the Biblical story-teller shifts to one or more off-line forms to retard the forward progress of the account and thereby create tension and focus.

Clause B. _____

Family relationship strings are hard enough to keep straight in English, you know, those wife's brother's mother's son-type statements! In this clause the phrase is בַּת־לָבָן אֲחִי אִמּוֹ We could say this in English *daughter of his maternal uncle Laban*. Look closely at אִמּוֹ *his mother*. It is not to be confused with עִמּוֹ *with him*.

Clause C. _____

A return to the mainline after a brief venture off the line recommends a *then* or *consequently* in translation. Do not forget to account for the *dagesh* in the *gimel*.

Clause D. _____

We saw this same root in Verses 3 and 8 as a qatal. This type of root with 2nd and 3rd letter the same is called a **geminate**, and they often have the same nikkud as hollow roots would (see Lessons 46-48).

Clause E. _____

Verse 11

Clause A. _____

Only the form and discourse functions of וַיִּשַׁק and וַיַּשְׁק are the same. They are not the same roots. Imagine the challenge of making sense out of a purely consonantal text. On the other hand, it is not so hard to figure out that Jacob was *not* watering Rachel, is it?

Clause B. _____

Clause C. _____

It is difficult to determine the root of the verb because it is one of the few verbs that does not follow the rules for determining missing letters. According to the rules, what missing letter does the *sere* under the prefixed pronoun indicate? _____ However, the root is the 3rd *heh* בכה meaning *weep*. בכה is part of a small group of 3rd *heh* roots that appear with inconsistent nikkud. Here they are:

root	nikkud that follow the rules	promiscuous nikkud
בכה	וַיִּבְכּוּ	וַיֵּבְךְּ
שתה	וַיִּשְׁתּוּ	וַיֵּשְׁתְּ
נטה	וַיִּטּוּ	וַיֵּט
רעה	וַיִּרְעוּ	וַיֵּרַע

357

In case you are wondering because of the examples, it is indeed the 3rd m. s. forms that tend to be promiscuous, and the 3rd m. p. forms that tend to follow the rule; however, even this pattern is not entirely consistent.

Verse 12

Clause A. _____

Clause B. _____
Sometimes the root נגד can be used to introduce direct speech, but the כי helps us realize that this is not direct speech. Remember the significance of the P-S word order here and in the next clause.

Clause C. _____

Clause D. _____
Do not be fooled into thinking this is a Qal weqatal. *Vav-patakh-dagesh forte* is not one of the alternative nikkud for the *vav* of a weqatal. What type of root does a *qamets* under a prefixed pronoun indicate? _____ The root will be one of your vocabulary words shortly.

Clause E. _____

Lesson 41—A major departure from the mainline

Verse 13

Clause A. _____
See 34.4 if you need help.

Clause B. _____
The clause contains the irregular infinitive of קרא which is here used in its sense *meet*.

Clause C. _____

Clause D. _____
We saw the same root in Verse 11 only in the Qal stem. The Piel stem often lends intensity to a root's meaning. Jacob embraced and kissed Laban in a very hearty manner that probably would have seemed forward if he treated Rachel in the same way.

Clause E. _____
The shortened vowel under the prefixed pronoun is customary when a pronominal suffix has been added.

Clause F. _____
The subject of the wayyiqtol string has switched from Laban to Jacob. This would be a common location for an X-qatal, or at least a mention of Jacob by name, but no such luxuries this time.

Verse 14

Clause A. _____

358

Do you remember the significance of the speech introduction formula used here? If not see the chart in Verse 5. It is consistent with the controlling nature which we find out characterizes Laban's character.

Clause B. _____

עֶצֶם means *bone, self*. Remember the grandiose style of Laban's overtures as the account reaches it climax.

Clause C. _____

חֹדֶשׁ יָמִים is an idiom, the meaning of which you can figure out.

Verse 15

Clause A. _____

This is typical dialogue initiation.

Clause B. _____

הֲכִי is made from interrogative *heh* and כִּי It means *because*, but the sense of a question is retained through the next clause.

Clause C. _____

The consequential relationship created by the *vav*-consecutive is very apparent here. חִנָּם means *gratis*.

Clause D. _____

Clauses B-E of this verse are actually all part of the Hortatory Discourse that this imperative suggests. The first two clauses are the reasoning behind the command. In Hortatory Discourse, the lower-ranked verb forms are used to provide motivation for and the consequences of the commands of the mainline.

Clause E. _____

Be careful! שָׂכַר and שָׁכַר are both fairly commonly attested roots.

Verse 16

Clause A. _____

The shift here to scene-setting verbless clauses creates a major break in the narrative like a וַיְהִי would do.

Clause B. _____

Verbless clause number 2. Of course the idea is not that Leah was literally bigger, only older.

Clause C. _____

Verbless clause number 3.

Verse 17

Clause A. _____

Verbless clause number 4. Is the adjective רַכּוֹת meaning *tender*, a predicate adjective or an attributive adjective? (18.2a)

Clause B. _____

יְפַת־תֹּאַר וִיפַת מַרְאֶה   is constructed adjective-noun and adjective-noun, and means *beautiful of form and beautiful of appearance*

Here the X-qatal of הָיָה punctuates the end of the series of four verbless clauses with the most emphatic construction possible. The momentary but complete halting of the narrative by four verbless clauses and the X-qatal creates a tension around the daughters of Laban that appropriately foreshadows Laban's ruse by elaborating upon them so heavily (by Biblical Hebrew standards). In addition, the string of off-the-line clauses creates a dramatic pause while we wait for Jacob's answer to Laban's question. The pause becomes like a look into the mind of Jacob as he contemplates his price for service. Good Biblical Hebrew story-telling has all the same qualities as good English story-telling albeit in a more compact version.

Verse 18
Clause A. _____

An X-qatal would have been appropriate here, but it would have put the viewpoint on Jacob as a lover. Rather, the story-teller wanted the focus on the loving as it emerged. Perhaps a good translation would be *And consequently, Jacob began to love Rachel.* You learned in Lesson 20.2 to use the word *then* with a wayyiqtol (or weqatal) when the subject of the mainline verbs switches. A good time to use the word *consequently* is after the narrative has left the mainline for some time in a lengthy elaboration of setting or participants. We can then take the mainline verb that resumes the narrative as a consequence of the preceding state of affairs.

Clause B. _____

Because of the pronominal suffix on אֶעֱבָדְךָ there is no lengthening of the verb to show us it is a cohortative. However, there is another way to tell. What is it? _____ (23.3d)

Verse 19
Clause A. _____

Clause B. : טוֹב תִּתִּי אֹתָהּ לָךְ מִתִּתִּי אֹתָהּ לְאִישׁ אַחֵר

This is a tough verbless clause made tougher by the words תִּתִּי and מִתִּתִּי You may recall that the irregular infinitive of נתן is תֵּת The addition of the pronominal suffix has shortened the vowel as usual. תִּתִּי means *my giving.*

Clause B uses the Biblical Hebrew comparative formula for saying "X is better than Y." Reading right to left, here is the formula:

$$\text{_____ "Y" } \text{מִ } \text{\_\_\_\_\_ "X" \_\_\_\_\_ } \text{טוֹב}$$

And a literal translation of Clause B using the formula:

My giving her to you is better than my giving her to another man.

In English it certainly is not very complimentary to Jacob. Whether it sounds so cold in Hebrew is difficult to say.

Clause C. _____

This is a clear acceptance of Jacob's proposal.

Verse 20

Clause A. _____

Clause B. _____

וַיִּהְיוּ בְעֵינָיו is an idiom meaning *they were to him* or *they seemed to him* אֲחָדִים has the sense *a few*.

Verse 21

Clause A. _____

Clause B. _____

הָבָה is a Qal imperative from the root יהב that means *give*. In thirty-two out of thirty-three uses in the Hebrew Bible it is used in the imperative form, often with the sense of the colloquial *C'mon*! or *Get going!* It is the first word of the famous Jewish song *Hava Nagila*.

Clause C. _____
Clause D. _____

This clause has the very familiar Biblical Hebrew root, used here to express the consummation of marriage.

Verse 22

Clause A. _____

Clause B. _____

מִשְׁתֶּה is another of the scores of Hebrew nouns made by adding *mem* to a root. Whether it is actually an accurate explanation is dubious, but as an aid to memory you may think of these nouns as having been made by adding the question words מָה or מִי to the root. *What* (מָה) has *drinking* (שׁתה)? *A banquet* (מִשְׁתֶּה)

Lesson 42—The conclusion

Verse 23

Clause A. _____

Clause B. _____

Clause C. _____

For this clause and the next one, copy the nikkud of the verbs. Take note of the minor differences between the Qal and Hiphil stems in these two clauses. Notice also that there is no difference between the two verbs in a purely consonantal text. Do you think the Masoretes were correct in their choice of nikkud?

Verse 24

There is only one clause in this verse.

To mention at this point in the narrative Laban's gift of Zilpah to Leah may seem incongruous with the rest of the account, particularly because it is not given as a parenthetical with off-line verb forms. You may be able to guess at a number of cultural, rhetorical, or thematic explanations for this detail.

שִׁפְחָה is a noun meaning *maid-servant*, and comes from the root שׁפח meaning *pour*. The connection is probably not because a maid waits on her mistress and pours drinks for her. It is more likely that a maid represents a figurative *outpouring* of the clan-head's estate as does the noun מִשְׁפָּחָה

Verse 25

Clause A. _____

Clause B. _____
Once again, we have the suspense-building departure from the mainline in this and the previous clauses.

Clause C. _____
Remember the significance of the speech introduction formula. If you need a reminder, see the chart in Verse 5, but you should be getting the idea by now. Remember the basis for the formulas: Specifying the speaker or addressee elevates his status in the dialogue.

Clauses D, E, and F are the subject of Lesson 15. What we can note here in the context of our discourse analysis is that paraphrasing is yet another discourse-slowing technique whereby the writer creates tension and focus.

Verse 26

Clause A. _____

Clause B. _____
The *sere* under the verb's prefix is critical for determining the word's stem.

Look up צער When Laban refers to his daughters as הַצְּעִירָה *the young one* and הַבְּכִירָה *the first-born*, he is also suggesting that Rachel is *the insignificant one*.

Of course, from Laban's perspective, it is a wonderfully convenient time to explain to Jacob the customs of their country! Jacob had only been living there for seven years!

Verse 27

Clause A. _____
See Lesson 20.5a for help with the verb. The root מלא is a good example of how the Piel stem changes the meaning of the Qal stem. In Qal מלא means *be full*, while in Piel it means *cause to be in a filled state, fill*. מלא is part of a group of verbs we refer to as stative verbs. They are the verbs which include the English *be* in their glosses as in *be full* for מלא

362

שָׁבֻעַ means *week*. Consummation of a marriage was a week long affair something like our American honeymoon.

Clause B. _____

Is the verb a weqatal or a sort of yiqtol? It can be either a 3rd f. s. Niphal weqatal or a 1st c. p. Qal cohortative. Does context settle the question? The existence of the DDO in the clause would necessitate the cohortative, but remember from Lesson 42.4 that the use of אֵת as a particle of emphasis for the subject of a clause is espoused by some.

For זֹאת you have to imagine Laban pointing to something or someone that is feminine.

Clause C. _____

This clause tells about the עֲבֹדָה not in the relative past as Jacob is expecting, but in the relative non-past, in this case, the future.

Verse 28

Clause A. _____

The previous clause, dependent Clause C of Verse 27 is the bombshell of the account as far as the extremity of the challenge Jacob must face for Rachel's hand in marriage. Yet, as is typical of Biblical Hebrew narrative, the challenge will now be resolved in a simple, compact series of wayyiqtols. There is no longer any need on the part of the writer to slow the narrative to create tension or focus. He will finish the narrative quickly and efficiently.

Clause B. _____

Clause C. _____

Verse 29

_____

There is only one clause. This verse increases the likelihood that the giving of a maid has some cultural significance to the ancient Hebrew. Does the gift bring some sense of justice to the account?

Verse 30

Clause A. _____

Clause B. _____

Watch out! Is מִלְאָה a Piel qatal or a proper name with a prefixed preposition? The 3rd f. s. Piel qatal is מִלְּאָה ! So close, yet so far! This time the prefixed *mem* is used to say something was done to Rachel more than Leah in similar fashion to the way it was used in the "better than" formula of Verse 19.

Clause C. _____

Did Jacob wed Rachel before or after his second tour of duty with Laban?

Thus ends one account among many in the book of Genesis which chronicle the origins of the nation of

Israel.

Outline of the discourse

This reading is over 100 clauses long so we will not plod through a clause-by-clause charting of the entire discourse. Rather we will list the major sections of the discourse, referring to the markers and functions of each section.

Section 1:   Clauses 1A-2A—A wayyiqtol string which describes Jacob's moving to the new setting of the episode.

Section 2:   Clauses 2B-3D—Two verbless clauses, a participle clause, and an embedded Procedural Discourse which together set the new scene.

Section 2^1:   Clause 2D and 3A-3D—An embedded Procedural Discourse. The entire discourse is made subordinate to the mainline by the X-yiqtol in the dependent clause.

Section 3:   Clause 4A-8E—A string of wayyiqtol speech introduction formulas which carry an extended dialogue between Jacob and those waiting by the well.

Section 3^1:   Clause 7B-7F—A Hortatory Discourse. Jacob reasons with a verbless clause and an irrealis in a dependent clause, and then gives the consequent commands in a string of three imperatives.

Section 3^2:   Clause 8C-8E—A Predictive Narrative of three clauses subordinated by the first one, a yiqtol in a dependent clause.

Section 4:   Clause 9A-10B—A major break at the arrival of Rachel. The break is created by a series of six off-the-line clauses.

Section 5:   Clause 10C-12E—A relatively uninterrupted string of wayyiqtols describing the actions of Jacob and Rachel. The interruptions are two dependent verbless clauses (12B and C).

Section 7:   Clause 13A-15E—Another fairly uninterrupted string of wayyiqtols. The first verb, a wayyiqtol of הָיָה sets this string apart from the previous one. Whereas the previous string features Jacob and Rachel, this one features Jacob and Laban.

Section 7^a: Clause 15B-15E—One of the interruptions of this section wayyiqtol string is a short Hortatory Discourse of one imperative and three supporting clauses.

Section 8:   Clause 16A-17B—Another major break created by four verbless clauses and an X-qatal of הָיָה The series elaborates upon the Rachel and Leah.

Section 9:   Clause 18A-20A—A string of wayyiqtols consequent to the previous break. Much of this string is the introduction of many short direct speech segments in which Jacob and Laban work out the details of their contract.

Section 10:   Clause 20B-22B—A string of wayyiqtols with an important embedded direct speech. Clause 20B's use of the wayyiqtol of היה is used to make a seven year jump in time.

Section 10¹: Clause 21B-21D—Jacob's Hortatory Discourse.

Section 11:   Clause 23A-24—This wayyiqtol string, set off by the transition marker, tells of Laban's ruse.

Section 12:   Clause 25A-27C—This stretch of dialogue, set off by the transition marker and a verbless clause, records the discussion pursuant to "the morning after."

Section 12¹: Clause 25D-25F—Jacob's three questions.

Section 12²: Clause 26B-27C—Laban's consequent Hortatory Discourse.

Section 13:   Clause 28A-30C—An uninterrupted string of wayyiqtols that resolves the account.

READING 7—*Ezekiel 37:1-14   Ezekiel's Valley of Dry Bones*

Lesson 43—*The intricate protocol of prophecy*

Introduction: Although there is a great deal of controversy about just how long, the Hebrew Bible was certainly written over a very long period of time, by a number of different writers from a number of different linguistic backgrounds. Because of its diverse origins, it must certainly contain several different dialects of Hebrew. In fact, it is remarkable that the Hebrew Bible is as uniform as it is from cover to cover. The book of Ezekiel is one part of the Hebrew Bible that was written relatively late, since it is about relatively late events in the history of Israel. And sure enough, the Hebrew of the book of Ezekiel seems to have some different patterns in it than the Hebrew of most of the other prose books you have studied. One of the main reasons for this reading is to expose you to Late Biblical Hebrew.

Macrostructure

Like many of the books which we categorize as "the Prophets," the message of the book of Ezekiel first condemns and then promises restoration. Ezekiel, the book's writer/narrator, spent the first part of his life in Jerusalem, presumably being trained to take a priestly office when he would come of age. He spent the latter part of his life as a deportee to Babylon. The experience of the prophet is mentioned here because it gives context to the three sections of his book.

The first twenty-five chapters of the book record the criticisms of *YHWH* that explain the deportation and *YHWH*'s promises of Jerusalem's eventual overthrow. The section concludes with the graphic vision of the caldron in chapter 24, symbolizing the siege of Jerusalem by the Babylonians. The second section of the book, chapters 25 through 32, then pronounces judgment on the nations surrounding Judah. And finally, the third section, chapters 33 through 48, prophesies the restoration of the Temple, the priesthood, and Jerusalem to a glory never before equaled. Our reading is therefore part of this third section, meant to give hope to the narrator's destitute people which he calls הַגּוֹלָה or *the captivity*.

Marking the boundaries of the discourse

Each writer of a biblical book, especially perhaps in the books of the Prophets, has his own style, part of which is the writer's particular method for segmenting his discourse. For instance one very common marker of discourse boundary in the Prophets is the "messenger of *YHWH*" formula, כֹּה אָמַר יהוה especially prevalent in Jeremiah. Another is the "prophetic utterance" formula, נְאֻם יהוה very common in Jeremiah, Amos, and Zechariah. Ezekiel, being heavily influenced by Jeremiah, does use both of these disjunctive phrases, but his preferred discourse marker is the "prophetic word" formula, used by him thirty-nine times, far more than anyone else. Translate it below.

וַיְהִי דְבַר־יהוה אֵלַי לֵאמֹר : _____

All this said, the discourse which we are about to analyze begins with yet another formula by which the prophet asserts the credibility of his call. Ezekiel 37:1 begins הָיְתָה עָלַי יַד־יְהוָה used twice by Ezekiel. Perhaps you can come up with a name for this formula yourself. The other end of our discourse is just as easy to spot because the next discourse begins in Verse 15 with Ezekiel's favorite, "the prophetic word" formula shown above.

Verse 1

Clause A. _____

The use of a clause-initial qatal in this clause is consistent with what common use of this construction? _____ (26.2)

As in our reading on 1Samuel 17:37, יַד in Ezekiel's introductory formula in this verse probably means *strength*. The idea is that Ezekiel was endowed with a special ability.

Clause B. _____

Clause C. _____

The root נוח has two conjugations attested for the Hiphil stem which have a slight difference in meaning. The word we are seeing in Verse 1 belongs to the "Hiphil A" conjugation meaning *cause to rest* as opposed to the "B" which means *lay, set down*. Other hollow roots also have alternative "A" and "B" conjugations in the Hiphil and Niphal stems, but the meaning of the roots are only affected in some of them. נוח is the only root in the Hebrew vocabulary for this course which has alternative "A" and "B" conjugations.

Both יַד יהוה and רוּחַ יהוה are technically feminine. So what is the subject of this and the preceding verb? The answer may have been a mystery to Ezekiel himself.

Clause D. _____

You only have to look backward one word to find the feminine noun to which הִיא refers.

Typical narrative may also have put the information in this clause in a dependent clause such as

$$\text{אֲשֶׁר מְלֵאָה עֲצָמוֹת}$$

However, this discourse is more than *set* in a valley. The topic of Ezekiel's vision *is this valley*. So the halt in the narration caused by the verbless clause is more appropriate.

Verse 2

Clause A. _____

The weqatal is clearly parallel with the preceding wayyiqtols and the וַיֹּאמֶר of the next verse. What is the function of a single weqatal that stands in for a wayyiqtol in a string of wayyiqtols? _____ _____ (37.2) However, the use of weqatal in the place of wayyiqtol may be a trend in the Hebrew language at the latter stage exhibited in Ezekiel. We'll explore this issue a bit more as we proceed.

Used twenty-five times in Ezekiel, the repetition of סָבִיב intensifies a single use as in *all around*.

Clause B. _____

Here is the second of three verbless clauses elaborating the vision. פְּנֵי is used in the sense of *surface*.

Clause C. _____

Verse 3

Clause A. _____

Clause B. _____

The vocative בֶּן־אָדָם is used extensively in Ezekiel and serves as a reminder to the prophet the distance between himself and the realm of his visions.

Is הֲתִחְיֶינָה Hitpael stem or Qal stem with an interrogative *heh*?

Clause C. _____

If you need help with the verb see 17.4f.

Clause D. _____

The use of אֲדֹנָי יְהוִה as a vocative parallels the use of בֶּן־אָדָם

Notice the fronting of אַתָּה

As is often the case, roots that refer to mental or emotional state or activity with a qatal need to be translated with our English present. We also saw this in our reading on Genesis 22:2 with the word אָהַבְתָּ

Verse 4

Clause A. _____

This is not the first time we have seen an auxiliary speech introduction formula used when there is not a change in speaker. Here it is used to re-direct the dialogue.

Clause B. _____

Fill out the verb analysis chart for הִנָּבֵא If you need help see 41.2.

root	stem	form	person, gender, number	function	basic root meaning

You may question where the passivity is in the meaning of this root, *prophesy*. This is a difficult question to answer because the root is only used in the Niphal and Hitpael stems, so there are no non-passive uses to use for comparison. It may be that the sense is *show oneself a prophet*.

Clause C. _____

This weqatal is a command/instruction, so it is a mainline verb. Whether this clause is Mitigated Hortatory or Instructional Discourse is hard to say.

Clause D. _____

The question is whether הָעֲצָמוֹת הַיְבֵשׁוֹת belongs with the previous clause or this one. Does the gender help link it with either אֲלֵיהֶם of the previous clause or שִׁמְעוּ of this clause? Nevertheless, הָעֲצָמוֹת הַיְבֵשׁוֹת is either a noun and adjective in apposition to the pronominal suffix הֶם-- or a vocative for the present clause's imperative. Vocatives and appositives are both often preceded by the definite article, so the definite article does not settle the question either way. English translations generally interpret the words as a vocative in which case it would be appropriate to add *O* as in *O, dry bones,...*

Verse 5

Clause A. _____

We have now arrived at a second level of embedding. Here is an outline:

```
___HOST:  The "Dry Bones Narrative" represented by a series of wayyiqtols
 |
 |          ___EMBEDDED:  The command to prophesy represented by an imperative and weqatal
 |         |
 |         |          ___EMBEDDED:  The message, to be introduced by the "messenger of YHWH"
 |         |         |               formula.
 |         |         |_____
 |         |_____
 |_____
```

Clause B. _____

Do you remember the common interpretation of a participle used in a +projection genre? (25.3b)

In this clause the more common construction [הִנֵּה + participle] is supplemented by אֲנִי

Which sense of רוּחַ seems most appropriate in this context: *wind, spirit,* or *breath*?

Clause C. _____

Verse 6

Clause A. _____

You will not be able to find גִדִים or even גִד in the *BDB*. Look under the plene spelling גִיד When using your dictionary, you should anticipate this type of spelling alteration.

Thus begins the series of weqatals you may have anticipated in a prophetic book. It took the writer five verses to work his way through the elaborate protocol typical of the Prophets. Spiritually, the protocol is carefully designed to create an ethos for the prophet, the credibility of which the prophet's audience cannot deny. Literarily, the protocol delays the onset of the anticipated prophecy, building suspense.

Clause B. _____

Clause C. _____

There are four roots with different derivations spelled עוּר one with a consonantal *vav* and three hollow roots. Our word in this clause is from hollow root III.

Clause D. _____

369

Clause E. _____

Clause F. _____

This is another oft-repeated formula in the book of Ezekiel, seen over fifty times. It lends cohesiveness to the entire book as do the prophetic introduction formulas.

We have rarely seen a "Clause F" in any verse in any of the readings we have done in this book. Such a high concentration of verbs is universally used by writers to heighten the audience's sense of urgency. The elaborate protocol preceding the prophecies puts the audience in suspense, but when the Predictive Narrative begins, it proceeds with a rush of activity. This discourse is characterized by several fast-moving concentrations of verbs.

Lesson 44—Late Biblical Hebrew

Verse 7

Clause A. _____

Fill out the verb analysis chart for וְנִבֵּאתִי :

root	stem	form	person, gender, number	function	basic root meaning

As for the verb's stem, you may recognize it as Niphal because you remember from Verse 4 that the root is only used in the Niphal and Hitpael stems. However, you should also understand the nikkud so you will be prepared to deal with other Niphal qatals and weqatals of 1st nun roots.

This second use of a weqatal to stand in for a wayyiqtol can be explained in the same manner as the first in Verse 2. However, both of them, together with the weqatals of Verses 8 and 10 may be a sign of an evolving language. The Hebrew Bible was written over a period of many centuries, so we cannot expect that the same language system which is at use in one part of the book is in operation, without any changes, in every other part of the book. Ezekiel is one of the later-written books of the Hebrew Bible, and it displays a much freer use of the weqatal for Historical Narrative than earlier books. Post-biblical Rabbinical writings continued the substitution of weqatal and qatal for the wayyiqtol. In Modern Hebrew, which has evolved into a Indo-European-style tensed language, the wayyiqtol has been entirely replaced by the qatal.

Another possibility, not necessarily exclusive of the first, is that the freer use of the weqatal is a function of the heightened dramatic style of prophetic ecstasy. You will notice that this and the next two Historical Narrative weqatals in Verses 8 and 10 have the prophet as their subjects. Two story lines therefore develop simultaneously, that of the prophet's actions carried by the weqatals and that of the events in the valley carried by the wayyiqtols.

370

Clause B. _____

The verb in this clause is a Pual qatal. Pual is the passive counterpart to the Piel stem, so this verb means *I was commanded*. You will study the Pual in Lesson 45.

Clause C. _____

Here the narrative transition marker begins a new segment of the discourse which tells the effects of the prophet's obedience.

Compare the Niphal imperative in Verse 4 with כְּהִנָּבְאִי from this clause. We could just about translate the word literally if it was prefixed with a *bet* בְּהִנָּבְאִי *in my prophesying*, but *as my prophesying* does not make any sense.. See 34.4 if you need help.

"Clause" D. _____

This is really a stylistic fragment such as we might use in English rather than a true clause.

Clause E. _____

עֲצָמוֹת has been treated as if it was a masculine plural noun consistently throughout this reading, but the verb does not agree with even this idiosyncratic use. The verb is neither the expected 3rd m. p. וַיִּקְרְבוּ nor the 3rd f. p. וַתִּקְרַבְנָה Such inconsistencies are fortunately somewhat uncommon.

Notice the transformation in the nikkud of עֶצֶם that result from its being made plural or its having a suffix attached.

Also notice yet another treatment of עֶצֶם as if it was masculine in the 3rd m. s. pronominal suffix ו—

Verse 8

Clause A. _____

For a comment on the verb form see clause 7A.

Clause B. _____

Clause C. _____

Clause D. _____

For עוֹר see Verse 6.

מִלְמָעְלָה is made from four parts as follows: הָ -- + מַעַל + לְ + מִ and means *above*.

Clause E. _____

Here the narrative stops and thereby creates suspense. The audience expects a complete fulfillment of the prophecies especially in view of the prophet's heretofore complete obedience. To the contrary, אֵין identifies the missing element.

Verse 9

Clause A. _____

Clause B. _____

Clause C. _____
Repetition, paraphrase, and elaboration are the tools of a skilled raconteur in any language as markers of peak suspense.

Clause D. _____

Clause E. _____

Clause F. _____
Fill out the verb analysis chart for בֹּאִי :

root	stem	form	person, gender, number	function	basic root meaning

As in Verse 4, the vocative is prefixed by the definite article.

Clause G. _____
Fill out the verb analysis chart וּפְחִי :

root	stem	form	person, gender, number	function	basic root meaning

Be flexible as you analyze a verb. Fill in the "form" column first this time. The best clue is the preceding verb with which this clause's verb is in series.

For the root you must of course determine the missing letter. פוח is an attested root that has an appropriate meaning *breathe, blow*, but the f. s. imperative of a hollow root would be וּפוּחִי פחה is also an attested root, but only as a noun פֶּחָה meaning *governor*. It is not fair thinking politicians blow a lot of hot air. Finally, נפח is also an attested root, and it does have a meaning that fits in the context.

It's ending and the following word tell you בַּהֲרוּגִים is functioning as a noun. The *shureq* after the second root letter (see 45.2) and discerning the root are the keys to analyzing it. The derivation of the word

372

is a key to interpreting the entire discourse because it suggests the origin of the bones. They are not identified by the more general Hebrew word הַמֵּתִים meaning *the dead*.

Clause H. _____

Fill out the verb analysis chart for וְיִחְיוּ :

root	stem	form	person, gender, number	function	basic root meaning

Use the word's clause-initial position to help you specify its form and function. See 23.3d if you need help.

Verse 10

Clause A. _____

See the note on Clause 7A.

Notice that the verb in this clause is different from the verb in 7A. Do not be fooled into thinking this clause's verb is Hiphil stem even though it has a pre-formed *heh* and dot vowel after the second root letter. The clue is the *dagesh forte* in the *nun*. First *nun* roots do not have this *dagesh* in their first root letter because the 1ˢᵗ *nun* itself assimilates into the 2ⁿᵈ root letter. For instance, a 3ʳᵈ m. s. Hiphil weqatal of נגד is וְהִגִּיד Rather, the *dagesh forte* is the assimilated *tav* of the Hitpael pre-formative. We do not distinguish between the meaning of Niphal of נבא and Hitpael.

Clause B. _____

This is the active variation of Clause 7B's passive version. What clues in the consonantal text did the Masoretes use to determine the respective nikkud for 7B and this clause?

Clause C. _____

Clause D. _____

Clause E. _____

Clause F. _____

Verse 11

Clause A. _____

The last section of a discourse about a prophetic vision like the one we are analyzing typically ends with a section which interprets the vision. The wayyiqtol of this clause begins this section with וַיֹּאמֶר which has, each time it is used in this discourse, introduced the speech of *YHWH*.

Clause B. _____

373

A verbless clause is expository or explanatory by nature. The fronting of הָעֲצָמוֹת הָאֵלֶּה directs the audience's focus while הֵמָּה is the resumptive pronoun (see the reading on 1 Samuel 17:37C) that makes the clause descriptive.

Clause C. _____

We have learned about the Hebrew word הִנֵּה when it is used with a participle in Lesson 25.3, except that in this verse, the pronominal suffix that is usually attached to הִנֵּה and functions as the participle's subject is missing. In a case like this, the subject is understood rather than written, and its gender and number are indicated by the ending on the participle. Translation: *Behold, they are saying*

Clause D. _____

The root יבשׁ is a "state of being" or stative verb in the Qal stem that is adjectival in and of itself, so that we do not need the customary *er*-word or gerund for translation of the qatal (see 33.2 for a review). Rather, we often use the English present and an adjective for this type of verb. Translation of יָבְשׁוּ : *They are dried*

Remember that some other Qal stative roots that you know are רוּם טמא כלה כבד מלא
חזק and אבד which you will see in the next verse.

Clause E. _____

תִּקְוָה is a noun made from the root קוה

Clause F. _____

Fill out the verb analysis chart for נִגְזַרְנוּ :

root	stem	form	person, gender, number	function	basic root meaning

Notice the doubly passive construction of the Niphal stem verb and the word לָנוּ

What does the series in this verse of two "state of being" verbs, as opposed to action verbs, and one passive verb grammatically indicate about the House of Israel's outlook on their situation as deportees in Babylon?

Verse 12

Clause A. _____

This is the third time in the discourse that the prophet is commanded to prophesy, but it is the first time that the word לָכֵן is used to set off the commands. This last Hortatory Discourse is thereby marked as the concluding Hortatory of the host discourse.

Clause B. _____

374

Clause C. _____

Here begins the Predictive Narrative that completes the prophet's responsibility for this particular instance of the hand of *YHWH* coming upon him. It also resolves all the literary tension that remains as to what the vision of the dry bones means.

Clause D. _____

Clause E. _____

The location of the vocative עַמִּי sets apart this third promise.

The construct chain אַדְמַת יִשְׂרָאֵל which is more familiar to you as אֶרֶץ יִשְׂרָאֵל is found exclusively in the book of Ezekiel, and may attest to a land in the humbled state to which the conqueror Babylon had brought it.

Verse 13

Clause A. _____

Compare this and the next clause to the same pair in Verse 6 which culminated the original Predictive Narrative of this discourse. It remains as the ultimate promise here.

Clause B. _____

Stop at יהוה

בְּפִתְחִי אֶת־קִבְרוֹתֵיכֶם

Although it is not technically a clause, deal with this adverbial phrase and the next as two separate units.

וּבְהַעֲלוֹתִי אֶתְכֶם מִקִּבְרוֹתֵיכֶם עַמִּי

Notice how the vocative is once again placed with the "bringing up" of the House of Israel as it is in Clause 12E.

Also notice the arrangement of the elements in this Predictive Narrative in Verses 12 and 13. They are labeled to make comparison easier.

A. פֹּתֵחַ אֶת־קִבְרוֹתֵיכֶם
  B. וְהַעֲלֵיתִי אֶתְכֶם מִקִּבְרוֹתֵיכֶם
    C. עַמִּי
      D. וְהֵבֵאתִי אֶתְכֶם אֶל־אַדְמַת יִשְׂרָאֵל
      E. וִידַעְתֶּם כִּי־אֲנִי יְהוָה
A¹. בְּפִתְחִי אֶת־קִבְרוֹתֵיכֶם
  B². וּבְהַעֲלוֹתִי אֶתְכֶם מִקִּבְרוֹתֵיכֶם
    C³. עַמִּי

This type of parallel ordering of elements is often done in Biblical Hebrew prose as well as poetry. It is often used to bring emphasis to the central element(s).

Another common arrangement of elements is A, B, C, D, C[1], B[2], A[1], called **chiasm** /KEE-az-m/ which focuses on the central element which may or may not be repeated. Since chiasm ends with the same element with which it began, we may say it is "closes the circle," something which is literarily satisfying. It is therefore not surprising that a chiastic arrangement of elements often marks closure of an episode or even an entire narrative. It reflects the kind of ordered ending that one would expect of a narrative which is controlled by the providential care of the Supreme Being. A considerable degree of variation and flexibility may be exercised in the number and structuring of the elements as shown in Genesis 41:54b-57 which closes the peak episode in the "Life of Joseph" narrative:[1]

A. וַיְהִי רָעָב בְּכָל־הָאֲרָצוֹת וּבְכָל־אֶרֶץ מִצְרַיִם הָיָה לָחֶם
And a famine happened in all the lands, and it was in all the land of Egypt that there was bread

B. וַתִּרְעַב כָּל־אֶרֶץ מִצְרַיִם
And all the land of Egypt hungered

C. וַיִּצְעַק הָעָם אֶל־פַּרְעֹה לַלָּחֶם
And the people cried to Pharaoh for bread

D. וַיֹּאמֶר פַּרְעֹה לְכָל־מִצְרַיִם לְכוּ אֶל־יוֹסֵף אֲשֶׁר־יֹאמַר לָכֶם תַּעֲשׂוּ
And Pharaoh said to all Egypt, "Go to Joseph. It is what he says that you will do."

A[2]. וְהָרָעָב הָיָה עַל כָּל־פְּנֵי הָאָרֶץ
And it was the famine that was on the whole face of the land

D[1]. וַיִּפְתַּח יוֹסֵף אֶת־כָּל־אֹצְרוֹת בַּר (based on textual variants)
And Joseph opened all the granaries

C[1]. וַיִּשְׁבֹּר לְמִצְרַיִם
And he sold to the Egyptians

B[1]. וַיֶּחֱזַק הָרָעָב בְּאֶרֶץ מִצְרַיִם
But the famine was strong in the land of Egypt

A[1]. וְכָל־הָאָרֶץ בָּאוּ מִצְרַיְמָה לִשְׁבֹּר אֶל־יוֹסֵף כִּי־חָזַק הָרָעָב בְּכָל־הָאָרֶץ׃
And it was all the land that were comers toward Egypt to buy from Joseph for the famine had become strong in all the land.

Verse 14

Clause A. _____

Clause B. _____

Clause C. _____
This clause uses the Hiphil B conjugation that was mentioned in Verse 1.

Clause D. _____

Clause E. _____
We are accustomed to seeing אֲנִי יְהוָה as a verbless clause, but it is not this time. We know because the qatal דִּבַּרְתִּי needs an "X."

[1] Longacre(1989), 31, 35-36.

Clause F. _____

נְאֻם־יְהוָה

This is not a clause, but we will consider it a separate unit. Notice how it and the preceding two clauses are used to put the final stamp of validity on the entire discourse. Throughout the discourse, the prophet is merely the "son of man" while the Hand of *YHWH* gives the prophet an extraordinary ability to see and interpret, and the Spirit of *YHWH* vitalizes and restores *YHWH*'s otherwise hopeless people. The prophet's words are only powerful inasmuch as they are said in obedience to *YHWH*'s commands.

READING 8--Genesis 43:1-45:28   Joseph Reveals Himself to His Brothers

Lesson 45—The denouement episode

Macrostructure

Our final reading in this course is again one episode, this time from the section of Genesis called תֹּלְדוֹת יַעֲקֹב found in Genesis 37-50. In fact, we do not even have time to read the entire episode which begins in Genesis 43 and is itself quite long. We may title our reading "Joseph Reveals Himself to His Brothers."

First , let us examine the layers of embedding to which our reading belongs. The episode we are reading is itself an embedded Historical Narrative in a series of episodes which are part of the "Life of Joseph" narrative. The "Life of Joseph" narrative is, in turn, part of the תֹּלְדוֹת יַעֲקֹב Finally, the תֹּלְדוֹת יַעֲקֹב is part of a series of Historical Narratives which make up the book of Genesis, and illustrate the providence of *YHWH* in the lives of His chosen. We may exhibit these levels of embedding schematically as follows:

```
__Historical Narrative: The Genesis history of YHWH's providential care for His chosen
|      __Historical Narrative: תֹּלְדוֹת יַעֲקֹב
|      |     __Historical Narrative: "Life of Joseph"
|      |     |     __Historical Narrative: Our Present Reading, "Joseph Reveals
|      |     |     |_____Himself to His Brothers"
|      |     |_____
|      |_____
|_____
```

In order to examine a discourse's macrostructure properly, we must describe both its meaning and its plan. The meaning and plan of תֹּלְדוֹת יַעֲקֹב much of which also applies to the "Life of Joseph" narrative, is revealed in several thematically parallel events. In Genesis 48, Joseph brings his sons Manasseh and Ephraim to their grandfather Jacob to be blessed by him. Much to Joseph's dismay, Jacob crosses his hands during the blessing, laying the right hand of blessing on the younger child rather than on the customary first-born. Jacob thereby illustrates what to the human mind seems like the arbitrariness of *YHWH's* choice.

Preference for the younger is also illustrated in the last verses of Genesis 42. Jacob refuses to allow his sons, who have already been to Egypt and back for grain, to bring their youngest brother Benjamin there for more. Jacob is worried about the intentions of the Egyptian vizier (he does not realize the vizier is actually his long-missing son Joseph) who has demanded to see Benjamin if the family is to be allowed to negotiate a second purchase of grain. But Jacob's emotional refusal is appalling: his son Simeon is already imprisoned in Egypt and waiting for the return of his brothers with Benjamin. It seems that Jacob can bear to lose Simeon but not Benjamin. In 42:36 he claims, apparently, a fear of losing a third son with fatalistic אֵין-clauses: יוֹסֵף אֵינֶנּוּ וְשִׁמְעוֹן אֵינֶנּוּ וְאֶת־בִּנְיָמִן תִּקָּחוּ

In another thematic parallel in Genesis 49, Jacob prophesies concerning his own re-united sons that the pre-eminence among them will not fall after the human tradition to the first-born Rueben, but to Judah and Joseph who we eventually find are the progenitors of the great Southern and Northern Kingdoms.

Finally, in our present reading, we see that Joseph's brothers must learn to accept their father's special love not only for Benjamin, but especially for Joseph. Ultimately, they must accept the special call of *YHWH* upon Joseph's life. Throughout the "Life of Joseph," the תֹּלְדוֹת יַעֲקֹב and in the broader arena of Genesis, we see the mystery of favor or choice, often the mystery of *YHWH*'s choice, and the providence of *YHWH* in carrying out His choice. ***Seeing YHWH's choice*** is exactly the point of the "Life of Joseph." The narrative unfolds before us in a masterpiece of story-telling art until Joseph as well as his brothers finally realize what *YHWH* has known all along.[1] Joseph reiterates the realization four times to his brothers in Genesis 45:5-9 and once again in 50:20, shown here:

$$\text{וְאַתֶּם חֲשַׁבְתֶּם עָלַי רָעָה אֱלֹהִים חֲשָׁבָהּ לְטֹבָה}$$

Marking the boundaries of the discourse

Recall that the episode just before our reading depicts Jacob refusing to allow his youngest son Benjamin to be brought to Egypt. Our reading then begins in 43:1-2 by describing the extreme circumstances that bend Jacob's will:

$$\text{וְהָרָעָב כָּבֵד בָּאָרֶץ: וַיְהִי}$$

But the famine was heavy upon the land, and then it happened...

Thus begins Jacob's sons' second fateful trip to Egypt. The episode is therefore comprised of those events which relate to this trip: the decision to go, the preparations for the trip, the dramatic events once there, and finally, the return.

The closing boundary of the episode which we are analyzing is not as clearly defined as the others we have worked with. There is a break at 45:16's X-qatal which also marks the beginning of an embedded Hortatory Discourse of Pharaoh to Joseph. We might think of this as the end of the episode since the attention switches to Pharaoh who has previously not been a participant in our episode. However, the Hortatory Discourse does not mark a real transition to another episode because the focus is brought right back to the brothers in Verse 21. The embedded Hortatory is actually necessary background within the host discourse.

We might also end the episode in Verse 25 because in Verse 26, the scene has switched from Egypt back to Canaan. On the other hand, the episode did begin in Canaan, and it is reasonable to think of the episode as a round trip. In addition, there is no overt transition marker or other off-the-line clause type to mark this as a boundary, only an uninterrupted string of wayyiqtols.

We also lack the overt markers we are used to at the beginning of Chapter 46, but we will consider this the end of the episode because Chapter 46 begins the new movement, Jacob's trip down to Egypt. Let us conclude that a new trip is a new episode. We will therefore be examining some excerpts from the episode that is located in Genesis 43:1 to 45:28.

---

[1] Alter(1981), 159-177.

Kinds of episode

Because time has constrained us in this course to reading only single episodes of major Historical Narratives, we have mostly been limited to examining the devices a Hebrew writer uses *within* an episode, but not how he creates cohesion, build-up of tension, peak, and resolution *from episode to episode*. Let us here try to pick up some of the slack by studying the five *kinds* of episode which often make up the plot of a full Historical Narrative discourse.[1] As you study the chart below, keep in mind that our present reading is excerpts from the **denouement episode** of the "Life of Joseph" narrative.

OPENING EPISODE: **An opening episode often contains the inciting incident which poses the problem around which the plan and meaning of the story will revolve.**	An opening episode may have a formulaic title or sentence such as $$\text{אֵלֶּה תֹלְדוֹת} \rule{2cm}{0.4pt}$$ It is also likely to introduce all of the main characters, often with a number of verbless clauses and/or X-qatals. In effect, the scene-setting is accomplished by embedded Expository Discourse(see Reading 3, V. 15). Genesis 37:2, which, it turns out, begins the opening episode of both the תֹלְדוֹת יַעֲקֹב and the "Life of Joseph" is a good example: אֵלֶּה תֹלְדוֹת יַעֲקֹב יוֹסֵף בֶּן־שְׁבַע־עֶשְׂרֵה שָׁנָה הָיָה רֹעֶה אֶת־אֶחָיו בַּצֹּאן וְהוּא נַעַר אֶת־בְּנֵי בִלְהָה וְאֶת־בְּנֵי זִלְפָּה נְשֵׁי אָבִיו In the opening episode for both תֹלְדוֹת יַעֲקֹב and the "Life of Joseph" narratives, the love of Jacob and hate of ten of his sons for his eleventh, Joseph, is presented in Hebrew as a most ominous state of affairs in 37:3-4: וְיִשְׂרָאֵל אָהַב אֶת־יוֹסֵף מִכָּל־בָּנָיו כִּי־בֶן־זְקֻנִים הוּא לוֹ וְעָשָׂה לוֹ כְּתֹנֶת פַּסִּים: וַיִּרְאוּ אֶחָיו כִּי־אֹתוֹ אָהַב אֲבִיהֶם מִכָּל־אֶחָיו וַיִּשְׂנְאוּ אֹתוֹ וְלֹא יָכְלוּ דַּבְּרוֹ לְשָׁלֹם: Notice for their scene-setting value, the two X-qatals, the isolated weqatal marking a pivotal event, and elaboration of the emerging וַיִּשְׂנְאוּ אֹתוֹ with the irrealis clause וְלֹא יָכְלוּ דַּבְּרוֹ לְשָׁלֹם The inciting incident of both תֹלְדוֹת יַעֲקֹב and the "Life of Joseph"? Genesis 37:28: וַיִּמְכְּרוּ אֶת־יוֹסֵף לַיִּשְׁמְעֵאלִים בְּעֶשְׂרִים כָּסֶף *And they sold Joseph to the Ishmaelites for twenty (pieces of) silver*

---

[1] The five kinds of episode are based on Longacre, *The Grammar of Discourse*(New York: Plenum, 1983), §4.

BUILD-UP EPISODES: **Build-up episodes explore, expand on, and complicate the problem that is incited in the opening episode.**	Build-up episodes are usually many in number, and they build up to the climax and/or denouement episode(s). The build-up episodes in the "Life of Joseph" feature the following: Joseph's stewardship in Potiphar's house, Joseph's ruin, and his experiences in Potiphar's prison. In a Historical Narrative, these episodes are ordered chronologically, and a consequential relationship between events is evident. A rhythm of action ebbs in and out of the wayyiqtol string. Temporal expressions such as הָאֵלֶּה אַחֲרֵי הַדְּבָרִים or the infinitive with the particles *bet* or *koph* are common devices for creating cohesion by referring back before the narrative proceeds forward. We have seen in our earlier readings how new episodes are often bounded by וַיְהִי or the description of a new scene or the switching of story participants using low-ranking clause types. (Of course, not every use of וַיְהִי indicates a new episode. Sometimes it only marks a new paragraph in a continuing episode.)
CLIMAX: **(peak 1)** **The climax is the episode in which the problem we have been following since the inciting incident becomes most developed and complicated.**	The climax episode can also be called the peak 1 episode because it has many of the same features as the denouement or peak 2 episode. Suspense is high. In the "Life of Joseph" narrative the climax is in Genesis 41 in which Joseph interprets Pharaoh's dreams and rises to the place of power in Egypt which his own dream foretold. Neither the climax peak nor the denouement peak is a point in time, or one event. Each of the two peaks is an episode that is highlighted by the Hebrew writer by his creating a "zone of turbulence."[1] The idea is that the verb forms, pacing, and density of description and elaboration used in the build-up episodes creates a pattern. This pattern is violated in the peak(s). Any of the following devices are likely to be used to create a "zone of turbulence" in Biblical Hebrew narrative: 1. Wayyiqtols that do not represent chronologically ordered and distinct events. Rather, one or more wayyiqtols may paraphrase or elaborate upon an earlier clause. 2. Paraphrase, repetition, and elaboration using an increase of non-mainline clause types like an isolated weqatal, X-qatal, participle, and verbless clause. 3. Leitwort or chiastic structures may be employed. 4. Lengthy dialogue or monologue. 5. "Packing the stage with actors." 6. A blending of the viewpoints of the story narrator and a story participant, often marked with a הִנֵּה (See the Reading on Gen 22:13)

---

[1] Longacre(1983), 22.

DENOUEMENT: **(peak 2)** The denouement is the episode in which the narrative's tension is released.	Many of the same devices which mark a climax peak or peak 1 of a Historical Narrative also mark the denouement peak or peak 2. The difference between the two may be expressed by the parameter called *release*. *Release* refers to the release of the tension which first began building with the inciting incident of the opening episode. In the climax peak, the tension is like a knot being interwoven in as complicated a way as possible and being pulled as tight as possible, so the climax is minus for release (-release). In the denouement, on the other hand, the tension is released. The audience at this point has a good idea whether what was put at risk in the inciting incident is rescued or lost. The denouement is +release. Remember that this present reading is the denouement episode of the "Life of Joseph" narrative. This is the episode that shows whether the hate and jealousy of the ten sons of Jacob has been corrected and whether the sale of Joseph to Egypt can be redeemed. Note: Considerable variety is to be expected in the design of Historical Narrative Discourses. No one puts a writer in jail if he fails to overtly mark one episode in his narrative as the climax and another as his denouement. Both may be present, one may be present, or neither may be present.
RESOLVING EPISODES: The resolving episodes, called collectively the resolution, more or less answer the audience's remaining questions.	A narrative is typically lop-sided around the peaks, weighted more heavily on the build-up side. The resolution is a shorter episode or series of episodes, typically relatively uninterrupted strings of wayyiqtols. The resolving episodes finish unraveling the answers to the questions that built up during the previous episodes. During the resolution of the "Life of Joseph" narrative, Jacob has a vision confirming that the trip to Egypt is God's will for him. The arrangements for and the experiences of Jacob in Egypt are then recounted including Jacob's blessing of Joseph's two sons.

As mentioned above, not every narrative contains every type of episode. However, perhaps a narrative with all these episode types can be represented by the flight of an arrow. The opening episode with its inciting incident is like the archer's letting an arrow fly. The arrow has begun a journey, and we the audience begin to wonder if the arrow can reach its mark. The long upward path of the arrow during which so many factors can affect the arrow's flight is like the build-up episodes. Just before the arrow reaches its highest point and slows almost to a stop is the climax peak as we may hope that the arrow can proceed only a bit farther. Just when the arrow changes its trajectory to begin down is the denouement peak. The suspense is largely released because we can now extrapolate whether the arrow can reach its mark. The short downward flight is like the resolution of the story.

Furthermore, remember that one episode in the major narrative may itself be considered an embedded discourse. One episode may therefore have its own "parts in miniature," that is, its own inciting incident, build-up of suspense, climax, denouement, and resolution. We shall see that this is exactly the case in our present reading. Genesis 47:1-50:28 is *both* the denouement episode of the "Life of Joseph" story *and* an embedded narrative in its own right with a fully developed episodic structure.[1]

Genesis 43:1-5, 8-10

Verse 1 and Verse 2 up to the *atnakh* are used to set the stage for the episode. Read it.

The remainder of Verse 2 begins a dialogue between Jacob and Judah that culminates in a decision to bring Jacob's young son Benjamin to Egypt. Jacob hesitates before allowing this course until, in Verse 13 he says וְאֶת־אֲחִיכֶם קָחוּ וְקוּמוּ שׁוּבוּ אֶל־הָאִישׁ The decision is the inciting incident of this embedded narrative. Much of the tension in the narrative is about whether Benjamin will be returned safely to his father. At the same time, the incident has an additional significance to the greater "Life of Joseph" narrative. Read Verse 2 after the *atnakh* through the end of Verse 5.

Notes:
Verse 2: See that אֹכֶל means *food,* not to be confused with אֱכֹל the imperative or אֹכֵל the participle.

Verse 3: If you have trouble determining the root used in הָעֵד הֵעִד see Lesson 28.3. If you have trouble with the sense of the *bet* in בָּנוּ see 26.4A.5.

Verse 4: The type of construction יֶשְׁךָ מְשַׁלֵּחַ also seen in Verse 5, is covered in 31.2.

These verses represent the third time in the "Life of Joseph" story that we have heard that the youngest brother Benjamin must be brought to Egypt as the condition for buying grain. First Joseph, whom his brothers did not yet recognize, made the demand in 42:15-20. The incognito Joseph means to remind his ten brothers of their earlier refusal to accept that one son may receive favor from his father and *YHWH* Himself that the others do not receive. Then the sons who return to Jacob repeat the condition for their return to Egypt in 42:33-34. Jacob refuses to meet the condition for fear of losing his youngest son even though one of his other sons is being held captive in Egypt. We can see that Joseph's intention is successful in that each time sending Benjamin to Egypt is brought up, the earlier (supposed) loss of Joseph is also brought up.

The point here in terms of discourse analysis is that the conspicuous repetition of the Benjamin condition loads thematic weight on this repeated detail. Recall that paraphrase often marks peak. In addition, the entire inciting incident of this embedded discourse is related to us in the form of direct speech. Lengthy passages of direct speech are also markers of peak.

When Judah offers himself in Verses 8-9 as the lad's protector, it is the first real glimpse that the sibling rivalry that incited the entire "Life of Joseph" narrative may be ready to unravel. Read Verses 8-10.

Notes:
Verse 8: Note the rhythm of the four cohortatives in a row, the fourth set off by לֹא Note also the emphatic use of the phrase גַם־אֲנַחְנוּ גַם־אַתָּה גַּם־טַפֵּנוּ

---
[1] Longacre(1989), §1.3.2.7.

383

Verse 9: The fronting of אָנֹכִי shifts the focus to Judah. אֶעֶרְבֶ֫נּוּ uses the root II of ערב in the sense of *go as a pledge for*, and you should remember the pronominal suffix. וְחָטָ֫אתִי seems to have the sense *I will be the bearer of blame*.

Verse 10: לוּלֵא means *except*. הִתְמַהְמָ֫הְנוּ comes from the geminate root, a root having 2nd and 3rd letters the same, מהה meaning *linger*. Yes, the הִת pre-formative does give the word a reflexive sense. The geminate root type is rather promiscuous and will be covered in Lessons 46-48.

Lesson 46—Repetition and monologue as a markers of peak, part 1
Summary of the skipped material

For time' sake, we have to skip reading some of the episode, so a summary of the skipped material follows.

Genesis 43:11-14—This is the Hortatory Discourse in which Jacob commands his sons to bring money and gifts to Egypt as well as their brother Benjamin. Out of the eight commands he gives, six are imperatives. Jacob may have given the commands with the mitigated weqatals, but it seems that he is attempting to affirm his place as patriarch in the face of circumstances that are controlling him.

Genesis 43:15-43:34—This is a long stretch of narration that is briefly and occasionally interrupted with direct speech. Wayyiqtols abound as Jacob's sons head to Egypt, are received by Joseph through his servant, re-unite with Simeon, and are entertained at a banquet. The brothers react when Joseph mysteriously knows how to seat them at the banquet in their birth-order:

וַיִּתְמְה֣וּ הָאֲנָשִׁים אִישׁ אֶל־רֵעֵ֑הוּ

We may think the verb here is from the same root we saw in Verse 10's הִתְמַהְמָ֫הְנוּ but מהה always has the characteristic sequence מהמה Rather, וַיִּתְמְהוּ is thought to be a Qal stative from the root תמה meaning *be astonished*. At the banquet, Joseph, who has now effectively demonstrated that he knows Benjamin is the last-born son, gives Benjamin five times the serving over his brothers. This is another in the series of calculations by Joseph to favor Benjamin before his other brothers. Apparently, he wants to see if his brothers had learned to accept that one may be favored above another.

This scene is the first time in the "Life of Joseph" narrative that all twelve sons of Jacob are in one scene together. Recall that "packing the stage with actors" is one marker of a peak in a Historical Narrative.

Genesis 44:1-17—These verses tell of the instructions for, and execution of Joseph's ruse. He sends his brothers back to Canaan with sacks of grain, but he also has his own silver cup planted in Benjamin's sack so that Benjamin can be framed for thievery. Joseph arranges for the men to be intercepted. Whoever has the silver cup, the brothers are told, is to be executed. The others can go free. The ruse gives the brothers a perfect opportunity to be rid of their another favored brother. Joseph, as if to warn his brothers to be careful, reminds them twice that he can divine the truth. To do so Joseph uses the infinitive absolute and yiqtol of the root נחש in Verses 5 and 15 as in נַחֵשׁ יְנַחֵשׁ This root also gives us the Hebrew word for *serpent*, נָחָשׁ the subtle creature of the Garden of Eden. Wise as a serpent, Joseph has constructed the perfect situation to either reprove his brothers of their sibling hate or reconcile with them because they have learned their lesson.

The first half of Judah's long monologue

Read Genesis 44:18-25 which is the first half of a very long monologue by Judah.

Notes:

Verse 18: For an explanation of בִּי אֲדֹנִי see the particle of entreaty in 23.4B.11. Notice the deferential use of the jussive and other third person forms that Judah uses in reference to himself, as well as the deferential phrasing.

Verse 19: Here the deferential style continues only Judah now refers to the Joseph in the third person. Judah is avoiding, even grammatically, any suggestion of a nose-to-nose relationship with Joseph.

Verse 20: This verse begins a series of wayyiqtols that Judah uses to recount past events. Here is a review of זָקֵן forms:

זָקָן *beard*

זָקֵן *be* or *grow old* (Qal qatal 3rd m. s.)

זָקֵן *old* (m. s. adjective)

זְקֻנִים *old age*

וְיֶלֶד זְקֻנִים קָטָן is a construct chain modified by an adjective.

You learned לְבַד as a single vocabulary item, but it is actually two parts. The word לְבַדּוֹ is three parts: וֹ + בַד + לְ and means *by himself. By herself* is לְבַדָּהּ and so on.

Verse 22: Judah seems to be shifting to an "abbreviated" colloquial style in the clauses וְעָזַב אֶת־אָבִיו וָמֵת The relationship between the clauses is "when(if)/then", but Judah uses the qatal as the plain expression of fact where the yiqtol would normally be used in an apodosis/paradosis.

Verse 23: Do not be fooled by the defectiva *holem* and paragogic *nun* in תֹסִפוּן It is a Hiphil yiqtol 2nd m. p. of the root יסף The root יסף often in conjunction with an infinitive, is used to express the idea of *again* as in תֹסִפוּן לִרְאוֹת *You will not again see.*

Lesson 47—Repetition and monologue as markers of peak, con't

We are only half way through reading Judah's long monologue, the longest direct speech in the entire "Life of Joseph" narrative, but it is worth mentioning two discourse issues now. First, *within the present episode,* the speech is the climax, marked by the departure from the host narrative's wayyiqtol string to the wayyiqtol string and direct speeches within Judah's direct speech. Thematically, Judah's speech emphasizes that he is not going to lie his way out of his present dilemma over the fate of his younger brother Benjamin. Rhetorically, the lengthy departure from the mainline of the host discourse underlines the details of the story for us once more, and delays the onset of the *denouement of the present episode,* all of which builds tension in the episode. The nagging question of the episode is "What will become of Benjamin?"

Second, at the same time the long speech marks the climax of the episode itself, in the larger "Life of Joseph" narrative, it helps mark the denouement. Remember, that both climax and denouement are marked as peaks 1 and 2 by the same characteristics. Here the marker is the long monologue which dutifully recounts almost the entire "Life of Joseph" narrative from the perspective of the ten brothers. This issue of perspective or viewpoint is very important. Previously the story has been narrated by a rather traditional third person omniscient narrator, in a sense, from God's perspective. In fact, it turns out, that "Life of Joseph" narrative is very much about men learning to see the way God sees. Even though Judah recounts the story faithfully from his view, we the audience, are acutely aware of Judah's ignorance of the whole picture, his desperate need to see what God sees. He does not even realize he is talking to his brother. Judah's monologue is an excellent example of how shifting from the established perspective of the detached narrator to the perspective of one of the story participants is used as a marker of peak.

Judah's long monologue is not the only device used to mark the denouement of the "Life of Joseph" narrative; several others are on the way. For now, finish reading Judah's monologue in Genesis 44:26-34.

Notes:
Verse 26: The conjugation of יֻכַל as a yiqtol is in Reading 3 on Judges 16:5. The repetition in לֹא נוּכַל לָרֶדֶת and לֹא נוּכַל לִרְאוֹת must be calculated to impress the Egyptian vizier that these aliens from Canaan have the greatest of regard for the Egyptian's strict instructions. At the same time, the repetition intensifies the highlighting of Benjamin, who has become a symbol for Joseph.

Verse 27: In case we were not sure whether Judah thinks of Joseph when he thinks of losing Benjamin, he reminds us here.

Verse 28: This is still the direct speech of Jacob. עַד־הֵנָּה means *since these (things)*.

Verse 29: The *vav* of וּלְקַחְתֶּם is a *vav*-consecutive remember. You might try *And so...* for your translation. You know the root קָרָא as having the meaning *encounter, befall*. The root קָרָה is a synonym. In this verse, the *heh* has dropped and the pronominal suffix הוּ-- has been added. The *heh* on the end of שְׁאֹלָה is not a regular part of the word, a noun.

Verse 30: Has the direct speech of Jacob ended? The word עַתָּה is a marker of discourse break. Judah has established the "given" for the Egyptian official (and re-established it for us in doing so). The עַתָּה marks a transition to his resulting dire predictions.[1] We have in the expression קְשׁוּרָה בְנַפְשׁוֹ וְנַפְשׁוֹ two pronominal *holems*. Each one refers to someone different. Who are the antecedents?

Verse 31: In כִּרְאוֹתוֹ made of preposition, infinitive construct, and pronominal suffix, you can see that the temporal adverb can be used in a future time context just as we have often encountered it in a past time context. For a review of this construction's use see 34.4a.

Verse 32: The root ערב is the same one we saw used in 43:9 above.

Verse 33: Once more, as in Verse 30, the word עַתָּה is used to break the discourse. What follows is Judah's request. His entire monologue is a carefully crafted Hortatory Discourse divided into three sections by the two עַתָּה s. The first section is the given, the second is the prediction, and the third is the request. The word נָא clearly identifies יֵשֶׁב as a jussive which in turn identifies יַעַל as a jussive by analogy with יֵשֶׁב The "X" before יַעַל shifts the focus from Judah in the previous clause to הַנַּעַר

---

[1] Niccacci(1990), §73. In fact, the Hebrew word עתה is a macro-syntactic marker for the conclusion of an argumentative speech.

386

Verse 34: For the definition of the word אֵיךְ you can look it up in the *BDB* as it is written. Then the *BDB* tells you what other word to see for the meaning. English translations generally treat בָרָע as the object of אֶרְאֶה However, it may be possible to see the word as adverbial, as in *lest I see in evil what will find my father*. The *evil* in this translation could be the blame or guilt upon Judah for not bringing home Benjamin.

Judah has now made it clear to Joseph and us that he is willing to accept the favor his father shows to Benjamin. Rather than take the perfect opportunity to dispose of his second favored brother, he says he is willing to be enslaved so Benjamin can return to his father. We can now extrapolate a happy ending. The only missing detail is Joseph's reaction.

Lesson 48—The revelation

Read Genesis 45:1-8.

Notes:

Verse 1: עַל can mean *near*. הוֹצִיאוּ can either be a Hiphil imperative or qatal. וַיִּקְרָא is a clue to which one it is here. After Joseph's direct speech there is a seeming avoidance of the wayyiqtol in the use of the irrealis and Hitpael infinitive of ידע Avoidance of wayyiqtols is a marker of peak in Historical Narrative. In addition, although we have had the twelve brothers "pack the stage" before as a marker of peak, in this detail, the emphasis is on how the twelve brothers are isolated on the stage.

Verse 2: To *give one's voice* in Hebrew is an idiom for being loud. בִּבְכִי is comprised of the preposition בְּ plus the noun בְּכִי meaning *weeping*. This verse's וַיִּשְׁמְעוּ and וַיִּשְׁמַע are a good example of how repetition and the use of wayyiqtols which *do not* represent successive events are used to mark peak.

Verse 3: The story's tension began unwinding when Judah made his speech to protect Benjamin, but Joseph's weeping and identifying himself releases the tension even more. Joseph uses S-P order for the verbless clause that identifies him because he knows his brothers know him. They just do not know that they know yet. The "Life of Joseph" narrative is a story about recognition, but recognition does not come easy.

Verse 4: Repetition has been used extensively to mark this denouement peak, but no instance of repetition is used so effectively as this simplest reiteration of the words אֲנִי יוֹסֵף Joseph puts emphasis on himself with the object pronoun אֹתִי which translates poorly into English.

Verse 5: The root עצב means *hurt, pain grieve* in Qal, but is the verb in this verse Qal stem? The *sere* under the prefix should answer the question. As for the second verb, there is not a *sere* or *qamets* under the prefix, so what letter must have dropped from the root? הֵנָּה means *hither*. You can easily figure out the root that gives us the feminine noun מִחְיָה which means *preservation*.

Verse 6: You will learn in Lesson 49 that the ending יִ ם -- means *dual, two*, so that שְׁנָתַיִם means *two years*. You can see that אֵין can refer to a future time as in *there will not be* as well as its more common present time reference *there is no*. The words חָרִישׁ וְקָצִיר mean *plowing time and harvest*.

Verse 7: Here we have an excellent example of the *vav*-consecutive of the wayyiqtol. The sense is, *And so God sent me*. Identifying the roots of פְּלֵיטָה and שְׁאֵרִית are fairly easy to identify, and the words are worth looking up.

Verse 8: This verse largely paraphrases and elaborates on Verses 5 and 7. Recall that paraphrase and elaboration are markers of peak. Notice also the fronting of אַתֶּם and the casus pendens הָאֱלֹהִים by which Joseph draws a distinction between who has been the vital agent at work in his life.

Probably the most critical marker of denouement peak in this assignment is suggested by Joseph's two uses of the word עַתָּה In each case Joseph then states that it has been God all along who has been the Controller of his life, not his brothers. It is at this point that Joseph's brothers, and most probably Joseph himself, recognize God's providential care of the תֹּלְדוֹת יַעֲקֹב as well as God's special part for Joseph within this care. The viewpoint of the twelve sons of Jacob shifts at this point from their limited, biased human perspective to the enlightened, pragmatic knowledge of God.

Lesson 49—The unraveling of denouement, pt. 1
Read Genesis 45:9-15.

Notes:
Verse 9: Key in on the nikkud under the first root letter of מַהֲרוּ lest you think it is a qatal. Joseph again reiterates, this time for his father that God has sent him to Egypt. This is the fourth repetition of this idea since Verse 5. This verse and the next illustrate the typical use of imperatives and a weqatal in Hortatory Discourse, the imperatives for the immediate commands and the weqatal for the more distant.

Verse 10: See the note above about the use of the weqatals here. You know קָרַב the verb and קֶרֶב the noun. קָרוֹב is the adjective. בָּקָר means *livestock*.

Verse 11: The weqatals of the previous verse may be predictive rather than hortatory. It's hard to say. The weqatal וְכִלְכַּלְתִּי which switches to a first person subject is definitely predictive, and therefore definitely off-the-line in Joseph's Hortatory Discourse. The sense is, *That I may...* It is probably best, because all the weqatals in Verses 9 through 11 as off-the-line weqatals in a Hortatory Discourse (see 22.3) giving purpose, as in, *That you may...* and *That I may...*

The word וְכִלְכַּלְתִּי is in the Pilpel stem which you learned in Lesson 48.5b. Fill out the verb analysis chart תִּוְרֵשׁ :

root	stem	form	person, gender, number	function	basic root meaning

We have not seen the root ירשׁ in this stem much. In the Qal it means *inherit*, and in the Hiphil it means *dispossess*. In the stem in which you see it in this verse it means *be impoverished*.

Verse 12: This verse as well as the next once again stress the theme of seeing. What significance do you think a special mention of Benjamin has?

Verse 13: The interruption of Verse 12 separates the weqatals of this verse from the off-the-line weqatals of Verses 9 through 11. These verses are Instructional Discourse. How do we know? They are now goal-oriented rather than agent (person)-oriented.[1] Remember that the root רָאָה can mean *understand* as well as *see*. It may well be, together with its synonym נכר (*recognize*), a Leitwort in the "Life of Joseph" narrative.

Verse 14: The wayyiqtol marks the end of Joseph's direct speech. Notice the two uses of the noun צַוָּאר It is hard to say why the first is in the plural construct.

Verse 15: The words וְאַחֲרֵי כֵן are an "X". It is an interesting departure from the wayyiqtol string used to emphasize just when it was that the brothers began speaking to Joseph. Some grammarians would refer to this qatal as an *ingressive* qatal because it marks the beginning of a situation.

Summary: Joseph's direct speech followed by all the hugs and weeping and kisses illustrate the release of tension that characterizes the denouement episode of a Historical Narrative. We can now predict that hate and jealousy that began the "Life of Joseph" narrative is not going to succeed in destroying this family. This is not to say that all the tension is released or that the narrative is resolved. The response of the brothers, except for Benjamin, is not yet clear. But resolution is now a viable possibility.

Lesson 50—The unraveling of denouement, pt. 2

Before you begin reading Verses 21-28, here is a summary of Verses 16-20. Pharaoh hears of the dramatic reunion of Joseph with his brothers, and there may be some doubt whether Pharaoh will receive Joseph's brothers favorably. Earlier in the account in Genesis 43:32, we had heard that Egyptians counted it an abomination to eat with Hebrews. However, Verses 16-20 completely allay any suspicions. Pharaoh provides Joseph's brothers with provision for the trip to Canaan and back to Egypt again including wagons. He tells them not even to worry about bringing all their possessions back to Egypt with them because, he says,

כִּי־טוּב כָּל־אֶרֶץ מִצְרַיִם לָכֶם הוּא
For the good of all the land of Egypt--it is yours

Read Verses 21 through 28.

Notes:

Verse 21: Notice that Jacob is referred to as Israel here, the princely name that *YHWH* Himself has given to him. He is only called Israel during three stretches in the entire "Life of Joseph" narrative. The first is before Joseph disappears in the first place when Israel's tribe is intact. The second and third are during the denouement episode that we are now reading, when he is commanding his sons about their return to Egypt with Benjamin, and in these last verses of the episode now that it is clear his family will once again be not

---

[1] Dawson(1994), §2.2.1.1.

only re-united but reconciled. The word *Israel* is one of two Leitwörter in this episode, helping to mark it as the denouement.

Verse 22: לְכֻלָּם is made of three parts as follows, preposition, כֹּל which has modified by the addition of a pronominal suffix, and the pronominal suffix. חֲלִפוֹת שְׂמָלֹת means *changes of garments*. How ironic that special garments for the youngest son are featured in both the opening and denouement episodes of this story. The repetition of this image is perhaps not a Leitwort, but certainly a Leitmotif. The repetition of the image brings the episode to a satisfying close.

Verse 23: In the phrase עֲשָׂרָה חֲמֹרִים נֹשְׂאִים ... וְעֶשֶׂר אֲתֹנֹת נֹשְׂאֹת we see a good example of gender agreement between number, noun, and participle. All the detail here is a characteristic of the peak episode we are reading. Here is the vocabulary:

חֲמוֹר	*donkey*
אָתוֹן	*she-ass*
בַּר	*grain*
מָזוֹן	*food*

Verse 24: In the word תִּרְגְּזוּ Joseph reveals that he has the same concern that we do over how his brothers will ultimately be willing to respond to their dramatic reunion with Joseph. He does not want them to get cold feet. It will be challenging for them to face their father as he will almost surely learn of their past evil and return to Egypt.

Verse 26: The nikkud under the prefixed subject pronoun tells you the missing letter in וַיָּפָג

Verse 27: The verses are carried by a high percentage of wayyiqtols as will be typical on the resolution side of a narrative. The repetition in these two clauses,

וַיְדַבְּרוּ אֵלָיו אֵת כָּל־דִּבְרֵי יוֹסֵף אֲשֶׁר דִּבֶּר אֲלֵהֶם

makes it clear that the brothers have completely relinquished to the need for an honest reconciliation.

Verse 28: When the adjective רַב appears without a noun to modify, hanging outside the grammatical structure of any clause, it is performing as an idiom, like an interjection, *enough!* or *It is enough!* The news in the previous verse that וַתְּחִי רוּחַ יַעֲקֹב אֲבִיהֶם together with Jacob's proclamation in this verse finish the release of tension in the "Life of Joseph" narrative. Jacob can finally and truly be called *Israel*.

WHERE DO YOU GO FROM HERE

If you have studied this text independently and wish to continue your studies but cannot do so in a formal setting, the basic advice is to build your vocabulary and to read as much Biblical Hebrew and as much about Biblical Hebrew as you can. Your limited vocabulary is probably the most severe limitation on your ability to read the Hebrew Bible, so building your vocabulary is probably the most efficient single effort you can make at this point. A good study guide to help you build your vocabulary is Larry Mitchel's *A Student's Vocabulary for Biblical Hebrew and Aramaic* (Grand Rapids: Zondervan, 1984). The books lists all Biblical Hebrew words and their glosses by frequency of use down to a frequency of ten.

As far as reading the Hebrew Bible is concerned, the books of Deuteronomy and 1 and 2 Samuel are excellent places to begin. Both have a fair amount of material that is both accessible to a fairly inexperienced reader and material that is challenging as well. The language of the book of Deuteronomy seems to have been very influential upon the language in much of the rest of the Bible.

As for reading about Hebrew, the first order of business is to work your way completely through a reference grammar. A clear, concise, modern reference grammar that is sensitive to discourse issues is *A Biblical Hebrew Reference Grammar* by Christo H.J. van der Merwe, Jackie Naude and Jan H. Kroeze (Sheffield: Sheffield Academic Press, 1999). *Gesenius' Hebrew Grammar*, edited by Kautzsch, translated by Cowley (Oxford: Clarendon, 1910) is probably the most widely referred to grammar in other scholarly literature. Another reference grammar that you may prefer because it is extensively cited with scholarly writings, illustrated with Biblical passages, and furnished with an outstanding bibliography is *An Introduction to Biblical Hebrew Syntax* by Bruce K. Waltke and M. O'Connor (Winona Lake: Eisenbrauns, 1990). Neither the Gesenius nor the Waltke and O'Connor reference grammars uses the discourse analytical approach that this text does.

If you want to expand on your understanding of the discourse analytical view of Biblical Hebrew, you may want to read two works which were highly influential in the preparation of this text, *Joseph: A story of Divine Providence: A Textlinguistic Analysis of Genesis 37 and 39-48* by R. E. Longacre (Winona Lake: Eisenbrauns, 1989) or "The Syntax of the Verb in Classical Hebrew Prose." *Journal for the Study of the Old Testament* by Alviero Niccacci (Sheffield: JSOT Press, 1990). Other works of interest are named throughout this work in its footnotes and in its bibliography.

One of the greatest benefits to learning Hebrew is in the reading of Biblical Hebrew poetry, a topic which has not been dealt with in this course. A thorough work on the qualities and workings of Biblical Hebrew poetry is *Classical Hebrew Poetry* by Wilfred G. E. Watson (Sheffield: JSOT Press, 1995).

Whatever course you wish to pursue, reading tends to beget reading whether Hebrew or about it.

לְמַּעַן יְבָרֶכְךָ יְהוָה אֱלֹהֶיךָ בְּכָל־מַעֲשֵׂה יָדְךָ אֲשֶׁר תַּעֲשֶׂה

Deuteronomy 14:29

VERB CHARTS

In the following verb charts the Hebrew root קָטַל is chosen as the paradigm strong root, even though it is used only four times in the Hebrew Bible. It is chosen as the paradigm root in this book for two reasons. First, it is the paradigm root which is commonly chosen in the charts and terminology of many of the reference grammars which you may encounter if you continue your Hebrew studies after this course. Second, קָטַל is the root which gives us the names of the four finite verb forms which are used throughout this book, wayyiqtol, yiqtol, weqatal, and qatal.

As for each type of weak root, a root is chosen as a paradigm which is both common and well represents its type.

The charts list qatal and yiqtol forms but not weqatal and rarely wayyiqtol forms. This is because the weqatal and wayyiqtol may be easily derived from their corresponding qatal or yiqtol forms. The exception is with a few root types which typically exhibit a shorter or apocopated form in wayyiqtol. If a root type uses an apocopated wayyiqtol, it is noted in the charts.

Throughout the charts, all the spaces in the charts are filled if that form is attested in any root of that type. The spaces are usually left blank if a combination root-type, stem, and form is not attested in the Hebrew Bible. For instance, there are no Pual or Hophal imperatives attested in the Hebrew Bible, so the corresponding spaces are blank. On the other hand, the charts occasionally include unattested forms when the unattested forms help to create continuity in the pattern being illustrated. In such a case the unattested form is marked by an *asterisk*[*].

Reminders:
1. "A" class roots, by far the most common are typically transitive; that is, they take a direct object. "E" and "O" class roots are typically stative and/or intransitive.
2. The *meteg,* the vertical slash next to some of the *qametses*, reminds us to pronounce the *qamets* as usual, like the *a* in *father* rather than as a *qamets khatuf* which is pronounced like the *o* in *boat.*

STRONG ROOTS

QATAL

	QAL "A"	QAL "E"	QAL "O"	NIPHAL
SING. 3rd M.	קָטַל	כָּבֵד	קָטֹן	נִקְטַל
3rd F.	קָטְלָה	כָּבְדָה	קָטְנָה	נִקְטְלָה
2nd M.	קָטַּלְתָּ	כָּבַדְתָּ	קָטֹנְתָּ	נִקְטַלְתָּ
2nd F.	קָטַלְתְּ	כָּבַדְתְּ	קָטֹנְתְּ	נִקְטַלְתְּ
1st C.	קָטַּלְתִּי	כָּבַדְתִּי	קָטֹנְתִּי	נִקְטַלְתִּי
PLUR. 3rd C.	קָטְלוּ	כָּבְדוּ	קָטְנוּ	נִקְטְלוּ
2nd M.	קְטַלְתֶּם	כְּבַדְתֶּם	קְטָנְתֶּם	נִקְטַלְתֶּם
2nd F.	קְטַלְתֶּן	כְּבַדְתֶּן	קְטָנְתֶּן	נִקְטַלְתֶּן
1st C.	קָטַּלְנוּ	כְּבַדְנוּ	קָטֹנּוּ	נִקְטַלְנוּ

YIQTOL

	QAL "A"	QAL "E"	QAL "O"	NIPHAL
SING. 3rd M.	יִקְטֹל	יִכְבַּד	יִקְטַן	יִקָּטֵל
3rd F.	תִּקְטֹל	תִּכְבַּד	like	תִּקָּטֵל
2nd M.	תִּקְטֹל	תִּכְבַּד	כבד	תִּקָּטֵל
2nd F.	תִּקְטְלִי	תִּכְבְּדִי		תִּקָּטְלִי
1st C.	אֶקְטֹל	אֶכְבַּד		אֶקָּטֵל
PLUR. 3rd M.	יִקְטְלוּ	יִכְבְּדוּ		יִקָּטְלוּ
3rd F.	תִּקְטֹּלְנָה	תִּכְבַּדְנָה		תִּקָּטַלְנָה
2nd M.	תִּקְטְלוּ	תִּכְבְּדוּ		תִּקָּטְלוּ
2nd F.	תִּקְטֹּלְנָה	תִּכְבַּדְנָה		תִּקָּטַלְנָה
1st C.	נִקְטֹל	נִכְבַּד		נִקָּטֵל

IMPERATIVE

	QAL "A"	QAL "E"	QAL "O"	NIPHAL
SING. M.	קְטֹל	כְּבַד		הִקָּטֵל
F.	קִטְלִי	כִּבְדִי		הִקָּטְלִי
PLUR. M.	קִטְלוּ	כִּבְדוּ		הִקָּטְלוּ
F.	קְטֹּלְנָה	כְּבַדְנָה		הִקָּטַלְנָה

INFINITIVE

	QAL "A"	QAL "E"	QAL "O"	NIPHAL
CONSTRUCT	קְטֹל			הִקָּטֵל
ABSOLUTE	קָטוֹל			הִקָּטֹל נִקְטֹל

PARTICIPLE

	QAL "A"	QAL "E"	QAL "O"	NIPHAL
SING. M.	קֹטֵל	כָּבֵד	קָטֹן	נִקְטָל
F.	קֹטְלָה קֹטֶּלֶת	כְּבֵדָה	קְטַנָּה	נִקְטָלָה נִקְטֶּלֶת
PLUR. M.	קֹטְלִים	כְּבֵדִים	קְטַנִּים	נִקְטָלִים
F.	קֹטְלוֹת	כְּבֵדוֹת	קְטַנּוֹת	נִקְטָלוֹת

394

STRONG ROOTS continued

QATAL

PIEL	PUAL	HIPHIL	HOPHAL	HITPAEL
קִטֵּל קִטַּל	קֻטַּל	הִקְטִיל	הָקְטַל	הִתְקַטֵּל
קִטְּלָה	קֻטְּלָה	הִקְטִילָה	הָקְטְלָה	הִתְקַטְּלָה
קִטַּלְתָּ	קֻטַּלְתָּ	הִקְטַלְתָּ	הָקְטַלְתָּ	הִתְקַטַּלְתָּ
קִטַּלְתְּ	קֻטַּלְתְּ	הִקְטַלְתְּ	הָקְטַלְתְּ	הִתְקַטַּלְתְּ
קִטַּלְתִּי	קֻטַּלְתִּי	הִקְטַלְתִּי	הָקְטַלְתִּי	הִתְקַטַּלְתִּי
קִטְּלוּ	קֻטְּלוּ	הִקְטִילוּ	הָקְטְלוּ	הִתְקַטְּלוּ
קִטַּלְתֶּם	קֻטַּלְתֶּם	הִקְטַלְתֶּם	הָקְטַלְתֶּם	הִתְקַטַּלְתֶּם
קִטַּלְתֶּן	קֻטַּלְתֶּן	הִקְטַלְתֶּן	הָקְטַלְתֶּן	הִתְקַטַּלְתֶּן
קִטַּלְנוּ	קֻטַּלְנוּ	הִקְטַלְנוּ	הָקְטַלְנוּ	הִתְקַטַּלְנוּ

YIQTOL

PIEL	PUAL	HIPHIL	HOPHAL	HITPAEL
יְקַטֵּל	יְקֻטַּל	יַקְטִיל	יָקְטַל	יִתְקַטֵּל
תְּקַטֵּל	תְּקֻטַּל	תַּקְטִיל	תָּקְטַל	תִּתְקַטֵּל
תְּקַטֵּל	תְּקֻטַּל	תַּקְטִיל	תָּקְטַל	תִּתְקַטֵּל
תְּקַטְּלִי	תְּקֻטְּלִי	תַּקְטִילת	תָּקְטְלִי	תִּתְקַטְּלִי
אֲקַטֵּל	אֲקֻטַּל	אַקְטִיל	אָקְטַל	אֶתְקַטֵּל
יְקַטְּלוּ	יְקֻטְּלוּ	יַקְטִילוּ	יָקְטְלוּ	יִתְקַטְּלוּ
תְּקַטֵּלְנָה	תְּקֻטַּלְנָה	תַּקְטֵלְנָה	תָּקְטַלְנָה	תִּתְקַטֵּלְנָה
תְּקַטְּלוּ	תְּקֻטְּלוּ	תַּקְטִילוּ	תָּקְטְלוּ	תִּתְקַטְּלוּ
תְּקַטֵּלְנָה	תְּקֻטַּלְנָה	תַּקְטֵלְנָה	תָּקְטַלְנָה	תִּתְקַטֵּלְנָה
נְקַטֵּל	נְקֻטַּל	נַקְטִיל	נָקְטַל	נִתְקַטֵּל

IMPERATIVE

PIEL	PUAL	HIPHIL	HOPHAL	HITPAEL
קַטֵּל		הַקְטֵל		הִתְקַטֵּל
קַטְּלִי		הַקְטִילִי		הִתְקַטְּלִי
קַטְּלוּ		הַקְטִילוּ		הִתְקַטְּלוּ
קַטֵּלְנָה		הַקְטֵלְנָה		הִתְקַטֵּלְנָה

INFINITIVE

PIEL	PUAL	HIPHIL	HOPHAL	HITPAEL
קַטֵּל		הַקְטִיל		הִתְקַטֵּל
קַטֵּל קַטֹּל	קֻטֹּל	הַקְטֵל	הָקְטֵל	הִתְקַטֵּל

PARTICIPLE

PIEL	PUAL	HIPHIL	HOPHAL	HITPAEL
מְקַטֵּל	מְקֻטָּל	מַקְטִיל	מָקְטָל מֻקְטָל	מִתְקַטֵּל
מְקַטֶּלֶת	מְקֻטֶּלֶת	מַקְטֶלֶת	מָקְטֶלֶת or מָ-	מִתְקַטֶּלֶת
מְקַטְּלִים	מְקֻטָּלִים	מַקְטִילִים	מָקְטָלִים or מָ-	מִתְקַטְּלִים
מְקַטְּלוֹת	מְקֻטָּלוֹת	מַקְטִילוֹת	מָקְטָלוֹת or מָ-	מִתְקַטְּלוֹת

WAYYIQTOL: וַיַּקְטֵל

FIRST GUTTURAL ROOTS
QATAL

	QAL	QAL	NIPHAL	HIPHIL	HOPHAL
SING. 3rd M.	עָמַד		נֶעֱמַד	הֶעֱמִיד	הָעֱמַד
3rd F.	עָמְדָה		נֶעֶמְדָה	הֶעֱמִידָה	הָעֶמְדָה
2nd M.	עָמַּ֫דְתָּ		נֶעֱמַּ֫דְתָּ	הֶעֱמַּ֫דְתָּ	הָעֱמַּ֫דְתָּ
2nd F.	עָמַדְתְּ		נֶעֱמַדְתְּ	הֶעֱמַדְתְּ	הָעֱמַדְתְּ
1st C.	עָמַּ֫דְתִּי		נֶעֱמַּ֫דְתִּי	הֶעֱמַּ֫דְתִּי	הָעֱמַּ֫דְתִּי
PLUR. 3rd C.	עָמְדוּ		נֶעֶמְדוּ	הֶעֱמִ֫ידוּ	הָעֶמְדוּ
2nd M.	עֲמַדְתֶּם		נֶעֱמַדְתֶּם	הֶעֱמַדְתֶּם	הָעֱמַדְתֶּם
2nd F.	עֲמַדְתֶּן		נֶעֱמַדְתֶּן	הֶעֱמַדְתֶּן	הָעֱמַדְתֶּן
1st C.	עָמַּ֫דְנוּ		נֶעֱמַּ֫דְנוּ	הֶעֱמַּ֫דְנוּ	הָעֱמַּ֫דְנוּ

YIQTOL

	QAL	QAL	NIPHAL	HIPHIL	HOPHAL
SING. 3rd M.	יַעֲמֹד	יֶחֱזַק	יֵעָמֵד	יַעֲמִיד	יָעֱמַד
3rd F.	תַּעֲמֹד	תֶּחֱזַק	תֵּעָמֵד	תַּעֲמִיד	תָּעֱמַד
2nd M.	תַּעֲמֹד	תֶּחֱזַק	תֵּעָמֵד	תַּעֲמִיר	תָּעֱמַד
2nd F.	תַּעַמְדִי	תֶּחֶזְקִי	תֵּעָמְדִי	תַּעֲמִ֫ידִי	תָּעֶמְדִי
1st C.	אֶעֱמֹד	אֶחֱזַק	אֵעָמֵד	אַעֲמִיד	אָעֱמַד
PLUR. 3rd M.	יַעַמְדוּ	יֶחֶזְקוּ	יֵעָמְדוּ	יַעֲמִ֫ידוּ	יָעֶמְדוּ
3rd F.	תַּעֲמֹ֫דְנָה	תֶּחֱזַ֫קְנָה	תֵּעָמַ֫דְנָה	תַּעֲמֵ֫דְנָה	תָּעֳמַ֫דְנָה
2nd M.	תַּעַמְדוּ	תֶּחֶזְקוּ	תֵּעָמְדוּ	תַּעֲמִ֫ידוּ	תָּעֶמְדוּ
2nd F.	תַּעֲמֹ֫דְנָה	תֶּחֱזַ֫קְנָה	תֵּעָמַ֫דְנָה	תַּעֲמֵ֫דְנָה	תָּעֳמַ֫דְנָה
1st C.	נַעֲמֹד	נֶחֱזַק	נֵעָמֵד	נַעֲמִיד	נָעֱמַד

IMPERATIVE

	QAL	QAL	NIPHAL	HIPHIL	
SING. M.	עֲמֹד	חֲזַק	הֵעָמֵד	הַעֲמֵד	
F.	עִמְדִי	חִזְקִי	הֵעָמְדִי	הַעֲמִ֫ידִי	
PLUR. M.	עִמְדוּ	חִזְקוּ	הֵעָמְדוּ	הַעֲמִ֫ידוּ	
F.	עֲמֹ֫דְנָה	חֲזַ֫קְנָה	הֵעָמַ֫דְנָה	הַעֲמֵ֫דְנָה	

INFINITIVE

	QAL		NIPHAL	HIPHIL	HOPHAL
CONSTRUCT	עֲמֹד		הֵעָמֵד	הַעֲמִיד	
ABSOLUTE	עָמוֹד		נַעֲמוֹד הֵאָסֹף	הַעֲמֵיד	הָעֲמֵד

PARTICIPLE

	QAL	QAL	NIPHAL	HIPHIL	HOPHAL
SING. M.	עֹמֵד	חָזֵק	נֶעֱמָד	מַעֲמִיד	מָעֳמָד
F.	עֹמֶ֫דֶת עֹמְדָה	חֹזֶ֫קֶת	נֶעֱמֶ֫דֶת	מַעֲמִידָה	
PLUR. M.	עֹמְדִים	חֲזָקִים	נֶעֱמָדִים	מַעֲמִידִים	מָעֳמָדִים
F.	עֹמְדוֹת	חֲזָקוֹת	נֶעֱמָדוֹת	מַעֲמִידוֹת	

WAYYIQTOL: וַיַּעֲמֵד

396

FIRST *ALEPH* ROOTS

The following 1ˢᵗ *aleph* roots deviate from the 1ˢᵗ guttural pattern for Qal yiqtol and Qal wayyiqtol: אבד

אפה אמר אכל אהב

YIQTOL

	QAL
SING. 3ʳᵈ M.	יֹאכַל
3ʳᵈ F.	תֹּאכַל
2ⁿᵈ M.	תֹּאכַל
2ⁿᵈ F.	תֹּאכְלִי
1ˢᵗ C.	אֹכַל
PLUR. 3ʳᵈ M.	יֹאכְלוּ
3ʳᵈ F.	תֹּאכַלְנָה
2ⁿᵈ M.	תֹּאכְלוּ
2ⁿᵈ F.	
1ˢᵗ C.	נֹאכַל

IMPERATIVE

	QAL
SING. M.	אֱכֹל
F.	אִכְלִי
PLUR. M.	אִכְלוּ
F.	

WAYYIQTOL: וַיֹּאכַל וַיֹּאמֶר

397

THIRD GUTTURAL ROOTS

QATAL

	QAL	NIPHAL	PIEL	PUAL
SING. 3rd M.	שָׁלַח	נִשְׁלַח	שִׁלַּח	שֻׁלַּח
3rd F.	שָׁלְחָה	נִשְׁלְחָה	שִׁלְּחָה	שֻׁלְּחָה
2nd M.	שָׁלַחְתָּ	נִשְׁלַחְתָּ	שִׁלַּחְתָּ	שֻׁלַּחְתָּ
2nd F.	שָׁלַחַתְּ	נִשְׁלַחַתְּ	שִׁלַּחַתְּ	שֻׁלַּחַתְּ
1st C.	שָׁלַחְתִּי	נִשְׁלַחְתִּי	שִׁלַּחְתִּי	שֻׁלַּחְתִּי
PLUR. 3rd C.	שָׁלְחוּ	נִשְׁלְחוּ	שִׁלְּחוּ	שֻׁלְּחוּ
2nd M.	שְׁלַחְתֶּם	נִשְׁלַחְתֶּם	שִׁלַּחְתֶּם	שֻׁלַּחְתֶּם
2nd F.	שְׁלַחְתֶּן	נִשְׁלַחְתֶּן	שִׁלַּחְתֶּן	שֻׁלַּחְתֶּן
1st C.	שָׁלַחְנוּ	נִשְׁלַחְנוּ	שִׁלַּחְנוּ	שֻׁלַּחְנוּ

YIQTOL

	QAL	NIPHAL	PIEL	PUAL
SING. 3rd M.	יִשְׁלַח	יִשָּׁלַח	יְשַׁלַּח	יְשֻׁלַּח
3rd F.	תִּשְׁלַח	תִּשָּׁלַח	תְּשַׁלַּח	תְּשֻׁלַּח
2nd M.	תִּשְׁלַח	תִּשָּׁלַח	תְּשַׁלַּח	תְּשֻׁלַּח
2nd F.	תִּשְׁלְחִי	תִּשָּׁלְחִי	תְּשַׁלְּחִי	תְּשֻׁלְּחִי
1st C.	אֶשְׁלַח	אֶשָּׁלַח	אֲשַׁלַּח	אֲשֻׁלַּח
PLUR. 3rd M.	יִשְׁלְחוּ	יִשָּׁלְחוּ	יְשַׁלְּחוּ	יְשֻׁלְּחוּ
3rd F.	תִּשְׁלַחְנָה	תִּשָּׁלַחְנָה	תְּשַׁלַּחְנָה	תְּשֻׁלַּחְנָה
2nd M.	תִּשְׁלְחוּ	תִּשָּׁלְחוּ	תְּשַׁלְּחוּ	תְּשֻׁלְּחוּ
2nd F.	תִּשְׁלַחְנָה	תִּשָּׁלַחְנָה	תְּשַׁלַּחְנָה	תְּשֻׁלַּחְנָה
1st C.	נִשְׁלַח	נִשָּׁלַח	נְשַׁלַּח	נְשֻׁלַּח

IMPERATIVE

	QAL	NIPHAL	PIEL	
SING. M.	שְׁלַח	הִשָּׁלַח	שַׁלַּח	
F.	שִׁלְחִי	הִשָּׁלְחִי	שַׁלְּחִי	
PLUR. M.	שִׁלְחוּ	הִשָּׁלְחוּ	שַׁלְּחוּ	
F.	שְׁלַחְנָה	הִשָּׁלַחְנָה	שַׁלַּחְנָה	

INFINITIVE

	QAL	NIPHAL	PIEL	
CONSTRUCT	שְׁלֹחַ	הִשָּׁלַח	שַׁלַּח	
ABSOLUTE	שָׁלוֹחַ	נִשְׁלוֹחַ	שַׁלֵּחַ	

PARTICIPLE

	QAL	NIPHAL	PIEL	PUAL
SING. M.	שֹׁלֵחַ	נִשְׁלָח	מְשַׁלֵּחַ	מְשֻׁלָּח
F.	שֹׁלַחַת	נִשְׁלַחַת נִשְׁלָחָה	מְשַׁלֶּחֶת	מְשֻׁלַּחַת
PLUR. M.	שֹׁלְחִים	נִשְׁלָחִים	מְשַׁלְּחִים	מְשֻׁלָּחִים
F.	שֹׁלְחוֹת	נִשְׁלָחוֹת	מְשַׁלְּחוֹת	מְשֻׁלָּחוֹת

THIRD GUTTURAL ROOTS continued

HIPHIL	HOPHAL	QATAL HITPAEL

הִשְׁלִיחַ — הָשְׁלַח — הִשְׁתַּלַּח
הִשְׁלִיחָה — הָשְׁלְחָה — הִשְׁתַּלְּחָה
הִשְׁלַחְתָּ — הָשְׁלַחְתָּ — הִשְׁתַּלַּחְתָּ
הִשְׁלַחַתְּ — הָשְׁלַחַתְּ — הִשְׁתַּלַּחַתְּ
הִשְׁלַחְתִּי — הָשְׁלַחְתִּי — הִשְׁתַּלַּחְתִּי
הִשְׁלִיחוּ — הָשְׁלְחוּ — הִשְׁתַּלְּחוּ
הִשְׁלַחְתֶּם — הָשְׁלַחְתֶּם — הִשְׁתַּלַּחְתֶּם
הִשְׁלַחְתֶּן — הָשְׁלַחְתֶּן — הִשְׁתַּלַּחְתֶּן
הִשְׁלַחְנוּ — הָשְׁלַחְנוּ — הִשְׁתַּלַּחְנוּ

Remember that in the Hitpael of roots that begin with ז ס צ שׁ or שׂ, the ת of the preformative and the 1st root letter will transpose. See Lesson 43.3 for a review.

YIQTOL

יַשְׁלִיחַ — יָשְׁלַח — יִשְׁתַּלַּח
תַּשְׁלִיחַ — תָּשְׁלַח — תִּשְׁתַּלַּח
תַּשְׁלִיחַ — תָּשְׁלַח — תִּשְׁתַּלַּח
תַּשְׁלִיחִי — תָּשְׁלְחִי — תִּשְׁתַּלְּחִי
אַשְׁלִיחַ — אָשְׁלַח — אֶשְׁתַּלַּח
יַשְׁלִיחוּ — יָשְׁלְחוּ — יִשְׁתַּלְּחוּ
תַּשְׁלַחְנָה — תָּשְׁלַחְנָה — תִּשְׁתַּלַּחְנָה
תַּשְׁלִיחוּ — תָּשְׁלְחוּ — תִּשְׁתַּלְּחוּ
תַּשְׁלַחְנָה — תָּשְׁלַחְנָה — תִּשְׁתַּלַּחְנָה
נַשְׁלִיחַ — נָשְׁלַח — נִשְׁתַּלַּח

IMPERATIVE

הַשְׁלַח — הִשְׁתַּלַּח
הַשְׁלִיחִי — הִשְׁתַּלְּחִי
הַשְׁלִיחוּ — הִשְׁתַּלְּחוּ
הַשְׁלַחְנָה

INFINITIVE

הַשְׁלִיחַ — הִשְׁתַּלַּח
הַשְׁלֵחַ — הָשְׁלֵחַ

PARTICIPLE

מַשְׁלִיחַ — מָשְׁלַח — מִשְׁתַּלֵּחַ
מַשְׁלַחַת — מָשְׁלַחַת — מִשְׁתַּלַּחַת
מַשְׁלִיחִים — מָשְׁלָחִים — מִשְׁתַּלְּחִים
מַשְׁלִיחוֹת — מָשְׁלָחוֹת — מִשְׁתַּלְּחוֹת
וַיַּשְׁלַח — (WAYYIQTOL)

399

FIRST *YOD* ROOTS *unattested forms

QATAL

	QAL	NIPHAL	HIPHIL	HOPHAL
SING. 3rd M.	יָשַׁב	נוֹשַׁב	הוֹשִׁיב	הוּשַׁב
3rd F.	regular	נוֹשְׁבָה	הוֹשִׁיבָה	הוּשְׁבָה
2nd M.		נוֹשַׁ֫בְתָּ	הוֹשַׁ֫בְתָּ	הוּשַׁ֫בְתָּ
2nd F.		נוֹשַׁ֫בְתְּ	הוֹשַׁ֫בְתְּ	הוּשַׁ֫בְתְּ
1st C.		נוֹשַׁ֫בְתִּי	הוֹשַׁ֫בְתִּי	הוּשַׁ֫בְתִּי
PLUR. 3rd C.		נוֹשְׁבוּ	הוֹשִׁיבוּ	הוּשְׁבוּ
2nd M.		נוֹשַׁבְתֶּם	הוֹשַׁבְתֶּם	הוּשַׁבְתֶּם
2nd F.		נוֹשַׁבְתֶּן	הוֹשַׁבְתֶּן	הוּשַׁבְתֶּן
1st C.		נוֹשַׁ֫בְנוּ	הוֹשַׁ֫בְנוּ	הוּשַׁ֫בְנוּ

YIQTOL

	QAL	NIPHAL	HIPHIL	HOPHAL
SING. 3rd M.	יֵשֵׁב	יִוָּשֵׁב	יוֹשִׁיב	יוּשַׁב
3rd F.	תֵּשֵׁב	תִּוָּשֵׁב	תּוֹשִׁיב	תּוּשַׁב
2nd M.	תֵּשֵׁב	תִּוָּשֵׁב	תּוֹשִׁיב	תּוּשַׁב
2nd F.	תֵּשְׁבִי	תִּוָּשְׁבִי	תּוֹשִׁ֫יבִי	תּוּשְׁבִי
1st C.	אֵשֵׁב	אִוָּשֵׁב	אוֹשִׁיב	אוּשַׁב
PLUR. 3rd M.	יֵשְׁבוּ	יִוָּשְׁבוּ	יוֹשִׁ֫יבוּ	יוּשְׁבוּ
3rd F.	תֵּשַׁ֫בְנָה	*תִּוָּשַׁ֫בְנָה	*תּוֹשֵׁ֫בְנָה	תּוּשַׁ֫בְנָה
2nd M.	תֵּשְׁבוּ	תִּוָּשְׁבוּ	תּוֹשִׁ֫יבוּ	תּוּשְׁבוּ
2nd F.	*תֵּשַׁ֫בְנָה	*תִּוָּשַׁ֫בְנָה	*תּוֹשֵׁ֫בְנָה	*תּוּשַׁ֫בְנָה
1st C.	נֵשֵׁב	נִוָּשֵׁב	נוֹשִׁיב	נוּשַׁב

IMPERATIVE

	QAL	NIPHAL	HIPHIL	HOPHAL
SING. M.	שֵׁב דַּע	הִוָּשֵׁב	הוֹשֵׁב	
F.	שְׁבִי	הִוָּשְׁבִי	הוֹשִׁ֫יבִי	
PLUR. M.	שְׁבוּ	הִוָּשְׁבוּ	הוֹשִׁ֫יבוּ	
F.	שֵׁ֫בְנָה	*הִוָּשַׁ֫בְנָה	*הוֹשֵׁ֫בְנָה	

INFINITIVE

	QAL	NIPHAL	HIPHIL	HOPHAL
CONSTRUCT	שֶׁ֫בֶת	הִוָּשֵׁב	הוֹשִׁיב	הוּשַׁב
ABSOLUTE	יָשֵׁב		הוֹשֵׁב	

PARTICIPLE

	QAL	NIPHAL	HIPHIL	HOPHAL
SING. M.	יֹשֵׁב	נוֹשָׁב	מוֹשִׁיב	מוּשָׁב
F.	יֹשֶׁ֫בֶת יֹדַ֫עַת	נוֹשָׁ֫בֶת	מוֹשֶׁ֫בֶת	מוּעֶ֫דֶת / מוּשֶׁ֫בֶת
PLUR. M.	יֹשְׁבִים	נוֹשָׁבִים	מוֹשִׁיבִים	מוּשָׁבִים

WAYYIQTOL: וַיֹּ֫שֶׁב

400

SECOND CLASS FIRST *YOD* ROOTS *unattested forms

QATAL

QAL	QAL	HIPHIL
יָטַב	יָרֵא	הֵיטִיב
regular	יָרְאָה	הֵיטִיבָה
	יָרֵאתָ	הֵיטַבְתָּ
	יָרֵאת	הֵיטַבְתְּ
	יָרֵאתִי	הֵיטַבְתִּי
	יָרְאוּ	הֵיטִיבוּ
	יְרֵאתֶם	הֵיטַבְתֶּם
	יְרֵאתֶן	הֵיטַבְתֶּן
	יָרֵאנוּ	הֵיטַבְנוּ

YIQTOL

QAL	QAL	HIPHIL
יִיטַב	יִירָא	יֵיטִיב
תִּיטַב	תִּירָא	תֵּיטִיב
תִּיטַב	תִּירָא	תֵּיטִיב
תִּיטְבִי	תִּירְאִי	תֵּיטִיבִי
אִיטַב	אִירָא	אֵיטִיב
יִיטְבוּ	יִירְאוּ	יֵיטִיבוּ
תִּיטַבְנָה	תִּירֶאנָה	*תֵּיטֵבְנָה
תִּיטְבוּ	תִּירְאוּ	תֵּיטִיבוּ
*תִּיטַבְנָה	תִּירֶאנָה	*תֵּיטֵבְנָה
נִיטַב	נִירָא	*נֵיטִיב

IMPERATIVE

QAL	QAL	HIPHIL
יְטַב	יְרָא	הֵיטֵב
יִטְבִי		הֵיטִיבִי
יִטְבוּ	יְראוּ	הֵיטִיבוּ
יְטַבְנָה		*הֵיטֵבְנָה

INFINITIVE

QAL		QAL	HIPHIL
יְטֹב	יְרָאָה יִרְאַת	הֵיטִיב
יָטוֹב	יְרֹא	הֵיטֵב

PARTICIPLE

QAL	QAL	HIPHIL
יֹטֵב	יָרֵא	מֵיטִיב
	construct: יְרֵאַת	
	יְרֵאִים	

WAYYIQTOL: וַיֵּיטֶב

401

FIRST *NUN* ROOTS *unattested forms
QATAL

	QAL	QAL	NIPHAL	HIPHIL	HOPHAL
SING. 3rd M.	נָגַשׁ	נָפַל	נִגַּשׁ	הִגִּישׁ	הֻגַּשׁ
3rd F.	regular		נִגְּשָׁה	הִגִּישָׁה	הֻגְּשָׁה
2nd M.			נִגַּשְׁתָּ	הִגַּשְׁתָּ	הֻגַּשְׁתָּ
2nd F.			נִגַּשְׁתְּ	הִגַּשְׁתְּ	הֻגַּשְׁתְּ
1st C.			נִגַּשְׁתִּי	הִגַּשְׁתִּי	הֻגַּשְׁתִּי
PLUR. 3rd C.			נִגְּשׁוּ	הִגִּישׁוּ	הֻגְּשׁוּ
2nd M.			נִגַּשְׁתֶּם	הִגַּשְׁתֶּם	הֻגַּשְׁתֶּם
2nd F.			נִגַּשְׁתֶּן	הִגַּשְׁתֶּן	הֻגַּשְׁתֶּן
1st C.			נִגַּשְׁנוּ	הִגַּשְׁנוּ	הֻגַּשְׁנוּ

YIQTOL

	QAL	QAL	NIPHAL	HIPHIL	HOPHAL
SING. 3rd M.	יִגַּשׁ	יִפֹּל	יִנָּגֵשׁ	יַגִּישׁ	יֻגַּשׁ
3rd F.	תִּגַּשׁ	תִּפֹּל	תִּנָּגֵשׁ	תַּגִּישׁ	תֻּגַּשׁ
2nd M.	תִּגַּשׁ	תִּפֹּל	תִּנָּגֵשׁ	תַּגִּישׁ	תֻּגַּשׁ
2nd F.	תִּגְּשִׁי	תִּפְּלִי	תִּנָּגְשִׁי	תַּגִּישִׁי	תֻּגְּשִׁי
1st C.	אֶגַּשׁ	אֶפֹּל	אֶנָּגֵשׁ	אַגִּישׁ	אֻגַּשׁ
PLUR. 3rd M.	יִגְּשׁוּ	יִפְּלוּ	יִנָּגְשׁוּ	יַגִּישׁוּ	יֻגְּשׁוּ
3rd F.	תִּגַּשְׁנָה	תִּפֹּלְנָה	תִּנָּגַשְׁנָה	תַּגֵּשְׁנָה	תֻּגַּשְׁנָה
2nd M.	תִּגְּשׁוּ	תִּפְּלוּ	תִּנָּגְשׁוּ	תַּגִּישׁוּ	תֻּגְּשׁוּ
2nd F.	*תִּגַּשְׁנָה	*תִּפֹּלְנָה	תִּנָּגַשְׁנָה	תַּגֵּשְׁנָה	*תֻּגַּשְׁנָה
1st C.	נִגַּשׁ	נִפֹּל	נִנָּגֵשׁ	נַגִּישׁ	נֻגַּשׁ

IMPERATIVE

	QAL	QAL	NIPHAL	HIPHIL	HOPHAL
SING. M.	גַּשׁ	נְפֹל	הִנָּגֵשׁ	הַגֵּשׁ	
F.	גְּשִׁי	נִפְלִי	הִנָּגְשִׁי	הַגִּישִׁי	
PLUR. M.	גְּשׁוּ	נִפְלוּ	הִנָּגְשׁוּ	הַגִּישׁוּ	
F.	גַּשְׁנָה	נְפֹלְנָה	הִנָּגַשְׁנָה	הַגֵּשְׁנָה	

INFINITIVE

	QAL	QAL	NIPHAL	HIPHIL	HOPHAL
CONSTRUCT	גֶּשֶׁת	נְפֹל	הִנָּגֵשׁ	הַגִּישׁ	הֻגַּשׁ
ABSOLUTE	נָגוֹשׁ	נָפֹל	הִנָּגֵשׁ	הַגֵּשׁ	הֻגַּשׁ

PARTICIPLE

	QAL	QAL	NIPHAL	HIPHIL	HOPHAL
SING. M.	נֹגֵשׁ	נֹפֵל	נִגָּשׁ	מַגִּישׁ	מֻגָּשׁ
F.	נֹגְשָׁה	נֹפְלָה נֹפֶלֶת	נִגֶּשֶׁת נִגָּשָׁה	מַגֶּשֶׁת	מֻגָּשָׁה
PLUR. M.	נֹגְשִׁים	נֹפְלִים	נִגָּשִׁים	מַגִּישִׁים	מֻגָּשִׁים

WAYYIQTOL: וַיִּגַּשׁ

402

GEMINATE ROOTS *unattested forms
QATAL

	QAL	QAL	NIPHAL	HIPHIL	HOPHAL	POLEL
SING. 3rd M.	סָבַב	תַּם	נָסַב נָמֵס	הֵסֵב הֵקַל	הוּסַב	סוֹבֵב
3rd F.	סָבְבָה	תַּמָּה	נָסַּבָּה	הֵסַּבָּה	הוּסַבָּה	סוֹבְבָה
2nd M.	סַבּוֹתָ		נְסַבּוֹתָ	הֲסִבּוֹתָ		סוֹבַבְתָּ
2nd F.	סַבּוֹת		נְסַבּוֹת	הֲסִבּוֹת		סוֹבַבְתְּ
1st C.	סַבּוֹתִי		נְסַבּוֹתִי	הֲסִבּוֹתִי		סוֹבַבְתִּי
PLUR. 3rd C.	סָבְבוּ	תַּמּוּ	נָסַבּוּ	הֵסַבּוּ הֵחֵלּוּ	הוּסַבּוּ	סוֹבְבוּ
2nd M.	סַבּוֹתֶם		נְסַבּוֹתֶם	הֲסִבּוֹתֶם		סוֹבַבְתֶּם
2nd F.	סַבּוֹתֶן		נְסַבּוֹתֶן	הֲסִבּוֹתֶן		סוֹבַבְתֶּן
1st C.	סַבּוֹנוּ		נְסַבּוֹנוּ	הֲסִבּוֹנוּ		סוֹבַבְנוּ

YIQTOL

	QAL	QAL	NIPHAL	HIPHIL	HOPHAL	POLEL
SING. 3rd M.	יָסֹב	Others are pat-	יִסַּב	יָסֵב יַסֵב	יוּסַב יֻסַּב	יְסוֹבֵב
3rd F.	תָּסֹב	terned after	תִּסַּב	תָּסֵב	תּוּסַב	תְּסוֹבֵב
2nd M.	תָּסֹב	the 3rd m. s.'s:	תִּסַּב	תָּסֵב		תְּסוֹבֵב
2nd F.	תָּסֹבִּי	יִסֹב	תִּסַּבִּי	*תָּסֵבִּי		*תְּסוֹבְבִי
1st C.	אָסֹב	יִמַּל	אֶסַּב	אָסֵב		*אֲסוֹבֵב
PLUR. 3rd M.	יָסֹבּוּ	יֵקַל	יִסַּבּוּ יִסֹבּוּ	יָסֵבּוּ יַסֵבּוּ	יוּסַבּוּ	יְסוֹבְבוּ
3rd F.	תְּסֻבֶּינָה		*תִּסַּבֶּינָה	תְּסֻבֶּינָה		*תְּסוֹבֵבְנָה
2nd M.	תָּסֹבּוּ		תִּסַּבּוּ	תָּסֵבּוּ		תְּסוֹבְבוּ
2nd F.	*תְּסֻבֶּינָה		*תִּסַּבֶּינָה	תְּסֻבֶּינָה		*תְּסוֹבֵבְנָה
1st C.	נָסֹב		נִסַּב	נָסֵב		*נְסוֹבֵב

IMPERATIVE

	QAL		NIPHAL	HIPHIL		POLEL
SING. M.	סֹב		הִסַּב	הָסֵב		סוֹבֵב
F.	סֹבִּי		הִסַּבִּי	הָסֵבִּי		
PLUR. M.	סֹבּוּ		הִסַּבּוּ	הָסֵבּוּ		
F.	סֻבֶּינָה		*הִסַּבֶּינָה	*הֲסִבֶּינָה		

INFINITIVE

	QAL		NIPHAL	HIPHIL	HOPHAL	POLEL
CONSTRUCT	סֹב		הִסֵּב	הָסֵב	הוּסַב	סוֹבֵב
ABSOLUTE	סָבוֹב		הִסּוֹב הִמֵּס	הָסֵב		סוֹבֵב

PARTICIPLE

	QAL		NIPHAL	HIPHIL	HOPHAL	POLEL
SING. M.	סֹבֵב		נָסָב	מֵסֵב	מוּסָב	מְסוֹבֵב
F.	סוֹבְבָה		נָסַבָּה	מְסִבָּה		מְסוֹבְבָה
PLUR. M.	סֹבְבִים		נְסַבִּים	מְסִבִּים		מְסוֹבְבִים
F.	סֹבְבוֹת		נְסַבּוֹת	מְסִבּוֹת		מְסוֹבְבוֹת
WAYYIQTOL:	וַיָּסָב			וַיָּסֵב		

QATAL

	QAL	QAL	QAL	QAL	QAL
SING. 3rd M.	קָם	בָּא	שָׂם	מֵת	בּוֹשׁ
3rd F.	קָ֫מָה	בָּ֫אָה	שָׂ֫מָה	מֵ֫תָה	בּ֫וֹשָׁה
2nd M.	קַ֫מְתָּ	בָּ֫אתָ	שַׂ֫מְתָּ	מַ֫תָּה	*בֹּ֫שְׁתָּ
2nd F.	קַמְתְּ	בָּאתְ	שַׂמְתְּ	*מַתְּ	בֹּשְׁתְּ
1st C.	קַ֫מְתִּי	בָּ֫אתִי	שַׂ֫מְתִּי	מַ֫תִּי	בֹּשְׁתִּי
PLUR. 3rd C.	קָ֫מוּ	בָּ֫אוּ	שָׂ֫מוּ	מֵ֫תוּ	בּ֫וֹשׁוּ
2nd M.	קַמְתֶּם	בָּאתֶם	שַׂמְתֶּם	*מַתֶּם	*בּוֹשְׁתֶּם
2nd F.	*קַמְתֶּן	*בָּאתֶן	*שַׂמְתֶּן	*מַתֶּן	*בּוֹשְׁתֶּן
1st C.	קַ֫מְנוּ	בָּ֫אנוּ	שַׂ֫מְנוּ	מַ֫תְנוּ	בֹּ֫שְׁנוּ

YIQTOL

SING. 3rd M.	יָקוּם	יָבוֹא	יָשִׂים	the same	יֵבוֹשׁ
3rd F.	תָּקוּם	תָּבוֹא	תָּשִׂים	as	תֵּבוֹשׁ
2nd M.	תָּקוּם	תָּבוֹא	תָּשִׂים	קום	*תֵּבוֹשׁ
2nd F.	תָּק֫וּמִי	תָּב֫וֹאִי	תָּשִׂ֫ימִי		תֵּב֫וֹשִׁי
1st C.	אָקוּם	אָבוֹא	אָשִׂים		אֵבוֹשׁ
PLUR. 3rd M.	יָק֫וּמוּ	יָב֫וֹאוּ	יָשִׂ֫ימוּ		יֵב֫וֹשׁוּ
3rd F.	תְּק֫וּמֶנָה	תָּבוֹאנָה	תְּשִׂ֫ימֶנָה		*תֵּב֫וֹשְׁנָה
2nd M.	תָּק֫וּמוּ	תָּב֫וֹאוּ	תָּשִׂ֫ימוּ		תֵּב֫וֹשׁוּ
2nd F.	תְּק֫וּמֶנָה	*תָּבוֹאנָה	*תְּשִׂ֫ימְנָה		*תֵּב֫וֹשְׁנָה
1st C.	נָקוּם	נָבוֹא	נָשִׂים		*נֵבוֹשׁ

IMPERATIVE

SING. M.	קוּם	בּוֹא	שִׂים	מוּת	*בּוֹשׁ
F.	ק֫וּמִי	ב֫וֹאִי	שִׂ֫ימִי	*מ֫וּתִי	בּ֫וֹשִׁי
PLUR. M.	ק֫וּמוּ	ב֫וֹאוּ	שִׂ֫ימוּ	*מ֫וּתוּ	בּ֫וֹשׁוּ
F.	קֹ֫מְנָה	*בֹּ֫אנָה	*שֵׂ֫מְנָה	*מֹ֫תְנָה	*בֹּ֫שְׁנָה

INFINITIVE

CONSTRUCT	קוּם	בּוֹא	שִׂים	מוּת	בּוֹשׁ
ABSOLUTE	קוֹם	בּוֹא	שׂוֹם	מוֹת	בּוֹשׁ

PARTICIPLE

SING. M.	קָם	בָּא	the same	מֵת	*בּוֹשׁ
F.	קָמָה	בָּאָה	as	מֵתָה	*בּוֹשָׁה
PLUR. M.	קָמִים	בָּאִים	קום	מֵתִים	בּוֹשִׁים
F.	קָמוֹת	בָּאוֹת		*מֵתוֹת	*בּוֹשׁוֹת

| WAYYIQTOL: | וַיָּ֫קָם | | וַיָּ֫שֶׂם | וַיָּ֫מָת | |

404

HOLLOW ROOTS continued *unattested forms

QATAL

NIPHAL	HIPHIL	HOPHAL	POLEL
נָקוֹם	הֵקִים		קוֹמֵם
נָק֫וֹמָה	הֵק֫ימָה		קוֹמָ֫מָה
*נְקוּמֹ֫ותָ	הֲקִימֹ֫ותָ		קוֹמַ֫מְתָּ
*נְקוּמֹות	הֲקִימֹות		*קוֹמַ֫מְתְּ
נְקוּמֹ֫ותִי	הֲקִימֹ֫ותִי		קוֹמַ֫מְתִּי
נָק֫וֹמוּ	הֵק֫ימוּ	הוּקְמוּ	קוֹמֵ֫מוּ
נְקוֹמֶתֶם	הֲקִימֹותֶם		*קוֹמַמְתֶּם
*נְקֹמֹותֶן	*הֲקִימֹותֶן		*קוֹמַמְתֶּן
*נְקוּמֹ֫ונוּ	הֲקִימֹ֫ונוּ		*קוֹמַ֫מְנוּ

YIQTOL

NIPHAL	HIPHIL	HOPHAL	POLEL
יִקּוֹם	יָקִים	יוּקַם	יְקוֹמֵם
תִּקּוֹם	תָּקִים	תּוּקַם	תְּקוֹמֵם
תִּקּוֹם	תָּקִים	*תּוּקַם	תְּקוֹמֵם
*תִּקּ֫וֹמִי	תָּק֫ימִי	*תּוּקְמִי	*תְּקוֹמֲמִי
אֶקּוֹם	אָקִים	*אוּקַם	אֲקוֹמֵם
יִקּ֫וֹמוּ	יָק֫ימוּ	יוּקְמוּ	יְקוֹמֲמוּ
תִּקּ֫וֹמֶנָה	תְּקֵ֫מְנָה	*תּוּקַ֫מְנָה	תְּקוֹמֵ֫מְנָה
תִּקּ֫וֹמוּ	תָּק֫ימוּ	*תּוּקְמוּ	תְּקוֹמֲמוּ
תִּקּ֫וֹמֶנָה	*תָּקֵ֫מְנָה	*תּוּקַ֫מְנָה	תְּקוֹמֵ֫מְנָה
נִקּוֹם	נָקִים	נוּקַם	*נְקוֹמֵם

IMPERATIVE

NIPHAL	HIPHIL	HOPHAL	POLEL
הִקּוֹם	הָקֵם		קוֹמֵם
*הִקּ֫וֹמִי	הָק֫ימִי		*קוֹמֲמִי
הִקּ֫וֹמוּ	הָק֫ימוּ		קוֹמֲמוּ

INFINITIVE

NIPHAL	HIPHIL	HOPHAL	POLEL
הִקּוֹם	הָקִים	הוּקַם	קוֹמֵם
הִקּוֹם	הָקֵם		

PARTICIPLE

NIPHAL	HIPHIL	HOPHAL	POLEL
נָקוֹם	מֵקִים		
נְקוֹמָה	מְקִימָה		
נְקוֹמִים	מְקִימִים		
נְקוֹמוֹת	מְקִימוֹת		

WAYYIQTOL: וַיָּ֫קֶם

THIRD *ALEPH* ROOTS *unattested forms

QATAL

	QAL	QAL	NIPHAL	PIEL
SING. 3rd M.	מָצָא	מָלֵא	נִמְצָא	מִצֵּא דִּכָּא
3rd F.	מָצְאָה	מָלְאָה	נִמְצְאָה	* מִצְּאָה
2nd M.	* מָצָּאתָ	מָלֵּאתָ	נִמְצֵּאתָ	מִצֵּאתָ
2nd F.	מָצָאת	מָלֵאת	נִמְצֵאת	* מִצֵּאת
1st C.	מָצָּאתִי	מָלֵּאתִי	נִמְצֵּאתִי	מִצֵּאתִי
PLUR. 3rd C.	מָצְאוּ	מָלְאוּ	נִמְצְאוּ	מִצְּאוּ
2nd M.	מְצָאתֶם	מְלֵאתֶם	נִמְצֵאתֶם	מִצֵּאתֶם
2nd F.	* מְצָאתֶן	* מְלֵאתֶן	* נִמְצֵאתֶן	* מִצֵּאתֶן
1st C.	מָצָּאנוּ	מָלֵּאנוּ	נִמְצֵּאנוּ	מִצֵּּאנוּ

YIQTOL

	QAL	QAL	NIPHAL	PIEL
SING. 3rd M.	יִמְצָא		יִמָּצֵא	יְמַצֵּא
3rd F.	תִּמְצָא		תִּמָּצֵא	תְּמַצֵּא
2nd M.	תִּמְצָא		תִּמָּצֵא	תְּמַצֵּא
2nd F.	תִּמְצְאִי		תִּמָּצְאִי	* תְּמַצְּאִי
1st C.	אֶמְצָא		אֶמָּצֵא	אֲמַצֵּא
PLUR. 3rd M.	יִמְצְאוּ		יִמָּצְאוּ	יְמַצְּאוּ
3rd F.	תִּמְצֶּאנָה		תִּמָּצֶּאנָה	תְּמַצֶּּאנָה
2nd M.	תִּמְצְאוּ		תִּמָּצְאוּ	* תְּמַצְּאוּ
2nd F.	תִּמְצֶּאנָה		תִּמָּצֶּאנָה	תְּמַצֶּּאנָה
1st C.	נִמְצָא		* נִמָּצֵא	נְמַצֵּא

IMPERATIVE

	QAL	QAL	NIPHAL	PIEL
SING. M.	מְצָא		הִמָּצֵא	מַצֵּא
F.	מִצְאִי			
PLUR. M.	מִצְאוּ			מַצְּאוּ
F.	מְצֶּאנָה			

INFINITIVE

	QAL	QAL	NIPHAL	PIEL
CONSTRUCT	מְצֹא		הִמָּצֵא	מַצֵּא
ABSOLUTE	מָצוֹא		נִמְצֹא	מַצֵּא

PARTICIPLE

	QAL	QAL	NIPHAL	PIEL
SING. M.	מֹצֵא		נִמְצָא	מְמַצֵּא
F.	מֹצֵאת		נִמְצָאָה	
PLUR. M.	מֹצְאִים		נִמְצָאִים	מְמַצְּאִים

QATAL

PUAL	HIPHIL	HOPHAL	HITPAEL
מֻצָּא קֹרָא*	הִמְצִיא		
	הִמְצִּיאָה	הֻמְצְאָה	
	הִמְצֵּאתָ		
	הִמְצֵאת		
	הִמְצֵּאתִי		הִתְמַצֵּאתִי
מֻצְאוּ	הִמְצִּיאוּ		הִתְמַצְּאוּ
	הִמְצֵאחֶם		
	הִמְצֵאחֶן*		
	הִמְצֵּאנוּ*		

YIQTOL

PUAL	HIPHIL	HOPHAL	HITPAEL
יֻמְצָא	יַמְצִיא		יִתְמַצֵּא
	תַּמְצִיא		תִּתְמַצֵּא
	תַּמְצִיא		תִּתְמַצֵּא
	תַּמְצִּיאִי		תִּתְמַצְּאִי*
	אַמְצִיא		אֶתְמַצֵּא*
	יַמְצִּיאוּ		יִתְמַצְּאוּ
	תַּמְצֶּאנָה		תִּתְמַצֶּאנָה*
	תַּמְצִּיאוּ		תִּתְמַצְּאוּ
	תַּמְצֶּאנָה		תִּתְמַצֶּאנָה*
	נַמְצִיא		נִתְמַצֵּא*

IMPERATIVE

PUAL	HIPHIL	HOPHAL	HITPAEL
	הַמְצֵא		
	הַמְצִּיאִי		
	הַמְצִּיאוּ		

INFINITIVE

PUAL	HIPHIL	HOPHAL	HITPAEL
	הַמְצִיא		הִתְמַצֵּא
	הַמְצֵא		

PARTICIPLE

PUAL	HIPHIL	HOPHAL	HITPAEL
מְמֻצָּא	מַמְצִיא		מִתְמַצֵּא
	מַמְצִיאָה		מִתְמַצֵּאָה*
מְמֻצָּאִים	מַמְצִיאִים		מִתְמַצְּאִים
מְמֻצָּאוֹת			מִתְמַצְּאוֹת

WAYYIQTOL: וַיַּמְצֵא

407

THIRD *HEH* ROOTS *unattested forms

QATAL

	QAL	NIPHAL	PIEL	PUAL
SING. 3rd M.	גָּלָה	נִגְלָה	גִּלָּה	גֻּלָּה
3rd F.	גָּלְתָה	נִגְלְתָה	גִּלְּתָה	גֻּלְּתָה
2nd M.	גָּלִיתָ	נִגְלֵיתָ נִגְלֵיתָ	גִּלִּיתָ	גֻּלֵּיתָ
2nd F.	גָּלִית	נִגְלֵית	גִּלִּית	*גֻּלֵּית
1st C.	גָּלִיתִי	נִגְלֵיתִי	גִּלִּיתִי גִּלֵּיתִי	גֻּלֵּיתִי
PLUR. 3rd C.	גָּלוּ	נִגְלוּ	גִּלּוּ	גֻּלּוּ
2nd M.	גְּלִיתֶם	*נִגְלֵיתֶם	גִּלִּיתֶם	*גֻּלֵּיתֶם
2nd F.	גְּלִיתֶן	*נִגְלֵיתֶן	*גִּלִּיתֶן	*גֻּלֵּיתֶן
1st C.	גָּלִינוּ	נִגְלֵינוּ	גִּלִּינוּ	*גֻּלֵּינוּ

YIQTOL

	QAL	NIPHAL	PIEL	PUAL
SING. 3rd M.	יִגְלֶה	יִגָּלֶה	יְגַלֶּה	יְגֻלֶּה
3rd F.	תִּגְלֶה	תִּגָּלֶה	תְּגַלֶּה	תְּגֻלֶּה
2nd M.	תִּגְלֶה	תִּגָּלֶה	תְּגַלֶּה	תְּגֻלֶּה
2nd F.	תִּגְלִי	*תִּגָּלִי	תְּגַלִּי	
1st C.	אֶגְלֶה	אֶגָּלֶה אִגָּלֶה	אֲגַלֶּה	
PLUR. 3rd M.	יִגְלוּ	יִגָּלוּ	יְגַלּוּ	יְגֻלּוּ
3rd F.	תִּגְלֶינָה	תִּגָּלֶינָה	תְּגַלֶּינָה	
2nd M.	תִּגְלוּ	תִּגָּלוּ	תְּגַלּוּ	
2nd F.	תִּגְלֶינָה	תִּגָּלֶינָה	תְּגַלֶּינָה	
1st C.	נִגְלֶה	*נִגָּלֶה	נְגַלֶּה	

IMPERATIVE

	QAL	NIPHAL	PIEL
SING. M.	גְּלֵה	הִגָּלֵה	גַּלֵּה גַּל
F.	גְּלִי	הִגָּלִי	גַּלִּי
PLUR. M.	גְּלוּ	הִגָּלוּ	גַּלּוּ
F.	גְּלֶינָה		

INFINITIVE

	QAL	NIPHAL	PIEL	PUAL
CONSTRUCT	גְּלוֹת	הִגָּלוֹת	גַּלּוֹת	גֻּלּוֹת
ABSOLUTE	גָּלֹה	הִגָּלֹה הִנָּפֹה	גַּלֹּה גַּלֵּה	

PARTICIPLE

	QAL	NIPHAL	PIEL	PUAL
SING. M.	גֹּלֶה	נִגְלֶה	מְגַלֶּה	מְגֻלֶּה
F.	גֹּלָה	נִגְלָה	מְגַלָּה	מְגֻלָּה
PLUR. M.	גֹּלִים	נִגְלִים	מְגַלִּים	מְגֻלִּים
F.	גֹּלוֹת	נִגְלוֹת	מְגַלּוֹת	מְגֻלּוֹת

WAYYIQTOL: וַיִּגֶל   וַיִּגָּל   וַיְגַל

THIRD *HEH* ROOTS continued *unattested forms

QATAL

HIPHIL	HOPHAL	HITPAEL
הִגְלָה	הָגְלָה	הִתְגַּלָּה
הִגְלְתָה	הָגְלְתָה	*הִתְגַּלְּתָה
הִגְלִיתָ הִגְלֵיתָ	הָגְלֵיתָ	הִתְגַּלִּיתָ
הִגְלֵית הִגְלִית	*הָגְלֵית	*הִתְגַּלִּית
הִגְלֵיתִי הִגְלִיתִי	הָגְלֵיתִי	הִתְגַּלֵּיתִי
הִגְלוּ	הָגְלוּ	הִתְגַּלּוּ
הִגְלֵיתֶם הִגְלִיתֶם	*הָגְלֵיתֶם	הִתְגַּלִּיתֶם
*הִגְלֵיתֶן	*הָגְלֵיתֶן	*הִתְגַּלִּיתֶן
הִגְלֵינוּ	*הָגְלֵינוּ	*הִתְגַּלֵּינוּ

YIQTOL

HIPHIL	HOPHAL	HITPAEL
יַגְלֶה		יִתְגַּלֶּה
תַּגְלֶה	only נכה is attested:	*תִּתְגַּלֶּה
תַּגְלֶה		תִּתְגַּלֶּה
תַּגְלִי		תִּתְגַּלִּי
אַגְלֶה		אֶתְגַּלֶּה
יַגְלוּ	יֻכּוּ	יִתְגַּלּוּ
תַּגְלֶינָה		*תִּתְגַּלֶּינָה
תַּגְלוּ	תֻּכּוּ	תִּתְגַּלּוּ
תַּגְלֶינָה		*תִּתְגַּלֶּינָה
נַגְלֶה		נִתְגַּלֶּה

IMPERATIVE

HIPHIL	HOPHAL	HITPAEL
הַגְלֵה		*הִתְגַּלֵּה הִתְגַּל
הַגְלִי		הִתְגַּלִּי
הַגְלוּ		הִתְגַּלּוּ

INFINITIVE

HIPHIL	HOPHAL	HITPAEL
הַגְלוֹת		הִתְגַּלּוֹת
הַגְלֵה	הָגְלֵה	

PARTICIPLE

HIPHIL	HOPHAL	HITPAEL
מַגְלֶה	מָגְלֶה מֻגְלֶה	מִתְגַּלֶּה
מַגְלָה	מֻגְלָה	
מַגְלִים	מֻגְלִים	מִתְגַּלִּים

WAYYIQTOLS:

HIPHIL	HOPHAL	HITPAEL
וַיַּגְל		וַיִּתְגַּל

409

SECOND GUTTURAL ROOTS *unattested forms

QATAL

	QAL	NIPHAL	PIEL	PUAL
SING. 3rd M.	נָאַל	נִגְאַל	בֵּרֵךְ בֵּרַךְ	בֹּרַךְ
3rd F.	נָאֲלָה	נִגְאֲלָה	בֵּרְכָה	* בֹּרְכָה
2nd M.	נָאַלְתָּ	נִגְאַלְתָּ	בֵּרַכְתָּ	בֹּרַכְתָּ
2nd F.	נָאַלְתְּ	נִגְאַלְתְּ	בֵּרַכְתְּ	בֹּרַכְתְּ
1st C.	נָאַלְתִּי	נִגְאַלְתִּי	בֵּרַכְתִּי	בֹּרַכְתִּי
PLUR. 3rd C.	נָאֲלוּ	נִגְאֲלוּ	בֵּרְכוּ	בֹּרְכוּ
2nd M.	גְאַלְתֶּם	נִגְאַלְתֶּם	בֵּרַכְתֶּם	בֹּרַכְתֶּם
2nd F.	גְאַלְתֶּן	נִגְאַלְתֶּן	*בֵּרַכְתֶּן	בֹּרַכְתֶּן
1st C.	נָאַלְנוּ	נִגְאַלְנוּ	בֵּרַכְנוּ	בֹּרַכְנוּ

YIQTOL

	QAL	NIPHAL	PIEL	PUAL
SING. 3rd M.	יִגְאַל	יִגָּאֵל	יְבָרֵךְ	יְבֹרַךְ
3rd F.	תִּגְאַל	תִּגָּאֵל	תְּבָרֵךְ	תְּבֹרַךְ
2nd M.	תִּגְאַל	תִּגָּאֵל	תְּבָרֵךְ	תְּבֹרַךְ
2nd F.	תִּגְאֲלִי	תִּגָּאֲלִי	תְּבָרְכִי	*תִּבֹרְכִי
1st C.	אֶגְאַל	אֶגָּאֵל	אֲבָרֵךְ	אֲבֹרַךְ
PLUR. 3rd M.	יִגְאֲלוּ	יִגָּאֲלוּ	יְבָרְכוּ	יְבֹרְכוּ
3rd F.	תִּגְאַלְנָה	תִּגָּאַלְנָה	תְּבָרֵכְנָה	תְּבֹרַכְנָה
2nd M.	תִּגְאֲלוּ	תִּגָּאֲלוּ	תְּבָרְכוּ	תְּבֹרְכוּ
2nd F.	תִּגְאַלְנָה	תִּגָּאַלְנָה	תְּבָרֵכְנָה	תְּבֹרַכְנָה
1st C.	נִגְאַל	נִגָּאֵל	נְבָרֵךְ	נְבֹרַךְ

IMPERATIVE

	QAL	NIPHAL	PIEL	
SING. M.	גְאַל	הִגָּאֵל	בָּרֵךְ	
F.	גַאֲלִי	הִגָּאֲלִי	בָּרְכִי	
PLUR. M.	גַאֲלוּ	הִגָּאֲלוּ	בָּרְכוּ	
F.	גְאַלְנָה	הִגָּאַלְנָה	בָּרֵכְנָה	

INFINITIVE

	QAL	NIPHAL	PIEL	PUAL
CONSTRUCT	גְאַל	הִגָּאֵל	בָּרֵךְ	
ABSOLUTE	גָאֹל	הִגָּאֵל נִגְאוֹל	בָּרֵךְ	בֹּרֹךְ

PARTICIPLE

	QAL	NIPHAL	PIEL	PUAL
SING. M.	גֹאֵל	נִגְאָל	מְבָרֵךְ	מְבֹרָךְ
F.	גֹאֶלֶת גֹאֲלָה	נִגְאֶלֶת נִגְאָלָה	מְבָרֶכֶת מְבָרָכָה	מְבֹרָכָה
PLUR. M.	גֹאֲלִים	נִגְאָלִים	מְבָרְכִים	מְבֹרָכִים
F.	גֹאֲלוֹת	נִגְאָלוֹת	מְבָרְכוֹת	מְבֹרָכוֹת

VOCABULARY

PARTICLES

Particles are the small words that provide some of the nuts and bolts of a language, that is, the connecting elements. In English, the particles include *the, a/an,* and the prepositions as well as others. In Hebrew, many of the particles are single letters that are always prefixed to another word. The list below is not an exhaustive list of the Hebrew particles, only the most commonly used ones. In the future, when more particles are introduced to you, they will be included as a regular part of the vocabulary list.

1. אֵת   אֶת   sign of a definite direct object

6. וְ   **and, but, then, so that**

2. אֶת   (preposition) **with**

7. כְּ   **as, like**

3. בְּ   **in, by, with, agains**

8. לְ   **to, for, of**

4. הַ   **the**

9. מִ   **from, out of, of** (derived from מִן)

5. הֲ   interrogative *heh* used for forming a question

PROPER NOUNS

Proper nouns, in other words, place and people names, will not be usually be included as part of the regular vocabulary list. Here are some of the most commonly used proper nouns:

1	יהוה	the LORD	11	יַעֲקֹב	Jacob
2	אֱלֹהִים	God, gods, magistrates	12	אַהֲרֹן	Aaron
3	יִשְׂרָאֵל	Israel	13	שְׁלֹמֹה	Solomon
4	דָּוִד	David	14	לֵוִי	Levi, Levite
5	יְהוּדָה	Judah	15	פְּלִשְׁתִּי	Philistine
6	מֹשֶׁה	Moses	16	פַּרְעֹה	Pharaoh
7	אֲדוֹנִי	Lord	17	בָּבֶל	Babylon
8	מִצְרַיִם	Egypt	18	יְהוֹשֻׁעַ	Joshua
9	יְרוּשָׁלַיִם	Jerusalem	19	אֵל	El, God
10	שָׁאוּל	Saul	20	יוֹסֵף	Joseph

VOCABULARY

The rest of your vocabulary is listed more or less by frequency in the Hebrew Bible. Some adjustments are made to coincide with the exercises in this book.

As in most lexicons, verbs are listed by their 3rd m. s. Qal qatal even if there is no such attested form. A verb's several senses in its several attested stems are listed, with the most commonly used sense in bold print.

1	כֹּל כָּל	**all, any, every**	4	אָמַר	Q: **say,** think, promise, command
2	אֲשֶׁר	**who, whom, that, which**	5	לֹא	**no, not**
3	אֶל	**to, toward, into, at**	6	בֵּן	**son**

7	עַל	on, upon, concerning, against	36	לָקַח	Q: take, receive
					N: be taken
8	כִּי	for, that, because, when, but	37	אֶחָד	one, first, once, each
9	הָיָה	Q: happen, become, be	38	יָדַע	Q: know
		N: be done			N: be known
10	עָשָׂה	Q: do, make			H: make known, declare
		N: be done, be made	39	אִם	if
11	בּוֹא	Q: enter, come	40	עָלָה	Q: go up
		H: bring, bring in			H: bring up, offer
12	מֶלֶךְ	king			N: be brought up, be taken away
13	אֶרֶץ	earth, land, country			
14	יוֹם	day, time	41	שָׁנָה	year
15	אִישׁ	man, husband, each one	42	שֵׁם	name, fame
16	פָּנִים	face, presence	43	אֲנִי	I
17	בַּיִת	house	44	עַיִן	eye, spring
18	נָתַן	Q: give, put, permit	45	שָׁלַח	Q: send
19	עַם	people			P: send forth, send away
20	יָד	hand, strength	46	מוּת	Q: die
21	הָלַךְ	Q: go, come, walk			H: kill, execute
		H: lead, bring	47	שָׁם	there
		Ht: walk to and fro	48	אָכַל	Q: eat, consume
22	דָּבָר	word, thing, matter			N: be eaten
23	הוּא	he, that one, that			H: feed, cause to eat
24	רָאָה	Q: see, look at, consider	49	עֶבֶד	slave, servant
		N: appear, be seen	50	צִוָּה	P: charge, command
		H: show, cause to see	51	אִשָּׁה	woman, wife
25	עַד	as far as, until, while	52	שְׁנַיִם	two
26	אָב	father		שְׁתַּיִם	(f.) two
27	שָׁמַע	Q: hear, listen to, understand, obey	53	גַּם	moreover, also, even
		H: proclaim, announce	54	נֶפֶשׁ	self, person, life
28	דִּבֶּר	P: speak	55	אַיִן	[there] is not, are not
29	זֶה	(m.) this one, this	56	אָדוֹן	master, lord, sir
30	עִיר	town, city	57	כֹּהֵן	priest
31	יָשַׁב	Q: sit, remain, dwell	58	אֵלֶּה	these
		H: set, place, cause to dwell	59	מָה	what? how?
32	יָצָא	Q: go out, come out	60	אַתָּה	(m. s.) you
		H: bring out, take out	61	קָרָא	Q: call, proclaim, read
33	שׁוּב	Q: turn back, return			N: be called
		P: bring back, restore	62	אַחַר	behind, after
		H: bring back, turn back	63	אַל	not
34	הִנֵּה הֵן	behold! lo! see! here!	64	דֶּרֶךְ	way, road, manner
35	עִם	with, beside			

65	כֵּן	thus, so		95	הִיא	she, (f.) that
66	רָעָה	evil, distress, harm		96	שָׁמַר	Q: keep, watch, preserve
67	נָשָׂא	Q: lift, carry, take				N: be on one's guard
		N: be lifted up		97	קֹדֶשׁ	sacredness, holiness
		P: lift, take up		98	מָצָא	Q: find
		Ht: lift up oneself				N: be found, be left
68	אָח	brother				H: present
69	קוּם	Q: arise, stand		99	עוֹלָם	eternity, antiquity
		P: confirm		100	עַתָּה	now
		H: raise, set up		101	נָפַל	Q: fall, lie
70	לֵב	heart, mind, will				H: fell, cause to fall
71	רֹאשׁ	head, chief, top		102	שְׁלֹשָׁה	(m.) three
72	בַּת	daughter			שָׁלֹשׁ	(f.) three
73	מֵאָה	hundred		103	רַב	many, much, great
74	זֹאת	(f.) this one, this		104	מִי	who?
75	שִׂים	Q: put, place		105	מִשְׁפָּט	justice, judgment, custom,
76	מַיִם	water, waters				manner, norm
77	כֹּה	thus, here		106	שָׁמַיִם	heaven(s), sky
78	גּוֹי	nation		107	שַׂר	ruler, chieftain
79	אָדָם	man, humankind, Adam		108	תּוֹךְ	midst, middle
80	הַר	mountain, hill		109	חֶרֶב	sword
81	עָבַר	Q: pass over, by, through		110	כֶּסֶף	silver, money
		H: bring over, by, through		111	נָא	"please," "now"
82	עֶשֶׂר	ten		112	מִזְבֵּחַ	altar
	עֲשָׂרָה	(f.) ten		113	מָקוֹם	(noun) place
83	גָּדוֹל	great, big		114	שִׁבְעָה	(m.) seven
84	עָמַד	Q: stand, stop, take one's			שֶׁבַע	(f.) seven
		stand		115	יָם	sea
		H: erect, make stand		116	זָהָב	gold
85	הֵם	they, those		117	יָרַד	Q: come down, go down
	הֵמָּה	(f.) they, those				H: bring down
86	קוֹל	voice, sound		118	יָרֵא	Q: fear, be afraid
87	נָכָה	H: smite, strike				N: be fearful
88	יָלַד	Q: bear, give birth to		119	רוּחַ	wind, spirit, breathe
		H: beget, father		120	אֵשׁ	fire
89	אֶלֶף	thousand, military unit		121	נְאֻם	"says," utterance, oracle
90	תַּחַת	under, in place of		122	בָּנָה	Q: build
91	חַי	alive, living				N: be built
92	עוֹד	still, yet, again		123	שַׁעַר	gate
93	פֶּה	mouth		124	נָגַד	H: declare, tell, inform
94	צָבָא	army, warfare, host		125	דָּם	blood

126	אָנֹכִי	I
127	מָלַךְ	Q: reign, rule, be king
		H: make king
128	אֹהֶל	tent
129	חֲמִשָּׁה	(m.) five
	חָמֵשׁ	(f.) five
130	טוֹב	(noun) benefit
		(adj.) good, pleasant
131	סָבִיב	around, circuit, surrounding
132	עֵץ	tree(s), wood
133	בָּרַךְ	Q: kneel
		N: bless oneself
		P: bless
		Ht: bless oneself
134	כְּלִי	vessel, utensil, article
135	אוֹ	or
136	מִלְחָמָה	battle, war
137	שָׂדֶה	field, country
138	אַרְבָּעָה	(m.) four
	אַרְבַּע	(f.) four
139	עָנָה	Q: answer, respond
140	עֶשְׂרִים	twenty
141	נָבִיא	prophet
142	מִשְׁפָּחָה	clan, family
143	פָּקַד	Q: visit, observe
		N: be missing, be visited
		P: muster
		H: appoint, deposit
144	סוּר	Q: depart from, turn aside
145	מְאֹד	very, exceedingly, strength
146	עֵת	time. season
147	לֶחֶם	bread, food
148	חַטָּאת	sin, sin offering
149	חָזַק	Q: be/grow strong
		P: strengthen, harden
		H: strengthen, seize
		Ht. strengthen oneself
150	כָּרַת	Q: cut off/down, make a covenant
		N: be cut off/down
		H: cut off, destroy

151	עָבַד	Q: work, serve
		H: compel to labor
152	עֹלָה	burnt offering
153	בְּרִית	covenant, agreement
154	אֹיֵב	enemy
		from participle of אָיַב be hostile to, treat as an enemy
155	חָיָה	Q: live
		P: preserve alive
		H: restore, resurrect
156	חֹדֶשׁ	month, new moon
157	קָרַב	Q: draw near, approach
		P: bring near
		H: bring near
158	אַתֶּם	(m. p.) you
159	אַף	anger, nostril, nose
160	אֶבֶן	stone
161	צֹאן	flock
162	לְמַעַן	for the sake of, in order that, on account of
163	מִדְבָּר	wilderness, plain
164	בָּשָׂר	flesh, meat
165	רָשָׁע	wicked, guilty
166	בֵּין	between
167	לֵבָב	heart, mind, will
168	מַטֶּה	rod, staff, tribe
169	מָלֵא	Q: be full
		N: be filled
		P: fill
170	חֶסֶד	goodness, kindness
171	רֶגֶל	foot
172	אַמָּה	cubit
173	חַיִל	strength, wealth, army
174	לַיְלָה	night
175	גְּבוּל	border, boundary, territory
176	נַעַר	boy, youth, servant
177	חָטָא	Q: sin, miss
		P: purify, make a sin offering
		H: cause to sin
178	שָׁלוֹם	welfare, peace, wholeness
179	מַעֲשֶׂה	deed, work

414

180	זָכַר	Q: remember, call to mind	
		N: be remembered	
		H: remind	
181	יָרַשׁ	Q: take possession of, inherit	
		H: inherit, dispossess	
182	עָוֹן	sin, guilt, punishment	
183	קֶרֶב	midst, among, inward part	
184	זֶרַע	seed, offspring	
185	רָבָה	Q: be/become many, much	
		H: make many, great	
186	אֲדָמָה	ground, land	
187	בָּקַשׁ	P: seek, desire	
188	נַחֲלָה	property, share, inheritance	
189	כָּתַב	Q: write	
		N: be written	
190	מוֹעֵד	appointed time, place, or meeting	
191	אֵם	mother	
192	תּוֹרָה	Torah, teaching, law	
193	כּוּן	N: be established, ready	
		H: establish, prepare	
194	שָׁתָה	Q: drink	
195	אָהֵב	Q: love	
196	שִׁשָּׁה	(m.) six	
	שֵׁשׁ	(f.) six	
197	נָטָה	Q: stretch out, extend	
		H: turn aside, incline, pervert justice	
198	בֹּקֶר	morning	
199	יָסַף	Q: add	
		H: add to, increase, do again	
200	מַחֲנֶה	camp, encampment	
201	מַלְאָךְ	messenger, angel	
202	עָזַב	Q: leave, abandon	
		N: be forsaken	
203	נָצַל	N: deliver oneself	
		P: strip off, plunder	
		H: snatch away, deliver	
204	שָׁכַב	Q: lie down	
205	בֶּגֶד	garment	
206	כָּלָה	Q: be complete, be finished	
		P: complete, finish	

207	צַדִּיק	just, righteous
208	יָשַׁע	N: be liberated, saved
		H: deliver, save, give victory to
209	אָרוֹן	ark, chest
210	אָסַף	Q: gather, remove
		N: assemble, be gathered
211	כָּבוֹד	glory, splendor, honor
212	רוּם	Q: be high, exalted, rise
		H: raise, lift up, erect
213	יָכֹל	Q: be able, prevail
214	כַּף	palm of hand, sole of foot
215	לָכֵן	therefore
216	שֶׁמֶן	oil, fat
217	גָּלָה	Q: uncover, depart, go into exile
		N: be uncovered
		P: uncover, disclose
		H: take into exile
218	שֵׁבֶט	rod, staff, tribe
219	אֹזֶן	ear
220	בְּהֵמָה	cattle, beast
221	רֵעַ	friend, companion
222	שָׁבַע	N: swear, take an oath
		H: cause to swear
223	סֵפֶר	letter, book
224	שָׁפַט	Q: judge, govern
		N: enter controversy
225	אָבַד	Q: perish, die, be lost
		P: destroy, kill
		H: execute
226	בָּקָר	cattle, herb, ox
227	רִאשׁוֹן	former, first
228	מִצְוָה	commandment
229	זָקֵן	(n.) old man, (adj.) old, (n.) elder
230	שָׂפָה	lip, speech, edge
231	שְׁלֹשִׁים	thirty
232	שָׁחָה	bow down; prostrate oneself—always attested in the sequence שׁתחו

233	קָדַשׁ	Q: be set apart	259	חָכְמָה	wisdom, skill
		N: show oneself sacred	260	שָׂמַח	Q: rejoice, be glad
		P: set apart, consecrate			P: gladden
		Ht: purify oneself	261	מִנְחָה	offering, gift, tribute
		H: consecrate	262	צָפוֹן	north
234	בָּחַר	Q: choose	263	כָּסָה	P: cover, conceal
		N: be chosen	264	כְּמוֹ	as, like, when
235	לָחַם	N: wage war, fight	265	נֶגֶד	in front of, opposite
236	שָׁאַל	Q: ask, inquire	266	רֹב	multitude, abundance
237	בִּין	Q: perceive, understand	267	שָׁחַת	P: spoil, ruin, corrupt
		N: be intelligent			H: spoil, ruin, corrupt
		H: teach, cause to understand	268	זָבַח	Q: slaughter, sacrifice
238	דּוֹר	generation, era			P: sacrifice
239	מְלָאכָה	work, business, occupation	269	נָצַב	N: take ones stand
240	רָעָה	Q: pasture, tend, graze			H: set up, erect
241	בַּעַל	Baal, owner, lord	270	אַשּׁוּר	Ashur (Assyria)
242	הָרַג	Q: kill, slay	271	עֵדָה	congregation, gathering
243	חוּץ	outside, street	272	שָׁבַר	Q: break
244	לָמָּה	why?			N: be broken
245	חֲמִשִּׁים	fifty			P: break, shatter
246	פֶּתַח	doorway, opening, entrance	273	נָסַע	Q: set out, journey
247	דָּרַשׁ	Q: seek, consult, frequent			H: lead out
		N: let oneself be consulted	274	חָצֵר	court
248	זֶבַח	(noun) sacrifice	275	עֲבֹדָה	labor, service
249	סָבַב	Q: turn about, go around, surround	276	שָׂנֵא	Q: hate
					P: hate
		N: turn oneself against	277	אָז	at that time, then
		H: turn, cause to turn, lead around	278	חָנָה	Q: encamp
			279	נוּחַ	Q: rest, be quiet
250	אַךְ	surely, only			H: give rest to, leave
251	מָוֶת	death	280	פָּתַח	Q: open
252	טָמֵא	Q: be/become defiled			N: be opened
		N: defile oneself, be defiled			P: set free, open, loosen
		P: defile	281	הָלַל	P: praise
		Ht.: defile oneself			Ht: glory, boast
253	נוּס	Q: flee, escape	282	יַיִן	wine
254	גִּבּוֹר	warrior, mighty man	283	רָדַף	Q: pursue, persecute
255	צְדָקָה	righteousness			P: pursue ardently
256	שֵׁנִי	second	284	מַעַל	upward, above
	שֵׁנִית	(f.) second	285	מִשְׁכָּן	tabernacle, dwelling
257	אַיִל	(animal) ram	285	יַחְדָּו	(adv.) together
258	לְבַד	alone, by oneself	286	נַחַל	stream, wadi, torrent

287	סוּס	horse	318	אוֹר	light
288	חָכָם	wise, skillful, clever	319	אֲנַחְנוּ	we
289	יָמִין	right hand	320	חֵמָה	heat, rage, fury
290	יֵשׁ	there is, there are	321	בָּטַח	Q: trust, be confident
291	נְחֹשֶׁת	copper, bronze	322	לָכַד	Q: capture, seize
292	קָרָא	Q: meet, encounter			N: be captured, seized
293	אַרְבָּעִים	forty	323	נָהָר	river, stream
294	פָּנָה	Q: turn, look	324	רֶכֶב	chariot, chariotry
		P: turn away, clear away	325	יָשָׁר	upright, just, straight
		H: turn	326	פְּרִי	fruit
295	אֲרָם	Aram (Syria)	327	אָמַן	N: be confirmed, faithful
296	חוֹמָה	wall			H: trust, believe
297	כִּסֵּא	throne, seat	328	חַיָּה	living being, animal
298	מִסְפָּר	number	329	פַּעַם	time, occurrence, foot
299	פֶּן	lest	330	צֶדֶק	righteousness, righteous
300	שָׁאַר	N: be left over, be left behind	331	לָשׁוֹן	tongue, language
		H: leave over, spare	332	שָׂרַף	Q: burn
301	שֶׁמֶשׁ	sun			N: be burned
302	פַּר	bull, young bull	333	תּוֹעֵבָה	abomination
303	קָבַר	Q: bury	334	מַמְלָכָה	kingdom, dominion
		N: be buried	335	קָדוֹשׁ	sacred, holy
304	עֶרֶב	sunset, evening	336	גָּדַל	Q: grow up, become great
305	שָׁכֵן	Q: settle down, abide			P: cause to grow, rear (a child)
		P: establish, settle			
		H: place, set			H: make great, magnify
306	חָלַל	P: defile, profane, pollute	337	קָטַר	P: burn sacrifices, incense
		H: begin			H: burn sacrifices, incense
307	נָשִׂיא	chief, prince	338	אָחוֹת	sister
308	חֹק	statute, ordinance	339	בָּכָה	Q: weep, bewail
309	יָתַר	N: be left over, remain	340	יָדָה	H: give thanks, praise
		H: leave over, leave			Ht: confess, give thanks
310	כֹּחַ	strength, power	341	נָבָא	N: prophesy
311	אֱמֶת	faithfulness, truth, stability			Ht: prophesy
312	עֶצֶם	bone, substance, self	342	בִּלְתִּי	not, except
313	שָׁלַךְ	H: throw, cast	343	כָּבֵד	Q: be heavy, honored
314	חָשַׁב	Q: think, account, plan			N: be honored
		N: be accounted, thought			P: honor, make insensible
		P: consider, devise			H: make heavy
315	חֲצִי	half, middle	344	שָׁפַךְ	Q: pour out
316	קָהָל	assembly, congregation			N: be poured out
317	בְּכוֹר	first-born	345	שֶׁקֶר	lie, falsehood
			346	רַק	only, surely

417

347	שַׁבָּת	Sabbath
348	כָּפַר	P: reconcile, cover over
349	לָבֵשׁ	Q: dress, put on clothes
		H: clothe (someone)
350	נֶגֶב	southland, Negeb
351	עַמּוּד	pillar, column
352	בּוֹשׁ	Q: be ashamed
		H: put to shame
353	כָּנָף	wing, extremity, skirt
354	שְׁמֹנָה	eight
	שְׁמֹנֶה	(f.) eight
355	עָפָר	dust, dirt
356	שְׁלִישִׁי	third
357	קָבַץ	Q: gather, collect, assemble
		N: be gathered
358	כֶּבֶשׂ	lamb
359	סָפַר	Q: count, number
		N: be counted, numbered
		P: recount (a tale), relate
360	נָחַם	N: be sorry, repent, comfort oneself
		P: comfort, console
361	עֳנִי	affliction, poor(one)
	עָנִי	afflicted, poor
362	צָרָה	distress, trouble, narrow
	צַר	
363	בַּעַד	through, behind, on behalf of
364	בָּמָה	high place, ridge, back
365	שָׁרַת	P: minister, serve
366	גָּאַל	Q: redeem, act as a kinsman
		N: redeem oneself, be redeemed
367	חֻקָּה	statute, enactment
368	רוּץ	Q: run
369	שָׁלֵם	Q: be complete, sound
		P: complete, make good, reward
370	תָּמִיד	continually, daily
371	יָטַב	Q: be well, be pleasing
		H: do good to, make good
372	מַרְאֶה	sight, appearance, vision
373	שָׁכַח	Q: forget
		N: be forgotten
374	מְעַט	a little, few
375	רֹחַב	breadth, width
376	רָעָב	famine, hunger
377	אֹרֶךְ	length

מראה (372)
משכן (285)
משפחה (142)
משפט (105)
נא (111)
נאם (121)
נוס (253)
נבא (341)
נביא (141)
נגב (350)
נֶגֶד (124)
נֶגֶד (265)
נהר (323)
נוח (279)
נחל (286)
נחלה (188)
נחם (360)
נחשת (291)
נטה (197)
נכה (87)
נסע (273)
נער (176)
נפל (101)
נפש (54)
נצב (269)
נצל (203)
נשא (67)
נשיא (307)
נתן (18)
סבב (249)
סביב (131)
סור (144)
סוס (287)
סֵפֶר (223)
סָפַר (359)
עֶבֶד (49)
עָבַד (151)
עבדה (275)
עבר (81)
עד (25)
עדה (271)
עוד (92)
עולם (99)
עון (182)
עזב (202)

כרת (150)
כתב (189)
לְ (particle 8)
לא (5)
מלאכה (239)
לב (70)
לבב (167)
לבד (258)
לבש (349)
לֶחֶם (147)
לָחַם (235)
לילה (174)
לכד (322)
לכן (215)
למה (244)
למען (162)
לקח (36)
לשון (331)
מִ (particle 9)
מאד (145)
מאה (73)
מדבר (163)
מה (59)
מועד (190)
מות (46)
מָוֶת (251)
מזבח (112)
מחנה (200)
מטה (168)
מי (104)
מים (76)
מלא (169)
מלאך (201)
מלחמה (136)
מֶלֶךְ (12)
מָלַךְ (127)
ממלכה (334)
מנחה (261)
מספר (298)
מעט (374)
מעל (284)
מעשה (179)
מצא (98)
מצוה (228)
מקום (113)

חרב (109)
חשב (314)
טוב (130)
טמא (252)
יד (20)
ידה (340)
ידע (38)
יום (14)
יחדו (285)
יטב (371)
יין (282)
יכל (213)
ילד (88)
ים (115)
ימין (289)
יסף (199)
יצא (32)
ירא (118)
ירד (117)
ירש (181)
יש (290)
ישב (31)
ישע (208)
ישר (325)
יתר (309)
כְּ (particle 7)
כבד (343)
כבוד (211)
כבש (358)
כה (77)
כהן (57)
כון (193)
כח (310)
כי (8)
כל (1)
כלה (206)
כלי (134)
כמו (264)
כן (65)
כנף (353)
כסא (297)
כסה (263)
כסף (110)
כף (214)
כפר (348)

ELEVEN HELPFUL CHARTS

I. QAL YIQTOL/WAYYIQTOL MISSING LETTER RULES:

1. ○○ ַ־וַ   **first *yod*** (or *heh* of הלך) See 3.2a

2. ○○ ־וַ   **third *heh*** See 8.3a

3. ○⊙ ־וַ   **first *nun*** (or *lamed* of לקח) See 9.2b

4. ○○ ־וַ   **hollow root** See 10.3a

II. QATAL/WEQATAL SUBJECT AFFIXES:

he (it)	∅---	they	וּ ---
she (it)	ה ---		
you (sing. masc.)	תָּ ---	you (plur. Masc.)	תֶּם ---
you (sing. fem)	תְּ ---	you (plur. Fem.)	תֶּן ---
I	תִּי ---	we	נוּ ---

III. YIQTOL/WAYYIQTOL SUBJECT PREFIXES AND COMPLEMENTS:

he (it)	--- י	they (masc.)	י --- וּ
she (it)	--- ת	they (fem.)	ת --- נָה
you (sing. masc.)	--- ת	you (plur. Masc.)	ת --- וּ
you (sing. fem.)	ת --- י	you (plur. Fem.)	ת --- נָה
I	--- א	we	נ ---

IV. SYNOPSIS OF STEM SIGNATURES FOR A STRONG VERB:

STEM / FORM	1. QAL	2. NIPHAL	3. PIEL
QATAL 3RD M. S.	○○○ָ	נ○○○	○○○ִ
YIQTOL 3RD M. S.	י○○○ְ	י○⊙○	י○⊙○
PARTICIPLE M. S.	○○ֹ○	נ○○○	מ○⊙○○
IMPERATIVE M. S.	○○○ְ	ה○○○	○○ֵ○
INFINITIVE CONST.	(לְ) ○○ֹ○	(לְ)ה○⊙○○	(לְ) ○○ֵ○

STEM / FORM	4. PUAL	5. HIPHIL	6. HOPHAL
QATAL 3RD M. S.	○⊙○	ה○○י○	ה○○○
YIQTOL 3RD M. S.	י○○⊙	י○○י○	י○○○
PARTICIPLE M. S.	מ○⊙○○	מ○○י○	מ○○○
IMPERATIVE M. S.		ה○○○	
INFINITIVE CONST.		(לְ) ה○○י○	(לְ) ה○○○

V. THE SYSTEM OF VERBAL STEMS

Agent: \ Patient:	NULL	PASSIVE	ACTIVE
ACTIVE	QAL: to act	PIEL: to cause to be in a state	HIFIL: to cause to act
PASSIVE	NIFAL: to be acted upon	PUAL: to be caused to be in a state	HOFAL: to be caused to act
REFLEXIVE (DOUBLE STATUS)	NIFAL: to act and consequently, be acted upon	HITPAEL: to cause oneself to act	

VI. PRONOMINAL SUFFIXES:

ִי	me, my	ָנוּ	us, our	
ְךָ	you, your (m.s.)	ְכֶם	you, your (m.p.)	
ֵךְ	you, your (f.s.)	ֵכֶן	you, your (f.p.)	
וֹ	him, it, his, its	ָם or ָהֶם	them, their (m.p.)	
ָהּ or ָהָ	her, it, hers, its	ֵהֶן	them, their (f.p.)	

VII. DISCOURSE SWITCH CUES

CUE	DISCOURSE GENRE
wayyiqtol	Historical Narrative
the root אמר	Direct Speech
X-yiqtol when inside direct speech	Predictive Narrative
X-yiqtol when outside direct speech	Procedural Discourse
an explicit reference to time duration	Procedural Discourse
volitional and clause-initial yiqtol	Hortatory or Instructional Discourse
verbless clause	Expository Discourse

VIII. HISTORICAL NARRATIVE DISCOURSE PROFILE SCHEME:

Mainline: 1a. Wayyiqtol

      1b. Pivotal/ climactic event on the mainline: Isolated Weqatal

Off-the-line:

2. Topicalization: X-qatal

   3. Embedded Direct Speech

      4. Relative past background: Qatal in a dependent clause

         5. Relative non-past background: Yiqtol in a dependent clause

            6. Backgrounded activities: Participle

               7. Embedded Procedural Discourse

                  8. Transition marker: Wayyiqtol of היה

                     9. Scene setting: Verbless Clause

                        10. Irrealis scene setting: Negation of any verb by לֹא

IX. PREDICTIVE NARRATIVE AND INSTRUCTIONAL DISCOURSE PROFILE SCHEME:
Note: The difference between Predictive Narrative and Instructional Discourse is often elusive. Instructional Discourse has an occasional imperative form. Whereas Predictive Narrative is participant oriented, Instructional Discourse is goal oriented.

1. Mainline: Weqatal (or in Instructional Discourse, an occasional Imperative to mark major procedures)

Off-the-line:
2. Topicalization: X-yiqtol
   3. Relative past background: Qatal in dependent clause
      4. Non-past background: Yiqtol in a dependent clause
         5. Backgrounded activities: Participle
            6. Transition marker: Mainline form of הָיָה
               7. Scene-setting: Verbless clause
                  8. Irrealis: Negation of any verb

X. HORTATORY DISCOURSE PROFILE SCHEME:

Mainline: 1a. Imperative
           1b. Jussive   Note: These four are equally ranked
           1c. Cohortative
           1d. Weqatal (for Mitigated Hortatory Discourse)

Off-the-line:
2. Topicalization: X-Imperative (or Jussive or Cohortative)
   3. Prohibitive commands: אַל or לֹא + Yiqtol
      4. Express possibility: Yiqtol
         5. Consequence, purpose: Weqatal
            6. Consequence, purpose: לֹא or פֶּן + Yiqtol
               7. Consequence, purpose: Embedded Predictive Narrative
                  8. Identification of problem: Embedded Historical Narrative
                     9. Backgrounded activities: Participle
                       10. Scene setting: Verbless Clause

XI. THE BOOKS OF THE BHS IN ORDER

הַתּוֹרָה **The Law**

בְּרֵאשִׁית	"In the beginning"
שְׁמוֹת	"Names"
וַיִּקְרָא	"And He called"
בְּמִדְבַּר	"In the wilderness"
דְּבָרִים	"Words"

נְבִיאִים **Prophets**

יְהוֹשֻׁעַ	Joshua
שֹׁפְטִים	Judges
שְׁמוּאֵל א	1 Samuel
שְׁמוּאֵל ב	2 Samuel
מְלָכִים א	1 Kings
מְלָכִים ב	2 Kings
יְשַׁעְיָהוּ	Isaiah
יִרְמְיָהוּ	Jeremiah
יְחֶזְקֵאל	Ezekiel
הוֹשֵׁעַ	Hosea
יוֹאֵל	Joel
עָמוֹס	Amos

עֹבַדְיָה	Obadiah
יוֹנָה	Jonah
מִיכָה	Micah
נַחוּם	Nahum
חֲבַקּוּק	Habakkuk
צְפַנְיָה	Zephaniah
חַגַּי	Haggai
זְכַרְיָה	Zechariah
מַלְאָכִי	Malachi

כְּתוּבִים **Writings**

תְּהִלִּים	Praises (Psalms)
אִיּוֹב	Job
מִשְׁלֵי	The Proverbs (of…)
רוּת	Ruth
שִׁיר הַשִּׁירִים	The Song of Songs
קֹהֶלֶת	Assembler (Ecclesiastes)
אֵיכָה	Wo! (Lamentations)
אֶסְתֵּר	Esther
דָּנִיֵּאל	Daniel
נְחֶמְיָה-עֶזְרָה	Ezra-Nehemiah
דִּבְרֵי הַיָּמִים	"The affairs of the days" (1 and 2 Chronicles)

BIBLIOGRAPHY

Alter, Robert. *The Art of Biblical Narrative*. New York: Basic Books, 1981.

_____. *The World of Biblical Literature*. New York: Basic Books, 1992.

_____. *Genesis*. New York: W. W. Norton, 1996.

Anderson, Francis I. *The Hebrew Verbless Clause in the Pentateuch*. Journal of Biblical Literature Monograph 14. Nashville: Abington, 1970.

_____. *The Sentence in Biblical Hebrew*. Janua Linguarum, Series Practica 231. The Hague: Mouton, 1974.

_____. "Salience, Implicature, Ambiguity, and Redundancy in Clause-Clause Relationships in Biblical Hebrew," in *Biblical Hebrew and Discourse Linguistics*, edited by Robert Bergen. Dallas: Summer Institute of Linguistics, 1994.

Bandstra, Barry L. "Word Order and Emphasis in Biblical Hebrew Narrative: Syntactic Observations on Genesis 22 from a Discourse Perspective," in *Linguistics and Biblical Hebrew* edited by Walter R. Bodine. Winona Lake: Eisenbrauns, 1992.

Barr, James. *The Semantics of Biblical Language*. Oxford: Oxford University Press, 1961.

Ben Zvi, Ehud, Maxine Hancock, Richard Beinert. *Readings in Biblical Hebrew: An Intermediate Textbook*. New Haven: Yale University, 1993.

Bergen, Robert. "Evil Spirits and Eccentric Grammar," in *Biblical Hebrew and Discourse Linguistics*, edited by Robert Bergen. Dallas: Summer Institute of Linguistics, 1994.

Bergsträsser, Gotthelf. 1983. *Introduction to the Semitic Languages: Text Specimens and Grammatical Sketches*. Trans., Peter T. Daniels. Winona Lake: Eisenbrauns.

Berlin, Adele. 1983. *Poetics and Interpretation of Biblical Narrative*. Sheffield: Almond Press.

de Beauregrande, Robert-Alain and Wolfgang U. Dressler. 1981. *Introduction to Text Linguistics*. London: Longman.

Biblical Hebrew and Discourse Linguistics. Edited by Robert Bergen. Dallas: Summer Institute of Linguistics, 1994.

Bodine, Walter R. "The Study of Linguistics and Biblical Hebrew," in *Linguistics and Biblical Hebrew*, edited by Walter R. Bodine. Winona Lake: Eisenbrauns, 1992a.

_____. "How Linguists Study Syntax," in *Linguistics and Biblical Hebrew*, edited by Walter R. Bodine. Winona Lake: Eisenbrauns, 1992b.

_____. "Discourse Analysis of Biblical Literature: What it is and What it Offers," in *Discourse Analysis of biblical Literature*, edited by Walter R. Bodine. Atalanta: Society of Biblical Literature, 1995.

Brockelmann, Carl. *Hebräische Syntax*. Neukirchen: Neukichener Verlag, 1956.

Brown, Francis, S. R. Driver, and C. A. Briggs. *A Hebrew and English Lexicon of the Old Testament*. Oxford: Clarenon, 1907.

Buth, Randall. "Methodological Collision between Source Criticism and Discourse Analysis," in *Biblical Hebrew and Discourse Linguistics*, edited by Robert Bergen. Dallas: Summer Institute of Linguistics, 1994.

_____. "Functional Grammar, Hebrew and Aramaic: An Integrated Textlinguistic Approach to Syntax," in *Discourse Analysis of Biblical Literature*, edited by Walter R. Bodine. Atlanta: Society of Biblical Literature, 1995.

_____. "Word Order in the Verbless Clause: A Generative-Functional Approach," in *The Verbless Clause in Biblical Hebrew*, edited by Cynthia L. Miller. Winona Lake: Eisenbrauns, 1999.

Chomsky, William. *Hebrew: The Eternal Language*. Philadelphia: Jewish Publication Society, 1957.

Colins, John C. "The *wayyiqtol* as 'Pluperfect': When and Why," in *Tyndale Bulletin, 46.1*, 1995.

Comrie, Bernard. *Aspect: An Introduction to the Study of Verbal Aspect and Related Problems*. Cambridge: Cambridge University, 1976.

_____. *Tense*. Cambridge: Cambridge University, 1985.

Crystal, David. *A Dictionary of Linguistics and Phonetics*, 4th ed. Malden, MA: Blackwell, 1997.

Dawson, David Allen. *Text-linguistics and Biblical Hebrew*. Sheffield: Sheffield Academic Press, 1994.

van Dijk, Teun A. *Text and Context: Explorations in the Semantics and Pragmatics of Discourse*. London: Longman, 1977.

_____. *Macro-Structures*. Hillsdale, NJ: Erlbaum, 1979.

Eskhult, M. *Studies in the Verbal Aspect and Narrative Technique in Biblical Narrative Prose.* Uppsala: Uppsala University, 1990.

den Exter Blokland, A. Francois. *In Search of Syntax: Towards a Syntactic Segmentation Model for Biblical Hebrew.* Amsterdam: VU University Press, 1995.

Fox, Everett. *The Five Books of Moses.* New York: Schocken, 1995.

Georgakopoulou, A. and Dionysis Goutsos. *Discourse Analysis. An Introduction.* Edinburgh: Edinburgh University, 1997.

Gesenius, Wilhelm and Emil Kautzsch. *Gesenius' Hebrew Grammar.* Trans. A. E. Cowley. Oxford: Clarendon, 1910.

Greenberg, Moshe. *Introduction to Hebrew.* Englewood Cliffs, New Jersey: Prentice-Hall, 1965.

Grimes, Joseph E. *The Thread of Discourse.* The Hague: Mouton, 1976.

Hatav, Galia. *The Semantics of Aspect and Modality: Evidence from English and Biblical Hebrew.* Philadelphia: John Benjamins, 1997.

Hetzron, Robert. "Hebrew," in *The World's Major Languages*, edited by Bernard Comrie. New York: Oxford, 1990.

Hopper, Paul J. "Aspect and Foregrounding in Discourse," in *Discourse and Syntax*, ed. Talmy Givon. New York: Academic, 1979.

Isaksson, Bo. "'Aberrant' Usages of Introductory *wehaya* in the Light of Text Linguistics," paper delivered at IOSOT at Cambridge, 1995.

Joosten, Jan. "The Indicative System of the Biblical Hebrew Verb and its Literary Exploitations," in *Narrative Syntax and the Hebrew Bible: Papers of the Tilberg Conference, 1996*, edited by Ellen van Wolde. Leiden: Brill, 1997.

Jouon, Paul, Takamitsu Muraoka. *A Grammar of Biblical Hebrew.* Rome: Editrice Pontifico Instituto Biblico, 1993.

Kittel, Bonnie Pedrotti, Vicki Hoffer, Rebecca Abst Wright. *Biblical Hebrew: A Text and Workbook.* New Haven: Yale University, 1989.

Lambdin, Thomas O. *Introduction to Biblical Hebrew.* New York: Scribner, 1971.

Linguistics and Biblical Hebrew. Edited by Walter R. Bodine. Winona Lake: Eisenbrauns, 1992.

The Literary Guide to the Bible. Edited by Robert Alter and Frank Kermode. Cambridge: Harvard University, 1987.

Lode, Lars. "Postverbal Word Order in Biblical Hebrew: Structure and Function (Part One: Genesis), in *Semitics X.* 24-39, 1984.

_____. "A Discourse Perspective on the Significance of the Masoretic Accents," in *Biblical Hebrew and Discourse Linguistics*, edited by Robert Bergen. Dallas: Summer Institute of Linguistics, 1994.

Longacre, Robert E. *The Grammar of Discourse.* New York: Plenum, 1983.

_____. *Joseph: A Story of Divine Providence.* Winona Lake: Eisenbrauns, 1989.

_____. "Discourse Perspective on the Hebrew Verb: Affirmation and Restatement," in *Linguistics and Biblical Hebrew*, edited by Walter R. Bodine. Winona Lake: Eisenbrauns, 1992.

_____. "*Weqatal* Forms in Biblical Hebrew Prose: A Discourse Modular Approach," in *Biblical Hebrew and Discourse Linguistics*, edited by Rodert Bergen. Dallas: Summer Institute of Linguistics, 1994a.

_____. "A Textlinguistic Approach to the Biblical Narrative of Jonah," in *Biblical Hebrew and Discourse Linguistics*, edited by Robert Bergen. Dallas: Summer Institute of Linguistics, 1994b.

_____. "Building for the Worship of God," in *Discourse Analysis of Biblical Literature*, edited by Walter R. Bodine. Atlanta: Society of Biblical Literature, 1995.

Lowery, Kirk. "The Theoretical Foundations of Hebrew Discourse Grammar," in *Discourse Analysis of Biblical Literature*, edited by Walter R. Bodine. Atlanta: Society of Biblical Literature, 1995.

_____. "Relative Definiteness and the Verbless Clause," in *The Verbless Clause in Biblical Hebrew: Linguistic Approaches*, edited by Cynthia L. Miller . Winona Lake: Eisenbrauns, 1999.

MacDonald, Peter J. "Discourse Analysis and Biblical Interpretation," in *Linguistics and Biblical Hebrew*, edited by Walter R. Bodine. Winona Lake: Eisenbrauns, 1992.

McFall, Leslie. *The Enigma of the Hebrew Verbal System: Solutions from Ewald to the Present Day.* Sheffield: The Almond Press, 1982.

van der Merwe, Christo. "From Paradigms to Texts: New Paradigms and New Tools for Interpreting the Old Testament," *Journal of Northwest Semitic Languages, XXII*, 1993.

_____. "Discourse Linguistics and Biblical Hebrew Grammar," in *Biblical Hebrew and Discourse Linguistics*, edited by Robert Bergen. Dallas: Summer Institute of Linguistics, 1994.

_____. "An Overview of Hebrew Narrative Syntax," in *Narrative Syntax and the Hebrew Bible*, edited by Ellen van Wolde. Leiden: Brill, 1996a.

_____. "A Critical Analysis of Narrative Syntactic Approaches, with Special Attention to their Relationship to Discourse," in *Narrative Syntax and the Hebrew Bible*, edited by Ellen van Wolde. Leiden: Brill, 1996b.

Mettinger, Tryggve N. D. "The Hebrew Verbal System: A Survey of the Recent Research," in *Annual of the Swedish Theological Intitute, IX*, 1973.

Mitchel, Larry A. *A Student's Vocabulary for Biblical Hebrew and Aramaic*. Grand Rapids: Zondervan, 1984.

Miller, Cynthia L. *The Representation of Speech in Biblical Hebrew Narrative: A Linguistic Analysis*. Atlanta: Scholars Press, 1996.

Muraoka, Takamitsu. *Emphatic Words and Structures in Biblical Hebrew*. Jerusalem: The Magna Press, 1985.

Narrative Syntax and the Hebrew Bible: Papers of the Tilburg Conference, 1996. Edited by Ellen van Wolde. Leiden: Brill, 1997.

Niccacci, Alviero. *The Syntax of the Verb in Classical Hebrew Prose*. trans. W. G. E. Watson. Sheffield: Sheffield Academic Press, 1990.

_____. "On the Hebrew Verbal System," in *Biblical Hebrew and Discourse Linguistics*, edited by Robert Bergen. Dallas: Summer Institute of Linguistics, 1994a.

_____. "Analysis of Biblical Narrative," in *Biblical Hebrew and Discourse Linguistics*, edited by Robert Bergen. Dallas: Summer Institute of Linguistics, 1994b.

_____. "Basic Facts and Theory of the Biblical Hebrew Verb System in Prose," in *Narrative Syntax and the Hebrew Bible: Papers of the Tilberg Conference 1996*, edited by Ellen van Wolde. Leiden: Brill, 1996.

_____. "Types and Functions of the Nominal Sentence," in *The Verbless Clause in Biblical Hebrew*, edited by Cynthia L. Miller. Winona Lake: Eisenbrauns, 1999.

Pike, Kenneth. *Linguistic Concepts: An Introduction to Tagmemics*. Lincoln: University of Nebraska, 1982.

Revell, E. John. "The System of the Verb in Standard Biblical Prose," in *Hebrew Union College Annual, LX*, 1989.

_____. *The Designation of the Individual: Expressive Usage in Biblical Narrative*. Kampen, The Netherlands: Kok Pharos, 1996.

Saenz-Badillow, Angel. *A History of the Hebrew Language*. Cambridge: Cambridge University, 1993.

Schneider, Wolfgang. *Grammatik des biblischen Hebräisch*. Munich: Claudius, 1974.

The Semitic Languages. Edited by Rodert Hetron. New York: Routledge, 1997.

Ska, Jean-Louis. *"Our Fathers Have Told Us": Introduction to the Analysis of Hebrew Narratives*. Rome: Pontifico Istituto Biblico, 1990.

Smith, Carlota. *The Parameter of Aspect*. Boston: Kluwer, 1997.

Smith, Mark S. *The Origins and Development of the* Waw-Consecutive. Atlanta: Scholars Press, 1991.

Sternberg, Meir. *The Poetics of Biblical Narrative; Ideological Literature and the Drama of Reading*. Bloomington: Indiana University, 1987.

Talmon, Shamaryahu. "The Old Testament Text," *The Cambridge History of the Bible, vol. 1, From the Beginnings to Jerome*. Cambridge: Cambridge University, 1970.

Talstra, Eep. "Text Grammar and Hebrew Bible," in *Bibliotheca Orientalis, vol. 35*, 1978.

_____. Text Grammar and Hebrew Bible, II: Syntax and Semantics," in *Bibliotheca Orientalis, vol. 39*, 1982.

Traugott, Elizabeth Closs and Mary Louise Pratt. *Linguistics for Students of Literature*. New York: Harcourt, Brace, and Jovanovich, 1980.

Turner, William. "The Tenses of the Hebrew Verb," in *Studies Biblical and Oriental*. Edinburg: Adam and Charles Black, 1876.

Waltke, Bruce and M. O'Connor. *An Introduction to Biblical Hebrew Syntax*. Winona Lake: Eisenbrauns, 1990.

Watson, Wilfred G. E. *Classical Hebrew Poetry*. Sheffield: JSOT Press, 1995.

Weingreen, Jacob. *A Practical Grammar for Classical Hebrew*. 2nd ed. Oxford: Clarendon, 1957.

Wendland, Ernst, ed. *Discourse Perspectives on Hebrew Poetry in the Scriptures*. New York: United Bible Societies, 1994.

Winther-Nielsen, Nicolai. "The Miraculous Grammar of Joshua 3-4," in *Biblical Hebrew and Discourse Linguistics*, edited by Robert Bergen. Dallas: Summer Institute of Linguistics, 1994.

INDEX

absolute
  of a construct chain, 32, 43, 283, 328
  of numbers, 217
absolute form of a noun, 39, 71, 72, 203, 312
accentual system, ix, 83
accusative case, 237
adjective
  attributive, 99, 100, 110, 281, 285, 317
  of nationality, 267, 344
  predicate, 99, 137, 359
  substantive, 100, 250, 282, 290, 300, 344
adverb, 287
  adverbial phrase, 237, 238, 375
  interrogative, 354
  marked by   , 237
  temporal, 197, 261
alphabet, ix
Alter, Robert, 192, 281, 379
Anderson, v, 10
apocopated forms, 96, 133, 168, 393
apodosis, 245, 246, 385
apposition, 58, 110, 368
assimilation, 42, 220, 223, 232, 243, 308, 310,
  335, 346, 373
atnakh, 83, 119
attributions, 22
augmenting roots, 4, 7, 18, 154, 155, 223, 236

Bandstra, Barry, 23, 28
BDB, 307
Berlin, Adele, 291
bet of hostility, 263
bet of instrumentality, 311, 313, 338
Biblia Hebraica Stuttgartensia, 314, 321
Buth, Randall, 10, 11

cardinal numbers, 217, 271
casus pendens, 169, 301
chiasm, 376
clause
  basic building block of discourse, 54, 281
  building block of discourse, 54
  clause initial, 22
  defined, 7
  dependent, 7, 17, 18, 54, 66
  independent, 7, 18
  marking boundaries between, 54
  predicate and subject, 10
  verbless clause, 10
clause-by-clause analysis, 281, 296, 327
clause-initial, 23, 54, 74, 134

qatal of oral Historical Narrative, 149
clause-initial position, 64
closed syllables, xiii
cohortative, 136, 138, 286, 300, 323, 348, 360
  ambiguity of X-yiqtol, 348
  in Gen 29, 363
comparative degree(formula for), 360, 363
comparative formula, 360
compound direct object, 38
compound shewa, xiii
conjunctive accents, 83
consonants, ix
construct
  defined, 32
  infinitive, 87
construct chain, 43
  defined, 32
  in Gen 17, 300
  in Gen 22, 292
  uses, 32
construct form, 36, 67, 68, 71, 72, 102, 108, 203,
  217
  of פה, 252
  of numbers, 217

dagesh, xi
  forte, 7, 26, 41, 52, 78, 81, 179, 223, 232, 233,
    236, 373
  forte absent in Piel wayyiqtol, 8
  forte defined, 3
  lene, 332
  lene defined, 3
Dawson, D. A., v, 62, 65, 102, 107, 319, 389
DDO, 15, 17
  as "particle of emphasis", 237
  as marker of accusative case, 237
  with pronominal suffixes, 67, 73, 108
defectiva spelling, xiii, 57, 88, 124, 146, 151,
  161, 250, 310, 329, 339, 344
definite article, 15, 29, 57, 281, 369
  assimilated into prepositions, 78, 284, 346
  on אלהים, 56, 281
  on attributive adjectives, 100, 317
  on participles, 228
  with time words, 321
definiteness, 15, 281, 291, 317
  defined, 29
  of attributive adjectives, 99
  of construct chains, 32
demonstrative
  adjectives, 100, 281, 291
  pronouns, 68

431

Procedural Discourse, 203, 206, 208, 318, 346, 353, 424
   discourse profile scheme, 209
promiscuous roots, 358
pronominal suffix, 67
   as resumptive pronoun, 348
   causes definiteness, 317
   creating euphony, 328, 331
   obscures cohortative, 360
   on מן, 302
   on הנה, 374
   on DDO, 108
   on infinitive construct, 195, 197
   on Niphal infinitive construct, 233
   on nouns, 67
   on prepositions, 150, 216, 217
   on verbs, 150, 302
   opposed to independent pronoun, 319
   use of mappiq, 308
   used objectively, 109
   used possessively, 108, 132
   variability, 204, 309
   vowel shortening, 174, 310, 332, 358
   with הנה, 143
pronominal suffix charts, 109
prophetic formulas, 366
protasis, 245

qamets khatuf, 14, 80, 393
qatal
   affix, 81, 422
   four component verbal system, 74
   Hiphil, 154, 155, 161, 312, 355
   Hishtaphel, 242, 243
   Hitpael, 243
   in a dependent clause, 18, 53, 54, 59, 103, 151, 210, 213, 282, 424, 425
   in Jdg 16, 317, 320, 323
   in question, 82
   meaning of, 58
   Niphal, 219, 220, 312, 313, 332, 352
   of נתן, 87
   of בוא, 355
   of עלה, 207
   of היה, 360, 364
   of 3rd *heh* roots, 166
   of hollow roots, 47, 143, 145, 160
   of stative roots, 368, 374
   opening oral Historical Narrative, 149, 150, 367
   Piel, 26, 157, 363
   Pual, 311
   setting time of scene, 261

topicalization, 23
translation of, 24
verbal meaning of, 21, 74, 89
X-qatal, 22, 28, 52, 53, 54, 59, 103, 130, 139, 210, 213, 282, 338, 347, 355, 356, 360, 364, 376, 424, 425
Qere, 321, 351

reflexive sense, 225, 237
resumptive pronoun, 348, 374
Revell, E. J., 75, 111, 123, 125, 138
root, 4

second class 1st yod roots, 122, 299, 316
second guttural roots, 157
segolate nouns, 316
Septuagint, 315
shewa
   silent, xiv
   vocal, xiv
shortened form of jussive, 133, 137
shortened vowels, 29, 36, 71, 174, 358
   of wayyiqtol, 96
sof passuq, 282
speech introduction, 9, 71, 209, 281, 310, 344, 348, 368
speech introduction formulas, 354
spelling peculiarities of the Hitpael stem, 242
stative roots, 190, 374
stem, 4, 8, 27, 153, 156, 163, 215, 251, 252
Sternberg, Meir, 2
subjunctive mood, 265
substantive, 100, 282
suspense, 10, 48, 280, 285, 288, 330, 362, 369, 370

temporal adverbs, 381
tetragrammaton, 3
textual variations, 315, 321, 329, 351
topicalization, 23, 28, 48, 53, 59, 73, 93, 103, 130, 138, 139, 145, 149, 210, 213, 267, 282, 287, 301, 302, 424, 425
transformation of letters, 72, 154, 172, 223, 243, 309
transitivity, 191
transposition of letters, 242, 399
Turner, Wm., 21

V1, 134
van der Merwe, Christo, v, 51, 197, 261
vav conjunctive, 92, 267, 317
vav consecutive
   defined, 92, 93
   in Deu 6, 329